Cognitive Psychology

and Its Implications

A Series of Books in Psychology

Editors:
Richard C. Atkinson
Jonathan Freedman
Gardner Lindzey
Richard F. Thompson

Cognitive Psychology
and Its Implications.

John R. Anderson

CARNEGIE-MELLON UNIVERSITY

W. H. Freeman and Company
San Francisco

Sponsoring Editor: W. Hayward Rogers

Project Editors: Nancy Flight, Dick Johnson

Manuscript Editor: Suzanne Lipsett

Designer: Sharon Smith

Production Coordinator: Fran Mitchell

Illustration Coordinator: Cheryl Nufer

Artists: Catherine Brandel and Victor Royer

Compositor: Graphic Typesetting Service

Printer: The Maple-Vail Book Manufacturing Group

Library of Congress Cataloging in Publication Data

Anderson, John Robert, 1947-
    Cognitive psychology and its implications.

    (A Series of books in psychology)
    Bibliography: p.
    Includes index.
    1. Cognition. I. Title.
BF311.A5895   153   80-14354
ISBN 0-7167-1197-4

BF
311
.A5895

Printed in the United States of America

    2   3   4   5   6   7   8   9

This book is dedicated to

Gordon H. Bower

who has inspired me in countless discussions and from whom I have learned the most about cognitive psychology.

Contents

Preface

To the Student

This is an exciting time to be a cognitive psychologist. While the status of cognitive psychology is not yet that of a mature science, we can bring into focus the emerging outline of its permanent scope. Using new and sophisticated techniques, researchers are generating a body of knowledge that when adequately developed will have enormous implications for understanding the structure of human experience. For many of you, the very concept of cognitive psychology will be a little unclear as you begin this book. I have attempted to explain as clearly as possible the theoretical and experimental foundations for our current understanding of higher mental process. Of equal importance are the many illustrations where the findings of the field are already being applied. I have tried to identify areas of current investigation that show promise for application to our daily lives.

While experimental results and concepts are analyzed and discussed, it has been necessary to impose some organization on the field, reflecting to some extent my own theoretical biases. At all times, particular attention has been paid to bridging the gap between the world of the laboratory and our experience in everyday living.

To the Instructor

The most troublesome problem educators face is ensuring long-term retention. The simple fact is that students forget most of what they learn in college courses. One reason is that teachers and textbook writers try to teach too much, spending valuable time on nonessential material. A reasonable overall objective for a course using a text such as this one might be: to communicate a core of facts, principles, and abilities (a couple of hundred) and, assuming that the students are cooperative and work hard, to guarantee that students will learn them. The criterion for "learn" should include the ability not only to display possession of this set on the final test, but also to display possession in a number of years. By this criterion, most educators would score poorly as teachers or textbook writers. (I certainly have failed in this regard in some courses I have taught.) Obviously, we usually strive to convey more than a couple of hundred facts in a course. However, some facts are central to a topic, and students must learn them to understand the area, while others are not as important and might be forgotten by students with no significant loss of overall understanding.

Accordingly, this text is structured on the basis of some informed guesses about how students' retention of important information can be facilitated. Because I have tried to identify clearly and focus on the few hundred most important facts in the field, the book does not pretend to cover every finding in cognitive psychology. However, a select set of details is presented to create redundancy (which improves memory) and to add interest and credibility to the main points. I have also tried to show how these general points relate to specific cases by the use of examples, particularly ones that incorporate everyday issues. Thus, most chapters contain discussions of the implications of the research.

If the research on human memory has shown one thing, it is that the organization of material is of central importance. And, since the only way to organize empirical results is by theory, this text is unabashedly theoretical. If there is a second thing we know about human memory, it is that associating multiple objects to the same stimulus is difficult. In particular, as any student will tell us, it is difficult to keep different theoretical accounts of the same phenomena straight. Therefore, I have tried to be selective regarding the theories recounted in this book.

In referring to the experimental work on memory we find that one important principle of retention is totally frustrated by standard textbook structure: The principle that spacing, or distributing, in one's study of a topic is important for retention. Because of the need for a logical organization, textbooks tend to confine discussion of a particular topic to one location, whereas students learn more efficiently by returning to a topic more than once over a period of time. This textbook, like any other, is naturally constrained by space limitations, and I hope instructors will try to remedy this problem by altering course structure—for instance, by incorporating review procedures.

This text can be covered in a one-semester course with class experimental projects and some outside readings. In a quarter course, not much time will be left over for special projects or supplemental readings. Instructors may choose to omit chapters or to cover chapters out of order. Some chapter cross-references help give the text coherence when it is read from beginning to end, but the only real obstacle is reordering the chapters is the material on semantic networks introduced in Chapter 4. These networks, which have been an important part of cognitive psychology for ten years and should be treated as significant in any text, do play major roles in some of the other chapters (6, 7, 13, and 14). Although covering these later chapters before Chapter 4 would cause some difficulty, even this order constraint could be overcome if some effort were made to help students with the networks.

The production systems introduced in Chapter 8 play a minor role in Chapters 9 and 10 and somewhat larger roles in Chapters 13 and 14. I have adapted the production-system formalism to make the productions quite readable without any introduction. In fact, I submit that the formalism in this text for describing procedural knowledge is the most readable in existence. Therefore, Chapter 8 is not a prerequisite for Chapters 9, 10, 13, and 14.

While the book is fairly selective in the theory and research covered, it is comprehensive with respect to the topics of cognitive psychology. Like any introductory text, this one greatly underrepresents the formal and technical sophistication of the field. To pursue the goals of cognitive psychology, it is often necessary to develop mathematical models, statistical analyses, formal analyses, or computer simulations. These analyses are often both complex and intellectually deep. Most students in introductory cognitive-psychology courses do not have the prerequisites for understanding these constructs. Therefore, theory and research are generally presented considerably less formally than I would have preferred. However, examples of complex analyses occur occasionally throughout the text where they are particularly relevant and relatively accessible through intuition. Perhaps in a generation's time a textbook writer in cognitive psychology will be able to assume that students possess considerable mathematical and technical skills, similarly as today such skills are prerequisites for a course in physics. It is certainly true now that any student intending to go on in cognitive psychology must acquire these skills. The examples in the text will serve to illustrate the kinds of background required.

More people have read and commented on this text than I will ever know, since many of the reviews were anonymous. The following people have, with my knowledge, commented on parts of the manuscript: Lyle Bourne, Jr., John Bransford, Bill Chase, Charles Clifton, Lynn Cooper, Robert Crowder, Susan Fiske, Marcel Just, Stephen Keele, Stephen Kosslyn, Elizabeth Loftus, Allen Newell, Donald Norman, Gary Olson, Allan Paivio, Jane Perlmutter, Peter Polson, Stephen Reed, Russell Revlin, Lance Rips, Miriam Schustack, Ed Smith, Kathryn Spoehr, and Tom Trabasso. The following are among the people who read and commented upon the book in its entirety or almost its entirety: Elizabeth Bjork, Ellen Gagne, Lynn Hasher, Lynne Hyatt, Clayton Lewis, Lynne

Reder, Charles Tatum, David Tieman, and Henry Wall. I can say that without exception the book has improved through their comments. I thank them all very much. The students in the Thinking classes I taught at Yale and Carnegie–Mellon also deserve thanks. They both convinced me that I had something worth saying and provided me with good feedback. A very special thanks goes to Vickie Silvis Wille, who was responsible for most of the manuscript preparation and coordination. Her efforts have been simply heroic. My own research, which is described on more than one occasion in this book, was supported by the National Science Foundation and the Office of Naval Research. In at least two instances, this text constitutes the first published reports of that research.

March 1980   John R. Anderson

Cognitive Psychology
and Its Implications

Part I

INTRODUCTION

Chapter 1

The Science of Cognition

Summary

1. Cognitive psychology attempts to understand the nature of human intelligence and how people think.

2. The study of cognitive psychology is motivated by scientific curiosity, by the desire for practical applications, and by the need to provide a foundation for other fields of social science.

3. People have speculated about human cognition for 2000 years. Only in the last 100 years, however, has cognition been studied scientifically. In the last 25 years, knowledge about human cognition has greatly increased.

4. Cognitive psychology is dominated by the *information processing approach,* which analyzes cognitive processes into a sequence of ordered *stages.* Each stage reflects an important step in the processing of cognitive information.

5. Theories in cognitive psychology are attempts to summarize large sets of data and to establish a basis for making predictions about new data. These theories are fairly successful in accounting for what we know about human cognition. To a certain extent, however, they are speculative and should not be treated as absolute truths.

Our species is referred to as *homo sapiens,* or "man, the intelligent." This term reflects the general belief that intelligence is what distinguishes us from other animals. The goal of cognitive psychology is to understand the nature of human intelligence and how it works. Subsequent chapters in this book discuss what cognitive psychologists have discovered about various aspects of human intelligence. This chapter attempts to answer the following preliminary questions:

> Why do people study cognitive psychology?
> Where and when did cognitive psychology originate?
> What are the methods of cognitive psychology as a science?

Motivations

Intellectual Curiosity

One reason for studying cognitive psychology motivates any scientific inquiry —the desire to know. In this respect, the cognitive psychologist is like the tinkerer who wants to know how a clock works. The human mind is a particularly interesting device that displays remarkable adaptiveness and intelligence. We are often unaware of the extraordinary aspects of human cognition. Just as we can easily overlook the enormous accumulation of technology that permits a sports event on television to be broadcast live from Europe, so we can forget how sophisticated our mental processes must be to enable us to understand and enjoy that sportscast. One would like to understand the mechanisms that make such intellectual sophistication possible.

The inner workings of the human mind are far more intricate than the most complicated systems of modern technology. The field of artificial intelligence (AI) is attempting to develop programs that will enable computers to display intelligent behavior. Despite the fact that this has been an active field of research for more than 20 years, AI researchers still have no idea how to create a truly intelligent computer. No existing programs can recall facts, solve problems, reason, learn, or process language with anything approximating human facility. This failure has occurred not because computers are inferior to human brains but because we do not yet know how human intelligence is organized.

In a discussion of human intelligence, it is profitable to consider someone truly exceptional. Professor A. C. Aitken was a mathematician at Edinburgh University. Besides being an accomplished and creative mathematical thinker, he was legendary for his feats of memory and his abilities as a lightning-fast calculator. He was studied by the psychologist I. M. L. Hunter (1966, 1977). In one example, Aitken was given the task of expressing 4/47 in decimals. After an initial pause of about 4 seconds, he began producing the following digits at the rate of about one digit every three-quarters of a second:"0 8 5 1 0 6 3 8 2 9

7 8 7 2 3 4 0 4 2 5 5 3 1 9 1 4." He discussed the problem for a minute and then picked up at the end of the sequence: "1 9 1 4 8 9. . . ." He paused for another 5 seconds: "3 6 1 7 0 2 1 2 7 6 5 9 5 7 4 4 5 8." At this point, he stopped and announced that the decimal sequence repeated itself every 46 places.

Aitken was able to give similar performances on an amazing variety of arithmetic problems. In general, his mental calculations were more rapid and accurate than the calculations of most people with pencil and paper. Aitken did not possess any unique cognitive gifts. Rather, his performance depended on his having developed normal mental abilities.

Practical Application

The desire to understand is an important motivation to the study of cognitive psychology, as it is in any science, but the practical implications of the field constitute an important secondary motivation. If we really understand how people acquire knowledge and intellectual skills and how they perform feats of intelligence, then we will be able to improve their intellectual training and performance accordingly. Throughout this book, I identify the implications of the areas of research under discussion. Because this book is addressed mainly to college students, the focus is generally on the kinds of intellectual problems students encounter in their course work, but occasionally the implications for a broader range of social problems and issues are considered.

It seems inevitable that cognitive psychology will prove beneficial to both individual and society. Many of our problems derive from an inability to deal with the cognitive demands placed on us. These problems are being exacerbated by the "information explosion" and the technological revolution we are presently experiencing. Cognitive psychology is just beginning to make headway on these issues, but some clear and positive insights with direct application to everyday life have already emerged. Students who read this text and learn the lessons it has to offer will improve the capacity of their intellects, at least modestly. And, on a larger scale, by the turn of the century the lessons of cognitive psychology will have momentous consequences for intellectual performance. So, one reason for studying cognitive psychology and for encouraging its development as a field is to enable people to be more effective in their intellectual pursuits.

Implications for Other Fields

Students and researchers interested in other areas of psychology or social science have another reason for following developments in cognitive psychology. Cognitive psychology attempts to understand the basic mechanisms governing human thought, and these basic mechanisms are important in understanding the types of behavior studied by other social science fields. For example, understanding how humans think is important to understanding why certain thought malfunctions occur (clinical psychology), how people behave with other individuals or in groups (social psychology), how persuasion works (political science), how economic decisions are made (economics), why certain ways of organizing groups are more effective and stable than others (sociology), or why natural languages have certain constraints (linguistics). Cognitive psychology studies the foundation on which all other social sciences stand.

It is certainly true, nonetheless, that much social science has developed without a grounding in cognitive psychology. Two facts account for this situation. First, cognitive psychology is not very advanced. Second, other areas of social science have managed to find higher order principles unrelated to cognitive mechanisms to explain the phenomena in which they are interested. However, much is unknown or poorly understood in these other fields. If we knew how these higher order principles were explained in terms of cognitive mechanisms and how to apply cognitive mechanisms directly to higher order phenomena, we might have a firmer grasp on the phenomena in question. Thus, throughout this text, the implications of cognitive psychology for other areas of social science are cited.

The History of Cognitive Psychology

Early History

In Western civilization, interest in human cognition can be traced to the ancient Greeks. Plato and Aristotle, in their discussions of the nature and origin of knowledge, speculated on memory and thought. These early discussions, which were essentially philosophical in nature, eventually developed into a centuries-long debate. The antagonists were the empiricists, who believed that all knowledge comes from experience, and the nativists, or rationalists, who argued that children come into the world with a great deal of innate knowledge. The debate intensified in the seventeenth, eighteenth, and nineteenth centuries, with such British philosophers as Locke, Hume, and Mill arguing for the empiricist view and such Continental philosophers as Descartes and Kant propounding the nativist view. Though these arguments were at their core philosophical, they frequently slipped into psychological speculations about human cognition. It will be clear throughout this book, but particularly in Chapter 12, on language, that this debate is still with us.

During this long period of philosophical debate, such sciences as astronomy, physics, chemistry, and biology developed markedly. Curiously, no concomitant attempt was made to apply the scientific method to the understanding of human cognition; this undertaking did not take place until the end of the nineteenth century. Certainly, no technical or conceptual barriers existed to studying cognitive psychology earlier. In fact, many of the experiments performed in cognitive psychology could have been performed and understood in the time of the Greeks. But cognitive psychology, like many other sciences, suffered because of our egocentric, mystical, and confused attitude about ourselves and our own nature. It had seemed inconceivable before the nineteenth century that the workings of the human mind could be susceptible to scientific analysis. As a consequence, cognitive psychology as a science is only 100 years old and lags far behind many other sciences in sophistication. We have spent much of the first 100 years freeing ourselves of the pernicious misconceptions that can arise when one engages in such an introverted enterprise as a scientific study of human cognition. It is the case of the mind studying itself.

Psychology in Germany

The date usually cited as marking the beginning of psychology as a science is 1879, when Wilhelm Wundt established the first psychology laboratory in Leipzig, Germany. Wundt's psychology was cognitive psychology (in contrast to other major divisions of psychology, such as physiological, comparative, clinical, or social), although he had far-ranging views on many subjects. The method of inquiry used by Wundt, his students, and a large portion of the early psychologists was *introspection*. In this method, highly trained observers reported the contents of their consciousness under carefully controlled conditions. The basic belief was that the workings of the mind should be open to self-observation. Thus, to develop a theory of cognition, one needed only to develop a theory that accounted for the contents of introspective reports.

Let us consider a sample introspective experiment. Mayer and Orth (1901) had their subjects perform a free-association task. The experimenters spoke a word to the subjects and then measured the amount of time the subjects took to generate responses to this word. Subjects then reported all their conscious experiences from the moment of stimulus presentation until the response was generated. To get a feeling for this method, try to generate an associate to each of the following words; after each association try to introspect on the contents of your consciousness during the period between reading the word and making your association: coat, book, dot, bowl.

In Mayer and Orth's experiment, many reports were given of rather non-describable conscious experiences. Whatever was in consciousness, it did not seem to involve sensations, images, or other things that subjects in these laboratories were accustomed to report. This result started a debate on the issues of *imageless thought*—whether conscious experience could really be devoid of concrete content. As we will see in Chapter 4, this issue is still very much with us.

Psychology in America

Introspective psychology was not well accepted in America. Psychology in America at the turn of the century was largely an armchair avocation, in which the only self-inspection was casual and reflective rather than intense and analytic. William James' (1890) *Principles of Psychology* reflects the best of this tradition, and many of its proposals are still relevant and cogent today. The mood of America was determined by the philosophical doctrines of pragmatism and functionalism. Many of the psychologists of the time were involved in education, and the demand was for an "action-oriented" psychology that would be capable of practical application. The intellectual climate in America was not receptive to a psychology focused on such questions as whether or not the contents of consciousness were sensory.

One of the important figures of early American scientific psychology was Edward Thorndike, who developed a theory of learning that was directly applicable to school situations. Thorndike was interested in such basic questions as the effects of reward and punishment on rate of learning. To him, conscious experience was just excess baggage, which could be largely ignored. As often as not, his experiments were done on infrahuman animals such as cats. Animals involved fewer ethical constraints than humans with regard to experimenting, and Thorndike was probably just as happy that such subjects could not introspect.

While introspection was being ignored at the turn of the century in America, it was getting into trouble on the Continent. Different laboratories were reporting different types of introspections—each type matching the theory of the particular laboratory from which it emanated. It was becoming clear that introspection did not give one a clear window onto the workings of the mind. Much that was important in cognitive functioning was not open to conscious experience.

These two factors, the "irrelevance" of the introspective method and its apparent contradictions, set the groundwork for the great behaviorist revolution in American psychology, which occurred around 1920. John Watson and other behaviorists led a fierce attack, not only on introspectionism, but also on any attempt to develop a theory of mental operations. Psychology, according to the behaviorists, was to be entirely concerned with external behavior and was not to try to analyze the workings of the mind that underlay this behavior:

> Behaviorism claims that consciousness is neither a definite nor a usable concept. The Behaviorist, who has been trained always as an experimentalist, holds, further, that belief in the existence of consciousness goes back to the ancient days of superstition and magic. [Watson, 1930, p. 2]

• • •

> . . . The Behaviorist began his own formulation of the problem of psychology by sweeping aside all medieval conceptions. He dropped from his scientific vocabulary all subjective terms such as sensation, perception, image, desire, purpose, and even thinking, and emotion as they were subjectively defined. [Watson, 1930, p. 5]

The behaviorist program and the issues it spawned all but eliminated any serious research in cognitive psychology for 40 years. The rat supplanted the human as the principal laboratory subject, and psychology turned to finding out what could be learned by studying animal learning and motivation. Quite a bit was discovered, but little was of direct relevance to cognitive psychology.

In retrospect, it is hard to understand how behaviorists could have taken an antimental stand and held out so long with it. Just because introspection proved to be unreliable did not mean that one could not develop a theory of internal structure and process. It only meant that other methodologies were required. In physics, a theory of atomic structure was developed, although that structure could not be directly observed but only inferred. But behaviorists argued that a theory of internal structure was not necessary to an understanding of human behavior, and, in a sense, they may have been right (see Anderson and Bower, 1973, pp. 30–37). However, a theory of internal structure makes understanding human beings much easier. The success of cognitive psychology during the past 25 years in analyzing complex intellectual processes testifies to the utility of such concepts as mental structures and processes.

In both the introspectionist and the behaviorist programs, we see the human mind struggling with the effort to understand itself. The introspectionists held a naive belief in the power of self-observation. The behaviorists were so afraid of falling prey to subjective fallacies that they refused to let themselves think about mental processes. Modern cognitive psychologists seem to be much more at ease with their subject matter. They have a relatively detached attitude toward human cognition and approach it much as they would any other complex system.

The Reemergence of Cognitive Psychology

Three main influences account for the modern development of cognitive psychology. The first was the development of what has been called the information-processing approach, which grew out of human-factors work and information theory. Human factors refers to research on human skills and performance. This field was given a great boost during World War II, when practical information on these topics was badly needed. Information theory is a branch of communication sciences that provides an abstract way of analyzing the processing of knowledge. The work of the British psychologist Donald Broadbent at the Applied Psychology Research Unit in Cambridge was probably most influential in integrating ideas from these two fields and developing the information-processing approach. He developed these ideas most directly with regard to perception and attention, but the analyses now pervade all of cognitive psychology. The characteristics of the information-processing approach are discussed later in this chapter. While other types of analysis in cognitive psychology exist, information-processing is the dominant viewpoint and the main one presented in this book.

Closely related to the development of the information-processing approach were developments in computer science, particularly artificial intelligence, which tries to get computers to behave intelligently. Allen Newell and Herbert Simon (at Carnegie–Mellon University) have spent 25 years educating cognitive psychologists as to the implications of artificial intelligence (and educating workers in artificial intelligence as to the implications of cognitive psychology). The direct influence of computer-based theories on cognitive psychology has always been minimal. However, the indirect influence has been enormous. A host of concepts has been taken from computer science and used in psychological theories. Probably more important, observing how we could analyze the intelligent behavior of a machine has largely liberated us from our inhibitions and misconceptions about analyzing our own intelligence.

The third field of influence on cognitive psychology is linguistics. In the 1950s, Noam Chomsky, a linguist at the Massachusetts Institute of Technology, began to develop a mode of analyzing the structure of language. His work showed that language was much more complex than previously believed and that many of the prevailing behavioristic formulations were incapable of explaining these complexities. Chomsky's linguistic analyses proved critical in enabling cognitive psychologists to fight off the prevailing behavioristic conceptions. George Miller, at Harvard University in the 1950s and early 1960s, was instrumental in bringing these linguistic analyses to the attention of psychologists and in identifying new ways of studying language.

Cognitive psychology has grown rapidly since the 1950s. A very important event was the publication of Ulric Neisser's book *Cognitive Psychology* in 1967. This book gave a new legitimacy to the field. The book consisted of six chapters on perception and attention and four chapters on language, memory, and thought. Note that this chapter division contrasts sharply with that of this book, which has one chapter on perception and twelve on language, memory, and thought. The chapter division in my book reflects the growing emphasis on higher mental processes. Following Neisser's work, another important event was the beginning of the journal *Cognitive Psychology* in 1970. This journal has done much to give definition to the field.

The Methods of Cognitive Psychology

The Need for an Abstract Analysis

How does one go about studying human cognitive functioning? An obvious but naive answer is that one studies the physiological mechanisms that underlie the behavior. For example, in this context, to understand how people do mathematics, why not simply inspect their brains and determine what goes on there when they are solving mathematics problems? Serious technical obstacles must be overcome, however, before the physiological basis of behavior could be studied in this way. But, even assuming that these obstacles could be properly handled, the level of analysis required is simply too detailed to be useful. The brain is composed of more than 10 billion nerve cells. Millions are probably involved in solving a mathematics problem. Suppose we had a listing that explained the role of each cell in solving the problem. Since this listing would have to describe the behavior of millions of individual cells, it would not offer a very satisfactory explanation for how the problem was solved. A neural explanation is too complex and detailed to adequately describe sophisticated human behavior. We need a level of analysis that is more abstract.

Computers offer an interesting analogy to help understand the need for an abstract analysis. Like the brain, a computer consists of millions of components. For any interesting computer task—for example, solving a problem in mathematics such as integration—trying to understand the overall behavior of the machine by studying the behavior of each of its physical components is hopeless. However, high-level programming languages exist for specifying the behavior of the computer. The computer has an *interpreter* for converting each statement in the higher level language into a large number of low-level statements that specify what the physical components of the computer should do. These high-level programming languages can be quite abstract and thus obviate the need to consider many of the physical details of the computer. One can often obtain a good understanding of the behavior of the computer by studying the high-level computer program. A cognitive theory should be like a computer program. That is, it should be a precise specification of the behavior, but offered in terms sufficiently abstract to provide a conceptually tractable framework for understanding the phenomenon.

As an example of an abstract term in a high-level programming language, consider the LISP programming language, used in creating artificial-intelligence programs, in which there is an associative-retrieval function called GET. One can use this function to retrieve concepts related to other concepts. For instance, to retrieve the capital of the United States, one might evoke the function GET, giving it the terms USA and CAPITAL (called arguments). The function will return WASHINGTON (called a value). One need not specify the detailed machine operations that underlie this act. The GET function identifies that portion of the computer's memory that stores information about the United States, searches that portion for the name of the capital, and then returns the answer Washington. This GET function is the sort of concept that would be useful in a cognitive theory. To a large degree, cognitive psychology has been engaged in a search for the right set of higher level concepts with which to describe human intelligence.

What, then, is the relationship between cognitive psychology and physiological psychology? Certainly, cognitive psychologists believe their concepts can be explained in physiological terms, even as computer scientists believe that their programming constructs can be explained in terms of the machine's components. Cognitive psychology is to physiological psychology much as computer science is to electrical engineering. The results from physiological experiments can set constraints on the form of cognitive theories but they do not prescribe these theories. For instance, knowledge about the amount of information the brain can store could serve to rule out certain theories of memory as impossible but would not suggest the correct theory of memory.

The task of the cognitive psychologist is a highly inferential one. The cognitive psychologist must proceed from observations of the behavior of humans performing intellectual tasks to conclusions about the abstract mechanisms underlying the behavior. Developing a theory in cognitive psychology is much like developing a model for the working of the engine of a strange new vehicle by driving the vehicle, being unable to open it up to inspect the engine itself.

Information-Processing Analysis

In this chapter the phrase *information processing* has already been bandied about, and you may well have encountered it elsewhere in psychology. What does it really mean? Again, let us begin to answer the question with an analogy. Suppose we followed a letter in a successful passage through the postal system. First, the letter would be put in a mailbox; the mailbox would be emptied and the contents brought to a central station. The letter would be sorted according to region, and the letters for a particular region shipped off to their destination. There they would be sorted again as to area within the postal district. Letters of the same destination would be given to a carrier, and the carrier would deliver the letter to the correct address.

Now, just as we traced the letter through the postal system, let us follow this question as it is processed through the human mind:

Where does your grandmother live?

First, you must identify each word and retrieve its meaning. Then you must determine the meaning of this configuration of words, that is, understand the question being asked. Next, you must search your memory for the correct answer. Upon finding the answer in memory, you have to formulate a plan for generating the answer in words, and then transform the plan into the actual answer:

She lives in San Francisco.*

---

*The fact that your grandmother probably does not live in San Francisco may not be the only inaccurate part of this example. The serial stages described would be somewhat controversial. This example is meant to illustrate the process of information processing, not specific stages.

What we did in this example was to trace the flow of information through the mind. We use the term *information* to refer to the various mental objects operated on—the question, the representation of its meaning, the memory of where your grandmother lives, the plan for generating an answer, and so on. These objects, while mental and abstract, are analogous to the letter in the postal example. An important aspect of the analogy is that there is a clear *sequence* or *serial ordering* to the mental operations just as there is to the postal operations. The important characteristic of an information-processing analysis, then, is that it involves a tracing of a sequence of mental operations and their products (information) in the performance of a particular cognitive task.

Such analyses are often given in flowchart form. A flowchart is a sequence of boxes where each box reflects a stage of processing. Arrows from one box to another indicate the temporal sequencing (flow) of the stages. Figure 1-1 is a sample flowchart specifying how one should process the information in a chapter in this text. Each chapter begins with a short summary of the information found there. The first box in the figure specifies the process of studying this summary. In box 2, readers ask themselves if they are interested in learning more about these points. If they are not, an arrow goes from the box to the instruction to quit (in many class situations students will not have this option). If interested, they go on. Note the decision boxes (diamonds in this figure), where students must decide between a number of different paths for further processing. The existence of decision boxes indicates that a fixed sequence of steps will not always be taken.

In the third box, students are to make up a set of questions from the summary to keep in mind while reading the chapter. For instance, one of the summary points for this chapter is:

> The study of cognitive psychology is motivated by scientific curiosity, by the desire for practical applications, and by the need to provide a foundation for other fields of social science.

In box 3, students might ask:

> What are the practical applications of cognitive psychology?

In box 4, students are to skim the chapter to identify the major sections. Then to each section, they apply steps 5 through 9. They make up specific questions for the section to be read (box 5)—for example, a question for this section on the information-processing approach might be:

> How do I interpret a flowchart such as Figure 1-1?

Next, students read the section fairly carefully (box 6) and determine whether the section questions can be answered (box 7). If not, students review the section (box 8) until the questions can be answered. If all the section questions can be answered, students go on, making up more questions if more sections remain to be read (box 9).

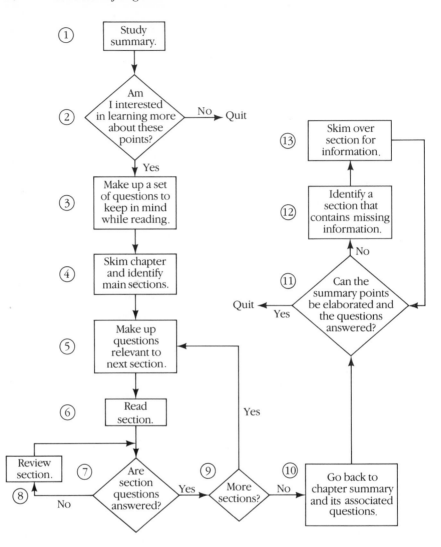

Figure 1-1   *A flowchart of the procedure recommended for studying this text.*

The final portion of the flowchart (boxes 10 through 13) involves an end-of-chapter review. Students check to see whether they can answer the questions written for the chapter (boxes 10 and 11). If they cannot, they go back and skim the sections containing the information relevant to the un-answered questions (boxes 12 and 13). Thus, this flowchart provides at a rather global level (in contrast to specifying how to read each sentence) a prescription for sequencing the processing of information in a chapter.

Actually, this flowchart contains considerable wisdom about how to read this textbook. The important ideas are (1) elaborating the summary into questions to be kept in mind while reading (box 3); (2) dividing the chapter into sections with special questions (boxes 4, 5, and 6); (3) testing one's memory after each section and rereading if one cannot answer the questions relevant to that section (boxes 7 and 8); (4) reviewing the chapter (boxes 10, 11, 12, and 13).

Measurement in Information-Processing Psychology

In the preceding section, we discussed how the information-processing approach analyzes a task. A few words are also required about how behavior is most frequently measured in information-processing psychology. The information-processing approach has strong roots in the practically oriented human-performance research that was developed during World War II. The great concern of this line of research was to develop measures of how *good* performance was in various tasks and to understand what factors prevented performance from being better. The emphasis on performance accounts for the two most popular measures in cognitive psychology—frequency of success on a task and performance speed. The performance orientation of information-processing psychology helps to make this study more directly applicable to issues of improving human cognition. This book relies heavily on experiments that collect measurements of success frequency and performance speed.

It is important to explain how these two dependent measures are interpreted. The frequency of success at a task is often expressed as the percentage of successful attempts out of all attempts. So, rather than saying that a subject got 12 answers correct, we refer to the performance as 75 percent correct (where the total was 16 questions). The arbitrary nature of the measures is thus removed and the numbers made more meaningful.

Some consensus seems to exist in the field as to how differences in percentage measures should be evaluated. For instance, suppose that subjects learned 70 percent of the vocabulary items in a foreign language by one study method and 75 percent by another study method. What should we make of the difference? Specific statistical measures are employed to determine if a difference is reliable—that is, whether the difference is likely to be reproducible. However, some differences, even if they are statistically significant, seem too small to be important. Roughly speaking, a performance difference between two conditions of 5 percent is considered fairly important; a difference greater than 10 percent is quite substantial. I frequently employ this rule of thumb in my grading practices; for example, I try to design examinations so that the difference between two letter grades is at least 10 percent.

With respect to performance speed, many tasks studied in cognitive psychology are completed in times well under a second. Therefore, the measure of this dependent variable is often referred to as *reaction time*. Because reaction times are often shorter than a second, they are frequently measured in milliseconds (msec, thousandths of a second). The 5 percent–10 percent rule seems to apply to reaction times as well as performance differences. Where reaction times differ between two conditions, a difference of 5 percent is considered fairly important; if the difference is greater than 10 percent it is considered to be substantial. Thus, the difference between 500 and 575 msec (75 msec is 15 percent of 500 msec) is usually regarded as quite substantial, whereas the difference between 3000 and 3075 msec (75 msec is 2.5 percent of 3000 msec) is usually considered relatively unimportant.

The Nature of the Theories in the Field

In this book, we will be considering a related set of theories about cognitive functioning. Thus, it is important to understand both what a theory is and what it is not. A theory is not a speculative conjecture; nor is it "the truth." Rather, a theory is a system for understanding various phenomena that have been researched and for making predictions about phenomena that have yet to be researched.

Psychologists perform laboratory experiments and observe natural experiments in the real world. These experiments provide a mass of data about human cognitive functioning. For instance, a psychologist may observe that under a certain condition, people retain 25 percent of what they learn when tested 24 hours after learning by a recall test but 50 percent when tested by a recognition test. Psychologists have accumulated great quantities of such data; one would need many lifetimes just to read about the results of all the experimental activity in psychology. Thus, to make these data accessible, we must have a way of summarizing and systemizing them. Moreover, psychological research, extensive as it is, has only scratched the surface of the experiments possible. Clearly, a way is needed to make predictions about new situations on the basis of past results. This predictive capability is particularly important with respect to the practical applications of cognitive-psychology research. Performing controlled experiments on, say, the effects of two different four-year curricula on foreign-language learning is extremely expensive. Such an experiment would also be somewhat unethical with respect to the students involved as guinea pigs. Rather, what is needed is a theory developed from simple laboratory situations that would allow us to predict the effects of different curricula in the classroom situation.

In common parlance, people who say "I have a theory about this" are usually advancing a speculative proposal. But theory in science is, or should be, based on a careful and systematic consideration of available data, not on mere speculation Still, a scientist is well aware of the difference between theory and truth. Often, competing theories do equally good jobs of accounting for available data—for example, the wave and particle theories of light in physics. Both provide an explanation of light but each assumes a very different conception of light.

Understanding the difference between theory and truth is particularly important in cognitive psychology. The cognitive psychologist proposes theories about what is happening inside a subject's head on the basis of the subject's external behavior. Clearly, there is no way to know for certain whether a cognitive theory describes what is actually going on inside. What is important is that the theory be accurate in predicting a subject's actions under a certain condition. For instance, where two study techniques are being compared, a good theory would predict which technique will result in subjects' learning more items.

A cognitive theory differs from the truth in two ways. First, even if the theory correctly predicts external behavior, we cannot know whether it accurately describes the internal processes. In fact, it is well understood from automata theory (an abstract field of study in computer science) that many different mechanisms can generate the same external behavior. Second, even if a theory correctly accounts for all the available data, the chance always exists that it will fail to predict the outcome of a new experiment and thus will have to be revised. For instance, Newtonian physics seemed a perfectly good theory of the universe until critical experiments were done that indicated that the theory of relativity was more accurate.

Little is known about how theories come to be created. In later chapters, we will discuss some things that are known about creativity and scientific-theory formation. For now, it is sufficient to understand that theories are attempts to account for existing sets of data. Once a theory is created, a scientist will perform new experiments that test predictions of the theory with respect to new situations. To the extent that these predictions are confirmed, the credibility of the theory is increased. When predictions are not confirmed by the experiments, the theory is rejected or at least revised. The older a science is, the less rapidly are its theories rejected and revised. Existing theories stay more or less unchanged for decades. Most new research in an established science serves to extend a theory to new situations or to slightly modify a theory.

The Nature of the Theories in This Book

Introductory textbooks for older sciences present the established theories, The controversial areas of research in these sciences are too advanced to be covered in an introductory text. But cognitive psychology is not an advanced science. Certain subdomains within the field—for example, perception, memory, problem solving, and language—are becoming well understood. Still, the form of a theory that would specify how all the subfields in cognitive psychology interconnect is still very unclear. Later chapters will present some of the theories that have been proposed to explain how these subareas are connected and will note the more controversial assumptions of these theories, but covering all the theoretical alternatives and their differences in detail is beyond the scope of this book.

It seems certain that the shape of the theories favored in this book will change over the years as new data come in, and that these theories will eventually be supplanted by better ones. However, the theories presented here are the best available means for understanding human cognitive functioning and they agree with opposing theories in many of their predictions. It is unlikely that the best theories 100 years from now will be very different in their predictions about cognitive behavior, although they might be quite different in their assumptions about the human mind. This point is important to appreciate: theories in a science tend to differ more radically in their assumptions than in their predictions. For instance, Newtonian physics and relativity theory largely agree in their predictions of external activity in the universe, but differ in their assumptions about the underlying laws of the universe.

A useful analogy can be made between our understanding of cognitive psychology and our understanding of the relationship between exercise and good health. For a long time, physical exercise has been held to be positively related to human health. Over the decades, many different theories about the exact nature of the relationship between exercise and health have been proposed. For example, in the past short, abrupt, strenuous exercises that benefit skeletal muscles were favored, but recently continuous "aerobic" exercises, which benefit the autonomic muscles such as the heart, are claiming attention. In addition, different theories are currently circulating as to whether exercising "until it hurts" is beneficial. While all these theories are based on assumptions about the functioning of the human body, the specific assumptions differ from theory to theory. Nonetheless, the theories have much in common, particularly their basic claim that exercise is healthful. It would be foolish to let the differences among the various theories serve as a justification for not exercising at all. While the theories might disagree about the relative merits of various exercise programs, they would all agree that almost any program is much better than nothing.

A text on the effects of exercise on the human body has a responsibility to present the common core of knowledge on which most theories agree. But to give a complete picture, a text must also take a stand on issues about which no consensus exists. A responsible text will acknowledge points of controversy and, as fully as possible within the constraints of brevity and nontechnicality, explain the issues underlying the controversies.

In the present text, I have tried to present cognitive-psychology theory in the same way I would like to see theory about the human body presented. I will try to indicate the kind of data on which a theory rests. Above all, I have emphasized a theory's implications for better cognitive functioning wherever relevant. However, the reader is urged to remember at all times that the material presented is scientific *theory* and that it lies somewhere between absolute truth and speculation with respect to its reliability. Trying to apply the principles of a theory to one's life makes sense, but where a theory does not seem to explain a particular phenomenon, one should suspect the theory, not the phenomenon. Persistence in applying principles that are not working does not make sense.

How to Use This Book

We turn now to the substance of Figure 1-1 as a guide to study rather than as an example of information processing. Obviously, you will be the final judge on how best to study this book. But I recommend that you seriously consider following the scheme outlined in the figure. The chapter summaries are extremely important in this approach. Students have a natural tendency to skip over summaries and get to the "meat" of a text right away. However, research in our laboratory (Reder and Anderson, in press) suggests that memory for a text is facilitated by initial study of a summary. The summaries are written in a deliberately terse style. Each point is central to the material, and each one is numbered. Take time to consider each point in the summary fully before starting the chapter text.

The summaries represent the most important points covered in the text. If you do not acquire and retain the information in the summary, there has been a serious failure of learning. Of course, I would hope you would learn more than this from the chapters. However, what more you should learn should depend, in part, on your purposes.

The summaries serve three functions. First, they reflect the overall structure in each chapter. If you have learned a summary, you will know how the more specific points in the chapter relate to one another. Second, they serve to identify and define the most important new concepts and principles. The first stages of Figure 1-1 are intended to enable you to fix in memory these summary points and to prepare yourself for how the text will relate to the summary. Third, the summaries provide criteria against which you can test your learning of the material. The last stages (11, 12, and 13) of Figure 1-1 are concerned with this function.

To use these summaries to the greatest advantage, you are advised to make up a set of questions, based on the summaries, to keep in mind as you read the text. When you finish a chapter, you should be able to answer these questions and be capable of elaborating each sentence of the summary with at least three or four sentences of additional detail. This question-generation process will encouarge you to think deeply about the text and to be aware of your goals in reading the text. Another function of the process is to introduce some spacing into your study of the text. You are encouraged first to study the main points, then to skim the chapter, next to carefully read each section and to review that section, and finally to review the chapter. This pattern will allow you to review major points throughout your study of the chapter. In Chapters 7 and 13, where reading is covered in detail, the importance of question making and spaced study will be discussed more fully.

Remarks and Suggested Readings

Boring's (1950) book is a classic review of the early history of psychology. A broad and up-to-date survey of current theory and research in cognitive psychology is the six-volume *Handbook of Learning and Cognitive Processes,* edited by Estes (1975–1979). This work is designed for a knowledgeable scientist not particularly familiar with cognitive psychology. A recent volume, *Cognition and Instruction,* edited by Klahr (1976), presents a sampling of research reflecting the growing concern with educational applications of cognitive psychology. Most effort in this regard has gone into problems of reading. *The Psychology of Reading,* a text by Gibson and Levin (1975), surveys this research.

A fairly readable cognitive theory is contained in *Explorations in Cognition,* by Norman and Rumelhart (1975). This book includes discussions of computer modeling and of a computer model of cognition developed at San Diego. Other recent theoretical monographs are Anderson (1976); Anderson and Bower (1973); Kintsch (1974); Miller and Johnson-Laird (1976); and Newell and Simon (1972).

Chapter 2

Perception and Attention

Summary

1. When information first enters the human system, it is registered in *sensory memories*. These sensory memories include an *iconic memory* for visual information and an *echoic memory* for auditory information. Sensory memories can store a great deal of information but only for brief periods of time.

2. Attention is a very limited mental resource that can only be allocated, at most, to a few cognitive processes at a time. The more frequently that processes have been practiced, the less attention they require; eventually they can be performed without interfering with other cognitive processes. Processes that are highly practiced and require little or no attention are referred to as *automatic*. Processes that require attention are called *deliberate*.

3. Two types of models have been proposed for describing how perceptual patterns are recognized. One involves *template matching,* in which a whole pattern is matched at once. The other involves *feature analysis,* in which components of the pattern are first recognized and then combined. The chapter will explain why feature analysis is a better psychological theory.

4. Pattern recognition can involve both automatic and deliberate processes (see point 2). The chapter will discuss how attention facilitates the nonautomatic, deliberate processes.

5. Pattern recognition involves an integration of *bottom-up processing* and *top-down processing*. Bottom-up processing refers to the use of sensory information in pattern recognition. Top-down processing refers to the use of the context of the pattern as well as general world knowledge in recognition.

6. A set of *Gestalt principles of organization* serves to impose an organization on stimuli. Organization based on these principles is not dependent on prior knowledge.

For most people, seeing and hearing are as effortless as breathing. We take for granted our ability to recognize objects and people, read words, and understand utterances almost instantaneously. However, an enormous amount of information processing underlies these feats. As Glass, Holyoak, and Santa (1979) argue, it becomes apparent that perceptual information processing is nontrivial when we consider people who cannot successfully process perceptual information. One case described in the literature concerns a soldier who suffered brain damage due to accidental carbon monoxide poisoning. He could recognize objects through their feel, smell, or sound, but was unable to discriminate a circle from a square or recognize faces or letters (Benson and Greenberg, 1969). One the other hand, he was able to discriminate light intensities and colors and tell in what direction an object was moving. Thus, his system was able to register visual information, but somehow his brain damage resulted in a loss of the ability to combine visual information into perceptual experience. This case shows that perception is much more than simply the registering of sensory information. In this chapter, we will review what is known about the ways sensory information is processed and patterns are recognized as well as the role of attention in guiding these information-processing activities.

Thus, this chapter is concerned with how information is initially structured as it comes into the human system. Subsequent chapters will be concerned with how information is processed after its initial analysis by the perceptual system; that is, they will be concerned with the processing of knowledge by higher level systems such as those of memory, reasoning, problem solving, and language.

Sensory Memory

Visual Sensory Memory

Many studies of visual-information processing have involved determining what a subject can extract from a brief visual presentation. A typical trial in such an experiment begins with the subject focusing on a dot in a blank white

X	M	R	J
C	N	K	P
V	F	L	B

Figure 2-1 *An example of the kind of display used in a visual-report experiment. Subjects are presented briefly with this display and are asked to report the letters it contains.*

field. By having the subject so fixate, the experimenter can control where the subject is focusing during stimulus presentation. The stimulus, perhaps a set of letters, is visually projected where the subject is looking. After a brief exposure (for example, 50 msec), the stimulus is removed.

A number of studies have been concerned with the capacity of the memory that first registers this sensory information. In such experiments, displays of letters such as that in Figure 2-1 are presented briefly and subjects are then asked to report as many items as they can recall from such displays. Usually, subjects are able to report three, four, five, or at most six items. Many subjects report that they saw more items but that the items faded away before they could be reported.

An important methodological variation on this task was performed by Sperling in 1960. He presented an array consisting of three rows of four letters, as shown in Figure 2-1. Immediately after this stimulus was turned off, the subject was cued to report just one row of the display. The cues were in the form of differential tones (high tone for top row, medium for middle, and low for bottom). Sperling's method was called the *partial-report procedure* in contrast with the *whole-report procedure,* which was used until then.

By using the number of letters that the subject was able to report from a particular row, Sperling was able to estimate the number of letters the subject had available the instant the display was turned off. Subjects were able to recall a little over three items from a row of four. Because subjects did not know beforehand which row would be cued, they had to have more than three items available from each of the three rows. The total number of items available, then, would be three rows times more than three items per row, which is more than nine items. This result contrasts sharply with the four or five items subjects typically recall in the whole-report procedure. So, subjects were correct in their claims that they could see more items than they could report before the items faded from the image of the display. Indeed, they probably could see all twelve letters. Sperling's estimate was less than twelve, however, probably due to subjects' failures to use the partial-report procedure perfectly.

In the procedure just described, the tone cue was presented immediately after offset of the display. Sperling also varied the length of the delay between the offset of the display and the tone. The results he obtained in terms of number of letters available out of twelve are presented in Figure 2-2. (Recall

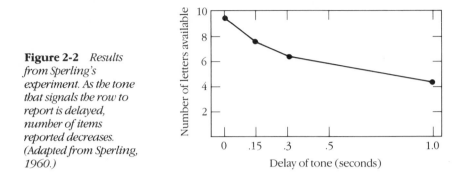

Figure 2-2 *Results from Sperling's experiment. As the tone that signals the row to report is delayed, number of items reported decreases. (Adapted from Sperling, 1960.)*

our estimate that the number of letters available is three times the number reported from a row.) As the delay increases to 1 second, subjects' performance decays back to the original whole-report level of four or five items. Thus, it appears that the memory for the actual display decays very rapidly and is essentially gone by the end of 1 second. All that is left after a second is what the subject has had time to more permanently encode.

Sperling's experiments indicate the existence of a brief *visual sensory store*—a memory that can effectively hold all the information in the visual display. While information is being held in this store, it can be processed by higher level mental routines such as those involved in making a report of the display's content. This sensory store appears to be particularly visual in character. In one experiment showing the visual character of sensory store, Sperling (1967) varied the postexposure field (the visual field after the display). He found that when the postexposure field was light the sensory information remained for only a second, but when the field was dark it remained for a full 5 seconds. Thus, a bright postexposure field tends to "wash out" memory for the display. Further, following the display with another display of characters effectively "overwrites" the first display and so destroys the memory for the letters. The brief visual memory revealed in these experiments is called an *icon* by Neisser (1967). Without such a visual icon, perception would be much more difficult. Many stimuli are of very brief duration. In order to recognize them, the system needs some means of holding onto them for a short while until they can be analyzed.

The brevity of the sensory register contrasts sharply with the duration of some of the higher level memories that we will discuss in later chapters. For instance, in Chapter 6 we will discuss *short-term memory,* which can, under some circumstances, hold information such as telephone numbers almost indefinitely. In the Sperling experiment, information is being recoded from the sensory memory into some more permanent form—such as this short-term memory. Presumably, subjects are able to report four or five letters even minutes after the display has disappeared because the visual information has been recoded. Subjects recode as many letters as they can into a more permanent form before the display disappears from the sensory register and are then able to retain the recoded items for relatively long periods.

Auditory Sensory Memory

Evidence for an auditory sensory memory similar to the visual memory comes from experiments by Moray, Bates, and Barnett (1965) and by Darwin, Turvey, and Crowder (1972). The setup of the Darwin, Turvey, and Crowder study is illustrated in Figure 2-3. The subject listened to a recording over stereo headphones, hearing three lists of three items read simultaneously. Because of stereophonic mixing, one list seemed to come from the left side of the subject's head, one from the middle, and one from the right side. The investigators compared results derived from a whole-report procedure, in which subjects were instructed to report all nine items, with a partial-report procedure, in which they were cued visually after the presentation of the lists as to whether they should report the items coming from the left, middle, or right locations.

A greater percentage of the letters were reported in the partial-report procedure than in the whole-report procedure. Thus, as with iconic memory, it appears that more information is immediately available in auditory memory than can be reported. Neisser has called this auditory memory the *echoic memory*. It is clear that we need such a memory to process many aspects of speech information. Neisser (1967, p. 201) gives the example of a foreign-

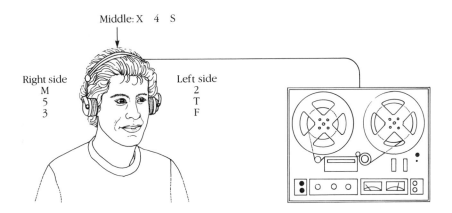

Figure 2-3 *The experimental situation in the Darwin, Turvey, and Crowder experiment. By stereophonic mixings, lists of digits are simultaneously presented to the left, middle, and right of the subject's head. (From Loftus and Loftus, 1976.)*

er who is told, "No, not zeal, seal." Foreigners would not be able to benefit from this advice if they could not retain the "z" long enough to compare it with the "s."

Attention and Sensory-Information Processing

A Model of Attention

The types of studies described above on sensory memory show that a large amount of information gets into sensory memory, but that it is quickly lost if not attended to. Thus, attention plays in important role in selecting sensory information for further processing. As Chapter 8 will show, attention is similarly involved at higher levels of cognition. However, introducing the concept of attention at this point is essential to an understanding of such phenomena as the report studies just described.

A great many theories of attention have been developed in cognitive psychology. In this section, we describe a recent kind of theory that has been quite successful in accounting for a wide range of attentional phenomena (Kahnerman, 1973; LaBerge and Samuels, 1974; Norman and Bobrow, 1975; Posner and Snyder, 1975; Shiffrin and Schneider, 1977; Schneider and Shiffrin, 1977). Attention is conceived of as being a very limited mental resource. Numerous metaphors can help one think about the limited-resource characteristic of attention. One is energy—imagine an energy limitation, as if attention were powered by a fixed electrical current. Given the fixed energy supply, attention would only be allocable to so many tasks. (If allocated to more, the performance would degrade or a fuse would blow.) A second metaphor is spatial: think of attention as a workspace in which only so many tasks can be performed. A third metaphor is animate: think of attention as a small set of agents, often called *demons,* which can perform tasks, but only one at a time; thus, attention cannot be assigned to more tasks than there are demons.

Attention is sometimes thought of as being single-minded. In terms of the metaphors cited above, this single-mindedness would mean that only enough energy, only enough workspace, or only a single attention demon was available for one task or process. Evidence for this single-minded character of attention is the fact that performing two attention-demanding tasks at once is difficult. For instance, it is difficult if not impossible to simultaneously do two addition problems, or to hold two conversations, or to hold a conversation and do an addition problem. However, rather than thinking of attention as single-minded, it is probably more accurate to think of it as not having the capacity to perform two *demanding* tasks simultaneously. Tasks that are practiced to the point at which they do not make excessive demands can be

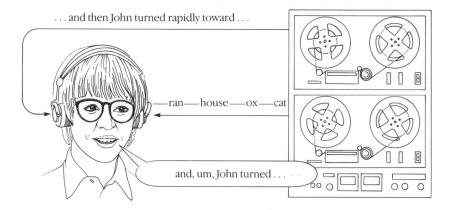

Figure 2-4   *A typical shadowing task. Messages are presented to the left and right ears and the subject attempts to shadow one ear. (From Lindsay and Norman, 1977.)*

performed simultaneously. For instance, we can walk and talk at the same time. Perhaps the reason we cannot simultaneously do mental addition and carry on a conversation is that each activity in itself involves multiple attention-demanding subcomponents. For instance, addition may involve reading, retrieving addition facts from memory, and writing—all three activities that make separate demands on attention. In any case, it is clear that whether or not attention is truly single-minded, its capacity is severely limited.

The limited capacity of attention is the root cause of the reporting limitations demonstrated in visual and auditory reporting tasks. All the information gets into sensory memory, but to be retained each unit of information must be attended to and transformed into some more permanent form. Given that attention has a limited capacity, all the elements in sensory memory cannot be attended to before they are lost. If subjects are immediately cued to report only a subset, they can attend to these items before they fade from memory. However, if the cue is delayed until the items have faded from memory, subjects will only be able to report those elements of the subset they were able to attend to and transform into a more permanent form.

Divided-Attention Studies

Considerable research has been done on how subjects select what sensory input they attend to. Most of this research has involved a dichotic listening task. In a typical dichotic listening experiment, illustrated in Figure 2-4, subjects wear a set of headphones. Subjects hear two messages, one entering each ear, and are asked to "shadow" one of the two messages (that is, report the words from one message as they hear them). Most subjects have remarkably little trouble in doing this. They tune out one message and attend to the other.

Figure 2-5   *An illustration of the shadowing task in the Gray and Wedderburn experiment. The subject follows the meaningful message as it moves from ear to ear. (Adapted from Klatzky,* Human Memory, *1st ed., W. H. Freeman and Company, copyright © 1975.)*

Psychologists have discovered that very little about the unattended message is processed in a shadowing task (e.g., Cherry, 1953; Moray, 1959). Subjects can tell if the unattended message was a human voice or a noise, if human whether male or female, and whether the sex of the speaker changed. However, this information is about all they can report. They cannot tell what language was spoken or report any of the words spoken, even if the same word was repeated over and over again. An analogy is often made between performing this task and being at a cocktail party, where one tunes into one message (a conversation) and filters out others.

One might think that the subject simply "turns one ear off," but a number of experiments have shown that this is not always the case. A couple of undergraduates at Oxford, Gray and Wedderburn (1960), demonstrated that subjects

Figure 2-6 *An illustration of the Triesman experiment. The meaningful message moves to the other ear, and the subject sometimes continues to shadow it against instructions. (Adapted from Klatzky,* Human Memory, *1st ed., W. H. Freeman and Company, copyright © 1975.)*

were quite successful in following a message that jumped back and forth between ears. Figure 2-5 illustrates the subject's task in their experiment. Suppose that part of the meaningful message that subjects were to shadow was "dogs scratch fleas." The message to one ear might be "dogs six fleas," while the message to the other might be "eight scratch two." Instructed to shadow the meaningful message, subjects will report "dogs scratch fleas." Thus, subjects are capable of shadowing a message on the basis of meaning rather than physical ear.

Triesman (1960) looked at a situation in which subjects were instructed to shadow a particular ear. The result is illustrated in Figure 2-6. The message in the to-be-shadowed ear was meaningful until a certain point, at which it turned into a random sequence of words. Simultaneously, the meaningful message switched to the other ear—the one to which the subject had not been attending. Some subjects switched ears, against instructions, and continued to follow the meaningful message. Thus, it seems that messages from both ears get into sensory memory, and that subjects choose certain features for selecting what to attend to in sensory memory. If subjects use meaning as the criterion (either according to or in contradiction to instructions), they will switch ears to follow the message. If subjects use ear of origin in deciding what to attend to, they will shadow the proper ear. The conclusion is that a lot of information gets into sensory memory, but that only a small portion of it is attended to and only that portion is later remembered.

Automaticity

Recall that the capacity of attention for separate tasks is limited and must be divided up among competing processes. The amount of attention required by a process depends on how practiced that process is. The more a process has been practiced the less attention it requires, and there is speculation that highly practiced processes require no attention at all. Such highly practiced processes that require little attention are referred to as *automatic*. While it is probably more correct to think of automaticity as a matter of degree rather than as a well-defined category it is useful to classify cognitive processes into two distinct types—*automatic processes,* which do not require attention, and *deliberate processes,* which do (LaBerge and Samuels, 1974, and Shiffrin and Schneider, 1977). Automatic processes complete themselves without subject control. In the visual and auditory report tasks reviewed earlier, the registering of the stimuli in sensory memory is an automatic process. Many aspects of driving a car and comprehending language appear to be automatic. Deliberate processing seems to require conscious control. In the report studies, reporting a row of items in the visual task or a spatial location in the auditory task is a deliberate process. Many higher cognitive processes, such as performing mental arithmetic, are deliberate.

This theory of attention attributes the loss of information in the whole-report procedure to attentional limitations on reporting the contents of sensory memory. Schneider and Shiffrin (1977) and Shiffrin and Schneider (1977) have been engaged in an extensive investigation of the ways in which subjects scan visual arrays and the role of automaticity in this activity. Figure 2-7 illustrates the Schneider and Shiffrin paradigm. Subjects are given a target letter or number and are instructed to scan a series of visual displays for the target. The displays consist of 20 different frames flashed on a screen; subjects are to report if the target occurred in one of these frames. Two factors are varied. First, each frame has one, two, or four characters on it. This factor is referred to as frame size. The other important variable is the relationship between the target item and the items on the frames. In the *same-category condition,* the target is a letter, as were all items on the frames. In the

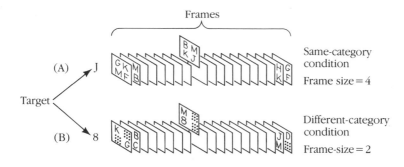

Figure 2-7 *Two examples of positive trials in the Schneider and Shiffrin experiment. (A) The same-category condition, in which the target is a letter, J, as are the distractors. (B) The different-category condition, in which the target is a digit, 8, and the distractors are letters. (Adapted from Schneider and Shiffrin, 1977. Copyright © 1977 by the American Psychological Association. Reprinted by permission.)*

different-category condition, the target is always a number and all nontargets on the frames are letters. Thus, in the different-category condition, either one number appears on 1 of the 20 frames, in which case it is the target and the subject is to respond *yes,* or no number occurs on any of the frames, in which case the subject is to respond *no.*

As reported in Schneider and Shiffrin (1977) performance was strikingly different between the different- and the same-category conditions. In the different-category conditions subjects required an exposure of only 80 msec per frame to achieve 95 percent accuracy, but in the same-category condition they needed 400 msec per frame to achieve the same degree of accuracy. In the different-category condition, the number of items per frame had little effect on performance. But in the same-category condition, subjects' performance deteriorated dramatically as the number of items per frame increased.

Schneider and Shiffrin argue that before coming into the laboratory, subjects were so well practiced at detecting a number among letters that this process was automatic. In contrast, when subjects had to identify a letter among letters, deliberate processing was needed. In this situation, subjects had to attend separately to each letter in each frame and compare it with the target. All these steps took time, and thus, subjects were able to inspect each frame properly and achieve respectable levels of performance only when the slides were presented slowly. Also, the more letters were in a frame, the more slowly the frames had to be presented, since subjects had to check each letter in the frame separately. In contrast, subjects could check all items simultaneously in the different-category situation to see if any were numbers. They were able to perform this processing simultaneously because the detection process was automatic.

Schneider and Shiffrin's results in the same-category condition are similar to Sperling's study reviewed earlier. Just as Sperling found limitations on ability to report, so Schneider and Shiffrin found limitations on ability to detect letters among other letters. However, when the task was a letter-number discrimination, subjects were able to revert to an automatic process that was not limited as to capacity.

Shiffrin and Schneider (1977) ran another experiment similar to the one described above but in which the target always came from one set of letters (B, C, D, F, G, H, J, K, L) and the distractors always came from another set (Q, R, S, T, V, W, X, Y, Z). After 2,100 trials, subjects were at the same levels of performance as in the different-category condition of the previous experiment. Thus, subjects need 2,100 trials of practice before discriminating between two different sets of letters had become as automatic as discriminating numbers from letters. This result demonstrates that processes can become automatic with enough practice. When they do, devoting attention to them is no longer necessary and performance is no longer affected by the number of processes being performed simultaneously.

Pattern Recognition

Thus far, we have considered how sensory information is first recorded and selected for processing by attentional mechanisms. We are now in a position to answer the critical question for a theory of perception: How is this information recognized for what it is? To a large extent, we will focus on a more specific, deceptively simple question: How do we recognize a presentation of the letter *A* as an instance of the pattern *A*?

Template-Matching Models

Perhaps the most obvious way to recognize a pattern is by means of template matching. Grasping this concept requires a little understanding of the flow of information through the visual system, given schematically in Figure 2-8. Light reflects off an object and enters the eye through the lens. When we look at the object, the lens will so focus that a sharp representation of the object falls, upside-down, on the back of the eye, called the retina. The retina is covered with light-sensitive cells. Through a series of neural transformations, the information received on the retina is registered and transmitted via the optic nerve to the brain.

The template-matching theory of perception assumes that this retinal image is faithfully encoded at the brain and that an attempt is made to compare it directly to various stored patterns. These patterns are called *templates*. The basic idea is that the perceptual system tries to compare the letter to templates it has for each letter and reports the template that gives the best match. Figure

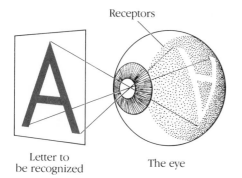

Receptors

Letter to
be recognized

The eye

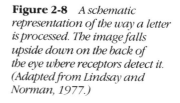

Figure 2-8 *A schematic representation of the way a letter is processed. The image falls upside down on the back of the eye where receptors detect it. (Adapted from Lindsay and Norman, 1977.)*

2-9 illustrates various attempts to make template matching work. In each case, an attempt is made to achieve a correspondence between the retinal cells stimulated by the *A* and the retinal cells specified for a template pattern. The first diagram in the figure (A) shows a case in which a correspondence is achieved and an *A* is recognized. The second diagram (B) shows that no correspondence is reached between the input of an *L* and the template pattern for an *A*. But *L* is matched in the third diagram (C) by the *L* template. However, things can go wrong very easily with a template. The fourth diagram (D) shows a mismatch that occurs when the image falls on the wrong part of the retina, and diagram E shows the problem when the image is a wrong size. Diagram F shows what happens when the image is in a wrong orientation, and diagrams G and H show the difficulty when the images are nonstandard *A*s. There is no known way to correct templates for all these problems.

A common example of template matching involves the account numbers printed on checks, which are read by check-sorting machines used by bank computers. Figure 2-10 shows my check blank (actually from a former account). The account number is the bottom line. A great deal of effort has gone into making the characters in this number maximally discernible. To assure standardization of size and position, they must be printed by machine; a check-sorter would not recognize hand-printed numbers. The very fact that a standardized system is needed for template matching to work reduces the credibility of this process as a model for human pattern recognition. In humans, pattern recognition is very flexible; we can recognize LARGE characters and small characters; characters in the wrong place; in strange orientations; in unusual SHaPes; blurred or broken characters, and even, with some effort, upside-down characters.

Feature Analysis

Partly because of the difficulties posed by template matching, psychologists have proposed that pattern recognition occurs through feature analysis. In this model, stimuli are thought of as combinations of elemental features. The

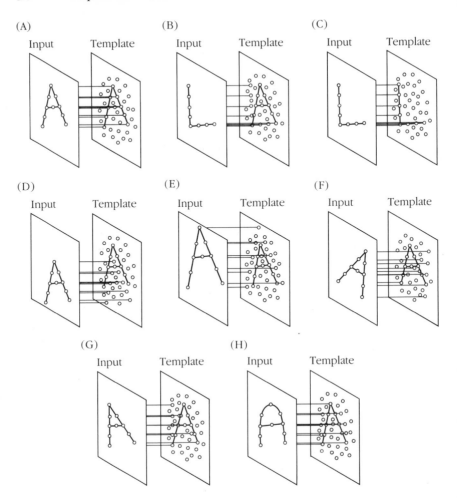

Figure 2-9 *Examples of template-matching attempts. A through C show successful template-matching attempts. D through H show failed attempts. (Adapted from Neisser, 1967.)*

features for the alphabet might consist of horizontal lines, vertical lines, lines at approximately 45-degree angles, and curves. Thus, the capital letter *A* can be seen as consisting of two lines at 45-degree angles (∧) and a horizontal line (–). The pattern for the letter *A* consists of these lines plus a specification as to how they should be combined.

The reader might wonder how feature analysis represents an advance beyond the template model. After all, what are the features but minitemplates? However, the feature model has a number of advantages over the template

Figure 2-10   *A typical blank check, with specially designed account numbers to permit successful template matching.*

model. First, since the features are simpler, it is easier to see how the system might try to correct for the kinds of difficulties caused by template models. Indeed, there is physiological evidence that the nervous system extracts such features as horizontal lines, and we have some idea about how the system does this (Hubel and Weisel, 1962; Lettvin, Maturana, McCulloch and Pitts, 1959). A second advantage of the feature-combination scheme is that it is possible to specify those relationships among the features that are most critical to the pattern. Thus, for *A*, the critical point is that the two approximately 45-degree lines intersect (or almost intersect) at the top and that the cross bar intersects both of these. Many other details are unimportant. Thus, all the following patterns are *As:* A, ⊿, 4, A, A. A final advantage is that use of features rather than larger patterns will reduce the number of templates needed. In the feature model, one would not need a template for each possible pattern but only for each feature. Since the same features tend to occur in many patterns, this would mean a considerable savings.

There is a fair amount of behavioral evidence for the existence of features as components in pattern recognition. For instance, where letters have many features in common—as with *C* and *G*—evidence suggests that subjects are particularly prone to confuse them (Kinney, Marsetta, and Showman, 1966). When such letters are presented for very brief intervals, subjects often misclassify one stimulus as the other. So, for instance, subjects in the Kinney, Marsetta, and Showman experiment made 29 errors when presented with the letter *G*. Of these errors, 21 involved misclassification as *C*, 6 misclassification as *O*, 1 misclassification as *B*, and 1 misclassification as *9*. No other errors occurred. It is clear that subjects were choosing items with similar feature sets as their responses. Such a response pattern is what we would expect using a feature-analysis model. If subjects could extract only some of the features in the brief presentation, they would not be able to decide among stimuli that shared these features.

Another kind of experiment that yields evidence in favor of features involves stabilized images. The eye has a very slight tremor, called *physiological nystagmus,* which occurs at the rate of 30 to 70 cycles per second. Also, the eye slowly drifts over an object. Consequently, the retinal image of an object on which a person tries to fixate is not perfectly constant; its position changes slightly over time. There is evidence that this retinal movement is critical for perception. When techniques are used to keep an image on the exact same position of the retina regardless of eye movement, the perception of the object disappears. It seems that if the exact same retinal and nervous pathways are constantly used they become fatigued and stop responding.

The most interesting aspect of this phenomenon is the way the stabilized object disappears. It does not simply fade away or disappear all at once. Rather, different portions drop out over time. Figure 2-11 illustrates the fate of one of the stimuli in an experiment by Pritchard (1961). The left-hand item was the image presented; the four others are various fragments that were reported. Two points are important to note. First, whole features such as "vertical bar" seemed to be lost. This finding suggests that features are important units in perception. Second, the stimuli that remained tended to constitute complete letter or number patterns. This result indicates that these features are combined together to define the recognized patterns. Thus, even though our perceptual system may extract features, what we perceive are patterns composed from these features. The feature-extraction and feature-combination processes underlying pattern recognition are not available to conscious awareness; what we are aware of are the patterns.

Speech Recognition

Up to this point, we have considered only recognition of written characters. Recognition of a spoken message poses some new problems. One major problem is segmentation. Speech is not broken up into discrete units the way printed text is. Well-defined gaps seem to exist between words in speech, but often this is an illusion. If we examine the actual physical speech signal, we often find undiminished sound energy at word boundaries. Indeed, a cessation of speech energy is as likely to occur within a word as between words. This property of speech becomes clear when we listen to a foreign language that we do not know. The speech appears to be a continuous stream of sounds with no obvious word boundaries. It is our familiarity with our own language that leads to the illusion of word boundaries.

Even within a single word segmentation problems exist. These intraword problems involve the identification of *phonemes.* Phonemes are the basic vocabulary of speech sounds; it is in terms of them that we recognize words. A phoneme is defined as the minimal unit of speech that can result in a difference in the spoken message. To illustrate, consider the word *bat*. This word is analyzed into three phonemes: [b], [a], and [t]. Replacing [b] by the phoneme [p], we get *pat;* replacing [a] by [i], we get *bit;* replacing [t] by [n], we get *ban*. Obviously, a one-to-one correspondence does not always exist between letters and phonemes. For example, the word *one* consists of the phonemes [w], [ə], and [n]; *school* consists of the phonemes [s], [k], [ú], and [l]; and *night* consists of [n], [ī], and t. It is the lack of perfect letter-to-sound correspondence that makes English spelling so difficult.

A segmentation problem arises when the phonemes composing a spoken word are to be identified. The difficulty is that speech is continuous and phonemes are not discrete the way letters are on a printed page. Segmentation at this level is like recognizing a written (not printed) message, where one letter runs into another. Also, as in the case of writing, different speakers vary in the way they produce the same phonemes. The variation among speakers is dramatically clear, for instance, when one first tries to understand a speaker with a strong and unfamiliar dialect—for instance, an American listener trying to understand an Australian speaker. However, examination of the speech signal will reveal that even among speakers with the same accent considerable variation exists. For instance, women and children normally have a much higher pitch than men.

It is fair to say that we do not yet understand how the human speech-perception system deals with problems of phoneme segmentation or phoneme identification. Attempts have been made in artificial intelligence to build speech-recognition systems that can take a spoken message and put out a printed version (e.g., Reddy, 1975; Reddy and Newell, 1974). Some progress has been made in this direction, and perhaps in ten more years we will have systems whose perception approaches human quality. When that happens, we might also gain a better understanding of how speech perception is accomplished in humans.

Table 2-1   The Classification of [b], [p], [d], and [t] According to Voicing and Place of Articulation

	Voicing	
Place of Articulation	Voiced	Voiceless
Bilabial	[b]	[p]
Alveolar	[d]	[t]

However, even now some things are clear about speech perception. Feature-analysis and feature-combination processes seem to underlie speech perception much as they do visual recognition. As with individual letters, individual phonemes can be analyzed as consisting of a number of features. It turns out that these features refer to aspects of how the phoneme is generated. Among the features for phonemes are the consonantal feature, voicing, and the place of articulation (Chomsky and Halle, 1968). *Consonantal* is the quality in the phoneme of having a consonantlike property (in contrast to vowels). *Voicing* is the sound of a phoneme produced by the vibration of the vocal cords. For example, compare the ways you produce *sip* and *zip*. The [s] in *sip* is voiceless but the [z] in *zip* is voiced. You can detect this difference by placing your fingers on your larynx as you generate these sounds. The larynx will vibrate for a voiced consonant.

Place of articulation refers to the place at which the vocal track is closed or constricted in the production of a phoneme. (It is closed at some point in the utterance of most consonants.) For instance [p], [m], and [w] are considered *bilabial* because the lips are closed during their generation. The phonemes [f] and [v] are considered *labiodental* because the bottom lip is pressed against the front teeth. Two different phonemes are represented by [th]—one in *thy* and the other in *thigh*. Both are *dental* because the tongue presses against the teeth. The phonemes [t], [d], [s], [z], [n], [l], and [r] are all *alveolar* because the tongue presses against the alveolar ridge of the gums just behind the upper front teeth. The phonemes [sh], [ch], [j], and [y] are all *palatal* because the tongue presses against the roof of the mouth just behind the alveolar ridge. The phonemes [k] and [g] are *velar* because the tongue presses against the soft palate, or velum, in the rear roof of the mouth.

Consider the phonemes [p], [b], [t], and [d]. All four share the feature of being consonants. However, the four can be distinguished according to voicing and place of articulation. Table 2-1 classifies these four consonants according to these two features.

Considerable evidence exists for the role of such features in speech perception. For instance, in 1955, Miller and Nicely had subjects try to recognize consonants such as [b], [d], [p], and [t] when presented in noise. Subjects

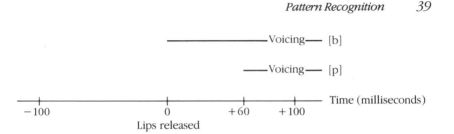

Figure 2-12   *The difference between [b] and [p], the delay between the release of the lips and voicing in the case of [p]. (From* Psychology and Language *by Herbert H. Clark and Eve V. Clark.* © *1977 by Harcourt Brace Jovanovich, Inc. Reproduced by permission of the publisher.)*

exhibited confusion, thinking they had heard one sound in the noise when actually another sound had been presented. Miller and Nicely were interested in what sounds subjects would confuse with what. It seemed likely that subjects would most often confuse consonants that were distinguished by just a single feature, and this prediction was confirmed. To illustrate, when presented with [p], subjects more often thought that they heard [t] than that they heard [d]. The phoneme [t] differs from [p] only in terms of place of articulation, while [d] differs in both place of articulation and voicing. Similarly, subjects presented with [b] more often thought they heard [p] than [t].

This experiment is an earlier demonstration of the kind of logic we saw in the Kinney, Marsetta, and Showman study on letter recognition. When the subject can only identify a subset of the features underlying a pattern (in this case the pattern is a phoneme), the subject's responses will reflect confusion among the phonemes sharing the same subset of features.

Voice-Onset Time

The features of phonemes refer to properties by which they are articulated. What are the properties of the acoustic stimulus that encode these articulatory features? This issue has been particularly well researched in the case of voicing. In the pronunciation of such consonants as [b] and [p], two things happen: the closed lips are opened, releasing air, and the vocal cords begin vibrating (voicing). In the case of the voiced consonant [b], the release and the vibration of the vocal cords are nearly simultaneous. In the case of the unvoiced consonant [d], the release occurs 60 msec before the vibration begins. What we are detecting when we perceive a voiced versus an unvoiced consonant is the presence or absence of a 60-msec interval between release and voicing. This period of time is referred to as *voice-onset time*. The difference between [p] and [b] is illustrated in Figure 2-12. Similar differences exist in other such voiced-unvoiced pairs, such as [d] and [t]. Again, the factor controlling the perception of a phoneme is the delay between the release of closure and vibration of the vocal cords.

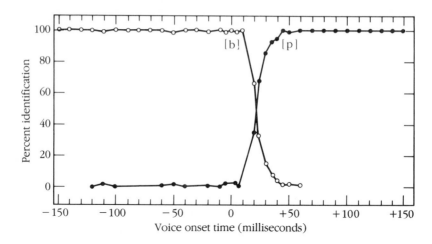

Figure 2-13   *Percentage identification of [b] versus [p] as a function of voice-onset time. A sharp shift in these identification functions occurs at about 25 msec. (From* Lisker and Abramson, 1970.)

Lisker and Abramson (1970) performed experiments with artificial (computer-generated) stimuli in which the delay between release of closure and voicing was varied from −150 msec (voicing 150 msec before release) to +150 msec (voicing 150 msec after release). The task was to identify which sounds were [b]s and which were [p]s. Figure 2-13 plots the percentage of [b] identifications and [p] identifications. Throughout most of the continuum, subjects agreed 100 percent on what they heard, but there is a sharp switch from [b] to [p] at about 25 msec. At a 10 msec voice onset, subjects are in nearly unanimous agreement that the sound is a [b]; at 40 msec they are in nearly unanimous agreement that the sound is a [p]. Because of this sharp boundary between the voiced and unvoiced phoneme, perception of this feature is referred to as *categorical.*

Other evidence for categorical perception of speech comes from discrimination studies (see Studdert-Kennedy, 1976, for a review). Subjects are very poor at discriminating between a pair of sounds that differ in voice-onset time but where both are identified as [b] or where both are identified as [p]. However, they are good at discriminating pairs that have the same difference in voice-onset time but where one is identified as a [b] and the other is identified as a [p]. It seems that subjects can only identify the phonemic category of a sound and are not able to make acoustic discriminations within that phonemic category. Thus, subjects are able to discriminate two sounds only if they fall on different sides of a phonemic boundary.

Another line of research showing evidence for such features in speech recognition involves an *adaptation paradigm*. Eimas and Corbit (1973) had their subjects listen to repeated presentations of *da* over and over again. This

Table 2-2   The Different Types of Trials in LaBerge's Experiment

Types of Stimuli	Test Is Familiar, Expected, Positive	Test Is Unfamiliar, Expected, Positive	Test Is Familiar, Unexpected, Positive	Test Is Unfamiliar, Unexpected, Positive
Prime	p	ʈ	a	a
Test	p	ʈ	qq	ʈ ʈ
	Test Is Familiar, Expected, Negative	Test Is Unfamiliar, Expected, Negative	Test Is Familiar, Unexpected, Negative	Test Is Unfamiliar, Unexpected, Negative
Prime	p	ʈ	a	a
Test	q	ʈ	bq	ʈ ʈ

sound involves a voiced consonant [d]. The experimenters reasoned that this constant repetition of the voiced consonant might fatigue or *adapt* the feature detector that responded to the presence of voicing. They then presented subjects with a series of artificial sounds that spanned the acoustic continuum —such as that between *ba* and *pa* (as in the Lisker and Abramson study mentioned earlier). Subjects had to indicate whether each of these artificial stimuli sounded more like *ba* or more like *pa*. (Remember, the only feature difference between *ba* and *pa* is voicing.) Eimas and Corbit found that some of the artificial stimuli subjects would normally have called the voiced *ba;* they now called the voiceless *pa.* Thus, the repeated presentation of *da* had fatigued the *voiced* feature detector and raised the threshold for detecting voicing in *ba,* making many former *ba* stimuli sound like *pa.*

Attention and Pattern Recognition

Earlier, we indicated that attention was not involved in automatic processes. One would think that the pattern recognition underlying perception of familiar characters, such as letters and numbers, would be automatic and not need the aid of attention. We seem to recognize familiar letters without ever attending to them. On the other hand, recognition of unfamiliar patterns might seem to require the intercession of attention.

Experiments by LaBerge (1973) nicely confirm these intuitions about the interaction between attention and pattern recognition. LaBerge wanted to compare recognition of a familiar set of characters *(p, q, b, d)* with an unfamiliar set (ʈ , ʈ , ʈ , ʈ). In his paradigm, subjects were presented with a *prime stimulus,* which lasted 1 second. The prime stimulus was then removed and a *test stimulus* was presented. Table 2-2 lists the various kinds of trials presented to subjects. The prime stimulus was always a single character, such as *p*. The test stimulus was usually a single character too; thus, subjects simply had to judge whether the two stimuli were the same. Occasionally, however, the test stimulus consisted of two characters and subjects had to judge whether the two characters were identical—a judgment that did not depend on the prime stimulus. It is to be emphasized that usually (75 percent of the time) subjects were tested with a single letter.

To clarify the paradigm, let us consider a couple of the conditions in Table 2-2. In the familiar, expected, and positive condition, subjects might first see a *p* as a prime. After 1 second to study the *p,* the stimulus would be removed and another *p* would be presented. Subjects were to respond *yes,* since the prime and the test were the same. This condition is called *familiar* because *p* is a familiar letter; it is called *expected* because the subject expected to see the single letter *p;* and it is called *positive* because a match occurred and a *yes* response was given. Now consider the unfamiliar, unexpected, and positive condition. Here subjects initially see the prime *a.* They expect the test stimulus to be either an *a* or some other single stimulus, since they usually see single stimuli. However, after the prime the subjects actually see ⅂⅂ . Because subjects see a pair, they know they must decide whether the two stimuli are identical. The stimuli are identical in this case, so the correct response is *yes.* The condition is called *unfamiliar* because the test judgment involves unfamiliar stimuli, *unexpected* because the subject did not expect two characters in the test, and *positive* because both of the test characters matched and a *yes* response was given.

We will just consider those trials where the response was positive. When the stimulus was expected, whether it was familiar or unfamiliar did not make any difference. Subjects made their positive judgments equally fast. They focused their attention on the test pattern and were ready to recognize it. However, when the stimulus was unexpected, a considerable difference in judgment speed was exhibited between familiar letters (530 msec) and unfamiliar letters (580 msec). Presented with unexpected familiar stimuli, subjects seem to recognize the items automatically and were able to compare their encoding of the two characters. With unfamiliar stimuli, however, it seemed that attention had to be shifted from the expected pattern to the presented patterns, and this shift took time. However, after 1 hour's practice for 5 days, subjects came to recognize the new characters when unexpected as quickly as they recognized the familiar characters when unexpected. Thus, this amount of practice made recognition automatic. In conclusion, these results indicate that familiar patterns are recognized automatically, but less familiar patterns need attention to be recognized.

Pattern Recognition: A Summary

It appears that patterns are not recognized as unanalyzed templates. Rather, patterns are broken down into smaller features that can be recognized more economically. These features are extracted individually. The patterns that we

TAE CAT

Figure 2-14 *A demonstration of context. The same stimulus is perceived as an H or an A depending on the context. (From Selfridge, 1955.)*

perceive are combinations of such features with certain interconnections. That is, we identify patterns by processes that recognize feature configurations. If the pattern is familiar, the stimulus will be recognized automatically without the intercession of attention; if the pattern is unfamiliar, attention must be directed to the stimulus to synthesize the features into a pattern. As we will see when we look at the role of context, there is more to pattern recognition than such feature combination alone, but feature combination is an important part of the story.

Context

Bottom-Up Versus Top-Down Processing

So far, visual perception has been discussed as if it were totally *bottom-up.* That is, detectors identified features, which were combined to identify patterns such as letters, which combined to form words, which combined to form sentences. A similar analysis was performed in the case of speech perception. This type of processing is referred to as *bottom-up* because information flows from little perceptual pieces (features), which serve as the foundation of perception, to larger units built from them. One might well wonder how we could possibly read or hear if perception were totally bottom-up. Assuming that a letter consists of, say, 5 features, this would mean that something on the order of 15,000 feature detections would be required in the reading of a page of text. For a fairly normal reader, this would amount to more than 100 feature detections per second; for very rapid readers, it could amount to 300 or more feature detections per second. On the surface, the amount of work appears enormous; it seems implausible that our minds could work that fast. However, it also seems clear that in normal reading we do not bother to detect every feature, every letter, or even every word. As we will discuss more extensively in Chapter 13, there are even some senses in which we can read without even processing every sentence.

Consider the example in Figure 2-14. We perceive this as *THE CAT* even though the *H* and the *A* are identical. The general context provided by the words force the appropriate interpretation. When context or general world knowledge guide perception, we refer to the processing as *top-down* processing, because high-level general knowledge determines the interpretation of the low-level perceptual units.

One important line of research on top-down, or contextual, effects comes from a series of experiments on letter identification, starting with the experiments of Reicher (1969) and Wheeler (1970). Subjects in these experiments were given a very brief presentation of either a letter (such as *D*) or a word (such as *WORD*). Immediately afterwards, they were given a pair of alternatives and instructed to report which they had seen. (The initial presentation was sufficiently brief that subjects made a good many errors in this identification task.) If they had been shown *D,* subjects might be presented with *D* or *K* as alternatives. If they had been shown *WORD,* they might be shown *WORD* or *WORK* as alternatives. Note that the two word choices differ only in the *D* or *K* letter. Subjects were about 10 percent more accurate in the word condition. Thus, they more accurately discriminated between *D* and *K* in the context of a word than as letters alone despite the fact that, in some sense, they had to process four times as many letters in the word context.

Rumelhart and Siple (1974) have provided one explanation for how this feat might have been accomplished. Suppose subjects are able to identify the first three letters as *WOR.* Now consider how many four letter words are consistent with a *WOR* beginning: *WORD, WORK, WORM, WORN, WORT.* Suppose subjects only detect the bottom curve ($\smile$) in the fourth letter. In the *WOR* context, they know the stimulus must have been *WORD.* However, when the letter is presented alone and subjects detect the curve, they will not know whether the letter was *B, D, C, O, or Q,* since each of these letters is consistent with the curve feature. Thus, in the *WOR* context subjects need only detect one feature (e.g., the $\smile$) to perceive the word, but when the letter is presented alone they must identify a number of features. Note that the Rumelhart and Siple analysis implies that perception is a highly inferential process. In the context of *WOR,* it is not the case that the subject sees the *D* better; rather the subject is better able to infer that *D* is the fourth letter.

This example illustrates the *redundancy* of many complex stimuli such as words. These stimuli consist of many more features than are required for recognition. Thus, perception can proceed successfully when only some of the features are recognized, with context filling in the remaining features. In language, this redundancy exists on many levels besides the feature level. For instance, redundancy occurs at the letter level. We do not need to perceive every letter in a string of words to be able to read it. To xllxstxatx, I cxn rxplxce xvexy txirx lextex of x sextexce xitx an x, anx yox stxll xan xanxge xo rxad xt—ix wixh sxme xifxicxltx. (This example is adapted from Lindsay and Norman, 1977.)

Effects similar to the Reicher-Wheeler effect have been shown at the multi-word level in an experiment by Tulving, Mandler, and Baumal (1964). The following are examples of the material they used:

> Countries in the United Nations form a military *alliance.*
> The political leader was challenged by a dangerous *opponent.*
> A voter in municipal elections must be a local *resident.*
> The huge slum was filled with dirt and *disorder.*

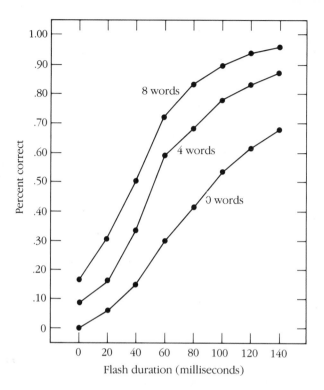

Figure 2-15 *Percent correct identifications of word strings as a function of the duration of its exposure and the number of preceding context words. (From Tulving, Mandler, and Baumal, 1964. Copyright © 1964 by the Canadian Psychological Association. Reprinted by permission.)*

Each sentence provides an eight-word context preceding a critical word. Subjects were either given none, four, or eight of the context words and then shown the target word for a brief period. So, in the various conditions subjects would see the following:

0-context	disorder
4-context	*Filled with dirt and* disorder
8-context	*The huge slum was filled with dirt and* disorder,

where the italicized words constitute the context first studied and *disorder* the critical word, presented after the context for a very brief period. The experimenters manipulated the duration of this critical word from 0 to 140 msec. They were interested in how bottom-up information (manipulated by exposure duration) interacted with context (manipulated by number of words).

Figure 2-15 presents the results of the experiment. It can be seen that the probability of a correct identification increases both as the amount of context increases and the exposure duration increases. Note that subjects benefit from context even in the zero-msec exposure condition, where they are clearly guessing. In this exposure condition, subjects are performing 16 percent better with an eight-word context than with a zero-word context. Note, however, that this benefit of context is larger with longer exposures—more than 40 percent at a 60-msec exposure and about 30 percent at the longest, the 140-msec, exposure. (The effect diminishes somewhat between 60 and 140 msec because subjects in the eight-word-context condition are performing almost perfectly and show little benefit of further exposure, while subjects in the zero-word condition continue to benefit from the longer exposure.) These results indicate that subjects can take advantage of the context to improve their identification of the words. As was the case in the Reicher-Wheeler letter-identification paradigm, subjects are using the context to reduce the amount of perceptual information they need in identifying the word.

The experiment by Tulving et al. shows that we can use sentence context to help identify words. With context we need to extract less information the word itself in order to identify it. In fact, we can use context to fill in words that did not even occur in the sentence, as the previous sentence illustrates. Presumably, you were able to fill in the missing *from* as you read the sentence and perhaps you did not even notice that it was missing. (This example was also adapted from Lindsay and Norman, 1977.)

Context and Speech

Equally good evidence exists for the role of context in the perception of speech. A nice illustration is the *phoneme-restoration effect,* demonstrated in an experiment by Warren (1970). He had subjects listen to the sentence, "The state governors met with their respective legislatures convening in the capital city," with 120 msec pure tone replacing the middle *s* in legislatures. However, only 1 in 20 subjects reported hearing the pure tone and that subject was not able to locate it correctly.

A nice extension of this first study is an experiment by Warren and Warren (1970). They presented subjects with sentences such as the following:

> It was found that the *eel was on the axle.
> It was found that the *eel was on the shoe.
> It was found that the *eel was on the orange.
> It was found that the *eel was on the table.

In each case, the * denotes a phoneme replaced by nonspeech. For the four sentences above, subjects reported hearing *wheel, heel, peel,* and *meal,* depending on context. The important feature to note about each of these sentences is that the sentences are identical through the critical word. The identification of the critical word is determined by what occurs after it. Thus, the

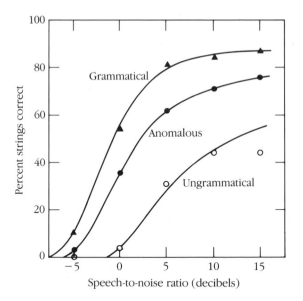

Figure 2-16
Percent correct identifications of word strings as a function of the type of string and the speech-to-noise ratio. (From Miller and Isard, 1963.)

identification of words is often not instantaneous but can depend on the perception of subsequent words.

These two experiments on speech perception illustrate how context can cause us to hear what is not there. We found instances of such illusory perception when we considered visual perception, but we also found clear instances (e.g., Reicher and Wheeler) of context appearing to facilitate the identification of what was actually presented. Facilitation has been similarly demonstrated in the domain of speech perception. For example, Miller and Isard (1963) presented sentences to subjects in noise; subjects were to listen to the sentences and report them back. Some sentences were perfectly normal:

> A witness signed the official document.
> Sloppy fielding loses baseball games.

Other sentences were what the experimenters called *anomalous:*

> A witness appraised the shocking company dragon.
> Sloppy poetry leaves nuclear minutes.

These sentences obey the rules of English grammar; they just do not make any sense. The third category of sentences was called *ungrammatical:*

> A legal glittering the exposed picnic knight.
> Loses poetry spots total wasted.

These sentences are basically just random strings of words.

Figure 2-16 shows the percent of correct perception of these three kinds of sentences. The data are plotted as a function of the speech-to-noise ratio—

naturally, subjects perceived less when there was more noise. However, what is critical in the figure is that at all levels of speech-to-noise ratio, the normal (grammatical) is clearly superior to the anomalous and the anomalous is superior to the ungrammatical. These results show that subjects were able to improve their speech perception both through the use of meaning constraints (differences between normal and anomalous) and grammar constraints (differences between anomalous and ungrammatical).

The Interaction of Bottom-Up and Top-Down Processing

Bottom-up processing, in which perceptual units combine to form larger units, is sometimes referred to as *data-driven processing* (e.g., Lindsay and Norman, 1977). In this kind of processing, the environment is really in control of the organism. The use of top-down information, such as context and general knowledge (examples are grammar and syntax) is sometimes referred to as *conceptually driven processing.* In such processing, the perceiver imposes its knowledge and conceptual structures on the environment to help decide what is out there. Without this top-down approach, pattern recognition would be extremely difficult, both because of the immense amount of processing required in a pure bottom-up system and because of the noisy and unreliable character of data from the environment. The importance of top-down processing to perception is the basis for the claim that has been made that perception really is an act of considerable intelligence. All one's knowledge about the world and one's ability to reason with this knowledge can be used to aid in bottom-up perceptual processing.

It should be clear that bottom-up or top-down processing alone would be insufficient. The burden of data would be unbearable if we only processed information in a bottom-up manner. And if we only used top-down processing, we would always be hallucinating. For instance, if we expected a person to say a particular thing, we would hear it no matter what was said. The two approaches must combine in some way for processing to occur. In fact, the two sources of information can combine in two ways. One was already discussed with respect to the Reicher-Wheeler phenomenon. The system can combine the constraints provided by both top-down and bottom-up sources to make identifications it was not able to make with just one source. Suppose we saw the following sentence but did not process the last word:

For dinner I had fried _____.

Even with the context available it is unlikely one would be able to guess the correct word. Thus, top-down processing alone is not enough. On the other hand, suppose some of the letters in a word were provided (bottom-up information) but the context were not:

tr––t

On the basis of these three letters alone one would be unlikely to identify the word (it could be *tract, trait, treat, trout, trust,* or *tryst*). So bottom-up information is not enough to permit word identification. However, suppose we had both the context (top-down information) and the letters (bottom-up information):

For dinner I had fried tr––t.

With this combination of bottom-up and top-down information, we can identify the word.

A second kind of interaction between top-down and bottom-up processes is the former processes informing the latter of what to attend to. Consider the following partial sentence:

The rock shattered the w––––––––.

How could this sentence possibly end? The two most likely candidates are *window* and *windshield.* Clearly, processing the next three letters makes no sense, because they would not tell us which the target word was. Rather, processing the missing word's length or its final letter would be useful. For instance, the following information should enable recognition:

The rock smashed the w––––––––d.

Thus, the sentence context can allow the system to selectively sample the information needed to complete perception.

Note that we have found another important involvement of attention in perception. When too much information exists to be sampled in rapid perceptual processing, the attentional resource is allocated to the processing of those features likely to be the most informative.

Attention, Perception, and the Teaching of Reading

We have been looking at how people recognize alphanumeric characters and words. It should come as no surprise that these results have strong implications for how reading should be taught. We will discuss reading from the point of view of higher cognitive processes in later chapters (7, 13). In this section, we consider several implications of research on attention and perception. (A great many more are reviewed in the book by Gibson and Levin, 1975.)

Earlier, we reviewed the research on how a skill became automatic with practice. Two consequences of automaticity are that the skill is performed more rapidly and that it no longer interferes with other ongoing behavior. Clearly, automaticity in letter recognition is critical if a child is to become a fluent reader. The child must be able to recognize characters quickly and to recognize many characters at once without the recognitions of individual letters interfering with each other. Moreover, as we will discuss in more detail in Chapter 13, successful reading requires that the processes of language comprehension occur simultaneously with those of character recognition. It is important that the character recognition be automatic so that it not interfere with comprehension. As LaBerge (1973) has shown, practice is the factor that strongly promotes automaticity in reading. Hence, a child must get a lot of practice reading and recognizing characters. The old drill and practice sessions, now in some disrepute, may not have been such a bad idea, though more enjoyable and creative ways for children to get reading practice probably exist. The important point is that school curricula be designed to allow children to spend a great deal of time reading.

In this chapter, we saw the importance of expectation and context in relieving the burden of bottom-up processing. Some evidence suggests that good readers are better able than poor readers to take advantage of the contextual constraints in a text. Basically, readers using context make inferences and venture hypotheses about what they are reading on the basis of what they have read. Thus, reading teachers should encourage beginning readers to make such inferences. Samuels, Dahl, and Archwamety (1974) found that training students to make such inferences was helpful. They presented third graders with such sentences as

My mother sleeps on her _____,

and encouraged them to rapidly guess a word that completes the sentence. This training resulted in faster word recognition and higher comprehension-test scores relative to control groups that did not receive training for hypothesis testing while reading.

Context and the Recognition of Faces and Scenes

So far, our discussion has focused almost entirely on the role of context in the perception of printed and spoken material. However, some work has been done on how more complex visual stimuli are perceived. In dealing with linguistic material, we are processing very highly overlearned patterns. When we process other highly overlearned patterns, such as faces, the same kind of interaction seems to take place between features and context that occurs with linguistic stimuli. Consider Figure 2-17, which is derived from work by Palmer (1975). He pointed out that in the context of a face, very little feature information is required for recognition of the individual parts, such as nose, eye, ear, or lips. In contrast, when these parts are presented in isolation, considerably more visual detail is required to permit their recognition.

Context also appears to be important for visual stimuli that are not highly

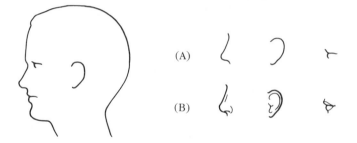

Figure 2-17 *Facial features in the context of a face and out of context. Minimal information is necessary in context, but features are not easily recognized in row A. More of the features' internal structure must be provided to permit recognition, as in row B. (Adapted from Palmer, 1975.)*

overlearned patterns. Biederman, Glass, and Stacy (1973) have looked at perception of objects in novel scenes. Figure 2-18 illustrates the two kinds of scenes presented to their subjects. Part A of the figure is a normal scene, while in B the same scene is jumbled. The scene was briefly presented to subjects on a screen, and immediately after the presentation an arrow was presented that pointed to a position on the screen where an object had been. Subjects were asked to identify the object that had been in that position of the scene. So, in the example scene, the object pointed to might have been the fire hydrant. Subjects were considerably more accurate in their identification with the coherent than with the jumbled pictures. Thus, as with their processing of written text or speech, subjects are able to recruit context in a visual scene to help their identification of an object.

Context and Expectation in Real Life

So far, we have discussed effects of context and expectation in a laboratory situation. Such effects are abundant in real life. For instance, Sommer (1959) discusses a typical hunting accident. A group of hunters saw something move in the bush. One of the party asked his friend if it was a deer. The friend answered yes. They fired three shots at the object and brought it down. It turned out that they had killed a member of their party who had gotten separated. The case was investigated and brought to trial. A policeman testified that he saw a man under the same conditions and clearly perceived that it was a man and not a deer. Had the hunters deliberately killed their companion? The conflicting reports of the hunters and the policeman are to be expected, given what we know about effects of context and expectation. The hunters were expecting to see a deer moving in the bush and that is what they saw. The policeman was expecting to see a man and that is what he saw.

Figure 2-18 *Scenes used in the study by Biederman, Glass, and Stacy (1973). (A) A coherent scene. (B) A jumbled scene. It is harder to recognize the fire hydrant in the jumbled scene. (From Biederman, Glass, and Stacy, 1973. Copyright © 1973 by the American Psychological Association. Reprinted by permission.)*

Gestalt Principles of Perceptual Organization

To this point, this chapter has considered the ways in which familiar objects and patterns are perceived. But what happens when we are presented with an unfamiliar object or pattern? How do we perceive it? Stimuli tend to organize themselves in accordance with a number of principles, referred to as Gestalt principles of perception, after the Gestalt psychologists who documented many of them. Consider the various figures in Figure 2-19. In part A, we perceive four pairs of lines rather than eight separate lines. This picture illustrates the principle of *proximity:* Elements close together tend to organize into units. Part B illustrates the same principle. We see five columns of dots rather than five rows because the dots in a column are closer together

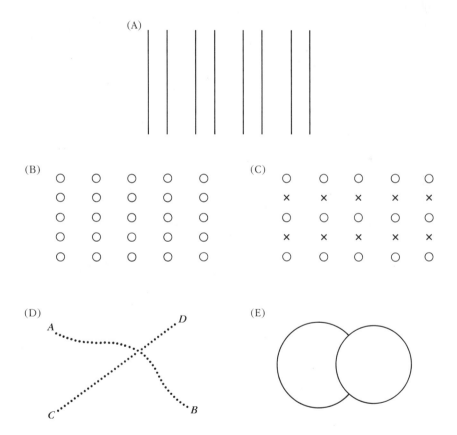

Figure 2-19 *Illustrations of the Gestalt principles of organization. (A and B) The principles of proximity. (C) The principle of similarity. (D) The principle of good continuation. (E) The principle of closure.*

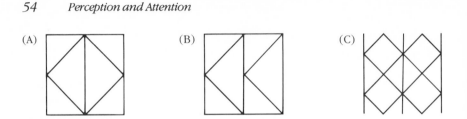

Figure 2-20 *Illustrations of the Gestalt principle of symmetry. A is better than B because it is symmetrical. The interpretation imposed on C is symmetrical.*

than the dots in a row. In part C, we tend to see five rows of alternating Os and Xs, even though the rows are spaced similar to those in B. This example illustrates the principle of *similarity:* Objects that look alike tend to be grouped together. Part D illustrates the principle of *good continuation.* We perceive part D as two lines, one from *A* to *B* and the other from *C* to *D,* although there is no reason why this could not represent another pair of lines, one from *A* to *D* and the other from *C* to *B.* However, the line from *A* to *B* displays better continuation than the line from *A* to *D,* which has a sharp turn. Part E illustrates the principles of *closure* and *good form.* We see the drawing as one circle occluded by another, although the occluded object could have many other possible shapes.

Another Gestalt principle is that of *symmetry.* Compare patterns A and B in Figure 2-20. Pattern A seems like a much "better" pattern because it is symmetrical. The principle of symmetry can also determine the way we perceive a pattern. Consider pattern C. We see this pattern as being composed of diamonds and vertical lines rather than many *K*s, though the latter is also true (half the *K*s are normal and half are inverted). The reason is simply that diamonds are symmetrical and *K*s are not.

One of the important Gestalt claims is that the whole is more than the sum of its parts. The rows, columns, lines, and circles seen in Figure 2-19 are more than just a sum of the parts that compose them. These whole units are emergent properties of the perception.

	Conditions	
	Configural	Part
Standard pattern presented first	( )	(
↓		
Two test patterns presented	( )))	( )
↓		
Subject must select the test pattern that is the same as the standard		

Figure 2-21 *The sequence of events is the experiment by Pomerantz et al. (1977). (Adapted from Glass, Holyoak, and Santa.)* Cognition. *Copyright © 1979 by Addison-Wesley, Reading, Massachusetts. Fig. 2.8. Reprinted with permission.)*

Figure 2-22   *A demonstration of the fact that by shifting attention we perceive different units of organization.*

There is some evidence to suggest that we actually perceive these larger configurations faster and more accurately than we perceive their components. An experiment by Pomerantz, Soyer, and Stoeven (1977) illustrated one situation in which subjects recognized a configuration faster than its components. Figure 2-21 illustrates the sequence of events in this experiment. The researchers presented their subjects with a standard pattern and then presented two test patterns. Subjects had to indicate which test pattern they had seen. The experiment consisted of two important conditions of contrast. In the *configural condition,* subjects saw a well-organized configuration as a standard and were tested on two well-organized configurations. In the *part condition,* subjects saw just a part of the stimulus in the configural condition and were only tested with parts of the configuration. However, in both the configural and the part condition, the difference between the test stimuli was always the same single element. That is, the configural-test patterns differed in the same way as the part-test patterns. However, subjects in the configural condition made their choices more quickly. Clearly, then, since a configuration can be recognized more quickly than its parts, perception of the configuration must be something more than the separate perception of the elements.

While Gestalt principles tend to favor a particular organization for a stimulus (as illustrated in Figures 2-19 and 2-20), we can reorganize a stimulus by appropriately shifting attention. Consider the stimulus in Figure 2-22. Probably you first perceive this stimulus as an 8 against a white background.

(A)   (B)

(C)   (D)

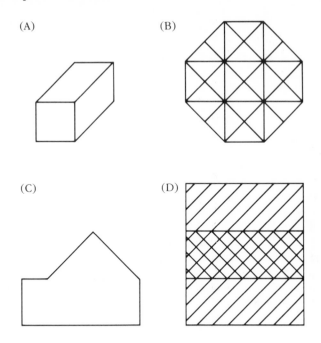

Figure 2-23   *Hidden figures. Try to find A in B and C in D. These tasks are hard because the Gestalt principles organize the stimuli differently. (Adapted from Witkin, "The Perception of the Upright." Copyright © 1959 by Scientific American, Inc. All rights reserved.)*

However, by appropriately shifting your attention you can perceive the figure as row upon row of dots, or, by again shifting attention, as a single rectangle.

The function of the Gestalt principles seems to be to quickly segment a stimulus into a set of objects and to organize these objects into larger configurations. By and large, the segmentation is successful and the appropriate patterns are isolated. For instance, in a written page, the Gestalt principle of proximity serves to identify the letters and words, the principles of proximity and good continuation identify the line. However, on occasion, Gestalt principles lead to the wrong organization and we have to call on attention to restructure the scene. Particularly striking examples of this phenomenon are hidden-figure tests, such as those in Figure 2-23.

General Conclusions

An enormous amount of sensory information comes into our system every moment. The major problem facing the perceptual system is that it must, with only limited resources, process this great load of information in such a way

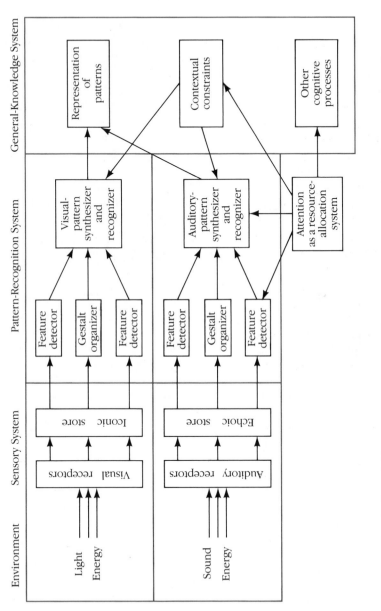

Figure 2-24 *The flow of information through the information-processing system from the environment to its perceptual representation in the general-knowledge system. The arrows from the attention box point to some of the processes attention controls. (Adapted from Rumelhart, 1977.)*

that the environment makes sense. Unless sensory information is encoded quickly, it is very rapidly lost from iconic and echoic stores. The system utilizes various pattern recognizers and some basic Gestalt principles of organization to structure this sensory input. The pattern recognizers appear to combine both sensory features and contextual information in identifying familiar configurations. Gestalt principles impose organization on both familiar and unfamiliar configurations. These two modes for perceptual structuring can sometimes come into conflict. FoR iNsTaNcE tHiS sEnTeNcE iS hArD tO rEaD. The reason is that the principle of similarity is trying to organize nonadjacent letters. At all levels, attention seems to play the role of manager, deciding what information to attend to and what patterns to try to recognize. Certain highly overlearned patterns (and probably the Gestalt principles too) are applied automatically, but with these exceptions attention determines what we will see and hear.

Figure 2-24 summarizes the sensory and perceptual systems in terms of the flow of information. This illustration is slightly modified from a similar flow-chart in Rumelhart (1977). Light and sound energy are registered by the visual receptors in the eye and the auditory receptors in the ear. This information is held temporarily in iconic and echoic stores. Then, through the operation of feature detectors and Gestalt principles of organization, information is extracted and used by the pattern recognizers and synthesizers. The recognizers and synthesizers identify patterns in the stimulus input and organize these patterns into an overall description of the environment. The output of these pattern synthesizers and recognizers is deposited as part of our general long-term knowledge. Also, our general long-term knowledge serves as a source of contextual constraints on the pattern-forming processes. Attention serves as a monitor, allocating resources to the various ongoing perceptual processes as well as to other, nonperceptual cognitive processes (such as deductive reasoning).

The remainder of this book will be concerned with that portion of Figure 2-24 headed General-Knowledge System. This term refers to our nonperceptual intellectual facilities, or higher level cognition. This chapter has presented an overview of how the information gets into this higher level system. We are now in a position to study the properties of these cognitive processes.

Remarks and Suggested Readings

The topics covered in this chapter are easily expanded into a full course; most colleges offer at least one course on this material. Such courses focus particularly on what is known about the elemental sensory processes. A fair amount of physiological evidence is available about these processes, and rather direct connections can be made between physiology and psychological experience.

Among the standard texts providing extensive surveys of the research on sensation and perception are Rock (1975) and Kaufman (1974).

James Gibson (e.g., 1950, 1966) has developed a very influential theory of perception, quite different from the one presented here. Ideas from this theory are beginning to appear in analyses of other higher level cognitive phenomena. For instance, Turvey and Shaw (1977), in their analysis of human memory, have been strongly influenced by Gibson. Neisser (1976) presents a view of perception, attention, and cognition that also shows the influence of Gibson.

A number of texts dealing with human information processing provide somewhat different, and also often more extensive, discussions of perception and attention. One should not think that the model of attention presented here is the only one in cognitive psychology. For discussions of a number of alternative attention models, read Massaro (1975) and Norman (1976). Other texts on attention and perception include Klatzky (1980), Lindsay and Norman (1977), Rumelhart (1977), and Wickelgren (1979). Clark and Clark (1977) contains good discussions of speech generation and perception. Two books edited by Solso (1973, 1975) contain recent papers on attention and perception. Very current research can be found in an annual series titled *Attention and Performance*. For information on attempts at making computers see, read Winston (1975), and on attempts at making computers recognize speech, read Reddy (1975).

Just as considerable variation exists among ideas about the nature of attention, so multiple views are held about the role of context in perception. Estes (1975) reviews some of the points of view and presents arguments against some of the views advanced here.

Part II
THE REPRESENTATION OF KNOWLEDGE

Chapter 3

Mental Imagery

Summary

1. The study of *mental imagery* is concerned with understanding the ways in which we internally represent and process information about spatial relations and about *continuously varying* quantities such as size.

2. Mental images can be considered *abstract-analog* representations of objects. They are *analogs* because they are capable of simulating continuous changes in external objects with continuous changes in themselves. They are *abstract* because they do not seem tied to the visual modality or any other modality.

3. When asked to perform a mental transformation on an image, such as rotating it 180 degrees, subjects imagine the image moving through the intermediate states in the transformation. The greater the transformation that must be performed the longer subjects take to perform it.

4. When subjects are asked to compare two mental objects on a dimension such as size, they engage in a process similar to that of discriminating between the size of two physically presented objects.

5. Although many people report experiences of visualizing objects in imagery tasks, an image does not seem to be a mental picture in the head. It differs from a picture in that it is not tied to the visual modality, it is not precise and can be distorted, and it is segmented into meaningful pieces.

6. The processes involved in mental imagery seem also to be involved with the understanding of one's environment and the use of maps.

7. People have difficulty both in reasoning about their environment and in using maps because of limitations on the amount of information that can be held in an image and because images are not precise but are subject to distortions.

Imagery and Perception

The last chapter was concerned with the ways in which we perceive various external stimuli. However, in many circumstances we process visual information (such as size) and spatial information (such as position in an array) in the absence of any external stimulus. The study of *mental imagery* is concerned with these processes. Although these imagery processes are similar to perceptual processes and perhaps overlap them, important differences distinguish the imagining of an object and the seeing of an object.

For an example of a task that appears to involve mental imagery, consider the following test from the Spatial Visualization II series, part of an Army–Air Force battery of aptitude tests constructed by Guilford, Fruchter, and Zimmerman (1952):

All surfaces of a 3-inch cube are painted red and it is then cut into twenty-seven 1-inch cubes.

Questions: 1. How many cubes have *three* faces painted red?
2. How many cubes have *one* face painted red?
3. How many cubes have *no* red faces?
4. How many cubes have *two* faces painted red?

How would you solve these problems? Most people experience a visual-spatial representation of the block in their "mind's eye." Obviously, they don't actually see the object, and they suffer no confusion about what is in their mind and what is in the real world. However, certain similarities exist between their experience of such visual imagery and their experience of viewing an object.

Imagery provides an important kind of knowledge representation because it enables us to represent and process physical properties of objects in the absence of these objects. For centuries, the idea has been advanced that images are merely faint versions of perceptions. An interesting, if methodologically questionable, attempt to show just this was an experiment by Perky (1910). She had subjects attempt to imagine a red tomato on a screen. A faint tomato was actually projected onto a screen; though faint, it was detectable under normal conditions. Perky's subjects failed to perceive that a picture was actually being projected on the screen, but rather thought it was part of their image. Thus, they appeared to confuse image and perception.

It is hard to know exactly what to make of Perky's experiment, but it seems unwise to think of an image as just a faint percept. Sometimes we can have very clear and vivid images but suffer no confusion about whether they are images. On the other hand, normally we do not confuse faint percepts for images. While images and perceptions are not identical, it seems they have a lot in common. Indeed, one way to study the structure of percepts is to study the structure of images.

In American psychology, imagery has long been a subject of controversy. (For a partial review of the conflict see Richardson, 1969.) The behaviorists attempted to banish all research on the concept as part of their purge of mentalistic concepts from psychology. Research on the topic only became respectable about 15 years ago, when behaviorism lost its grip on psychology. Much research has simply tried to show that mental imagery existed—which would seem a strange endeavor except that it was needed as a defense against behaviorist prejudice. More recently, considerable debate has ensued over the nature of the information representation underlying imagery. There is a general tendency to think of images as involving pictures in the head. Most researchers agree that this picture-in-the-head interpretation is inadequate— that an image is less precise and more abstract than a picture. However, considerable disagreement exists as to how the information in an image is to be understood.

Although personal biases no doubt color this chapter, the intention is to present what we know about imagery without taking a stand regarding the precise nature of representation. This chapter is concerned mainly with the kinds of operations that can be performed on mental images. We begin with research on mental rotation, which has played a key role in stirring renewed interest in mental imagery. Next, we touch on a number of transformations other than rotation, which subjects appear able to perform on mental objects. We go on to discuss research on the comparison of analog quantities, and, finally, applications of this mental-imagery research to spatial cognition. The next chapter covers image representations as one of the possible codes for information in long-term memory.

Mental Rotation

The Rotation of Three-Dimensional Objects

Roger Shepard and his colleagues have performed a long series of experiments on mental rotation. The first experiment was that of Shepard and Metzler (1971). Subjects were presented with pairs of two-dimensional repre-

(A)

(B)

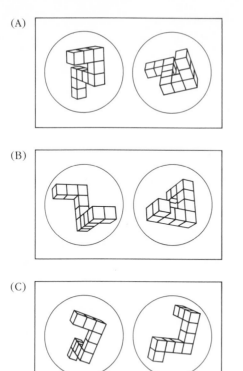

(C)

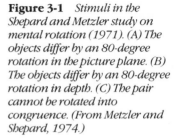

Figure 3-1 *Stimuli in the Shepard and Metzler study on mental rotation (1971). (A) The objects differ by an 80-degree rotation in the picture plane. (B) The objects differ by an 80-degree rotation in depth. (C) The pair cannot be rotated into congruence. (From Metzler and Shepard, 1974.)*

sentations of three-dimensional objects like those in Figure 3-1. Their task was to determine if the objects were identical except for orientation. The two figures in Figures 3-1A and 3-1B are identical; they are just presented at different orientations. Subjects report that to match the two shapes they rotated one of the objects in each pair mentally until it was congruent with the other object. Figure 3-1C is a foil pair: there is no way of rotating one object so that it is identical with the other.

The graphs in Figure 3-2 show the time required for subjects to decide that the members of pairs such as those in Figures 3-1A and B were identical. The reaction times are plotted as a function of the angular disparity between the two objects presented to the subject. This angular disparity represents the amount one object would have to be rotated to match the other object in orientation. Note that the relationship is linear—for every equal increment in amount of rotation, an equal increment in reaction time is required. Reaction time is plotted for two different kinds of rotation. One is for two-dimensional rotations (Figure 3-1A), which can be performed in the picture plane (that is, by rotating the page). The other is for depth rotations (Figure 3-1B), which

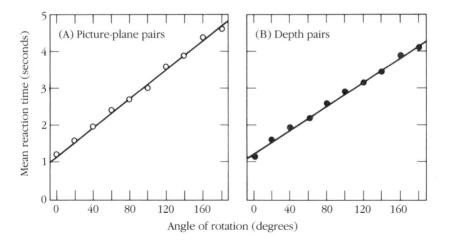

Figure 3-2   *Mean time to determine that two objects have the same three-dimensional shape as a function of the angular difference in their portrayed orientations. (A) Plot for pairs differing by a rotation in the picture plane. (B) Plot for pairs differing by a rotation in depth. (From Metzler and Shepard, 1974.)*

require the subject to rotate the object *into* the page. Note that the two functions are very similar. Processing an object in depth (in three dimensions) does not appear to take longer than processing in the picture plane. Hence, subjects must be operating on three-dimensional representations of the objects both in the picture-plane and depth conditions.

These data might seem to indicate that subjects rotate the object in a three-dimensional space within their heads. The greater the angle of disparity between the two objects, the longer subjects take to complete the rotation. Of course, subjects are not actually rotating an object in their heads. However, whatever the actual mental process is, it appears to be an *analog* of a physical rotation.

Mental rotation has also been studied in a series of experiments by Cooper and Shepard (1973), who used letter stimuli such as those in Figure 3-3. The six items on the left are well-formed Rs that have been rotated varying numbers of degrees from the vertical. The six items to the right are backwards Rs, which have also been rotated varying numbers of degrees. The subjects were presented with one of the 12 stimuli in Figure 3-3 and had to decide whether the stimulus was a normal or a backwards R. Figure 3-4 presents the times subjects took to judge that a letter was normal as a function of its deviation in orientation from upright. Subjects' judgment times increase with deviation from the upright up to 180° This result suggests that a mental-rotation process took place in which the stimulus was rotated in the plane until it was upright and then judged as normal or backward. The fact that subjects are

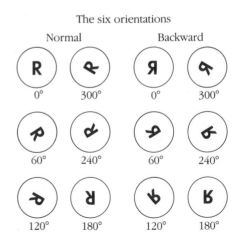

Figure 3-3 *Normal and backwards versions of one of the stimuli in the mental-rotation study by Cooper and Shepard (1973).*

slowest at 180° indicates that they will rotate clockwise or counterclockwise —whichever way is shorter. Note that the rotation times for this experiment are much faster than those in the Shepard and Metzler study. Subjects seem to be rotating at a rate of more than 300°/second (as opposed to only 50°/second in Shepard and Metzler). Although the exact reason for this difference in rotation rates is somewhat in dispute, it is probably related to the greater complexity of the Shepard and Metzler figures.

Analog Representations

A distinguishing feature of imagery representations and processes is that they appear to be *analogs* of corresponding physical processes. Before we review imagery studies further, we need to clarify the notion of representations and processes as analogs. One process is an analog of another when it mimics or simulates the structure of the other process. Many examples of analogs of processes exist. The road simulators used in driver's education are analogs. They are not actual driving situations, but they try to preserve much of the structure of an actual driving situation. A movie is an analog. Even though some people lose track of the distinction, the action on the screen is not identical with that in the real world. However, it does preserve much of the structure of a real-world experience. Often, analogs are much more abstract than these two examples. For instance, a bathroom scale represents weight by position on a disk, with every change in weight resulting in a change in the position of the disk. Analog computers represent numbers by amount of voltage; the larger the number, the greater the voltage.

In discussing knowledge representation, it is useful to make distinctions between three kinds of representations—concrete analogs, abstract analogs,

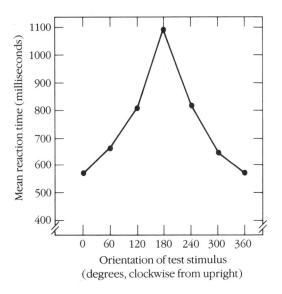

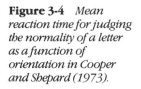

Figure 3-4 *Mean reaction time for judging the normality of a letter as a function of orientation in Cooper and Shepard (1973).*

and symbolic representations. Consider a person's weight. We might choose to represent this value with an object that weighs 1 ounce for every pound. So, the weight of a person who weighed 150 pounds would be represented by a 9-pound, 6-ounce weight. Such an object would be a *concrete analog,* since representation of the information is concretely tied to what we are representing. An abstract analog of a person's weight would be a length of a line: different line lengths would mirror different weights, but the connection between the dimensions of line length and weight is arbitrary. Finally, a *symbolic representation* of a person's weight would be the printed expression *150 pounds.* In the symbolic representation, no connection exists between variation in the structure of the phrase and variation in what is being represented. For instance, the phrase *151 pounds* is not larger as a printed message than *150 pounds.*

Much of the controversy about mental imagery concerns whether the representations in imagery tasks should be thought of as concrete analogs, abstract analogs, or symbolic representations. Experiments such as those by Shepard and Metzler and by Cooper and Shepard provide evidence that the representation is an analog, since there appears to be a strong connection between variations in the mental representation of the objects and variations in physical orientation. We will present evidence in this chapter that image representations must be abstract analogs.

A distinction related to the analog-symbolic distinction is whether imagery representations are discrete or continuous. A good illustration of the difference between discrete and continuous representations is the difference between digital watches and sweep-hand watches. Digital watches are discrete: they can only represent a specific number of times: 12:00, 12:01, 12:02, and so on. In contrast, a sweep hand can continuously vary, representing all the times between 12:00 and 12:01. Because times in Figures 3-2 and 3-4 appear to be continuous functions of angle, it is argued that the representation of an object must vary continuously as it is rotated. The problem with this conclusion is that it is difficult to distinguish between continuous change and very small discrete changes. Therefore, pursuing the discrete-continuous distinction does not appear to be profitable. The research on mental rotation can be better interpreted as showing that imagery representations are analogical.

More Evidence for Mental Rotations

Returning to the Shepard and Metzler studies (Figures 3-1 and 3-2), one can question whether subjects were really continuously transforming their internal representation of a stimulus. Perhaps the increases in time merely reflected the fact that the farther apart two objects are in rotation the more dissimilar they appear and the harder it is to see their underlying identities. Thus, according to this alternate explanation, subjects would not be engaged in the process of continuously rotating an image but would only be using up more time in pondering problems of increased difficulty. In contrast to this alternate explanation, subjects often report that they are rotating an image, but there has long been a tendency to distrust subjects' introspective reports in this field.

Among the best evidence for continuous transformation is that reported by Metzler (1973). She calculated from plots such as those in Figure 3-2 the rate at which each subject was rotating a figure. Suppose it took a subject 3.5 seconds longer to judge a stimulus when it was at 180° disparity than when it was at 0° disparity. This would mean that the subject was rotating at a rate of 180°/3.5 second, or approximately 50°/second. Metzler then presented her subjects with one stimulus, *a,* and instructed them to start rotating it in a specified direction. At various times after they had started their rotation, she presented a second test stimulus, *b,* which was rotated a certain number of degrees from *a.* Subjects were to judge whether *a* was identical to *b.* Metzler determined the exact point in time at which to present *b* to match the subject's rotating image of *a.* So, if she calculated that a particular subject was rotating at 50°/second and that the test stimulus was 135° removed from the original, she would present the test stimulus at 135°/50 = 2.7 second delay. If subjects were actually rotating their mental images of *a* when *b* was introduced, their reaction times should have been short and unaffected by the degree of rotation between *b* and the original orientation of *a.*

Figure 3-5 shows Metzler's results. The left-hand panel displays data for

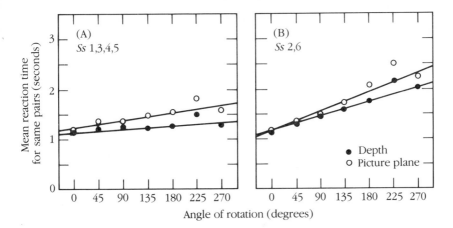

Figure 3-5 *Mean reaction time to judge a mentally rotating figure is identical to a second figure as a function of angle of rotation. (A) Data for the four subjects with relatively small variability in rotation time. (B) Data for the two subjects with much greater rotation-time variability. (From Metzler, 1973.)*

four of her six subjects. For these subjects, there is virtually no dependence of reaction time on the angular separation between the original and test figure. In the right-hand panel, which shows reaction times for the other two subjects, some dependence is demonstrated, but it is much reduced from that in Figure 3-2. We would expect to see some effect of angle of rotation for subjects that were variable in their rate of rotation. This is because variable subjects would often not be at the calculated point in their rotation; they would have rotated the figure either too far or not far enough. The two subjects in part B had been determined to be more variable than the four in part A by a prior experiment. Thus, Metzler's data show that subjects are continuously rotating a mental object and, if the second figure is presented at the right moment in the rotation, the two objects will match.

Other Image Transformations and Operations

Paper Folding

Researchers have looked at a number of other tasks which seem to show that when subjects are performing certain mental computations they are operating on a visual image the way one might perform continuous operations on a physical object. Shepard and Feng (1972) looked at a task in which subjects were required to make judgments about paper cubes that had been unfolded into patterns of six squares. Figure 3-6 illustrates some of their problems. Subjects were asked to determine from a two-dimensional pattern whether

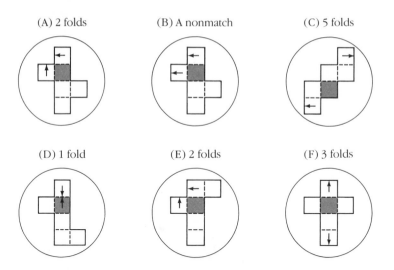

Figure 3-6 *Six illustrative problems adapted from Shepard and Feng (1972). The overall task was to determine whether the heads of arrows would meet when the patterns were folded into cubes.*

the heads of the two arrows marked on the pattern would or would not meet if the squares were folded into a cube. The time subjects took to answer the questions were recorded. Subjects reported going through the mental process of refolding the squares to answer these questions. Moreover, their reaction-time data were consistent with these reports. Figure 3-7 plots decision times as a function of the number of folds required to bring the arrows into correspondence. These data approximate a linear function of the number of folds. Thus, it seems that processing time is a function of the amount of movement that must be performed on the image.

Image Scanning

An experiment by Kosslyn, Ball, and Reiser (1978) shows that processing time increases with the amount of movement the image goes through. These investigators presented subjects with a map of a fictitious island (see Figure 3-8) containing a hut, a tree, a rock, a well, a lake, sand, and grass. Subjects were trained on this map until they could draw it with great accuracy. Then an object was named aloud and subjects were asked to picture the map mentally and focus on the object named. Five second later, a second object was named. Subjects were instructed to scan the map for this second object and to press a button when they had mentally focused on it.

Figure 3-9 presents the times subjects needed to perform this mental oper-

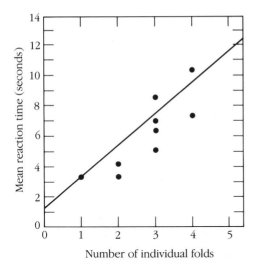

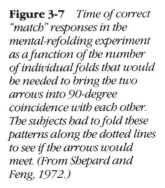

Figure 3-7 *Time of correct "match" responses in the mental-refolding experiment as a function of the number of individual folds that would be needed to bring the two arrows into 90-degree coincidence with each other. The subjects had to fold these patterns along the dotted lines to see if the arrows would meet. (From Shepard and Feng, 1972.)*

ation as a function of the distance between the two objects in the original map. There are 21 possible pairs of points, and each point is represented in Figure 3-9. The abscissa gives the distance between each pair. The farther apart the two objects were, the greater was the reaction time. Clearly, subjects did not have the actual map in their heads and therefore were not moving from one location in their heads to a second location. However, again, they were going through a process analogous to this physical operation.

Figure 3-8 *The fictitious map used by Kosslyn, Ball, and Reiser (1978) to determine differences in processing time relative to the distance between images to be recalled. Subjects had to commit this map to memory and then mentally scan from point to point on the map. (Copyright © 1978 by the American Psychological Association. Reprinted by permission.)*

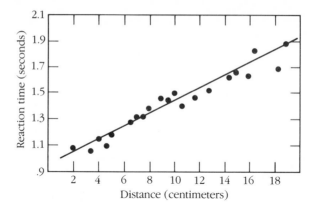

Figure 3-9   *Time to scan between two points in Figure 3-8 as a function of the distance between the points. (From Kosslyn, Ball, and Reiser, 1978. Copyright © 1978 by the American Psychological Association. Reprinted by permission.)*

Interference and Image Scanning

Brooks performed an important series of experiments in 1968 on the scanning of visual images. He had subjects scan imagined diagrams such as the one in Figure 3-10. For example, the subject was to scan around an imagined block F from a prescribed starting point and in a prescribed direction, categorizing each corner as a point in the extreme top or bottom (assigned a "yes" response) or as a point in between (assigned a "no" response). In the example, the correct sequence of responses is yes, yes, yes, no, no, no, no, no, no, yes. For a nonvisual contrast task, Brooks also gave subjects sentences such as,

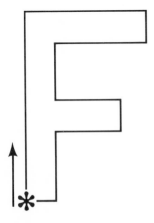

Figure 3-10   *An example of a simple block diagram used by Brooks (1968) to study the scanning of mental images. The asterisk and arrow showed the subject the starting point and the direction for scanning the image. (Copyright © 1968 by the Canadian Psychological Association. Reprinted by permission.)*

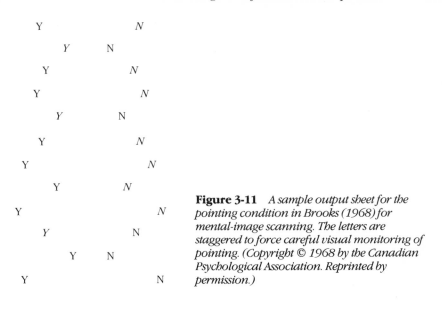

Figure 3-11 *A sample output sheet for the pointing condition in Brooks (1968) for mental-image scanning. The letters are staggered to force careful visual monitoring of pointing. (Copyright © 1968 by the Canadian Psychological Association. Reprinted by permission.)*

A bird in the hand is not in the bush. Subjects had to scan through such a sentence while holding it in memory, classifying each word as a noun or not. A second experimental variable was how subjects made their responses. Subjects either (1) said "yes" and "no"; (2) tapped with the left hand for yes and the right hand for no; or (3) pointed to successive Ys or Ns on a sheet such as that in Figure 3-11. The two variables of stimulus material (diagram or sentence) and output mode were crossed to yield six conditions.

Table 3-1 gives the results of Brooks' experiment in terms of the mean time spent in classifying the sentences or diagrams in each output condition. The important result for our purposes is that subjects took much longer for diagrams in the pointing condition than in any other condition. This was not the case for sentences. Apparently, scanning a sheet, as in Figure 3-11, conflicted with scanning a mental array. Thus, this result strongly reinforces the conclusion that when subjects are scanning a mental array, they are scanning a representation that is an analog of a physical array. Requiring the subject to

Table 3-1 Mean Classification Times in Brooks, 1968 (seconds)

Stimulus Material	Output		
	Pointing	Tapping	Vocal
Diagrams	28.2	14.1	11.3
Sentences	9.8	7.8	13.8

engage in a conflicting scanning action on an external physical array causes great interference to the mental scan.

It is sometimes thought that Brooks' result was due to the conflict between engaging in a visual pointing task and scanning a visual image. However, subsequent results make it clear that the interference is not due to the visual character of the task. Rather, the problem is more abstract, arising from the conflicting directions in which they had to scan the physical array versus the image. Thus, the conflict is *spatial,* not visual per se. In another experiment, Brooks found evidence of similar interference when subjects had their eyes closed and indicated yes and no by scanning an array of raised Ys and Ns, as in Figure 3-11, with their fingers.

Baddeley and Lieberman (reported in Baddeley, 1976) performed an experiment that strongly supports the view that the nature of the interference in the Brooks task is spatial rather than visual. Subjects were required to perform two tasks simultaneously. All subjects performed the Brooks letter-image task. However, subjects in one group simultaneously monitored a series of stimuli of two possible brightnesses. Subjects had to press a key whenever the brighter stimulus appeared. This task involved the processing of visual but not spatial information. Subjects in the other condition were blindfolded and seated in front of a swinging pendulum. The pendulum emitted a tone and contained a photocell. Subjects were instructed to try to keep the beam of a flashlight on the swinging pendulum. Whenever they were on target, the photocell caused the tone to change frequency, thus providing auditory feedback. This test involved the processing of spatial but not visual information. The spatial-auditory tracking task produced far greater impairment in the image-scanning task than did the brightness-judgment task. This result also indicates that the nature of the impairment in the Brooks task was spatial, not visual. These results reinforce the conclusion that though an image is an analog of a physical structure, it is an abstract analog.

Comparisons of Analog Quantities

Judgments of Remembered Quantities

The point made time and again in these mental-imagery experiments is that processes performed on images tend to vary continuously with the properties of the images—for instance, with angular disparity in the rotation studies or with distance in the scanning studies. At an abstract level, we can summarize these results as follows: when subjects transform a mental object spatially, processing time increases continuously with the amount of the spatial transformation. However, another set of imagery results in the literature shows mental distance exerting the reverse effect: when subjects try to discriminate between two objects, their time to make this discrimination decreases continuously with the amount of difference between the two objects.

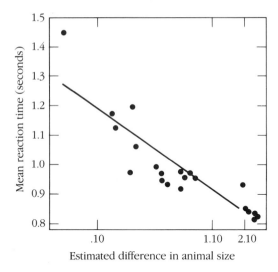

Figure 3-12 *Results from Moyer (1973). Mean time to judge which of two animals is larger as a function of the estimated difference in the size of the two animals. The difference measure is plotted on the abscissa in a logarithmic scale.*

One experiment illustrating this result was performed by Moyer (1973). He was interested in the speed with which subjects could judge the relative size of two animals from memory. For example, *Which is larger, moose or roach?* and *Which is larger, wolf or lion?* Many people report that in making these judgments, particularly for the items that are similar in size, they experience images of the two objects and seem to compare the size of the objects in their image.

In Moyer's experiment, he also asked subjects to estimate the absolute size of these animals. He plotted the reaction time for making a mental-size-comparison judgment between two animals as a function of the difference between the two animals' estimated sizes. Figure 3-12 reproduces these data. The individual points in the figure represent comparisons between pairs of items. In general, the judgment times decrease as the difference in estimated size increases. The graph shows that a fairly linear relation exists between the scale on the abscissa and the scale on the ordinate. Note, however, that on the abscissa of Figure 3-14 the differences have been plotted logarithmically. (A log-difference scale makes variations among small differences large relative to the same variations among large differences). Thus, the linear relationship in Figure 3-14 means that increasing the size difference has a diminishing effect on reaction time.

Significantly, very similar results are obtained when subjects make comparisons of actual physical magnitudes. For instance, Johnson (1939) had subjects judge which of two simultaneously presented lines were longer. Figure 3-13 plots subject judgment time as a function of the log difference in line length. Again a linear relation is obtained. It is reasonable to expect perceptual judgments to take longer the more similar the quantities being

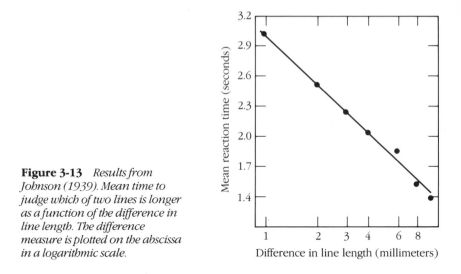

Figure 3-13 *Results from Johnson (1939). Mean time to judge which of two lines is longer as a function of the difference in line length. The difference measure is plotted on the abscissa in a logarithmic scale.*

compared are, since discriminating accurately is more difficult in such circumstances. The fact that similar functions are obtained when mental objects are compared indicates that making mental comparisons involves difficulties of discrimination similar to those involved in perceptual comparisons.

Many other studies have shown that the time required to determine the difference between two objects is a function of the magnitude of their difference. Paivio (1975) showed that Moyer's result extended to mental-size judgments for all kinds of objects besides animals (e.g., *Is a drum larger than a chair?*). Holyoak and Walker (1976) showed similar effects for mental judgments of time (e.g., *Which is longer: a minute or year?*), temperature, and quality. Another experiment, by Moyer and Landauer (1967), showed this same effect for judgments about the larger of two digits from the set 1 through 9. Again judgment time was a function of the logarithm of the difference between the two digits. In an important follow-up to this study, Buckley and Gillman (1974) replicated the finding of a logarithmic function of difference for number judgments. They found the same logarithmic function whether subjects were comparing numeric symbols (i.e., the digits 1 through 9) or clusters of one to nine dots. Again, it seems that whatever comparison process is being evoked in the symbolic situation, there is a similar comparison process evoked in the perceptual situation.

Judgments of Abstract Qualities

A number of experiments have required that subjects make quantitative comparisons of qualities with no obvious physical representation. For instance, Banks and Flora (1977) had one group of subjects rate animals on a 1–10 scale as to intelligence. The mean ratings of the eight animals rated were ape (9.20), dog (7.36), cat (6.57), horse (5.57), cow (3.58), sheep (3.42), chicken (3.36), and fish (1.68). A second, independent group of subjects was then presented with pairs of these animals and asked to judge which member of the pair was the more intelligent. Banks and Flora found that judgment time decreased as the distance in rated intelligence between the two animals increased. Similar distance effects are found when subjects make judgments as to ferocity of animals (Kerst and Howard, 1977) or pleasantness of words (Paivio, 1978). Even though such judgments do not involve picturable quantities, Paivio (1978) has argued that the imagery system is involved in making these judgments just as it is in making judgments about concrete quantities. The implication again is that visual imagery is not tied to the visual modality but involves a more general ability for processing analog information.

Thus, similar inverse distance functions are found at three levels, varying from the perceptual to the abstract:

1. When the objects being compared are physically presented to subjects, as when two lines are being compared with respect to length.
2. When the physical attributes of mental objects are being compared —for instance, size of animals.
3. When quantities that cannot be visualized are being compared—for instance, pleasantness of objects.

This array of results points to the conclusion that the process for making comparisons between qualities mentally is abstract in that it is not tied to a perceptual modality. This conclusion corresponds to our earlier conclusion that the processes for performing continuous transformations on an imagined object are abstract. Thus, images behave like abstract analogs.

Judgments of Linear Orderings

Suppose you learn such information as the following:

> John is taller than Fred.
> Fred is taller than Bill.
> Bill is taller than Herb.
> Herb is taller than Dave.
> Dave is taller than Alex.

If you learn these items so that you can recite them perfectly in correct order—John, Fred, Bill, Herb, Dave, and Alex—you will have learned what is called a *linear ordering*.

Next suppose you are asked, "Who is taller, Dave or Fred?" How would you go about answering this question? Some evidence suggests that subjects

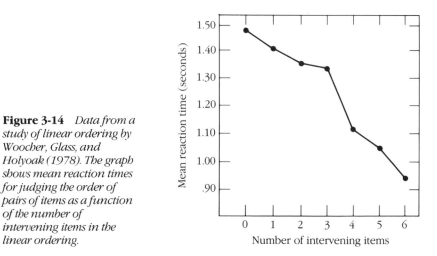

Figure 3-14 *Data from a study of linear ordering by Woocher, Glass, and Holyoak (1978). The graph shows mean reaction times for judging the order of pairs of items as a function of the number of intervening items in the linear ordering.*

answer such a question by engaging in the same processes they use in making comparison judgments about the size of items in natural categories such as lions and wolves. Many experiments have been performed using linear orderings, such as Potts (1972, 1975) and Trabasso and Riley (1975). In this section, we consider a recent experiment by Woocher, Glass, and Holyoak (1978), in which subjects were to learn quite long linearly ordered lists. The results of this experiment are typical. Subjects learned about the linear ordering on the dimension of height of 16 people, referred to by name, and were asked to judge the relative heights of various pairs of items in the list. Interest focused on the amount of time subjects took to answer these questions as a function of the distance between the two items in the list. The latter varied from a distance of no intervening items (members of the pair were adjacent in the ordering) to a distance of six intervening items. Figure 3-14 plots the subjects' reactions times as a function of this distance. Note that a decreasing function was obtained similar to that obtained when subjects make magnitude estimates of natural categories. A particularly striking feature of these data concerns the results for pairs with no intervening items. These are the pairs subjects were trained on to learn the linear orderings. Despite the fact that subjects were directly trained on only these pairs, they were slowest in judging these pairs.

These results can be interpreted as indicating that subjects perform this task by comparing two quantities. Perhaps subjects associate a height with each individual. When asked to compare two individuals, they retrieve the heights of each and compare them. Often subjects report imagining the individuals ordered from left to right or top to bottom on an imaginary line in front of them. When asked to make a comparison, they try to imagine which individual comes before or above the other. If subjects were comparing continuously varying quantities, we would expect their reaction times to decrease with ordinal distance, and this is indeed what we find.*

An experiment by Potts (1977) serves nicely to illustrate the close connection between the work on artificial linear orderings and that on natural orderings such as sizes of animals. Potts had different groups of subjects study the following assertions, which order three artificial animals (JAL, FIB, and KIB) relative to the size of known animals:

Group 1	*Group 2*
blue whale is larger than JAL	blue whale is larger than JAL
JAL is larger than elephant	JAL is larger than elephant
zebra is larger than FIP	bullfrog is larger than FIP
FIP is larger than cougar	FIP is larger than scorpion
bee is larger than KIB	bee is larger than KIB
KIB is larger than flea	KIB is larger than flea

The size of a FIP was being implicitly manipulated for the two groups. That is, FIP was between a zebra and cougar in size for group 1 and between a bullfrog and a scorpion in size for group 2. After learning these orderings, subjects had to make judgments about the ordering of various animals. Of particular interest were the judgments involving the category FIP. Subjects were asked to make judgments about the relationship of the FIP category to the animals they had studied as well as to new animals. One group of new animals included the following, all of which were larger than FIPs for either group: rhino, hippo, bison, camel, and moose. A second group of new animals included the following, all of which were smaller than FIPs for either group: roach, ladybug, termite, housefly, and gnat.

Figure 3-15 shows the times subjects in the two groups took to make size comparisons of FIPs to animals in the large and small categories. Group 1 found it harder to compare FIPs to the large category, and group 2 found it harder to compare FIPs to the small category. Presumably, the source of difficulty for group 1 was that FIP was close in size to the large category; for group 2, it was that FIP was close in size to the small category. Subjects found it hard to make size comparisons between objects that were similar in size. These results are consistent with the idea that when subjects acquire a linear ordering they are associating analog quantities with members of the linear ordering to represent members' position on the ordering.

---

*Because there are ordinal distances rather than distances on an interval scale, it is not easy to explore the issue of whether these are logarithmic functions such as the ones in Figures 3-12 and 3-13, where we could assign interval values to the distances.

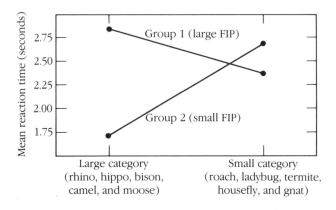

Figure 3-15   *Time to make comparisons of size of FIPS (imaginary animals) to large and small animals when subjects have learned large or small animals bracketing the size of a FIP. (Adapted from Potts, 1977.)*

Images Versus Mental Pictures

We have reviewed the ample evidence showing that images are analogs that vary continuously with properties of the objects they represent. People have a natural tendency to think of images as "pictures in the head." Most theorists in the area resist this temptation and for good reason. Let us review their reasons for distinguishing between images and mental pictures.

First, as we have emphasized, images are abstract and not tied to visual properties. Properties associated with visual images can derive from tactile as well as visual experience (Brooks). Also, we can process in imagelike manner such quantities as intelligence.

Also, some operations are easy to perform on a picture but hard to perform on an image. Consider the following example (adapted from Simon, 1978):

> Imagine but do not draw a rectangle 2 inches wide and 1 inch high, with a vertical line cutting it into two 1-inch squares. Imagine a diagonal from the upper left-hand corner to the lower right-hand corner of the 2 × 1-inch rectangle. We will call this line diagonal *A*. Imagine a second diagonal from the upper right-hand corner to the lower left-hand corner of the right *square*. Call this line diagonal *B*. Consider where diagonal *A* cuts diagonal *B*. What is the relationship of the length of *B* above the cut to the length of *B* below the cut?

This is very difficult imaginal task. To the extent that we can answer the question accurately, we have to call on abstract knowledge about geometry. However, if presented with a physical picture of the figure described, we could quickly and fairly accurately report the length relation between the two

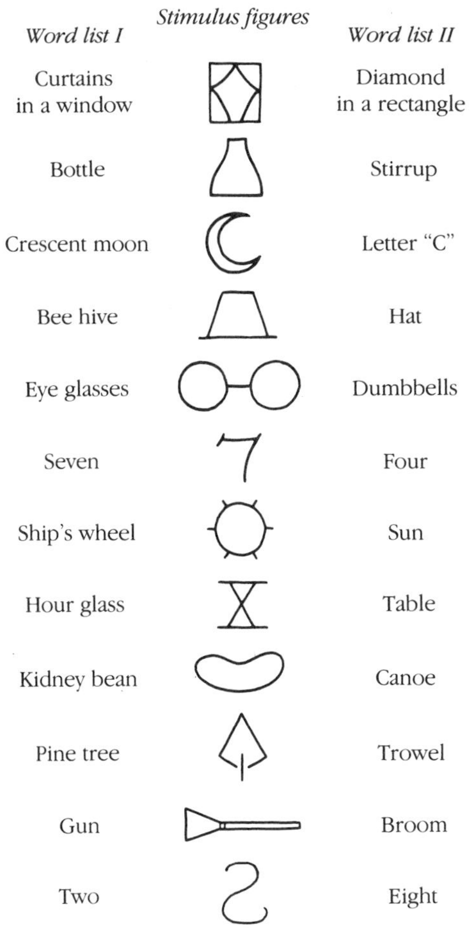

Word list I	Stimulus figures	Word list II
Curtains in a window		Diamond in a rectangle
Bottle		Stirrup
Crescent moon		Letter "C"
Bee hive		Hat
Eye glasses		Dumbbells
Seven		Four
Ship's wheel		Sun
Hour glass		Table
Kidney bean		Canoe
Pine tree		Trowel
Gun		Broom
Two		Eight

Figure 3-16 *Materials used in the Carmichael, Hogan, and Walter (1932) experiment in which subjects were shown figures accompanied by cue words and were then asked to reproduce the figures. Subjects studied the stimulus figures with one of the two verbal labels.*

segments of line *B*. This example shows that an image cannot always be inspected like a picture.

A third point of distinction is that images can be distorted by general knowledge. Consider the classic study by Carmichael, Hogan, and Walter (1932). Subjects were exposed to the shapes in Figure 3-16 along with one of the two verbal descriptions. Thus, the fifth object might be described to the subject as *eye glasses* or *dumbbells*. In either case, subjects were to remember the exact drawing. However, when asked to draw the objects from memory, their drawings were distorted in the direction of the named category. For instance, given *eye glasses,* the subject might put a bend in the shaft, but given *dumbbells,* a subject might put a double shaft between the two circles. Thus, subjects' memory for the physical properties of the drawings was distorted by

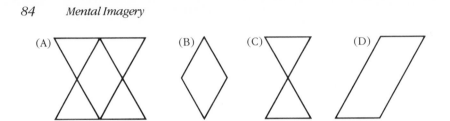

Figure 3-17   *Forms used by Reed in his studies concerning the components of images. Figures B, C and D are all contained in A. However, subjects appear to see B and C more easily as part of A than they can see D as part of A. (From Reed, 1974.)*

general knowledge about a category. A true picture would not be distorted by knowledge of the object pictured. Thus, images seem to be more malleable than pictures.

Finally, images consist of pieces while pictures do not. Consider Figure 3-17A. Reed presented subjects with such forms and asked them to hold images of the forms in their minds (Reed, 1974; Reed and Johnson, 1975). The form was removed and subjects were presented with pieces of the form such as Figures 3-17B, C, and D. Subjects were able to identify B and C as parts of A 65 percent of the time but were successful with D only 10 percent of the time. The reason for the difference was that subjects' image of A consisted of such pieces as B and C but not D. A picture would not show this property. All pieces of A would be equally represented in a picture. (A similar point is made in a different paradigm by Palmer, 1977.)

General Properties of Images

If an image is not a picture, what is it? This is an issue about which many cognitive psychologists have strong opinions but little good evidence. My own opinion is that an image is a representation basically like the propositional network representations discussed in the next chapter. However, this is a view so controversial that I feel I cannot develop it in an introductory text. However, even if we are unable to define imagery representation precisely, we can specify some of the properties of images:

1. They are capable of representing continuously varying information.
2. They are capable of having operations performed on them that are analogs of spatial operations.
3. They are not tied to the visual modality but seem to be part of a more general system for representing spatial and continuously varying information.

4. Quantities, such as size, are harder to discriminate in images the more similar they are.

5. Images are more malleable and less crisp than pictures.

6. Images of complex objects are segmented into pieces.

It is informative to consider when images, having the properties reviewed, will prove to be useful to cognition and when they will not. Earlier, we contrasted analog representation (e.g., representing a weight by a quantity such as a line length) with symbolic representations (e.g., representing a weight by a phrase like *150 pounds*). Imaginal structures, because of their analog properties, represent the external world much more faithfully than do symbolic structures. The relationship between symbolic structures and the external world is quite arbitrary. It is not possible to continuously vary symbolic structures in the way that it is possible to continuously vary imaginal or analog structures. We saw in the work on mental comparisons that the more similar two analog quantities were to each other, the harder it was to discriminate between them. No corresponding confusion occurs with respect to two symbolic structures—they either match each other or they do not.

Symbolic structures are more useful for some intellectual purposes, while analog structures are more useful for others. For example, in attempting to recall a phone number, clearly we want to be dealing with a discrete symbolic structure—the actual numbers. We have to be able to dial the number exactly; it would not do to remember a number that is merely close. Here we do not want a representation that is an analog of a physical quantity. It is interesting to speculate as to whether the emergence of human intelligence as we know it depended on the development of symbolic representation—whether the capacity for symbolic representation is what separates man from other animals. The uniqueness of human intelligence is often ascribed to the fact that humans have an advanced language system that can process symbols effectively. This issue will be explored further in the next chapter and in Chapter 12.

Whether it is part of a more primitive representational system or not, an imaginal analog representation is more advantageous than a symbolic representation in many situations. One has only to compare the effectiveness of a map versus a set of verbal instructions as a guide to an unfamiliar city. Clearly, in some situations we need a representation that is an analog of the external world. And, intriguingly, analog representations are used in situations other than just those requiring us to reason about continuously varying physical features of the external world. For example, we have seen that such analogs seem to be used in reasoning about intelligence and pleasantness. Analog representations also seem to find their way into the thought patterns of experts in very symbolic areas. Mathematicians are famous for reporting that imagery helps them reason about their field. For instance, mathematicians in abstract algebra often report that they think of the groups they study in terms of networks or other spatial metaphors. Indeed, in the next chapter we will represent abstract propositions in network form.

We probably tend to convert symbolic structures into spatial analogs because we are particularly well practiced at operating on analogs of spatial structures. We get such practice during every moment of our perceiving lives. Whenever it is possible to mirror the essential aspects of a symbolic structure in an analog structure, it is to our advantage to do so.

Mental Imagery and Spatial Cognition

Cognitive Maps

A number of efforts are now underway to determine how the work on mental imagery applies to the practical problems of map interpretation and finding one's way in the environment. Back in the heyday of behaviorism, Tolman (e.g., 1948) caused a stir with his claims, considered quite radical, that rats had "cognitive maps." Cognitive maps are internal representations of the spatial layout of one's environment. Such mentalistic constructs were not popular with behaviorists. Nowadays it seems quite clear that, whatever the situation with respect to rats, humans make important use of cognitive maps for guiding themselves through their environments. Often, these cognitive maps are formed from memories of "paper" maps. A recent surge of research has been concerned with the nature of these cognitive maps and the ways in which people use them as well as the ways in which people use real paper maps.

It is now becoming clear that the same kinds of processes are involved in the processing of cognitive maps as are involved in the imagery tasks discussed earlier. One illustration of this point is a study by Maki, Maki, and Marsh (1977). The experimenters had subjects make judgments about American states from their memory of the U.S. map. Subjects had to decide either which of a pair of states was to the north or south or which of a pair of states was to the east or west. In line with other research on mental comparisons, the researchers found that judgment time decreased with the distance between the two states. And they found another significant effect: that east–west judgments were generally harder to make. The U.S. map is, of course, standardly oriented with the north to the top. The disadvantage for east–west judgments is just one instance of a rather general difficulty people have in making left–right judgments relative to above–below judgments. For instance, people are slower to judge an object that is to the left of another in an array than to judge an object above another.

In another study, Loftus (1978) examined subjects' facility in comprehending compass directions. Subjects were given a direction (e.g., 220°) and were instructed to indicate this direction on a circle relative to north (or 0°) at the

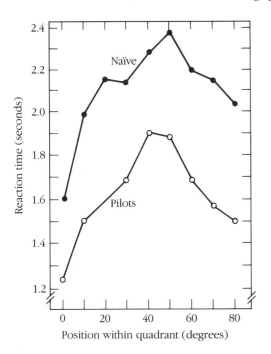

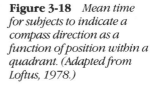

Figure 3-18 *Mean time for subjects to indicate a compass direction as a function of position within a quadrant. (Adapted from Loftus, 1978.)*

top. The investigator compared this facility in experienced pilots, who have to comprehend such directions regularly, with that in relatively naive subjects. The pilots comprehended the instructions much more rapidly than the naive subjects, but both groups showed similar effects. All subjects gave their fastest response times for the standard compass points (north, east, south, and west). Figure 3-18 presents response times to indicate the directions as a function of number of degrees past the standard point. Note that reaction time increases until about 50°. The result is consistent with the subjects' reports. They claimed to go to one of the four standard reference points and then to mentally rotate forward or backward until they reached the specified point. The reason that the reaction-time function does not increase beyond 50° is that subjects would often rotate back from the next quadrant to these points. So, it seems that the mental-rotation processes identified and studied in the laboratory also operate in compass-direction comprehension. It is important to note, however, that subjects given a direction such as 220° managed to avoid having to rotate all 220°. They went directly to a reference point (e.g., to due south or 180°) and rotated from there.

A study by Jonides and Baum (1978) illustrates that another aspect of image processing is involved in understanding the environment. These investigators had students at the University of Michigan estimate the distance between objects on their campus. They found that the time required to make the distance judgments increased with the distance between two objects—the results were similar to those reported by Kosslyn, Ball, and Reiser discussed earlier. In another study, Baum and Jonides (1977) had subjects judge which of two distances on campus was shorter. Here they found that subjects took longer the closer the two distances were—again, results in line with other research on the comparison of analog quantities.

If we accept the premise that the understanding of maps and our environment involves the same processes as those involved in imagery studies, then the question arises as to how we might apply our knowledge about imagery to practical problems of using maps and getting around the environment. It is clear that finding one's way in the environment is sometimes difficult. Our environment is often organized like a maze, and maps of this environment can be like mazes too. It is not always easy to use one maze (the map) to guide oneself through another maze (e.g., a city). Finding one's way in cities organized on a simple grid formula—such as much of Manhattan—is easy, but most regions have more complex structures. We are clearly limited in how quickly we can process imaginal information and how much such information we can process at once. To make matters worse, our environments are usually very complex and large. We should be able to use findings from cognitive-psychology research to determine the best ways for dealing with the high information-processing demands created by the environment or to alert ourselves to the kinds of mistakes we are likely to make in map cognition.

Three possible solutions apply in problems of finding one's way around the environment. These solutions represent overall approaches to difficulties experienced by the general population in a given environment.

1. Change the environment. This can be a real possibility for city planners.
2. Improve the auxiliary devices (maps, road signs, directions) for finding one's way around.
3. Improve individuals' skills in using existing devices in the environment as it is.

Whatever combination of these solutions is ultimately used, it should be based on an understanding of the mental processes used in reasoning about spatial regions.

One important consideration in spatial reasoning is the importance of *landmarks,* or *reference points.* We saw a simple case of using reference points in Loftus's study, where subjects used the four standard compass points as references. Since one's environment is typically very large and complicated, having to mentally search through and process an entire area can be very time-consuming. The alternative is to organize the environment in terms of reference points or landmarks so that one can mentally go quickly to a

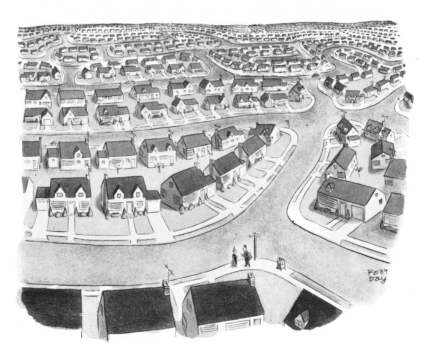

"I'm Mrs. Edward M. Barnes. Where do I live?"

Figure 3-19   *Cartoon from* The New Yorker *illustrating the problem of finding one's way around the environment. (Drawing by Robt. Day; © 1954 The New Yorker Magazine, Inc.)*

relevant landmark and focus processing on the immediate area around it. The concept of landmarks leads to the following recommendations, one for each of the approaches listed on the previous page.

1. City planners should create prominent landmarks at regular points in the city—for instance, at major choice points (intersections) in the road systems. It would be particularly helpful to make these landmarks visible at a distance so that individuals could prepare themselves for the decisions ahead.

2. Map makers should highlight the presence of these landmarks.

3. In trying to understand an area, individuals should locate major landmarks around which to organize their spatial understanding.

Route Maps Versus Survey Maps

There is evidence (Hart and Moore, 1973) that as children develop, their cognitive maps progress from what are called *route maps* to *survey maps*. Adults often show the same sequence in learning about a new area. A route map is a path that indicates specific places but contains no two-dimensional information. Thus, with a route map, if your route from location 1 to location 2 were blocked, you would have no general idea of where location 2 was, so you would be unable to construct a detour. If you knew (in the sense of a route map) two routes from a source, you would have no idea whether these routes were at a 90° angle or a 180° angle from each other. A survey map, in contrast, contains this information.

To understand the limitations of route maps, consider the directions I have memorized for getting from my home to Chatham Center in Pittsburgh:

1. Go two blocks south on Amberson.
2. Turn right on Fifth.
3. Follow Fifth for a mile or so until the road forks.
4. Turn left and go two or three blocks.
5. After the Playhouse, turn right.
6. Go a block and turn right onto the Boulevard of the Allies.
7. Follow the Boulevard for about a mile and a half.
8. Turn right on the Cross-Town Boulevard and follow it for maybe a quarter of a mile.
9. Chatham Center has been reached; follow directions for parking.

This is a route map. Using this information alone, are you able to determine the relative direction from my house to Chatham Center? If you try to calculate the direction, you will probably judge that it is north by northwest. In fact, Chatham Center is almost due west but slightly southwest. (Some of the roads take jogs, and some turns are not 90°.) There is no way of determining this fact from a route map. One would need at least some survey-map knowledge of Pittsburgh to be able to determine this direction.

Thorndyke and Hayes-Roth (1978) investigated secretaries' knowledge of the Rand building, a large, mazelike building, in Santa Monica, California. They found that secretaries quickly acquired an ability to find their ways from one specific place in the building to another—for example, from their offices to the photocopy room or from their offices to the lunch room. This knowledge represents a route map. However, typically secretaries had to have ten years' experience in the Rand building before they were capable of making such survey-map determinations as the direction of the lunch room from the photocopy room.

Survey maps tend to be organized around landmarks. For children, the first prominent landmark is their home. Later, others evolve, such as their school. There is evidence that many species, ranging from bees to humans, use such maps anchored around a reference point, particularly the home. It may be that the use of reference points taps some very basic and primitive capabilities for spatial cognition. This is one of many issues that needs more research.

Misinterpretations of Cognitive Maps

One of the most heavily studied phenomena in spatial cognition involves distortions in people's mental maps. People try to regularize their cognitive maps. For instance, Milgram and Jodelet (1976) showed that Parisians think the Seine makes a much gentler arc through Paris than it does. Consequently, they actually get confused about Right Bank districts, placing them mentally on the Left Bank. Stevens and Coupe (1978) documented a set of misconceptions people have about North American geography. Consider the following questions, taken from their research:

> Which is farther east: San Diego or Reno?
> Which is farther north: Seattle or Montreal?
> Which is farther west: The Atlantic or the Pacific entrance to
> the Panama Canal?

The first choice is the correct answer in each case, but most people hold the wrong opinion. Reno seems to be farther east because Nevada is east of California, but this reasoning does not account for the slope in California's coastline. Montreal seems to be north of Seattle, since Canada is north of the United States, but the border dips in the east. And the Atlantic is certainly east of the Pacific, but consult a map if you need to be convinced about the Panama Canal. The geography of North American is quite complex, and subjects resort to abstract facts about relative locations of large physical bodies (e.g., California and Nevada) to make judgments about smaller locations (e.g., San Diego and Reno). These outcomes are similar to results of Carmichael, Hogan, and Walter (1932) that we reviewed earlier and demonstrate again the close connection between imaginal information and more general knowledge.

Stevens and Coupe were able to demonstrate such confusions with experimenter-created maps. Figure 3-20 illustrates the maps that different groups of subjects learned. The important feature of the incongruent maps is that the relative location of the Alpha and Beta counties is inconsistent with the X and Y cities. After learning the maps, subjects were asked a series of questions about the locations of cities including, *Is* X *east or west of* Y? for the left-hand maps, and, *Is* X *north or south of* Y? for the right-hand maps.

Subjects were in error 18 percent of the time on the $X-Y$ question for the congruent maps and 15 percent for the homogeneous maps, but they were in error 45 percent of the time for the incongruent maps. Subjects were using information about the location of the counties to help them remember the

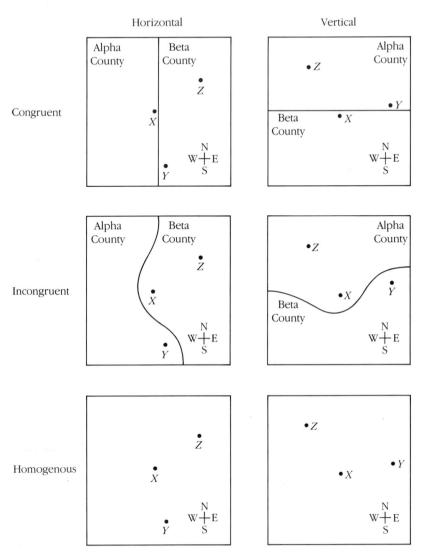

Figure 3-20 *Maps studied by subjects in the experiments of Stevens and Coupe (1978), in which the effects were studied of "higher order information" (location of county lines) on subjects' recall of city locations.*

city locations. This reliance on "higher order" information led them to make errors, just as similar reasoning can lead to errors in questions about North American geography.

Another major source of difficulty with an environment, particularly when one is new to it, are left-right confusions. If you are following on a paper map a road headed north, comprehending the map is fairly easy, since the direction corresponds to map orientation. However, when your direction is not north, you may experience confusion. Should you rotate the map or yourself? Is it safe to attempt this rotation mentally or should you do it physically? The informal evidence is that experts in map reading (for example, generals trained to direct troops in novel terrain) always orient the map so that north is at the top whereas novices orient the map to match the direction in which they are headed. Perhaps experts do not suffer left-right confusions and are better able to process the global properties of maps if they are kept in constant orientation. The problem of orientation would seem to be an important area for continuing work in mental rotation.

Remarks and Suggested Readings

The nature of the representation for mental imagery is currently being hotly debated. References to this controversy are given at the end of Chapter 4. I have avoided getting embroiled in this issue in this chapter and have simply tried to draw common-sense conclusions from the existing research. Shepard and Podgorny (1978) provide a good overview of the research on mental imagery and some discussion of this controversy. The research on imagery has suffered from a lack of explicit theories regarding the exact processes and representations involved. One attempt to remedy this deficit is the computer simulation program of Kosslyn and Schwartz (1977).

An influential study of our understanding of our environment is provided by Lynch (1960) in his book *The Image of the City,* where he contrasts Boston, Jersey City, and Los Angeles and the conception of each city held by its inhabitants. He also discusses cultural differences in the representation of the environment. Hintzman (1979) has just completed a major series of studies of the ways in which people orient themselves in somewhat familiar environments. Interestingly, he concludes that subjects solve this problem by using not mental images but propositions, which are discussed in the next chapter.

Chapter 4

The Representation of Information in Memory

Summary

1. The *dual-code theory* claims that information is stored in long-term memory in terms of visual images and verbal representations. This theory contrasts with the *propositional code theory,* which holds that representation in memory is abstract and is not tied to a particular sensory modality.

2. Evidence for the propositional position comes from experiments showing that memory for a verbal communication retains not the exact wording but just the meaning of the communication, and from experiments showing that memory for a picture does not retain the visual details but rather a meaningful interpretation of the picture.

3. This chapter explains how a sentence is analyzed into its underlying propositions and how a network representation of these propositions is created. Such representations reveal in graphical form the associative connections between concepts.

4. Part of the meaning of a concept can be represented in terms of its connections to other concepts. This portion of the meaning is referred to as the *configurational meaning* of a sentence. Configurational meaning can be represented by a propositional network.

5. Propositional networks can be used to represent the meaningful information from pictures that subjects are good at remembering.

6. The closer together the concepts in a propositional network are, the better cues they are for each other's recall.

7. Initial memory for an event contains both verbal and visual details. However, information about these details tends to be rapidly forgotten within the first minute following the stimulus, leaving only memory for the meaning of the event.

8. Because memory for meaning is longer lasting than memory for physical details, individuals can improve their memories by converting meaningless to-be-remembered information into a more meaningful form. A number of mnemonic techniques based on this principle are discussed.

Propositional Versus Dual-Code Theories

I once sat down to have a gyro sandwich with an astrophysicist:

He: So you study memory. What are the current hot issues in memory?

Me: Well, one issue is how information is represented in long-term memory. It might seem esoteric to a layman, but consider. . . .

He: We have verbal memories and we have visual memories, but the question is do we have memories that are neither verbal nor visual?

Me: Yes, that is the hot issue.

The astrophysicist nicely illustrated the layperson's intuitions, which agree with a thesis in psychology called the *dual-code theory of memory.* Currently, this theory's strongest advocate is Allan Paivio, of the University of Western Ontario (e.g., Paivio, 1971). The theory holds that information is represented in memory in two ways—as visual images and as verbal memories. We discussed the properties of images in the previous chapter. There we reviewed evidence that images are more spatial than visual per se; however, dual-code theorists have generally maintained that images are basically visual. A verbal memory is auditory (that is, memory for the sounds) or articulatory (that is, memory for the motor acts of speech) in character; it is memory for a string of words, and resembles the original auditory perception or articulatory generation of a string of words. Proponents of the dual-code hypothesis do not deny that other codes may exist for other modalities, such as touch, taste, and smell. However, they consider the verbal and visual codes to be the dominant ones for hearing, seeing humans. And proponents do insist that all information is represented as sensory or motor experiences. Thus, they would deny that we have memories that are not tied to a particular sensory modality.

In this chapter, we will consider further these verbal and visual codes. We will also present evidence for an abstract, nonsensory code and consider how this abstract information might be represented. We will then return to visual and verbal information, considering how this information is dealt with in memory.

Memory for Verbal Information

There should be little doubt that we have some verbatim memories, that is, memories of the exact words we have heard, read, or spoken at certain times. We can remember verbatim lines from poems, songs, plays, and speeches. However, considerable doubt exists as to whether all or even most of our memory for verbal communication can be accounted for in terms of memory for the verbatim (auditory or written) message.

The real difficulty with the verbatim-memory hypothesis is that typically people seem to remember the gist or meaning of what they read and not the exact words. Consider the previous chapter on imagery in this book. I hope you have read it carefully and remember much from it, but can you recall much or anything of its exact wording? I am not sure I can, and I wrote it! Thus, it seems that the dual-code hypothesis is wrong in its claims that verbatim memories are dominant.

An experiment by Wanner (1968) illustrates circumstances under which people do and do not remember information about exact wording. Wanner had subjects come into the laboratory and listen to tape-recorded instructions. For one group of subjects, "the warned group," the tape began this way:

> The materials for this test, including the instructions, have been recorded on tape. Listen very carefully to the instructions because you will be tested on your ability to recall particular sentences which occur in the *instructions.*

The second group received no such warning and so had no idea that they would be responsible for verbatim memory for the instructions. After this point, the instructions were the same for both groups. At a later point in the instructions, one of four possible critical sentences occurred:

1. When you score your results, do nothing to correct your answers but mark carefully those answers which are wrong.
2. When you score your results, do nothing to correct your answers but carefully mark those answers which are wrong.
3. When you score your results, do nothing to your correct answers but mark carefully those answers which are wrong.
4. When you score your results, do nothing to your correct answers but carefully mark those answers which are wrong.

Immediately after presentation of this sentence, all subjects (warned or not) heard the following conclusion to the instructions:

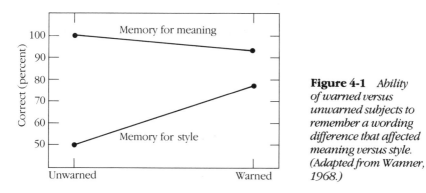

Figure 4-1 *Ability of warned versus unwarned subjects to remember a wording difference that affected meaning versus style. (Adapted from Wanner, 1968.)*

To begin the test, please turn to page 2 of the answer booklet and judge which of the sentences printed there occurred in the instructions you just heard.

On page 2 they found the critical sentence they had just heard plus a similar alternative. Suppose they had heard sentence 1. They might have to choose between 1 and 2 or between 1 and 3. Both pairs differ in the ordering of two words. However, the difference between 1 and 2 does not contribute critically to the meaning of the sentences; the difference is just stylistic. On the other hand, sentences 1 and 3 clearly do differ in meaning. Thus, by looking at subjects' ability to discriminate between different pairs of sentences, Wanner was able to measure their ability to remember the meaning versus the style of the sentence and to determine how this ability interacted with whether or not they were warned. The relevant data are displayed in Figure 4-1.

In this display, the percentage of correct identifications of sentences heard before is a function of whether subjects had been warned. The percentages correct for subjects who were asked to discriminate a meaningful difference in wording and for subjects who were asked to discriminate a stylistic difference are plotted separately. If subjects were just guessing, they would have scored 50 percent correct by chance; thus, we would not expect any values below 50 percent.

The implications of Figure 4-1 are clear. First, memory is better for changes in wording that result in changes of meaning than just in changes of style. The superiority of memory for meaning indicates that people normally extract the meaning from a linguistic message and do not remember its exact wording. Moreover, memory for meaning is equally good whether subjects are warned or not. (The slight advantage for unwarned subjects does not approach statistical significance.) Thus, subjects retain the meaning of a message as a normal part of their comprehension process. They do not have to be especially cued to memorize the sentence. In Chapter 7, we will see more evidence showing that intention to learn is often irrelevant to good memory.

The second implication of these results is that the warning did have an effect on memory for the stylistic change. Subjects were almost at chance in remembering stylistic change when unwarned, but they were fairly good at remembering when warned. This result indicates that we do not naturally retain much information about exact wording but that we can do so when we are especially cued to pay attention to such information. However, even with such a warning, memory for stylistic information is much poorer than memory for meaning.

Other experiments dramatically make the point that we remember the meaning rather than the exact wording of a verbal communication. These experiments contrast memory for meaningful sentences with that for random word strings. Consider an experiment by Pompi and Lachman (1967). They had subjects study either a coherent paragraph or the words that appeared in the paragraph scrambled into a random order. The result is so obvious it hardly needs reporting: subjects in the paragraph condition were able to recall more of the words than subjects in the scrambled condition. Clearly, we normally remember the meaning and not just the words. When we cannot extract the meaning of a passage, we have difficulty remembering the words.

Memory for Visual Information

On many occasions, our memory capacity seems much greater for visual information than for verbal information. A representative experiment was reported by Shepard (1967), in which he had subjects study a set of magazine pictures one picture at a time. After studying the pictures, subjects were presented with pairs of pictures consisting of one they had studied and one they had not studied. The subjects' task was to recognize which of each pair was the studied picture. This task was contrasted with a verbal situation, in which subjects studied sentences and were similarly tested on their ability to recognize studied sentences when presented with pairs containing one new and one studied sentence. Results exhibited 11.8 percent errors in the sentence condition but only 1.5 percent errors in the picture condition. Recognition memory was fairly high in the sentence condition, but it was virtually perfect in the picture condition.

What is it that subjects are remembering when they remember a picture? It seems that, in contrast to the claims of the dual-code hypothesis, they are not remembering the picture as an exact visual object. Instead they are remembering some rather abstract representation that captures the picture's meaning. That is, it proves useful to distinguish between the meaning of a picture and the physical picture, just as it proves important to distinguish between the meaning of a sentence and the physical sentence. A number of experiments point to the utility of this distinction with respect to picture memory and to the fact that we tend to remember the picture's meaning, not the physical picture. For example, subjects show poor memory for pictures that they are

Figure 4-2   *An apparently meaningless picture. Subjects show better memory for this picture when they can recognize the dog. (From Ronald James.)*

unable to interpret meaningfully. Consider the picture in Figure 4-2, which appears to be a random collection of ink blobs. The picture seems to have no meaning, and subjects show poor memory for it. However, if you look carefully, you will see a dog hidden in the picture. If people are able to detect the hidden figure in pictures like these, they will show much better memory for the picture (Wiseman and Neisser, 1974).

Figure 4-3 contains some of the material from the experiment of Bower, Karlin, and Dueck (1975), which makes the same point as Wiseman and Neisser's experiment. These investigators had subjects study such pictures, called *droodles,* with or without an explanation of their meaning. After subjects had studied the pictures, they were given a memory test in which they had to redraw the pictures. Subjects who had been given labels with which to study the pictures showed better recall of these pictures (70 percent correctly reconstructed) than subjects who were not given the verbal labels (51 percent).

It seems that people normally extract and remember the meaning from a picture just as they do with sentences. A recent experiment by Mandler and

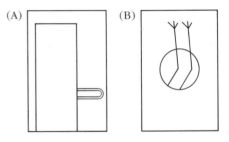

Figure 4-3 *"Droodles" used in Bower, Karlin, and Dueck (1975). (A) A midget playing a trombone in a telephone booth. (B) An early bird who caught a very strong worm.*

Ritchey (1977) made this point in yet another way. The experimenters had subjects study pictures of scenes, such as the classroom scene in Figure 4-4A. After studying eight such pictures for ten seconds each, subjects were tested for their recognition memory of the pictures. In the test, subjects were presented with a series of pictures and instructed to identify which pictures they had studied in the series. The series contained the exact pictures they had studied as well as distractor pictures such as Figures 4-4B and C. A distractor such as B was called a *token distractor*. It differs from the target only with respect to the pattern on the teacher's dress, a visual detail relatively unimportant to the meaning of the picture. In contrast, the distractor (C) involves a *type change*—from a world map to an art picture used by the teacher. This visual detail is relatively more important to the meaning of the picture, since it indicates the subject being taught. All eight pictures shown to subjects contained possible token changes and type changes. In each case, the type change involved a more important change to the picture's meaning than did the token change. There was no systematic difference in the amount of physical change involved in a type versus a token change. Subjects were able to recognize the original pictures 77 percent of the time, reject the token distractors only 60 percent of the time, but reject the type distractors 94 percent of the time. Chance guessing performance would have been 50 percent.

The conclusion in this study is very similar to that in the Wanner experiment reviewed earlier. Just as Wanner found that subjects were much more sensitive to meaning-significant changes in a sentence, so Mandler and Ritchey have found that subjects are sensitive to meaning-significant changes in a picture. It may be that subjects have better memory for the meanings of pictures than for the meanings of sentences, but that they have poor memory for the physical details for both. Thus, while people may remember visual and verbal details, in contradiction to the dual-code hypotheses the mainstay of human memory seems to be neither the verbal code nor the visual code. Rather, the mainstay is an abstract representation that preserves only the meaning of the item studied. Such a representation is referred to as a *propositional representation*.

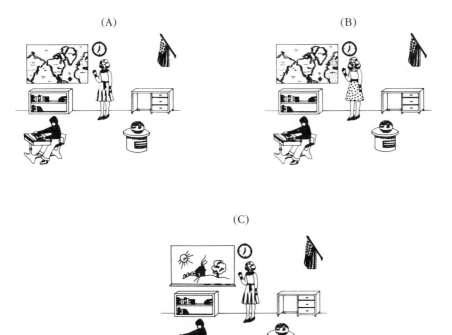

Figure 4-4 *Pictures similar to those used in Mandler and Ritchey (1977). (A) Subjects studied this target picture. Later they were tested with a series of pictures that included the target (A) but also token distractors such as B and type distractors such as C. (Copyright © 1976 by the American Psychological Association. Reprinted by permission.)*

Propositional Representations

Analysis into Propositions

The idea that information is represented in terms of propositions is currently the most popular concept of how meaning is represented in memory. In a propositional analysis, only the meaning of an event is represented. The unimportant details—details that humans tend not to remember—are not represented. This idea has been incorporated into such contemporary theories as Anderson (1976), Anderson and Bower (1973), Clark (1974), Fredericksen (1976), Kintsch (1974), and Norman and Rumelhart (1975). The concept of a *proposition,* borrowed from logic and linguistics, is central to this analysis. A proposition is the smallest unit of knowledge that can stand as a separate assertion, that is, the smallest unit about which it makes sense to make the judgment true or false. Propositional analysis most clearly applies to linguistic information, and it is with respect to this information that the topic is developed here. In a later section, propositional analysis will be discussed with respect to representing the meaning of a picture.

Consider the following sentence:

1. Nixon gave a beautiful Cadillac to Brezhnev, who is leader of the USSR.

This sentence can be seen to be composed from the following simpler sentences:

2. Nixon gave a Cadillac to Brezhnev.
3. The Cadillac was beautiful.
4. Brezhnev is leader of the USSR.

If any of these simple sentences were false, the complex sentence would not be true. These sentences closely correspond to the propositions that underlie the meaning of the sentence. Each simple sentence expresses a primitive unit of meaning. One criterion we have for our meaning representations is that each separate unit in them correspond to a unit of meaning.

However, the propositional-representation theory does not claim that a person remembers in exact sentences such as 2 through 4. Past research indicates that subjects do not remember the exact wording of such underlying sentences any more than they remember the exact wording of the original sentences. For instance, Anderson (1972) showed that subjects would show poor ability to remember whether they heard sentence 2 or another sentence, labeled 5:

5. Brezhnev was given a Cadillac by Nixon.

Thus, it seems that information is represented in memory in a way that expresses the meaning of the primitive assertions but does not preserve exact wording. A number of propositional notations represent information in this abstract way. One, used by Kintsch (1974), represents each proposition as a list containing a *relation* followed by an ordered list of *arguments*. The relations correspond to the verbs (in this case, *give*), adjectives *(beautiful)*, or other relational terms *(is leader of)* in the sentences, while the arguments correspond to the nouns *(Nixon, a Cadillac, Brezhnev,* and *USSR)*. The relations assert connections among the entities referred to by these nouns. As an example, sentences 2 through 4 would be represented by these lists:

6. *(Give,* Nixon, Cadillac, Brezhnev, *Past)*

7. *(Beautiful,* Cadillac*)*

8. *(Leader-of,* Brezhnev, USSR*)*

Kintsch standardly embeds a list of relations plus arguments in parentheses as above. Whether the subject had heard sentence 1 or sentence 9 below:

9. The leader of the USSR, Brezhnev, was given a Cadillac by Nixon and it was beautiful.

the meaning of the message would be represented by lists 6 through 8. Note that various relations take different numbers of arguments. For instance, the relation *give* is assumed to take four arguments—the agent of the giving, the object of the giving, the recipient of the giving, and the time of the giving.

Propositional Networks

There is another way to represent the meaning of the sentence labeled 1 in the preceding subsection—by means of a *propositional network.** Figure 4-5 illustrates the structure of a propositional network. In such a network, each proposition is represented by an ellipse, which is connected by labeled arrows to its relation and arguments. The propositions, the relations, and the arguments are called the *nodes* of the network, and the arrows are called the *links* because they connect nodes. The labels on the arrows indicate the type of connection between the nodes. For instance, the ellipse labeled 6 in Figure 4-5A represents proposition 6. This ellipse is connected to the relation *give* by a link labeled *relation,* to indicate it is pointing to the relation node. *Nixon* by an *agent* link, to *Cadillac* by an *object* link, to *Brezhnev* by a *recipient* link, and to *past* by a *time* link. The three network structures in Figure 4-5A/C represent the individual propositions 6 through 8 listed in the preceding subsection. Note that these different networks contain the same nodes (for example, A and B both contain *Cadillac.*) This overlap indicates that these networks are really interconnected parts of a larger network. This larger network is illustrated in Figure 4-5D.

The spatial location of elements in a network is totally irrelevant to the interpretation of network. A network can be thought of as a tangle of marbles connected by strings. The marbles represent the nodes, and the strings represent the links between the nodes. The network represented on a two-

---

*The propositional-network representation used here is a slight variant of a system proposed by Rumelhart, Lindsay, and Norman (1972). Many variations on and sophistications of these ideas exist (e.g., Anderson, 1976; Anderson and Bower, 1973; Norman and Rumelhart, 1975; Quillian, 1969), but this system has the virtue of simplicity.

(A)

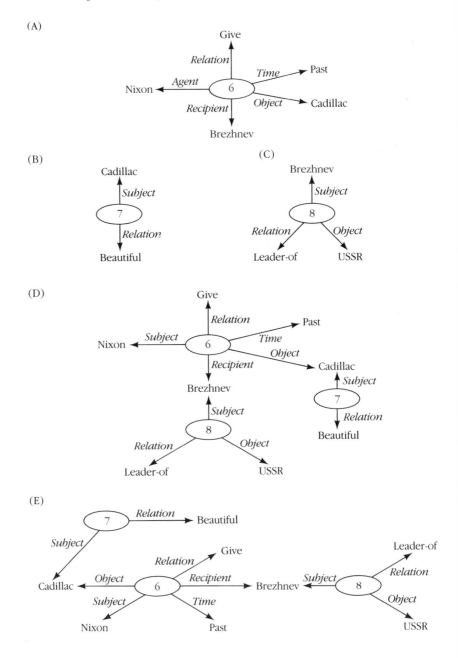

(B)

(C)

(D)

(E)

Figure 4-5 *Examples of propositional-network representations. A through C represent propositions 6 through 8. D illustrates the networks in A through C combined. E is another way of displaying the network in D.*

dimensional page is that tangle of marbles laid out in a certain way. We try to lay the network out in a way that facilitates its interpretation, but any order is possible. Thus, Figure 4-5E is another way of representing the network shown in Figure 4-5D. All that matters is which elements are connected to which, not where the components lie.

We have now two ways of representing the same propositional information: with a set of linear propositions, as in propositions 6 through 8, or with a network, as in Figure 4-5. Since the information represented is abstract, either notational convention will work. The linear representation is somewhat neater and more compact, but the network representation reveals the connections among elements. As we will see, this connectivity proves useful for understanding certain memory phenomena.

Besides the basic propositional structure, some other structures are needed to create adequate meaning representations. Suppose we wanted to represent the following three sentences.

10. Nixon gave Brezhnev a Cadillac.

11. Fred owns a Cadillac.

12. Fred shouted "Nixon."

(We will assume that Fred is the same person in sentences 11 and 12.) Given the representational concepts discussed so far, we would represent this information with the network in Figure 4-6A. However, this network exhibits a number of inadequacies. First, it is not the case that the object of Fred's shouting in sentence 12 is the same as the agent of the giving in sentence 10. In one case we are dealing with the person, and in the other case we are dealing with his name. Therefore, we need to distinguish between words and the concepts they refer to. This distinction is made in Figure 4-6B where words and concepts have different nodes. In this network (and as a general rule) words are represented with quotation marks, whereas concepts are represented by words without the quotation marks. A link labeled *word* indicates the connection between the concept and the word.

Another problem with Figure 4-6A is that only one node exists for Cadillac, which implies that the Cadillac Nixon gave is the one Fred owns. This example illustrates the need for a distinction between specific objects, such as the particular Cadillacs, and general classes, such as the category Cadillac. In Figure 4-6B, the distinction is made: two instance nodes, X and Y, stand for the two Cadillacs. Links labeled *isa* indicate that each node is a Cadillac.

Building Propositional Networks

Learning how to interpret and think about propositional networks is very useful. Such networks are becoming increasingly important in cognitive psychology. These representations will reappear in discussions of other phenom-

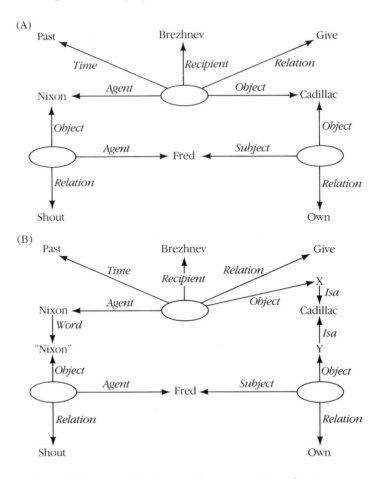

Figure 4-6   *Propositional-network representations of sentences 10 through 12. A is inadequate. B is more accurate because it distinguishes between words and concepts and between classes and instances.*

ena in subsequent chapters of this book. A good way to gain an understanding of propositional networks is actually to learn to construct propositional networks representing the meanings of sentences. Below is a list of the steps involved in the building of a propositional network. The list does not cover all possible sentence types, but it does cover the kinds of sentences most frequently encountered.

1. Identify all the relational terms. Mainly these will be verbs, adjectives, expressions such as *captain of* or *father of,* and some prepositions such as *above* or *on top of.*

2. Write simple sentences for each relation. These simple sentences will involve only the relation and its noun arguments. Each sentence will correspond to one of the sentence's propositions.

3. To begin constructing the network, draw an ellipse to represent the node for each proposition.

4. Write the relation for each proposition beside its node. Connect the proposition node to the relation via an arrow labeled *relation.*

5. Create nodes for each of the nounlike units in the propositions. Two kinds of nouns must be distinguished. If the noun refers to a specific object, such as *Nixon,* simply write this noun. If the noun refers to an instance of a class noun, such as a *man,* create a new node (call it something arbitrary such as X) and connect this new node to the class node by an *isa* label. In creating these nodes, be careful to avoid duplicating the same node. If *Nixon* appears in two or more propositions, it should be represented by only one node.

6. Draw arrows between each proposition node and the noun nodes it involves. Label these arrows with an appropriate semantic label such as *subject, agent, object, recipient, location, time,* and so on.

7. Rearrange the network to make it neat.

Let us work through this list by applying the process it describes to the following sentence.

1. The hungry lion ate Max, who starved it.

Step 1 requires that we identify the relational terms: *hungry, ate,* and *starve.* In step 2, we are to write the simple propositions involving only these relations:

2. The lion was hungry.
3. The lion ate Max.
4. Max starved the lion.

Steps 3 and 4 involve creating oval nodes for each proposition and connecting them to the relations. Figure 4-7A shows the network structure at this point. Step 5 involves creating nodes for all the noun units in the propositions. *Lion* is not a specific object. Therefore, a new node is created and arbitrarily called X to represent the specific lion. This node is attached by an *isa* link to *lion.* On the other hand, *Max* refers to a specific individual and an *isa* link is not required. Figure 4-7B illustrates the result of this stage. Step 6 requires that the propositions be connected to their noun-unit arguments. For proposition 2, *lion* has one *subject* link; for proposition 3, *lion* has an *agent* link and *Max*

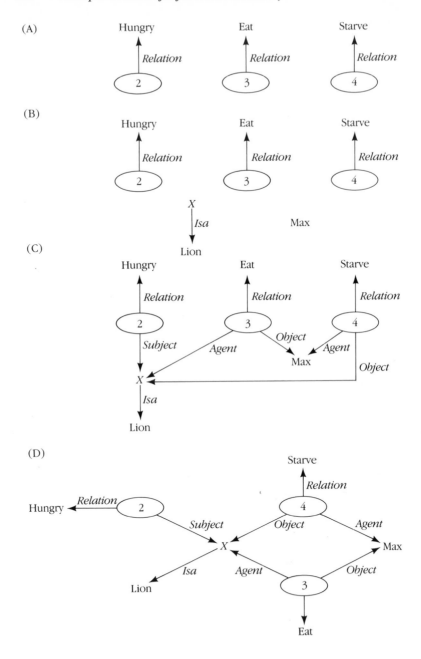

(A)

(B)

(C)

(D)

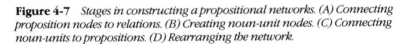

Figure 4-7 *Stages in constructing a propositional networks. (A) Connecting proposition nodes to relations. (B) Creating noun-unit nodes. (C) Connecting noun-units to propositions. (D) Rearranging the network.*

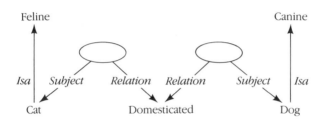

Figure 4-8 *Propositional-network representations for the meaning of* cat *and* dog.

an *object* link; for proposition 4, *Max* has an *agent* link and *lion* an *object* link. Figure 4-7C illustrates the product of this step. When propositions share arguments, they must point to the same node. Thus, the *subject* link from proposition 2 and the *agent* link from proposition 3 both point to *X*. Also, the *object* link from 3 and the *agent* link from 4 both point to *Max*. The final step, performed in Figure 4-7D, involves rearranging the nodes and links to make the network neater.

As an exercise, try constructing propositional networks for the following sentences:

1. The early bird catches the worm.
2. John drove from Los Angeles to San Francisco.
3. Lincoln was born in a log cabin and was president of the United States.

Possible networks for these sentences are given in Figure 4-18, at the end of the chapter.

Representing the Meaning of Concepts

So far, we have illustrated how to represent information that describes various events and features of people and objects. These representations tend to terminate in concepts such as *car* or *dog,* that is, simple nouns. It is important to ask how the meanings of these concepts are represented in such a network. I asked a friend what the concepts *dog* and *cat* meant. The following are the definitions that she gave:

> *Dog:* a member of the canine species that is domesticated.
>
> *Cat:* a member of the feline species that is domesticated.

Figure 4-8 illustrates the network form of these definitions. However, on inspection the definitions in Figure 4-8 might seem to be a "cheat," since they are merely defining the meaning of one concept such as *dog* in terms of other concepts such as *canine, domesticated,* and so on. This leaves the meaning of the other concepts (e.g., *canine*) undefined; hence, it might seem that *dog* has not really been defined. Let us see what happens if we ask our informant to define these associated terms. The set of definitions in the following list represents an attempt by the informant to track down the meaning of *canine.*

1. *Canine:* A mammal with a long snout and sharp teeth that tends to socialize with other members of its kinds.
2. *Mammal:* a milk-producing vertebrate with a four-chambered heart.
3. *Vertebrate:* an animal with a spinal cord and bilateral symmetry.
4. *Animal:* a living organism that moves.
5. *Organism:* matter that ingests, expels, and reproduces.
6. *Matter:* a conglomeration of molecules.
7. *Molecules:* a conglomeration of atoms.
8. *Atom:* a conglomeration of protons and neutrons.
9. *Proton:* a physiochemical building block.
10. *Building block:* something from which you construct other things.
11. *Thing:* its meaning depends on the context.

We find *canine* is defined in terms of *mammal, mammal* in terms of *vertebrate, vertebrate* in terms of *animal, animal* in terms of *organism, organism* in terms of *matter, matter* in terms of *molecules, molecules* in terms of *atoms, atoms* in terms of *protons, protons* in terms of *building blocks, building blocks* in terms of *things.* Finally, at *things,* my informant had to give up. She was trying desperately not to be circular in her definitions, and so finally reached the point where she could go no further.

Consider now a dictionary definition (Webster's *Seventh New Collegiate Dictionary,* 1973) of dog:

Dog: a highly variable carnivorous domesticated mammal probably descended from common wolf.

Consider a dictionary definition of *wolf:*

Wolf: any of various large mammals that resemble the related dogs.

The dictionary is openly circular: it uses *wolf* to define *dog* and *dog* to define *wolf.*

A propositional network is like a dictionary: it defines one concept in terms of another, either going in circles or eventually resorting to terms, such as *thing,* which really have no meaning. This definition of a concept in terms of

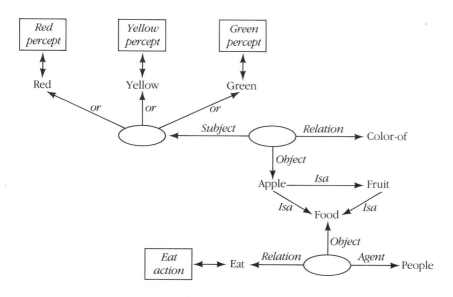

Figure 4-9 *A portion of a hypothetical propositional-network structure for* apple.

its relations to other concepts is referred to as the *configurational meaning* of a concept. The configurational meaning of a term such as *dog* consists of the configurations of propositions and concepts attached to the word in the network.

These configurations, however, do not constitute the whole meaning of *dog.* No number of such definitions will tell a blind person what a dog looks like. Part of the meaning of a concept must make reference to real, sensory qualities and real, performable actions. Thus, we assume that some connections exist between certain nodes in a propositional networks and sensory qualities and body actions. Such connections are contained in Figure 4-9, which represents a portion of the propositional-network structure connected to *apple* in a hypothetical person's mind. (As an exercise, try to work all the information contained in this propositional network into a narrative paragraph.) Note that connected to apple are primitive sensory qualities such as red, yellow, and green. These percepts contain the kind of information that our system registers when we actually see a color such as red. Note also that the *eat* concept is connected to the *eat* action. If no such connections existed in our networks for foods, we would not really know what it means to perform eating actions on the food objects. In summary, then, the total meaning of a concept is not just the other nodes it is connected to but also the sensory and motor information connected to some of these nodes.

Figure 4-10   *A cartoon from* The New Yorker. *A portion of the propositional-network structure for the meaning of the cartoon is given in Figure 4-11. (Drawing by W. Steig; © 1970 The New Yorker Magazine, Inc.)*

Representing the Meaning of Pictures

We reviewed evidence that subjects tend to remember the meaning of a picture rather than exact visual details. Consider the picture in Figure 4-10. Figure 4-11 is a portion of the propositional network that might represent this picture in a subject's memory. This network encodes the following information: "A clown is in a rowboat. He is wearing a polka-dotted suit and a hat. He is smiling. The rowboat is on an ocean." Note that this representation of the picture leaves out a lot of physical details. If the subject committed only this information to memory, he or she would be unable to report many details of the picture, for example, that waves are on the ocean or that a moon is above the ocean. In fact, subjects are poor at remembering just such details.

It would be wrong to think that the information represented in Figure 4-11 is exactly what everyone who sees this cartoon would commit to memory. Such a picture is a complex object, and different people would commit different aspects of the picture to memory. For instance, one person might

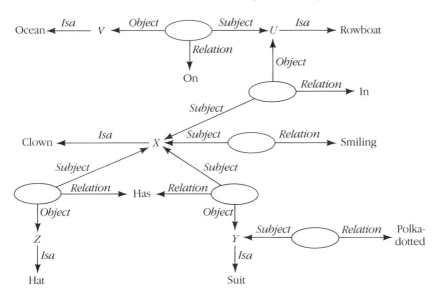

Figure 4-11   *A portion of the proposition-network representation assumed to be used by a hypothetical person of some of the information conveyed in Figure 4-10.*

notice the moon but might not notice that the clown's suit is polka-dotted. However, in all cases people tend to encode the more meaningful aspects of a picture and to ignore the less meaningful details.

Propositional Networks as Associative Structures

It is useful to think of the nodes in a semantic network as ideas and to think of the links between the nodes as associations between the ideas, as a number of experiments suggest. Consider an experiment by Weisberg (1969). He had subjects study and commit to memory such sentences as, *Children who are slow eat bread that is cold.* The propositional network representation for this sentence is illustrated in Figure 4-12. After learning a sentence, subjects were administered free-association tasks in which they were given a word from the sentence and asked to respond with the first word from the sentence that came to mind. Subjects cued with *slow* almost always free associated *children* and almost never *bread,* although *bread* is as close to *slow* in the sentence as *children.* However, Figure 4-12 shows that *slow* and *children* are nearer each other (three links) than *slow* and *bread* (five links). Similarly, subjects cued with *bread* almost always recalled *cold* rather than *slow,* although in the sentence *bread* and *slow* are as close as *bread* and *cold.* This is because *bread* and *cold* are closer to each other in the network than are *bread* and *slow* (five links). (A similar point has been made in a recent experiment by Ratcliff and McKoon, 1978.)

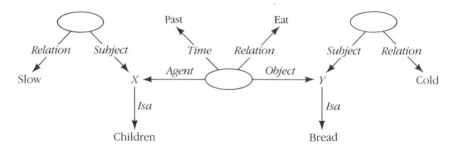

Figure 4-12 *A propositional-network representation of the sentence* Children who are slow eat bread that is cold.

This associative analysis of propositional structures has proved to be very useful in understanding variations in the times subjects take to retrieve information from memory. Collins and Quillian (1969) had subjects judge the truth of assertions about concepts such as the following:

1. Robins eat worms.
2. Robins have feathers.
3. Robins have skin.

Subjects were shown facts such as these as well as false assertions, such as, *Apples have feathers.* They were asked to judge whether a statement was true or false by pressing one of two buttons. The time from presentation of the statement to the button press was measured.

Figure 4-13 illustrates the kind of network structure that Collins and Quillian assumed represented the information in subjects' memories. Sentence 1 is directly stored with *robin.* However, sentence 2 is not directly stored at the *robin* node. Rather, the *have feathers* property is stored with *bird,* and sentence 2 can be inferred from the directly stored facts that *a robin is a bird* and *birds have feathers.* Again, sentence 3 is not directly stored with *robin;* rather, the *have skin* predicate is stored with *animal.* Thus, sentence 3 can be inferred from the facts *a robin is a bird* and *a bird is an animal* and *animals have skin.* Thus, with sentence 1, all the requisite information for its verification is stored with *robin;* in the case of sentence 2, subjects must traverse one link from *robin* to *bird* to retrieve the requisite information. And in sentence 3, subjects would have to traverse two links from *robin* to *animal.*

If our memories were structured like Figure 4-13, we would expect statement 1 to be verified more quickly than statement 2, which would be verified more quickly than statement 3. This is just what Collins and Quillian found. Subjects required 1310 msec to make judgments about statements like statement 1, 1380 msec for questions like 2, and 1470 for statements like 3.

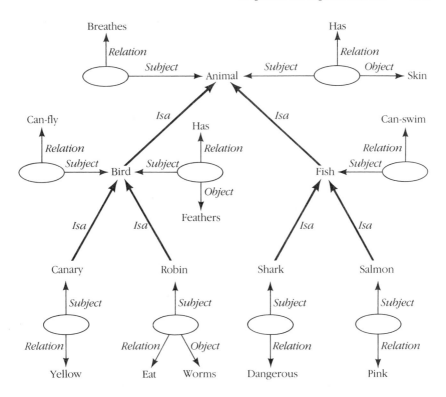

Figure 4-13 *The network of concepts assumed by Collins and Quillian (1969) in their experiment to compare reaction times in making true-false judgments about statements. A hierarchy of concepts and associated properties can be seen in the figure.*

These scores differ by fewer than a couple of hundred milliseconds. Therefore, the differences would be virtually impossible to detect by self-examination. However, with modern reaction-time methodology they can be quite reliably assessed in a psychology laboratory. Reaction-time methodology enables us to measure distance in a semantic network.

Subsequent research on the retrieval of information from memory has somewhat complicated the conclusions drawn from the initial Collins and Quillian experiment. The frequency with which facts are experienced has been observed to have strong effects on retrieval time (e.g., Conrad, 1972). Some facts such as *Apples are eaten,* for which the predicate could be stored with an intermediate concept such as food but which are experienced quite frequently, are verified as fast as or faster than facts such as *Apples have dark seeds,* which must be stored more directly with the *apple* concept. It seems that if a fact about a concept is frequently encountered, it will be stored with that concept even if it is also stored with a more general concept. The following statements about the organization of facts in propositional memory and their retrieval times seem to be valid conclusions from the research:

1. If a fact about a concept is frequently encountered, it will be stored with that concept even if it could be inferred from a more distant (in the network) concept.

2. The more frequently encountered a fact about a concept is, the more strongly that fact will be associated with the concept. And the more strongly associated with concepts are facts, the more rapidly are they verified.

3. Verifying facts that are not directly stored with a concept but that must be inferred takes a relatively long time.

Thus, both the strength of the connections between facts and concepts (determined by frequency of experience) and the distance between them propositionally have effects on retrieval time. We will have much more to say about the strength factor in Chapter 6, which discusses memory retrieval.

We can use the following facts (still all true in 1980) to illustrate the conclusions listed above:

1. Jimmy Carter raises peanuts.
2. Jimmy Carter lives in the White House.
3. Jimmy Carter likes classical music.
4. Jimmy Carter has a hot line.

We would expect fact 1 to be verified very rapidly because it is stored directly with the concept Jimmy Carter and is frequently encountered. Fact 2 should be quickly verifiable, even though it could be retrieved indirectly from the facts *Jimmy Carter is president* and *The president lives in the White House.* However, because fact 2 is frequently associated with Carter, it should be directly associated to Carter. Verifying fact 3 should take longer, even though this fact is directly stored with Jimmy Carter, since one does not encounter it frequently (in fact, many people may not know it is true). Fact 4 should also take a long time, since it is probably not stored with Carter but must be inferred from the fact that he is president.

Multiple Codes in Memory

Evidence for Visual and Verbal Codes

We have now considered the dual-code model, which asserts that information is stored either as visual or verbal images, and a propositional model, which asserts that information is stored in an abstract propositional network. We found that memory tends to retain the meaning and not the physical details of an input. This finding is predicted by the propositional model but is difficult to explain within the dual-code model. We also saw reaction-time data, such as those reported by Collins and Quillian, which are explained by the propositional model but are not obviously interpreted by the dual-code model. It is also the case that propositional models have been developed more rigorously than dual-code models. For example, they have been implemented in computer-simulation programs. In contrast, dual-code models have generally been left incompletely and vaguely specified.

All this success seems to have gone to the heads of the propositional theorists. They (this author included) have advanced what seems, on the face of it, to be an implausible claim: that human memory is exclusively propositional and that what appear to be verbal or visual memories are really fundamentally propositional. A number of problems arise when propositional codes are used by memory researchers to represent the physical detail of verbal or visual memories. For one thing, the necessary propositional encodings (e.g., networks) can become extremely complex. Moreover, predictions derived from these networks tend not to be borne out regarding memory for physical detail. The properties of visual representations differ from those of verbal representations, and both sets of properties differ from the properties of abstract propositional representations. Specifically, visual representations have a strong spatial structure and verbal representations have a strong sequential structure.

An experiment by Santa (1977) nicely illustrates the difference between spatial and verbal representations. The two conditions of Santa's experiments are illustrated in Figure 4-14. In the geometric condition, subjects studied a spatial array of three geometric objects, two geometric objects above and one below. As the figure shows, this array had a facelike property—without much effort one can see eyes and a mouth. After subjects studied it, this array was removed and subjects were immediately presented with one of a number of test arrays. The subjects' task was to verify that the test array contained the same elements, though not necessarily in the same spatial configuration, as the study array. Thus, subjects should respond positively to the first two arrays in the figure and negatively to the other two arrays. Interest was focused on the contrast between the two positive test arrays. The first array is identical to the study array, but in the second array the elements are arrayed linearly. Santa predicted that subjects would make a positive judgment more quickly in the first case where the configuration was identical, since, he hypothesized, the visual memory for the study stimulus would preserve spatial information. The results for the geometric condition are displayed in Figure 4-15. As can be seen, Santa's predictions were confirmed. Subjects were faster when the geometric test array preserved the configuration information in the study array.

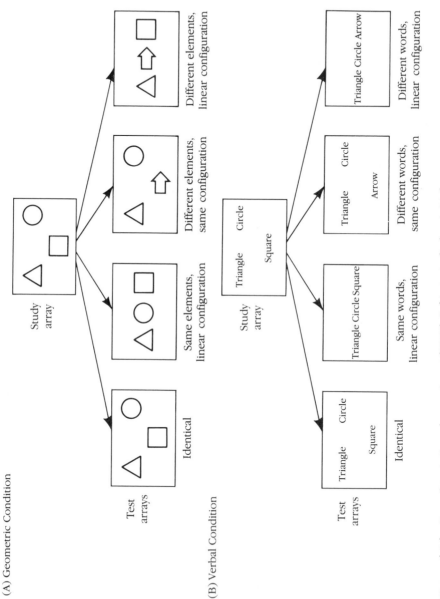

Figure 4-14 *Procedure in Santa's experiment (1977). Subjects studied an initial array and then had to decide whether one of a set of arrays contained the same elements.*

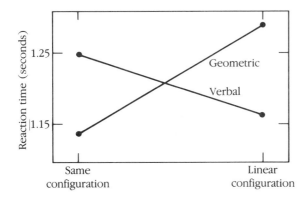

Figure 4-15 *Reaction times for Santa's experiment (1977) showing an interaction between type of material and test configuration.*

The results from the geometric condition are more impressive when they are contrasted with the results from the verbal condition, illustrated in Figure 4-14B. Here subjects studied words arranged in spatial configurations identical with geometric objects in the geometric condition. However, because it involved words, the study stimulus did not suggest a face or have any pictorial properties. Santa speculated that subjects would encode the word array according to normal reading order—that is, left to right and top to bottom. So, given the study array in Figure 4-14B, subjects would encode it "triangle, circle, square." Following the study stimulus, one of the test stimuli was presented. Subjects had to judge whether the words in the test stimulus were identical with those in the study stimulus. All the test stimuli involved words, but otherwise they presented the same possibilities as the tests in the geometric condition. In particular, the two positive stimuli exhibited the same configuration and a linear configuration, respectively. Note that the configuration of linear array is the same as that in which Santa predicted subjects would encode the study stimulus. Santa predicted that, since subjects had encoded the words linearly from the study array, they would be fastest when the test array was linear. As Figure 4-15 illustrates, his predictions were again confirmed. The verbal and the geometric conditions display a sharp interaction.

In conclusion, Santa's experiment indicates that linear order is very important for a verbal memory but spatial configuration is important for a visual memory. Neither factor would be expected to be important if the information were encoded propositionally.

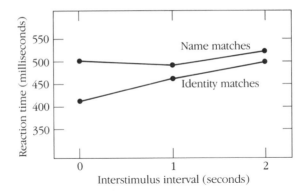

Figure 4-16   *Reaction times for matching successively presented letters as a function of the interstimulus interval. Functions for identity matches and name matches are shown. (Adapted from Posner, 1969.)*

Forgetting Visual and Verbal Information

Note that Santa's experiment involved immediate memory for the material. There is evidence that if subjects are asked to hold information in memory for any length of time, they tend to lose the spatial structure of visual material and the sequential structure of verbal material. Once these structures are lost, information representation becomes abstract. A classic experiment making this point was performed by Posner (1969). He presented subjects with two letters, with the presentations separated by varying intervals of time (called interstimulus intervals). The subjects' task was to decide as quickly as possible if the second letter—the *probe*—was the same as the first. The letters could be upper or lower case, but this did not matter for their judgment; an *A* followed by an *a* required a *same* response. The first letter was always upper case, but the second letter was either upper or lower. Thus, there were two *same* possibilities—*AA* and *Aa*—and two *different* possibilities—*AB* and *Ab*. (Of course, more letters than *A* and *B* were used.) Of principal interest was the difference between *AA*, called an *identity match*, and *Aa*, called a *name match*. One would expect subjects to be faster at making an identity match if they had exact visual information available. Figure 4-16 presents the subjects' reaction times in making their judgments as a function of the interstimulus interval. Note that initially there is a large advantage for the identity match but that after 2 seconds this advantage has almost completely disappeared. This alteration indicates that memory for the initial stimulus is rapidly transformed into an abstract code that does not retain specific visual information.

An experiment by Anderson (1974) made the same point in the verbal domain. Subjects listened to a story, which contained various critical sentences that would be tested, for instance:

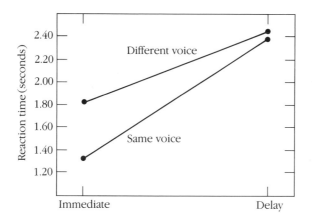

Figure 4-17   *Time to judge that a test sentence has the same meaning as a studied sentence. Times are shown as a function of delay in testing and as a function of whether study and test sentences have the same voice.*

1. The missionary shot the painter.

Later, subjects were asked to judge whether any of the following sentences followed logically from the story they had heard:

2. The missionary shot the painter.
3. The painter was shot by the missionary.
4. The painter shot the missionary.
5. The missionary was shot by the painter.

The first two sentences require a positive response and the last two require a negative response. Sentence 2 is analagous to Posner's identity match, whereas sentence 3, the passive transform, is analogous to Posner's name match. Here these sentences were called *same voice* (sentence 2) and *different voice* (sentence 3). As in Posner's test, the delay between the initial stimulus and the test probe was manipulated: subjects were tested either immediately after hearing the sentences or at a delay of about 2 minutes. The delay was filled with a presentation of more of the story. The manipulated delay of 2 minutes in this design is much longer than Posner's 2-second delay, since longer delay manipulations seemed necessary with verbal material.

The results of this experiment are reported in Figure 4-17. As in the Posner experiment, same-voice probes exhibit a large reaction-time advantage immediately but little advantage with delay. So, it seems that verbal information, like visual information, tends to be short-lived and that at delays we mainly remember abstract information.

However, one should not conclude from these findings that people have no memory for physical features at long delays. With effort, we can remember verbatim passages and exact visual details. In a series of clever experiments, Kolers (1979) has shown that under the appropriate circumstances we can retain visual details about the typography of a page of print for months! However, it does seem that after long delays most exact physical information is lost and that we are mainly left with a general characterization of the meaning of the stimulus.

One might think that the experiments cited in this section addressed the same visual and auditory sensory stores covered in Chapter 2. However, there are a number of arguments against this conclusion. First, the visual and verbal information considered here lasts longer than that typically measured in sensory-store studies. Note that even at the longest delays in Figures 4-16 and 4-17 some advantage is found for an identity match. Indeed, some advantage has been found for an identity match after days-long delays (Keenan, 1975), suggesting that exact verbal and visual information might be capable of being memorized permanently. Second, the identity information in the Posner task seemed impervious to masking by an interfering stimulus. For instance, a random black-and-white mask is known to erase a visual icon, but it does not eliminate the advantage of an identity match in the Posner task. Third, it has been shown that subjects do not require a visual presentation to make an identity match. For instance, Posner, Boies, Eichelman, and Taylor (1969) simply told their subjects, "It is a capital A," rather than visually presenting the first letter. They still found an "identity" advantage when they visually presented an *A* as the probe over an *a,* given a slight probe delay. Subjects, given a little time, are able to generate their own visual images of the stimulus. Together, these data seem to indicate that the visual and verbal images being tapped in these memory studies are distinct from the visual icons and auditory echoes studied in Chapter 2.

General Conclusions

As my conversation with the astrophysicist, cited earlier, indicated, people generally believe intuitively that information is represented both visually and verbally in memory. Paivio's dual-code hypothesis is an expression of the layperson's common sense. While the common-sense approach is not wrong, evidence suggests that an abstract propositional code tends to dominate in long-term memory. Since the principal concern of this book is long-term knowledge, a propositional-network system for representing this abstract knowledge has been proposed and described in detail. One might ask, however, why, if the abstract representation is the dominant one, we have so strong an introspective awareness of imagery and verbal codes but hardly any introspective evidence of an abstract code. This discrepancy might be due to the fact that when we recall information from long-term memory we tend to verbalize it or construct an image of it. Thus, even if the long-term knowledge is abstract, we represent it to ourselves in our consciousness in more concrete terms.

We may count this accumulating evidence for an abstract code, which is largely unsuspected by the layperson, as one of the major accomplishments of modern cognitive psychology. It is a significant breakthrough in our understanding of the nature of human intelligence. An interesting question, which needs to be explored, is whether other animals have a similar abstract code for their long-term knowledge. If not, abstractness of the memory code may be an important feature accounting for the uniqueness of human intelligence.

Implications: Using Mnemonic Techniques

I can still remember the traumatic experience I had in my first paired-associate experiment. It was part of a sophomore class on experimental psychology. For reasons I have long since forgotten, we had designed a class experiment that involved learning 16 memorable pairs such as DAX–GIB. That is, our task was to be able to recall GIB when prompted with the cue DAX. I was determined to outperform other members of my class. My personal theory of memory at that time, which I intended to apply, was basically that if you try hard and intensely you will remember well. In the impending experimental situation, this meant that during the learning period I would say (as loud as was seemly) the paired associates over and over again, as fast as I could. My theory was that by this method the paired associates would be forever "burned" into my mind. To my chagrin, I wound up with the worst score in the class.

My theory of "loud and fast" was directly opposed to the true means of improving memory. I was trying to commit a meaningless auditory pair to memory. But the material in this chapter suggests that we have best memory for meaningful information, not meaningless verbal information. I should have been trying to convert my memory task into something more meaningful. For instance, DAX is like *dad* and GIB is the first part of *gibberish*. So I might have created an image of my father speaking some gibberish to me. This would have been a simple *mnemonic* (memory-assisting) *technique* and would have worked quite well as a means of associating the two.

We do not often have the need to learn pairs of nonsense syllables outside the laboratory situation. However, in many situations we have to associate various combinations of terms that do not have much inherent meaning. We have to learn shopping lists, names for faces, telephone numbers, rote facts in a college class, vocabulary items in a foreign language, and so on. In all cases, we can improve memory if we transform the task into one of associating the items meaningfully. Transforming meaningless information into meaningful information is a prime trick of the memory experts who give nightclub acts.

Let us consider a couple examples of how difficult memory tasks can be transformed into more meaningful and easier ones.

As a first example, consider the memorizing of a telephone number. A good technique is to associate letters with numbers. Consider the following number-letter associations, which must first be committed to memory before the technique can be applied:

1 = t or d	6 = sh, or ch
2 = n	7 = k
3 = m	8 = f or v
4 = r	9 = p or b
5 = l	0 = z or s

Now, suppose you wanted to remember the number of the White House (202-456-1414). This number gives the sequence of letters n, s, n, r, l, sh, t, r, t, r, which you would then convert into a sequence of words by inserting vowels: for instance, *nose on a relish traitor.* Now you have something potentially more meaningful. You need only to associate this phrase with the White House to make it yet more meaningful. You might imagine the president twisting the nose on a tycoon who has given state secrets in exchange for rights to sell relish in Russia. By recalling this episode, and then the phrase, you have a means of reconstructing the White House telephone number. Committing the number-letter correspondences to memory takes effort, and becoming facile in converting the letters into words takes practice. The technique might seem to be more trouble than it is worth, but it is an excellent one for improving memory if you are willing to make the initial investment in learning and practice.

Another mnemonic technique is the *key-word method* for learning vocabulary items. Consider, for instance, the Italian *formaggio* (pronounced FOR MODGE JO), which means "cheese." No inherently meaningful connection exists between the Italian and English equivalents, but the key-word method forces one. The first step is to transform the foreign word into some English sound-alike phrase—for example, FOR MODGE JO sounds like "for much dough." The second step is to invent a meaningful connection between the two. In this case, we might imagine an expensive cheese that sold for much money, or "for much dough." Or consider, *carciofi* (pronounced CAR CHOW FE), which means "artichokes." We might transform CAR CHOW FE into "car trophy" and imagine a winning car at an auto show with a trophy shaped like an artichoke. Atkinson and Raugh (1975) studied such a key-word technique in language learning and showed it to be very effective. They claimed that as students become familiar with a foreign language, their consciousness of the key words drops out. Thus, it appears that the key word provides a helpful crutch for getting started but does not stay around to clutter up memory.

One might wonder what these mnemonic techniques have to offer for the learning of material that is already meaningful—for instance, the material in this textbook. Consider one of the important facts in this chapter: Memory for the exact wording of a sentence is rapidly lost. We might try translating this statement into a concrete image. For instance, we could imagine a screen inside a subject's head. The sentence is brightly displayed on the screen when it is heard and then rapidly fades away. However, it seems unlikely that such attempts to make more concrete the abstract lessons of a text will be very successful. The material in a textbook should already be quite meaningful. Converting such material into concrete images has been advocated by some popular writers on mnemonic techniques, but informal research in our laboratory does not support this practice. Basically, memory for meaningful text is not improved by techniques whose effect is to make meaningless material meaningful.

Thus, the best advice a student could follow who is attempting to remember meaningful text material is quite simple: try to understand it. Above all else, do not try to commit the contents to memory in a rote fashion. Techniques do exist for improving one's memory for text material, but they require an understanding of the dynamics of human memory. We will discuss such techniques in Chapter 6 and particularly in Chapter 7.

Of course, it is not the case that all the material in a text is meaningful. Suppose, you wanted to be able to reproduce Figure 4-1, from this chapter. (This seems to me to be far too detailed a memory to aspire towards; so I am certainly not recommending this as a study goal.) To perform this difficult task, you would have to commit to memory such facts such as "subjects warned about the test were 75 percent correct on memory for style." The exact number 75 is not particularly meaningful in itself. However, by referring to the number-to-consonant translation table, you might change 75 to *coal*. Then you might imagine a child in a class, writing a composition with a piece of *coal* while the teacher *warned* him to improve his *style*. This is a bizarre image, but the evidence is that bizarre images work at least as well as normal ones.

These mnemonic techniques work by converting the less meaningful into more meaningful material. They often involve the development of a visual image, an important function of the mental-imagery system. However, it seems that the meaningful relationship introduced by the imagery, not the imagery per se, is significant. Bower (1970) compared three conditions of noun-noun, paired-associate learning. In one condition, subjects merely said a pair, such as *car–fish,* over and over again to themselves. In a second condition, they developed an image of a car beside a fish. In a third condition, they had to create an interactive image (e.g., a big tuna driving a Cadillac!). Subjects were much better in this third condition than either of the other two. These results bear out the point made earlier that memory for visual information can be particularly good but only when it is memory for a meaningful interpretation of the visual material.

Remarks and Suggested Readings

The dual-code theory has been given its modern exposition in papers by Paivio (1969) and Bower (1972) and in a comprehensive book by Paivio (1971). Two expositions of the abstract propositional point of view and criticisms of the dual-code view were given by Anderson and Bower (1973) and by Pylyshyn (1973). For more recent discussions on this issue, see Kosslyn and Pomerantz (1977), Palmer (1978), Paivio (1975), and Anderson (1978). Much of this controversy is focused on the status of mental imagery and on various attempts to provide propositional-code versus visual-code explanations of the phenomenon. The status of the encoding of verbal information has been somewhat slighted in this controversy. There has been an unfortunate tendency to equate a propositional code with a verbal code.

The exact details of the propositional network given in this paper differ from those described in any of the specific proposals in the literature. See Anderson (1976), Anderson and Bower (1973), Kintsch (1974), and Norman and Rumelhart (1975) for some of these specific proposals about how propositional information is represented. Lindsay and Norman (1977) provide another introductory exposition of propositional networks.

Interestingly, researchers seem to be strongly divided into two camps: those claiming that there is only a propositional-code representation and those claiming that there is only a dual-code representation. Out of what is probably a false sense of parsimony, no one seems willing to admit that there might be three codes—abstract, verbal, and visual. For a proposal that comes close to this eclectic point of view, see a report by Kosslyn and Schwartz (1977) on their computer-simulation model for visual imagery.

Any number of popular books on mnemonic techniques are available. Perhaps the best is the book by Harry Lorayne and Jerry Lucas (1974), but the reader is warned that the techniques detailed there are at times difficult to acquire and that some of the recommendations might be simply incorrect. For a historical perspective on mnemonic techniques, read Yates (1966). For examples of the scientific study of mnemonic techniques, see Bower (1970) or Atkinson and Raugh (1975).

Appendix

On page 109, three sentences were to be represented in propositional-network form as an exercise. Figure 4-18 illustrates acceptable network representations for each of these sentences.

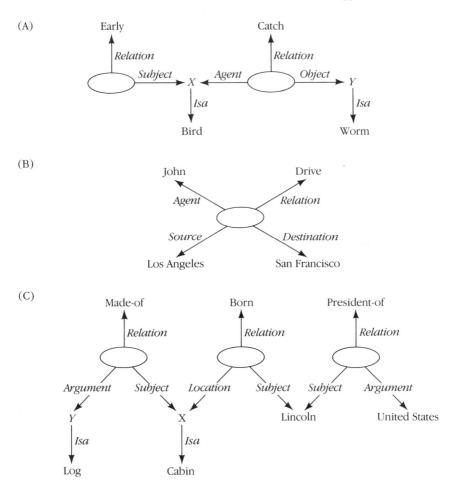

(A)

(B)

(C)

Figure 4-18 *Propositional-network representations of sentences 1 through 3 on p. 109. The labels on the links and the spatial array of the networks are somewhat arbitrary.*

Chapter 5

Schemas and Prototypes

Summary

1. *Schemas* are large, complex units of knowledge that organize much of what we know about general categories of objects, classes of events, and types of people.

2. With respect to natural categories such as birds or fruits wide variation exists in how typical instances are of their categories. Instances are typical of a category to the extent that they share properties with other members of the category. Instances that are very typical of a category are referred to as *prototypes.*

3. The members of large natural categories do not all share the same set of defining features. Rather, the members of a category tend to be related by a *family-resemblance structure,* in which instances share different features with different members of the category.

4. Through exposure to instances of a category, we learn which sets of features tend to occur together in many members of the category. Our knowledge of the category is composed of these *feature sets.* Each feature set can be thought of as a schema.

5. Schemas can represent stereotypic sequences of actions, such as going to a restaurant. Such event schemas are referred to as *scripts.* Scripts play an important role in the understanding and memory of stories.

6. Schemas can also represent our knowledge about individuals or groups. Schemas that are used to encode information about ethnic groups are referred to as *stereotypes*.

7. Schematic thought is a powerful way to process complex sets of information. However, schematic thought is subject to biases and distortions.

The previous two chapters were concerned with images and propositions that encode rather small units of knowledge. Increasingly, evidence suggests that larger and more complex units of knowledge exist that embody much of what we know about general categories of objects, classes of events, and types of people. These knowledge structures are referred to as *schemas*. Schemas may be simply collections of images or propositions or they may be more complex. It is not yet clear exactly how schemas are structured, but it is obvious that they have many interesting properties.

This chapter will review some of the evidence about the nature of schemas. First, it will consider natural categories. *Natural categories* refers to the classes of things that occur in the real world, such as *birds* or *sports*. We will review the research on the structure of such categories and then the research on their acquisition. Next, we will discuss what is known about event schemas and their role in story comprehension. Finally, we will consider schemas about groups of people and how these schemas lead to social stereotyping.

Natural Categories

Typicality Judgments

As we all know, both robins and chickens are birds. Taxonomically, robins and chickens are equally good birds. However, most people have definite opinions about what birds are like, and they would generally agree that robins are more consistent with these opinions than chickens. In fact, people have strong conceptions about what a "good" or typical member of a category is for most categories.

Much of the research documenting such category biases has been done by Rosch. In one experiment (1973), Rosch had subjects rate the typicality of various members of a category on a 1-to-7 scale, where 1 meant very typical and 7 meant very atypical. Subjects were extremely consistent in their responses. In the bird category, *robin* got an average rating of 1.1 and *chicken* a rating of 3.8. In reference to sports, *football* was thought to be very typical (1.2) while *weightlifting* was not (4.7). *Murder* was rated a very typical crime (1.0), while *vagrancy* was not (5.3). *Carrot* was a very typical vegetable (1.1), while *parsley* was not (3.8).

Figure 5-1   *"Which is the most typical bird?" (Adapted from Clark and Clark,* Psychology and Language; © *1977 by Harcourt Brace Jovanovich, Inc. Reproduced by permission of the publisher.)*

Using a rather different experimental paradigm, Battig and Montague (1969) had subjects list members of various categories and found that some members were much more likely to be listed than others. To give the frequencies for the examples listed above for Rosch, 377 subjects listed *robin* when asked to name birds but only 40 subjects listed *chicken;* 396 subjects gave *football* as a sport but only 3 gave *weightlifting;* 387 subjects gave *murder* while 3 gave *vagrancy;* and 316 gave *carrot* as a vegetable but only 15 gave *parsley.*

These differences in judged typicality are fairly intuitive, but what consequences do they have for performance? One experiment used by Rosch (1973) was simply to ask children or adults to judge whether an item was an instance of a category. She was interested in whether judgment times would be different for typical members (which she called central) and atypical members (which she called peripheral). Figure 5-2 presents subjects' reaction times in making these judgments. Children were much slower than adults, but both groups were slower to judge peripheral-category members. Also, the difference between central and peripheral questions was much larger for children than for adults. Recall that in Chapter 4 we also looked at category-membership judgment tasks and found that subjects took longer to make judgments about instances less strongly associated with a category. The result in Figure 5-2 seems to indicate that less typical members of a category are less well associated with that category.

Rosch (1975) has shown similar effects when subjects are asked to judge actual pictures of objects rather than to judge words. Subjects are faster to

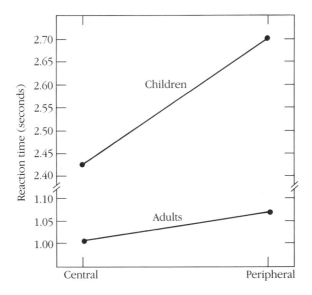

Figure 5-2   *Reaction times for correctly answered sentences about central-category and peripheral-category members in Rosch (1973).*

judge a picture as an instance of a category when it is a typical member of the category. For instance, apples are more rapidly seen as fruits than are watermelons, and robins are more rapidly seen as birds than are chickens. Thus, typical members of a category appear also to have an advantage in perceptual recognition.

Rosch (1977) demonstrated another way in which central members of a category are more typical. She had subjects compose sentences for category names. For *bird,* subjects generated sentences such as these:

> I heard a bird twittering outside my window.
>
> Three birds sat on the branch of a tree.
>
> A bird flew down and began eating.

Rosch replaced the category name in these sentences with a central member (robin), a less central member (eagle), or a peripheral member (chicken) and asked subjects to rate the sensibleness of the resulting sentences. Sentences involving central members got high ratings, sentences with less central members got lower ratings, and sentences with peripheral members got the lowest ratings. So, the evidence is that when people think of a category member, they generally think of typical instances of that category.

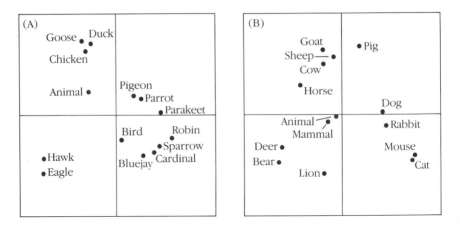

Figure 5-3   *The scaling solution for (A) birds and (B) mammals based on subject's similarity ratings. Distance between points is proportionate to the similarity of items as judged by subjects. (From Rips, Shoben, and Smith, 1973.)*

The existence of a range of typicality was demonstrated in yet another way by Rips, Shoben, and Smith (1973). They had subjects rate the similarity of various items to each other and to their category names. Subjects performed the task separately for birds and mammals. The similarity measures were then used in a multidimensional scaling analysis. The goal of such an analysis is to position the objects graphically, with the distance between objects proportionate to their similarity. In other words, the more similar two objects are judged to be, the closer together they are in the display. Figure 5-3 presents the two-dimensional scaling solutions for mammals and birds. Let us focus on the scaling solution for birds, since both solutions suggest similar conclusions. The two dimensions in the display are both fairly meaningful. From right to left, the birds appear to increase in size. The meaning of the top-to-bottom scale is not as clear, but it can be interpreted as indicating an increase in ferocity or perhaps a decrease in domesticity. Note that such birds as *robin* and *sparrow,* close together in this display, are relatively small and nondomestic. Close to *robin* and *sparrow* is the word *bird.* This can be taken as evidence that the typical bird is similar to robin in terms of its domesticity and size.

Schemas Versus Prototypes

The research reviewed in the preceding subsection suggests that for many natural categories people have strong preconceptions that define a typical category member. These preconceptions include notions of the appearance, behavior, typical habitat, and quality (goodness or badness) of a category member. This set of preconceptions about a category is referred to as a *schema* or a *prototype.* These two terms are sometimes used interchangeably in the literature, but there are subtle distinctions between them that can be important. A prototype is like an instance in that it has all values filled in, while in a schema some values may be omitted. Thus, a prototypical bird would be like any other bird, while a schematic bird might be a description with certain features such as color or food preference left out. A prototype, then, is a construct of a hypothetical, most typical instance of a category, while a schema is a construct composed of an often incomplete set of features that frequently occur together in the category. For now, however, we will simply use the terms *prototype* and *schema* to denote organized bodies of beliefs about what constitute instances of a category without committing ourselves to the issue of whether this knowledge is stored as a description of a specific event.

A schema is a kind of knowledge different from the *propositions* and *images* discussed in earlier chapters. The difference is partly one of degree. A schema is a much larger piece of knowledge than an image or proposition; it might be thought of as equivalent to a set of propositions and images. The difference is also one of kind: a schema is general rather than specific; that is, a schema does not represent a specific object but rather a large number of specific objects. We have propositions and images for specific people, places, things, and events. For instance, we have images or propositions about Neil Armstrong walking on the moon. In contrast, we have schemas only about general categories. It makes no sense to talk about a schema or prototype for Neil Armstrong walking on the moon. We could, however, talk about a schema or prototype for an astronaut or a space trip. The terms *schema* or *prototype* denote an averaging of a set of specific items or events. It should be noted that, while a schema is necessarily general, a proposition can be either specific or general.

Research on schemas is a new area of concern in cognitive psychology compared with research on propositions or images. Relatively little is known about these constructs, but they have generated considerable excitement as potentially proving to be very important in human cognition. Also, some controversy exists in cognitive psychology as to whether schemas are really anything but a collection of propositions and images or whether they are a fundamentally different knowledge representation. At this point, this controversy is a profitless feud with respect to what is known, and will therefore be side-stepped in this book. However, my particular biases may show through as the discussion progresses.

Family Resemblances

Rosch's work has been very important in understanding the organization of schemas for natural categories. From her work she has articulated the very influential concept of *family resemblance.* Let us consider some background to this concept. Rosch has emphasized that no fixed set of features defines whether an item is an instance of a category. As an example, she refers to Wittgenstein's (1953) discussion of what a *game* is. No set of features that we can list covers all the things we would think of as a game—soccer, tennis, chess, bridge, poker, solitaire, and so on. Some games have teams; others do not. Some involve physical skill; others do not. Some games involve luck; others do not. What organizes the separate instances into the *game* category is a set of *family resemblances* among the members. Soccer has some things in common with tennis, tennis with chess, chess with bridge, bridge with poker, and poker with solitaire, but soccer and solitaire seem very different things. The resemblance between category members is the same as that between family members—a son might be like his mother and the mother like her sister but in a different way. The nephew and aunt may have little in common. Poker is considered a game because it is similar to other activities that are considered games. Rosch argues that subjects will consider a member more typical of a given category if it is similar to many members of that category and not similar to members of other categories.

A study by Rosch and Mervis (1975) measured the similarity of category members. The experimenters considered 20 instances from each of 6 categories (furniture, vehicles, fruit, weapons, vegetables, and clothing). One group of subjects was asked to list attributes of each instance. So, given apple as an instance of fruit, a subject might list these attributes: *is red, grows on trees, can be eaten,* and *is round.* For rhubarb, subjects might give *grows in stalks, is sour,* and *can be eaten.* Subjects listed very few attributes for all 20 categories. For 4 of the categories, one common attribute was given for all 20 instances and for 2 categories no common attribute was listed. However, many attributes were listed for well over half of the instances.

A second group of subjects in the Rosch and Mervis study was asked to rate the typicality of each instance of the category. The investigators then compared typical and atypical members with respect to the attributes listed for them. They found that the more typical members tended to share features with more other instances. To take our apple–rhubarb contrast, most fruits are like apples in growing on trees, whereas few fruits are like rhubarb in growing in stalks. Apple is a more typical instance of fruit because it overlaps with other fruits in more ways.

A prediction that derives from the concept of family resemblance is that natural categories do not have fixed boundaries. People should have great difficulty and should be quite inconsistent in judging whether items at the periphery of a category are actually members of that category. McCloskey and Glucksberg (1978) looked at people's judgments as to what were or were not members of various categories. They found that while subjects did agree on some items, they disagreed on many. For instance, while all 30 subjects agreed *cancer* was a disease and *happiness* was not, 16 thought *stroke* was a disease and 14 did not. Again, all 30 subjects agreed *apple* was a fruit and

Figure 5-4 *The various cuplike objects used in the experiment by Labov studying the boundaries of the* cup *category (1973). (Reprinted with permission from W. Labov. "The Boundaries of Words and Their Meaning." In* New Ways of Analyzing Variation in English. *Edited by C.-J. N. Bailey and R. W. Shuy. Washington, D.C. Georgetown University Press. Pages 354 and 356. © 1973 by Georgetown University.)*

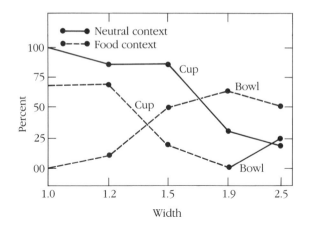

Figure 5-5   *The frequency with which subjects used the terms* cup *or* bowl *to describe the objects shown in Figure 5-4 as a function of the ratio of cup width to cup depth and as a function of the context in which the objects are imagined. The solid line is for the neutral-context condition; the dotted line is for the food-context condition (Reprinted with permission from W. Labov. "The Boundaries of Words and Their Meaning." In* New Ways of Analyzing Variation in English. *Edited by C.-J. N. Bailey and R. W. Shuy. Washington, D.C. Georgetown University Press. Pages 354 and 356.* © *1973 by Georgetown University.)*

chicken was not, but 16 thought *pumpkin* was and 14 disagreed. Once again, while all subjects agreed that a *fly* was an insect and a *dog* was not, 13 subjects thought a *leech* was and 17 disagreed. Thus, it appears that subjects do not always agree among themselves. McCloskey and Glucksberg tested the same subjects a month later and found that many had changed their mind about the disputed items. For instance, 11 out of 30 reversed themselves on *stroke,* 8 reversed themselves on *pumpkin,* and 3 reversed themselves on *leech.* Thus, disagreement as to category boundaries does not just occur *among* subjects. Subjects are very uncertain *within* themselves exactly where the boundaries of a category should be drawn.

Figure 5-4 illustrates a set of material used by Labov (1973). He was interested in which items subjects would call cups and which they would not. Which do you consider to be cups? The interesting point is that these concepts do not appear to have clear-cut boundaries. In one experiment, Labov used the series of items 1 through 4. These items reflect an increasing ratio of width of the cup to depth. For the first item the ratio is 1, while for item 4 it is 1.9. Labov also used an item (not shown) where the ratio was 2.5 to 1. Figure

5-5 shows the percentage of subjects calling each of the five objects a cup and the percentage calling it a bowl. The solid lines indicate the classifications when subjects were simply presented with pictures of the objects (the neutral context). As can be seen, the percentages of *cup* responses gradually decreased with increasing width, but there is no clear-cut point where subjects stopped using *cup*. At the extreme 2.5-width ratio, about 25 percent of the subjects still used the *cup* response, while another 25 percent used *bowl*. (The remaining 50 percent used other responses.) The dotted lines give classifications when subjects were asked to imagine the object filled with mashed potatoes and placed on a table. In this context, fewer *cup* responses and more *bowl* responses were given but the data show the same gradual shift from *cup* to *bowl*. Thus, it appears that subjects' classification behavior varies continuously not only with the properties of an object but also with the context in which the object is imagined or presented.

Schema Abstraction

Studies of Category Formation

How do we come to form schemas for categories such as bird and to note their typical features? How are such schemas organized and defined? Considerable research in cognitive psychology has recently addressed the *schema-abstraction* process by which subjects develop new category concepts by observing instances of the category. Consider the following experiment by Reed (1972), which illustrates the phenomena of schema abstraction with respect to faces. Reed trained subjects to categorize the ten cartoon faces in Figure 5-6. The five faces in the top row belong to category 1 and the lower five faces to category 2. The faces vary in terms of height of mouth, length of nose, distance between eyes, and height of forehead. These faces were presented to subjects one at a time and in random order; subjects were to classify each of them as members of one or the other category. After indicating their category choice for a given face, they were presented with the correct category label. This procedure was repeated with 12 passes through the 10 faces. On each pass, subjects studied the faces in a new random order.

After this study phase, subjects were presented with 24 new faces similar to the studied faces and asked to judge whether these new faces were members of category 1 or category 2. Among the 24 new faces were 2 faces that Reed called the category prototypes. These 2 faces are illustrated in Figure 5-7. Each of these prototypes had the average mouth height, length of nose, distance between eyes, and height of forehead for members of their category. Reed compared the number of correct classification judgments for these prototypes with the number of correct classifications for the other control faces in the set of 24 that the subject had not studied. Subjects were 90 percent correct in

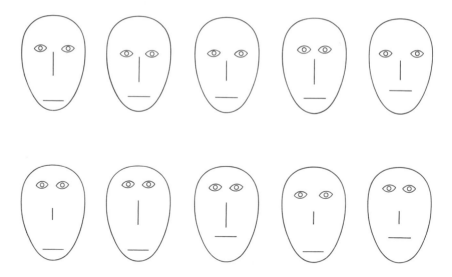

Figure 5-6 *The faces in the two artificial categories in Reed's experiment (1970) studying schema abstraction with respect to faces. The faces in the top row are from category 1, and the faces in the bottom row are from category 2. (From Reed, S. K. Pattern recognition and categorization.* Cognitive Psychology, *1972, 3, 382-407.)*

their classifications of the prototypes, but only 61 percent accurate (chance performance would be 50 percent) in their classification of the control faces. This result demonstrates that subjects can extract out the central tendency of a set of studied instances and then use this central tendency to help judge whether new members belong to the category. The prototype faces were more accurately categorized because they were close to this extracted central tendency, while the control faces were quite different. Basically, in the study phase subjects were forming impressions about the artifical categories and these impressions guided their judgments just as our impressions of natural categories such as birds guide our judgments about natural-category members.

Another experiment that illustrates the same points was conducted by Hayes-Roth and Hayes-Roth (1977). These investigators had subjects study exemplars of two clubs. Subjects might be given the following description of a club 1 member:

Joe Doe, 30 years old, junior high education, single, plays chess.

A member of club 2 might be described this way:

Bill Jones, 50 years old, college education, married, collects stamps.

The relevant variables for club classification were age, education, and marital status. Subjects studied 51 members of each club. The 51 members of each club are given in Table 5-1. By examining this table, you can see that a

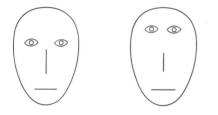

Figure 5-7 *The prototypes for category 1 and category 2 in Figure 5-6. (From Reed, S. K. Pattern recognition and categorization.* Cognitive Psychology, *1972, 3, 382-407.)*

majority of the members of club 1 were 30 years old, a majority were junior-high educated, and a majority were married. However, no member of club 1 possessed all three of these attributes—that is, no one was 30 years old, junior-high educated, and married. Still, we refer to this combination as the club 1 prototype. Similarly, a majority of club 2 was 50 years old, a majority was college educated, and a majority was single. However, again no member of club 2 had all three of these attributes. Still, we refer to this combination as the club 2 prototype.

Table 5-1 Constitution of Club 1 and Club 2 in Hayes-Roth and Hayes-Roth (1977)

	Club 1		Club 2
A.	10 instances of 30 years, junior high, single	M.	10 instances of 50 years, college, married
B.	10 instances of 30 years, college, married	N.	10 instances of 50 years, junior high, single
C.	10 instances of 50 years, junior high, married	O.	10 instances of 30 years, college, single
D.	1 instance of 30 years, junior high, divorced	P.	1 instance of 50 years, college, divorced
E.	1 instance of 30 years, senior high, married	Q.	1 instance of 50 years, senior high, single
F.	1 instance of 40 years, junior high, married	R.	1 instance of 40 years, college, single
G.	1 instance of 30 years, senior high, divorced	S.	1 instance of 50 years, senior high, divorced
H.	1 instance of 40 years, junior high, divorced	T.	1 instance of 40 years, college, divorced
I.	1 instance of 40 years, senior high, married	U.	1 instance of 40 years, senior high, single
J.	5 instances of 30 years, senior high, single	V.	5 instances of 30 years, senior high, single
K.	5 instances of 40 years, college, married	W.	5 instances of 40 years, college, married
L.	5 instances of 50 years, junior high, divorced	X.	5 instances of 50 years, junior high, divorced

After studying the 102 instances from the two clubs, subjects began a test phase in which they were presented with descriptions of this form:

1. 30 years, junior high, single
2. 50 years, college, single

For each description, the subjects had to rate (1) whether they had studied an individual with these characteristics and (2) whether the individual was a member of club 1 or 2. In the test phase, subjects had to rate all the descriptions they had previously studied and also a number they had not studied. Among the new descriptions were the prototypes of club 1 and club 2. Of principal interest was how performance on these nonstudied prototypes compared with performance on the studied descriptions. On the recognition question, subjects rated highest such descriptions as A, J, and M in Table 5-1, which had been studied many times. However, they rated next highest the prototypes—their ratings were higher than for any of the instances they had only studied once. On the club-membership judgment, subjects were more confident that the prototypes were in the category than they were about any studied instance.

These results once again demonstrate subjects' ability to extract the central tendency of a set of instances and to form a schematic description of a category from this central tendency. Further, this experiment shows that subjects do not completely lose track of the instances they study, since they gave the highest recognition ratings to members they had studied many times. However, subjects were so strongly influenced by their abstraction of the schema for the category that they were more likely to think they studied it than some of the category members that they actually did study. Just as we have a strong conception of what a good bird is like, so subjects in this experiment evolved strong conceptions of what a club 1 person was like.

One of the most impressive demonstrations of subjects' ability to extract the central tendency of a set of instances is a series of experiments performed by Posner and Keele (1968, 1970). These investigators used as their stimuli random dot patterns such as those in Figure 5-8. Subjects saw four instances of each of four "patterns," a pattern being defined with respect to a prototype dot pattern. The prototype was just a random 9-dot pattern. Subjects studied not the prototype but rather distortions from it. These distortions were the result of each dot being moved a random distance in a random direction. A prototype and two distortions of the prototype are shown in Figure 5-8. Subjects studied four distortions of each of the prototypes. As the reader may verify, these distortions appear on first glance to be relatively unrelated. The subjects studied the sixteen distortions until they were able to perfectly sort them into four piles of four to reflect the four categories.

After the study phase, subjects were given a transfer task in which they had to classify as to category membership the previously studied distortions, new

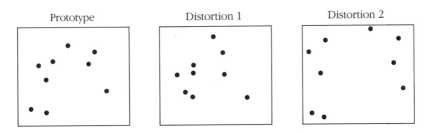

Figure 5-8   *Examples of the stimuli used in the experiments by Posner and Keele (1970), which demonstrated subjects' ability to extract a central category from a series of instances. Subjects studied distortions of a prototype such as the two examples on the right.*

unstudied distortions, and the prototypes. Their results showed 20 percent errors in classifying the previously studied, or old, patterns, 32 percent errors on the prototypes, and 50 percent errors on the new distortions (chance performance would be 75 percent errors). Posner and Keele also measured classification time, and this measure showed similar results: old patterns, 2.89 seconds; prototypes, 2.93 seconds; and new distortions, 3.69 seconds. Thus, even with such meaningless stimuli, subjects were able to extract the central tendency from each group of patterns. While their classifications of the prototype were not better than those of the studied instances in this experiment, subjects clearly showed better performance on the prototype than on other new instances.

What Is Learned?

In discussing natural categories, we introduced Rosch's notion of family resemblance. Her claim was that people learned the feature combinations that were most typical of a category. However, this is a very descriptive assertion and really does constitute an explanation of the phenomenon. What can we say about the actual knowledge structures that underlie one's conception of a category? A large number of theories have been developed about how this knowledge is represented. Up to now, in this text, we have not considered a range of competing theories, but in this case such an approach is useful. An understanding of what is wrong with individual theories can lead to a better understanding of the nature of the information that subjects learn and of the actual structure of categories.

Instance Theory

One class of theories regarding knowledge structures is the *instance theories* (e.g., Medin and Schaffer, 1978). These theories hold that subjects remember only the individual instances they have studied. To judge whether a new member is an instance of a category, they measure the similarity between it and the instances they have actually studied. A number of difficulties regarding instance theories have been identified. Particularly serious is the fact that subjects often rate new prototypes higher than the actual instances they have studied (as in the Hayes-Roth and Hayes-Roth study discussed in the preceding subsection), which suggests that subjects often forget the instances and remember the central tendencies. Posner and Keele (1968) have shown that subjects' ratings of the instances drop quite sharply after a week but that their ratings for the prototypes remain high, findings that are also consistent with the idea that subjects can forget instances and retain the central tendency. Thus, subjects would seem to have some sense of the central tendency of the category that does not depend on its specific instances. (However, see Medin and Schaffer, 1978, for a counter to these criticisms.)

Prototype Theory

Prototype theories (e.g., Franks and Bransford, 1971; Reed, 1972) reflect the view at the extreme opposite of that expressed in instance theories. They propose that we form a description of a single ideal instance of the category. We form this instance from the average, or most frequently encountered features of the category. For instance, the prototype of club 1 in the Hayes-Roth and Hayes-Roth experiment was someone who was 30 years old, junior-high educated, and married. The prototype for Posner's dot patterns would have been the average of the studied dot patterns. Instances are rated according to how similar they are to the prototype. The difficulty with prototype theories is opposite of that with instance-only theories. Prototype theories fail to explain the finding that subjects prefer studied instances over new instances that are the same distance from the prototype. Sometimes they prefer old instances to the prototype itself. It seems clear that subjects remember something about the specific instances.

Prototype-Plus-Instance Theory

The obvious alternative to the two types of theories reviewed so far is a theory that assumes that subjects both develop a prototype and remember the individual instances that gave rise to it. Though such an alternative is much more adequate, it still has some difficulties in accounting for certain facts about category structure. For example, it does not properly explain the family-resemblance structure of many categories. For natural categories such as *games,* no single central tendency can be captured by a prototype. That is, no set of properties is common to all games. We would need many prototypes to capture different clusters of features.

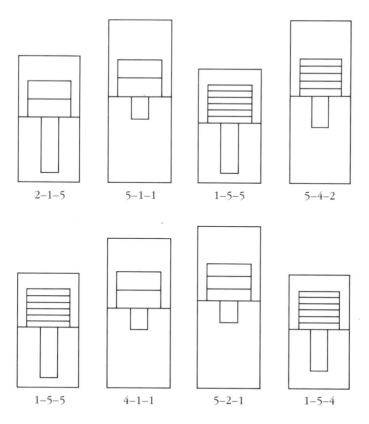

Figure 5-9 *Examples of study material in Neumann's experiment (1977) to study whether subjects would form multiple prototypes from a category. These stimuli vary in size of the main rectangle, size of the lower rectangle, and number of stripes of the upper rectangle.*

An experiment by Neumann (1977) illustrates how subjects can learn that more than one prototypical stimulus or central tendency exists in a set of information. He had subjects study geometric patterns consisting of large rectangles each with two rectangles within it. Figure 5-9 illustrates some of the geometric stimuli presented to subjects for study. These stimuli can be considered a large rectangle, divided in half, with smaller rectangles in the upper and lower halves. The outer and the lower rectangle could vary independently in length. The upper rectangle varied in terms of its number of stripes. Thus, there were three dimensions of variation. For the first dimension, size of outer rectangle, the values varied from 200 to 300 mm in increments of 25 mm. For the second dimension, size of lower rectangle, the values varied from 37.5 to 87.5 mm in increments of 12.5 mm. For the third dimension,

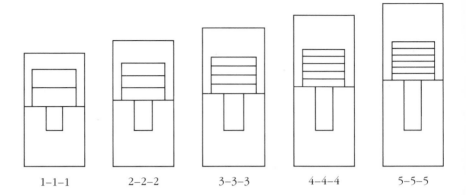

1-1-1   2-2-2   3-3-3   4-4-4   5-5-5

Figure 5-10   *Illustrations of the correlated test materials in Neumann's experiment (1977).*

number of stripes, values varied from 1 to 5. In what follows, I will refer to the five values on any dimension by the numbers 1, 2, 3, 4 and 5, where 1 denotes the smallest value on the dimension and 5 the largest. The stimuli in Figure 5-9 are labeled with three digits to indicate their values on the three dimensions. For instance, the first is labeled 2-1-5 (2 for the 225 mm length of the large rectangle; 1 for 1 stripe on the upper rectangle; and 5 for the 87.5 mm length of the lower rectangle). Neumann also used another set of stimuli in which the differences among values on a dimension were smaller and hence less discriminable.

Each set of stimuli was presented to a separate group of subjects. Each group studied eight stimuli. In that population of eight, values 1 and 5 on each dimension were present three times each, values 2 and 4 one time each, and value 3 not at all. Figure 5-9 illustrates one set of eight geometric stimuli that a subject might study. Within this frequency constraint, the features were combined randomly to create stimuli. The important feature of this manipulation was that subjects studied a preponderence of stimuli with extreme values and few intermediate values. Value 3, the average value, was not presented at all. After studying these patterns, subjects were presented with test patterns, which they rated according to how confident they were that they had studied them. Their confidence ratings varied from 1 ("I am sure that I did not see it") to 5 ("I am sure that I did see it").

Of particular interest are the subjects' ratings of the five "correlated" test patterns illustrated in Figure 5-10. One of these patterns had the same value 1 on all three dimensions; it was denoted 1-1-1. The other correlated patterns are 2-2-2, 3-3-3, 4-4-4, and 5-5-5. A tendency to prefer the 3-3-3 stimulus would indicate that subjects were remembering a single average value for each dimension. A tendency to prefer the extreme stimuli 1-1-1 or 5-5-5 would

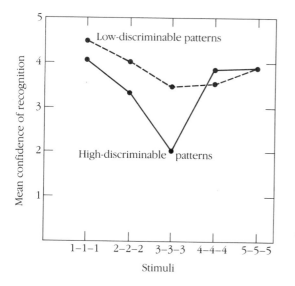

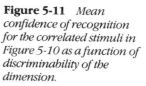

Figure 5-11 *Mean confidence of recognition for the correlated stimuli in Figure 5-10 as a function of discriminability of the dimension.*

indicate that subjects encoded that both large and small values had occurred on the dimensions.

The mean confidences for these stimuli are plotted in Figure 5-11. For our current purposes, the most interesting result occurs with the high-discriminable patterns. Here subjects rated the extremes (1-1-1 and 5-5-5) much higher than the mean value (3-3-3), showing that they could extract out multiple foci of centrality in a stimulus set. The confidence function is much flatter for the low-discriminable items. Thus, it seems that the ability to identify multiple prototypes or central tendencies in a set of instances depends on the discriminability of the different central tendencies. For instance, German shepherds may come in two distinct sizes, with very few German shepherds falling in between, but if they do, the difference is too small for non-German-shepherd owners to notice. On the other hand, determining that multiple foci exist for poodle sizes—toy, approximately 6 pounds; miniature, approximately 15 pounds; and standard, approximately 45 pounds—is much easier.

Multiple Prototypes–Multiple Instances Theory

An investigator who still wanted to hold onto the prototype concept in the face of this evidence could propose that subjects extracted multiple prototypes from the instances and, in addition, remembered multiple instances. However, even this model has its weakness. This weakness relates to the definition of a prototype. A prototype is like an instance in that the values of all its dimensions are filled in. The value chosen for each dimension of the prototype is, in some sense, an average value. The problem is that some dimensions of a concept are irrelevant and in no sense can they be assigned an average value. For instance, color seems irrelevant to the concept of a chair although every individual chair has a color. Shape of ears is relatively unimportant to one's concept of a dog although every specific dog's ears have some shape. As a final example, marital status seems irrelevant to our concept of a policeman, although every policeman has some marital status. However, a prototype must specify a value on these irrelevant dimensions, since a prototype, like an instance, has all its values filled in. It would be better to have a schema, which can have certain dimensions without specified values.

The problem with the concept of prototype, as we have been developing it, is that it has no measures built in of what Rosch and others have called *cue validity*. Some features, or *cues*, are very highly related to a category and others are less so; we need some way to weigh the validity of a cue. Only cues with high validity should be considered significant in determining category membership. Rosch has shown that the more prototypical members of a category are those with the most valid cues. The Rosch and Mervis analysis (1975) discussed earlier demonstrates this conclusion. The study showed that a prototypical fruit, such as *apple,* shares features with many other fruits; thus, the features, or cues, that apple possesses are highly valid.

Feature-Count Theory

One proposal as to how concepts are formed that does weigh the validity of cues is the *feature-count theory.* In this type of model, subjects are assumed to remember how frequently they have seen the various features in the instances. The more frequently a feature has been seen the more valid it is assumed to be. How well an instance fits a category depends on the frequency rating of its features. Such a theory would have to be supplemented with memory for the individual instances because, as we already noted with respect to the prototype model, subjects sometimes give higher ratings to instances they have actually seen.

The feature-count model is at an advantage over the prototype model in that it can weigh different dimensions with respect to their validity. For instance, if most chairs have four legs, four-leggedness will have a high feature count. Similarly, if chairs come in all colors, any color will have a relatively low feature count. However, feature-count theories are at a disadvantage to prototype theories in that they do not specify which features tend to go together. Some experiments (e.g., Medin and Schaffer, 1978) have shown that subjects tend to remember common feature combinations.

To further illustrate the fact that we remember feature combinations, consult your knowledge of dogs and you may discover that you are aware of various clusters of features. For example, there are very large dogs with short noses and floppy ears; these include Newfoundlands and St. Bernards. There are dogs ranging in size from medium to large that have relatively long hair and floppy ears; these include the spaniels, setters, and some of the other retrievers. Then there are the short and hairy dogs such as the Pekingese and toy terriers. And there are the large, multicolored dogs with medium-length hair and pointed ears; these include the German shepherds and huskies.* Thus, no one expects all dogs to be one size and to have one hair length and one ear shape. Instead, people know that certain clusters of features exist within the dog category. From one's knowledge of these features, one might be able to predict that though not all large dogs have short noses, one that does will tend to have floppy ears as well.

Feature-Set or Schema Theory

The most adequate model of the information underlying knowledge of categories is what has been called the feature-set model. Variations on this model have been developed by a number of theorists (Anderson, Kline, and Beasley, 1979; Hayes-Roth and Hayes-Roth, 1977; Reitman and Bower, 1973). This model proposes that people have a basic sensitivity to correlations of features in the environment—that they notice and remember what sets of features tend to occur together in a category. A special case of this phenomenon would be the remembering of a specific instance—that is, the remembering of a complete set of features.

To see how the feature-set model might apply, let us go back to the Hayes-Roth and Hayes-Roth material in Table 5-1, confining our attention to club 1 members, and compare the ratings given to the following description:

1. 30 years old, junior high, divorced
2. 30 years old, senior high, divorced

To evaluate these two descriptions, we should determine how often their feature sets have been studied. First, let's consider description 1. The complete combination of three features was studied once in D in Table 5-1. We also have to consider the three pairs of features that are contained in description 1: 30 years and junior high, 30 years and divorced, junior high and divorced. The first pair of features (30 years and junior high) occurs 11 times in Table 5-1 (10 times in A and once in D). The second pair (30 years and divorced) is found 2 times in Table 5-1 (once in D and once in G). The third pair (junior high and divorced) is also found 7 times (once in D, once in H, and 5 times in L). So, there are a total of 20 instances of the feature pairs. As

---

*Note that some dogs (for example, Great Danes and chihuahuas) do not fit any of these clusters. These breeds would receive lower typicality ratings because they do not have feature clusters typical of other breeds.

for single features, we have 28 instances of 30 years, 28 instances of junior high, and 8 instances of divorced, making a total of 64. Let us summarize our feature-set count for description 1:

triples:	1
pairs:	20
singles:	64

Similarly, we can perform this count for description 2. You should confirm that the following counts are correct:

triples:	1
pairs:	10
singles:	44

While descriptions 1 and 2 have the same triple count, 1 is ahead on the pair and single count. Thus, overall, the feature sets contained in description 1 are more frequent. Correspondingly, we would expect ratings to be higher for 1 than for 2, which is what Hayes-Roth and Hayes-Roth found.

Schema Abstraction: A Summary

This section has been concerned with how schemas are formed. The answer in the research we reviewed is that our minds seem especially tuned to pick out correlations of features in the environment and to develop categories around these correlations. Thus, the reason people generally agree that robins are better birds than are chickens is not due to any inherent goodness of robins. Rather, it derives from the fact that robins are more like the other kinds of birds we typically encounter and, therefore, are more likely than chickens to share feature sets with other frequently encountered birds. Presumably, someone whose principle encounters with birds involved turkeys, chickens, and ducks would have a rather different opinion about what constituted a good bird.

The term *schema* (the Greek plural is *schemata*) is used to refer to collections of feature sets. A schema is distinguished from a prototype in that all the features of the former need not be specified. Thus, if certain dimensions are not relevant (if no valid cues or features exist on those dimensions), then those dimensions need not be represented in the schema. The term *schema* is being widely used in the study of cognition to denote a variety of knowledge structures. One common aspect of these knowledge structures is that they are incomplete in the sense that they leave features unspecified. Another common aspect is that they can encode very complex bodies of knowledge. One of the areas where the schema notion has been applied is in the understanding of story comprehension. In the next section, we will discuss some of this story-comprehension research to show how the idea of a schema can be extended to a domain considerably different and perhaps more complex than that of category formation.

Story Schemas

Scripts

How do people comprehend stories? Recently, a considerable amount of research has addressed this question, in part, because the topic is perceived to be relevant to the applied question of how people read textbooks and similar material. Stories rather than textbooks are studied because they are simpler. One important concept to come out of this work has been the notion of *scripts,* developed by Roger Schank and Robert Abelson at Yale University (Schank and Abelson, 1977). These investigators used scripts—organized structures of stereotypic knowledge—as part of a model of how stories are comprehended. They pointed out that many circumstances involve stereotypic sequences of actions. For instance, the list below shows their hunch as to what the stereotypic aspects of dining at a restaurant might be, and represents the components of a script for such an occasion. Scripts arise from our recognition of the common characteristics of individual instances of restaurant-going episodes. Thus, the notion of script is an extension to episodes of the schema or prototype notion, which we have discussed so far with respect to object categories.

Bower, Black, and Turner (1979) report a series of experiments in which the psychological reality of the script notion was tested. They had subjects name what they considered the 20 most importants events in an episode such as going to a restaurant. With 32 subjects, they failed to get complete agreement on what these events were. No action was listed as part of the episode by all of the subjects. However, considerable consensus was reported. Table 5-2 lists those events named. The items in roman were listed by at least 25 percent of the subjects. The italicized items were named by at least 48 percent of the subjects, and the items in capitals were given by at least 73 percent. Using the 73 percent as a criterion, we find the stereotypic sequence was *sit down, look at menu, order, eat, pay bill,* and *leave*. It appears that the restaurant script has something of the family resemblance-structure we saw with objects. That is, different features are more or less part of the restaurant script, no fixed set of restaurant features would cover all restaurant-going episodes.

Scene I: Entering
    Customer enters restaurant.
    Customer looks for table.
    Customer decides where to sit.

Customer goes to table.
Customer sits down.

Scene 2: Ordering

Customer picks up menu.
Customer looks at menu.
Customer decides on food.
Customer signals waitress.
Waitress comes to table.
Customer orders food.
Waitress goes to cook.
Waitress gives food order to cook.
Cook prepares food.

Scene 3: Eating

Cook gives food to waitress.
Waitress brings food to customer.
Customer eats food.

Scene 4: Exiting

Waitress writes bill.
Waitress goes over to customer.
Waitress gives bill to customer.
Customer gives tip to waitress.
Customer goes to cashier.
Customer gives money to cashier.
Customer leaves restaurant.

Bower, Black, and Turner went on to show a number of effects of such action scripts on memory for stories. They had subjects study stories that included some but not all of the typical events from a story. Subjects were then asked to recall the stories (in one experiment) or to recognize (in another experiment) whether various statements came from the story. When recalling these stories, subjects tended to report statements that were part of the script but that had not been presented as part of the stories. Similarly, in the recognition test, subjects thought they had studied script items that had not actually been in the stories. However, subjects showed a greater tendency to recall actual items from the stories or to recognize actual items than to falsely recognize foils not in the stories. So, they still had some memory for the particular sentences of the stories. However, their memories were distorted in the direction of the general schema.

In another experiment, these investigators read to subjects stories composed of 12 prototypical actions in an episode. Eight of the actions occurred in their standard temporal position, but four were rearranged. Thus, in the restaurant story the bill might be paid at the beginning and the menu read at the end. In recalling these stories, subjects showed a strong tendency to

Table 5-2   Empirical script norms at three agreement levels.

Going to a Restaurant

Open door.
Enter.
Give reservation name.
    Wait to be seated.
    Go to table.
BE SEATED.
Order drinks.
    Put napkins on lap.
LOOK AT MENU.
Discuss menu.
ORDER MEAL.
Talk.
    Drink water.
Eat salad or soup.
    Meal arrives.
EAT FOOD.
    Finish meal.
Order dessert.
Eat dessert.
    Ask for bill.
    Bill arrives.
PAY BILL.
Leave tip.
    Get coats.
LEAVE.

Adapted from Bower, Black, and Turner, 1979.
Note: The items in capitals were mentioned by the most subjects (73 percent), items in italic by fewer subjects (48 percent), and items in lower case roman by still fewer subjects (25 percent).

put the events back in their normal order. In fact, about half of the statements were put back. This experiment serves as another demonstration of the powerful effect of general schemas on memory for stories.

These experiments indicate that new events are encoded with respect to these general schemas and that subsequent recall is influenced by the schemas. We have talked about these effects as if they were "bad"; that is, as if subjects were misrecalling the stories. However, it is not clear that these results should be classified as acts of misrecall. Normally, if a certain standard event such as paying a check is omitted in a story, we are supposed to assume it occurred. Similarly, if the storyteller says the check was paid at the beginning of the restaurant episode, one has some reason to doubt the storyteller. Scripts or schemas exist because they encode the predominant sequence of events in a particular kind of situation. Thus, they can serve as valuable bases for predicting missing information and for correcting errors in information.

Much of story and text comprehension cannot involve scripts, however. The hallmark of a good story or text is that it is not stereotypic but involves interesting, new combinations of events and facts. In comprehending these more sophisticated stories, more powerful cognitive processes (such as those we will study in subsequent chapters) have to be called upon. However, even the finest novels include various stereotypic subepisodes. Scripts can reduce the information-processing burden of encoding these episodes and thus free the system for processing the more complex, interesting aspects of the story.

"The War of the Ghosts"

Probably the most famous story in cognitive psychology is "The War of the Ghosts," which was used by Bartlett (1932) in research with English subjects before World War I. It has been used in research on many subsequent occasions and is still a popular research item today. The story is reproduced in its entirety below:*

The War of the Ghosts

One night two young men from Egulac went down to the river to hunt seals, and while they were there it became foggy and calm. Then they heard war-cries, and they thought: "Maybe this is a war-party." They escaped to the shore, and hid behind a log. Now canoes came up, and they heard the noise of paddles, and saw one canoe coming up to them. There were five men in the canoe, and they said:

"What do you think? We wish to take you along. We are going up the river to make war on the people."

One of the young men said, "I have no arrows."

"Arrows are in the canoe," they said.

"I will not go along. I might be killed. My relatives do not know where I have gone. But you," he said, turning to the other, "may go with them."

So one of the young men went, but the other returned home.

And the warriors went on up the river to a town on the other side of Kalama. The people came down to the water, and they began to fight, and many were killed. But presently the young man heard one of the warriors say: "Quick, let us go home: that Indian has been hit." Now he thought: "Oh, they are ghosts." He did not feel sick, but they said he had been shot.

So the canoes went back to Egulac, and the young man went ashore to his house, and made a fire. And he told everybody and said: "Behold I accompanied the ghosts, and we went to fight. Many of our fellows were killed, and many of those who attacked us were killed. They said I was hit, and I did not feel sick."

He told it all, and then he became quiet. When the sun rose he fell down. Something black came out of his mouth. His face became contorted. The people jumped up and cried.

He was dead.

---

*Frederic C. Bartlett, *Remembering: A Study in Experimental and Social Psychology* (New York: Cambridge University Press), 1967, p. 65. (Originally published in 1932.)

Presumably, you find this a rather bizarre story. Certainly, it appeared bizarre to Bartlett's subjects, accustomed as they were to the world of upper-class Victorian England. This story, however, would be perfectly reasonable to the people from which it was taken. It was part of the oral literary tradition of Indians on the West Coast of Canada a century ago. It fit in very well with their schemas for how the world worked. It does not fit in well with our cultural schemas or with the schemas of Bartlett's subjects.

Bartlett was interested in how subjects would remember a story that fit in so poorly with their cultural schemas. He had his subjects recall the stories after various delays, from immediately after study to years later. To get a feeling for their task, you might put this book aside and try to write down all you can remember from this story.

Bartlett's subjects showed clear distortions in their memory for the story and these distortions appeared to grow with time. Below is a representative recall given 20 hours after hearing the story:*

The War of the Ghosts

Two men from Edulac went fishing. While thus occupied by the river they heard a noise in the distance.

"It sounds like a cry," said one, and presently there appeared some in canoes who invited them to join the party on their adventure. One of the young men refused to go, on the ground of family ties, but the other offered to go.

"But there are no arrows," he said.

"The arrows are in the boat," was the reply.

He thereupon took his place, while his friend returned home. The party paddled up the river to Kaloma, and began to land on the banks of the river. The enemy came rushing upon them, and some sharp fighting ensued. Presently someone was injured, and the cry was raised that the enemy were ghosts.

The party returned down the stream, and the young man arrived home feeling none the worse for his experience. The next morning at dawn he endeavoured to recount his adventures. While he was talking something black issued from his mouth. Suddenly he uttered a cry and fell down. His friends gathered round him.

But he was dead.

Subjects omitted much of the story, changed many of the facts, and imported new information. Such inaccuracies in memory are not particularly interesting in and of themselves. The important observation is that these inaccuracies were systematic: the subjects were distorting the story to fit with their own cultural stereotypes. For instance, "something black came from his mouth" in the original story became "he frothed at the mouth" or "he vomited" in some stories. In the recall above, we find "hunting seals" changed to "fishing" and "canoe" changed to "boat." The hard-to-interpret aspects are omitted, includ-

---

*Ibid., p. 66.

ing the hiding behind the log and the connection between the Indian's injury and the termination of the battle. Further, this subject has the role of the ghosts completely turned around. Thus, Bartlett's prediction was borne out: when subjects read a story that does not fit with their own schemas, they will exhibit a powerful tendency to distort the story to make it fit.

Social Cognitions

Stereotypes

People can be thought of as being comprised of sets of features. If we perceive people in terms of feature sets, it is only natural that we should detect regularities in these sets. Our impression of a friend is probably a set of schemas formed from our numerous interactions with him or her. We come to expect a particular person to display certain physical features and have certain mannerisms, likes, dislikes, and so on. When friends violate these expectations, we tend to say that they are not "themselves." Professional mimics have their effect by capturing the prototypical features of famous people.

We have impressions of groups just as we have impressions of individuals. For example, we have definite impressions of what a typical doctor is like or what a typical taxi driver is like. These impressions are based in part on experience, but they also are based in part on images projected by the media. Students have impressions about what professors are like and professors have impressions about students. As is the case with other categories, our group impressions often do not have single prototypes. Thus, professors come in different types—old, clean-shaven, and conservative, or younger, bearded, and liberal (professors are stereotyped as male). Similarly, among the prototypes we have of students are the strong, dumb, and loud jocks and the smart, ambitious and dull premeds. Of course, not all instances conform to any of our prototypes, and, indeed, perfect instances of prototypes may be rare.

Social psychologists have not concerned themselves much with the emergence of group of individual schemas or the effects of such schemas on information processing. There are a few recent exceptions to this generalization (e.g., Abelson, 1976; Cantor and Mischel, 1977; Tesser, 1978), but the main focus in social psychology has been on the formation of general evaluative impressions (e.g., Anderson, 1974) rather than the identification of richer clusters of features.

The one major exception to the lack of interest in complex impressions is social psychology's fascination with *stereotypes*. One might well characterize the impressions of the doctor, taxi driver, professor, and student described above as stereotypes. However, social psychology has used *stereotype* to refer to sets of beliefs about ethnic groups that the believer has little good reason for holding but that often serve to justify bigotry. It is interesting to speculate to what degree these stereotypes resemble the kinds of schemas we have been discussing so far in this chapter.

A famous series of studies, started by Katz and Braly in 1933 and followed up by Gilbert in 1951, and by Karlins, Coffman, and Walters in 1969, focused on the changing racial stereotypes held by three generations of Princeton University undergraduates. In these experiments, subjects were given a list of 84 adjectives from which to select 5 adjectives that best described a particular ethnic group. The subjects could also give any additional adjectives they thought of. The ethnic groups rated were Americans, Chinese, English, Germans, Irish, Italians, Japanese, Jews, Negroes, and Turks. (The last study was done in 1967 when *Negro* was still a more common term than *black*.) Table 5-3 gives the most common adjectives used for Americans, Germans, Japanese, and Negroes.

The 1933 ratings displayed strong, negative stereotypes for Negroes, and similar negative stereotypes were found for Chinese, Irish, Jews, and Turks. Of the Princeton undergraduates tested, 84 percent thought Negroes were superstitious and 75 percent thought they were lazy. This stereotype apparently dissolved over the succeeding two generations, and by 1967 a new, somewhat more positive stereotype was beginning to emerge involving such terms as sensitive, musical, pleasure loving, and gregarious, although some of the old stereotype features remained. Another interesting finding was that the German and Japanese images deteriorated in 1951 after World War II but had been considerably rehabilitated by 1967. In contrast, the American self-image had deteriorated steadily, falling behind the image of Germans and Japanese in 1967.

In general, a fair degree of consensus existed among the subjects as to the character of various ethnic groups—a much greater agreement than would have occurred by chance. The amount of stereotyping (measured in terms of amount of agreement as to adjectives used) was almost as large in 1967 as it was in 1933 and was larger than in 1951. One phenomenon, first exhibited in 1951 and seen to be much stronger in 1967, consisted of students complaining and refusing to participate in the ratings. One subject in 1967 wrote,

> I must make it clear that I think it ludicrous to attempt to classify various ethnic groups. Perhaps my answers are a factor of the stereotypes that arise from individual interactions I have had with various members of these groups. I don't believe that any people can accurately be depicted as having, in total, certain characteristics. I have, however, attempted to relate my impression of the members of each of whom I have met. I would point out that in several instances, the number of such members is rather low.

So by 1967, while students still appeared to possess ethnic stereotypes, they were much more aware of the potential inaccuracies in these stereotypes.

Table 5-3   Comparisons of Stereotype Trait Frequencies

	Percent Checking Trait				Percent Checking Trait		
Trait	1933	1951	1967	Trait	1933	1951	1967
Americans				*Germans*			
Industrious	48	30	23	Scientifically minded	78	62	47
Intelligent	47	32	20	Industrious	65	50	59
Materialistic	33	37	67	Stolid	44	10	9
Ambitious	33	21	42	Intelligent	32	32	19
Progressive	27	5	17	Methodical	31	20	21
Pleasure loving	26	27	28	Extremely nationalistic	24	50	43
Alert	23	7	7	Progressive	16	3	13
Efficient	21	9	15	Efficient	16	—	46
Aggressive	20	8	15	Jovial	15	—	5
Straightforward	19	—	9	Musical	13	—	4
Practical	19	—	12	Persistent	11	—	4
Sportsmanlike	19	—	9	Practical	11	—	9
Individualistic	—	26	15	Aggressive	—	27	30
Conventional	—	—	17	Arrogant	—	23	18
Scientifically minded	—	—	15	Ambitious	—	—	15
Ostentatious	—	—	15				
Japanese				*Negroes*			
Intelligent	45	11	20	Superstitious	84	41	13
Industrious	43	12	57	Lazy	75	31	26
Progressive	24	2	17	Happy-go-lucky	38	17	27
Shrewd	22	13	7	Ignorant	38	24	11
Sly	20	21	3	Musical	26	33	47
Quiet	19	—	14	Ostentatious	26	11	25
Imitative	17	24	22	Very religious	24	27	8
Alert	16	—	11	Stupid	22	10	4
Suave	16	—	0	Physically dirty	17	—	3
Neat	16	—	7	Naive	14	—	4
Treacherous	13	17	1	Slovenly	13	—	5
Aggressive	13	—	19	Unreliable	12	—	6
Extremely nationalistic	—	18	21	Pleasure loving	—	19	16
Ambitious	—	—	33	Sensitive	—	—	17
Efficient	—	—	27	Gregarious	—	—	17
Loyal to family ties	—	—	23	Talkative	—	—	14
Courteous	—	—	22	Imitative	—	—	13

Stereotype Formation

How do such stereotypes arise? In keeping with the implications of the research reviewed earlier in this chapter, we might assume that stereotypes result from one's experiences with people from each group. However, this assumption would seem to contradict the commonly held belief that stereotypes are inaccurate and are often motivated by racial bias. For instance, LaPierre (1936) investigated stereotypes of Armenian laborers in southern California. Armenians were seen by other Californians to be liars, thieves, and troublemakers. In fact, Armenians appeared less often in legal cases, applied less often for charity, and had credit ratings as good as those received by other ethnic groups.

An important factor in ethnic stereotypes is the image of a group portrayed by the media. Few of the 1933 Princeton undergraduates had had much contact with blacks, yet most thought them to be lazy and superstitious. If one looks at movies from the 1920s and 1930s, it is clear where this idea came from. The image is the one Hollywood and other media choose to portray of black people. These features disappeared from the students' stereotype at a rate almost proportionate to that at which they disappeared from the movie screen. Similarly, World War II movie and newspaper characterizations of Germans and Japanese probably accounted in large part for the negative features that had been incorporated into their stereotypes by 1951. Inaccurate stereotypes can be fostered by in-group stories as well as by external media. For instance, if one's parents always tell stories of greedy Jews, this influence might have a strong effect on one's Jewish stereotype. Thus, it seems that one reason that stereotypes are often inaccurate and reflective of prejudice is that in many instances their development has little basis in direct, first-hand experience. Rather, stereotypes are often based on second-hand experience, possibly filtered through biased sources. One major motivation behind the forced integration of schools is to provide students with first-hand experience about other ethnic groups, thereby, it is hoped, dissipating inaccurate stereotypes.

There is also reason to believe that even stereotypes based on representative experience can show some distortions. The reason is simply that the mechanics underlying schema abstraction might not produce prototypes that perfectly reflect the population's characteristics. For instance, it is known in the impression-formation literature (e.g., N. Anderson, 1974) that the first information learned about an individual is weighted much more heavily in the formation of a judgment about that person than later information. Thus, there is every reason to expect that in stereotype formation first contacts will be weighted particularly heavily, which explains why early exposure to other ethnic groups may be so important.

Hamilton and Gifford (1976) have shown that stereotypes tend to over-emphasize unusual feature combinations. They had subjects study good and bad traits about two groups, A and B. Twice as many instances existed in group A as in group B, and in both groups twice as many instances had good traits as had bad. Thus, the ratio of good attributes to bad was equal in both groups. Nonetheless, subjects estimated that bad traits were more prevalent in group B than group A. In a second study, there were still twice as many instances presented in group A than in group B, but this time there were twice as many bad as good traits. Again the proportion of good traits was equal in both groups, but now subjects estimated that the proportion of good traits was greater in group B. Thus, subjects overestimated the frequency of the more unusual trait in the less frequently encountered group. Hamilton and Gifford argue that because group B was less frequently encountered and the trait less frequent, the combination was particularly memorable and so was given undue weight in the formation of an impression of the group. If similar processes occur in real life, they could lead to rather distorted stereotypes of minorities. For example, if Turks are relatively rare in one's experience and cruel behavior relatively infrequent, any instance of a cruel Turk will be particularly memorable and will lead to an illusory stereotype of the terrible Turk.

General Conclusions

Humans have a powerful ability to detect correlations among stimulus events and to build schemas to embody these correlations. Such schemas serve to help us recognize objects, make judgments, comprehend stories, and otherwise act in the world. Schemas are important knowledge structures that enable us to deal effectively with the information-processing demands of a large and complex world. They serve to extract and categorize clusters of experiences in that world.

Stereotyping reflects the dark side of schema abstraction. The mechanisms underlying schema abstraction are not particularly judicious about the sources of the information processed, and they are subject to statistical fallacies such as those illustrated in Hamilton and Gifford's illusory-correlation study. It appears that the price we pay for the power of schema abstraction is the potential for inaccuracies entering schemas. Schemas might be described as enabling "quick and dirty" methods of thinking. Thus, though it would seem unwise to deny ourselves the information-processing power inherent in schemas, we should be careful in applying that power. It is important that we realize, as did some Princeton undergraduates of the 1960s, that our impressions can vary in validity. And it is particularly important to be circumspect in judgments involving categories when (1) we have had little direct experience with the particular category, (2) we have reason to believe that our experience is biased, and (3) we are making judgments about uncommon categories or attributes.

An interesting example of the pros and cons of prototypes was demonstrated in a study by Rosenhan (1973). The experimenters in this study complained, falsely, that they were hearing voices and had themselves committed to various mental hospitals, but once in the hospitals they behaved normally. Nonetheless, these experimenter–patients had great difficulty in convincing members of hospital staffs they were normal, and they spent an average stay of three weeks before they could get out of the various facilities. Members of the hospital staffs insisted on viewing them in accordance with the mental-patient prototype, often interpreting their claims about being psychology experimenters as classical delusions consistent with clinically abnormal behavior. This study is often seen as an indictment of mental institutions, but the staff people may have been behaving as best they could under the circumstances. Consider Lindsay and Norman's (1977) interpretation of the staff predicament:

> The task is really a difficult one for the staff of the hospital. Imagine that you are in charge of a large group of mental patients, some of whom usually show no abnormal signs. One person walks around talking to herself, another repeats the same unessential operation over and over again, evidently unaware that he has done that operation before. Other patients play games or read or watch television. Some patients keep telling you that they are really normal (although they are very accurate at diagnosing the problems of others). And one patient walks around claiming to be in a psychological experiment, stating that he is really normal, and writing down everything that happens in a notebook. Who is to say which patients are normal? [Lindsay and Norman, 1977, p. 625]

Perhaps the experimenters matched the hospital staff personnel's prototype of a mental patient quite well. Generally, such a prototype might suffice for the staff members as long as it accurately reflected what the average patient is like; the staff does not normally have to deal with psychologists playing such games. There is no way that hospital personnel could take seriously and investigate carefully every outrageous claim made by every patient. The risk in processing patients according to prototypes is that patients who do not fit the prototype get lost, but it is unclear that there is an alternative that is both better and more feasible.

Remarks and Suggested Readings

The research and development of schemas have been phenomena almost exclusively of the 1970s (the most notable exception being that early work by Bartlett). A recent book edited by Rosch and Lloyd (1978) presents a number of papers discussing research in this area. In contrast to the activity in the domains of propositional knowledge and imagery, relatively little thought has been given to the mechanisms underlying schemas. Schank and Abelson's (1977) scripts model is specifically directed to story processing. A number of programmatic statements have been offered concerning more general schema (or frame) models—Minsky, 1975; Rumelhart and Ortony, 1977; Rumelhart and Norman, 1978; Bobrow and Winograd, 1977. Anderson, Kline, and Beasley (1979) presents a model for how simple schemas are abstracted and applied.

Cantor and Mischel (1977, 1978) report research that uses prototype notion for understanding the development of personality impressions. Other recent research on impression formation and social judgment that shows the influence of prototypes includes Nisbett and Ross (1980); Hastie, Ostrom, Ebbesen, Wyer, Hamilton, and Carlston (1979); and Taylor and Crocker (1978). Tesser (1978) describes a good deal of his research on the effects of schemas on impression formation and attitude change. Brigham (1971) reviews the classic work on stereotyping. Recent ideas and research on the process of stereotyping can be found in Hamilton (1979), and Taylor, Fiske, Etcoff, and Ruderman (1978).

Part III
Memory and Learning

Chapter 6

Human Memory: Basic Concepts and Principles

Summary

1. *Short-term memory* refers to a capacity for keeping a limited amount of information in a special *active* state. Information can only be used when it is in this active state.

2. Short-term memory holds nodes from the *long-term memory network* and connections among these nodes. The connections, in contrast to the nodes, may be temporary and will disappear when the information leaves the active short-term state.

3. To be recalled or retrieved from long-term memory, information must be activated. Activation must *spread* along paths through the network from the currently active portion of memory to the to-be-retrieved portion.

4. The speed at which activation spreads along a path depends directly on the strength of the path and inversely on the number of competing paths. The detrimental effect of competing paths on the rate of spread along a path is referred to as *associative interference*.

5. If the rate of activation along a path is sufficiently slow, because of either low strength or associative interference, then there will be failure of recall.

6. Performance is usually better on recognition tests than on recall tests. This fact illustrates that information can be in long-term memory but not avail-

able for recall. A recognition question is easier than a recall question because it offers more ways (network paths) in which memory can be searched for the queried information.

The First Memory Experiment

Hermann Ebbinghaus, an early experimental investigator of human memory, published a significant research monograph in 1885. The research reported in this monograph was probably the first rigorous experimental investigation of human memory. No pools of subjects were available when Ebbinghaus was doing his research. Therefore, he used himself as his sole subject. He taught himself series of nonsense syllables, consonant-vowel-consonant trigrams such as DAX, BUP, and LOC. In one of his many experiments, Ebbinghaus required himself to learn lists of 13 syllables to the point of being able to repeat the lists twice in order without error. Then he tested his retention for these lists at various delays. He counted the amount of time he took to relearn the lists, using the same criterion of two perfect recitations. Of interest was how much faster the second learning was than the first. Suppose it took him 1,156 seconds to learn the list initially and only 467 seconds to relearn the list. This meant he had saved 1156 − 467 = 689 seconds in the relearning. This savings can be expressed as a percentage of the original learning: 689/1156 = 64.3 percent. Ebbinghaus used percent-savings scores as the standard measure of his retention. Figure 6-1 plots these percent-savings scores as a function of retention intervals. As this figure clearly shows, rapid forgetting occurs initially, but some forgetting still occurs up to 30 days following the learning of the material.

Using a 24-hour retention interval, Ebbinghaus considered what would happen if, after learning the list to the criterion of two perfect recitals, he rehearsed it 30 additional times. Without this overlearning, Ebbinghaus achieved a savings score of 33.8 percent, but with this amount of overlearning, his savings on a subsequent 24-hour retention test was 64.1 percent. So, the additional study trials resulted in increased savings on a subsequent retention test.

Over the decades, the basic experimental results of Ebbinghaus have been reproduced by many other researchers using a large variety of techniques and measures. In all cases, subjects show rapid initial forgetting of the material they have learned. The effect of extra study time is to protect the memory against the process of forgetting.

While Ebbinghaus was correct in identifying delay and amount of study as two important determinants of recall, his research left many important factors undiscovered. Also, Ebbinghaus was not very successful at identifying the

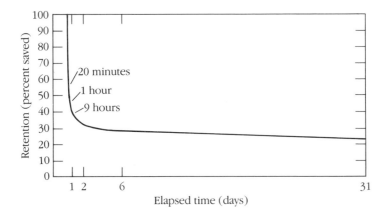

Figure 6-1 *Ebbinghaus' forgetting function. Retention of nonsense syllables is measured by savings in relearning. Retention decreases as retention interval (the time between initial learning and the retention test) increases but the rate of forgetting slows down.*

mechanisms underlying the effects of study time and retention interval. In this chapter, we will review the more recent research and theories that serve to broaden the picture of the mechanisms underlying the retention of information in memory.

Short-Term Memory

In his experiments, Ebbinghaus studied a list many times before he achieved the criterion of one perfect recital. However, he discovered that if the list was short enough—say, had fewer than five items—he could achieve the criterion of a perfect recital in a single study. We have all had the experience of holding a seven-digit phone number in memory long enough to dial it. There appears to be a transient memory, which can temporarily encode information perfectly after a single study. This transient memory is to be contrasted with the more permanent *long-term memory* (LTM), which holds information for hours, days, and years. Ebbinghaus' research basically addressed long-term memory. The transient memory is referred to as *short-term memory* (STM).

A now classical experiment by Peterson and Peterson (1959) illustrates the transient character of short-term memory. These investigators had subjects study three letters and then asked for recall of the letters after various intervals of time up to 18 seconds. Normally, subjects would have no difficulty performing this task perfectly. However, to prevent the subjects from rehearsing the material, Peterson and Peterson had subjects count backwards by

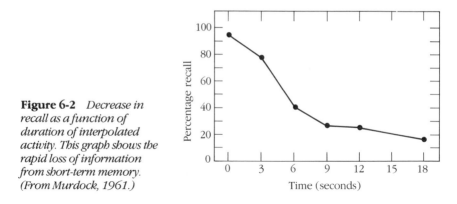

Figure 6-2 *Decrease in recall as a function of duration of interpolated activity. This graph shows the rapid loss of information from short-term memory. (From Murdock, 1961.)*

threes during the retention interval. Thus, following presentation of the letters, subjects might be asked to count backwards by threes as fast as possible from 418: 415, 412, and so on. Figure 6-2 illustrates recall at various retention intervals up to 18 seconds from a similar experiment by Murdock (1961). At 18 seconds, subjects are only recalling less than 20 percent of the three letters—or an average of less than 1 letter. The decay in recall to this level is rapid, largely complete after only 9 seconds. After this point the recall level appears *asymtope,* that is, it does not decrease much more. We can conclude from these results that when subjects are distracted from rehearsing, they will lose information very rapidly. People are only able to keep a telephone number in short-term memory when they can rehearse it to themselves. The 20 percent asymptotic recall displayed in Figure 6-2 probably reflects the amount of information subjects were able to successfully transform into a long-term-memory form. Of course, as we saw in the Ebbinghaus experiment, information is forgotten from long-term memory too, but at a much slower rate than the loss that occurred in the short-term-memory experiment of Peterson and Peterson.*

An important conclusion drawn from this work on short-term memory is that we can temporarily have information available that will not become a permanent part of memory. It is useful to think of short-term memory as a *working memory* holding only knowledge currently in use. The amount of information that we can hold in short-term memory represents a fundamental limitation on our mental capacity. A mental process cannot properly function unless we can keep in working memory the knowledge required by the process. For instance, if we lose track of the telephone number, we are unable to dial it.

Numerous attempts have been made to determine the number of items that

---

*The very low levels of performance at a delay, such as those in the Peterson and Peterson task, are possible only when the stimuli are presented over and over (see Keppel and Underwood, 1962).

short-term memory can hold. For instance, it has been found that people can hold in immediate memory seven or eight digits (a convenient fact given the length of phone numbers!). However, reasoning from such facts to the exact size of short-term memory is difficult. Suppose I hold in memory that Mary's phone number is 436-8071. How many items am I holding in short-term memory? There are reasons to suspect that I am holding fewer than seven items. I may encode "80" as "eighty," in which case it is perhaps one item. I may not encode 43 at all, since I know that this is the prefix for all Yale numbers and that Mary is at Yale. On the other hand, there is also reason to wonder if I have not encoded more than seven items. I have also encoded the knowledge that *this is Mary's telephone number*—how many items does this fact represent? I may also be holding other information in short-term memory simultaneously, such as the location of the telephone on which I am dialing the number, my reason for dialing the number, and so on. Thus, while it is clear that the capacity of short-term memory is limited, how to measure that capacity is not at all clear. Cognitive psychology is still working at developing adequate measures of the capacity of short-term memory.

Chunking

A fundamental question is whether the information in short-term memory is in a different mental location than that in long-term memory, or whether it is in the same location as the knowledge in long-term memory but is just in a special state. The evidence favors the latter conclusion. Particularly compelling here is the fact that the capacity of short-term memory varies with the meaningfulness of the material. Thus, subjects are usually able to successfully repeat back four nonsense syllables—

DAX   JIR   GOP   BIF—

but not six—

PID   LOM   FIK   GAN   WUT   TIB.

They are able to repeat back six one-syllable words—

TILE   GATE   ROAD   JUMP   BALL   LIME—

but not nine one-syllable words—

HAT   SAINT   FAN   RUN   GAIN   LIKE   NAIL   RICE   LAKE.

And they can repeat three four-syllable words (which equal twelve syllables)—

AMERICAN   DICTIONARY   GEOLOGY

but not six four-syllable words—

CONSTITUTION   MAJORITY   OPTIMISTIC   TERMINALLY
DOMESTICATE   CANADIAN.

Finally, they are able to repeat back a nineteen-word sentence:

> Richard Milhous Nixon, former president of the United States, wrote a book about his career in the White House.

The way to make sense of what seems to be an extreme variability in the size of short-term memory is to realize that the units remembered are different in each case. In the case of nonsense syllables, the units are individual letters or letter pairs. In the case of words, they are words or meaningful parts of words. And in the case of sentences, they are the meaningful phrases. George Miller (1956) introduced the term *chunk* to describe these units of memory. He argued that memory was limited not by the number of physical units (letters, syllables, words) in the stimulus but rather by the number of meaningful chunks. Miller contended that subjects remembered approximately seven chunks. But where are these chunks (letters, words, meaningful phrases) stored as units? The answer is that they are defined as units in long-term memory. In fact, in a network representation such as that discussed in Chapter 4, these chunks would be nodes. Therefore, it is assumed that when subjects remember a stimulus such as those displayed above, they are placing these long-term memory units (nodes) in a special state in which they are immediately accessible. This state is referred to as *active,* and the process of bringing nodes into the active state is called *activation.*

We now have three terms for referring to different aspects of the same phenomena. The empirical term *short-term memory* connotes the transient character of the memory. The term *working memory* conveys the fact that information is being held for use by mental procedures. Finally, the technical phrase *active memory* implies the fact that the units of this memory are in a special active state.

Note that while the items of short-term memory are long-term memory items, the connections among these items are not necessarily permanent. By *connections* I mean the associations or network links connecting the items or network nodes. When these connections are not permanent, the particular configuration of short-term information will not be permanently retained. So, after dialing we may lose memory for the string of digits that is a particular phone number. What are lost in this case are not the digits themselves, but their interconnections, which define the telephone number. However, sometimes new connections in STM do become permanent LTM connections, as when we permanently commit to memory a telephone number.

Let us summarize our conclusions about short-term memory:

1. The contents of STM are LTM nodes and connections between these nodes. These nodes may be considered to be chunks in that they may be connected to a lot of information.

2. STM has a limited capacity to keep the elements in an active state. If this information becomes inactive it will be lost unless it is also in long-term memory.

3. Information about connections among elements can be transformed into a permanent LTM state while the information is being held in STM.

4. STM serves as a repository for knowledge that is required by cognitive processes being performed. These procedures cannot function if the knowledge is not in STM.

5. STM contains the information of which we are immediately aware. That is, we have direct access to the contents of STM.

Activation should be thought of as synonymous with short-term memory. However, the term *short-term memory* as it contrasts with *long-term memory* can be confusing. The phrase *short-term* indicates that some of the information in the active state may be lost when it becomes inactive. Thus, information in short-term memory may not become a permanent part of long-term memory. However, short-term memory and long-term memory are not opposites. Short-term memory can contain information from long-term memory. To see this, consider a fact such as *George Washington was the first president*. This sentence expresses a permanent fact from long-term memory, but the fact is active in short-term memory when it is being focused upon. Thus, short-term and long-term memory are not opposites; rather, they overlap. *Short-term memory* refers to a small amount of information that is in a transient, active state. *Long-term memory* refers to a large body of information that is relatively permanently encoded. In other words, the two terms can refer to different aspects of the same information.

Retrieval from Long-Term Memory

The Need to Reactivate Information

We do not have direct access to any information that is not in short-term memory. Before we can recall or otherwise use knowledge in long-term memory, that knowledge must be activated. The proccess of activation takes time, and, hence, recall of information already in the STM state should be faster than recall of information that starts out in the LTM state. That this is true is illustrated by an experiment from my laboratory.

In the experiment, subjects studied two paired associates such as *dog–3* and *vanilla–8*. After studying such a pair for 2 seconds, subjects were either immediately tested for their memory or given 48 seconds of arithmetic tasks and then tested. In either case, a test consisted of presenting *dog* or *vanilla* and requiring the subject to recall the second item in the pair. Subjects were 98 percent correct immediately and only 48 percent correct after the 48-second delay. This result is quite similar to the result from Murdock shown in Figure 6-2. Again, it illustrates that information is lost rapidly from short-term memory if the subject is distracted from rehearsing the information. After a 48-second delay in which other activities intervene, the information is very unlikely to be active in short-term memory. Therefore, the 48 percent correct recall at this delay reflects information that was encoded into a long-term memory state and successfully recalled.

The point of interest in this experiment was the amount of time subjects took to recall, when they could do so, in the immediate condition versus the 48-second delay condition. Subjects took 1.31 seconds in the immediate condition but 1.96 seconds in the delayed condition, the difference being almost two-thirds of a second. This extra time reflects the amount of time needed to return the information from long-term memory to the short-term-memory state. The recall information is dependent on the reactivation of the information.

Retrieving Well-Known Information

We have been focusing on changes in memory for information subjects have learned in the minute prior to testing. What about memory for information that is well established in long-term memory? Are large temporal fluctuations demonstrated in its availability as well? An experiment by Loftus (1974) nicely answers this question. She looked at the time subjects required to retrieve well-learned information about categories such as fruit. She had subjects retrieve instances of a category that began with a certain initial letter. For instance, subjects might have to retrieve a fruit beginning with *p*. She found that subjects took an average of 1.53 seconds to perform this task the first time they were asked about a category. Then at varying delays she asked subjects to retrieve from the same category another member beginning with a different letter. Thus, she might ask subjects to retrieve a fruit beginning with *b*. She manipulated delay by inserting tests on other unrelated categories between the two tests on a category. For instance, during a two-item delay, subjects might be asked to retrieve a dog that began with *c* and a country that began with *r*. Looking at 0, 1, and 2 intervening items, she found retrieval times of 1.21 seconds, 1.28 seconds, and 1.33 seconds, respectively. The first time they were tested, subjects took 1.53 seconds to generate an associate. So, relative to this initial retrieval time, we see strong facilitation if the category is tested again immediately, when the memory about the category is still in an active short-term state. However, with increasing delay the probability increases that this portion of memory will drop out of its active state and will have to be reactivated. Hence, the times increase with delay.

Degree of Learning

From the Loftus experiment, we can estimate the time required to activate knowledge from long-term memory by subtracting the 0 delay question (1.21 seconds) from the time to answer the first question about the category (1.53 seconds). The difference of .32 seconds is much smaller than the estimate of .65 obtained in the paired-associate experiment previously discussed. The material in the paired-associate experiment was considerably less well learned than the category information in the Loftus study. There is evidence that material can be more rapidly activated if it is better learned and hence more strongly encoded.

Another experiment from my laboratory (Anderson, 1976) illustrates how speed of retrieval varies with strength of the memory trace.* In the first phase of this experiment, subjects committed to memory facts about locations of various people. For instance, the subject might learn the following sentences:

> The sailor is in the park.
>
> The lawyer is in the church.

Subjects were drilled over and over again on these sentences until they knew them by heart. Later, subjects were presented with sentences and asked to say whether each sentence was among the sentences they had studied. Thus, subjects might see,

> The sailor is in the park,

which would require a positive response. Negative items were created by recombining people and locations in ways that had not been studied. For example, the subject might be presented with the following negative test item:

> The sailor is in the church.

Subjects had not studied this sentence and therefore were required to give a negative response. Since subjects knew the material well enough to be correct almost all the time, we were interested only in the speed with which subjects made their correct recognition judgments. Reaction time was measured from the appearance of the item on a screen to the depression of one of two buttons indicating positive and negative judgments.

We were interested in two variables. One was differences in the amount of study applied to different sentences before testing. Some sentences were studied twice as frequently as others. We would expect frequency to be related to the strength of the encoding of a sentence and hence that more frequently encountered information would be retrieved more quickly from

---

*A *memory trace* is the encoding of a memory. For instance, a network representation of a remembered event would be a memory trace.

Table 6-1   The Effects of Delay of Repetition and Frequency of Exposure on Recognition Time for Second Presentation of a Sentence

	Delay	
Degree of Study	Short (0 to 2 Intervening Items)	Long (3 or more Intervening Items)
Less study	1.11 seconds	1.53 seconds
More study	1.10 seconds	1.38 seconds

From Anderson, 1976.

long-term memory. The second variable was the delay between any two presentations of a particular sentence. We compared the situation in which 0 to 2 items intervened between repetitions and the sentence was still likely to be in the active short-term memory with the situation in which 3 or more items intervened and the sentence probably had to be reactivated. We were interested in the effect of this delay between tests on recognition time for the second presentation of a sentence. The difference between the short delay and the long delay is a measure of the amount of time that activation of the information takes.

Table 6-1 displays judgment times for the second sentence in a repetition classified according to these two variables. At short test delays, frequency of study had very little effect on recognition time. On the other hand, following a long delay between repetitions, subjects were considerably faster on the more frequently studied sentence. Time to activate a sentence in long-term memory can be estimated as the difference between 3 or more intervening items and 0 to 2 intervening items. Using this estimate, it takes $1.53 - 1.11 = .42$ seconds to activate the less frequently studied items from long-term memory but only $1.38 - 1.10 = .28$ seconds to activate the more frequently studied items. Thus, as expected, it takes longer to reactivate the weaker memories.

At the beginning of this chapter, we saw in Ebbinghaus' research that frequency of exposure affected probability of recall. The data in Table 6-1 show that frequency also affects retrieval time. A major objective of this chapter is to show that effects on retrieval time and effects on retention are manifestations of the same underlying memory mechanisms. In this regard, several other properties of the activation process must be discussed.

Spread of Activation

It is informative to think about the activation concept within the propositional-network framework developed in Chapter 4. Consider Figure 6-3, which illustrates part of the propositional network surrounding the concept *dog*.

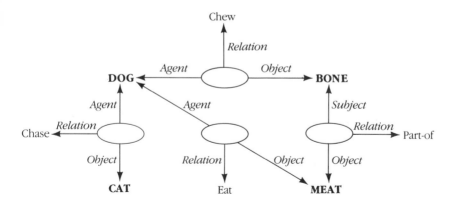

Figure 6-3 *A representation of* dog *in memory and some of its associated concepts. Presenting* dog *will prime these concepts.*

Note that *dog* is connected to the concept *bone.* Thus, when the word *dog* is presented to the subject, not only will that concept become active, but activation should spread to the concepts surrounding *dog,* so that terms such as *bone* become active as well. Evidence for spread of activation through such a network is drawn from an experiment by Jane Perlmutter and myself (unpublished). Subjects were presented with a sequence of words and asked to generate associates that began with specific letters. We were interested in contrasting such sequences as the two following:

Priming	*Control*
dog–c	gambler–c
bone–m	bone–m

In the first case, the subject might generate *cat* as the associate to *dog* and then be presented with *bone* and generate *meat* as an associate. In the second case, the control case, the responses might be *card* and *meat.* The important feature of the priming condition is that an already existing associative path leads from *dog* to *bone* and to *meat.* Therefore, activating the network structure to answer the first associate should help activate the structure needed to answer the second. The first associate (dog–c) serves to prime the second (bone–m). In contrast, no priming connection exists in the second case. Therefore, subjects were expected to generate the second associate faster in the priming condition. This expectation was confirmed: subjects took 1.41 seconds to generate an associate in the priming case as contrasted with 1.53 seconds in the control case.

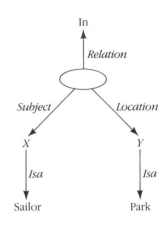

Figure 6-4 *A propositional-network representation for the statement* A sailor is in the park. *This structure must be activated for the proposition to be recognized.*

The notion of *spread of activation,* illustrated in this and other experiments, is fundamental to an understanding of recall from long-term memory. Activation spreads through long-term memory from active portions to other portions of memory, and this spread takes time. Consider the results in Table 6-1, drawn from the experiment in which subjects were required to recognize sentences of the form *A sailor is in the park.* Figure 6-4 is the propositional-network representation of such a sentence. This sentence, presented as a test probe, should activate the words *sailor, in,* and *park.* Activation spreads from link to link through the structure shown in Figure 6-4 like water flowing through irrigation channels. Before the sentence can be recalled, the whole structure in Figure 6-4 must be activated. Thus, the time spent in the retrieval of a memory structure would reflect the time taken for the spread of activation through that structure.

If one concept is activated, a good many associated concepts will become active because of spreading activation. Thus, the amount of active information resulting can be much greater than the "approximately seven" measure that was ascribed to short-term memory earlier in this chapter. We saw that the exact size of short-term memory was difficult to measure. The existence of the spreading activation phenomenon is one reason for this difficulty. The figure "approximately seven" refers to the amount of information that can be maintained in an active state. However, a great deal more information can be active momentarily. For instance, I can rehearse to myself Mary's phone number—which conforms to the seven-unit approximation—and keep it in short-term memory for minutes while I am finding a phone. However, while I am holding this information in short-term memory other associations generated through the spreading activation process temporarily enter and leave my short-term memory. In addition to the free-association information, observations of my environment can temporarily enter my short-term memory. Thus, the "approximately seven" figure represents the core focus of my

Table 6-2   Examples of the Pairs Used to Demonstrate Associative Pairing

Positive Pairs		Negative Pairs		
Unrelated	Related	First Nonword	Second Nonword	Both Nonwords
Nurse	Bread	Plame	Wine	Plame
Butter	Butter	Wine	Plame	Reab
940 msec	855 msec	904 msec	1087 msec	884 msec

From Meyer and Schvaneveldt, 1971.

immediate attention, while factors such as spreading activation and external stimulation create wide fluctuations in activation around this core.

Note that the spread-of-activation process is not entirely under an individual's control. For example, when subjects generated an associate to *dog* in the Perlmutter and Anderson experimenter described above, they had no reason to *want* to activate the *bone-meat* association. Still, some activation spread to this part of the network and helped to prime knowledge of the connection between *bone* and *meat*. Many experiments in cognitive psychology have demonstrated this unconscious priming—called *associative priming*—of knowledge through spreading activation.

Meyer and Schvaneveldt (1971) performed what has become a classic demonstration of associative priming. They had subjects judge whether or not pairs of items were words. Table 6-2 shows examples of the materials used in their experiments and subjects' judgment times. The items were presented one above the other. If either item in a pair was a nonword, subjects were to respond *no*. It appears from examing the negative pairs that subjects judged first the top item and then the second. Where the top item was a nonword, subjects were faster to reject the pair than when only the second item was a nonword. Where the top item was not a word, subjects did not have to judge the second item and so could respond sooner.

The major interest in this study was in the positive pairs. There were unrelated items such as *nurse* and *butter,* and pairs with an associative relation such as *bread* and *butter*. Subjects were 85 milliseconds faster on the related pairs. This result indicates that because subjects judged the first item to be a word, activation spread from that word and primed information about the second, associatively related item. If a subject is to make a judgment about whether an item is a word, the representation of the word has to be active in short-term memory. The implication of this result is that the associative spreading of activation through memory can facilitate the rate at which words are read. Thus, we can read material that has a strong associative coherence more rapidly than incoherent material in which the words are unrelated.

Interference

The Fan Effect

So far, we have treated activation as if it spreads down a network path (a sequence of links in the network) at a constant rate. However, various experiments indicate that this is not so. In one experiment (Anderson, 1974) we had subjects memorize 26 facts, again of the form *A person is in a location.* Some persons were paired with only one location and some locations with only one person. Other persons were paired with two locations and other locations were paired with two persons. For instance, suppose that subjects studied these sentences:

1. The doctor is in the bank. (1-1)
2. The fireman is in the park. (1-2)
3. The lawyer is in the church. (2-1)
4. The lawyer is in the park. (2-2)

Each statement is followed by two numbers, reflecting the number of facts associated with the subject and the location. For instance, sentence 3 is labeled 2-1 because its subject occurs in two sentences (sentences 3 and 4) and its location occurs in one (sentence 3).

Subjects were drilled on this material until they knew it more or less perfectly. Before beginning the reaction-time phase, subjects were able to recall all the locations associated with a particular type of person (e.g., doctor) and all the people associated with a particular location (e.g., park). Then they began a speeded-recognition phase of the experiment, during which they were presented with sentences and had to judge whether they recognized them from the study set. New foil sentences were created by the re-pairing of people and locations from the study set. The reaction times involving sentences such as those listed above are displayed in Table 6-3. This table classifies the data as a function of the number of facts associated with a person and a location. As can be seen, recognition time increases both as a function of the number of facts studied about the person and the number of facts studied about the location.

Figure 6-5 shows the network representation for sentences 1 through 4.* By applying the activation concept to this representation, we can nicely account for the increase in reaction time. Consider how the subject might recognize

---

*For simplicity, we have not represented the distinction between instances and concepts in the figure. As indicated in Chapter 4, this distinction is important. Therefore, the representation in Figure 6-5 is only an approximation of the true underlying representation. However, the figure highlights the features of the propositional network that are significant for an understanding of this experiment.

Table 6-3 Mean Recognition Time for Sentences as a Function of Number of Facts Learned About Person and Location

Number of Sentences Using a Specific Location	Number of Sentences about a Specific Person	
	1 Sentence	2 Sentences
1 sentence	1.11 seconds	1.17 seconds
2 sentences	1.17 seconds	1.22 seconds

From Anderson, 1974.

such a probe as *A lawyer is in the park.* First, suppose that the presentation of the terms *lawyer, in,* and *park* serves to activate their representations in memory. To recognize the sentence, a subject would have to bring the representation of the sentence into the short-term active state, and, therefore, activation must spread from the nodes to the total structure. The critical assumption is that the rate at which activation spreads from a source such as *lawyer* is inversely related to the number of links leading from it. So, given a structure like Figure 6-5, subjects should be slower to recognize a fact involving *lawyer* and *park* than one connecting *doctor* and *bank* because more paths emanate from the first set of concepts. That is, in the *lawyer* and *park* case two paths point from each of the concepts to the two propositions in which each was studied, whereas, only one path leads from each of the *doctor* and *bank* concepts.

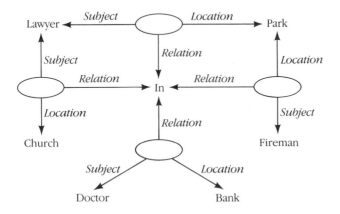

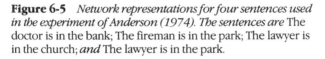

Figure 6-5 *Network representations for four sentences used in the experiment of Anderson (1974). The sentences are* The doctor is in the bank; The fireman is in the park; The lawyer is in the church; *and* The lawyer is in the park.

This is one experiment of many that points to a *limited-capacity feature* of the spreading-activation process. The nodes, such as *lawyer* and *park,* from which the spread of activation starts can be called *source nodes.* A source node has a certain fixed capacity for emitting activation. This capacity is divided among all the paths emanating from that node. The more paths exist, the less activation will be assigned to any one path and the slower will be the rate of activation. The *fan effect* is the name given to this increase in reaction time related to an increase in the number of facts associated with a concept. It is so named because the increase in reaction time is related to an increase in the fan of facts emanating from the network representation of the concept.

Interference is the more general term used to refer to such phenomena. The term conveys the fact that additional information about a concept interferes with memory for a particular piece of information. As we will see, such interference affects a wider range of measures than just recognition time. The term *fan effect* is reserved for interference effects as measured by recognition time.

Interference and Historical Memories

An experiment by Lewis and Anderson (1976) investigated whether the fan effect could be obtained with material the subject knew before the experiment. We had subjects learn fantasy facts about public figures—for example, *Napoleon Bonaparte was from India.* Subjects studied from zero to four such fantasy facts about each public figure. After learning these "facts," they proceeded to a recognition-test phase. In this phase they saw three types of sentences: (1) statements they had studied in the experiment, (2) true facts about the public figures (such as *Napoleon Bonaparte was an emperor*), and (3) statements about the public figure that were false both in the experimental fantasy world and in the real world. Subjects had to respond to the first two types of facts as true and the last type as false.

Figure 6-6 presents subjects' reaction times in making these judgments as a function of the number of fantasy facts (the fan) studied about the person. Note that reaction time increased with fan for all types of facts. Also note that subjects responded much faster to actual truths than to experimental truths. The advantage of actual truths can be explained, because these true facts would be much more strongly encoded in memory than the fantasy facts because of greater prior exposure. The most important result to note in Figure 6-6 is that the more fantasy facts subjects have learned about an individual such as Napoleon Bonaparte, the longer subjects take to recognize a fact that they already know about the individual, for example, *Napoleon Bonaparte was an emperor.* Thus, we can produce interference with preexperimental material.

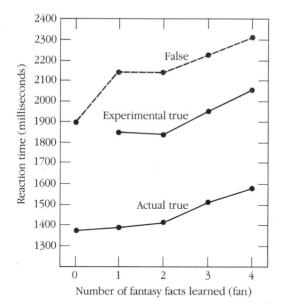

Figure 6-6 *Reaction times from Lewis and Anderson (1976). The task was to recognize true and fantasy facts about a public figure and to reject statements that were neither true nor fantasy facts. This figure shows that the time subjects took to make all three judgments increased as subjects learned more fantasy facts about public figures.*

Interference and Retention

So far, we have considered how interference from other information associated with a concept can slow down the speed with which the fact can be retrieved. The effects have been a matter of a few hundred milliseconds. We will now consider what happens as these interfering effects get more extreme —either because the to-be-recalled fact is very weak or the interference is very strong. There is evidence that the subject simply fails to remember the information under both circumstances. Results showing such failures of memory have been traditionally obtained with paired-associate material, although similar results have been obtained with other material. The effects of interference have been extensively studied, and many classic experiments have been performed by researchers such as Arthur Melton (now deceased), Leo Postman (University of California, Berkeley), and Benton Underwood (Northwestern University). More recent perspectives in the field come from James Greeno (University of Pittsburgh), Edwin Martin (University of Kansas), and Wayne Wickelgren (University of Oregon). We will not describe any one particular experiment here, but rather the prototypical experiment.

In the typical interference experiment, two critical groups are defined; these are illustrated in Table 6-4. The *A–D* experimental group learns two lists of paired associates, the first list designated *A–B* and the second designated *A–D*. The lists are so designated because they share common stimuli

Table 6-4   Experimental and Control Groups Used in a Typical Interference Paradigm

A–D Experimental		C–D Control	
LEARN	A–B	LEARN	A–B
LEARN	A–D	LEARN	C–D
TEST	A–B	TEST	A–B

(the *A* terms). For example, among the pairs that the subject studies in the *A–B* list might be *cat–43* and *house–61,* and in the *A–D* list *cat–82* and *house–37.* The *C–D* control group also first studies the *A–B* list, but then studies a different, second list, designated *C–D,* which does not contain the same stimuli as the first list. For example, in the *C–D* list subjects might study *bone–82* and *cup–37.* After learning their respective second lists, both groups are retested for their memory of their first list, in both cases the *A–B* list. Often this retention test is administered after a considerable delay, such as 24 hours or a week. In general, the *A–D* group does not do as well as the *C–D* group regarding both rate of learning of the second list and retention of the original *A–B* list.

These results are to be expected given our understanding of interference. Figure 6-7 shows the network representation of the knowledge structures for the two groups. Part A illustrates the assumed memory structure for the experimental group. Members of this group have *A* stimuli in both lists and so have learned interfering associations to these stimuli. Part B of the figure illustrates the assumed memory structure for the control group. There were different stimuli in the two lists—in list 1 subjects associated *43* to *cat* while in list 2 they associated *82* to *bone.* Thus, the experimental group has an extra list 2 association to interfere with the *cat–43* memory while the control group does not. In the reaction-time experiments discussed earlier, such interference (two associations rather than one) resulted in increased reaction time, but not failure to recall. However, in those experiments the items had been highly overlearned before reaction time was tested. In the interference experiments, subjects are tested as they are learning the paired associates. Here the strengths of associations are much weaker. When the exposure to the pairs has been minimal and their associations barely learned, the interference of associates learned in the second list will result in failure to recall. The implication is that failure to recall is the extreme case of a long retrieval time. Thus, it is not the case that the forgotten information is not in memory, but rather that it is in memory but is too weak to be activated in the face of the interference from other associations. In this view, forgetting is not actual loss of information from memory but rather loss of the ability to activate that information.

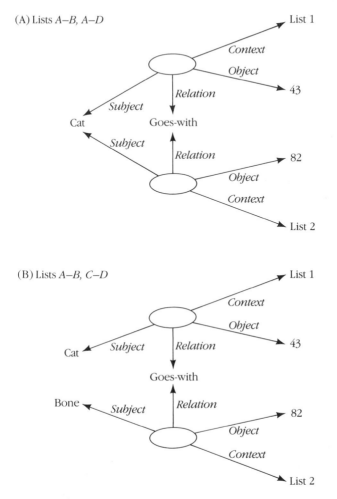

(A) Lists *A–B, A–D*

(B) Lists *A–B, C–D*

Figure 6-7   *Network representations for the two conditions identified in Table 6-4. (A) This network represents the encodings of the A–B and A–D associations in the experimental condition. (B) This network represents the encodings of the A–B and C–D associations in the control condition.*

Recall Versus Recognition

Consistent with the hypothesis that information exists in memory that we cannot recall is the fact that we can recognize many things we cannot recall. This phenomenon suggests that information can be in memory even though it cannot be activated in the recall-test situation. The memory-network analysis

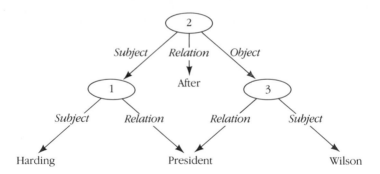

Figure 6-8   *A proposition-network representation of the information that Harding was president after Wilson.*

we have been developing makes clear the reason that recognition often works even when recall fails. For example, let us compare the efforts of students trying to answer the following questions:

1. Who was the president after Wilson?
2. Was Harding the president after Wilson?

Figure 6-8 illustrates the memory structure that is being addressed by the questions. The first question, a recall question, provides subjects with Wilson as a probe from which to search memory. The question requires that subjects access memory from Wilson and search to Harding. To do this the subject must activate the Wilson node and have activation spread to the Harding node. Suppose, however, that the network link between proposition 3 and 2 is too weak to be activated. Then there will be failure of recall. However, when asked the recognition question, that is, question 2, subjects might be able to search from Harding to Wilson even if they were unable to search from Wilson to Harding. That is, they might be able to retrieve proposition 3 from proposition 2 even though they were not able to retrieve 2 from 3. A recognition question is easier than a recall question because it offers the subject more ways to search memory.

Note that in our analysis of Figure 6-8 we assumed that subjects might be able to activate the association between propositions 2 and 3 but not the association between 3 and 2. In distinguishing between recall and recognition, it is useful to think of a link between two nodes as consisting of two separate associations going in opposite directions, with the possibility existing for one association to be available but not the other. The idea of associations different in two directions has played an important role in the paired-associate literature where subjects have to learn pairs such as *house–46*. The connection from *house* to *46* is referred to as a *forward association,* and the connection from *46* to *house* is referred to as the *backward associa- tion.* Usually the forward association (as indexed by subjects' ability to recall *46* when given a cue of *house*) is stronger than the backward association (as indexed by subjects' ability to recall *house* when given the cue of *46*). Howev- er, in line with our analysis above, subjects rate highest in a recognition test where they are given *house–46* and can use either the forward or backward associations.

A Mathematical Analysis

The analysis above of recall versus recognition memory has been nicely confirmed by a series of experiments by Wolford (1971). He had subjects commit to memory noun-number paired associates such as *girl–62.* Subjects were tested in a number of ways. In a *forward-recall condition,* they were presented with the word *girl* and asked to recall the response. Responses were correctly recalled 38 percent of the time in this condition. In a *back- ward-recall condition,* subjects were presented with the number *62* and asked to recall the word. In this condition, they gave 21 percent correct recall. Interest focused on a *two-alternative forced-choice recognition condition,* in which subjects were presented with the probes *girl* (71 or 62) and had to recognize the correct number. (The number 71 had occurred with another word.) Wolford reasoned that subjects would identify the correct response if the forward association from *girl* was intact (we will call the probability of this association being intact P_f). Or, if this association was not intact, they would still be able to tell if the backward association from *62* was intact (this probability is P_b). Or, if this association was not intact, subjects would still be able to tell if the association from *71* was intact; since they could reject *girl* as its stimulus (the probability of this response is also P_b). Finally, if this association was not intact, the subject would be able to guess and be correct half the time. From these possible responses, we come up with the following formula for probability correct on the forced-choice list:

Probability of correct recognition   =   probability of a forward association

    + probability of no forward association but a backward association from 62

    + probability of no forward association nor a backward association from 62 but a backward association from 71

    + probability of no forward association nor backward associations from 62 or 71 but a correct guess

Substituting probabilities for the components in equation 1, we obtain the following:

$$P_f = \text{Probability of a forward association;}$$

$$(1 - P_f)P_b = \text{Probability of no forward} \qquad (2)$$
$$\text{association but a backward}$$
$$\text{association from 62;} \qquad (3)$$

$$(1 - P_f)(1 - P_b)P_b = \text{probability of no forward}$$
$$\text{association nor a backward}$$
$$\text{association from 62 but a backward}$$
$$\text{association from 71;} \qquad (4)$$

$$(1 - P_f)(1 - P_b)(1 - P_b).50 = \text{probability of no forward}$$
$$\text{association nor a backward}$$
$$\text{association from 62 or 71 but a}$$
$$\text{correct guess.} \qquad (5)$$

Substituting equations 2 through 5 into 1 we get:

$$\text{Probability of a correct recognition} = P_f + (1 - P_f)P_b$$
$$+ (1 - P_f)(1 - P_b)P_b$$
$$+ (1 - P_f)(1 - P_b)(1 - P_b).50. \qquad (6)$$

Wolford was able to use the forward and backward recall probabilities to estimate the probability of a forward association, $P_f = .38$, and the probability of a backward association, $P_b = .21$. Substituting these values into the above expression we get the following results:

$$(.38) + (1 - .38)(.21) + (1 - .38)(1 - .21).21$$
$$+ (1 - .38)(1 - .21)(1 - .21).5 = .806.$$

The observed probability of correct recognition was .80! This analysis illustrates beautifully how recognition can be conceived of as a combination of forward and backward associations.

The Nature of Forgetting

Forgetting and Interference

We have shown how one memory trace can interfere with the retrieval of a second memory trace. And we have shown, in our comparison of recognition and recall, that information can be in memory in a state such that it will be recognized but not recalled. Finally, we have shown that a reason for this deficit in recall is interference at a node in memory, and that this deficit can be circumvented in recognition by retrieval from another node. All these points naturally lead to a conjecture about the nature of forgetting: Is it true that one never really loses information from memory but only loses access to this information? Moreover, is such a loss of access always due to interference from multiple associations to a node in memory? That is, whenever we forget information that we once knew, is the loss due to the acquisition or rehearsal of interfering information in the interval between original learning and the retention test.* Together these conjectures result in an extraordinarily bold hypothesis about the nature of forgetting and, unfortunately, one that proves to be extraordinarily difficult to test.

On the surface, it might appear that if people forgot items without explicitly studying interfering material, this result would be enough to refute the hypothesis. It is easy enough to demonstrate that forgetting occurs without experimental interference. For example, an experimenter could have subjects learn a single paired-associate list. On a retest a month later, subjects would have forgotten part of the list. These subjects would not have experienced any explicit experimenter-provided interference. However, such a result would not necessarily imply that the forgetting was *not* due to interference. The subjects' forgetting might have been caused by uncontrolled things that they learned or thought about during the retention interval. So, one difficulty in experimentally determining whether all forgetting is due to interference lies in creating a retention situation in which one can be sure no interference exists.

A number of attempts have been made at minimizing the amount of interference present in an experimental situation. In a famous study, Jenkins and Dallenbach (1924) compared retention by subjects over intervals in which the subjects were either waking or asleep. They reasoned that sleeping subjects would encounter less interference. Their subjects learned lists of ten nonsense syllables. The investigators found that subjects retained more than 50 percent of learned material for eight hours if they spent the time sleeping but only 10 percent if they spent their time awake. Of course, both groups forgot. We might attribute the forgetting of the sleep subjects to the activities of going to sleep, waking, dreaming, and so forth.

The experiment by Grissom, Suedfeld, and Vernon (1962) also addressed this issue by using sensory deprivation. Test subjects were given a prose passage to study and then were confined to bed in individual, soundproof, dark rooms and required to stay silent for 24 hours. Control subjects studied the same passage and were then allowed to continue their normal activities. Control subjects forgot 12.6 percent of the passage while the sensory-deprived subjects actually improved 1.8 percent over their performance on an immediate recall.

---

*Note that all new information is not expected to interfere—only that which overlaps with the original material in the concepts (nodes) from which retrieval must take place. For instance, in the paired-associate experiment, interference occurs when other facts about the same stimulus are learned.

Are Forgotten Memories Truly Lost?

One implication of the hypothesis that all forgetting is due to interference is that we never do really lose our memories—that forgotten memories are still there but are too weak to be revived. The results reported by Penfield (1959) are consistent with this notion. As part of a neurosurgical procedure, Penfield electrically stimulated portions of patients' brain and asked patients to report what they experienced (patients were conscious during the surgery and the stimulation technique was painless). In this way Penfield was able to determine the function of various portions of the brain. Stimulation of the temporal lobes of the brain led to reports of memories that patients were unable to report in normal recall—for instance, events from their childhood. It was as if Penfield's stimulation activated portions of the memory network that spreading activation could not reach. Unfortunately, it is hard to know whether the patients' memory reports were accurate, since going back in time to check on whether the events reported actually occurred was nearly impossible. Therefore, while suggestive, the Penfield experiments are generally discounted by memory researchers.

A better experiment, conducted by Nelson (1971), also indicates that "forgotten" memories still exist. He had subjects learn 20 digit-noun paired associates; they studied the list until they reached a criterion of one errorless trial. Subjects returned for a retest two weeks later, recalling 75 percent of the items on this retention test. However, interest focused on the 25 percent of the items for which the subjects were unable to recall the noun response to the digit stimulus. Subjects were given new learning trials on the 20 paired associates. The paired associates they had missed were either kept the same or changed. In the changed case, a new response was associated to an old stimulus. If subjects had learned *43–dog,* but failed to recall the response to *43,* they might now be trained on either *43–dog* (unchanged) or *43–house* (changed). They were tested after studying the new list once. If subjects had lost all memory for the forgotten pairs, there should be no difference between changed and unchanged pairs. However, subjects correctly recalled 78 percent of the unchanged items formerly missed but only 43 percent of the changed items. This large advantage for unchanged items indicates that subjects had retained something about the paired associates even though they had been unable to recall them initially. This retained information was reflected in the savings displayed in relearning.

Nelson (1978) also looked at the situation in which the retention test involved recognition. Four weeks after learning, subjects failed to recognize 31 percent of the paired associates they had learned. As in the previous experiment, Nelson had subjects relearn the missing items. For half the stimuli the responses were changed and for the other half they were left unchanged. After one relearning trial, subjects recognized 34 percent of the unchanged items but only 19 percent of the changed items. The recognition-retention test should have been very sensitive to whether the subject has anything in memory. However, even when subjects fail this sensitive test, there appears to be some evidence that a record of the items is still in memory—the evidence that relearning was better for the unchanged than changed pairs. The implication of the Nelson studies is that, if we can come up with a sufficiently sensitive measure, we can show that apparently forgotten memories are still there.

General Conclusions

We have reviewed a wide range of facts regarding human memory—specifically, regarding short-term memory, retrieval from memory, and forgetting. The unifying concept that spans these domains is activation. The active portion of long-term memory defines that knowledge to which we have immediate access. The limitations of short-term memory are limitations in keeping information active. Retrieval from long-term memory is achieved through the spread of activation to the desired portion of long-term memory. Forgetting occurs when activation can no longer spread into some portion of memory.

Implications of the Research

In the preceding sections, we reviewed a set of basic principles about memory. It is natural to ask what these principles imply about good memory. Many of the immediate implications are obvious, but a few are subtle.

Holding Information in Short-Term Memory

Two observations can be made about keeping information (e.g., a phone number) in short-term memory. One has to do with the power of rehearsal: constantly reviving information in one's mind can keep it available. This fact is unlikely to come as a surprise to most readers of this book. There is evidence that children spontaneously discover the utility of such rehearsal strategies around the age of ten (Flavell, Beach, and Chinsky, 1966; Keeney, Cannizzo, and Flavell, 1967).

The second observation has to do with the importance of chunking. When the amount of information to be remembered exceeds short-term capacity it can still be retained if it can be combined into fewer units. Consider the task of remembering the following ten-digit phone number: 201-255-1071. By utilizing the number-letter correspondence technique described in Chapter 4 (p. 124) we can convert this number into *nst-nll-tskt* and thence into *nasty nail late skate*. Thus, we have converted a task of holding ten items in short-term memory into one of holding four items.

Learning

This chapter has shown that a rather direct relationship exists between amount of study and amount of information committed to long-term memory. Even after the point where the information can be perfectly recalled in an immediate test, further study serves to make the material more impervious to forgetting. However, it would be a mistake to assume that increased study is the only factor in improved learning. As we will review in the next chapter, the way study time is spent can be critically important.

Forgetting

A peculiar recommendation can be drawn from this chapter as to how to avoid forgetting. Often, *not* learning certain material can be beneficial. And forgetting certain material (or at least not rehearsing it) can also prove advantageous. As we have shown, material in memory can interfere with the acquisition and retention of other material that overlaps it. Thus, if certain material is not important it is best not learned or not rehearsed. This advice implies that to learn and retain what is important, we should lead rather austere lives, refraining from learning about the trivial or unimportant. This idea has not been totally unavailable to the layperson. We find Sherlock Holmes recommending it quite explicitly:

> I consider that a man's brain originally is like an empty attic, and you have to stock it with such furniture as you choose. A fool takes in all the lumber of every sort that he comes across, so that the knowledge which might be useful to him gets crowded out, or at best is jumbled up with a lot of other things, so that he has a difficulty in laying his hands upon it. Now the skillful workman is very careful, indeed, as to what he takes into his brain-attic. He will have nothing but the tools which may help him in doing his work, but of these he has a large assortment, and all in the most perfect order. It is a mistake to think that that little room has elastic walls and can distend to any extent. Depend upon it, there comes a time when for every addition of knowledge you forget something that you knew before. It is of the highest importance, therefore, not to have useless facts elbowing out the useful ones. [Arthur Conan Doyle, 1904, p. 16]

Sherlock Holmes may well be right. If one can accurately judge what is important and if one is willing to pay the price of austerity in life, refraining from learning the unimportant could be an efficient way of remembering. However, I neither recommend such a memory strategy nor practice it myself.

As we will see in the next chapter, at least one theoretical complication does arise with respect to Holmes' recommendation. It may actually be beneficial to learn information that is redundant or related to the target material. Memory for important facts about a concept is interfered with mainly by

Figure 6-9   *The picture studied by the subjects in the experiment by Haber and Erdelyi in which effects of relaxation and free association on recall were studied. (From Haber and Erdelyi, 1969.)*

learning irrelevant facts about the concept. So, for instance, if one wanted to learn the ways in which World War II was rooted in World War I, details about clothing preferences of the political figures of that era would probably interfere with remembering.

Retrieval

Regarding revival of memories, the recommendations to be gleaned from this chapter are much more palatable than those cited above. As noted earlier, there is evidence that many memories are too weak to be sufficiently activated and hence cannot be recalled. Thus, techniques should probably be practiced that increase the degree of activation converging on the memory. Relaxation and free-association techniques have proven quite effective in helping to revive memories. Consider an experiment by Haber and Erdelyi (1969). They presented subjects with the picture in Figure 6-9 for a brief period and then had subjects try to recall what was in the picture. After concluding their first attempt at recall, subjects were instructed to relax and free-associate about the picture. After 35 minutes of free association, subjects were able to recall additional items from the picture.

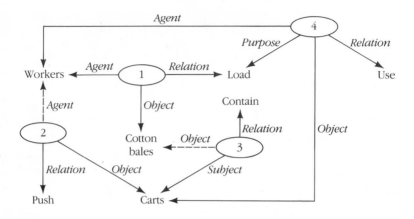

Figure 6-10   *An approximate network representation of a portion of the information conveyed by Figure 6-9.*

The effectiveness of such free-association techniques can be explained in terms of spreading activation. Figure 6-10 shows the network encoding for part of Figure 6-9. The information contained in that network is the following:

1. Workers are loading bales of cotton.
2. A worker is pushing a cart.
3. The cart contains some bales of cotton.

Also represented in Figure 6-10 is a general fact from long-term memory.

4. Workers use carts for the purposes of loading.

The connection between proposition 2 and *workers* and the connection between proposition 3 and *cotton bales* are dotted to indicate that these paths are weak (in the case of this hypothetical memory structure) and may not be usable for purposes of making propositions 2 and 3 accessible. Suppose subjects are able to recall fact 1 about the picture in the initial recall. Because the links to facts 2 and 3 are weak, subjects will be unable to recall these facts from fact 1. If they just focus on fact 1, thereby allowing activation to spread from it alone, they will never be able to recall facts 2 and 3.

On the other hand, if subjects free-associate about the picture, they might recall general fact 4, that carts are used by workers for loading bales of cotton. Activation can then spread from fact 4 through the *carts* concept to activate missing propositions 2 and 3. These facts will then be available for recall.

It is difficult to relax and free-associate in such situations as a time-pressured examination, but in other circumstances, when one is trying to remember the details of an accident, for instance, the technique can definitely be useful. I find it most useful in trying to remember the details of professional discussions or of research presentations.

Remarks and Suggested Readings

Many different views have been expressed regarding the nature of short-term memory. Melton (1963) put forth the thesis that short-term memory as distinct from long-term memory does not exist. Atkinson and Shiffrin (1968) originated many of the ideas about short-term memory reviewed in this chapter. However, ideas about short-term memory have evolved considerably in the past 12 years. For more recent discussions of the nature of short-term memory, see Bjork (1975), Craik and Jacoby (1975), Shiffrin (1975), and Wickelgren (1973, 1974). The ideas presented in this chapter have strong similarities to Shiffrin's recent proposals. A thorough review of this topic is in Crowder (1976).

The concept of spreading activation became popular in cognitive psychology with work on computer-simulation models by Quillian (1966, 1969) and by Reitman (1965). A comprehensive statement of the application of Quillian's ideas to psychological issues is to be found in Collins and Quillian (1972). A more up-to-date discussion is in Collins and Loftus (1975). My own ideas on this topic are more fully expressed in Anderson (1976).

The research on interference in long-term memory has had a very long research tradition. Many current issues could not be considered in this chapter. For discussions of the current ideas about forgetting, see the relevant chapters in Anderson and Bower (1973) and Crowder (1976). See also the papers by Postman and Underwood (1973) and by Wickelgren (1976).

Chapter 7

Memory Elaboration and Reconstruction

Summary

1. When information is committed to memory it is often *elaborated* with additional redundant information. Those elaborations facilitate recall by providing additional retrieval paths and by permitting recall by inference and reconstruction.

2. Memory for a piece of information can be improved by manipulations that increase the amount of elaboration performed by a subject. Such manipulations are said to affect the *depth* to which the material is processed.

3. *Intention to learn* is irrelevant to the amount learned. What is relevant is the way in which the information is processed.

4. Recall is often an act of *reconstruction,* in which are combined information from the to-be-recalled event, the elaborations of the event, the context of the events, and general relevant knowledge. As a result of such an act, subjects often recall things that they have not studied.

5. Information is better recalled if it is presented in an *organizational framework* that will make retrieval more systematic.

6. Memory performance improves the more closely the context at test matches the context at study. This has been shown to be true with respect to physical context, emotional and internal context, and the context provided by other study materials.

7. Studying material at widely *spaced* intervals tends to lead to better long-term retention because the material is learned in more different contexts.

8. Methods for studying textbooks such as the *PQ4R method* are effective because they impose a retrieval structure structure on the text, because they enforce spaced study, and because they promote deeper processing of the text.

Elaborations and Their Network Representations

In the previous chapter, we assumed, for simplicity's sake, a rather impoverished conception of the material that is typically committed to memory. Now, consider an experiment where a subject must commit to memory the following sentence.

1. The doctor hated the lawyer.

Figure 7-1A illustrates the kind of memory-network representation that we have been assuming for such a sentence. However, a subject presented with sentence 1 is unlikely to deposit only this structure in memory. Figure 7-1B is a network representation of what a subject might really think while studying the sentence. The difference between this structure and the simplified one is that the subject has elaborated upon the sentence with new thoughts or propositions. Since the subject thinks these propositions upon being presented with the sentence, they might be committed to memory—just as the studied proposition is. In such a case, in addition to the studied proposition, the subject would have stored the following information:

2. The subject studied this sentence in the psychology laboratory one dreary morning.
3. The lawyer had sued the doctor for malpractice.
4. The malpractice was the source of the doctor's hatred.
5. This sentence is unpleasant.

Another fact, representing some relevant information, was probably already in memory:

6. Lawyers sue doctors for malpractice.

Such structures as that in Figure 7-1B—called *elaborated structures,* since they incorporate *elaborations* on the original proposition—can have profound effects on memory. The function of this chapter is to review research that studies these effects.

One effect we would expect is that memory for any event would improve the more it is elaborated. Elaborations can lead to better memory in a least two ways. First, they provide redundant retrieval routes for recall. To see this, contrast Figures 7-1A and B. Suppose the link from node X (the doctor node) to the target proposition (node 1) is too weak to be revived at recall. If this were true and if the subject only had in memory structure A, he or she would be unable to recall proposition 1 prompted with *doctor*. On the other hand in representation B, even if the first link were too weak, there are other ways of retrieving the target proposition. For instance, the subject could recall from X the proposition that the lawyer sued the doctor for malpractice (node 3). From proposition node 3, the subject could recall the proposition that the malpractice suit led to the doctor's hating the lawyer (node 4). From here the subject would be able to recall node 1, which he or she had been unable to recall directly from X. That is, although the subject could not traverse the direct path from X to 1, he or she would be able to go from X to 3 to 4 to 1. Thus, this elaborated structure would help recall by providing the subject with *alternate retrieval routes* through the network to be used should the more direct ones fail.

Now, suppose the subject completely failed to encode the target proposition 1. Then, no matter what the attempts, recall would fail. However, if the subject were able to recall the elaborations on the target proposition, his or her knowledge state would be the following:

> I cannot remember the target sentence but I can remember conjecturing that it was caused by the lawyer suing the doctor for malpractice and I can remember it was a negative sentence.

With this information the subject might infer that the target sentence had been *The doctor hated the lawyer*. Thus, a second way in which elaboration aids memory is that it helps individuals to infer what they can no longer actually remember.

Both of these processes can be said to work because elaborations increase the *redundancy* with which information is encoded in memory. *Redundant elaboration* means that additional information is encoded in memory that provides more paths for retrieving and bases for inferring the to-be-remembered information. One would predict that experimental manipulations that increase the amount of redundant elaboration should increase the amount of recall.

In the last chapter, we studied interference manipulations, by which subjects' memory was shown to be poorer the more information was learned about a concept. Here the argument is that memory is being improved by redundant elaborations. The difference is that in the former case the additional information is irrelevant. To illustrate, if we wanted to learn (1) *The doctor*

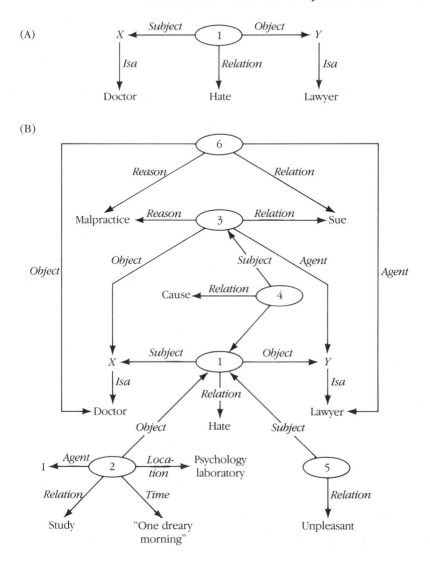

Figure 7-1 *A comparison of an unelaborated encoding (A) and an elaborated encoding (B) of the sentence* The doctor hated the lawyer.

hated the lawyer, learning an irrelevant fact such as (2) *The doctor vacationed in Guadalupe* would represent an interference. However, it would be facilitating to embellish sentence 1 with a relevant fact such as (3) *The lawyer sued the doctor.* In this case, the relevant fact provides an alternate retrieval path (like those we analyzed with respect to Figure 7-1, which the interfering sentence 2 did not.

Depth of Processing

Representative Studies

A number of experiments have appeared in the literature that can be interpreted as illustrating that more fully elaborated material results in better memory. These experiments have sometimes been viewed as illustrating the principle of *depth of processing*. Fergus Craik at the University of Toronto has promoted the term *depth of processing* (e.g., see the paper of Craik and Lockhart, 1972), but a great many independent researchers have been involved. They have shown in various ways that manipulations to increase the depth with which information is processed result in better memory. *Depth* here is used as an intuitive term to reflect how fully the subject processes the meaning of the material to be learned. There are a number of theoretical interpretations of depth of processing, but we will pursue the one that relates the phenomenon to network elaboration.

A classic demonstration of depth of processing comes from the 1969 experiments of Bobrow and Bower. These investigators had subjects try to commit to memory simple subject-verb-object sentences. There were two conditions of interest. In condition 1, subjects were provided with sentences written by the experimenters. In condition 2, subjects had to generate a sentence to connect the subject noun and object noun. After studying the sentences, subjects were prompted with the first *(subject)* noun and were required to generate the second *(object)* noun. Levels of recall in the two conditions were these: in condition 1 (sentences provided by experimenter), 29 percent; in condition 2 (sentences provided by subject), 58 percent. Presumably, in generating their own sentences subjects had to think more carefully about the meaning of the two nouns and their possible interrelationships. They probably considered a number of tentative connections between the two nouns before they chose one. This extra mental effort or deeper processing would have led to more elaborations of the nouns, and particularly to more elaborations that served to connect the two nouns.

A number of devices are known to improve subjects' memory for sentences provided by an experimenter. One is to ask the subject to generate a logical continuation to the sentence. So, given the sentence *The fireman stabbed the dancer,* a subject might continue *in a lovers' quarrel.* Another technique is simply to ask subjects to develop a vivid visual image of the situation described by the sentence. As with the Bobrow and Bower manipulation, both of these techniques encourage the subject to process the sentence more deeply and more elaborately.

These depth-of-processing results are not limited to sentences. One important experiment, reported by Hyde and Jenkins (1973), involved memory for individual words. Subjects saw groups of 24 words presented at the rate of 3 seconds per word. One group of subjects was asked to check whether each

Table 7-1 Percent of Words Recalled as a Function of Orienting Task and Whether Subjects Were Aware of Learning Task

Learning-Purpose Conditions	Orienting Task	
	Rate Pleasantness	Check Letters
Incidental	68	39
Intentional	69	43

word had an *e* or a *g.* The other group of subjects was asked to rate the pleasantness of the words. These two tasks were called *orienting tasks.* It is reasonable to assume that the pleasantness rating involved deeper and more elaborate processing than the letter-verification task. Another manipulation in the experiment was whether subjects were told that the true purpose of the experiment was to learn the words. Half the subjects in each group were told the true purpose of the experiment. These subjects were said to be in the intentional-learning condition. The other half in each group, who thought the true purpose was to rate the words or check for letters, were said to be in the incidental-learning condition. Thus there are altogether four conditions: pleasantness-intentional, pleasantness-incidental, letter-checking-intentional, and letter-checking-incidental.

After studying the list, all subjects were asked to recall as many words as they could. Table 7-1 presents the results from the Jenkins and Hyde experiment in terms of percent of the 24 words recalled. Two results are noteworthy. First, subjects' knowledge of the purpose of learning the words (of whether they would be tested for recall) had relatively little effect. Second, a large depth-of-processing effect was demonstrated; subjects showed much higher recall in the pleasantness-rating condition independent of whether they believed word learning to be incidental or intentional. In rating a word for pleasantness, subjects had to think about its meaning, which gave them an opportunity to elaborate upon the word. For instance, a subject presented with *duck* might think "Duck—oh yes, I used to feed the ducks in the park; that was a pleasant time."

Incidental Versus Intentional Learning

The Hyde and Jenkins experiment illustrates an important finding that has been proven over and over again in the research on intentional versus incidental learning: whether one intends to learn or not really does not matter (see Postman, 1964, for a review). What matters is how one processes the material during its presentation. If one engages in identical mental activities when not intending as when intending to learn, one gets identical memory performance in both conditions. People typically show better memory when they intend to learn because they are likely to engage in activities more conducive to good memory, such as rehearsal and elaborative processing. The small advantage of intentional subjects in the Jenkins and Hyde experiment may reflect some small variation in processing. Experiments that take great care to control processing find that intention to learn or amount of motivation to learn have no effect (see Nelson, 1976).

In fact, in some experiments in which processing is not carefully controlled, subjects actually do better in an incidental condition. One such study was a sentence-memory experiment by Anderson and Bower (1972). We had two groups of subjects generate short continuations to sentences. So, a subject might see *The minister hit the landlord* and add *with a cross.* One group of subjects was informed that there would be a memory test, and the other group was not. The intentional group recalled 48.9 percent of the sentences, while the incidental group recalled 56.1 percent. Later, interviews of the subjects revealed that the intentional subjects performed less well because some of them were busy employing poor memorization strategies such as saying the sentences over and over again to themselves. The incidental subjects simply elaborated on the sentences and were not hampered by poor theories of what makes for good memory. Brown (1979) also reported situations in which children were hampered in an intentional-learning situation by their mistaken ideas about memory.

Text Material

Frase (1975) has found evidence for the benefit of elaborative processing with text material. He compared two groups of subjects on their memory for a text: one that had been given topics to think about before reading the text and a control group that simply studied the text without advance topics. The topics given to the test group were similar to the summaries beginning the chapters in this book. They are sometimes called *advance organizers,* and in the Frase experiment were in the form of questions that the subjects must answer.* The subjects were to find answers to the advance questions as they read the text. This requirement should have forced them to process the text more carefully and to think about its implications. The advance-organizer group answered 64 percent of the questions correctly in a subsequent test, while the control group answered 57 percent correctly. The questions in the final test could be divided into those relevant to the advance organizers and those not relevant. For instance, if a test question was about an event that precipitated America's entry into World War II, it would be considered relevant if the advance questions directed the subject to learn why America entered the war. Such a test question would be considered not relevant if the advance question

---

*Ausubel (1968) introduced the term *advance organizers* to refer to general statements of information such as those in the chapter summaries here.

directed students to learn about the economic consequences of World War II. The advance-organizer group answered 76 percent of the relevant questions correctly and 52 percent of the irrelevant. Thus, they did only slightly worse than the control group on those topics for which they had not been given advance warning but much better on topics for which they had been given advance warning.

The evidence is quite clear that elaborative processing produces better memory for all sorts of material. This conclusion would be expected from the network model described earlier. Thus, students should elaborate on the material that they are learning in a course. This recommendation should please most teachers because it coincides with the recommendation that students think about the implications of what they are learning.

Deep or elaborative processing seems to be an important component in the mnemonic techniques such as those recommended by Lorayne and Lucas (1974) for learning relatively meaningless material. Consider Lorayne's discussion of the key to all mnemonic techniques:

> One of the fundamentals of a trained memory is what I call Original Awareness. Anything of which you are Originally Aware *cannot* be forgotten. And, applying my systems of association will *force* Original Awareness. [p. 6]

Lorayne never defines *Original Awareness,* but the recommendations for achieving it seem to imply that it involves elaborative processing:

> Learn how to make any intangible thing, any abstract piece of information, tangible and meaningful in your mind. [p. 6]

> • • •

> You can remember any piece of information if it is associated to something you already know or remember. [p. 7]

Reconstruction in Recall

Let us return to the discussion of subject's memory for this sentence:

1. The doctor hated the lawyer.

Elaborations improve memory for this sentence by increasing the redundancy of its encodings. Note that redundancy is not created by the subject simply making multiple mental copies of the sentence. Rather, redundancy is created by the storing of additional propositions that weakly or strongly imply the target sentence, as the following propositions do:

2. The lawyer sued the doctor for malpractice.
3. The doctor cursed the lawyer in court.

4. The doctor glared at the lawyer.

5. The lawyer assailed the doctor with a stream of questions.

Suppose subjects are no longer able to remember the studied sentence at test but are able to recall two of their elaborations, say:

2. The lawyer sued the doctor for malpractice.

4. The doctor glared at the lawyer.

In this case, the subject might well infer that the doctor hated the lawyer. Note, however, that this inference need not be true. For instance, the doctor and lawyer might be in cahoots, trying to defraud the doctor's malpractice-insurance company.

Thus, if we use elaborations to improve recall performance, we must be willing to make inferences and risk being wrong. Bartlett (1932), whose study involving "The War of the Ghosts" we reviewed in Chapter 5, found evidence for this *reconstructive* aspect of memory. He found that subjects recalled inferences that were not in the original story. Such "misrecalls" are just what we would expect if subjects were trying to reconstruct the original story on the basis of the elaborations in memory. The schema mechanisms discussed in that chapter provide one means for making such inferences.

A more recent demonstration of the inferential character of memory comes from Bransford, Barclay, and Franks (1972). They had subjects study one of the following sentences:

1. Three turtles rested beside a floating log, and a fish swam beneath them.

2. Three turtles rested on a floating log, and a fish swam beneath them.

Subjects who had studied sentence 1 were later asked whether they had studied this sentence:

3. Three turtles rested beside a floating log, and a fish swam beneath it.

Not many subjects thought they had studied this. Subjects who had studied sentence 2 were tested with

4. Three turtles rested on a floating log, and a fish swam beneath it.

Many more subjects thought they had studied this sentence than thought they had studied sentence 3. Of course, sentence 4 is implied by sentence 2, whereas sentence 3 is not implied by sentence 1. Thus, we have another case of subjects thinking they have actually studied what is implied from the studied material.

A study by Sulin and Dooling (1974) provides another illustration of how elaboration can bias subjects' memory for a text. They had subjects read the following passage:

Carol Harris's Need for Professional Help

Carol Harris was a problem child from birth. She was wild, stubborn, and violent. By the time Carol turned eight, she was still unmanageable. Her parents were very concerned about her mental health. There was no good institution for her problem in her state. Her parents finally decided to take some action. They hired a private teacher for Carol.

A second group of subjects read the same passage except that the name *Helen Keller* was substituted for *Carol Harris*. A week after reading the passage, subjects were given a recognition test in which they were presented with a sentence and asked to judge whether it had occurred in the passage. One of the critical sentences was *She was deaf, dumb, and blind*. Only 5 percent of the subjects who read the Carol Harris passage accepted this sentence, but a full 50 percent of the Helen Keller subjects thought they had read the sentence. This is just what we would expect. The second group of subjects had elaborated the story with facts they knew about Helen Keller. Thus, it would seem reasonable to them at test that this sentence had occurred in the studied material, but in this case their inference would have been wrong.

It is interesting to inquire whether such an inference as *She was deaf, dumb, and blind* was made while the subject was studying the passages or only at the time of the test. This is a subtle issue to get at, and subjects certainly do not have reliable intuitions about the matter. However, a couple of techniques are generally considered to yield evidence that inferences are being made at test. One is to determine whether the inferences increase in frequency with delay. With delay, subjects' memory for the studied passage should deteriorate and they will have to do more reconstruction, which will lead to more inferential errors. Both Dooling and Christiaansen (1977) and Spiro (1977) have found evidence for increased inferential intrusions with increased delay of testing.

Dooling and Christiaansen (1977) used another technique with the Carol Harris passage to show that inferences were being made at test. They had the subjects study the passage and told them a week later, just before test, that Carol Harris really was Hellen Keller. In this situation, subjects also made many inferential errors, accepting such sentences as *She was deaf, dumb, and blind*. Since they did not know Carol Harris was Helen Keller until test, they must have made such inferences at test. Thus, it seems that subjects do make reconstructive inferences at time of test.

Reder (1979) and Spiro (1977) have argued that in typical real-life memory situations a great deal of inference is involved in the act of recall. For instance, to adapt an example from Reder, in deciding that Darth Vador was evil in *Star Wars* one does not search memory for the specific proposition that Darth

Vador was evil, although the proposition may well have been directly asserted in the movie. One recalls that Darth Vador was evil by inference from memories about his behavior. The typical memory experiment overestimates the amount of direct retrieval involved in recall and underestimates the amount of inference. This is because the typical memory experiment emphasizes exact recall in a way that real life seldom does. Experiments are important for uncovering the basics of memory, but we should not lose sight of the fact that in many real-life situations recall is much more a matter of reconstruction.

The Interaction of Elaboration and Reconstruction

We have discussed inferential processes by which subjects elaborate a memory at study and inferential processes by which they reconstruct the memory at test. One would expect that the more a subject embellished a sentence at study the more inferential reconstruction would be possible at test. In fact, to use elaborations at study to improve memory performance, subjects often have to go from these elaborations to inferences about what was studied. Thus, we expect elaborative processing to lead both to an improvement in memory for what was studied and an increase in the number of inferences recalled. An experiment by Owens, Bower, and Black (1979) confirms this prediction. Subjects studied a story that followed the principle character, a college coed, through a day in her life: making a cup of coffee in the morning, visiting a doctor, attending a lecture, going shopping for groceries, and attending a cocktail party. The following is a passage from the story:

> Nancy went to see the doctor. She arrived at the office and checked in with the receptionist. She went to see the nurse who went through the usual procedures. Then Nancy stepped on the scale and the nurse recorded her weight. The doctor entered the room and examined the results. He smiled at Nancy and said, "Well, it seems my expectations have been confirmed." When the examination was finished, Nancy left the office.

Two groups of subjects studied the story. The only difference between the groups was that the theme group had read the following additional information at the beginning:

> Nancy woke up feeling sick again and she wondered if she really were pregnant. How would she tell the professor she had been seeing? And the money was another problem.

College students who read this additional passage characterized Nancy as an unmarried coed who is afraid she is pregnant as a result of an affair with a college professor. Subjects who had not read this opening passage had no reason to suspect that there is anything special about Nancy. We would expect

Table 7-2   Number of Propositions Recalled

Mean Number of Propositions Inferred	Theme Condition	Neutral Condition
Studied Propositions	29.2	20.2
Inferred Propositions	15.2	3.7

Adapted from Bower, Owens, and Black (1979).

the subject in the theme condition to make many more theme-related elaborations of the story than subjects in the neutral condition.

Subjects were asked to recall the story 24 hours after studying it. Subjects in the theme condition introduced a great many more inferences that had not actually been studied. For instance, subjects often reported that the doctor told Nancy she was pregnant. Intrusions of this variety are expected if subjects reconstruct the story on the basis of their elaborations. Table 7-2 reports some of the results from the study. Many more inferences are added in recall for the theme condition than for the neutral condition. However, a second important observation is that subjects in the theme condition also remembered more of the propositions they had actually studied. Thus, because of the additional elaborations made by subjects in the theme conditions, they were able to recall more of the story.

One might question whether subjects really benefited from their elaborations, since they also "misrecalled" many things that did not occur in the story. However, it is probably wrong to characterize the intruded inferences as misrecalls. Given the theme information, subjects were perfectly right to make these inferences and to recall them. In a nonexperimental setting (e.g., recalling information on an exam) one would expect subjects to treat such inferences as facts that were actually studied.

Advertisers often capitalize on our tendency to embellish what we hear with plausible inferences. Consider the following portion of a Listerine commercial:

> "Wouldn't it be great," asks the mother, "if you could make him coldproof? Well, you can't. Nothing can do that. [Boy sneezes.] But there is something that you can do that may help. Have him gargle with Listerine Antiseptic. Listerine can't promise to keep him coldfree, but it may help him fight off colds. During the cold-catching season, have him gargle twice a day with full-strength Listerine. Watch his diet, see he gets plenty of sleep, and there's a good chance he'll have fewer colds, milder colds this year."

A verbatim text of this commercial, with the only change that of the product name to "Gargoil," was used by Harris (1977). After hearing this commercial, all 15 of his subjects checked that "gargling with Gargoil Antiseptic helps

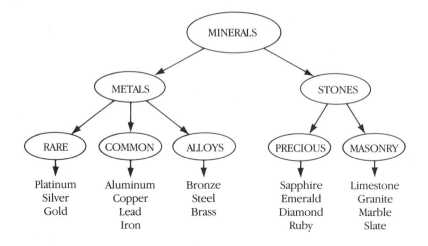

Figure 7-2   *A hierarchical tree presented to subjects in the free-recall experiment of Bower et al. The relationships among the items in the tree are categorical. (From Bower, Clark, Lesgold, and Winzenz, 1969.)*

prevent colds," although this assertion was clearly not made in the commercial. The Federal Trade Commission explicitly forbids advertisers from making false claims, but does the Listerine ad make a false claim? In a potential landmark case, the lower courts have ruled against Warner-Lambert, makers of Listerine, for implying false claims in this commercial. The case is still in appeal and may finally be decided in the U.S. Supreme Court.

A Perception-Recall Analogy

In Chapter 2, we learned that pattern recognition results from the combination of bottom-up information from the stimulus and top-down information from context and expectation. One way of describing perception is to say that we combine information from these multiple sources to *infer* what we must be seeing. A similar sort of combination seems to occur in recall. We combine information from our encoding of the to-be-recalled event (analogous to the stimulus in perception), of elaborations, of surrounding events (analogous to context), and of general knowledge (analogous to expectations) to infer what it is we are to recall. The similarity between perception and recall has been noted by many researchers who have proposed that similar mechanisms underlie the two processes (e.g., Bartlett, 1932; Neisser, 1967; Rumelhart and Ortony, 1976; Shaw and Bransford, 1977; Kolers, 1979). While suggestions about what these common mechanisms might be have so far been inexplicit, we can expect important breakthroughs in this area during the next decade.

Table 7-3 Average Number of Words Recalled Over Four Trials as a Function of Organization

Conditions	Trials			
	1	2	3	4
Organized	73.0	106.1	112.0	112.0
Random	20.6	38.9	52.8	70.1

Adapted from Bower, Clark, Lesgold, and Winzenz, 1969.

Organization and Recall

Hierarchical Structures and Other Organizations

Numerous manipulations have been shown to improve subjects' memory in recalling a long list of items. Many such devices involve organizing the material in such a way that subjects can systematically search their memories for the items. A nice demonstration of this use of organization is an experiment by Bower, Clark, Lesgold, and Winzenz (1969). They had subjects learn all the words in four hierarchies such as the one in Figure 7-2. Two conditions of learning were compared. In the *organized condition,* the four hierarchies were presented in upside-down trees as in Figure 7-2. In the *random condition,* subjects saw four trees, but the words in the trees were filled by random combinations of words from the four categories. Thus, instead of seeing separate trees for animals, clothing, transportation, and occupation, subjects saw four trees each containing some items from each category.

Subjects were given a minute to study each tree, and after studying all four trees they were asked to recall all the words in the four trees in any order. This study-test sequence was repeated four times. The performance of the two groups over the four trials is given in Table 7-3 in terms of number of words recalled. The maximum possible recall was 112. The organized group was shown to have an enormous advantage. Analysis of the order in which the organized group recalled the words indicated that subjects had organized their recall according to the tree hierarchies and recalled the words going down a tree from the top—for example, using Figure 7-2, first they would recall *minerals* and then *metals.*

The associative-network explanation of this result is straightforward: in the organized condition subjects were forming a memory network during the study phase similar to the hierarchy in Figure 7-2. To do this they only had to elaborate on connections already in memory. Thus, to return to the main topic of this chapter, another important function of elaborations can be imposing a hierarchical organization on memory. Such a hierarchical organization allows one to structure the search of memory and to retrieve information more efficiently.

Table 7-4 Chapter Outline to This Point

Elaborations and reconstruction
    Network representation
        Inferences and embellishments
        Contextual elements
        Connections to past knowledge
        Alternate retrieval routes
        Inferences at time of test

    Depth of processing
        Sentence memory
            Bobrow and Bower—self-generation
            Use of continuations
        Imagery
        Incidental versus intentional learning
            Hyde and Jenkins—rating of pleasantness
            Anderson and Bower—continuation generation
        Text material (Frase; advance organizers)
            Effect of questions on relevant material
            Effect of questions on irrelevant material
        Mnemonic techniques

    Reconstructive processes
        Inferential recall
        Bartlett's "War of the Ghosts"
        Bransford, Barclay, and Franks (three turtles)
        Dooling's studies with the Hellen Keller passage
        Interaction between elaboration and reconstruction

    Effects of organization
        Hierarchies
            Bower, Clark, Lesgold, and Winzenz
            This example

The implication of the result in Bower et al. for study habits is both important and clear. Course material can often be organized into hierarchies just as word lists can. Table 7-4 is a hierarchical organization for the material up to this point in the chapter. (In actually studying this material, students would be better off deriving their own organizations, as this will force deeper processing of the material). For readability, levels of the hierarchy are represented by levels of indentation. Note that in this hierarchy the connections are often not categorical, unlike those in Figure 7-2. For instance, the relation of *network representation* to *elaborations and reconstructions* is not one of an instance to a category. Rather, *network representation* serves as an explanation or mechanism for describing a phenomenon.

Bower et al. have shown that an individual need not utilize a strict categorial organization to derive the benefits of hierarchical structure. They investi-

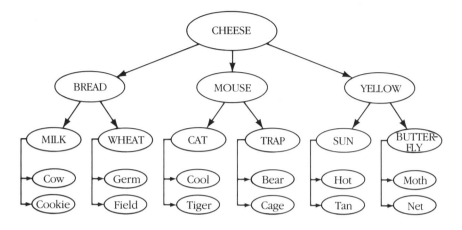

Figure 7-3 *A second type of hierarchical tree presented to subjects in the free-recall experiment of Bower et al. Here the relationships among the items are general associative rather than strictly categorical, as in Figure 7-2. (From Bower, Clark, Lesgold, and Winzenz, 1969.)*

gated hierarchies such as that in Figure 7-3, where the organization involves a loose associative structure. The presentation of information in such a hierarchy resulted in a considerable advantage over a random presentation.

Another demonstration of the importance of organization to recall was provided by Bower and Clark (1969). They required subjects to commit to memory lists of 10 unrelated nouns. The experimental group was told to study these nouns by constructing a narrative story around them. An example story generated by one subject with the to-be-recalled words capitalized is given below.

> A LUMBERJACK DARTed out of a forest, SKATEd around a HEDGE past a COLONY of DUCKs. He tripped on some FURNITURE, tearing his STOCKING while hastening toward the PILLOW where his MISTRESS lay.

A control group was given the same amount of time to study the 10 nouns but no special instructions. Both groups were tested immediately after the list was studied; immediate recall was almost perfect for both groups. However, a final test was given after the two groups had learned 12 lists in this manner. This final test was for all 120 words in all 12 lists. The experimental group recalled 94 percent while the control group recalled 14 percent!

The Method of Loci

A classic mnemonic technique, *the method of loci,* has its effect by promoting good organization in recall situations. This technique, used extensively in ancient times when speeches were given without written notes, is still used today. Cicero (in *De Oratore*) credits the method to a Greek poet, Simonides. Simonides had delivered a lyric poem at a banquet. Following his delivery, he was called from banquet hall by the gods Castor and Pollax, whom he had praised in his poem. While he was absent the roof fell in, killing all the participants at the banquet. The corpses were so mangled that relatives could not identify them. However, Simonides was able to identify each corpse according to where the person had been sitting in the banquet hall. This feat of total recall convinced Simonides of the usefulness of an orderly arrangement of locations into which one could place objects to be remembered. This story may be rather fanciful, but whatever the true origin of the method of loci, it is well documented (e.g., Christen and Bjork, 1976; Ross and Lawrence, 1968) as a useful technique for remembering an ordered sequence of items, such as the points one wants to make in a speech.

Basically, to use the method of loci one imagines a fixed path through a familiar area with some fixed locations along the path. For instance, if there were such a path on campus from the bookstore to the library one might use it. To remember a series of objects, one simply mentally walks along the path associating the objects with the fixed locations. As an example, consider a grocery list of six items—milk, hot dogs, dog food, tomatoes, bananas, and bread. To associate the milk with the bookstore, we might imagine a puddle of milk in front of the bookstore with books fallen into the milk. To associate hot dogs with the record shop (the next location in the path from the bookstore), we might imagine a package of hot dogs spinning on a record player turntable. The pizza shop is next, and to associate it with dog food we might imagine a pizza with dog food on it (well, some people even like anchovies). Then we come to the intersection; to associate this with tomatoes we can imagine an overturned vegetable truck and tomatoes splattered everywhere. Then we come to the administration building—and an image of the president coming out wearing only a hula-type skirt made of bananas. Finally, we reach the library and associate it to bread by imagining a huge loaf of bread serving as a canopy under which one must pass to enter. To recreate the list, we need only take an imaginary walk down this path, reviving the associations to each location. This technique works well with very much longer lists; one only needs more locations. There is considerable evidence (e.g., Christen and Bjork) that the same loci can be used over and over again in the learning of different lists.

Two important principles underlie the effectiveness of the method of loci. First, the technique imposes organization on an otherwise unorganized list. We are guaranteed that if we follow the mental path at time of recall, we will pass all the locations for which we created associations. The second principle is that generating connections between the locations and the items forces us to process the material deeply and so to produce redundant elaborations. The process of self-generation is very important. Thus, we should not use someone else's generated associations, but always make up our own.

The Effects of Encoding

Context

A clear implication of the network representation in Figure 7-1B is that reviving the experimental context in which items have been studied should aid recall. Note that such concepts as *psychology laboratory, one dreary morning,* and *unpleasant* are associated with the experimental memory. If at test such contextual stimuli and concepts could be revived, the subject would have additional ways to reactivate the target memory. There is ample evidence that context can greatly influence memory. This section will review some of the ways in which context influences memory. These context effects are often referred to as *encoding effects* because the context is affecting what is encoded into the memory trace that records the event.

Smith, Glenberg, and Bjork (1978) performed an experiment that showed the importance of physical context. In their experiment, subjects learned two lists of paired associates on different days and in different physical settings. On day 1, subjects learned the paired associates in a windowless room in a building near the University of Michigan campus. The experimenter was neatly groomed, dressed in a coat and a tie, and the paired associates were shown on slides. On day 2, subjects learned the paired associates in a tiny room with windows on the main campus. The experimenter was dressed sloppily in a flannel shirt and jeans (it was the same experimenter but some subjects did not recognize him) and presented the paired associates via a tape recorder. A day later, subjects made their recall, half in one setting and half in the other setting. Subjects could recall 59 percent of the list learned in the same setting as tested, but only 46 percent recall of the list learned in the other setting. Thus, it seems that recall is better if the context at test is the same as the context at study.

A perhaps more extreme version of this experiment was performed by Godden and Baddeley in 1975. They had divers learn a list of 40 unrelated words either on the shore or 20 feet under the sea. The divers were then asked to recall the list either in the same or a different environment. Figure 7-4 displays the results of this study. Subjects clearly showed superior memory when they were asked to recall in the same context in which they studied. So, it seems that contextual elements get associated to memories and that memory is improved when subjects are provided with these contextual elements again.

Some recent research by Bower, Montiero, and Gilligan (1978) shows that emotional context can have the same effect as physical context. They also had subjects learn two lists. For one list they hypnotically induced a positive state by having subjects review a pleasant episode in their lives, and for the other list they hypnotically induced a negative state by having subjects review a traumatic event. A later recall test was given under either a positive or nega-

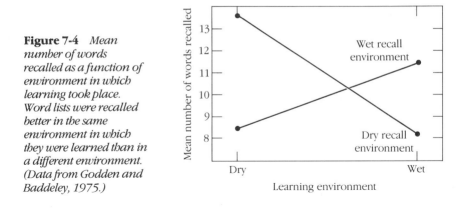

Figure 7-4 *Mean number of words recalled as a function of environment in which learning took place. Word lists were recalled better in the same environment in which they were learned than in a different environment. (Data from Godden and Baddeley, 1975.)*

tive emotional state (again hypnotically induced). Better memory was obtained when the emotional state at test matched the emotional state at study.

As an aside it is worth commenting that, despite popular reports, the best evidence is that hypnosis per se does nothing to improve memory (see Hilgard, 1968, for a discussion of hypnosis), though it can help memory to the extent that it can be used to recreate the contextual factors at the time of test. However, much of a learning context can also be recreated by nonhypnotic means, such as through free-association about the circumstance of the to-be-remembered event.

A related phenomenon is referred to as *state-dependent learning*. People find it easier to recall information if they can return to the same emotional and physical state they were in when they learned the information. For instance, it is often casually claimed that heavy drinkers when sober are unable to remember where they hid the alcohol when drunk and when drunk they are unable to remember where they hid the money when sober. In fact, some experimental evidence does exist for this state dependency of memory with respect to alcohol, but the more important factor seems to be that alcohol has a general debilitating effect on the acquisition of information (Parker, Birnbaum, and Noble, 1976). Marijuana has been shown to have similar state-dependent effects. In one experiment (Eich, Weingartner, Stillman, and Gillin, 1975), subjects learned a free-recall list after smoking either a marijuana cigarette or an ordinary cigarette. Subjects were tested 4 hours later—again after smoking either a marijuana cigarette or a regular cigarette. Subjects who learned in the marijuana condition recalled 12 percent of the items when tested while nonintoxicated and 23 percent when tested while intoxicated. Subjects who learned in the ordinary-cigarette condition recalled 25 percent of the items when tested while nonintoxicated and 20 percent when tested after smoking a marijuana cigarette.

Encoding Specificity

The effects of general environmental and internal context are fairly easy to understand intuitively, but evidence suggests that there can be less obvious effects of the context in experimental situations. For example, there is now good evidence that memory for to-be-learned material can be heavily dependent on the context of other to-be-learned material in which it is embedded. Consider a recognition-memory experiment by Thomson (1972). He had subjects study pairs of words such as *sky blue.* Subjects were told that they were only responsible for the second item of the pair—in this case *blue;* the first word represented context. Later, they were tested by either being presented with *blue* or *sky blue.* In either case, they were asked whether they had originally seen *blue.* In the single-word case they recognized *blue* 76 percent of the time, while in the pair condition their recognition rate was 85 percent. This difference indicates a dependence of memory on the context in which a to-be-recognized item is studied.

A series of experiments (e.g., Tulving and Thomson, 1973; Watkins and Tulving, 1975) has dramatically illustrated how memory for a word can depend on how well the test context matches the original study context. In one experiment (1975), Watkins and Tulving had subjects learn pairs of words such as *train–black* and told them that they were only responsible for the second word, referred to as the *to-be-remembered word* (again, the first word in the pairs served as the context). After this study phase, subjects were given words such as *white* and asked to generate four free associates to the word. So, a subject might generate *snow, black, wool,* and *pure.* The stimuli for the associate task were chosen to have a high probability of eliciting a to-be-remembered word. For instance, *white* has a high probability of eliciting *black.* Overall, the to-be-remembered word was generated 66 percent of the time as one of the four associates. After they had generated their associates, subjects were told to indicate which of the four associates was the one they had studied. They were forced to indicate a choice even if they thought they had not studied any of the words. In cases where the to-be-remembered word was generated, subjects correctly chose the word 54 percent of the time. Since subjects were always forced to indicate a choice, some of these correct choices must have been lucky guesses, meaning that true recognition was even lower. Following this test in which subjects free-associated and then recognized study words, subjects were presented with the original context words and asked to recall the to-be-recalled words. Subjects recalled 61 percent of the words—higher than their recognition rate without any correction for guessing! Moreover, Tulving and Watkins found that 42 percent of the words recalled had not been recognized earlier when the subjects gave them as free associates.

As we saw in the previous chapter, recognition is generally superior to recall. Conversely, we would expect that if subjects could not recognize a word, they would be unable to recall it. Usually, one expects to do better on a multiple-choice test than on a recall-the-answer test. Experiments such as the one described above have provided some very dramatic reversals of such standard expectations. Their results can be understood in terms of the similarity of the test context to the study context. The context in which the word *white* and its associates were studied was quite different from that in which *black* had originally been studied. In contrast, in the cued recall task, subjects were given the original context *(train)* with which they had studied the word. Thus, if the contextual factors are sufficiently weighted in favor of recall, as they were in these experiments, recall can be superior to recognition. Tulving offers these results as illustrating what he calls the *encoding-specificity principle:* The probability of recalling a item at test depends on the similarity of its encoding at test and its original encoding at study.

These experiments are confined to the study of single words because such research is much more tractable than that on larger units. However, it seems very important to know if similar results could be obtained with larger units such as text. It is something of an embarrassment to the field that no researcher seems to have looked for extensions of these results on encoding specificity to text material. However, one would expect that the same results would be obtained, since other results with single words have been shown to generalize to larger units of analysis. If the encoding-specificity results do generalize, the implication would be that memory for text depends in part on whether retesting is conducted in the context in which study took place. In particular, students' memory for a text should be improved by testing for facts that are couched in the same surrounding material in which they were presented in the text. Thus, examinations that test facts in isolation may seriously underestimate what the subjects "know" in one sense. Still, while such an underestimation might be *serious,* it is not clear that it is *grievous,* since memories that are so context dependent are not particularly valuable. Students ought to be able to remember the facts in multiple contexts. The research covered in the following subsection is concerned with how memory can be made independent of context.

Encoding Variability and the Spacing Effect

When facts are studied on multiple occasions, their encodings will be slightly different on each occasion. An important factor determining the measure of difference among the various encodings is the measure of difference among the learning contexts on each occasion. An obvious factor influencing the differences among learning contexts is the spacing over time of these contexts. The importance of spacing is illustrated in an experiment by Madigan (1969), again on the free recall of single words. Forty-eight words were presented at the rate of 1.5 second/word. Some words were presented once and others twice. After study, subjects were asked to recall as many words as

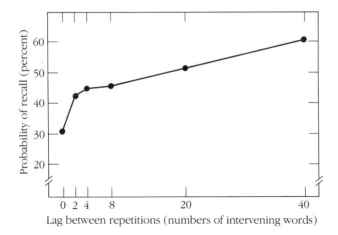

Figure 7-5 *Recall probability of twice-presented words as a function of the lag between the two occurrences of the work in Madigan (1969). Memory improves as the lag between repetition increases.*

they could. They recalled 28 percent of the words that appeared once and 47 percent of the words that appeared twice. Figure 7-5 shows an analysis of Madigan's data in the twice-presented condition. The data for the twice-presented condition are plotted as a function of *lag,* or the number of inter-vening words between the two presentations. Probability of recall increases systematically with lag. There is a very rapid increase over the initial lag and the benefit increases, if more slowly, to lags of 40 intervening items. To date, no evidence suggests that there is an amount of spacing after which recall will not further improve. Memory improves with the increase in lag between study episodes, although the advantage diminishes as the spacing is increased. This result is known as the *spacing effect.*

The spacing effect, illustrated in Figure 7-5, is an extremely robust and powerful phenomenon, and it has been repeatedly shown with many kinds of material. Spacing effects have been demonstrated in free recall, in cued recall of paired associates, in the recall of sentences, and in the recall of text material. It is important to note that these spacing results do generalize to textbook materials (Rothkopf and Coke, 1963, 1966; Reynolds and Glaser, 1964).

It is probable that a number of factors combine to produce the spacing effect. For instance, subjects may do poorly at short lags simply because of inattention. That is, they may regard a second study at such a short lag as unnecessary and ignore it. Rundus (1971) asked subjects to rehearse material out loud and found that they spent less rehearsal time on the second presentation of items at short lags. While other factors are probably involved (e.g., see Hintzman, 1974), an important factor in the lag effect, especially at long lags, is that suggested at the start of this subsection: *encoding variability* due to change of context. Probability of recall depends in part on study context matching test context. At long lags, it is likely that the two study contexts will be quite different from each other. The greater the difference between the two study contexts, the greater is the probability that one of the contexts will overlap with the test context. On the other hand, at short lags the two study contexts will be more similar, and the probability of study context matching test context will be not much greater than in the single-presentation condition.

The importance of encoding variability to the spacing effect is nicely demonstrated in some of the other analyses reported by Madigan (1969). He presented subjects with pairs of words but told them they were only responsible for remembering the second—the first just provided context (as in the previously described studies of Thomson and of Watkins and Tulving). Some target words were presented twice and some only once. When items were repeated, they occurred each time either with the same context word or with different context words. For example, the target word *chill* might occur twice in a list, separated by a lag of four intervening items. In the *different condition,* it might occur the first time with *fever* and the second time with *snow.* In the *same condition,* it would occur both times with *fever.* Madigan found that subjects performed better in the different condition. Moreover, the different condition did not show as large a spacing effect as the same condition. That is, the advantage of long lags over short lags was smaller in the different condition.

Madigan's results would be expected from the encoding-variability interpretation of the spacing effect. By providing different context words, Madigan forced a change in the encoding context. This change should be particularly important at short lags when large variations in context do not occur naturally. Note that the Madigan experiment demonstrates that it is possible to make repetition at short lags more effective by taking measures to create a change in the context. The implications of these results for study habits are almost too obvious to require comment: we should space our study of particular material over time. And, when such spacing is impossible, we should change the context of repetitive study. At a physical level, we can change the location in which we study. At a more abstract level, we can try to change the perspective we take on the to-be-learned material.

The encoding-variability analysis of the spacing effect does not imply that spaced study and variable encoding will always result in superior memory. What is really important is that one of the contexts in which the material is studied overlap with the context in which the material is tested. When students are not sure how the material is to be tested, they should study it in contexts as varied as possible. Spacing study is one way of ensuring a variety of contexts, but, as we have noted, other ways are also effective, such as changing the physical environment, mental set, and so on. However, when students know the context in which they are to be tested, then variable encoding may not be such a good idea. In this case, the ideal study location would be the location in which the test is to be administered. Of course, with respect to college exams this ideal may be hard to achieve. Gaining access to an exam room is often difficult, and, in any case, the difference between an empty exam room and one filled with anxious students and a monitor pacing slowly around the room is considerable.

Study Lag Versus Test Lag

The implication is that spacing should be beneficial when one is uncertain about when testing will occur. However, if the time of test is known, better test performance will result if all the study is massed just before the test. The reason for this is that just before a test one is in a context that is almost identical to the test context in some ways (mood and mental set). Glenberg (1976) has proposed a general relationship between study lag and test lag. Suppose you are going to study material twice. Let *study lag* refer to the delay between the two studies and let *test lag* refer to the delay between the second study and test. The rule is the following: The longer the expected test lag, the more advantageous is a long study lag. The reason is that the longer the test lag, the less the second study context will overlap with test and the more important it is that the first study context differ from the second, thus ensuring that the former will overlap in different ways with the test context.

To make Glenberg's proposal more concrete, suppose that you studied some experimental material twice before a test. We will focus on the second study context and consider the effects of varying the lag from it to the first study and to the test. In the second study context you were sleepy, thinking of a movie you had seen, liked the experiment, and were uncomfortable in your chair; these would constitute the contextual features. At a long test lag, the test context might be quite different. Now you might be alert, still thinking of the movie, disliking the experiment, and still physically uncomfortable. Note that the study context would overlap with test only in two ways—the movie and lack of comfort. If the study lag were short, the first study context would probably be identical to the second and so overlap in the same two ways with the test context as did the second study context. On the other hand, if the study lag were long, the first study context might be quite different—in this study period, you might be alert, like the experiment, be thinking about a movie, and be comfortable in your chair. Note that this first study context would also overlap with the test context in two ways, but one feature, alertness, would be different from those on which the second study context overlapped. Thus, the two study contexts combined would overlap with the test context in three ways, an improvement on the short study-lag situation, in which both study contexts overlapped with the test on the same two features.

On the other hand, when the test lag is short the second study context would overlap maximally with the test context. In this situation, a short study lag would be advantageous, since the first study context would overlap maximally with the second and hence with the test. To return to our concrete example, with a short test lag, you might be alert, dislike the experiment, be thinking of the movie, and feel uncomfortable in both the second study period and the test. With a short study lag, the first study context would also be the same. However, with a long study lag, during the first study period you might be sleepy, like the experiment, be thinking of the movie, and feel uncomfortable. Thus, with a short test lag, all that a long study lag would accomplish would be an increase in the difference between the first study context and the test context.

These ideas were tested by Glenberg (1976) in an experiment on continuous paired-associate learning. On each trial, subjects either saw a stimulus-response pair, which they were instructed to remember, or a stimulus from a past pair, for which they had to recall the associate. These study and test events alternated in an irregular fashion. Glenberg presented the pairs for study twice at varying lags identified by number of intervening study or test events. Subjects were tested at varying lags from the second study. Figure 7-6 presents his data. Each curve in that figure gives proportion of items recalled as a function of study lag. Different curves represent different test lags. Lag in this experiment is defined as number of intervening events where an event is either a study or test trial. Of course, subjects show best memory at short test lag, but more interesting is the interaction between study and test lag. At all test lags subjects displayed their worst memory at study lags of 0 or 1 intervening events. The poor performance at these very short lags probably reflects inattentiveness due to close repetitions. However, with respect to study lags of 4 to 40 events, we find the predicted interaction between study lag and test lag. For short test lags (2 and 8 intervening events), performance is a decreasing function of study lag. For long test intervals (32 and 64 events), performance is an increasing function of study interval.

Although Glenberg's results have not been shown experimentally to occur on the time scale of an academic course, they do suggest some study procedures. First, it is a bad idea to study the same fact over and over again with no spacing. Beyond this, the spacing of one's studying depends on one's specific purposes. Although I hate to admit this, if one's purpose is to pass an exam, concentrating a lot of study the night before the exam should be advantageous; in other words, it's best to cram. Of course, cramming will lead to poor long-term retention, as frequently noted by students a year after a course. Studying throughout the term does have some benefit, though this method is just not as

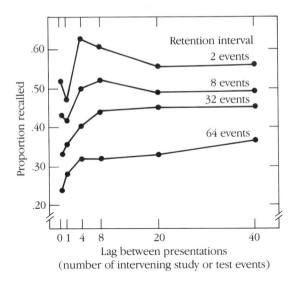

Figure 7-6 *The effect of study lag (delay between studies) on recall probability as a function of test lag (retention interval). Short study lags are optimal at short test lags, while long study lags are optimal at long test lags. (Data from Glenberg, 1976.)*

efficient as cramming. The strategy that will result in the best grade combines the techniques of studying during the term and cramming the night before.

The best course design for purposes of retention would space study and testing over the term. Thus, the preferred examination method is the administering of short quizzes throughout the course. However, the quizzes should cover not just the most recent material, as most short quizzes do, but material that goes back to the beginning of the course. Students being tested in this way would benefit from spacing of their study. Another useful teaching technique, to be used in conjunction with periodic quizzing, would be coverage of all material twice, once in the first half of the course and once in the second half (as suggested by Bjork, 1979).

General Conclusions

Consider again Figure 7-1, which compares the simplified conception of the information deposited in memory with an elaborated conception. The research reviewed in this chapter indicates that the elaborative conception is more accurate. Subjects elaborate the information they study with the following:

1. Connections to prior knowledge.
2. Imaginings and inferences about the material.
3. Features from the current context.

The evidence we have reviewed indicates that this process of elaboration leads to improved memory in the following ways:

1. It increases the redundancy of interconnections among the to-be-remembered information.

2. It imposes an organization on the information that can be used to guide the retrieval process.

3. It can increase the number of contextual elements that will overlap between study and test.

The PQ4R Method

Many college study-skills departments as well as private firms offer courses designed to improve students' memory for text material. These courses mainly teach study techniques for such texts as those used in the social sciences, not the more dense texts used in the physical sciences and mathematics or less dense, literary materials such as novels. The study techniques from different programs are fairly similar, and their success has been documented to some extent. Two of the more publicized and publicly accessible techniques are the *SQ3R method* (Robinson, 1961) and the later *PQ4R method* (Thomas and Robinson, 1972). Other techniques are quite similar and are often adaptations of these methods. These methods are strongly supported by the ideas covered in this chapter. We will examine the PQ4R method as an example.

The PQ4R method derives its name from the six phases it advocates for studying a chapter in a textbook:

1. *Preview.* Survey the chapter to determine the general topics being discussed. Identify the sections to be read as units. Apply the next four steps to each section.

2. *Questions.* Make up questions about the section. Often, simply transforming section headings results in adequate questions. For example, a section heading might be *Encoding Variability,* resulting in such questions as "What is encoding variability?" and "What are the effects of encoding variability?"

3. *Read.* Read the section carefully, trying to answer the questions you have made up about it.

4. *Reflect.* Reflect on the text as you are reading it, trying to understand it, to think of examples, and to relate the material to prior knowledge.

5. *Recite.* After finishing a section, try to recall the information contained in it. Try answering the questions you made up for the section.

If you cannot recall enough, reread the portions you had trouble remembering.

6. *Review.* After you have finished the chapter, go through it mentally, recalling its main points. Again try answering the questions you made up.

A slight variation on this technique for studying this text is detailed in Chapter 1. Clearly, one of the reasons for the success of this kind of technique is that all the passes through the material serve as spaced study of the material. Another probable effect is to make the subject aware of the way the material is organized. As we have seen, organization leads to good memory, especially on free-recall-type tests.

The central feature of the PQ4R technique, however, is the question-generation and question-answering characteristics. There is reason to suspect that the most important aspect of this feature is that it encourages (perhaps *forces* would be a better word) deeper or more elaborative processing of the text material. Earlier, we reviewed the experiment by Frase that demonstrated the benefit of reading a text with a set of advance organizers in mind. It seems that the benefit of that activity was specific to test items related to the questions.

The distinction between test items related to the study questions and those not related is important. Suppose that a study question in a text on African economics was, "What were the effects of the transition from colonialism on economic growth?" A *related* test question might then be, "Did the rate of foreign investment decrease as a result of the transition from colonialism?" An *unrelated* test question might be, "What factors limit the rate of development of the forestry industry in Africa?" Clearly, study questions related to test questions would be expected to aid memory more effectively than unrelated ones. Therefore, creating study questions that tap the most important topics is an important aspect of the study technique.

Another experiment by Frase (1975) compared the effects of making up questions and answering them. He had pairs of subjects study a text, which was divided into halves. For one half, one subject in the pair read the passage and made up study questions as he or she went along. These questions were given to the second subject, who then read the text while trying to answer them. The subjects switched roles for the second half of the text. All subjects answered a final set of test questions about the passage. A control group, who just read without doing anything special, answered correctly 50 percent of the set of questions that followed. Experimental subjects, when they read to make up questions, answered correctly 70 percent of the test items that were relevant to their questions and 52 percent of the irrelevant test items. When they read to answer questions, experimental subjects answered correctly 67 percent of the relevant test items and 49 percent of the irrelevant items. Thus, it seems that both question generation and question answering contribute to good memory. If anything, question making contributes the most. T. H. Anderson (1978), in a review of the research literature, finds further evidence for the particular importance of question making.

In another study lending support to the PQ4R techniques, Richards (1976) looked at the effect of different types of questions as advance organizers for reading. He had subjects study a passage about a fictitious African nation called Mala. The experiment compared the effectiveness of conceptual questions, which required the subjects to process a general issue such as exploitation of the people, and verbatim questions, which required subjects to recall a specific fact. Subjects responding to the conceptual questions showed better recall. Such results are the justification for prefacing each chapter in this book with general statements about the chapter contents. You should be using these statements to form general conceptual questions.

Reviewing the text with the questions in mind is another important component of the PQ4R technique. Rothkopf (1966) compared the benefit of reading a text with questions in mind and the benefit of considering a set of questions after reading the text, which enabled subjects to review the text. Rothkopf had subjects read a long text with questions interspersed every three pages. The questions were relevant to the three pages either following or preceding the questions. In the former condition, subjects were supposed to read the subsequent text with these questions in mind. In the latter condition, they were to review what they had just read and answer the questions. The two experimental groups were compared with a control group, which read the text without any special questions. This control group answered 30 percent of the questions correctly in a final test of the whole text. The experimental group whose questions previewed the text answered correctly 72 percent of the test items relevant to their questions and 29 percent of the irrelevant items—basically the same results as those Frase obtained in comparing the effectiveness of relevant and irrelevant test items. The experimental group whose questions reviewed the text answered correctly 72 percent of the relevant items but actually 42 percent of the irrelevant items. Thus, it seems that reviewing the text with questions in mind is more generally beneficial.

Remarks and Suggested Readings

The topics of this chapter are discussed more fully in a number of sources. The elaboration analysis comes from work by myself and Reder (Anderson, 1976, Ch. 10; Anderson and Reder, 1978; Reder, 1976, 1979). An up-to-date survey of research and opinion about depth of processing is found in the book edited by Cermak and Craik (1979). Shaw and Bransford (1977) provides another perspective of the integrative and constructive nature of cognition. Good reviews of research on organizational factors in memory is to be found in Bower (1970) and Mandler (1967, 1972). Good sources for Endel Tulving's opinions on encoding specificity are Watkins and Tulving (1975) and Flexser and Tulving (1978). The book edited by Melton and Martin (1972) is a collection of papers on encoding effects, especially effects of encoding variability. Crowder's 1976 memory text provides excellent surveys of many of these topics.

With respect to mnemonic techniques, I again refer the reader to the popular book of Lorayne and Lucas. A number of recent papers set forth recommendations from memory research for learning and teaching techniques. Among these are Bower (1970), Bjork (1978), Greeno (1974), and Norman (1973). Frase (1975), R. C. Anderson and Biddle (1975), and Rothkopf (1972) provide reviews of a good deal of research that is relevant to evaluating the PQ4R method. Gibson and Levin (1975, Ch. 11) provide a review of memory research relevant to reading. Also, the book by Thomas and Robinson (1972) sets forth the PQ4R method, and an earlier book by another Robinson (1961) describes the SQ3R method, which seems to have been the source for the PQ4R method.

Chapter 8

Cognitive Skills

Summary

1. Our knowledge can be categorized as *declarative knowledge* and *procedural knowledge.* Declarative knowledge comprises the facts we know; procedural knowledge comprises the skills we know how to perform.

2. Skill learning occurs in three steps: (1) a *cognitive stage,* in which a description of the procedure is learned; (2) an *associative stage,* in which a method for performing the skill is worked out; and (3) an *autonomous stage,* in which the skill becomes more and more rapid and automatic.

3. As a skill becomes more automatic, it requires less attention and we may lose our ability to describe the skill verbally.

4. Skills can be represented by sets of *productions.* Each production consists of a *condition* and an *action.* The condition is a general description of the circumstances under which the production should apply. The action consists of both the external behavior and the changes to be made in memory if the production applies.

5. Some of the *dynamic properties* of procedures are that procedures can be held in a short-term memory state, that different procedures can interfere with or facilitate one another, and that procedures undergo processes of generalization and discrimination.

6. Research on skill acquisition has implications for the learning of a cognitive skill such as computer programming. These implications involve the issues of spacing of practice, part versus whole learning, automating subskills, transfer among related skills, and effects of knowledge of results (feedback).

Procedural Knowledge

This chapter represents a watershed in the book. To this point, we have been mainly concerned with knowledge as "static" information and not with the processes that use this information. That is to say, we have been concerned with the knowledge underlying the recall of facts rather than the knowledge underlying the performance of various intellectual tasks. For instance, we have been interested in what people know about a history text rather than about how to program a computer. The distinction between *knowing that* and *knowing how* is fundamental to modern cognitive psychology. In the former, what is known is called *declarative knowledge;* in the latter, what is known is called *procedural knowledge.* The term *cognitive skill* is used here to refer to the ability to perform various intellectual procedures. This chapter reflects a shift in this text from a concern with declarative knowledge to a concern with procedural knowledge, or cognitive skill.

The next six chapters will cover a variety of cognitive skills in detail. The function of this chapter is to review what is known about procedural knowledge or cognitive skills in general—how they are represented, learned, and retained. In a sense, this chapter serves the function for procedural knowledge that the previous five chapters served for declarative knowledge. The severe imbalance in page allocation reflects the fact that cognitive psychology has much more fully studied declarative knowledge than it has procedural knowledge.

The Declarative–Procedural Distinction

As the term suggests, declarative knowledge tends to be information that can be verbally communicated. A typical instance of declarative knowledge is a fact such as *John MacDonald was the first prime minister of Canada.* However, declarative knowledge need not be verbal. As we saw in Chapter 4, it often takes the form of abstract propositions. And in Chapter 3 we saw that it often takes the form of mental imagery.

While the distinction is not absolute, most declarative knowledge can be expressed verbally while much procedural knowledge cannot. A good example of procedural knowledge that cannot be described is riding a bike. Most of us know quite well how to ride a bike but cannot put that knowledge into words. Indeed, it is common folklore that trying to analyze such a skill is disastrous. Someone trying to explain the action of executing a golf swing while performing the action stands a good chance of ruining the swing.

Other examples exist of procedural knowledge that are not motor in character, for example, knowledge of one's native language. Almost everyone possesses this knowledge, but stating the rules of the language is very difficult for most people. Consider, for instance, a set of rules relating to active and passive sentences such as the following:

> The girl hit the boys.
>
> The boys were hit by the girl.
>
> and
>
> The boys like the girl.
>
> The girl is liked by the boys.
>
> and
>
> The girl will tease the boy.
>
> The boy will be teased by the girl.

People can generate such active and passive equivalents without difficulty, but most people have no idea what the general rules are that relate the two forms. Indeed, professional linguists are still debating as to exactly what these rules are.

When we learn a foreign language in a classroom situation, we are aware of the rules of the language, especially just after a lesson that spells them out. One might argue that our knowledge of the language at that time is declarative. We speak the learned language by using general rule-following procedures applied to the rules we have learned, rather than speaking directly, as we do in our native language. Not surprisingly, applying this knowledge is a much slower and more painful process than applying the procedurally encoded knowledge of our own language. Eventually, if we are lucky, we can come to know a foreign language as well as we know our native language. At that point, we often forget the rules of the foreign language. It is as if the class-taught declarative knowledge had been transformed into a procedural form.

As we use the same knowledge over and over again in a procedure, we can lose our access to it and thus lose the ability to report it. An example here concerns telephone numbers. When we first learn a phone number, we can report it and dial it by means of a general telephone-dialing procedure that takes that telephone number as data. That is, the number initially has a declarative form. However, some people report that if they dial a number often enough, they lose the ability to recall the number verbally. The only way they are able to retrieve the number is to dial it. In fact, that knowledge can be specific to a particular telephone. For example, there was a time when my ability to recall the Michigan Computer number was specific to my home touch-tone phone.

Another personal example involves learning to drive. I became particularly aware of this a number of years ago when my wife taught me how to use a stick shift. One of the questions I asked her was whether I should take my foot off the gas when shifting gears. She said that I should keep my foot on the gas, but we did not like the results. So she took the driver's seat and we both watched what she did when she shifted—she did take her foot off the gas. Here was a case in which procedural and declarative knowledge were in direct conflict. Declaratively my wife thought her foot should stay on the gas but procedurally she knew better. The only way to tap the procedural knowledge was to observe herself performing the procedures. When I first shifted, I was using declarative knowledge exclusively—I retrieved the instructions from memory and followed them (sometimes saying the steps to myself). Now, after years of practice, I find it harder to report what is involved in shifting, although my performance is somewhat smoother.

Yet another example of the distinction between procedural and declarative knowledge, from Posner (1973), involves skilled typing:

> If a skilled typist is asked to type the alphabet, he can do so in a few seconds and with very low probability of error. If, however, he is given a diagram of his keyboard and asked to fill in the letters in alphabet order, he finds the task difficult. It requires several minutes to perform and the likelihood of error is high. Moreover, the typist often reports that he can only obtain the visual location of some letters by trying to type the letter and then determining where his finger would be. These observations indicate that experience with typing produces a motor code which may exist in the absence of any visual code. [p. 25]

This chapter begins with an overview of the stages involved in acquiring a skill. Next, it covers *production systems* as a way of representing the knowledge underlying cognitive skills. Using this form of knowledge representation, we will review some more detailed research and ideas about the acquisition of skills. Finally, we will review the implications of the work on skill acquisition for learning a cognitive skill such as computer programming.

Little systematic research has been done on cognitive procedures and our conclusions as to the nature of cognitive skills must remain tentative. Motor skills, which are strongly related to cognitive skills, have been researched heavily. However, a number of factors are involved with motor skills that are not relevant to cognitive skills. First, because motor skills involve the musculature, their performance depends on peripheral as well as central (brain, mind) characteristics. Thus, the training and building of muscles are often important in the learning of motor skills. A second important difference is that motor performance usually involves the monitoring of a behavior that must go on continuously, whereas most cognitive procedures tend to be symbolic and discrete. This means that important considerations in motor performance are the establishing of exact parameters to guide the action and the constant monitoring of these parameters in case the action gets off course and has to be adjusted. In the domain of cognitive skills, little seems comparable to this need for continuous monitoring. On the other hand, issues do arise in the study of cognitive skills that are not of much concern in understanding motor skills—such as how these skills draw on and use general factual knowledge. Because of these different concerns, only a rather small fraction of the research on the learning of motor skills can be used in understanding the character of cognitive skills.

The Stages of Skill Learning

It is useful to distinguish between three stages in learning a skill (e.g., as is done in Fitts and Posner, 1967). For adults, most skill learning begins with an instructional or study phase in which the learner is either instructed in the task or studies it himself and tries to understand it. The outcome of this *cognitive stage,* as it is called, is an internal and probably declarative representation of what the learner must do. For instance, I memorized the gear locations and the rules for shifting gears. In this stage I was basically learning a set of facts.

The knowledge acquired in the cognitive stage is quite inadequate for skilled performance. There follows what is called the *associative stage.* Two main things happen in this second stage. First, errors in the initial understanding are gradually detected and eliminated. So, I slowly learned to coordinate the release of the clutch in first gear with the application of gas in order not to kill the engine. Second, the connections among the various elements required for successful performance are strengthened. Thus, I no longer had to sit for a few seconds trying to remember how to get to second gear from first. Basically, the outcome of the associative stage is successful procedure for performing the skill. In this stage, the declarative information is transformed into a procedural form. However, it is not always the case that the procedural representation of the knowledge replaces the declarative. Sometimes the two forms of knowledge can coexist side by side, as when we can speak a foreign language fluently and still remember many rules of grammar. However, it is the procedural, not the declarative, knowledge that governs the skilled performance.

The third stage in the standard analysis of skill acquisition is the *autonomous stage.* In this stage, the procedure becomes more and more automated and rapid. No sharp distinction exists between the autonomous and associative stages. The autonomous might be considered an extension of the associa-

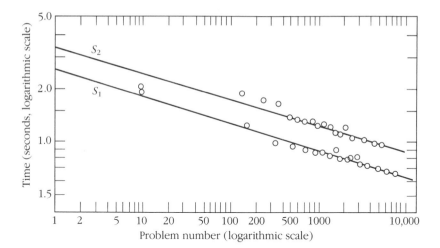

Figure 8-1 *Improvement with practice in time taken to add two numbers. Data are given separately for two subjects. Plot by Crossman (1959) of data by Blackburn (1936). Both time and problem number are plotted on a logarithmic scale.*

tive stage. Because facility in the skill increases, verbal mediation in the performance of the task often disappears at this point. In fact, the ability to verbalize knowledge of the skill can be lost altogether. This was the case with my wife, who had lost ability to say whether she took her foot off the gas during a shift. This autonomous stage appears to extend indefinitely. Throughout it, the skill gradually improves.

Research on the Autonomous Stage

Figure 8-1 is a graph of some data from Blackburn (1936) showing the improvement in performance of mental addition as a function of practice. Blackburn had two subjects, S_1 and S_2, perform 10,000 addition problems! The data are plotted on a log-log scale. That is, the abscissa is the logarithm of practice (number of additions) and the ordinate is the logarithm of time per addition. On this log-log plot, the data for two subjects approximate a straight line. Similar straight-line functions relating practice to performance time have been found over a wide range of tasks. In fact, virtually every study of skill acquisition has found a straight-line function on a log-log plot.* There is usually some limit to how much improvement can be achieved, determined by the capability of musculature involved, age, level of motivation, and so on.

---

*Such a straight line on a log-log plot implies that a power law exists relating time to practice. That is $T = aP^b$ where T is time and P is amount of practice.

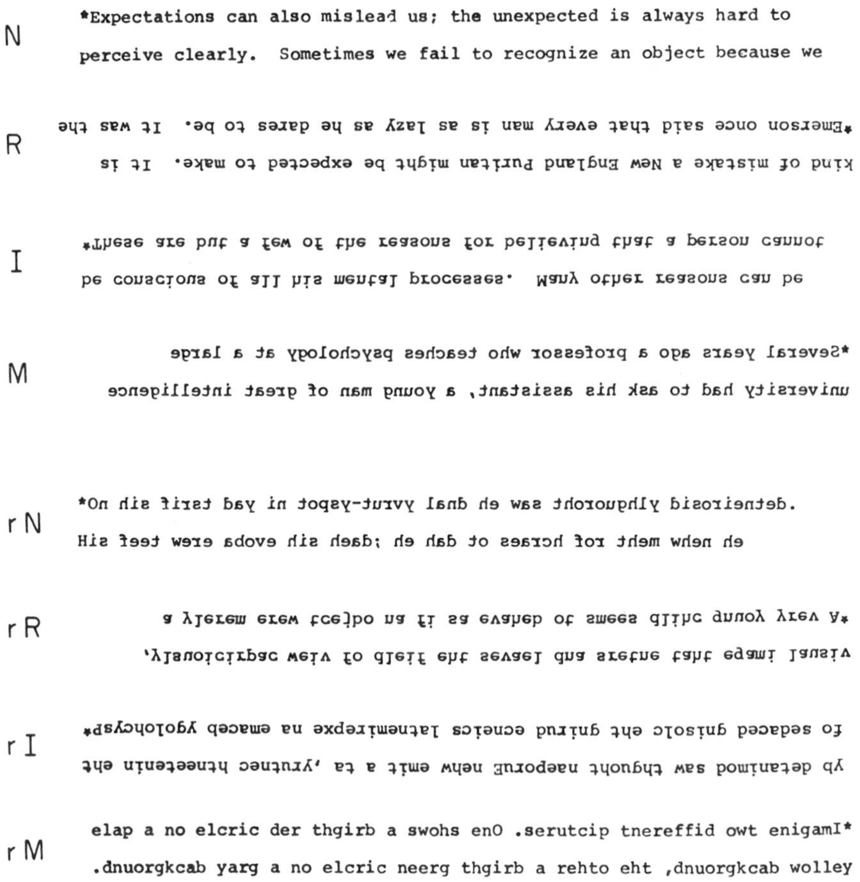

N   *Expectations can also mislead us; the unexpected is always hard to
perceive clearly. Sometimes we fail to recognize an object because we

R   *Emerson once said that every man is as lazy as he dares to be. It was the
kind of mistake a New England Puritan might be expected to make. It is

I   *These are but a few of the reasons for believing that a person cannot
be conscious of all his mental processes. Many other reasons can be

M   *Several years ago a professor who teaches psychology at a large
university had to ask his assistant, a young man of great intelligence

r N   *On his first day in Junior-Varsity Lab he was thoroughly disoriented.
His feet were above his head; he had to force not raise when he

r R   *A very young child seems to devalue as it an odd-job were merely a
visual imagery of very little self seance and arctue that agamt lateral

r I   *to sedaced an ecneics conscious during experience an ecneics lateral psychology
the fourteenth century, at a time when important thought was determined by

r M   *Imagine two different pictures. One shows a bright red circle on a pale
yellow background, the other a bright green circle on a gray background.

Figure 8-2   *Some examples of the spatially transformed texts used by Kolers' studies of the acquisition of reading skills. Kolers measured the effect of practice on reading speed involving these sorts of text transformations. The asterisk indicates the starting point. (From Kolers and Perkins, 1975.)*

There do not appear to be any cognitive limits on the speed with which a skill can be performed. In fact, one famous study followed the improvement of a woman whose job was to roll cigars in a factory. Her speed of cigar making followed this log-log relationship over a period of 10 years. When she finally stopped improving, it was discovered that she had reached the physical limit of the machinery with which she was working!

Kolers (1979) investigated the acquisition of reading skill using materials such as those illustrated in Figure 8-2. The first type of text *(N)* is normal, but the others have been transformed in various ways. In the *R* transformation,

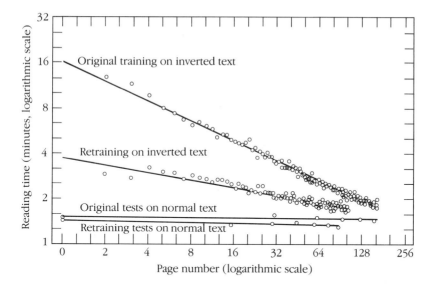

Figure 8-3 *The results for readers in Kolers' reading-skills experiment (1979) on two tests more than a year apart. Subjects were trained with 200 pages of inverted text with occasional pages of normal text interspersed. A year later they were retrained with 100 pages of inverted text, again with normal text occasionally interspersed. The results show the effect of practice on the acquisition of the skill. Both reading time an number of pages practiced are plotted on a logarithmic scale. (From Kolers, 1976. Copyright © by the American Psychological Association. Reprinted by permission.)*

the whole line has been turned upsidedown; in the *I* transformation, each letter has been inverted; in the *M* transformation, the sentence has been set as a mirror image of standard type. The rest are combinations of the several transformations. In one study, Kolers looked at the effect of massive practice on reading inverted *(I)* text. Subjects took more than 16 minutes to read their first page of inverted text as compared with 1.5 minutes for normal text. Following the initial test of reading speed, subjects practiced on 200 pages of inverted text. Figure 8-3 provides a log-log plot of reading time against amount of practice. In this figure, practice is measured in terms of number of pages read. The change in speed with practice is given by the curve labeled *original training on inverted text*. Kolers interspersed a few tests on normal text; data for these are given by the curve labeled *original tests on normal text*. We see the same kind of improvement for inverted text as in the Blackburn study (i.e., a straight-line function on a log-log plot). After reading 200 pages, Koler's subjects were reading at the rate of 1.6 minutes per page, almost at the same rate as subjects reading normal text.

Kolers brought his subjects back a year later and had them read inverted text again. These data are given by the curve in Figure 8-3 labeled *retraining on inverted text*. This time for the first page of the inverted text, subjects took about 3 minutes. Compared with their performance of 16 minutes on their first page a year earlier, subjects were displaying an enormous savings, but it was now taking them almost twice as long to read the text as it did after their 200 pages of training a year earlier. They had clearly forgotten something. As Figure 8-3 illustrates, subjects' improvement on the retraining trials obeyed a log-log relationship between practice and performance as had their original training. Subjects took 100 pages to reach the same level of performance that they had initially reached after 200 pages of training.

Attention and Automatization

The character of a skill seems to change with extensive practice during the autonomous stage. We refer to this change in character by saying a skill has become "automatic." Consider the changes that happen after years of driving a car. Although we once were intently focused on driving, we come to report that we drive long stretches without any conscious awareness. We find ourselves more and more able to carry on other tasks, for example, having a conversation, while we drive. This everyday example illustrates two important features associated with a skill after it has become automatic—it requires less attention and it interferes less with other ongoing behaviors.

Spelke, Hirst, and Neisser (1976) provide an interesting demonstration of how a highly practiced skill ceases to interfere with other ongoing behaviors. Their subjects had to perform two tasks—read a text silently for comprehension while simultaneously copying words dictated by the experimenter. These tasks are extremely difficult to do simultaneously at first. Subjects read much more slowly than normal. However, after six weeks of practice, subjects were reading with normal speed. They had become so skilled that their comprehension scores were the same as for normal reading. For these subjects, reading while copying had become no more difficult than reading while walking. It is of interest that subjects reported no awareness of what it was they were copying. Much as with driving, the subjects lost their awareness of the automated activity.*

We discussed the concepts of attention and automatization in Chapter 2, on perception and attention. There we found that attention becomes less and less important as a perceptual process becomes more automatic. The same conclusion appears to be true for automatization of nonperceptual cognitive skills. However, before considering evidence at higher levels, let us review

---

*When given further training with the intention of remembering what they were transcribing, subjects were also able to recall this information.

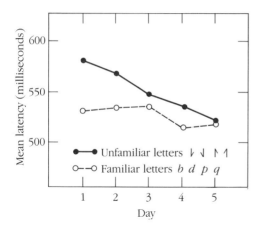

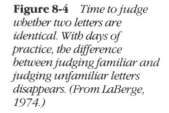

Figure 8-4 *Time to judge whether two letters are identical. With days of practice, the difference between judging familiar and judging unfamiliar letters disappears. (From LaBerge, 1974.)*

the LaBerge experiment that was important to establishing this conclusion for perception. LaBerge contrasted speed of recognizing the familiar letters *p, d, q, b* with the speed of recognizing a new set of characters on which subjects received special training: Ⱶ, ⱶ, Ⱶ, Ⱶ . Subjects' ability to recognize these two character sets was tested in two ways. In one condition, subjects first saw a letter and then, after the letter had been removed from the screen, a second letter below the place where it had appeared. Their task was to determine whether the second letter was the same as the first. Their reaction time was measured from the presentation of the second letter to their response. Under this condition, there was little difference in speed of recognition between the familiar character set and the unfamiliar character set. LaBerge assumed that presentation of the first letter primed the subject to focus attention on the recognition of the second letter. Thus, with attention focused on a particular character, familiarity has little effect.

However, occasionally subjects saw as the second item a pair of characters rather than a single character. In these cases, they might have first seen an *a* and then pairs such as Ⱶ Ⱶ, Ⱶ Ⱶ, *pp,* or *pq.* The character pair always differed from first, priming character. The subjects' task was to indicate whether the two letters in the pair were the same. In this case, the subjects' attention was presumably focused on the *a* and not on the characters to be matched. The results showed a clear disadvantage when the surprise characters where unfamiliar (e.g., Ⱶ Ⱶ) rather than familiar (e.g., *pp*). Subjects practiced making these judgments for 5 days. Figure 8-4 displays subjects' reaction times to make these judgments as a function of practice. As can be seen, the reaction-time difference decreased with practice. Thus, as the recognition of these unfamiliar characters became more automatic, subjects became better able to process the novel characters without the aid of attention.

The Recognition of Symbolic Expressions

I have recently extended the LaBerge result to a more purely cognitive task involving judgments of whether certain symbolic expressions were correctly formed. To take a familiar example, consider arithmetic expressions containing parentheses. Such expressions are formed according to certain well-known rules. Expressions such as

$$(8 + 2); ((3 + 4) \times 5); (8 - (3 - 2)); 7; ((5 \times 3) - (4 + 2))$$

are correctly formed, while others such as

$$8(+ 2); (3 + 4) \times 5); (- 8(3 - 2))$$

are not. One can formalize the rules for arithmetic expressions in the following way:

1. An arithmetic expression can be a number.
2. An arithmetic expression can be of the form: left parenthesis, followed by an arithmetic expression, followed by an operator (+, −, ×, ÷), followed by an arithmetic expression, followed by a right parenthesis.

Statement 2 is called a *recursive definition,* because it defines an arithmetic expression in terms of itself. This definition captures the fact that one arithmetic expression can occur within another and also that such an expression can be indefinitely large.

It is unlikely that most people learn the structure of arithmetic expressions from such a definition. However, such recursive definitions for other kinds of expressions are found in texts on higher mathematics and computer programming. Learning to analyze such expressions is an important component of acquiring expertise in such fields. We conjectured that the factors governing the application of such abstract definitions were similar to the factors governing the perceptual judgments in LaBerge's study. To test this hypothesis, we had subjects learn a new symbol structure, which we called DAX, to distinguish it from the arithmetic expressions, which we call MATH.

1. A DAX can be a number.
2. A DAX can be a letter followed by a left parenthesis, followed by a DAX, followed by another DAX, followed by a right parenthesis.

The following are examples of correctly formed DAXes:

H(42)
G(3K(42))
H(A(12) B(14))

Table 8-1 Example of Positive Trials in Anderson's Experiment on Judging Symbolic Expressions

What Subject Sees	Familiar Expected	Unfamiliar Expected
Subject first sees:	MATH	DAX
Then subject sees:	$((4 + 2) \times 3)$	G(K(42)3)

What Subject Sees	Familiar Surprise	Unfamiliar Surprise
Subject first sees:	DAX	MATH
Then subject sees:	$((4 + 2) \times 3)$	G(K(42)3)

Let us consider the last example, H(A(12) B(14)), and determine why it is a DAX. As definition 1 requires, this expression consists of a letter *H,* followed by a left parenthesis, followed by a DAX, A(12), followed by another DAX, B(14), and followed by a right parenthesis. Both A(12) and B(14) can be shown to be DAXes by similar analysis. For instance, A(12) begins with a letter, followed by a left parenthesis, followed by a number that is a DAX (definition 1), followed by a number that is a DAX, followed by a right parenthesis.

The following are examples of incorrectly formed DAXes:

> H4(2)
> G(3 K (42)
> H(A(1 B) 2(A 2))

In the first example, the 4 lies outside the parenthesis; in the second, a right parenthesis is missing; in the third, numbers appear where letters should be and letters appear where numbers should be.

Subjects were shown MATH and DAX expressions and were instructed to identify them as correctly formed or incorrectly formed. As in the LaBerge experiment, they were warned before a trial as to what judgment they were likely to make—that is, they were either warned that they would see a DAX-like expression and would have to judge its form, or that they would see a MATHlike expression and would have to judge its form. In this experiment, just the word DAX or MATH would appear on the screen as a warning. One quarter of the time, subjects were surprised with a test on an item from the category opposite the one for which they had been warned. That is, on these surprise trials, subjects would be warned to prepare for MATH but would see DAX, or vice versa. Table 8-1 illustrates the different types of positive trials. Of course, negative trials also occurred in which the symbolic expressions were incorrectly formed.

Table 8-2   Time (Seconds) to Judge Whether Familiar and Unfamiliar Expressions
Are Correctly Formed

	Type of Expression		
Type of Trial	Familiar (MATH)	Unfamiliar (DAX)	Deficit Due to Lack of Familiarity
Expected	2.63	2.88	0.25
Surprise	2.95	3.45	0.50
Benefit due to Warning or (Deficit due to Surprise)	0.32	0.57	

This experiment was designed to determine whether the same interaction occurs between practice and attention for such symbolic judgments as for perceptual judgments. The processes that analyze arithmetic expressions should be well practiced and not benefit from attention as much as the newly acquired procedures for analyzing DAX expressions. And if this hypothesis is true, a smaller deficit should occur because of a surprise on a MATH trial (i.e., when the subject is warned with DAX but has to judge an arithmetic expression) than on a DAX trial (i.e., when the subject is warned with MATH but has to judge a DAX expression). Table 8-2 presents the data from this experiment, classified according to whether subjects had to judge MATH (familiar) or DAX (unfamiliar) and according to whether the judgment was expected or unexpected. Note that subjects judged more quickly on MATH than on DAX, which reflects a greater preexperimental familiarity. Subjects were also faster when the type of judgment was expected and they could shift attention ahead of time to the relevant processes. As in the study by LaBerge, warning has the greatest benefit for judgments of the less familiar DAX expressions. The experiment provides a more purely cognitive demonstration of the fact that attention is more important for less practiced skills.

Implications of the Research on Skill Automatization

We have seen that as a skill becomes more practiced and automatic, it requires less and less attention. As a consequence, it can be performed rapidly and reliably should a sudden unexpected need for it arise. Also, because it needs less attention, the automatic skill interferes less with other skills. A person who aspires to be an expert in a particular area must practice the component subskills in that area until they are highly overlearned. For instance, pianists must practice a piece until memory is "in the fingers" and the piece can be performed without thinking about it. Once the mechanics of the piece are automated, the musician is able to concentrate on interpretation. The situation is similar for skilled athletics such as tennis. Players must drill themselves on the details of the subskills until they become automatic. When automaticity is achieved, players can concentrate on the higher level aspects of the game such as strategy. We will return to the importance of practice in the next chapter, on problem solving. An enormous amount of practice seems essential to achieving mastery in areas as diverse as sport, music, chess, and science. No one can enter these fields and become an instant master. Mastery takes concentrated practice for periods on the order of ten years (I. R. Hayes, personal communication).

Representations for Procedural Knowledge

One of the difficulties with developing effective theories of procedural knowledge for cognitive skills has been understanding how complex cognitive skills are represented in the human. Recently, artificial intelligence has made an important contribution to cognitive psychology in developing a set of procedural formalisms that can serve as models for how cognitive skills are represented. One of the possibilities, *production systems,* is described in this section. However, first it will be useful to review a similar proposal for representing procedures, developed earlier in psychology, termed *stimulus–response theory.* This theory is simpler than that of production systems and serves as a good basis for an understanding of the more complex theory.

Stimulus–Response Theory

In psychology, one of the earliest and most enduring ideas about the representation of procedural knowledge has been the *stimulus–response (S–R) bond,* the idea that learning proceeds through the connecting of specific stimuli to specific responses. This analysis has been particularly popular in the analysis of the behavior of nonhuman organisms. Consider one classic research paradigm, which involved teaching rats to run mazes. Figure 8-5A shows the simple T-maze that a rat might be taught to run. The rat is placed in a START box, a door opens to release it into the maze, it runs to the choice point and then chooses to run one way or the other. At the end of the maze it comes to a box that may or may not contain food, and a door drops locking it in the box. This procedure is repeated many times. At first the rat makes its choices haphazardly but, with time it learns that one side contains food. The hungry rat learns to run to the side that contains the food. What is the nature of the knowledge underlying this behavior? We might say the rat has learned

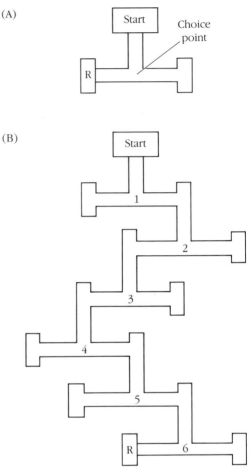

Figure 8-5 *Mazes for running of starved rats. (A) A simple T-maze. (B) A complex T-maze. R stands for the reward at the end of the maze.*

to associate the stimuli in the maze with the response of making the correct (right) turn. We can represent this knowledge as a stimulus–response bond, denoted as

maze

→

turn right,

where by *maze* we mean the sensory stimulation in the maze. By → we mean that the maze leads to the right turning response.

Consider now the more complex maze in Figure 8-5B. This maze offers six choice points: the rat must make a left turn, two rights, two lefts, and a right.

Hungry rats can learn to run this maze too. Here a more complex set of stimulus–response connections are necessary:

S1: first turn

→

turn left

S2: second turn

→

turn right

S3: third turn

→

turn right

S4: fourth turn

→

turn left

S5: fifth turn

→

turn left

S6: sixth turn

→

turn right

where *first turn, second turn,* and so on stand for the stimuli at these locations. It was frequently conjectured that prior responses served as part of the stimuli for the responses following. For instance, the aftertraces of making the first turn would serve as part of the stimulus for the second turn in the stimulus–response bond S2. In this way, subjects could learn to link together a long series of responses. Each response in the chain would serve as part of the stimulus for the next response.

Whether this stimulus–response analysis is accurate has long been in dispute in psychology. One argument against stimulus–response theory has been the claim that subjects are often not responding to external stimuli but rather are responding to internal, mental stimuli. Traditionally, stimulus–response theories have insisted that the controlling stimuli for behavior be external, perceivable conditions or events. There have been numerous demonstrations (e.g., Tolman, 1948) and arguments to the effect that rats learn cognitive "maps" for these mazes and use these mental structures to guide their behaviors. Such maps resemble the survey maps discussed in Chapter 3 in that they enable the rats to work from an internal representation of the general spatial layout.

The idea of simple stimulus–response connections has been even more problematical for human behavior. Lashley (1951) has pointed out that, in very skilled human behaviors (e.g., the performance by a pianist), the interval between successive responses seems too brief for each response to be occurring in response to the aftertrace of the previous one. Rather, the pianist seems to execute a sequence of responses as a unit. Also, for many cognitive skills (e.g., writing a computer program or doing mental arithmetic), humans seem to be responding to activated memories and not to external stimuli in the environment. These memories are often not even related to environmental events, but rather involve abstract knowledge.

Although there are exceptions, traditionally stimulus–response theories treat organisms as responding to a single stimulus at a time. Another criticism of stimulus–response theories, then, is that humans often respond to a *configuration* of events or stimuli rather than to any single stimulus. This is probably true even for rats in the maze. If we investigated what *second turn* really represented for the rat, we would probably find that it was a configuration of stimuli such as color, smell, texture of the maze, plus some memory for past body movements. Any of these stimuli alone would not be able to evoke the response.

Yet another criticism of stimulus–response theory is that S–R bonds are very *specific,* whereas our cognitive skills seem quite *general.* For instance, my skill at driving a stick-shift car will generalize to any three-speed shift. As another example of the generality of cognitive skills, consider the subjects who learned to recognize DAX in the experiment described in the preceding section. They acquired a skill that permitted recognition of a great many stimuli as DAXES. As a third example, consider language. In this domain, the evidence that our cognitive skills are general seems particularly compelling. We appear to be able to use our language skills to understand and generate a great many novel utterances. For instance, when I heard a robot in *Star Wars* referred to as a *droid,* I knew what the plural form of this would be—*droids.* This is an instance of a general cognitive rule—for pluralization—applying to the special case of a new word, *droid.*

In an extension of the concept of a stimulus–response connection called a *production,* the deficiencies of stimulus–response bonds are avoided. The notion of a production, as applied to psychology, was developed at Carnegie–Mellon University by Allen Newell and Herbert Simon. The notion of production systems has had a long history in mathematics and computer science, but has been applied extensively in psychology only since 1970. It is certainly not a universally accepted way of representing procedural knowledge. However, it is the most extensively developed and adequate representation of human cognitive skills.

Production Systems

Let us consider what a *production* in a system representing a cognitive skill looks like. The following might be the production to govern the shift from first to second gear in a three-speed car (an explanation of its structure follows the display):

> IF a car is in first gear
> and the car is going faster than 10 miles an hour
> and there is a clutch
> and there is a stick
> THEN depress the clutch
> and move the stick to the upper right position
> and release the clutch

Each production has a *condition* and an *action.* The condition contains a set of clauses preceded by IF, and the action a set of clauses preceded by THEN. In the production above, the condition has four clauses. The four clauses test for a *configuration* of events: (1) the car is in first gear; (2) the car is going faster than 10 miles an hour; (3) the clutch has been identified; (4) the stick shift has been identified. Their ability to test for a configuration of events is one important way in which productions differ from stimulus–response bonds. Note also that it is possible to perform a sequence of actions rather than a single action by following this production. This feature addresses Lashley's remarks about the unitizing of behavioral sequences.

Note that such productions are quite general. The production above will apply to any three-speed stick shift, not just to a particular car. Such generality of the condition is an important feature of productions and represents an important improvement over the concept of stimulus–response bonds. As another example, consider the following production, which encodes one of the rules for pluralization:

> IF the goal is to generate a plural of a noun
> and the noun ends in a hard consonant
> THEN generate the noun + *s*

This rule generates the plural for any noun that obeys the +*s* pluralization rule. Note that the condition for this production refers to an internal goal (the goal is to generate the plural of a noun) and some internal knowledge (the noun ends in a hard consonant). This characteristic illustrates the fact that production systems can refer to mental objects as well as external objects.

We noted that stimulus–response theories have four deficits: (1) stimulus–response bonds respond only to external, and not to mental, events; (2) they cannot treat sequences of responses as a unit; (3) they cannot respond to a configuration of features; and (4) they are not general. We have seen that productions remedy these deficits. Productions have proved to be very useful for modeling many aspects of human cognition. Learning how to interpret them is important. As an example of the application of productions to a very different cognitive domain, consider Gordon Bower's (1977) somewhat tongue-in-cheek use of them to model some of the maladaptive thinking associated with various clinical syndromes:

Paranoid-aggressive productions

IF   a person compliments me
THEN   the person is manipulating me

IF   a person is manipulating me
         and the person is smaller than me
THEN   punch the person

IF   a person is manipulating me
         and the person is bigger than me
THEN   insult the person

Depressive productions

IF   a person compliments me
THEN   the person pities me

IF   a person pities me
THEN   I am unlovable

IF   I am unlovable
THEN   I do not deserve to live
           and feel sad

The first set of productions models suspicious or paranoid inferences, in which a compliment is interpreted as an attempt to manipulate and manipulations are answered with a punch or an insult (depending on the size of the manipulator). The second set of productions models an aspect of depressive thinking called *distortion,* whereby a compliment is interpreted as insincere and thus an indication that the complimenter pities the individual. Notice how the sequence of productions leads the depressed thinker from a compliment to the interpretation that he is being pitied, hence that he is an unlovable person, and finally that he does not deserve to live. As Bower notes, "These productions would move the stream of thought along automatically to its inexorable, morbid conclusion" (p. 7).

The clauses that make up conditions and actions of productions can be interpreted as referring to propositional-network structure in memory. Thus, for instance, consider the following production for adding two digits. It is intended to model behavior in response to very simple problems such as 7 + 4.

IF   the goal is to add two digits
         and a number is the sum of the two digits
THEN   the goal is to write out the number.

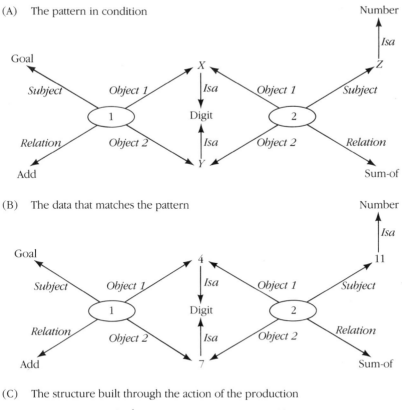

(A)   The pattern in condition

(B)   The data that matches the pattern

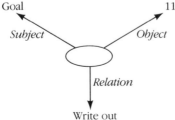

(C)   The structure built through the action of the production

Figure 8-6   *Network structures involved in the production on p. 240. (A) The general network pattern being referred to. (B) A propositional network that matches the pattern. (C) The structure added to memory as a function of the production applying to the network in B.*

Figure 8-6A illustrates the pattern described by the two clauses in the production's condition. The first clause is represented by proposition 1: the goal is to add X and Y where X and Y are digits (encoded by the *Isa* links). The second clause is represented by proposition 2 in Figure 8-6A: Z is the sum of X and Y

where Z is a number. The production is looking for a pattern in memory such as that represented in Figure 8-6A. Figure 8-6B illustrates a piece of long-term memory that will match this pattern. The first clause in the pattern will match the goal of adding 4 and 7. The second clause will match the fact that 11 is the sum of 4 and 7. In matching this pattern, 4 serves the function of the first digit X, 7 serves the function of the second digit Y, and 11 serves the function of the number Z. Productions can build new structure in memory through their actions. The action of this production calls for a memory structure to be built of the form *the goal is to write out the sum.* Figure 8-6C illustrates the network structure that the production would add to memory if its condition in A matched the network structure in B. This new structure records that the new goal is to write out the sum 11.

We could represent productions in terms of their network patterns and actions. However, they are rendered in pseudo English to make them more readable. You should try studying productions until you feel you can understand them. They will come up many times in subsequent chapters as models for cognitive skills. However, you should not feel responsible for actually being able to write productions, as you should for propositional networks. Information adequate for creating your own production systems can be found in the references at the end of this chapter. However, you should understand how production systems work.

A Production Set for Adding

Productions usually operate in sets, in which each production of the set performs part of the behavior for a larger task. Table 8-3 gives part of a production system for doing mental addition. To facilitate its interpretation, I have included with each production an explanation of what it does. It is very hard to understand such a set of productions simply by reading through them. It is easier to understand a set of productions by seeing how they apply to a problem. So, let us consider how this production set would apply to the following addition problem:

$$\begin{array}{r} 32 \\ +18 \\ \hline \end{array}$$

We assume this problem is encoded by a set of propositions that may be rendered approximately in this way:

> The goal is to add number1 and number2
> Number1 begins with 3
> The 3 is followed by a 2
> Number1 ends with this 2
> Number2 begins with a 1
> The 1 is followed by an 8
> Number2 ends with this 8

Table 8-3   A Set of Productions for Adding Two Numbers

Productions	Explanations

P1

IF the goal is to add two numbers and the first number ends with a digit and the second number ends with a digit THEN the subgoal is to then add the two digits	This production responds to the main goal of adding two numbers. It sets as the subgoal to add the digits in the first column.

P2

IF the subgoal is to add two digits and a number is the sum of the two digits THEN the subgoal is to put out the number	This production finds the sum of two digits and sets the subgoal to put out this sum.

P3

IF the subgoal is to put out a number and there is a carry flag and a second number is the sum of the first number plus 1 THEN the subgoal is to put out the second number and remove the carry flag	When there is a carry, this production adds 1 to the number to be put out and removes the carry flag.

P4

IF the subgoal is to put out a number and there is no carry flag and the number is less than 10 THEN write the number and the subgoal is to do the two digits in the next column	When there is no carry and the number is less than 10, this production writes the number out.

P5

IF the subgoal is to put out a number and there is no carry flag and the number is the sum of 10 plus a digit THEN write the digit and set the carry flag and the subgoal is to do the digits in the next column.	When there is no carry and the number is 10 or greater, this production writes out the difference between the number and 10 and sets the carry flag.

P6

IF the subgoal is to do the digits in the next column and the first number contains a digit in that column and the second number contains a digit in that column THEN the subgoal is to add the two digits	This production shifts attention to the digits in the next column.

P7

IF the subgoal is to do the digits in the next column and the first number does not contain a digit in that column and the second number does not contain a digit in that column THEN the problem is finished	This production recognizes when the last column of digits has been processed and the problem is at an end.

The condition P1 in Table 8-3 is satisfied when the following correspondences are made between elements of the condition and propositions in the data base above:

The goal is to add two numbers = the goal is to add number1 and number2

The first number ends with a digit = number1 ends with a 2

The second number ends with a digit = number2 ends with an 8

The action of P1, *the subgoal is to add the two digits,* becomes, given that 2 and 8 are the two digits matched in the condition, an instruction to add to memory the proposition, *the subgoal is to add 2 and 8.* By adding this proposition to memory, production P1 is able to invoke production P2 that will actually add 2 and 8.

Next, P2 applies. As a consequence of the execution of P1, the first element of the condition of P2 is satisfied:

The subgoal is to add two digits = the subgoal is to add 2 and 8

The remaining condition of P2 matches a proposition in memory about integer addition:

A number is the sum of the two digits = 10 is the sum of 2 and 8

The action of P2 adds to the data base *the subgoal is to put out 10.*
    The next production to apply is P5, whose condition is matched as follows:

The subgoal is to put out a number = The subgoal is to put out 10

The number is the sum of 10 plus a digit = 10 is the sum of 10 plus 0

The condition of P5 also contains a test that the carry flag has not been set. The action of P5 writes out the digit (which is 0 in this case) as part of the answer, sets a carry flag, and places a proposition in memory: *the subgoal is to do the digits in the next column* (to the effect that this column is finished).

It is worth considering why P5 and not others applies here. Production P3 failed because there is no carry. Production P4 failed because the number to put out was not less than 10. One might wonder why P1 or P2 do not apply again, since their conditions were satisfied once by memory elements that have not been changed. They cannot apply again because production systems do not allow production conditions to match twice to exactly the same database propositions. This constraint serves to prevent unwanted repetitions of the same productions.

Production P6 applies next, adding *the subgoal is to add 3 and 1* to the data base so that the next (10s) column can be added. Production P2 next applies, finds the sum, and adds *the subgoal is to put out 4* to the data base. Production P3 then adds 1 to 4 because of the carry. Production P4 will then apply and write out the second digit of the answer, 5. P7 applies last, noting that the problem is finished.

The similarities between this production system and the S–R system described earlier should be apparent. Note that a chain of productions—P1, P2, P5, P6, P2, P3, P4, and P7—was evoked here just as a chain of S–R bonds was evoked for the rat running the maze. As in the S–R case, the action of one production served to provide part of the stimulus for the next production. Consider, however, the important differences: the production system was responding to abstract propositions stored in memory rather than to external stimuli. The productions are general rather than specific to a particular situation and can apply to many memory elements. Finally, the productions respond to configurations of propositions and not to single features of the environment.

The reader is invited to simulate the operation of this production system on the following problem as an exercise:

$$\begin{array}{r} 495 \\ + 482 \\ \hline \end{array}$$

Can you specify the order of the productions that apply?

The Dynamics of Procedures

Having presented this formalism for representing procedural knowledge, we will now turn to considering in more detail the various *dynamic* properties of procedures. The term *dynamic* refers to the properties that determine how productions are acquired, retained, and retrieved. In this section, then, we will review what is known about the acquisition, retention, and retrieval of procedures. This section does for procedural knowledge what Chapters 6 and 7 did for declarative knowledge.

Short-Term Memory for Procedures

It appears that there is a short-term memory for the productions underlying a procedure just as there is a short-term memory for propositions. When a procedure is in short-term memory, it can be applied more reliably and more rapidly than when it must be retrieved from a longer term store. A number of experiments on motor skills have shown that a short-term component exists in the retention of procedures. Adams and Dijkstra (1966) used a task in which a subject had to learn to move a slide to a prescribed location on a metal bar. Subjects did not actually see the target position. Rather, they moved the slide until it came to a stop. Then subjects returned their slides to the start position and the retention interval began. After the retention interval, their task was to reproduce the movement with nothing to stop the slide at the

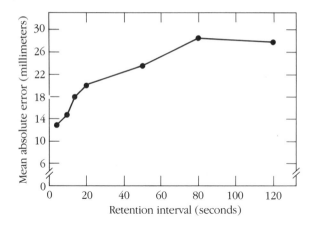

Figure 8-7 *Accuracy in performance of a simple linear motor response as a function of retention interval. Accuracy deteriorates as the short-term memory for the response is lost. (From Adams and Dijkstra, 1966. Copyright © 1966 by the American Psychological Association. Reprinted by permission.)*

correct position. Figure 8-7 maps the magnitude of subjects' error as a function of retention interval. This figure is very similar to figures showing the effects of delay on short-term retention of verbal material (such as Figure 6-2 in Chapter 6). As in the case of verbal retention, subjects showed an initial rapid loss of accuracy in performing the motor movement. This suggests that, as in the case of verbal retention, there is a short-term memory for a skill, and performance of the skill is best while it is still in short-term memory.

The Transfer of Practice

We saw in the declarative domain (Chapter 6) that one fact could interfere with another. Can one procedure also interfere with another? Unfortunately, no work with cognitive procedures has been done on this issue, and we must look once again to the research on motor skills. Lewis, McAllister, and Adams (1951) have shown for motor skills that procedures do interfere with each other. Their subjects used what is called a Modified Mashburn Apparatus, which was used for pilot selection in World War II. This apparatus simulates an aircraft, containing a stick about the size of an airplane's for two-dimensional manipulation and a rudder bar for one-dimensional foot operation.

A set of display lights defined the amount that the stick and rudder were to be moved. After they spent 30 trials learning to make the prescribed movement, subjects were switched to a second task, during which movements were required that were antagonistic to original movement. This second task, or *interpolated learning,* involved 10, 20, 30, or 50 trials. Then subjects were transferred back to the original task. It was found that their performance of the original skill had deteriorated and that this deterioration increased with an increase in interpolated learning. Thus, interfering effects occur with the learning of procedures like those found for declarative facts.

Such interference, or *negative transfer* as it is often called, among skills can be quite significant when a skill is placed in direct conflict with a well-engrained old skill. For instance, Conrad and Hull (1968) considered two spatial layouts for labeling numbers on machine keys. One is used with adding machines and the other with touch telephones:

Adding Machine	Telephone
7 8 9	1 2 3
4 5 6	4 5 6
1 2 3	7 8 9
0	0

The second layout corresponds to the standard left-to-right, top-down manner of reading. That is, if the telephone array is read left-to-right and top-down it is in the order 1–2–3–4–5–6–7–8–9, whereas the adding machine would come out in the order 7–8–9–4–5–6–1–2–3. The telephone array also incorporates the common practices of ordering 0 after 9 (e.g., on typewriters) and starting the series with 1. Conrad and Hull found that the telephone layout resulted in fewer errors in the keying of eight-digit sequences. Thus, learning to key numbers is easier on a telephone than on an adding machine because the numbers are ordered on the telephone in the generally practiced order, while this is not the case for the adding machine. Thus, in the adding machine case, there is negative transfer from prior habits.

While negative interference can be obtained, the more frequent outcome is beneficial transfer from one skill to another. For instance, one study investigated the transfer for three pairs of skills involved in sports: (1) from a badminton volley to a tennis volley; (2) from a volleyball tap for accuracy to a basketball tap for accuracy; and (3) from a track starting stance to a football starting stance. In each case, it was found that learning the first skill benefited subjects in learning the second. This benefit probably occurs because the skills require that many of the same components be learned. It is more common for two skills to share components than for them to involve antagonistic actions. Therefore, positive transfer is more common than negative transfer.

Generalization and Discrimination

Procedures must be capable of dealing with new examples. The process of extending a procedure to apply to new examples is called *generalization.* Generalization is particularly important in understanding language acquisition. For instance, children learn rules for pluralizing particular nouns or signaling the past tense of certain verbs. Later, they generalize the pluralization rule (i.e., add *s*) to nouns they have never encountered in the plural, and they generalize the past-tense rule (i.e., add *ed*) to verbs they have never encountered. In fact, they overgeneralize and generate words such as *mans* and *doed*. Thus, an inflectional procedure that develops from training on certain words generalizes to new words.

Generalization of procedures occurs in many situations besides language. Consider motor skills involved in a sport. For instance, by practicing shooting baskets from a number of positions, players improve their ability to shoot baskets from other positions. The acquisition of social skills offers another familiar example. Many social skills are learned and generalized: how to interact with students, teachers, deans, bosses, employees, lovers, children, door-to-door salesmen, and so on. It would be disastrous if we had to relearn our social skills for each new person we met.

There is some evidence that skills learned under variable circumstances generalize better to new situations than do skills learned in very rigid situations. For instance, Duncan (1958) studied lever positioning to show the effect of variability in the training situation. He varied the number of ways the positioning was performed but kept constant the total number of trials. For Duncan's task, the amount of transfer to a new version of the task was a function of the amount of variability in the original learning. Thus, it seems that ability to generalize a skill depends on practicing that skill in a wide range of situations.

Because people overgeneralize skills, a complementary process, *discrimination,* is needed. Discrimination restricts the range of situations and objects to which procedures may apply. Again, examples of discrimination can be seen quite clearly in language acquisition. In acquiring their language, children have to learn to deal with exceptions to rules—for example, the plural of *man* is *men.* Children can be observed to go through a period in which they apply a rule too generally—such as generating *mans*—and later to learn the exception to this rule. In languages that have noun declensions, a slightly different form of discrimination occurs. In such languages, nouns in different declensions are inflected for plural in different ways. Children begin by thinking that all nouns obey a single pluralization rule (taken from one of the dominant declensions) and only later discriminate a different rule for each declension (Slobin, 1973).

There are also good examples of discrimination that do not involve language. One important set of examples has to do with problem-solving skills. We are trained in many very general procedures for solving problems—for instance, integrating by parts in calculus. One of the skills in problem solving is knowing in which situations trying to apply such a procedure is appropriate. For instance, integration by parts is likely to be useful if the integral involves an exponential. Part of the skill in problem solving involves knowing when it is appropriate to apply a procedure.

We can conceive of discrimination and generalization in terms of operations on the productions that underlie procedures. Recall that productions consist of conditions and actions, where the conditions specify certain properties that should be true of the current information. If the properties specified in a condition are satisfied, then the production can be executed. Thus, it is the condition that controls whether or not a production applies in a particular situation. By making the condition of the production more general, we can generalize the procedure, and by making the condition more specific we can force discrimination into the procedure.

Consider a particular production for generating the nominative plural of *farmer* in Latin, a language with a strong declensional structure:

> IF   the goal is to generate the plural of *agricol*
> THEN   say *agricolae*

As another example, consider a pluralization rule for girl:

> IF   the goal is to generate the plural of *puell*
> THEN   say *puellae*

On the basis of individual productions like these, it is possible to create a new rule for a more general rule for pluralization:

> IF   the goal is to generate the plural of a word
> THEN   say the word plus *ae*

Note that this rule has been generalized over the individual words *agricol* and *puell* and now applies to any noun. However, it is only correct for first-declension nouns in Latin. It would, for instance, give the incorrect plural of horses, *equae*—rather than the correct *equi*. We can make the rule more specific and force it to apply only to first-declension nouns by making its condition more discriminate:

> IF   the goal is to generate the plural of a word
>   and the word is first declension
> THEN   say the word plus *ae*

The extra clause in the condition constrains this production to first-declension nouns.

Applications: Learning Cognitive Skills

Although research on cognitive skills is just beginning, the potential implications for skill learning appear to be very significant. Consider the implications for learning how to program computers. As we all know, computers are becoming a more and more integral part of our lives. Soon, computer programming may be as important and common a skill as typing—it will be very widespread, the degree of proficiency in it will vary greatly, and the skill itself will be of great aid in everyday life. Many readers of this text will not yet have had a programming course, so some of the concepts may be unfamiliar, but the basic implications about skill learning should be clear. Despite this potential unfamiliarity, the ideas examined here will be important, since most of us, whatever our exposure to computer programming so far, will find ourselves learning new computer or programming skills in the next ten years.

While the points to follow should be clear in any case, it would be helpful to say a few words about what the skill of computer programming involves. Programming involves preparing a set of instructions that tell the computer what it must do in a language it can understand. Programming is hard because (1) the programming languages, unlike English, are hard to work in and force one to be explicit; (2) it is often hard to think of a set of instructions that will solve a given problem; and (3) it is important to create a set of instructions which will enable the computer to perform the task efficiently.

In the following recommendations for teaching and learning programming, two types of extrapolations are employed. First, research on motor skills is extrapolated to cognitive skills. Second, research on cognitive facts is extrapolated to applications for cognitive skills. Because they rest on inferences rather than proven facts, the suggestions that follow are proposed tentatively.

The Spacing of Practice

We discussed in Chapter 7 the powerful effects that spaced study can have on the learning of verbal materials. Spacing appears to have even more profound effects on skill learning. The inefficiency of massed practice was shown in one study involving intensive training in Morse code during World War II (reported in Bray, 1948). Students were found to learn as rapidly with 4 hours a day practice as with 7 hours of practice. The 7-hour subjects were effectively wasting the 3 extra hours of practice crammed into the day.

In discussing effects of spacing, it is useful to distinguish between two issues involving practice: practicing one aspect of programming rather than other aspects and practicing programming rather than doing other things. Concentrated practice with respect to the first issue involves doing the same type of problem over and over again—for instance, when a person writes a series of programs all involving a loop* to calculate a sum. Because in massed practice the skills involved in constructing the loop are being associated to similar contextual cues, the skills will show less long-term benefit of the practice. This point has interesting implications for textbook writers, since the standard strategy in textbooks is to place similar exercises together. A certain amount of repetition may be beneficial in allowing the student to apply a lesson

---

*A loop is a programming mechanism for performing the same operation over and over again.

learned in one problem to the next. However, after the lesson is learned, it is unlikely that further repetition yields much benefit. In keeping with this analysis, Gay (1973) has shown that spaced practice of algebra rules results in better retention than massed practice.

The second kind of practice concerns work on a general topic, such as programming. Is it better to concentrate the study of programming into one long session or to study programming in short intervals interspersed with study sessions on other topics, such as history? In the literature on perceptual-motor skills, there is evidence that short, spaced periods of practice almost universally lead to much better learning and performance than long, concentrated practice. Therefore, spending too much time on programming at any one stretch is probably unwise. Many people find computer programming a particularly seductive activity and once into it will spend long hours at it. Therefore, it is important to keep in mind the advantage of spaced practice.

However, computer programming serves as a good example in arguing against extreme spacing of effort. An individual who only spent 5 minutes at a time on programming would probably never learn much and would probably never succeed in writing a program. Programming is a complex skill and a good deal of time must be spent in a session to enable all the relevant factors to be activated in memory and brought to bear in the writing of the program. Quitting at certain points in writing a program would be disastrous, because recreating the situation leading up to any particular point in the programming sequence could take half an hour. Although the issue requires further research, it appears that, either in learning to program or in programming itself, one should work for no longer than a couple of hours, if possible, but in that time should try to complete a well-defined problem.

Part Versus Whole Learning

Students working to acquire a skill frequently ask whether it is better to try to learn and practice the whole skill or to learn and practice parts of the skill, putting them together later. In the area of motor skills, the answer to this question depends on whether the parts to be practiced are independent. If they are, it is better to practice the parts separately. For instance, Koch (1923) taught subjects a rather bizarre skill—to type finger exercises using two typewriters simultaneously, one hand per typewriter. There were two groups of subjects—those who practiced each hand first and those who tried immediately to use both hands. The group that started by practicing with separate hands were better when they switched to both hands than the group that started with both hands, and they maintained this superiority with further practice. In contrast, experiments on tasks that require careful integration show superiority for whole learning over part learning. For example, in playing the piano it is better to try to learn the whole sequence rather than trying to integrate subsections of a sequence.

Computer programming, fortunately, seems to be an ideal domain for practicing subcomponents of a complex skill, because good programming languages and good programming style leads to the isolation of independent pieces of a program to do independent subtasks. Part training seems to be adopted in most texts on programming. The attempt is made to focus instruction on specific subskills—for instance, one lesson will be on performing arithmetic operations and a separate lesson on doing input and output of information.

Automatizing Subskills

Computer programs tend to be hierarchical in structure, with components embedded within components. For instance, within a program to do accounting operations for a business there may be embedded a sorting operation, within the sorting operation a looping operation, and within a looping operation a series of arithmetic operations. In trying to design an accounting program, programmers will have more capacity to work at the problems specific to accounting programs if their programming of the subcomponents is automatic. This rather intuitive prediction follows from the research on the relationship between attention and automaticity. The research explains, at least in part, why programmers become more sophisticated by sheer practice without further study of programming techniques. That is, as the subcomponents of a programming procedure become more automatic, programmers are able to focus more attention on higher level problems.

Transfer

As we noted, the transfer among related skills is mostly positive. Only in cases of rather direct incompatibility is any interference encountered. This situation implies that a mathematics education is good preparation for computer programming, since mathematics involves many subskills also needed in programming. Indeed, a great many undergraduate whizzes in computer science were math whizzes in high school, and a large number of graduate students in computer science have undergraduate degrees in mathematics.

Some notorious cases do exist of negative transfer or interference among different programming languages. For instance, knowing the primitive GOTO control structure of FORTRAN makes it harder to learn the more sophisticated *if-then-else* structure characteristic of other languages. Thus, students are well advised to choose their first programming language with an eye to the types of languages they will eventually want to use. The first language should be compatible with these.

Designers of programming languages should consider more carefully potential incompatibility with existing skills. For instance, in a number of programming languages all counting operations start with 0, whereas typically in other real-life situations counting begins with 1. This discrepancy probably accounts for more errors by beginners in these languages than anything else.

Knowledge of Results

Subjects learn a skill more rapidly if they receive feedback as to whether their skill attempts are correct and how they are in error (for a review of research on feedback see Bilodeau, 1969). The amount of time between the action and the feedback is important, an expected relationship, since for feedback to be useful, the action must be active in memory. After a delay, it may be hard to recall just what led to incorrect action. Computer systems that interact directly with their users are making it possible to provide more rapid feedback on one's programming efforts. In older computer systems, one would submit a program and wait hours or days before getting feedback on the correctness of the program. Now it is often possible to see a program run immediately.

Also important is the delay between the feedback and the next attempt, which utilizes the feedback. This interval is important probably because much of the feedback can be utilized only when the skill is applied. Therefore, it is important that the next skill application occur while the feedback is still in active memory. This point is typically ignored in the structuring of courses on computer programming. Usually students turn to other courses after getting back their graded assignments, but it is just at this point that they should be required to apply the lessons learned. This is a case where too much spacing can be counterproductive.

Internalizing an Ideal Model

Many skills do not require external feedback for their development. If the learners have a good model of what the skilled behavior should be like, they can use this model to correct their attempts. For instance, in learning to shoot baskets, a learner can perform a great deal of self-correction by noting how the ball misses the basket. In some tasks, much can be learned by observing experts perform the skill. In so doing, observers are able to internalize criteria by which to monitor their own attempts to perform the skill.

Keele (1973) cites several examples in support of the importance of an internalized model. One example involves the development of birdsong in some species such as white-crowned sparrows. It has been shown that in this species birdsong will not develop in individual birds that are never exposed to adult birdsong. On the other hand, if the bird is exposed to adult song during its first few months and then reared in isolation, the adult birdsong pattern will develop naturally when the birds are about nine months old. It seems that the early exposure enables the bird to encode the song, thus supplying it with an internal model against which it can compare and correct its own productions.

Another example cited by Keele is Pronko's (1969) description of the Suzuki method of teaching children to play the violin. Starting at infancy, the children hear the same selections over and over again until they are extremely well-encoded. When the children are old enough to have sufficient motor coordination, they are given a violin and given lessons at playing the encoded music. The children can then compare their produced sounds with their internalized models for the music and thus more easily make corrections. The results of this procedure appear to be amazingly successful.

Students of computer programming are particularly likely to benefit from the study of ideal programs and perhaps the memorizing of these programs. It is easy for novice programmers to develop sloppy habits if left to create their own programs. More meticulous habits might develop if novices had programs in memory against which to compare and correct their attempts. Admittedly, the generalization from birdsongs and the Suzuki method to computer programming represents quite a leap. And the correspondence is not perfect, since in the programming situation we would want students to use the memorized programs as analogs for creating new programs rather than in a verbatim fashion.

Remarks and Suggested Readings

Production systems are a popular representational medium for procedural knowledge. For further discussion of production systems and their relationship to stimulus–response theory, see Anderson (1976). Discussions of production systems are to be found in Newell and Simon (1972), Newell (1973), and Rychener and Newell (1978). Some people appear to view production systems as in competition with another kind of theoretical formalisms, variously called schemas, frames, and scripts. In Chapter 5, we reviewed empirical research relevant to these formalisms, which represent procedural and declarative knowledge in larger packets. Sources for this work include Bobrow and Winograd (1977), Minsky (1975), Rumelhart and Ortony (1976), and Schank and Abelson (1977). It is my personal view that the production system and schema formulations should not be viewed as competitors. Production systems are models for skills while schemas are patterns for recognizing recurring sets of features.

As indicated in this chapter, considerable research has been done on motor skills. Reviews of this research can be found in Fitts and Posner (1967), Keele (1973), Keele and Summers (1976), Pew (1974), and Welford (1968). These sources also review some of the research on cognitive skills. Work on acquisition of cognitive skills seems to be receiving a renewed interest. See Rumelhart and Norman (1977) for one perspective on the issues that need to be addressed in research on skill acquisition. See Anderson, Kline, and Beasley (1978) for another proposal.

Part IV

PROBLEM SOLVING AND REASONING

Chapter 9

Problem Solving

Summary

1. Problem solving is defined as any *goal-directed sequence of cognitive operations*. Problem solving that requires the development of new procedures is called *creative problem solving;* problem solving that uses existing procedures is called *routine problem solving.*

2. Problem solving can be conceived of as a search of a *problem space.* The problem space consists of *physical states* or *knowledge states,* achievable by the problem solver. The problem-solving task involves finding a sequence of operations, or *operators.* that transforms the *initial state* into a *goal state,* in which the goal is satisfied.

3. Subjects often choose operators that will transform the current state into a state more similar to the goal state. In such a case similarity is a *heuristic.* A heuristic is a "rule of thumb" that often but not always facilitates solution.

4. *Means-ends analysis* is one way of guiding the search of a problem space. It involves selecting operators to reduce the differences between the current state and the goal state as well as transforming the current state so that needed operators can apply.

5. Other ways of guiding a search through problem space include working backward from the goal state and planning by solving a simpler problem.

6. The key to solving problems in many cases is to represent them in a way that the needed operators can apply. *Functional fixedness* is the failure to solve problems due to an inability to represent the objects in one's environment in novel ways.

7. The amount and type of knowledge available for solving a problem will vary with one's problem-solving experience. By increasing the availability of relevant knowledge, one can facilitate problem solving; conversely, one can inhibit problem solving by increasing the availability of irrelevant knowledge. Effects of knowledge availability on problem solving are referred to as *set effects*.

8. An individual becomes expert in many problem-solving domains by making routine through practice many tasks that initially require creative problem solving. Practice can also improve creative problem solving.

A Definition

I once put this advertisement out:

Wanted: Secretary. Skilled typist. Must be good at solving office problems.

An applicant called on me.

HE: I am especially good at solving problems in typing.

ME: What do you mean, "problems in typing"?

HE: I often have a great problem in finding the right key to hit but I can always solve the problem by hunting around.

Forgetting the question of what this fellow was doing applying for the job, we can wonder about his use of the term *problem solving*. In fact, it is quite difficult to specify just what is meant by problem solving. Let us consider some examples of mental activities that are not problem-solving activities, decide why these are not instances of problem solving, and by this means build up a set of features to define problem solving.

1. *Goal-Directedness.* Daydreaming is generally not problem solving, although it can be as mentally complex as many activities that are considered problem solving. What daydreaming lacks is any explicit goal. So, one important feature of problem-solving activity is that it be *goal-directed.*

2. *Sequence of Operations.* Recalling a friend's phone number is not normally an instance of problem solving, even though it is directed to the goal of recalling that number. The problem with this sort of recall is that the process is too simple; only a single retrieval from memory is required. A behavior must involve a sequence of mental steps in order to qualify as problem solving. Thus, a second feature of problem solving is that it should involve a *sequence of operations.*

3. *Cognitive Operations.* Knotting a tie when you already know how do to it is not generally considered an instance of problem solving, even though it involves a sequence of steps with a clear goal. Dealing out a deck of cards in bridge is again not generally an instance of problem solving. These examples are basically physical activities without any important cognitive component. A third criterion for problem solving, then, is that the goal-directed activity depend on *cognitive operations.* The job applicant quoted above was using the term *problem solving* to refer to a simple visual search of the keyboard, without any significant cognitive component.

To summarize, an activity must satisfy these three criteria to be called problem solving: it must be goal-directed, it must involve a sequence of operations, and these operations must have a significant cognitive component. By these criteria, a large class of mental activities would be called problem solving. It is not uncommon to find *problem solving* equated with *thinking.* While this may attribute too much to problem solving (for instance, we might want to consider daydreaming or remembering a phone number to be examples of thinking but not of problem solving), it is not very far from accurate. It is for this reason that I have started the discussion of cognitive activities with problem solving. In subsequent chapters we will see that problem solving is an important component of deductive reasoning, inductive reasoning, and many aspects of language processing.

Insight and Creativity

Before we focus on problem solving per se, it is useful to consider one other potential criterion for problem solving—namely, whether the behavior is creative. Are we doing problem solving when we perform highly cognitive activities such as multiplying numbers on paper, repeating a sentence backwards, translating a sentence from one language to another, scanning a chapter for information about a topic, or performing a mental rotation (as described in Chapter 3)? All these activities involve a sequence of cognitive operations intended to achieve a goal. However, some people feel a hesitancy in calling these behaviors true instances of problem solving. This is because the sequences of operations involved can be routine or well practiced. In terms of a production system (Chapter 8), the productions for performing

Figure 9-1   *Köhler's ape solving the two-stick problem: he combines two short sticks to form a pole long enough to reach the food. (From Köhler, 1956.)*

these behaviors may already be well encoded. Some people would like to reserve the term *problem solving* for tasks that require novel solutions and the creation of new procedures. Better examples of problem solving tasks would be writing a term essay, proving a new theorem in mathematics, playing a game of chess, solving a mathematical puzzle, thinking of new uses for a company's product, or writing a song. Clearly, these tasks are more creative and often require that the problem solver develop new procedures.

One of the classic studies of problem solving illustrates the distinction between creative and routine problem solving (Köhler, 1927). Köhler, a famous German Gestalt psychologist who came to America in the 1930s, found himself trapped on Tenerife in the Canary Islands during World War I. On this island he found a colony of captive chimpanzees, which he studied, taking particular interest in the problem-solving behavior of the animals. His prize subject was a chimpanzee named Sultan. One problem posed to Sultan was to get some bananas that were outside his cage. Sultan had no difficulty if he was given a stick that could reach the bananas. He simply used the stick to pull the bananas into his cage. However, the critical problem occurred when Sultan was provided with two poles, neither of which would reach the food. After vainly reaching with the poles, the frustrated ape sulked in his cage. Suddenly, he went over to the poles and put one inside the other, creating a pole long enough to reach the food; with this extended pole, he was able to reach his prize (see Figure 9-1). This was clearly a creative problem-solving activity on the part of Sultan. Köhler used the term *insight* to refer to the ape's discovery. The ape later repeated his solution when presented again with the same problem. These later solutions are examples of routine problem solving.

In keeping with established terminology, both the first creative solution and the later repetitions are referred to as problem solving. Thus, creativity should not be thought of as one of the defining features of problem solving. We will use the terms *creative problem solving* and *routine problem solving* to refer to the two types of problem solving (for a recent discussion of this distinction, see Greeno, in press). Thus, creative problem solving tends to involve the learning or acquisition of new procedures. The ape's first solution to Köhler's problem was creative and resulted in the learning of a solution that enabled the ape to solve repetitions of the problem routinely. Subsequent repetitions of the solution are no longer creative.

The distinction drawn here between creative problem solving and routine problem solving is not absolute. Solutions to problems can be seen on a continuum, being classified as more creative to the extent that they require novel behavior or the learning of new procedures. Research on problem solving has focused both on creative problem solving, or insight, and on the transition of a problem-solving activity from being creative to being more routine. However, a third major focus of research in this area has been concerned with characterizing features of problem solving that are independent of this creative-routine distinction. We will review this third type of research first because it will serve to articulate further our conception of the nature of problem solving.

Searching the Problem Space

States in the Problem

Problem solving is an attempt to achieve a *goal*. The ape in Köhler's study was attempting to get the food. The task of the problem solver is to find some sequence of operations that will achieve this goal. In the terminology of problem solving, the initial situation of the problem solver is referred to as the *initial state,* the situations on the way to the goal as *intermediate states,* and the goal as the *goal state.* Starting from the initial state, there are many ways the problem solver can choose to change his or her state. Sultan could reach for a stick, stand on his head, sulk, and so on. Suppose the ape reaches for the stick. Now he is in a new state. He can transform this to another state, for example, by letting go of the stick (thereby returning to the earlier state), reaching with the stick for the food, throwing the stick at the food, or reaching for the other stick. Suppose he reaches for another stick. Again he is in a new state. From this state Sultan can choose to try, say, walking on the sticks, putting them together, or eating the sticks. Suppose he chooses to put the sticks together. He can then choose to reach for the food, throw the sticks away, or undo them. If he reaches for the food, he will achieve his goal state.

The states in this example are actual physical states of the world. However, often in problem solving, the term *states* refers to states of knowledge. For instance, consider the following problem:

> The country of Marr is inhabited by two types of people, liars and truars (truth tellers). Liars always lie and truars always tell the truth. As the newly appointed United States ambassador to Marr, you have been invited to a local cocktail party. While consuming some of the native spirits, you are engaged in conversation with three of Marr's most prominent citizens: Joan Landill, Shawn Farrar, and Peter Fant. At one point in the conversation, Joan remarks that Shawn and Peter are both liars. Shawn vehemently denies that he is a liar, but Peter replies that Shawn is indeed a liar. From this information can you determine how many of the three are liars and how many are truars? [From Wickelgren, 1974, p. 36]

Stop reading for a few minutes and try to solve this problem.

To solve this problem, we must consider different possible states of knowledge about Joan, Shawn, and Peter. For instance, we might start out with the following knowledge state:

1. Assume that Joan is a truar.

From this, since Joan asserts that Shawn and Peter are both liars, we can infer the following knowledge state:

2. If Joan is a truar, Shawn and Peter are liars.

However, Peter claims Shawn is a liar. Since Peter is a liar, Shawn must actually be a truar, but this conclusion contradicts the above assumption that Shawn is a liar. Because of the contradiction, we can now infer that assumption 1 is false. Hence:

3. Joan must be a liar.

If so, her assertion that Shawn and Peter are both liars must be false. Hence, we have the following knowledge state:

4. Joan is a liar and Shawn or Peter or both are truars.

To further explore the issue, we assume the following knowledge state:

5. Suppose that both Shawn and Peter are both truars.

Again, with this assumption we run into the problem that Peter claims that Shawn is a liar. If Peter is a truar, Shawn must be a liar. Therefore state 5 leads to a contradiction. Combining states 4 with 5, we get

6. Joan is a liar and only one of Shawn and Peter is a truar.

From state 6 we can reach the knowledge state that is the answer to the problem.

7. Two of the three are liars and one is a truar.

Just as Sultan found his way through states of the physical world to solve his problem, in this example the problem solvers must find their ways through states of knowledge 1 through 7.

The Problem Space

The various states that the problem solver can achieve are referred to as defining a *problem space,* or *state space.* The various ways of changing one state into another are referred to as *operators.* The problem is to find some possible sequence of state changes that goes from the initial state to the goal state in the problem space. One can conceive of the problem space as a maze of states and of the operators as paths for moving among the states. In this conception, the solution to a problem is achieved through a *search* process; that is, the problem solver must find an appropriate path through a maze of states. This conception of problem solving as a search through a state space was developed by Allen Newell and Herbert Simon of Carnegie–Mellon University and has become the dominant analysis of problem solving, both in cognitive psychology and artificial intelligence.

A problem-space characterization consists of a set of states and operators for moving among states. A good problem for illustrating the problem-space characterization is the 8-tile puzzle, consisting of 8 numbered, movable tiles set in a 3 × 3 frame. One cell of the frame is always empty, making it possible to move an adjacent numbered tile into the empty cell and thereby "moving" the empty cell as well. The goal is to achieve a particular configuration of tiles, starting from a different configuration. For instance, a problem might be to transform

2	1	6
4	*	8
7	5	3

into

1	2	3
8	*	4
7	6	5

The possible states of this problem are represented as configurations of tiles in the 8-tile puzzle. So, the first configuration shown is the initial state, and the second is the goal state. The operators that change the states are movements of tiles into empty spaces. Figure 9-2 reproduces an attempt of mine to solve this problem. This solution required 26 moves, each move being an operator that changes the state of the problem. This sequence of operators is considerably longer than necessary. Try to find a shorter sequence of moves. (The shortest sequence possible is given at the end of the chapter, in Figure 9-16.)

Similarity as a Basis for Selecting Operators

How do people choose operators? For instance, in the 8-tile-puzzle problem presented in the last subsection, four options were possible for the first move. One possible operator was to move the 1 into the empty square, another was to move the 8, a third was to move the 5, and the fourth was to move the 4. I chose the last operator. Why? The answer is that it seemed to get me closer to my end goal. I was moving the 4 tile closer to its final destination. Human problem solvers are often strongly governed by *similarity*. They choose operators that transform the problem state into a state that resembles the goal state more closely than the initial state.

The move from state 1 to state 2 was governed by immediate similarity. However, this criterion did not help in state 2. The state would be less similar than before to the final configuration whether I moved the 2 or the 7 tile into the empty position (and it seemed silly to back up by moving the 4 again). I made my choice on the basis of a more distant goal—if I moved the 2, I would then be able to move the 1 into its correct position. This choice reflects the use of *look-ahead* or *planning* behavior. I was choosing a move now because it would eventually enable me to come closer to the goal.

The early part of this sequence reflects an attempt on my part to come closer and closer to the goal. States C and D got the tile 1 in position. States E

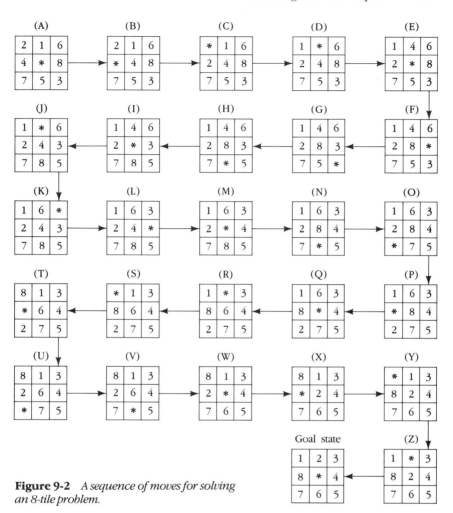

Figure 9-2 *A sequence of moves for solving an 8-tile problem.*

through H got the 5 tile in position. States I through L got the 3 tile in position. State M put the 4 tile in position. But then I was stuck. There was no way to get the 2, 6, or 8 tiles in position without moving a tile out of position. I decided to leave the 3, 4, 5 column alone and just randomly moved the tiles about until I achieved state W. Then I had the sequence 3, 4, 5, 6, and 7 in place. The moves to get the remaining tiles into position were "obvious."

So, my behavior was partially planful and partially random. It was organized by an overall attempt to reduce differences or increase similarity. This type of reliance on similarity is prevalent in many problem-solving situations. One way problem solvers often improve is by using more sophisticated measures

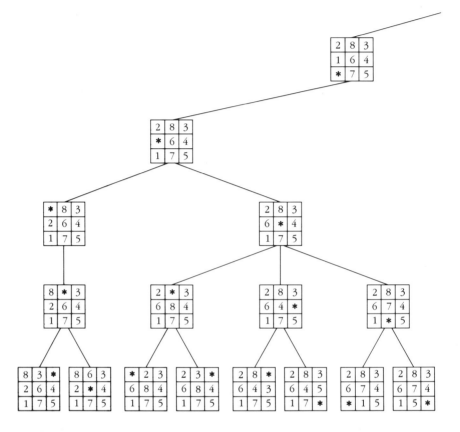

Figure 9-3 *Part of the search tree, 6 moves deep, for an 8-tile problem. (From Nilsson, 1971.)*

of similarity. After working with many tile problems, one begins to notice the importance of *sequence*—that is, whether noncentral tiles are followed by their appropriate successors. For instance, in state O of Figure 9-2, the 3 and 4 tiles are in sequence because they are followed by their successors 4 and 5, but the 5 is not in sequence because it is followed by 7 rather than 6. In trying to solve the problem, I was only considering the distance of titles from their final positions, and not whether they were in sequence. However, trying to move tiles into sequence proves to be more important (see Nilsson, 1971 for further discussion).

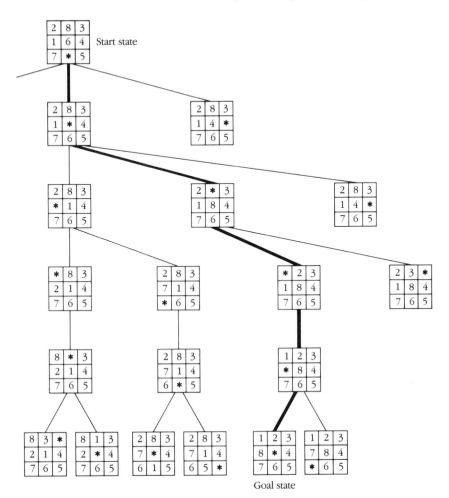

Often, discussions of problem solving involve the use of *search graphs* or *search trees*. Figure 9-3 gives a partial seárch tree for the following 8-tile problem:

2	8	3
1	6	4
7	*	5

into

1	2	3
8	*	4
7	6	5

Figure 9-3 is like an upside-down tree with a single trunk and branches leading out from that. This tree begins with the *start state,* represents all states reachable from this state, then all states reachable from those states, and so on. Any path through such a tree represents a possible sequence of moves that a problem solver might make. By generating a complete tree, one can also find the shortest sequence of operators between the start state and the goal state. Figure 9-3 illustrates some of the problem space. Frequently, in discussions of such examples, only the path through the problem space that leads to the solution is presented (for instance, in Figure 9-2). Figure 9-3 gives a better idea of the size of the space of possible moves that exist for a problem.

Heuristics Versus Algorithms

The various similarity measures used to guide solutions of the 8-tile problem are examples of *heuristics.* Heuristics are methods that tend to lead to successful solutions but that are not guaranteed to do so. Because heuristics only tend to lead to solutions, they can be thought of as "rules of thumb." Heuristics are contrasted with *algorithms,* which are defined as methods guaranteed to provide a solution. The 8-tile problem can serve as a means of demonstrating the contrast between algorithms and heuristics. To solve this problem, one could generate the complete search tree, as has been partly done in Figure 9-3. In doing so, the problem solver would be guaranteed to find a solution path, and the shortest path, if a solution existed at all. Generating the search tree is an example of an algorithm for solving the problem. However, such an algorithm is rather cumbersome. An example of a heuristic search method would be trying moves that seem to reduce the differences from the goal state, as in Figure 9-2. The heuristic method may never lead to the solution, since it is not systematic like the algorithm, but it is often much faster. In many problem situations, subjects use heuristic methods either because algorithms do not exist or the existing algorithms are too cumbersome. However, there are also problems for which perfectly good algorithms exist, such as long-division problems.

As a rather different example of the difference between an algorithm and a heuristic, suppose you arrive in a strange town and want to find out if your family has any relations there. Your family has been so prolific that you have lost track of all your second cousins, great aunts, and such. One solution would be to call up everyone in the phone book and interrogate them as to their family tree. Assuming that all the townsfolk were cooperative and listed in the phone book, you would have an algorithm for finding your lost relatives. However, this could cost you a lot of time. A heuristic would be to call up only those townsfolk in the phone book who have your family name. You might miss relatives who have changed their name through marriage or for other reasons, but the procedure would certainly be much less costly and would have a good chance of turning up a lost relative if one existed in the town. (Just how good a heuristic it is depends on how common your family name is; compare Anderson with Reder.)

Where Similarity Is Wrong

Similarity is a heuristic frequently used by subjects in many problems. In using this heuristic, subjects select operators that get them to states that are the most similar to the goal state. Problem solving improves as more effective measures of similarity are developed. However, in some problem-solving situations, a correct solution involves going against the grain of similarity. A good example is called the hobbits and orcs problem:

> On one side of a river are three hobbits and three orcs. They have a boat on their side that is capable of carrying two creatures at a time across the river. The goal is to transport all six creatures across to the other side of the river. At no point on either side of the river can orcs outnumber hobbits (or the orcs would eat the outnumbered hobbits). The problem, then, is to find a method of transporting all six creatures across the river without the hobbits ever being outnumbered.

Stop reading and try to solve this problem.

Figure 9-4 shows a correct sequence of moves for solution of this problem. Illustrated there are the locations of hobbits (H), orcs (O), and the boat (b). The boat, the three hobbits, and the three orcs all start on one side of the river. This condition is represented in state 1 by the fact that all are above the line. Then, a hobbit, an orc, and the boat proceed to the other side of the river. The outcome of this action is represented in state 2 by placement of the boat (b), the hobbit (H), and the orc (O) on the other side of the line. In state 3, one hobbit has taken the boat back, and the diagram continues in the same way. Each state in Figure 9-4 represents another configuration of hobbits, orcs, and boat. Subjects (e.g., those studied by Greeno, 1974) have a particular problem with the transition from state 6 to state 7 (see also Jeffries, Polson, Razran, and Atwood, 1977). One reason for this difficulty is that the action involves moving two creatures back to the wrong side of the river. The move seems to be away from a solution. At this point, subjects will often back up and look for some other solution.

Atwood and Polson (1976) provide another experimental demonstration of subjects' reliance on similarity and how that reliance can be beneficial or harmful. Subjects were given the following water-jug problem:

> You have three jugs which we will call A, B, and C. Jug A can hold exactly 8 cups of water, B can hold exactly 5 cups, and C can hold exactly 3 cups. A is filled to capacity with 8 cups of water. B and C are empty. We want you to find a way of dividing the contents of A equally between A and B so that both have four cups. You are allowed to pour water from jug to jug.

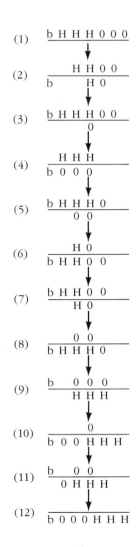

Figure 9-4   *A diagram of the successive states in a solution to the hobbits and orcs problem.*

Figure 9-5 illustrates two paths of solution to this problem. At the top of the figure, all the water is in jug *A*—represented *A*(8); no water is in jug *B* or *C*—represented *B*(0) *C*(0). The two possible actions are to pour *A* into *C,* in which case we get *A*(5) *B*(0) *C*(3) or to pour *A* into *B,* in which case we get *A*(3) *B*(5) *C*(0). From these two states more moves can be made. Numerous other sequences of moves are possible besides the two paths illustrated in Figure 9-5. However, Figure 9-5 does illustrate the two shortest sequences to the goal.

Atwood and Polson used the representation in Figure 9-5 to analyze subjects' behavior. For instance, Atwood and Polson asked which move subjects

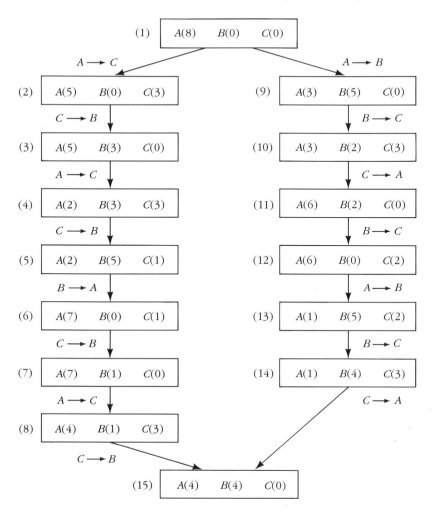

Figure 9-5 *Two paths of solution for the water-jug problem posed in Atwood and Polson (1976). Each state is represented in terms of the contents of the three jugs. The transitions between states are labeled in terms of which jug is poured into which.*

would prefer in starting from the initial state 1. That is, would they prefer to pour *A* into *C* and get state 2, or *A* into *B* and get state 9? The answer is that subjects preferred the latter move. Twice as many subjects moved to state 9 as moved to state 2. Note that state 9 is quite similar to the goal. The goal is to have 4 cups in both *A* and *B* and state 9 has 3 cups in *A* and 5 cups in *B*. In contrast, state 2 has no cups of water in *B*. Throughout their problem, Atwood and Polson found a strong tendency for subjects to move to states that were similar to the goal state. Usually, similarity was a good heuristic, but there are critical cases where similarity is misleading. For instance, the transitions from states 5 to 6 and from states 11 to 12 both lead to significant decreases in similarity to the goal. However, both transitions are critical to their solution paths. Atwood and Polson found that more than 50 percent of the time subjects deviated from the correct sequence of moves at these critical points. Rather, subjects chose some move that seemed closer to the goal but actually took them away from the solution.

These examples illustrate the heuristic character of similarity. While it frequently does a good job in leading one to a solution, in some situations it does not work and can even be misleading. To repeat, heuristics are only rules of thumb and can be wrong on occasion.

Ways of Guiding Search

So far, we have treated problem solvers as if they looked ahead only one step at a time. Trying to solve a problem in this way is like trying to reach the top of a hill blindfolded, where one chooses each step by feel, in accordance with the greatest rise in height. Obviously, a much more efficient solution would be to remove the blindfold, survey the surroundings, locate the top of the hill, and plan how to make the ascent of the hill. Problem solvers frequently look ahead in this spirit. In fact, we saw in my solution of the 8-tile puzzle in Figure 9-2 that I engaged in sequences of moves organized to achieve a subgoal some number of moves in the future. We will discuss a number of methods by which problem solvers can guide their solution efforts: means-ends analysis, working backwards, and planning by simplification.

Means-Ends Analysis

Means-ends analysis is one method of organizing problem solving and introducing an element of planning into it. This method has been extensively studied by Newell and Simon, who have used it in a computer-stimulation program, called the General Problem Solver (GPS), which models human problem solving. The following is Newell and Simon's description of means-ends analysis.

> The main methods of GPS jointly embody the heuristic of means-end analysis. Means-end analysis is typified by the following kind of common-sense argument:

> I want to take my son to nursery school. What's the difference between what I have and what I want? One of distance. What changes distance? My automobile. My automobile won't work. What is needed to make it work? A

new battery. What has new batteries? An auto repair shop. I want the repair shop to put in a new battery; but the shop doesn't know I need one. What is the difficulty? One of communication. What allows communication? A telephone . . . and so on.

The kind of analysis—classifying things in terms of the functions they serve and oscillating among ends, functions required, and means that perform them—forms the basic system of heuristic of GPS. More precisely, this means-ends system of heuristic assumes the following:

1. If an object is given that is not the desired one, differences will be detectable between the available object and the desired object.

2. Operators affect some features of their operands and leave others unchanged. Hence operators can be characterized by the changes they produce and can be used to try to eliminate differences between the objects to which they are applied and desired objects.

3. If a desired operator is not applicable, it may be profitable to modify the inputs so that it becomes applicable.

4. Some differences will prove more difficult to affect than others.

It is profitable, therefore, to try to eliminate "difficult" differences, even at the cost of introducing new differences of lesser difficulty. This process can be repeated as long as progress is being made toward eliminating the more difficult differences. [Newell and Simon, 1972, p. 416]

Figure 9-6 displays in flowchart form the procedures used in the means-ends analysis employed by GPS. A general feature of this means-ends analysis is that it breaks a larger goal into subgoals. GPS creates subgoals in two ways. First, in flowchart 1, GPS breaks the current state into a set of differences and sets the reduction of each difference as a separate subgoal. It chooses to try to eliminate first what it perceives as the most important difference. Second, in flowchart II, GPS tries to find an operator that will eliminate the difference. However, this operator may be unable to apply immediately because a difference exists between the operator's condition and the state of the environment. Thus, before the operator can be applied, eliminating another difference may be necessary. To eliminate the difference that is blocking the operator's application, flowchart II will have to be called again to find another operator relevant to eliminating that difference.

The Tower of Hanoi Problem

Means-ends analysis has proved to be an extremely general and powerful method of problem solving. Ernst and Newell (1969) discuss its applications to the modeling of monkey and bananas problems (such as Sultan's predicament described at the beginning of the chapter), algebra problems, calculus problems, and logic problems. However, we will illustrate means-ends analy-

Flowchart I Goal: Transform current state into goal state

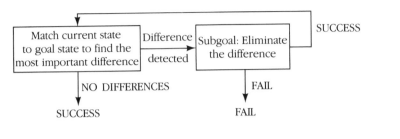

Flowchart II Goal: Eliminate the difference

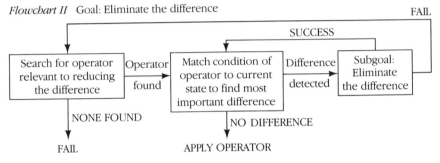

Figure 9-6 *The application of means-ends analysis by Newell and Simon's General Problem Solver. Flowchart I breaks a problem down into a set of differences and tries to eliminate each. Flowchart II searches for an operator relevant to eliminating a difference.*

sis here by applying it to *the tower of Hanoi problem*. A simple version of this problem is illustrated in Figure 9-7. There are three pegs and three disks of differing sizes, *A, B,* and *C.* The disks have holes in them so they can be stacked on the pegs. The disks can be moved from any peg to any other peg. Only the top disk on a peg can be moved and it can never be placed on a smaller disk. The disks all start out on peg 1, but the goal is to move them all to peg 3, one disk at a time, by means of transferring disks among pegs.

Bourne, Dominowski, and Loftus (1979) suggest a way to mimic this problem with some coins and papers. First, draw circles on a sheet of paper and label them 1, 2, 3. Now select three coins varying in size, such as a quarter, a nickel, and a dime. Place them in order of decreasing size on circle 1. Now you have an analog of the tower of Hanoi problem, in which the circles are the pegs and your coins are the disks. The task is to move the three coins from circle 1 to circle 3, moving a coin from one circle to another, under the constraint that you never place a larger coin on a smaller coin.

Figure 9-8 traces out the application of the GPS techniques to this problem. The first line gives the general goal of moving *A, B,* and *C* to peg 3. This goal

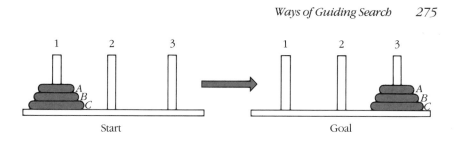

Figure 9-7 *The three-disk version of the tower of Hanoi problem.*

leads us to the first flowchart of Figure 9-6. One difference between the goal and the current state is that *C* is not on 3. This difference is chosen first because GPS tries to remove the most important differences first, and we are assuming that the largest misplaced disk will be viewed as the most important difference. Therefore, a subgoal is set up to eliminate this difference. This takes us to the second flowchart, which tries to find an operator to reduce the difference. The operator chosen is to *move C to 3*. The condition for applying a move operator is that nothing be on the disk. Since *A* and *B* are on *C*, there is a difference between the condition of the operator and the current state. Therefore, a new subgoal is created to reduce one of the differences—*B* on *C*. This subgoal gets us back to the start of flowchart II, but now with the goal of removing *B* from *C* (line 6 in Figure 9-8). Note that we have gone from I to II and back to II. This action is called *recursion* because to use flowchart II (to find a way to move *C* to 3) we need to go back to flowchart II (to find a way to remove *B* from *C*). Thus, one procedure is using itself as a subprocedure.

The operator chosen the second time in flowchart II is to move *B to 2*. However, we cannot immediately apply the operator of moving *B* to 2, since *B* is covered by *A*. Therefore, another subgoal is set up—that of removing *A*—and flowchart II is used to remove this difference. The operator relevant to achieving this is to *move A to 3*. There are no differences between the conditions for this operator and the current state. Finally, we have an operator we can apply (line 12 in Figure 9-8). Thus, we achieve the subgoal of moving *A* to 3. Now we return to the earlier intention of moving *B* to 2. There are no more differences between the operator for this move and the current state, so the action takes place. The subgoal of removing *B* from *C* is then satisfied (line 16 in Figure 9-8).

We have now returned to the original intention of moving *C* to 3. However, disk *A* is now on peg 3, which prevents the action. Thus, we have another difference to be eliminated between the now current state and the operator's condition. We move *A* onto peg 2 to remove this difference. Now the original operator of moving *C* to 3 can be applied (line 24 in Figure 9-8).

The state at this point is that disk *C* is in peg 3 and *A* and *B* are on peg 2. At this point, GPS returns to its original goal of moving the three disks to 3. It

1. Goal: Move *A*, *B*, and *C* to Peg 3
2.   :Difference is that *C* is not on 3
3.   :Subgoal: Make *C* on 3
4.   :Operator is to move *C* to 3
5.   :Difference is that *A* and *B* are on *C*
6.   :Subgoal: Remove *B* from *C*
7.   :Operator is to move *B* to 2
8.   :Difference is that *A* is on *B*
9.   :Subgoal: Remove *A* from *B*
10.   :Operator is to move *A* to 3
11.   :No difference with operator's condition
12   :Apply operator (move *A* to 3)
13.   :Subgoal achieved
14.   :No differences with operator's condition
15.   :Apply operator (move *B* to 2)
16.   :Subgoal achieved
17.   :Difference is that *A* is on 3
18.   :Subgoal: Remove *A* from peg 3
19.   :Operator is to move *A* to 2
20.   :No difference with operator's condition
21.   :Apply operator (move *A* to 2)
22.   :Subgoal achieved
23.   :No difference with operator's condition
24.   :Apply operator (move *C* to 3)
25.   :Subgoal achieved
26.   :Difference is that *B* is not on 3
27.   :Subgoal: Make *B* on 3
28.   :Operator is to move *B* to 3
29.   :Difference is that *A* is on *B*
30.   :Subgoal: Remove *A* from *B*
31.   :Operator is to move *A* to 1
32.   :No difference with operator's condition
33.   :Apply operator (move *A* to 1)
34.   :Subgoal achieved
35.   :No difference with operator's condition
36.   :Apply operator (move *B* to 3)
'37.   :Subgoal achieved
38.   :Difference is that *A* is not on 3
39.   :Subgoal: Make *A* on 3   .
40.   :Operator is to move *A* to 3
41.   :No difference with operator's condition
42.   :Apply operator (Move *A* to 3)
43.   :Subgoal achieved
44.   :No difference
45. Goal Achieved

Figure 9-8   *A trace of the application of GPS to the tower of Hanoi problem in Figure 9-7.*

Given state

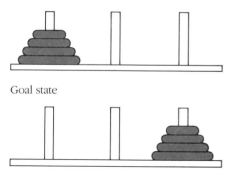

Goal state

Figure 9-9   *The four-disk version of the tower of Hanoi problem.*

notes that another difference is that *B* is not on 3 and sets up another subgoal of eliminating this difference. It achieves this subgoal by first moving *A* to 1 and then *B* to 3. This gets us to line 37 in the trace. The remaining difference is that *A* is not on 3. This difference is eliminated in the lines 38 through 42. With this step, no more differences exist and the original goal is achieved.

This type of procedure for reaching a solution is also referred to as a *problem-reduction procedure* because it breaks a problem into subproblems. Note that subgoals are created in service of other subgoals. For instance, to achieve the subgoal of moving the largest disk, a subgoal is created of moving the second largest disk, which is on top of it. We indicated this logical dependency of one subgoal on another in Figure 9-8 by indenting the processing of the dependent subgoal. At line 9 of Figure 9-8, four goals and subgoals had to be remembered. As Simon (1975) has pointed out, the number of subgoals that must be remembered simultaneously will increase as we increase the number of disks. With every disk added to the problem, another subgoal will have to be maintained. From what we studied earlier about the limitations of short-term memory (Chapter 6), we can predict that subjects should have difficulty keeping many goals and subgoals active in short-term memory. In fact, the evidence is that when subjects try to use such problem-reduction methods, they often fail because they lose track of the subgoals and how they interrelate. These problems are less taxing to short-term memory if solvers use paper and pencil to keep a chart like Figure 9-8 to indicate where they are in the problem. (Of course, the degree of detail in Figure 9-8 is not necessary.) As an exercise, you might try applying this GPS procedure to the four-disk problem in Figure 9-9. The tower of Hanoi problem gets dramatically harder with each additional disk, but the same general GPS procedure will work in all cases.

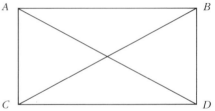

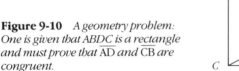

Figure 9-10 *A geometry problem: One is given that ABDC is a rectangle and must prove that AD and CB are congruent.*

Working Backward

A useful way to solve some problems is to work backward from the goal. This can be a particularly useful search heuristic in areas such as finding proofs in mathematics. Consider the geometry problem illustrated in Figure 9-10. The student is given that *ABDC* is a rectangle and is asked to prove that $\overline{AD}$ and $\overline{CB}$ are of the same length (are congruent). In working backward, the student would ask, "What would prove that $\overline{AD}$ and $\overline{CB}$ are congruent? I could prove this if I could prove that the triangles *ACD* and *BDC* are congruent." Thus, the student would work backward from the goal of proving line congruence to that of proving triangle congruence. The next step is reasoning, "I could prove that triangles *ACD* and *BDC* are congruent if I could prove that two sides and an included angle (the side-angle-side postulate) are congruent." Thus, the student would reason back from this subgoal to another subgoal. It is not obvious to all students that they should work backward in finding a proof, since they are required to reason in a forward manner in writing the proof:

Statement	*Reason*
$\overline{AC} \cong \overline{BD}$	Definition of rectangle
$\overline{CD} = \overline{CD}$	Identity
$\angle ACD, \angle BDC$ are right angles	Definition of rectangle
$\angle ACD \cong \angle BDC$	Right angles are congruent
$\triangle ACD \cong \triangle BDC$	Side-angle-side
$\overline{AD} \cong \overline{CB}$	Corresponding parts of congruent triangles are congruent.

It is useful to compare working backward with means-ends analyses. Both involve considering the goal and determining what operations will achieve the goal. However, means-ends analysis considers the difference between the goal and the current state, whereas pure working backwards does not. Therefore, means-ends analysis is a more constrained way of searching the problem space. As a consequence, it can lead to a solution more quickly with fewer false paths being considered. Working backward is useful when many paths in the problem space lead from the initial state but few paths lead to the goal state. This is true of the geometry case. Any number of inferences can be derived from the initial problem (such as $\angle BCD = \angle ABC$), but relatively few inferences are relevant to establishing the goal of $\overline{AD} = \overline{CB}$. In contrast, in the tower of Hanoi problem, as many paths lead to the goal state as lead from the start state. Here we need a more powerful search heuristic such as means-ends analysis.

Planning by Simplification

Another way of solving a problem is to develop a plan. Plans serve two functions. They help prevent costly mistakes and they serve to simplify the problem solving. Consider an architect's plan for a house. It is certainly much cheaper for the architect to design the house on paper than it would be for the builder to design a house with wood and concrete. If the architect makes a mistake and forgets the kitchen, starting over again would be relatively inexpensive. It would, of course, be absurd for the builder to construct the house, discover there is no kitchen, and then start over again.

The other function of plans, to simplify problem solving, is less obvious. An architect's plan ignores many details that need to be resolved. As any builder will testify, an enormous amount of problem solving remains to be done after an architect's plans are received. Thus, the architect's plan provides an overall structure for the detailed problem solving that the builder must carry out. Because this overall structure is sound, it is likely (but not assured) that the builder will not run into any insurmountable problems in following the plan. In solving intellectual problems, this simplifying function of planning is its important feature. The other consideration, that of reducing the cost of errors, does not often weigh heavily in more intellectual problems. Here, the problem solving usually requires only relatively cheap material such as paper and pencil.

In planning by simplification, one abstracts the problem into a simpler form, solves the problem in the simpler form, and then uses this solution to guide problem solving in the more complex form. Hayes (1978) gives the following example. Suppose our task is to express X in terms of Y given the following five equations:

$$R = Z^2$$
$$X = R + 3$$
$$2M = 3L + 6$$
$$Y = M + 1$$
$$R = 3L$$

Student performance is often quite haphazard. It helps to abstract these equations to indicate the connections among the variables:

$$R\text{———}Z$$
$$X\text{———}R$$
$$M\text{———}L$$
$$Y\text{———}M$$
$$R\text{———}L$$

In this abstract representation, the problem of expressing X in terms of Y reduces to finding a path connecting X and Y. This path is

$$X\text{———}R\text{———}L\text{———}M\text{———}Y$$

This abstract solution can now be used to guide a solution for the original problem.

To apply the abstract solution, we first combine the equations for the first link $(X\text{———}R)$ and the second link $(R\text{———}L)$. These equations are

$$X = R + 3$$
$$R = 3L$$

Their combination is $X = 3L + 3$. Next, we combine this equation with the equation for the next link $(2M = 3L + 6)$, derive a new equation, and continue this process until the equation is derived relating X and Y.

$$X = 2Y - 5$$

As another example of planning by simplification, consider the problem of preparing a large dinner party. One might try to use a successful small dinner party as a plan to guide organization of the large dinner party. Perhaps a helper had been hired through a local employment agency to prepare the small party. One might now go to the same agency for two or three helpers, since the agency had provided good help before. It had taken a day to prepare the small party successfully. Thus, for the large party one might set aside two full days. The guests had been asked two weeks in advance for the small party. Given that it is better to give longer notice for a large party, the guests might be asked three weeks in advance.

At the small party, the hors d'oeuvres had been carrots, celery, cheese and crackers. The dinner started with paté de fois gras followed by a green salad. The main course had been chicken Kiev, rice pilaf, and a spinach ring. A California white wine had been served. Afterwards, there had been chocolate mousse and coffee. The table had been covered with a new tablecloth, candles, and a centerpiece of tulips and crocuses from the garden.

Assuming that the large party was to take place in the same season as the small one, the partygiver might want to keep the table decorations and the same kind of centerpiece arrangement but remove the chairs and use the table for a buffet. The paté de fois gras might be used to supplement the hors d'oeuvres rather than as a special course. To simplify matters, the green salad could be served with the main course. Naturally, the quantities would be much larger. The chicken Kiev could still be served, but it would have to be prepared in advance and heated up before being served. And the spinach ring might be supplemented with a second vegetable, such as broccoli in a cheese sauce. The same wine might be served, but perhaps purchased in gallon bottles and served in carafes as a economy move. And the recipe for chocolate mousse would probably be enlarged or else supplemented or replaced by pastries from a bakery to cut down on the amount of preparation. A large coffee maker might be borrowed or rented.

This dinner-party example illustrates that translating from a plan to a solution may not always be direct. One could not use the same times, quantities, and arrangements for the large party as for the small party. Rather, the party giver would simply use the small dinner party as a guide, adjusting many of the parameters to meet the needs of the large party.

Representation

The Importance of the Correct Representation

We have analyzed problem solution into problem states and operators for changing states. So far, we have discussed problem solving as if the only problem were operator selection. Similarity measures, means-ends analysis, working backwards and planning methods all serve to help the problem solver select the right operator. However, the way in which states of the problem are represented also has significant effects.

A famous example illustrating the importance of representation is the *mutilated-checkerboard problem.* Suppose we have a checkerboard in which the two diagonally opposite corner squares have been cut out. Figure 9-11 illustrates this mutilated checkerboard. Sixty-two squares remain on this board. Now suppose that we have 31 dominos, each of which covers exactly two squares of the board. Can we find some way of arranging these 31 dominos on the board so that they cover all 62 squares? If it can be done, explain how. If it cannot be done, prove that it cannot. Perhaps the reader would like to ponder this problem before reading on. Few people are able to solve this problem and very few see the answer quickly.

The answer is that the checkerboard cannot be covered by the dominos. The trick to seeing this is to include in your representation of the problem the fact that each domino must cover one black and one red square, not just any two squares. There is just no way to place a domino on two squares of the checkerboard without having it cover one black and one red square. This means that with 31 dominos we can cover 31 black squares and 31 red squares. But the mutilation has removed two black squares. Thus, there are 32

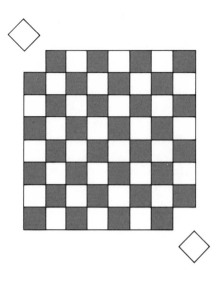

Figure 9-11   *The mutilated checkerboard. (Adapted from Wickelgren,* How to Solve Problems. *W. H. Freeman and Company. Copyright © 1974.)*

red squares and 30 black. It follows that the mutilated checkerboard cannot be covered by 31 dominos.

Why is the mutilated-checkerboard problem easier to solve when we represent each domino as covering a red and black space? The answer is that in so representing the problem we are encouraged to count and compare the number of red and black squares on the board. Thus, the effect of the problem representation is that it allows the critical operator to apply (that is, counting red and black squares to check for parity).

Another problem that depends on correct representation is the *27-cubic apples problem.* Imagine 27 apples, each of which is shaped as a perfect cube. They are packed together in a crate 3 apples high, 3 apples wide, and 3 apples deep. A worm is in the center apple. Its life's ambition is to eat its way to all the apples in the crate, but it does not want to waste time by visiting any apple twice. The worm can move from apple to apple only by going from the side of one into the side of another. It cannot go from the corner of one apple to the corner of another or from the edge of one into the edge of another. Can you find some path by which the worm, starting from the center apple, can reach all the apples without going through any apple twice? If not, can you prove it is impossible? The solution is left to the reader. Hint: the solution is based on a partial 3-dimensional analogy to the solution for the mutilated-checkerboard problem. (The solution is given at the end of the chapter.)

Functional Fixedness

Often, solutions to problems depend on the solver's ability to represent the objects in one's environment in novel ways. This fact has been demonstrated in a series of studies by different experimenters. A typical experiment in the

Figure 9-12   *The two-string problem used by Maier.*

series is the two-string problem of Maier (1931), illustrated in Figure 9-12. Two strings hanging from the ceiling are to be tied together, but they are so far apart that the subject cannot grasp both at once. Among the objects in the room are a chair and a pair of pliers. Subjects try various solutions involving the chair but these do not work. The only solution is to tie the pliers to one string and set that string swinging like a pendulum, and then to get the second string, bring it to the center of the room, and wait for the first string to swing close enough to grasp. Only 39 percent of Maier's subjects were able to see this solution within 10 minutes. The difficulty is that subjects do not perceive the pliers as a weight that can be used as a pendulum. This phenomenon is called *functional fixedness*. It is so named because subjects are fixed on representing the object according to its conventional function and fail to represent its novel function.

Another demonstration of functional fixedness is an experiment by Duncker (1945). The task he posed to subjects is to support a candle on a door, ostensibly for an experiment on vision. The problem is illustrated in Figure 9-13. On the table are a box of tacks, some matches, and the candle. The correct solution is to tack the box to the door and use the box as a platform

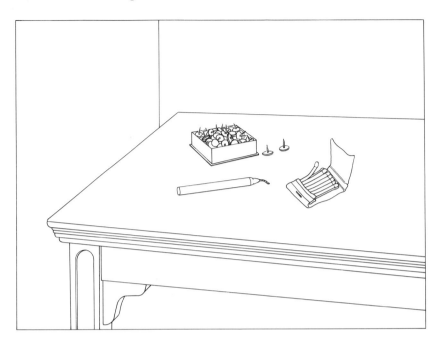

Figure 9-13 *The candle problem used by Dunker. (Adapted from Glucksberg and Weisberg, 1968. Copyright © 1968 by the American Psychological Association. Reprinted by permission.)*

for the candle. This task is difficult for subjects because they see the box as a container, not as a platform. Subjects have greater difficulty with the task if the box is filled with tacks, reinforcing perception of the box as a container.

Another demonstration of functional fixedness, introduced by Glucksberg and Danks (1968), involved a problem that required a screwdriver blade to function as wire in an electric circuit. Again, the solution is difficult to conceive because subjects do not normally perceive a blade as having this function. In an interesting follow-up to this study, Teborg (1968) gave subjects practice classifying objects such as paper clips and crayons according to their conducting properties. This practice turned out to be very useful in dissipating the functional fixedness and enabling subjects to perceive the needed function of the screwdriver blade. This experiment illustrates the importance of practice on problem-solving—a point to which we will be returning.

These demonstrations of functional fixedness are consistent with the interpretation that representation has its effect on operator selection. For instance, in Duncker's candle problem (Figure 9-13), subjects had to represent the match box so that it could be used by the problem-solving operators that were looking for a support for the candle. When the box was conceived of as a container and not as a support, it was not available to the support-seeking operators.

Encodings of Problem-Solving Skills

Production Systems

Problem solving involves the application of mental procedures to achieve a goal. These procedures can be encoded as production systems. For problems with which we have had prior experience, we already have working procedures. (For instance, Table 8-3 of Chapter 8 gives a production system for solving arithmetic problems.) On the other hand, when we are faced with a novel problem we have to create a new production system for solving it. On some occasions, such as the insight experiments described above, creating a production system that will work can be a major problem. But on other occasions the production system needed can be fairly obvious. Such an occasion involves the water-jug problem studied by Luchins (1942; Luchins and Luchins, 1959).

In Luchins' water-jug experiments, a subject was given a set of jugs of various capacities and unlimited water supply. The subject's task was to measure out a specified quantity of water. Two examples are given below:

Problems	Capacity of Jug A	Capacity of Jug B	Capacity of Jug C	Desired Quantity
1	5 quarts	40 quarts	18 quarts	28 quarts
2	21 quarts	127 quarts	3 quarts	100 quarts

Assume that subjects have a tap and a sink so that they can fill jugs and empty them. The jugs start out empty. Subjects are only allowed to fill the jugs, empty them, and pour water from one jug to another. In problem 1, subjects are told that they have three jugs—jug A, with a capacity of 5 quarts; jug B, with a capacity of 40 quarts; and jug C, with a capacity of 18 quarts. To solve this problem, subjects would fill A and pour it into B, fill A again and pour it into B, and fill C and pour it into B. The solution to this problem is denoted 2A + C. The solution for the second problem is to first fill jug B with 127 quarts; fill A from B so that 106 quarts are left in B; fill C from B so that 103 quarts are left in B; empty C; fill C again from B so that the goal of 100 quarts in B is achieved. The solution to this problem can be denoted B − A − 2C.

When subjects first encounter these water-jug problems, they must analyze the character of the problems, create some procedures to deal with them, and start to apply these procedures. Table 9-1 shows four productions that a subject might create for these problems. Problem 1 (with the A + 2C solu-

Table 9-1   Four Productions for Solving Water-Jug Problems

FILL	IF	a jug is empty and the capacity of the jug is greater than the goal
	THEN	fill the jug
ADD	IF	one jug has capacity greater than the goal and a second jug has capacity less than the goal
	THEN	fill the second jug and pour it into the first jug
SUBTRACT	IF	one jug contains more than the goal and the capacity of a second jug is less than the contents of the first jug
	THEN	empty the second jug and pour the first jug into it
STOP	IF	a jug contains the desired quantity
	THEN	stop

tion) above would be solved by applying the ADD production three times —once filling C and adding it to B and twice adding A to B. Problem 2 (with the $B - A - 2C$ solution) would be solved by first applying the FILL production to jug B and then applying the subtract production three times—one time subtracting out jug A from jug B and twice subtracting out jug C.

The productions in Table 9-1 are not the most sophisticated productions one might construct for the task, but they have some selectivity built into their operation. Consider the FILL production: its function is to set up a large jug for a series of subtractions. It does not indiscriminately fill any jug—rather, it only fills jugs whose capacities are greater than the goal. The ADD production will only apply if there is a jug with a capacity greater than the goal and a second jug with a capacity smaller than the goal. It fills the first jug with the second. The SUBTRACT production looks for a jug that contains more than the goal and a second jug that, when subtracted from the first, will not leave the first empty. The STOP production simply recognizes when the goal has been achieved.

Set Effects

Luchins studied the effect of giving subjects a series of problems, all of which could be solved by addition. This created an "addition set" such that subjects solved new addition problems faster than control subjects, who had no practice, and solved subtraction problems more slowly. These set effects can be explained with respect to the productions in Table 9-1. By repeatedly giving subjects problems that required addition solutions, Luchins was strengthening productions such as ADD relative to productions such as SUBTRACT. Thus, the ADD production would come to apply more quickly and reliably. The SUBTRACT production, suffering interference from the ADD production, would come to apply less rapidly and reliably.

Table 9-2   Luchin's 1939 Water-Jug Problems

Problems	Capacity of Jug A	Capacity of Jug B	Capacity of Jug C	Desired Quantity
1	21	127	3	100
2	14	163	25	99
3	18	43	10	5
4	9	42	6	21
5	20	59	4	31
6	23	49	3	20
7	15	39	3	18
8	28	76	3	25
9	18	48	4	22
10	14	36	8	6

The set effect that Luchins is most famous for demonstrating is the *Einstellung effect,* or *mechanization of thought,* which is illustrated by the series of problems in Table 9-2. Subjects were given these problems in this order and required to find solutions for each. Take time out from reading this text and try to solve each problem.

All problems except 8 can be solved using the $B - 2C - A$ method (that is, filling B, twice pouring B into C to fill C, and once pouring B into A). For problems 1 through 5, this solution is the simplest, but for problems 7 and 9 the simpler solution of $A + C$ applies. Problem 8 cannot be solved by the $B - 2C - A$ method, but can be solved by the simpler solution of $A - C$. Problems 6 and 10 are also solved more simply as $A - C$ than $B - 2C - A$. Of Luchins' subjects who received the whole setup of ten problems, 83 percent used the $B - 2C - A$ method on problems 6 and 7, 64 percent failed to solve problem 8, and 79 percent used the $B - 2C - A$ method for problems 9 and 10. The performance of subjects who worked on all 10 problems was compared with the performance of control subjects who only saw the last five problems. These control subjects did not see the biasing $B - 2C - A$ problems. Fewer than 1 percent of the control subjects used $B - 2C - A$ solutions and only 5 percent failed to solve problem 8. Thus, the first five problems can create a powerful bias for a particular solution. This bias hurt solution of problems 6 through 10.

Note that the Einstellung effect does not involve creating a general bias for subtraction over addition. The critical problem, 8, involved subtraction too. Rather, subjects are remembering a particular sequence of operations, and it is memory for this sequence that is blinding them to other possibilities. While these effects are quite dramatic, they are relatively easy to reverse with the exercise of cognitive control. Luchins found that simply by warning subjects by saying, "Don't be blind," after problem 5, more than 50 percent of the subjects overcame set for the $B - 2C - A$ solution.

Another kind of set effect in problem solving has to do with the influence of general semantic factors. This effect is nicely illustrated in the experiment of Safren (1962) on anagram solution. Safren presented subjects with lists such as the following in which each set of letters was to be unscrambled and made into a word:

kmli
recma
graus
foefce
teews
ikrdn

This is an example of an organized list, in that the individual words are all associated with drinking coffee. Safren compared solution times for organized lists such as these with those for unorganized lists. Median solution time was 12.2 seconds for anagrams from unorganized lists but 7.4 seconds for anagrams from organized lists. Presumably, the facilitation was due to the fact that the earlier items in the list associatively primed, and so made more available, the later words. Note that this anagram experiment contrasts with the water-jug experiment in that no particular procedure is being strengthened. Rather, what is being strengthened is part of the subject's factual (declarative) knowledge about spellings of associatively related words.

In general, set effects occur when some knowledge structures become more available at the expense of others. These knowledge structures can either be procedures, as in the water-jug problem, or declarative facts, as in the anagram problem. If the available knowledge is what subjects need for solving the problem, their problem solving will be facilitated. If the available knowledge is not what is needed, problem solving will be inhibited. It is good to realize that set effects can sometimes be easily dissipated (as with Luchins "don't be blind" instruction). If you find yourself stuck on a problem and you keep generating similar, unsuccessful approaches, it is often useful to force yourself to back off, change set, and try a different kind of solution.

Incubation Effects

Problem solvers frequently report that after trying and getting nowhere on a problem, they can put the problem aside for hours, days, or weeks and then, upon returning to it, can see the solution quickly. Numerous examples of this pattern were reported by the famous French mathematician Poincare (1929), for instance the following:

> Then I turned my attention to the study of some arithmetical questions apparently without much success and without a suspicion of any connection with my

Given state   Goal state

Chain *A*

Chain *B*

Chain *C*

Chain *D*

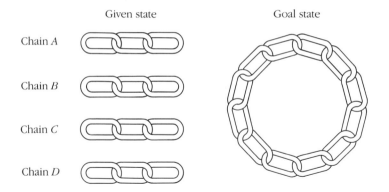

Figure 9-14 *The cheap-necklace problem. (Figure 4-5 from Wickelgren,* How to Solve Problems. *W. H. Freeman and Company. Copyright © 1974.)*

preceding researches. Disgusted with my failure, I went to spend a few days at the seaside, and thought of something else. One morning, walking on the bluff, the idea came to me, with just the same characteristics of brevity, suddenness and immediate certainty, that the arithmetic transformations of indeterminate ternary quadratic forms were identical with those of non-Euclidean geometry. [p. 388]

Such phenomena are referred to as *incubation effects.* An incubation effect was nicely demonstrated in an experiment by Silveira (1971). The problem she posed to subjects, called the cheap-necklace problem, is illustrated in Figure 9-14. Subjects were given the following instructions:

> You are given four separate pieces of chain that are each three links in length. It costs 2¢ to open a link and 3¢ to close a link. All links are closed at the beginning of the problem. Your goal is to join all 12 links of chain into a single circle at a cost of no more than 15¢.

Try to solve this problem yourself. A solution is provided in the section headed "Appendix" at the end of this chapter. Silveira tested three groups. A control group worked on the problem for half an hour; 55 percent of these subjects solved the problem. For one experimental group, their half hour spent on the problem was interrupted by a half-hour break in which they performed other activities; 64 percent of these subjects solved the problem. A third group had a four-hour break; and 85 percent of these subjects solved the problem. Silveira required her subjects to talk aloud as they solved the cheap-necklace problem. She found that subjects did not come back to the problems with solutions completely worked out. Rather, they started out trying to work out the problem much as before.

The best explanation for incubation effects relates them to set effects.

During initial attempts on a problem, subjects set themselves to think about the problem in certain ways and bring to bear certain knowledge structures. If this initial set is appropriate, subjects will solve the problem. However, if the initial set is not appropriate, subjects will be stuck throughout the session with inappropriate procedures. By going away from the problem, the activation of the inappropriate knowledge structures will dissipate and subjects will be able to take a fresh approach to the problem.

Numerous other attempts have been made to display incubation effects by interrupting problem solving, only some of which have proven successful (see Dominowski and Jenrick, 1972; Murray and Denny, 1969 for discussions). Sometimes worse performance is found with an interruption. A good example of a situation in which interruption is harmful is in the solving of a set of simultaneous equations. The only effect of interruption here would be subjects losing their places in the solution. Incubation effects are most likely to be found, in problems such as the cheap-necklace problem, which depend on a single key insight. As we discussed with respect to the issue of spacing in computer programing (Chapter 8), achieving the optimal balance of rest and work on a problem can be a delicate matter.

The Implications of Problem-Solving Research

The Nature of Expertise

Two types of recommendations can be made regarding the improvement of problem-solving abilities. One relates to creative problem solving and the other to routine problem solving. Many of the problems discussed in this chapter involve facing novel situations that require considerable amounts of insight. In these situations, people are usually painfully slow and frequently get on the wrong track. There are a number of ways of facilitating creative problem solving, which will be discussed below. However, first we will consider a very different way of dealing with problem solving. Experts in a specific problem domain tend to deal with problem-solving difficulties by doing away with the need for creative problem solving as much as possible. What distinguishes someone who is very successful in a problem area from someone who is not is the acquisition and practiced application of a lot of knowledge relevant to the problem domain. There is just no substitute for experience.

The importance of practice to expertise has been best documented for chess. No matter how intelligent a person is, becoming a chess expert takes years of practice. Indeed, many chess masters are not particularly intelligent in other dimensions. De Groot (1965, 1966) attempted to determine what separated expert chess players from novices. He found hardly any difference between expert players and weaker players, except of course, that the expert

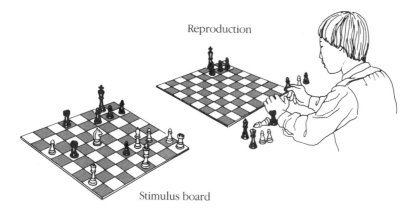

Reproduction

Stimulus board

Figure 9-15   *The reproduction task in Chase and Simon (1973). Subjects were to reproduce the configuration of pieces on the reproduction board. (Adapted from Klatzky, 1975.)*

players chose much better moves. For instance, chess masters consider about the same number of possible moves before selecting their move. In fact, if anything, masters consider fewer moves than chess duffers.

However, de Groot did find one intriguing difference between masters and weaker players. He presented chess masters with chess positions (i.e., chessboards with pieces in a configuration that occurred in a game) for just 5 seconds and then removed the chess position. The chess masters were able to reconstruct the positions of more than 20 pieces after just 5 seconds of study. In contrast, the chess duffer could reconstruct only 4 or 5 pieces—an amount much more in line with the traditional capacity of short-term memory (see Chapter 6). It appears that chess masters build up chunks of 4 or 5 pieces that reflect common board configurations as a function of their massive amount of experience with the task. Thus, they remember not individual pieces but rather chunks. In line with this analysis, if the players are presented with random chessboard positions rather than ones that are actually encountered in games, no difference is demonstrated between masters and duffers. Both types of subjects can only reconstruct a few chess pieces. The masters complain about being very uncomfortable and disturbed by such chaotic board positions.

Chase and Simon (1973) examined the nature of the chunks used by masters. They used a chessboard-reproduction task as illustrated in Figure 9-15. The subject's task was simply to reproduce the positions of pieces of a target chessboard on a test chessboard. In this task, subjects glanced at the target board, placed some pieces on the test board, glanced back to the target board, placed some more pieces on the test board, and so on. Chase and Simon defined as a chunk those pieces that subjects moved following one glance.

They found that these chunks tended to define meaningful game relations among the pieces. For instance, more than half of the master's chunks were pawn chains (configurations of pawns that occur frequently in chess).

Simon and Gilmartin (1973) estimate that masters have acquired on the order of 50,000 different chess patterns, that they can quickly recognize such patterns on a chessboard, and that this ability is what underlies their superior memory performance in chess. This 50,000 figure is not unreasonable when one considers the years of devoted study that becoming a chess master takes.

What might be the relationship between memory for so many chess patterns and superior performance in chess? Newell and Simon (1972) speculated that, in addition to learning many patterns, masters have also learned what to do in the presence of such patterns. Basically, they must have something on the order of 50,000 productions in which the condition of a production is a chess pattern and its action is the appropriate response to that pattern. For instance, if the chunk pattern is symptomatic of a weak side, the response of the production might be to suggest an attack on the weak side. Thus, masters effectively "see" possibilities for moves; they do not have to think them out. This explains why chess masters do so well at "lightning chess," in which they only have a few seconds to move.

So, to summarize, chess experts have stored the solutions to many problems that duffers must solve as novel problems. Duffers have to analyze different configurations, try to figure out their consequences, and act accordingly. Masters have all this information stored in memory, thereby claiming two advantages. First, they do not risk making errors in solving these problems, since they have stored the correct solution. Second, because they have stored the correct analysis of so many positions, they can focus their problem-solving efforts on more sophisticated aspects and strategies of chess. It bears repeating that chess players only become masters after years of playing. They have to be able to store a great deal of information about chess to be experts. Native intelligence is no substitute for knowledge.

To become an expert in any problem-solving field requires years of study. The effect of this study is to transform solution by creative problem solving into solution by the simple retrieval of stored answers. One becomes an expert by making routine many aspects of a problem that require creative problem solving for novices. Thus, one's behavior is less error prone and more attention can be focused on those aspects of the problem that cannot be routinized.

Improving Creative Problem Solving

A clear implication of our conclusions regarding expertise is that we cannot become expert problem solvers in all fields. Becoming an expert in any one field takes a great deal of time. Therefore, we are certain to be forever running into novel situations that require creative solutions, in the fields in which we are not experts as well as in the advanced areas of fields in which we are experts. The question is how to find solutions in these novel situations.

Can one become a better creative problem solver? Many people believe it is possible to improve one's creative problem-solving ability with practice. It has been informally observed that people such as mathematicians who solve many problems are better as creative problem solvers because of their experience. A number of books contain advice for effective problem solving (Adams, 1974; Polya, 1957; and Wicklegren, 1974). These are based on the premise that practice and training can lead to better creative problem solving. The issue clearly needs careful research, but it does seem that judicious application of our knowledge about problem solving should lead to better performance. For instance, many of the recommendations in Wicklegren's book appear to have their foundation in the ideas that we have reviewed in this chapter. Among these recommendations are the following:

1. It is often useful to make oneself explicitly aware of both the problem space for a problem and the operators for moving among states in that problem space.

2. It is important to be aware of the various techniques for attacking a problem. Among the techniques we considered are (a) working forward according to a similarity heuristic; (b) working backwards; (c) means-ends analysis; and (d) planning. The best technique to use will vary with the problem.

3. It is important to seek out the right representation for a problem.

4. There are dangers in becoming set on incorrect approaches to a problem. These dangers can be overcome by consciously changing set.

Like many of the implications from cognitive psychology, it is not enough to know the above principles in the abstract. One needs to practice their application to problems. Presumably, it is this area in which books such as those by Adams, Polya, or Wicklegren are useful. They provide abundant problems for practicing problem solving and advice about how these problems should be approached.

Remarks and Suggested Readings

A number of textbooks provide extensive reviews on problem solving. Many exhibit a certain tendency to equate the topic of thinking with problem solving. So, texts with the topic *thinking* in their title, such as Johnson (1972) or Vinacke (1974), include extensive discussions of the traditional problem-solving literature. A more modern review of problem-solving research is to

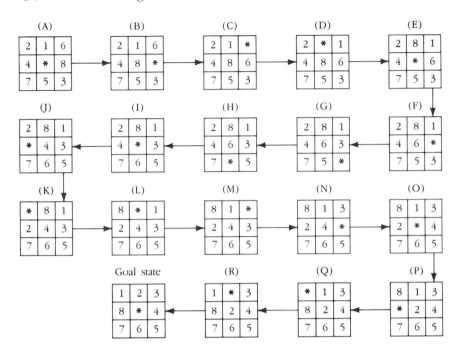

Figure 9-16 *The minimum-task solution for the 8-tile problem solved less efficiently in Figure 9-2.*

be found in Hayes (1978). Newell and Simon have been the most influential workers on problem solving in the modern era. Their work is extensively presented in their 1972 book. A more thorough discussion of GPS is to be found in Ernst and Newell (1969). Recent overviews of the problem-solving literature are to be found in Greeno (1978) and Simon (1978). Gregg (1974) edited a collection of papers on problem solving.

A great deal of research in artificial intelligence could be classified under the topic of problem solving. This work has had particularly strong influence on the thinking of cognitive psychologists, partly because of the efforts of Newell and Simon. The texts by Hunt (1975), Nilsson (1971), and Winston (1977) all provide discussions of the problem-solving techniques in artificial intelligence.

Appendix

A number of problems were presented in this chapter without solution. Figure 9-16 gives the minimum-path solution to the problem solved less efficiently in Figure 9-2.

With regard to the problem of the 27 cubic apples, the worm cannot succeed. To see that this is the case, imagine that the apples alternate in color, green and red, in a three-dimensional checkerboard pattern. If the center apple, from which the worm starts is red, there are 13 red apples and 14 green apples in all. Every time the worm moves from one apple to another, he must change colors. Since the worm starts from the red, this means that he cannot reach more green apples than red apples. Thus, he cannot visit all 14 green apples if he also visits each of the 13 red apples just once.

Solve the cheap-necklace problem in Figure 9-13 by opening all three links in one chain (at a cost of 6¢) and then using the three open links to connect together the remaining three chains (at a cost of 9¢).

Chapter 10

Deductive Reasoning

Summary

1. Research on deductive reasoning has frequently compared reasoning behavior in human beings with the prescriptions of a *logical system.* A logical system consists of *rules of inference,* which permit true conclusions to be derived from true premises.

2. *Sentential logic* is concerned with rules of inferences for statements built from simple propositions and from logical connectives such as *if, and, or,* and *not. Truth tables* prescribe the means of determining the truth of a complex statement in sentential logic from the truth of its component propositions.

3. *Conditional reasoning* is deduction involving statements of the form *If A then B,* where *A* and *B* are propositions. Subjects make errors in conditional-reasoning tasks because they misinterpret the meaning of the connective *if* and because they do not use the rule of inference known as *modus tollens.* Modus tollens allows one to reason from the premises *If A then B* and *B is false* to the conclusion *A is false.*

4. When the conclusion is not obvious in a reasoning task, subjects engage in problem-solving behavior to come up with a conclusion and to evaluate the conclusion.

5. *Categorical syllogisms* are reasoning problems involving the quantifiers *all, some, no,* and *some not. Venn Diagrams,* in which the categories are represented by circles, can be helpful in reasoning about categorical syllogisms.

6. Subjects make many errors on categorical syllogisms, particularly errors that involve the acceptance of invalid conclusions. This pattern of errors is partially accounted for by the *atmosphere hypothesis,* which asserts that subjects are inclined to accept conclusions similar to the premise.

7. In dealing with categorical syllogisms, subjects appear to be relying on a number of problem-solving heuristics that result in fairly good performance but that produce errors on certain critical problems.

8. Subjects' reasoning behavior deviates from the prescriptions of standard logic in that subjects frequently misinterpret statements, fail to recognize certain conclusions as valid, accept contingent conclusions as valid, and use problem-solving heuristics rather than rules of inference. This "lack of logic" can be explained in terms of deficits in logical training and of the fundamental intractability of logical deduction.

Logic and Reasoning

Deductive reasoning refers to the processes by which people evaluate and generate logical arguments. *Logic* is a subdiscipline of philosophy and mathematics that tries to formally specify what it means for an argument to be logically correct. To understand the psychological research on deductive reasoning, one has to understand the relationship of this research to logic. Until the twentieth century, logic and the psychology of thought were often considered one and the same. The famous Irish mathematician George Boole (1854) called his book on logical calculus *An Investigation into the Laws of Thought,* and designed it "in the first place, to investigate the fundamental laws of those operations of the mind by which reasoning is performed." Of course, humans did not always operate according to the prescriptions of logic, but such lapses were seen as the malfunctioning of mental machinery that was logical when it worked properly. In trying to improve one's mind, one tried to train oneself to be logical. A hundred years ago, a section on "cognitive processes" in a psychology text would have been about "logical thinking." The fact that only one of the three chapters in this section is on deductive reasoning reflects the current understanding that a large portion of human thought is not logical reasoning in any useful sense. However, the belief persists that in studying deductive reasoning we are dealing with mental operations that are fundamentally logical in nature.

Systems of Logic

Much of the research on deductive reasoning has been explicitly designed to compare human performance with the prescriptions of logic. In such experiments, the reasoning problems presented to subjects are analyzed in the terms used in logic. Therefore, it is essential to have some familiarity with the nature of systems of logic and the terminology of logic. In addition to its main purpose of discussing human reasoning, this chapter will explain some of the more important concepts of logic. This discussion is also intended to familiarize the student new to formal logic with some fundamental logical techniques. As will be argued at the end of the chapter, practicing logical techniques is a good way to improve one's reasoning ability. However, this chapter does not contain a complete exposition of formal logic; you must go to a logic text for that.

A logical system basically consists of certain *rules of inference,* statements that authorize certain conclusions if certain premises are true. A valid deduction in a logical system involves only correct applications of rules of inference. A particularly useful rule of inference is *modus ponens.* It states that given the proposition A *implies B* and given A, one may infer B. The statement A *implies B* is often rendered *If A then B.* So, suppose we are told the following:

1. If it rains tomorrow, then the game will be cancelled.
2. If the game is cancelled, then our team will surely lose the pennant.
3. It will rain tomorrow.

From 1 and 3 we can infer 4 by modus ponens:

4. The game will be cancelled.

From 2 and 4 we can infer 5:

5. Our team will surely lose the pennant.

This example is an instance of a valid deduction. By *valid* we mean that if premises 1 through 3 are true, the conclusion 5 must be true. Of course, the premises might not be true, in which case the conclusion need not be true. Logic and deductive reasoning are not concerned with examining the truth of the premises in a logical argument. Rather, the concern is with whether the premises logically imply the conclusions.

Another rule of inference is *modus tollens.* This rule states that if we are given the proposition A *implies B* and the fact that B is false, then we can infer that A is false. Below is an inference exercise that requires the use of modus tollens. Suppose we are given the following premises:

6. If it snows tomorrow, then we will go skiing.

7. If we go skiing, then we will be happy.

8. We are not going to be happy.

Then it follows from 7 and 8 by modus tollens that

9. We will not be going skiing,

and it follows from 6 and 9 by modus tollens that

10. It is not going to snow tomorrow.

Is Human Deduction Logical?

Determining whether human deduction is logical might seem quite easy. One could give people logical problems such as the ones above and see if they went through the same steps of deduction as in the logical system just illustrated. However, subjects' failures to make deductions of logic corresponding to those above would not mean that their reasoning—and hence human reasoning—was illogical. Many different logics exist besides the one sketched in the preceding section, and these logics would provide different sequences of deductive steps. One sequence of deductive steps is not inherently more logical than another. When we ask whether human reasoning is logical we are not asking whether it can be equated with any particular logic; rather, we are asking whether it has a property that all logics have in common, the property of *soundness*. By soundness we mean that the logic does not deduce untrue conclusions from true premises.

In a certain sense it is clear that human reasoning is not logical by the soundness criterion. People are forever making mistakes in reasoning and will often admit they are wrong when the mistakes are pointed out. However, if the only errors were "slips of the mind," we still might argue that there was a sense in which human reasoning was basically sound. That is, people really "know better" and could do better, but they are sometimes sloppy. The real question is whether there are situations in which humans will insist that a certain conclusion follows when it does not. The answer to this question is that such situations apparently do exist. Consider the validity of the following syllogism:

> Some members of the labor party are self-educated.
>
> No Wallonians belong to the labor party.
>
> Therefore, at least some Wallonians are not self-educated.

Begg and Denny (1969) found that 55 percent of their subjects considered this kind of syllogism to be logically valid, which it is not. This percentage is far too high and consistent to be a random "slip of the mind."

However, as an indication of the difficulties involved in this issue, even this example does not mean that people are illogical. Consider the predicament of subjects trying to decide whether the conclusion in the above example followed from the two premises. They might really be unable to decide and might just be guessing. The assertion that subjects are logical does not require that they be able to successfully complete every deduction. It only requires that they not think that an answer logically follows when it does not. The critical question is whether a subject will accept an illogical conclusion such as that above and firmly believe it to be true. The answer to this question appears to be yes. In an experiment (Anderson, 1976, chap. 9) subjects were encouraged to indicate when they were uncertain as to the validity of conclusions. Still, a full 40 percent insisted on accepting an invalid conclusion such as the one above, and some were so adamant in their belief that they entered into heated debates with the experimenter.

Pragmatic Deduction

As has been suggested by a number of writers (e.g., Chapman and Chapman, 1959; Henle, 1962), humans often do not even attempt to be logical in their reasoning. Rather, their deduction is often better characterized as *pragmatic* or *probabilistic*—that is, it is based on inferences that are likely to be true and that function well in the practical world. People learn that when certain facts (premises) are true, other facts (conclusions) have a high probability of being true. They have rules for predicting the truth of the conclusions given the truth of the premises. It is useful to think of these pragmatic rules as being cast in the form of productions such as those we studied in Chapter 8. Thus, a person might have the following rule:

> IF   a dog sees a cat
> THEN   the dog will chase the cat

If Rover sees Boots, then the production will apply and predict that Rover will chase the cat. Of course, this deduction is hardly necessarily true, but a person would have some reason to believe it. Note that such productions behave in accordance with modus ponens. That is, they predict a consequence given the truth of certain antecedent propositions. Indeed, we have even chosen to represent productions in *if–then* form.

People very often do not distinguish logical conclusions from highly likely inferences. This fact was shown quite clearly in some ratings gathered by Reder (1976). She had subjects read stories and judge the plausibility of inferences from the stories. For example, in one story, this line appeared:

> The teacher dragged the jock to the podium by his hair.

Subjects were asked to judge the plausibility of the following two statements, given the assertion above:

1. The jock was at the podium.
2. The teacher did not like the jock.

Subjects judged the two to be equally plausible although 1 follows logically from the definition of *drag to* and 2 could conceivably be false. Reder found that throughout her data subjects tended not to discriminate between necessary deductions and highly plausible conclusions. Presumably, they had productions for making both kinds of inferences. Thus, for sentence 1 above their production might be

P1:   IF   one person drags a second person to a location
         THEN   the second person is at the location

And for 2, their production might be

P2:   IF   one person drags a second person by the hair
         THEN   the first person does not like the second person

For purposes of getting around in the world and understanding discourse, there is no practical purpose in making a distinction between the kinds of inferences exemplified by P1 and P2. Both are almost certain to be true, and the difference between an inference that is 100 percent certain and one that is 99 percent certain is negligible. If a stranger approaches me, puts a gun in my face, and asks for my wallet, the inference that he wants to steal my wallet is likely to be true. The inference is in no way a necessary one, but I would not want my system to refuse to make it because of niceties of logical necessity.

The fact that often no practical distinction exists between logical necessity and high plausibility does not refute the usefulness of logical deduction. Many situations require precise rather than probabilistic reasoning. Much of science, mathematics, and engineering rests on logical deduction. The enormous contribution of these fields to modern life demonstrates the potential importance of the distinction between a logical necessity and a highly probable inference. It is also clear that many of society's decision-making bodies, such as the U.S. Congress, could do with a greater infusion of logical reasoning.

Despite the prevalence of pragmatic reasoning, we will focus in this chapter on research concerning people's efforts to reason logically. Most research on reasoning has involved logical reasoning, and this research has provided some interesting findings. In the next chapter, on inductive reasoning, we will discuss some aspects of pratmatic reasoning.

Conditional Reasoning

Conditional reasoning refers to how people reason with implicational or conditional statements, for example,

> If the maid hid the gun, then the butler was not at the scene of the crime.

Such conditional statements are important in mathematics and science, and, as the above example suggests, they can be significant in the evaluation of evidence. Therefore, it is important to understand how people tend to reason about such statements and what errors they are prone to in their reasoning.

The Logical Connectives

This section is concerned with how subjects reason with the conditional connective *if–then,* and, to a lesser degree, with the other logical connectives, *and, or,* and *not* (or *is false*). These connectives are often represented in logic by the symbols ⊃ , &, ∨, and ∼, respectively. Thus, the sentence

> If John goes to school or Mary stays home, then their father will be happy and their mother will not be happy.

would be represented in this way:

> [(John goes to school) ∨ (Mary stays home)]
> ⊃ [(father is happy) & ∼ (mother is happy)]

Note that brackets are used to indicate which elements belong together. Often, in formal analysis as well as in some experiments, propositions are represented by single capital letters. Thus, the above might be represented

$$[(P \vee Q)] \supset [(R \, \& \sim S)],$$

where

$$P = \text{John goes to school}$$
$$Q = \text{Mary stays home}$$
$$R = \text{father is happy}$$
$$S = \text{mother is happy}$$

Truth Tables

One way of analyzing the meaning of expressions in standard logic is by means of *truth tables.* A truth table specifies means of determining the truth of a complex expression from the truth of its components. Table 10-1 gives the truth tables for ∼ (negation), & (conjunction), ∨ (disjunction), and ⊃ (implication). These tables specify whether a combination is true (T) or false (F) for every combination of the component propositions.

Table 10-1   Truth Table Analysis

A. Negation		B. Conjunction			C. Disjunction			D. Implication or Conditional		
P	$\sim P$	P	Q	$P \& Q$	P	Q	$P \vee Q$	P	Q	$P \supset Q$
T	F	T	T	T	T	T	T	T	T	T
F	T	T	F	F	T	F	T	T	F	F
		F	T	F	F	T	T	F	T	T
		F	F	F	F	F	F	F	F	T

Negation, in part A of Table 10-1, involves just one component proposition, and it reverses the truth of that proposition. The truth table for $\sim P$ (read *not P* or *P is false*) contains just two lines to represent the two possible truth values of P. The first line indicates that if P is true, $\sim P$ is false, while the second line indicates that if P is false $\sim P$ is true.

A *conjunction,* in part B of Table 10-1, involves two propositions, and it is true only if both its component propositions are true. In the truth table for $P \& Q$, four lines are required to represent the possible combinations of truth values for the component propositions P and Q. The first line tells us that if both P and Q are true then $P \& Q$ is true. The second line tells us that if P is true and Q is false then $P \& Q$ is false. The last two lines present the other possible combinations of truth values for P and Q. For both combinations $P \& Q$ is false.

Disjunction, in part C of Table 10-1, is referred to as the *nonexclusive or,* since it is true when either or both of the components is true. Thus, $P \vee Q$ is true in the first line, where P and Q are both true, in the second, where only P is true, and in the third, where only Q is true. Disjunction is only false in the fourth line, where both P and Q are false. The nonexclusive use of *or* contrasts with the frequent use of the *exclusive or* in everyday language, which is read as being true if just one of the components is true. For instance, with respect to the sentence

John loves Mary or he loves Fred,

we would usually assume that he only loves one or the other, not both.

The interpretation of an implication in part D of Table 10-1 deviates from the way *if* is frequently interpreted in natural language. Note that an implication is considered true if the first clause (called the *antecedent; P* in Table 10-1) is false, no matter what the truth of the second clause (called the *consequent; Q* in Table 10-1). Thus, $P \supset Q$ is true in lines 3 and 4 of Table 10-1D, where the antecedent P is false. $P \supset Q$ is only false in line 2 where P is true and Q is false. In ordinary language it seems more natural to consider expressions whose antecedent is false as lacking any truth value. For instance, consider this statement:

> If John Kennedy is alive, then he is living in South America.

Given that the antecedent about Kennedy is false, it does not make a lot of sense to speak of the truth of the whole sentence. Certainly, it seems unnatural to say that the sentence must be true. Research into human reasoning investigates the ways in which such reasoning deviates from standard truth-table definitions and also the success with which subjects reason according to their own definitions.

Conditional Syllogisms

A considerable amount of research has focused on reasoning with conditional syllogisms (e.g., Marcus and Rips, 1979; Rips and Marcus, 1977; Staudenmayer, 1975; Taplin, 1971; Taplin and Staudenmayer, 1973). Examples of conditional syllogisms include the following:

1. If the ball rolls left, the green lamp comes on.
   The ball rolls left.
   Therefore, the green lamp comes on.
2. If God exists, life will be beautiful.
   God does not exist.
   Therefore, life is not beautiful.

Or, more abstractly, we may represent these syllogisms in the following way:

$$1. \quad \frac{\begin{array}{l} P \supset Q \\ P \end{array}}{\therefore Q}$$

$$2. \quad \frac{\begin{array}{l} P \supset Q \\ \sim P \end{array}}{\therefore \sim Q}$$

Conditional syllogisms involve such arguments as these, where one premise is an implication between two propositions, the second premise is one of these propositions or its negation, and the conclusion is the other proposition or its negation. Subjects are asked to determine whether these syllogisms are logically valid. In the above case, syllogism 1 is valid and 2 is not.

The correct evaluation of conditional syllogisms is critical to proper performance in such academic areas as science and mathematics. The importance of such reasoning probably accounts for the considerable amount of study it has received. One might imagine that logicians and scientists would be better than the average population at evaluating conditional syllogisms.

However, researchers typically use untrained college undergraduates in their experiments rather than trained mathematicians or logicians. Often, undergraduates with explicit training in logic are excluded from these experiments. Therefore, research on this kind of reasoning is designed to understand how fairly intelligent people reason about implications when their only contact with the logical connective *if* has been in ordinary life.

Consider a representative experiment by Rips and Marcus (1977) in which subjects from the University of Chicago were asked to evaluate eight types of syllogisms. Though the syllogisms are presented abstractly in Table 10-2, the subjects were actually tested with concrete propositions. An example would be

> If the ball rolls left, the green lamp comes on.
> The green lamp comes on.
> Therefore, the ball rolled left.

Subjects were asked to judge whether the conclusion was always true, sometimes true, or never true given the premises. Table 10-2 gives the percentage of responses in each category for each type of syllogism.

Problems 1 and 2 in Table 10-2 indicate that subjects could apply modus ponens quite successfully. However, they had much greater difficulty with the other form of the conditional syllogism permitting a valid conclusion. This is the form in problems 7 and 8, which required application of the rule of modus tollens. Here more than 30 percent of the subject population failed to realize that one can reason from the negation of the second term in a conditional to the negation of the first term. Syllogisms 3 and 4 display evidence for a fallacy in conditional reasoning known as *denial of the antecedent* (the first term in the conditional). Almost 20 percent of the subject population believed that one can conclude that Q is not true if one knows that *P implies Q* and that P is not true. Problems 5 and 6 display a tendency for a fallacy known as *affirmation of the consequent* (the second term in the conditional). On these problems almost 20 percent of the subject population believed that one can conclude that P is true from knowing *P implies Q* and Q.

It seems that one source of the fallacies displayed in problems 3 through 6 originates from the fact that subjects do not interpret conditionals in the same way that logicians do. This discrepancy has been demonstrated in a series of experiments by Taplin (1971), Taplin and Staudenmayer (1973), and Staudenmayer (1975). They showed that many subjects interpreted the conditional as being what logicians would call the *biconditional*. The biconditional is rendered in English unambiguously by the rather awkward construction *if and only if*. For instance,

> Israel will use atomic weapons if and only if it is faced with annihilation.

Table 10-2   Percent of Total Responses for Eight Types of Conditional Syllogisms

Syllogism	Always	Sometimes	Never
1. $P \supset Q$ $\underline{P}$ $\therefore Q$	100[a]	0	0
2. $P \supset Q$ $\underline{P}$ $\therefore \sim Q$	0	0	100[a]
3. $P \supset Q$ $\underline{\sim P}$ $\therefore Q$	5	79[a]	16
4. $P \supset Q$ $\underline{\sim P}$ $\therefore \sim Q$	21	77[a]	2
5. $P \supset Q$ $\underline{Q}$ $\therefore P$	23	77[a]	0
6. $P \supset Q$ $\underline{Q}$ $\therefore \sim P$	4	82[a]	14
7. $P \supset Q$ $\underline{\sim Q}$ $\therefore P$	0	23	77[a]
8. $P \supset Q$ $\underline{\sim Q}$ $\therefore \sim P$	57[a]	39	4

[a]The correct response.

Adapted from Rips and Marcus, 1977.

With the biconditional, if either the first or second premise is true, the other will be true. Similarly, if either the first or second premise is false the other will be false. The truth table for the biconditional (denoted ↔) is given below:

P	Q	$P \leftrightarrow Q$
T	T	T
T	F	F
F	T	F
F	F	T

Note that under the biconditional interpretation, if the first clause *(P)* is false, then the second *(Q)* must also be false. This relationship can be verified on the truth table for the biconditional: when *P* is false and *P*↔*Q* is true, then *Q* must be false. Thus, denial of the antecedent is not a fallacy if one is using a biconditional interpretation. Also under the biconditional analysis, if the second clause *(Q)* is true, then the first *(P)* must also be true. Thus, affirmation of the consequent is not a fallacy either if one is using a biconditional interpretation.

The Failure to Apply Modus Tollens

The hypothesis that subjects interpret the conditional as a biconditional explains why some subjects display the fallacies of affirming the consequent or denying the antecedent, but it leaves unexplained the difficulty they have in applying modus tollens in problems 7 and 8 of Table 10-2. Modus tollens is a valid inference even if the conditional is interpreted as a biconditional. Table 10-2 actually is a rather mild case of failure to apply modus tollens. In other situations the failure can be much more grievous.

A very striking demonstration of failure to apply modus tollens comes from a series of experiments performed by Wason (for a review see Wason and Johnson-Laird, 1972, chap. 13 and 14). In one of the principal experiments from this research, four cards showing the following symbols were placed in front of subjects:

Subjects were told that a letter appeared on one side of each card and a number on the other. The task was to judge the validity of the following rule, which referred only to these four cards:

> If a card has a vowel on one side, then it has an even number on the other side.

The subjects' task was to turn over only those cards that had to be turned over for the correctness of the rule to be judged. Forty-six percent of the subjects elected to turn over both E and 4, which is a wrong combination of choices. The E had to be turned over, but the 4 did not have to be turned over, since neither a vowel nor a consonant on the other side would have falsified the rule. Only 4 percent elected to turn over E and 7, which are the correct choices. An odd number behind the E or a vowel behind the 7 would have falsified the rule. Another 33 percent of the subjects elected to turn over the E only. The remaining 17 percent of the subjects made other, incorrect choices.

So, subjects displayed two types of errors in this task. First, they often turned over the 4, another example of the fallacy of affirming the consequent. Again, this response might just have reflected an interpretation by subjects of the conditional as biconditional. However, even more striking was the almost

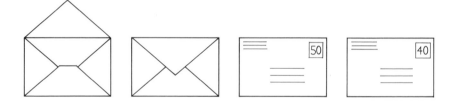

Figure 10-1 *Material used in the envelope experiment by Johnson-Laird, Legrenzi, and Legrenzi (1972). Subjects were asked which envelopes should be turned over to test the rule* If a letter is sealed, then it has a 50-lire stamp on it.

total failure to take the modus tollens step of disconfirming the consequent and determining whether the antecedent was also disconfirmed (in other words, turning over the 7).

These failures of reasoning have been observed over a wide range of situations, but interesting exceptions have been demonstrated. Johnson-Laird, Legrenzi, and Legrenzi (1972) presented subjects with the material in Figure 10-1. They asked subjects to imagine that they were Post Office workers engaged in sorting letters. The task was to discover whether the postal regulation requiring an extra 10 lire of postage on sealed letters had been violated. Thus, subjects were to test this rule:

> If a letter is sealed, then it has a 50-lire stamp on it.

They were asked which letters should be turned over. Here, 21 of the 24 subjects made the right choice, turning over the sealed letter and the letter with the 40-lire stamp. The fact that they had little difficulty in seeing that the 40-lire envelope should be turned over indicated that use of a rule such as modus tollens can depend on context. While the rule of modus tollens may not be generally available, it does seem available in the context where one is trying to "catch cheaters."

Inability to reason with modus tollens is a major weakness of human deduction. For instance, students coming into college math courses, where they need to be able to use the rule, often need special coaching on the rule. This widespread failure to use modus tollens probably reflects the fact that we are not practiced in thinking about what is not the case. The rule requires us to realize $P \supset Q$ is equivalent to $\sim Q \supset \sim P$. While we are not generally practiced in reasoning about negation of a proposition, the experimental results cited above illustrate that we are practiced in certain contexts. The fact that availability of an inference rule depends on context illustrates another way in which human reasoning is different from logical deduction. Such a rule as modus tollens would apply in all appropriate situations in logic.

Deductive Reasoning as Problem Solving

We are often faced with problems of deduction for which no ready-made rules of inference exist. Consider the following type of problem (adapted from Johnson-Laird, 1975), which often stumps subjects:

1. All people who live on Vancouver Island are members of the Social Credit Party.
2. No Doukabours live on Vancouver Island.
3. What can you say about the relationship between members of the Social Credit Party and Doukabours?

Certainly, no immediate answer comes to my mind. This kind of question creates a problem-solving situation. To answer the question, I have to find a combination of inferences that clearly applies. Try to solve the question for yourself and then consider the following sequence, which does successfully result in an answer for me:

1. Consider someone who lives in Vancouver Island and is a Social Credit party member. Statement 1 implies that such people exist.*
2. Statement 2 implies that such a person is not a Doukabour since he lives on Vancouver Island.
3. Therefore, some Social Credit party members are not Doukabours.

Finding such a sequence of steps can be a major problem. Indeed, in mathematics and logic many famous examples of conjectures have defied all attempts at proof for decades or centuries. Some of the most brilliant minds have failed to find the sequence of steps that would prove or disprove such conjectures. To the extent that it is not obvious what follows logically from a set of statements, subjects have to engage in various problem-solving behaviors to arrive at their deductions. In the remainder of this chapter, we will consider situations where subjects must engage in considerable amounts of problem solving to perform their deductions.

Deductive-Reasoning Protocols

Newell and Simon (1972) reexamined some logic tasks first studied by Moore and Anderson (1954). These tasks were presented to subjects in the form of abstract propositions denoted by letters such as *P*, *Q*, and *R*. The subject's task

---

*I am assuming here that the universal permits the assumption of the existence of at least some.

was to derive a conclusion from certain assumed premises. For instance, one problem given to a subject was the following:

$$\text{ASSUME} \quad 1. \ R \supset \sim P$$
$$2. \ \sim R \supset Q$$
$$\text{PROVE} \quad 3. \ \sim(\sim Q \ \& \ P)$$

They asked subjects to reason out loud as they attempted to prove the conclusion. They recorded their subjects' reasoning. Such records are referred to as *protocols*. After making a few frustrated stabs at the problem, one subject settled into a means-ends analysis. First, he noted that Q and P were together in the same proposition in the to-be-proven conclusion and that they were not together in the premise clauses. In his protocol he said,

> Oh, I don't have Q and P together in either expression so I have to get them together somehow.

Thus, the subject was setting as his first subgoal the reduction of a major difference between the premises and the conclusion. He had been given a number of rules of inference for manipulating these logical expressions and now he turned to consider those rules that served to change the composition of expressions. He hit upon the following, called the *chaining rule:*

> a. If you have $A \supset B$ and $B \supset C$, you may infer $A \supset C$.

However, he realized that he could not apply this rule because the premises were not in correct form:

> But before I can do that . . . I have to . . . um . . . interchange, or make an R into a $\sim R$.

Next, he applied one of the rules of inference he had been given, which was

> b. If you have $A \supset B$ you may infer $\sim B \supset \sim A$.

Applied to premise 1 this rule yielded

$$4. \ P \supset \sim R.$$

Now the subject had reached the point where he could apply the chaining rule, which he had previously intended to use. Applying it to 4 and 2, he derived

$$5. \ P \supset Q.$$

From this point, the subject appeared to move directly to the solution without any further planning. He first applied the following inference rule from the set he had been given:

> c. If you have $A \supset B$, you may infer $\sim A \lor B$,

which, applied to 5, yielded

6. $\sim P \lor Q.$

Then he recalled the following rule:

d. If you have $A \lor B$, then you may infer that $\sim(\sim A \And \sim B)$,

which, applied to 6, gave him his target expression:

7. $\sim(\sim Q \And P).$

What is striking about the above episode is that it displays many features that are characteristic of problem-solving behavior. The subject searches a state space, uses similarity to guide his search, forms plans, and performs means-ends analysis. As evidence of the fact that subjects were solving these logic problems in a means-ends fashion, Newell and Simon report considerable success in applying their General Problem Solver model (discussed in Chapter 9) to simulating the behavior of subjects in such tasks.

Subjects in these experiments were reasoning with formal logic. They were given abstract expressions and asked to make inferences according to certain transformation rules. They were not even informed as to the meaning of such operational symbols as $\lor$; therefore, they were clearly manipulating abstract symbols. It remains to be shown that in situations where they are reasoning about natural-language expressions rather than abstract logical formulae, subjects also behave in a clear problem-solving mode. The next section, on reasoning with quantifiers, will provide this needed evidence for the problem-solving character of human deduction.

Reasoning About Quantifiers

Much of human knowledge is cast with logical quantifiers such as *all* or *some.* Witness Lincoln's famous statement: "You may fool all the people some of the time; you can even fool some of the people all of the time; but you can't fool all of the people all the time." Our scientific laws are cast with such quantifiers also. It is extremely important to understand how people reason with such quantifiers.

The Categorical Syllogism

Modern logic is greatly concerned with analyzing the meaning of quantifiers such as *all* and *some,* as in, for example, the statement *All philosophers read some books.* At the turn of this century, the sophistication with which such quantified statements were analyzed increased considerably (see Church, 1956, for a historical discussion). This more advanced treatment of quantifiers is covered in most modern logic courses. However, most of the research on

(A)   All *A*'s are *B*'s.

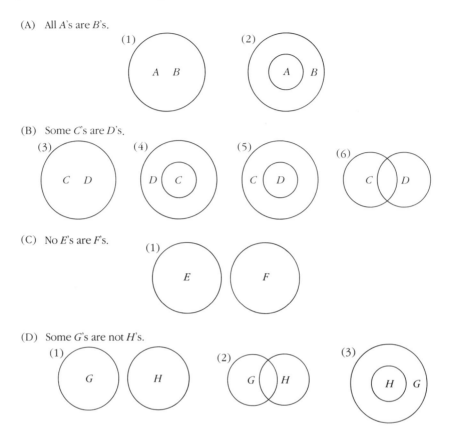

(B)   Some *C*'s are *D*'s.

(C)   No *E*'s are *F*'s.

(D)   Some *G*'s are not *H*'s.

Figure 10-2   *Venn-diagram interpretations of categorical statements 1' through 4'.*

quantifiers in psychology has focused on a simpler and older kind of quantified deduction, called the *categorical syllogism.* Much of Aristotle's writing on reasoning concerned the categorical syllogism. Extensive discussion of categorical syllogisms can be found in textbooks on logic as recent as that of Cohen and Nagel (1934).

Categorical syllogisms involve statements containing the quantifiers *some, all, no,* and *some not.* Examples of such categorical statements are

      1. All doctors are rich.

      2. Some lawyers are dishonest.

      3. No politician is trustworthy.

      4. Some actors are not handsome.

In experiments, the categories (for example, doctors, rich people, lawyers, dishonest people, and so on) in such statements are frequently represented by letters, say *A, B, C.* This system serves as a handy shorthand for describing the material. In the traditional analysis of categorical statements, the sentences above would be analyzed into *subject* and *predicate,* the first category (for example, doctor) being the subject and the second category (rich people) the predicate. Thus, the above statements might be rendered in this way:

1.' All *A*s are *B*s.
2.' Some *C*s are *D*s.
3.' No *E*s are *F*s.
4.' Some *G*s are not *H*s.

A *Venn diagram* is a graphic interpretation of such a categorical statement. Figure 10-2 presents Venn diagrams for the four types of statements above (parts A through D correspond to 1' through 4' above). In the Venn diagrams, each category is represented by a circle, and the area within a circle represents all the individuals in the category. Where two circles overlap, this overlap represents individuals in both categories.

There are four possible Venn diagrams. First, the circles for the two categories can be identical. This means that the two categories contain the same individuals. Second, one circle can be within the other. This means that all the individuals in the first category are in the second but some individuals in the second are not in the first. Third, the two circles can partially overlap. This means that some individuals are in both categories but some individuals in each category are not in the other category. Finally, the two circles can be completely disjoint. This means that there are no indidivuals who are in both categories.

Figure 10-2A illustrates that the quantifier *all* can have two possible interpretations: either (1) *A* and *B* are identical or (2) *B* includes *A* and things other than *A* (i.e., the *B* circle contains the *A* circle). Part B shows that *some* has four possible interpretations. People often interpret *some* as only implying the meaning conveyed by Venn diagram 6, in which *C* and *D* overlap, but some *C* are not *D* and some *D* are not *C.* However, the standard logical meaning of *some* allows the ambiguity in Figure 10-2B. In reasoning experiments, subjects often have to be told explicitly that *some* has this broader meaning. Part C of the figure gives the one interpretation for *no.* Finally, part D illustrates the three meanings of *some not.* We will return to these Venn diagrams after discussing results from some experiments studying how subjects reason with categorical syllogisms.

A categorical syllogism typically contains two premises and a conclusion.

All three statements are of a categorical nature. The following is a simple example:

1.   All *A*s are *B*s.

All *B*s are *C*s.

∴ All *A*s are *C*s.

This syllogism, incidently, is one that most people correctly recognize as valid. On the other hand, people accept with almost equal frequency the following invalid syllogism:

2.   Some *A*s are *B*s.

Some *B*s are *C*s.

∴ Some *A*s are *C*s.

The conclusion in syllogism 2 is neither necessarily true nor false; rather, it is *contingent.* A set of rules exists that can be used to determine whether the conclusions of syllogisms are valid. The rule relevant to syllogism 2 above involves the concept of a particular premise. A particular premise is one that uses *some* or *some not:*

1. From two *particular* (quantified by *some, some not*) premises nothing can be derived.

Other such rules follow:

2. From two *negative* premises, nothing can be derived.
3. If one premise is particular, the conclusion cannot be *universal* (quantified by *all, no*).
4. If one premise is negative, the conclusion cannot be positive.

Some contingent syllogisms are not caught by these rules, however. For example, the following syllogism is not valid:

3.   All *A* are *B.*

All *C* are *B.*

∴ All *A* are *C.*

Traditional texts on logic such as Cohen and Nagel (1934) list even more rules to help spot fallacies such as 3 above. For instance, example 3 reflects the error of the *undistributed middle.* The rule is a little complex, but the basic idea is that the middle term, *B,* which occurs in both premises, must occur at least once as either the subject in a universal premise or the predicate in a negative premise. In the above, *B* occurs both times as the predicate in universal affirmative statements. It is clear, however, that average subjects do not have these kinds of rules, which would allow them to catch such fallacies.

The Atmosphere Hypothesis

The general problem subjects seem to have with categorical syllogisms is that they are too willing to accept false conclusions. Many syllogisms, such as 2 and 3 above, are available, but subjects accept their conclusions as valid anyway. However, subjects are not completely indiscriminate in their acceptance of syllogisms. That is, while they will accept 3 they will not accept 4, and while they will accept 5 they will not accept 6.

> 4. All *A*s are *B*s.
>   All *C*s are *B*s.
>   ∴ No *A*s are *C*s.
>
> 5. No *A*s are *B*s.
>   No *B*s are *C*s.
>   ∴ No *A*s are *C*s.
>
> 6. No *A*s are *B*s.
>   No *B*s are *C*s.
>   ∴ All *A*s are *C*s.

To account for this pattern of errors, Woodworth and Sells (1935) proposed the *atmosphere hypothesis*. This hypothesis stated that the logical terms *(some, all, no, not)* used in the syllogism created an "atmosphere" which predisposed subjects to accept conclusions with the same terms. There are two parts to the atmosphere hypothesis. One part asserts that subjects would accept a positive conclusion to positive premises and a negative conclusion to negative premises. When the premises were mixed, the subjects would prefer a negative conclusion. Thus, they would tend to accept the following conclusion:

> 7. No *A*s are *B*s.
>   All *B*s are *C*s.
>   ∴ No *A*s are *C*s.

The other part of the atmosphere hypothesis concerns a subject's response to particular statements *(some, some not)* versus universal statements *(all* or *no)*. As the above examples illustrate, subjects will accept a universal conclusion if the premises are universal. They will accept a particular conclusion if the premises are particular. So they tend to accept syllogisms 8 and 9 but not 10 and 11.

> 8. Some *A*s are *B*s.
>   Some *B*s are *C*s.
>   ∴ Some *A*s are *C*s.
>
> 9. Some *A*s are not *B*s.
>   Some *B*s are not *C*s.
>   ∴ Some *A*s are not *C*s.

10.   Some *A*s are *B*s.
        Some *B*s are *C*s.
        ∴ All *A*s are *C*s.

11.   Some *A*s are not *B*s.
        Some *B*s are not *C*s.
        ∴ No *A*s are *C*s.

When one premise is particular and the other universal, subjects prefer a particular conclusion. So they will accept the following:

12.   All *A*s are *B*s.
        Some *B*s are *C*s.
        ∴ Some *A*s are *C*s.

It has been suggested that this tendency represents a "principle of caution." A particular statement involving *some* is less extreme and therefore more likely to be safe.

Consider the following invalid syllogism:

13.   No *A*s are *B*s.
        Some *B*s are *C*s.
        ∴ Some *A*s are not *C*s.

This syllogism seems to compact all of the atmosphere principles into one. Unfortunately, subjects do not always prefer the particular negative conclusion, given these premises. Chapman and Chapman (1959) found that for this set of premises the universal negative conclusion is preferred, that is, *No As are Cs*. However, Woodworth and Sells (1935) and Begg and Denny (1969) have found that the particular negative conclusion is preferred for these premises, in support of the atmosphere hypothesis.

Limitations of the Atmosphere Hypothesis

The atmosphere hypothesis has been quite successful in capturing many of the main trends in the data on syllogistic reasoning. However, it is becoming increasingly clear that this hypothesis does not represent the whole story. For one thing, according to the atmosphere hypothesis, subjects would be just as likely to accept the atmosphere-favored conclusion when it was contingent as when it was valid. That is, it predicts that subjects would be just as likely to accept

All *A*s are *B*s
Some *B*s are *C*s,
∴ Some *A*s are *C*s,

which is not valid, as they would be to accept

> Some As are Bs,
> All Bs are Cs,
> ∴ Some As are Cs,

which is valid. In fact, subjects are more likely to accept the conclusion in the valid case. Thus, subjects do display some ability to evaluate a syllogism accurately.

An even more serious limitation of the atmosphere hypothesis is that it fails to predict the effects that the form of a syllogism has on subjects' validity judgments. For instance, the hypothesis predicts that subjects would be no more likely to erroneously accept

> Some As are Bs,
> Some Bs are Cs,
> ∴ Some As are Cs

than they would to erroneously accept

> Some Bs are As,
> Some Cs are Bs,
> ∴ Some As are Cs.

In fact, it has now been established (Johnson-Laird and Steedman, 1978) that subjects are more willing to erroneously accept the conclusion in the former case. In general, subjects are more willing to accept a conclusion from *A* to *C* (that is, one that involves *A* as subject and *C* as predicate) if they can find a chain leading from *A* to *B* in one premise and *B* to *C* in the second premise. Other effects of the form of the argument rather than the quantifiers have been shown by Dickstein (1978).

In conclusion, while the atmosphere hypothesis clearly describes many qualitative features of the data on syllogism evaluation, the hypothesis obviously does not constitute the whole story. As the next section will argue, subjects appear to be using a variety of problem-solving heuristics in evaluating syllogisms, and the atmosphere hypothesis simply captures descriptively the central tendency of many of these heuristics.

Problem Solving and Categorical Syllogisms

To return to our problem-solving framework, it appears again that subjects are frequently unable to find the steps of inference that let them reason through to the truth or falsity of a conclusion. Consider one of the valid syllogisms that subjects often have great difficulty with:

> Some Bs are As,
> No Cs are Bs,
> ∴ Some As are not Cs.

In a study I did on problems like this with University of Michigan undergraduates as subjects, only 60 percent agreed that the above conclusion was valid. To help subjects reason through to the conclusion, I gave them a couple of intermediate steps on the way to the conclusion:

1. Some *B*s are *A*s.
2. No *C*s are *B*s.

From 1 it follows	3. Some *A*s are *B*s.
From 2 it follows	4. No *B*s are *C*s.
From 3 and 4 it follows	5. Some *A*s are not *C*s.

In this form, 80 percent of the subjects got this problem right.

Similarly, subjects have problems with contingent syllogisms because they tend to have no systematic way of showing that the conclusion need not be true. The way to prove that a syllogism is contingent is to look for counterexamples where the premises are true but the conclusion is not. One way to do this is by means of Venn diagrams. By considering various possible combinations of Venn diagrams, we are able to find counterexamples to categorical syllogisms.* To illustrate how this works, consider the following invalid syllogism:

No *A*s are *B*s,
All *B*s are *C*s,
∴ No *A*s are *C*s.

Figure 10-3 gives the only Venn diagram of the first premise (1) and the two Venn diagrams of the second premise, 2 and 3. In the Venn diagram (1) for the first premise, the two categories *A* and *B* are disjoint. In the Venn diagram (2) for the second premise, the category *B* is contained within *C*. In the other Venn diagram (3), for the second premise, *C* and *B* are identical. Venn diagrams 4 through 7 represent various possible combinations of diagram 1 for the first premise, with one of diagrams 2 and 3 for the second premise. In diagram 4, 1 and 2 are combined such that the circle for *C* in 2 does not touch *A*. In this diagram, *A* and *C* are disjoint. However, as 5 illustrates, it is also possible for the circle for *C* to overlap with *A*, and as 6 illustrates, it is even possible for *C* to include *A* completely. Diagram 7 represents the combination of 1 and 3. There is only one possibility for this combination. Since *C* and *B* are identical in 3, and *A* is disjoint from *B* in 1, *A* must be disjoint from *C* in 7. The conclusion *No A are C* in the above syllogism, while it describes combinations 4 and 7, does not describe diagrams 5 and 6. Thus, diagrams 5 and 6 are counterexamples to the conclusion; they show that possible interpretations of the premises are incompatible with the conclusion.

---

*Quine (1950) suggests a different way of using Venn diagrams in evaluating categorical syllogisms.

No *A*'s are *B*'s.

All *B*'s are *C*'s.

Possible combinations

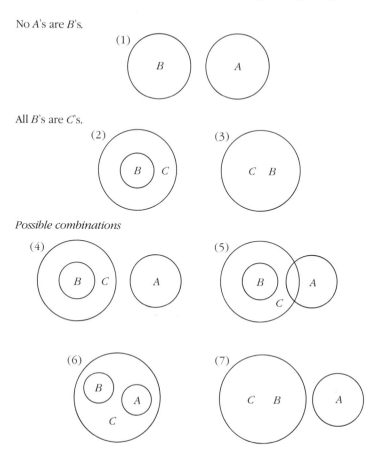

Figure 10-3 *Combinations of Venn-diagram representations of premises. If a valid conclusion follows from the premises, it must be consistent with all Venn-diagram combinations.*

Even if subjects do reason in terms of some model such as Venn diagrams, they may find it hard to construct a model that contradicts the conclusion. Consider the following syllogism:

Some *A*s are *B*s,
Some *B*s are *C*s.
∴ Some *A*s are *C*s.

Figure 10-4 shows that each premise has four Venn-diagram interpretations. Thirty-three distinct combinations of these premise diagrams are shown! (You

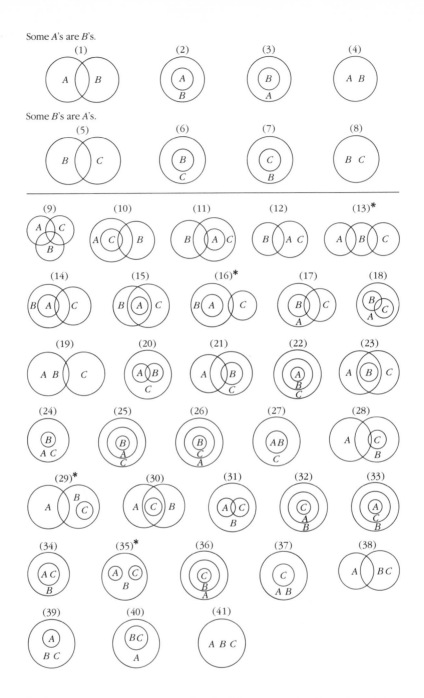

Figure 10-4 *Four Venn diagrams of each of the two premises* Some As are Bs *(1 through 4) and* Some Bs are Cs *(5 through 8) and 33 possible combinations of these implementations (9 through 41). By inspecting these combinations, one can determine if any conclusions are valid. The asterisks indicate combinations that violate the conclusion* Some As are Cs.

are not seriously expected to work through all these.*) Of these diagrams, only four (13, 16, 29, and 35) violate the conclusion. It would not be hard for a subject to miss these combinations and conclude that the syllogism was valid.

Simply stated, then, categorical syllogisms pose difficult problem-solving demands on a subject. A *representation problem* exists (see Chapter 9) in that subjects often do not know how to represent a state space for the problem (that is, steps in a deduction, combinations of Venn diagrams) so that they can solve the problem. Even if they do know of a state space for representing the problem, they will have difficulty in searching the space. Subjects often face a large space of possibilities to search and do not know how to conduct the search.

Errors Resulting from Heuristics

While it is understandable that subjects make as many errors as they do, it remains to be explained why they only accept some, and not all, contingent syllogisms. This phenomenon also seems to have a problem-solving explanation. Subjects use various heuristics (discussed in Chapter 9) to help them in their representation and search. These heuristics lead to errors on a few problems only, as with any good heuristic. Many of the heuristics that researchers have attributed to subjects lead to atmosphere errors. Indeed, rules 3 and 4 on p. 314, while perfectly correct, could lead to atmosphere errors if they were the only ones a subject used.

It may be that when the problem gets hard, some subjects don't think about the meaning of the statement but rather simply use the words *all, some, some not,* and *no* to evaluate the conclusion—just as the atmosphere hypothesis suggests. In itself, the atmosphere hypothesis proves not to be a bad heuristic. Using this method, subjects reject about 75 percent of the contingent syllogisms and identify most of the valid syllogisms. Thus, used by itself, the atmosphere heuristic leads to a performance more than 80 percent correct. This is not bad for such a crude heuristic.

Another explanation of errors is known as the *conversion hypothesis* (Henle, 1962; Chapman and Chapman, 1959). According to this explanation, subjects interpret *All As are Bs* to mean *A is the same as B. Some As are Bs* will be interpreted as meaning *Some As are Bs but not all As are Bs and not all Bs are As. Some As are not Bs* will get the same interpretation as *Some As are Bs.* Figure 10-5 shows the Venn-diagram representations of these favored interpretations. Each statement now is interpreted by a single Venn diagram. In contrast, as illustrated in Figure 10-2, the correct interpretation of these statements often involves multiple Venn diagrams. Thus, subjects have simpli-

---

*Actually, it is not entirely clear how many distinct Venn diagrams might be constructed. Figure 10-4 illustrates all the distinct relations between *A* and *C* consistent with each pairing of an interpretation of *A* and *B* with an interpretation of *B* and *C.* Many other set relations exist among *A, B,* and *C* (someone has estimated 64).

(A)

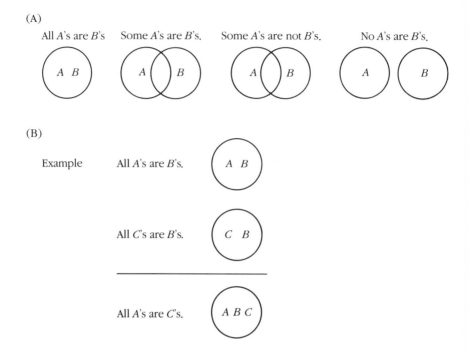

(B)

Figure 10-5 *(A) Venn-diagram representations of the favored interpretations of each of the categorical statements. (B) An example of the combination of these interpretations.*

fied the Venn-diagram interpretations of the statements by conversion. These simplified interpretations make reasoning about syllogisms easier if less correct. Figure 10-5 also shows how, given these representations, subjects would make an atmosphere error of accepting the following syllogism:

> All *A*s are *B*s.
> All *C*s are *B*s.
> ∴ All *A*s are *C*s.

Ceraso and Provitera (1971) have shown that when the premises were stated less ambiguously, subjects made many fewer errors. For instance, in their experiment, *All As are Bs* was stated as *All As are Bs but some Bs are not As.* This more explicit expression should discourage subjects from making erroneous conversions.

Like the atmosphere heuristic itself, this conversion heuristic will lead to fairly good performance but yield errors on certain critical problems. These errors will tend to be in accord with the atmosphere hypothesis.

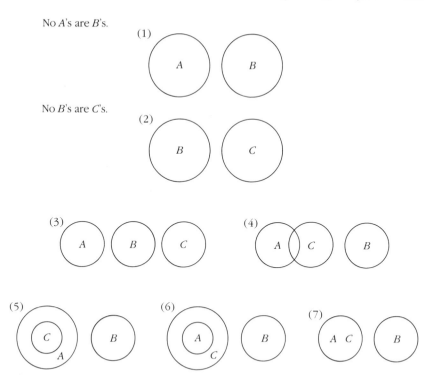

No *A*'s are *B*'s.

No *B*'s are *C*'s.

Figure 10-6   *Various Venn-diagram combinations for the syllogism below.*

Yet another way in which heuristics might come into play is in the search for a contradictory model. For example, some of the more sophisticated subjects actually try to reason by combining Venn diagrams in their head. (They have probably picked up Venn diagrams in some course on mathematics, set theory, or logic.) Consider the following syllogism:

> No *As* are *Bs*.
> No *Bs* are *Cs*.
> ∴ No *As* are *Cs*.

Figure 10-6 shows that each premise can be represented in only one way, so this problem is fairly simple. Still, there are five possible ways in which the premises can be combined. Subjects may not be able to search this space effectively in their heads. The disjointed Venn interpretation of the premises may lead subjects to try only combination 3. In general, if subjects use some sort of similarity heuristic in combining premises and only consider combinations similar to the premises, they will make atmosphere errors. This tendency will be borne out even if subjects are not biased in the premise combinations they try. We saw that in Figure 10-4 only 4 of the 33 possible combinations violated the atmosphere conclusion. Therefore, it is quite possible that subjects would miss the critical four if they only sampled a few. Most Venn-diagram combinations do not contradict particular conclusions. This may be why subjects give particular conclusions more readily than universal conclusions. Erickson (1974) has shown that many specifics of subjects' reasoning can be explained by the hypothesis that subjects engage in only a partial search of a space of Venn diagrams.

Another explanation of subjects' reasoning behavior, developed by Johnson-Laird and Steedman (1978), is that the subject actually creates a little world that satisfies the premises. (A similar idea has been proposed by Guyote and Sternberg, 1978). Consider these premises:

> All the artists are beekeepers.
>
> Some of the beekeepers are chemists.

A subject might imagine a group of artists who are beekeepers, perhaps add some additional beekeepers who are not artists, and then imagine that some of the beekeepers are chemists. To illustrate this possibility more specifically, let us suppose that for the premises above the subject imagines four individuals. Individuals 1, 2, and 3 are artists but 4 is not. All four are beekeepers. Individuals 2 and 4 are chemists. The subjects inspects this group, notes that individual 2 is an artist and a chemist and concludes,

> Some artists are chemists.

Thus, the subject is building a specific model for the premises and inspecting this to see what is true in that model. Again, this kind of reasoning pattern is a fairly good heuristic but will lead to errors, as in the example above. Johnson-Laird has developed this idea to explain why subjects are more likely to come up with conclusions when the premises have one form rather than another (refer to the discussion on p. 317).

Yet another hypothesis, suggested by Chapman and Chapman (1959) and Henle (1962), is that subjects decide not to work within the difficult framework of logical reasoning but that they revert to the probabilistic kind of reasoning that serves them well in many natural-world situations. For instance, they might reason

> Some plants with leaves of three are poisonous.
>
> Some of the plants in my yard have leaves of three.
>
> Therefore, some of the plants in my yard are probably poisonous.

This kind of reasoning pattern is very useful in a world where little is certain. Such a reasoning pattern might be imported into the laboratory situation when the subject cannot find any other way to reason. Again, this probabilistic heuristic will lead to atmosphere errors.

Categorical Syllogisms: A Summary

Current theory on categorical syllogisms is quite fragmented. One researcher will propose that subjects use an atmosphere heuristic, another that they search Venn-diagram-like models, and another that they use probabilistic reasoning. Many baroque combinations and variations of these hypotheses appear as well. It seems clear to me that subjects use many different heuristics. Dominowski (1977), looking at patterns of response for individual subjects, found evidence that different subjects were using different heuristics.

General Conclusions

Reasoning and Logic

We have seen ample evidence for the conclusion that humans are in some senses illogical in their deductive reasoning. By this, we mean a number of different things:

1. People do not always interpret statements the way logicians prescribe they should. For instance, they sometimes interpret *if* as *if and only if* and they interpret *All As are Bs* as *A equals B*.

2. They fail to recognize certain logical conclusions as valid, either because they have not learned the appropriate rule of inference (for instance, modus tollens) or because they cannot figure out how to combine a number of steps in a deduction (for instance, in the hard categorical syllogisms).

3. They accept certain contingent conclusions as valid. In part this acceptance may reflect a misinterpretation of the premises (point 1 above) but in part it reflects an inability to find counterexamples to the conclusions.

4. Faced with the difficulties identified in points 2 and 3, subjects often fall back on various heuristics for solving logical problems. These heuristics often succeed but sometimes they do not.

So, subjects' "lack of logic" reflects a refusal to reason according to the rules of logic plus an inability to do so.

In closing, it is worth noting that modern logic has cast this problem in an interesting light. It has been shown that no logical procedure is capable of identifying all possible conclusions as valid or contingent. Basically, the full class of logical problems is just too difficult. Problems will always exist for which any logical procedure would have to conclude "I don't know." Some experiments (e.g., Anderson, 1976) have allowed subjects the possibility of saying that they don't know. In my study, over a range of categorical problems designed to be tricky, subjects were correct 62 percent of the time, wrong 17 percent of the time, and claimed not to know 21 percent of the time. Clearly, if they had been forced to give answers they would have made many more errors. Still, 17 percent is a fairly high error rate, but is understandable, since the response, "I don't know" is often unsatisfactory in everyday life. So we have to fall back on heuristics and hope they will work. Usually these heuristics do work, but in most experiments on deductive reasoning the problems are designed so that the heuristics often fail.

While humans are not quite logical, they seem to do their best given their limited knowledge of logic. They would do better if they had more logical training and knew more rules of inference and techniques for analyzing a conclusion. However, in the end, even the most highly trained logicians have to fall back on heuristic techniques to guide their problem-solving efforts in finding a proof. Reasoning is fundamentally a matter of problem solving, not a logical activity.

Implications

This chapter contains a good deal of information to help one in logical reasoning. A number of techniques were identified that can serve well in reasoning. These include the notion of a valid deduction where each step involves application of a correct rule of inference, truth-table analysis, the use of a contradictory model to show that a conclusion is contingent, and the use of Venn diagrams. (A former undergraduate in one of my classes, Larry Birn-baum, was able to improve subject performance from 66 percent correct to 92 percent correct by instructing them in the use of Venn diagrams.)

A number of rules that subjects often lack were also identified. These include modus tollens and the rules for evaluating categorical syllogisms. Certainly, one's arsenal of techniques would be improved by taking a course in logic. However, modern logic courses tend to emphasize the abstract (and intellectually deeper) aspects of the domain rather than practical applications. Knowing the principles of logic in the abstract is not enough. One needs to practice the techniques in the situations where they are to be used. Logicians are notorious for often failing to use modus tollens in the Wason card problem (although not as frequently as average subjects). The need for practice in the relevant context follows directly from what we learned about skill acquisition (Chapter 8). There we found that skills narrowly practiced in one context tended to be invoked only in that context. It was a virtue of the more traditional approach to logic, whatever its faults, that it tried to stress the transfer to practical situations. A "logical mind" is not something given at birth; a logical mind must be trained.

There is evidence that simply being aware of the typical kinds of fallacies leads to better performance. Traditional courses in logic used to spend time labeling and analyzing the kinds of fallacies people typically make. Simpson and Johnson (1966) gave subjects instructions against making atmosphere errors. These instructions involved explaining the character of the atmosphere error and presenting some training syllogisms on which subjects could practice avoiding atmosphere errors. A few minutes of training resulted in a considerable decrease in atmosphere errors (from 57 percent to 39 percent). Similarly, Wason (1969) was able to devise training devices that increased subjects' tendency to use modus tollens. Perhaps we should not be surprised that practice makes perfect in reasoning, but these results are important news in the areas of deductive reasoning. These results are newsworthy because the field has been confused by the belief that thought should be naturally logical.

An important insight of cognitive psychology has been that deductive reasoning is a special case of problem solving rather than some special faculty of the mind. It is to be hoped that, together with the more abstract developments in logic, cognitive psychology has banished the traditional view that failure to make logical deductions reflects a particularly grievous intellectual deficit. Rather, such failures reflect in part a lack of knowledge about appropriate problem-solving strategies and techniques, and in part the fact that deduction can pose fundamentally intractable problems. The identification of deduction with problem solving has also led to the suggestion that problem-solving techniques (for example, planning, heuristic search, and representation) are applicable to deductive reasoning.

Remarks and Suggested Readings

A good introduction to logic is Suppes (1957). A number of texts offer a more formal and technical development in logic, including Mendelson (1964), Church (1956), Kleene (1952), Schoenfield (1967), and Robbin (1969). Church's text is particularly significant as a standard in the field and provides discussions of many of the important conceptual issues. It is probably better to study mathematical logic as part of a formal course than just out of a textbook. Such courses are offered by many college departments including philosophy, mathematics, and computer science.

A number of books and some recent edited collections of papers review research on deductive reasoning. Among these are Wason and Johnson-Laird (1972) and Falmagne (1975). Other important recent papers in the field include Erickson (1974), Johnson-Laird and Steedman (1978), Taplin (1971), Taplin and Staudenmayer (1973), and Rips and Marcus (1977). Among the important "classic" papers are those by Woodworth and Sells (1935), Chapman and Chapman (1959), and Henle (1962). The work of Newell and Simon provides a distinctive approach to logic and is extensively presented in their 1972 book. Newell (1980) has recently written a paper forcefully advancing the view that deductive reasoning is problem solving. Osherson, in a series of books and perhaps most clearly in his 1975 paper, has argued for a logiclike analysis of human deduction.

Chapter 11

Inductive Reasoning

Summary

1. For an argument to be *inductively valid,* the conclusion must be probable if the premises are true. This criterion contrasts with that for *deductively valid* argument, in which the conclusion must be certain if the premises are true.

2. The components of the inductive-reasoning process are *hypothesis forma- tion* and *hypothesis evaluation.*

3. Hypothesis formation has been most thoroughly studied in the research on concept formation. This research addresses the ways in which subjects form hypotheses about the definition of a concept when they are given instances of the concept.

4. In concept-formation studies, subjects differ in terms of the *strategies* they use for testing hypotheses about the concept. Subjects try to develop strate- gies that will lead to rapid identification of the concept but minimize cognitive strain. Subjects often evolve more effective strategies as they become more sophisticated at concept identification.

5. Subjects have particular difficulty in acquiring and utilizing *negative infor- mation* in forming hypotheses. *Negative information* refers to data that are inconsistent with a hypothesis.

6. *Bayes' theorem* prescribes a way for evaluating a hypothesis. It updates the probability of a hypothesis in light of new evidence. In the terminology of Bayes' theorem, the original probability of a hypothesis is referred to as the *prior probability,* the updated probability as the *posterior probability,* and the probability of the evidence given the hypothesis as the *conditional probability.*

7. In evaluating hypotheses, human beings deviate from the norm prescribed by Bayes' theorem in that they do not adjust the posterior probabilities as radically as they should and they tend to ignore information about prior probabilities.

8. When subjects cannot directly observe the probability of a particular type of event, they try to estimate its probability by means of various heuristics. These heuristics are biased and can lead to serious distortions in probability estimates. It is the use of such heuristics that accounts for the deviations from the prescriptions of Bayes' theorem.

Induction Versus Deduction

Consider the following argument:

> Mary and John live in the same house.
> John has the same last name as Mary.
> <u>Mary has a picture of John on her desk at work.</u>
> Therefore, Mary and John are married.

The above is an example of an inductively valid argument; its conclusion is not necessarily true, but only highly probable. After all, it is possible that Mary and John are just siblings, or that Mary and John were married but got a divorce for tax purposes, or that Mary and John are lovers who just happen to have the same name. I am sure you can think of other possible, if improbable, states of affairs (pun intended) that would account for the premises but contradict the conclusion. Thus, we would say that the above conclusion is *inductively valid* (it is probable) but not *deductively valid* (it does not necessarily follow).

To illustrate the difference between inductively valid and deductively valid conclusions, consider the following argument:

> The Abkhasian Republic of the USSR has 10 men over 160.
> <u>No other place in the world has a man over 160.</u>
> 1. The oldest man in the world today is in the USSR.
> 2. The oldest man in the world tomorrow will be in the USSR.

Conclusion 1 is deductively valid. If the premises are true (and I don't know if they are, but this is irrelevant), then the conclusion must be true. However, conclusion 2 is only inductively valid; that is, it is a highly likely conclusion if the premises are true, but it is conceivable that all 10 men could die before tomorrow.

In the last chapter, we noted that subjects often do not discriminate between a deductively valid conclusion and a highly plausible one. They fail to make such discrimination in everyday life for good reason. It makes no practical difference whether a conclusion is certain or is only true 999 times out of 1,000. However, philosophers and logicians consider the distinction extremely significant. They have developed relatively satisfactory systems for understanding deductive logic, but they are still tearing their hair out about how to understand inductive logic. Our concerns in this chapter will not be with the philosopher's view of induction, however. Rather, we will focus on the actual difficulties people have in reasoning inductively.

Two major difficulties can be identified with respect to inductive reasoning. First, evaluating a particular inductive conclusion is often hard. Consider the predicament of Jane as she tries to evaluate the following argument:

> Often when Jane turns around in class, Dick is looking at her.
> Dick keeps asking Jane for suggestions on his homework.
> Dick has stopped seeing Janice.
> Therefore, Dick has a crush on Jane.

Many other possible explanations for Dick's behavior certainly exist, and evaluating the probability of the conclusion given the premises is extremely difficult for Jane. Indeed, in trying to evaluate that hypothesis, basically Jane would be engaging in a problem-solving activity.

The second difficulty in inductive reasoning occurs when only the premises are provided and one must come up with a conclusion. This is the process of hypothesis formation. As with deductive reasoning, deciding on what conclusion, if any, should be drawn can be quite difficult. Consider the following premises:

> The first number in the series is 1.
> The second number in the series is 3.
> The third number in the series is 7.

What conclusion follows? One possible conclusion is that

1. The fourth number in the series is 15.

However, a better conclusion would probably be

2. The nth number in the series is $2^n - 1$

This conclusion seems better because it is general and so describes the whole series. However, it might not be the correct conclusion. For instance, the series might actually obey the following rule:

3. The nth number is $n^2 - n + 1$

Of course, this conclusion predicts that the fourth number in the series will be 13, whereas conclusion 2 predicts that the fourth number will be 15. However, the original three premises provide no means of selecting between the two extrapolations. This fact reflects the important feature of induction: one can never know for sure whether a conclusion is true or whether some other conclusion would be better. Thus, it is often hard to find an inductive conclusion and, once a set of possible conclusions has been found, it is often hard to decide which is the best of the set.

Research in cognitive psychology has tended to study separately each of these two aspects of inductive reasoning, *hypothesis formation* and *hypothesis evaluation*. The two major sections of this chapter will cover these two major research domains. In the final section, we will consider a real-world domain, scientific-theory formation, in which hypothesis formation and hypothesis evaluation must occur together.

Hypothesis Formation

A very common kind of inductive-reasoning task involves going from particular evidence to the conclusion of more general statements. For instance, consider the following set of premises and one possible conclusion:

> Fred is allergic to apples.
> Fred is not allergic to potatoes.
> Fred is not allergic to bananas.
> Fred is allergic to plums.
> Fred is not allergic to oranges.
> Fred is allergic to grapes.
> <u>Fred is allergic to cherries.</u>
> ∴ Fred is allergic to the skin of fruits.

This inductive conclusion seems reasonable (assuming that Fred peels his oranges and bananas). Note that each of these premises specifies a particular fruit but the conclusion is general and refers to all possible types of fruit. The great importance of inductive reasoning is illustrated by this argument. Induction can allow us to proceed from a few examples to a conclusion that will help us make predictions about new examples. In this case, we can now make predictions about the kinds of food Fred can eat safely. However, this example also makes clear the risk inherent in any inductive inference. There is just no way of knowing for sure that a general inductive conclusion will be true of other instances. It may turn out that Fred is not allergic to pears and is allergic to celery, in which case we would have to search for another inductive conclusion.

In the analyses that follow, we will view hypothesis formation principally as a matter of problem solving. Recall from Chapter 9 that problem solving can be analyzed as a search through a set of possible states for a goal state. In the case of hypothesis formation, the set of states to be searched is a set of possible hypotheses. The goal state corresponds to a hypothesis that accounts for all the available evidence.

We will refer to the different schemes subjects use for searching the problem space as *strategies*. Different subjects use different strategies; their choices of strategies are a function of the information-processing demands involved in the problem and their own sophistication at the problem-solving task. Subjects tend to choose strategies that minimize the amount of information-processing effort required to solve the problem. The ability to find the most efficient strategies appears to be a function of subjects' experience and sophistication with respect to particular kinds of induction problems.

Concept Identification

We begin our discussion of hypothesis formation with a review of some of the significant results from the *concept-identification* or *concept-formation* literature. This material derives from one of the older research traditions in cognitive psychology. Historically, this domain is important not only because it studies hypothesis formation, but also because it was one area in which cognitive psychology first successfully broke from the predominant behaviorist traditions of the 1950s and early 1960s. As an example of a concept-formation task, consider the following:

> A dax can be large, bright, red, and square.
> A dax can be large, dull, red, and square.
> A dax cannot be small, dull, red, and square.
> A dax cannot be large, bright, red, and triangular.
> A dax can be large, dull, blue, and square.
> What is a dax?

The best answer is probably that a dax is a large square. This example is very similar to the allergy-hypothesis example above, except here artificial materials with arbitrary features such as large, bright, red, and square are used. With carefully controlled material such as that in the concept-formation example above, researchers have discovered a good deal about how people form inductive hypotheses.

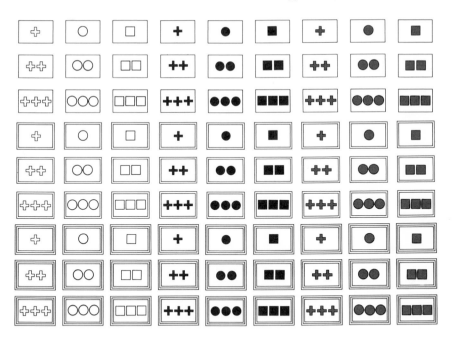

Figure 11-1 *Material used by Bruner, Goodnow, and Austin in one of their studies of concept identification (1956). The array consists of instances of combinations of four attributes, each exhibiting three values. Open figures are in green, solid figures in black, and gray figures in red. (*A Study of Thinking. *Copyright © 1956. Reprinted by permission of John Wiley & Sons, Inc.)*

A classic series of studies of concept identification was reported by Bruner, Goodnow, and Austin (1956). Figure 11-1 illustrates the kind of material that they used. The stimuli were all rectangular boxes containing various objects. The stimuli varied on four dimensions: number of objects (one, two, or three); number of borders around the boxes (one, two, or three); shape (cross, circle, or square); and color (green, red, and black, represented here as open, solid, and gray. Subjects were told that they were to discover some concept that described a particular subset of these instances. For instance, the concept might have been black crosses. Subjects were to discover the correct concept on the basis of information they were given about what were and what were not instances of the concept.

Figure 11-2 contains three illustrations (the three columns) of the information subjects might have been presented. Each column consists of a sequence of instances identified either as members of the concept (positive, +) or not (negative, −). Each column represents a different concept. Subjects would be presented with the instances in a column one at a time. From these instances

Concept 1   Concept 2   Concept 3

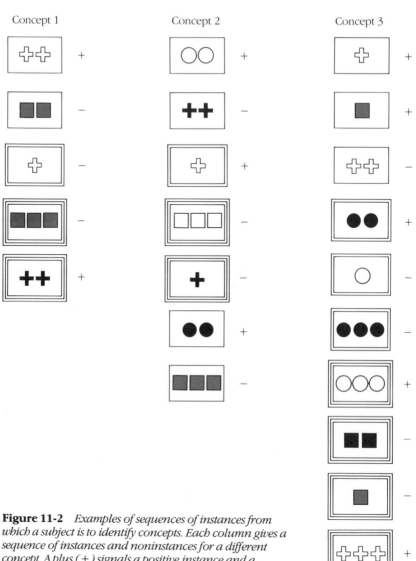

Figure 11-2   *Examples of sequences of instances from which a subject is to identify concepts. Each column gives a sequence of instances and noninstances for a different concept. A plus (+) signals a positive instance and a minus (−) a negative instance.*

subjects would determine what the concept was. Stop reading and try to determine the concept for each column.

The concept in the first example is *two crosses*. This concept is referred to as a *conjunctive* concept, since the conjunction of a number of features (in this case the features are *two* and *cross*) must be present for the instance to be positive. Subjects typically find conjunctive concepts easiest to discover. In some sense conjunctive hypotheses seem to be the most "natural" kind of hypotheses and the type that has been researched most extensively. The solution to the second example is *two borders or circles.* This kind of concept is referred to as a *disjunctive concept,* since an instance is a member of the concept if either of the features is present. In the final example, the solution is that the number of objects must equal the number of borders. This example is a *relational concept,* since it specifies a relationship between two dimensions.

The problems in this series are particularly difficult, because to identify the concepts a subject must both determine which features are relevant and discover the kind of rule that connects the features (e.g., conjunctive, disjunctive or relational). The former problem is referred to as *attribute identification* and the latter as *rule learning* (Haygood and Bourne, 1965). In many experiments, either the form of the rule or the relevant attributes are identified for the subject. For instance, in the Bruner, Goodnow and Austin (1956) experiments, subjects only had to identify the correct attributes. They knew that they would be identifying conjunctive concepts.

Two Concept-Formation Strategies

Bruner et al. were interested in how subjects would go about identifying a concept. One of the experimental situations in which they studied concept formation is referred to as the *reception paradigm.* In this paradigm, subjects see instances one at a time and are asked to judge at presentation whether each is a member of the category. After making their classifications, subjects are given feedback as to whether their classifications were correct. It is inferred that subjects have identified the concept when they make no more errors in their classification. Bruner et al. discovered that in this paradigm most of their subjects spontaneously adopted one of two strategies to identify the concept. The optimal strategy, called the *wholist strategy* and described in Table 11-1, was adopted to some degree by 65 percent of the subjects. Table 11-1 is a 2 × 2 matrix in which the situations are classified according to whether a positive or negative instance of the concept has been presented (columns) and whether the subject has correctly or incorrectly classified the instance (rows).

Table 11-1 is a bit abstract and is best understood when applied to an example. Suppose, then, that the first stimulus the subject sees is

one border, one green square,

and that this is a positive instance. The table specifies that all the features in this first positive instance be taken as the hypothesis. That is, subjects will hypothesize that the concept is defined by the conjunction of the features *one*

Table 11-1   The Wholist Strategy for Concept Identification

Summary of Strategy:
Take the set of all the features of the first positive instance as the initial hypothesis. Then, as more instances are presented, eliminate any feature in this set that does not occur with a positive instance.

Classifications	Positive Instance	Negative Instance
Correct	Maintain the hypothesis now in force.	Maintain the hypothesis now in force.
Incorrect	Take as the next hypothesis what the old hypothesis and the present instance have in common.	Impossible unless one has misreckoned.

border, one object, green color, and *square shape.* If subjects are then presented with

one border, two red circles,

they would judge this instance not to be a member of the category because it does not match the hypothesis. Suppose this judgment is correct; this condition is described in the upper right cell of Table 11-1, and the hypothesis is kept. Then suppose subjects are presented with

two borders, one green square.

They would also judge this instance not to be a member of the category. But suppose they are wrong and that this is a positive instance. This case is described in the lower left cell, and subjects take as their new hypothesis what the old hypothesis and the current instance have in common:

one green square.

Suppose they are now presented with

three borders, one green square.

They would classify this as an instance of the category and would be told that they are correct. They would then be in the condition described by the upper left cell, and would keep the hypothesis. Finally, assume that subjects are presented with

one border, two green crosses.

They would say that this is not an instance of the category, but suppose it is.

Table 11-2 Partist Strategy for Concept Identification

Summary of Strategy

Begin with part of the first positive instance as a hypothesis (i.e., choose just a subset of the features in the instance). Then, as more instances are presented, retain the hypothesis or change it to be consistent with the instances.

Classifications	Positive Instance	Negative Instance
Correct	Maintain hypothesis now in force.	Maintain hypothesis now in force.
Incorrect	Change hypothesis to make it consistent with past instances; in other words, choose a hypothesis not previously disconfirmed.	Change hypothesis to make it consistent with past instances; in other words, choose a hypothesis not previously disconfirmed.

Again, the situation is that of the lower left cell of Table 11-1, and subjects would make a new hypothesis,

green,

the feature that the old hypothesis and new instance have in common.

It is impossible, if subjects follow this wholist strategy faithfully, for them ever to make an error on a negative instance (lower right cell of Table 11-1). Note that subjects only have to revise the hypothesis when they fail to identify an instance (lower left cell). They never have to change the hypothesis when they are correct (upper cells). The wholist strategy is relatively easy to follow, for it requires that subjects remember only the current hypothesis, not past instances. Of the subjects who attempted to follow the wholist strategy in the Bruner et al. study, 47 percent were able to do so without ever deviating from the prescriptions of Table 11-1.

The other common subject strategy Bruner et al. detected they called the *partist strategy*. In this strategy, subjects started with a conjunctive hypothesis that was consistent with the first positive instance. It would involve some subset of the features contained in that instance. Thus, this strategy differs at the start from the wholist strategy, where subjects take as their first hypothesis *all* the features in the first positive instance. Table 11-2 describes the behavior of an "ideal" partist subject after the first trial (I use the word *ideal* because subjects often did not conform perfectly to this strategy). Subjects' behavior is presented in the same format as in Table 11-1 in order to facilitate comparison. When subjects are correct, they maintain the hypothesis. Here the partist strategy does not differ from the wholist strategy. However, when subjects are wrong they try to select a new hypothesis consistent with the past items. This process requires memory for all the past items, and subjects often fail at this point because they are unable to remember past items. Bruner et al. classified 35 percent of their subjects as following a partist strategy. Of these, only 38 percent were able to behave in accord with Table 11-2 consistently over five trials.

The reason that the partist strategy is less useful than the wholist strategy for identifying conjunctive concepts lies in the initially formed hypothesis. In wholist strategy, all the potentially relevant information from the first instance is kept in the initial hypothesis, whereas in the partist strategy some potentially relevant features are dropped out. In the wholist strategy, a feature is dropped from the hypothesis only when it is proven irrelevant. The partist strategy can be seen as the outcome of an inappropriate application of a similarity heuristic (discussed in Chapter 9) to the task of hypothesis search. Subjects believe that the correct concept will involve a conjunction of one, two, or at most three of the features in the first instance. Therefore, they try to maximize the similarity between the first hypothesis and the eventual correct hypothesis by including only one, two, or three features in the initial hypothesis.

More Studies of the Reception Paradigm

In contrast to Bruner et al. (1956), most other research has found that subjects tend to use a partist strategy much more often than a wholist strategy. Evidence for a variant of the partist strategy comes from a series of concept-formation experiments using a reception paradigm performed by Trabasso and Bower (e.g., Bower and Trabasso, 1964; Trabasso and Bower, 1968). In a typical experiment, subjects learned concepts about material consisting of five-letter strings. In each of the five positions, one of two letters might appear. Thus, there were five dimensions (the five positions) and two values on each dimension. The concepts that subjects had to identify were defined by a value on a single dimension—for instance, the concept might be R in third position. Moreover, subjects knew they were looking for a value on a single dimension. Thus, the concepts to be identified were quite simple.

Trabasso and Bower were interested in testing two aspects of the hypothesis-testing view of concept formation. The first was the assumption that subjects change their hypotheses only after trials on which they make errors. Given this assumption, subjects could only identify the correct hypothesis after making an error. The second point of interest was the assumption that subjects learn in an all-or-none fashion. Until subjects try the correct hypothesis, they essentially know nothing about that concept. An alternate viewpoint would be that subjects gradually identify the concept.

Some early research on concept formation had yielded data that seemed, on the surface, to favor the gradual-learning rather than the all-or-none-learning assumption of hypothesis-testing models. In the typical reception

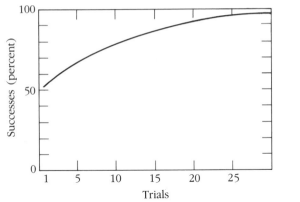

Figure 11-3 *Probability of correctly classifying an instance as a function of trial in the typical concept-identification experiment. The probabilities in this hypothetical curve have been averaged over subjects.*

paradigm, during one trial a subject is shown a stimulus, is asked to indicate if it is in the category, and is then given feedback as to whether his or her classification is correct. Such trials are repeated over and over again. Figure 11-3 is a typical plot of probability of a correct response as a function of trial number. The percent correct is averaged over all the subjects in the experiment. This figure shows a continuous approach to perfect performance, suggesting that subjects gradually accumulate the evidence necessary to identify the correct response. The apparent gradualness in Figure 11-3 would seem to contradict the hypothesis-testing explanation. According to this explanation, subjects identify the correct hypothesis or concept on a single trial. Therefore, this explanation predicts that subjects would perform at a chance level (which is 50 percent) for a while and then abruptly jump to 100 percent on the trial on which they identified the correct hypothesis.

Bower and Trabasso (1964) wondered whether the apparent gradualness of concept discovery might be the result of averaging over subjects. They thought that one subject might have selected the correct concept after an error on trial 10 and showed an abrupt jump to perfect categorization, another subject might have selected the correct concept on trial 6, and still another on trial 20, and so on. Averaging different subjects together would give the illusion of gradual improvement. The increase in average probability of correct classification would just reflect the growing percentage of subjects who had identified the concept and who were responding perfectly. To test for this possibility, Bower and Trabasso identified for each subject the last trial on which he or she made an error and then plotted probability of correct categorization back from that trial. Figure 11-4 shows those data. Suppose the last error a subject made was on trial 9. For this subject, trial 1 in Figure 11-4 would come from trial 8, trial 2 would come from trial 7, and so on; finally, trial 8 would come from trial 1. For a subject whose last error was on trial 21, trial 1 in Figure 11-4 would come from trial 20, trial 2 would come from trial

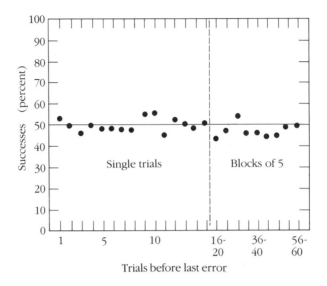

Figure 11-4   *A backwards learning curve. Trial numbers represent number of trials before last error. After trial 15, average data are plotted for successive blocks of five trials. (From Bower and Trabasso, 1964.)*

19, and so on; finally, trial 20 would come from trial 1. Thus, in Figure 11-4, trial 1 is the trial just prior to the last error for all subjects, trial 2 is the second trial before the last error for all subjects, and so on. The curve illustrated in Figure 11-4 is called a *backwards learning curve.*

If each subject had been gradually learning the concept, we would see a gradual improvement in this backwards learning curve as it approached trial 1 (the trial prior to the last error for all subjects). However, probability correct hovers around the chance level of 50 percent right up to the trial just prior to the last error (trial 1 in Figure 11-4). These data are good evidence for *all-or-none-learning.* That is, individual subjects displayed the all-or-none learning postulated by the hypothesis-testing theory. A very important lesson is contained in this analysis: an average learning curve (Figure 11-3) apparently displaying gradual learning can actually be hiding all-or-none learning, uncovered with a backwards learning curve (Figure 11-4).

Trabasso and Bower have advanced what has been called the *hypothesis-sampling theory* to account for their data. (This theory was a variant of some ideas that had been put forward by Restle in 1962.) The assumption is that all values on all dimensions are available as possible hypotheses for the concept. Subjects select or sample one of these hypotheses at random and respond according to it. As long as their responses are correct, they stay with their hypothesis. However, as soon as the hypothesis leads to an incorrect prediction, they discard it and sample another hypothesis at random that is consistent with the current trial. This process continues until subjects finally select the correct hypothesis. The Trabasso and Bower hypothesis-sampling strategy is quite similar to the partist strategy (Table 11-2) described by Bruner, Goodnow, and Austin. According to both strategies, subjects only change their hypotheses after trials on which they make errors. Both strategies predict all-or-none learning. A difference, however, is that according to the partist strategy, subjects try to use their memory for the past trials to select the best hypothesis after an error. In the hypothesis-sampling strategy of Bower and Trabasso, subjects do not use past trials to help select a better hypothesis. Their only constraint is that the hypothesis be consistent with the current trial. Bruner et al. noted that their subjects had a hard time remembering past instances. The Trabasso and Bower theory incorporates the extreme version of this difficulty—i.e., the total inability to recall past instances.

Memory for Past Instances

The Trabasso and Bower theory claims that when subjects make errors and so discover that their hypotheses are wrong, they do not use memory for the past instances to form new hypotheses about the concept. Bower and Trabasso (1963) provided a number of striking confirmations of this *no-memory assumption*. In these experiments, they gave subjects feedback consistent with one hypothesis for a while and then, not telling the subject of the switch, began giving them information consistent with a second hypothesis. According to their no-memory assumption, subjects would not be hindered in identifying the second concept even though they had earlier received information consistent with a different hypothesis. Since, according to their prediction, subjects would not use past instances in forming a new hypothesis, when subjects made an error after the concept had been switched, the inconsistent information from the past would have no influence on the next hypothesis they choose.

One of the experiments used by Bower and Trabasso to demonstrate this phenomenon involved three conditions. In the *reversed* condition, subjects were given feedback for the first 10 trials consistent with a concept that was the opposite of the hypothesis that would be correct after trial 10. For instance, if the correct hypothesis after trial 10 was *red*, subjects would be told for the first 10 trials that a stimulus was in the category only when it was *blue*— that is, when it had another value on the same dimension. In the *non-reversed condition*, subjects were given feedback for the first 10 trials according to an irrelevant dimension. For instance, if the correct hypothesis after trial 10 was *red*, they might be told an instance was in the category only when it was *square*. In the *control condition*, subjects were given feedback in the

Figure 11-5   *An example of the stimulus material used by Levine (1966) in his experiment to test the no-memory assumption.*

first 10 trials according to the correct hypothesis (*red* in this example). For all groups, after the tenth trial feedback was consistent with the correct hypothesis.

Bower and Trabasso were interested only in subjects who made errors after the tenth trial, that is, subjects who had not selected the correct hypothesis by trial 10. According to their theory, all three groups would take an equal number of extra trials after trial 10 to solve the problem. Since subjects would have no memory for past events, the reversed and nonreversed groups would not be hurt by the inconsistent feedback from the first 10 trials. In fact, no detectable difference occurred among the three groups, as Bower and Trabasso had predicted.

Subsequent research has indicated that the no-memory proposal of Bower and Trabasso is too extreme for some situations. Perhaps the clearest contrary evidence comes from Levine (1966). He presented subjects with stimuli such as those in Figure 11-5. The stimuli consisted of two objects varying on four binary dimensions: position (left or right), size (large or small), form (X or T), and color (black or white). As in the Trabasso and Bower experiments, the correct concept was a single value of one dimension. Subjects in Levine's experiment had to identify which of the two stimuli was an instance of the concept. He gave subjects a series of trials, and between each trial he interrogated subjects to determine their hypotheses.* He found, in accordance with hypothesis-sampling strategy and the more general partist strategy, that subjects kept their hypotheses on 95 percent of the trials in which they had been correct and switched 98 percent of the time after an error trial. Interest focuses on how well subjects do at selecting another hypothesis after an error trial.

Figure 11-6 presents the performance of subjects in Levine's experiment and compares it to various theoretical possibilities. If subjects choose at random one of the eight possible hypotheses (left, right, large, small, X, T, black, or white), their chances of selecting a correct hypothesis would be one in eight. On the other hand, subjects could do much better if they considered the trial just previous in selecting a hypothesis for the current trial. Suppose the correct response was a large black T on the left. Then they could limit their hypothesis to four (large, black, T, and left) and have a 1 in 4 chance of

---

*His method was to give subjects a series of instances without feedback and to infer their hypotheses from their responses.

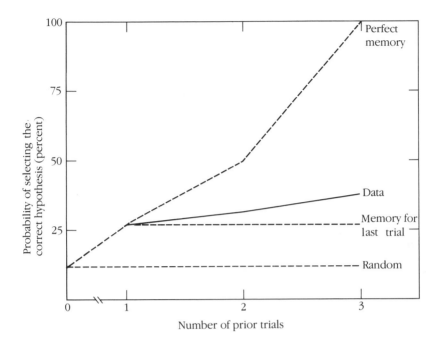

Figure 11-6 *Probability of selecting the correct hypothesis following a wrong response on trials 1, 2, and 3. The data (solid line) are contrasted with various theoretical ideals (broken lines).*

selecting the correct hypothesis. This is the curve labeled *memory for last trial*. However, if subjects could remember earlier trials, they would be able to do still better. Suppose the sequence of correct responses on three trials was as follows:

> large black T on the left
> large white T on the right
> small white T on the left

If subjects made an error after the second trial and could remember the previous two trials, they could restrict their choice of a new hypothesis to large or T. After the third trial, if they could remember all three trials, subjects could restrict their hypothesis to just T. The probability of correct choice is given in the curve called *perfect memory*. As can be seen, subjects' actual performance is between perfect memory and memory for just the last trial. Thus, subjects are able to remember a little more about past instances than they would according to the hypothesis-sampling strategy of Trabasso and Bower.

Concept-Identification Research: A Summary

Subjects' behavior in concept-identification tasks can be seen to fall on a continuum of effectiveness. Most subjects seem to start out in such a task performing according to the primitive Bower and Trabasso hypothesis-testing strategy, trying one hypothesis at a time and not using memory for past instances. However, as they become more familiar with the task, subjects may start to use memory for past events to help revise their hypotheses, behaving more in accord with the partist model developed by Bruner et al. Still, this view is inherently unsatisfactory, because subjects can only recall a few of the past stimuli (shown also by Trabasso and Bower, 1964, who explicitly asked subjects to try to recall past stimuli). Perhaps the frustration inherent in the strategy is what leads subjects to reorganize their strategies in accordance with the wholist model conceived by Bruner et al. Such a model allows the subject to compress all the relevant information from past stimuli into a single hypothesis. The transition to the wholist strategy is clearly an act of insight in the problem-solving sense (see Chapter 9). It should be noted in this regard that the subjects in the Bruner et al. experiments who displayed the wholist strategy were both relatively sophisticated (Harvard graduate students) and relatively practiced at the task. Bourne (1963) has also reported that subjects do tend to shift to this strategy over trials. Dominowski (1974) has also shown how the strategies adopted by subjects change with the characteristics of the concept-formation task.

This research on concept formation has frequently been compared with the research reviewed in Chapter 5 on the acquisition of schematic concepts. As the chapter organization of this book indicates, I think these two research traditions should be treated independently. The research in Chapter 5 is relevant to the acquisition and use of a particular knowledge structure, the schema. The research reviewed in this section demonstrates subjects' strategies for solving problems of hypothesis formation. The important distinction is the approach taken by the subject to the learning situation. In paradigms that study prototype formation or schema abstraction, the subject is passive and often does not realize that a rule underlies the examples; often, in fact, there is no real rule. In the concept-formation process, the subject is actively searching for a hypothesis. The first paradigm is probably an appropriate model for the way a child learns a concept; the second is probably an appropriate model for the way a doctor diagnoses a disease.

Using Negative Information

Simple Concepts

Subjects have particular difficulty in the proper use of negative information, that is, information about what is *not* an instance of a category. Consider a concept-learning experiment in which the stimuli vary on three binary (two-valued) dimensions—size (large and small), shape (circle and triangle), and color (red and yellow). Suppose subjects are trying to learn a concept defined on a single feature (e.g., small) and are presented with the following negative instance:

large red triangle.

It is the case that subjects could calculate from this negative instance that the following is a positive instance:

small yellow circle,

which is just the opposite of the first instance on each dimension. The relationship of these instances illustrates a general rule applying to single-feature concepts with binary dimensions:

Each negative instance is equivalent to a positive instance with all values switched.

This rule also means that if subjects are presented with

small yellow triangle

as a positive instance, they can know that one negative instance is the stimulus with the above values switched:

large red square.

Thus, in this experimental situation, positive and negative examples are perfectly equivalent in the information they offer subjects. However, subjects do better given positive evidence, examples of the category, than given negative evidence, nonexamples of the category (Hovland and Weiss, 1953; Johnson, 1972). Subjects obviously are not aware of the informational equivalence of positive and negative instances, and they find it difficult to use examples that violate the concept to infer what the concept is.

Relational Concepts

An experiment by Wason (1960) shows that, in addition to being poor at using negative information, subjects fail to seek negative information. In his experiment, subjects were told that three numbers—2, 4, and 6—conformed to a simple relational rule. Subjects were to discover that rule by generating various triads of numbers and giving their reason for each of their choices. They were told whether each triad generated conformed to the rule. They were to announce the rule when they thought they had identified it. The protocol below comes from one of Wason's subjects. Each triad the subject produced and the reason for the choice is included along with the experimenter's feedback as to whether the triad conformed to the rule. The sequence of triads was occasionally broken when the subject decided to announce a hypothesis. The experimenter's feedback for each hypothesis is given in parentheses.

Triad	Reason Given for Triad	Feedback
8 10 12	Two added each time.	yes
14 16 18	Even numbers in order of magnitude	yes
20 22 24	Same reason.	yes
1 3 5	Two added to preceding number.	yes

Announcement: *The rule is that by starting with any number two is added each time to form the next number.* (Incorrect)

2 6 10	The middle number is the arithmetic mean of the other two.	yes
1 50 99	Same reason.	yes

Announcement: *The rule is that the middle number is the arithmetic mean of the other two.* (Incorrect)

3 10 17	Same number, seven, added each time.	yes
0 3 6	Three added each time.	yes

Announcement: *The rule is that the difference between two numbers next to each other is the same.* (Incorrect)

12 8 4	The same number is subtracted each time to form the next number.	no

Announcement: *The rule is adding a number, always the same one, to form the next number.* (Incorrect)

1 4 9	Any three numbers in order of magnitude	yes

Announcement: *The rule is any three numbers in order of magnitude.* (Correct)

The important feature to note about this protocol is that the subject tested the hypothesis by generating sequences mainly consistent with it. The correct procedure would have been to try sequences that were inconsistent also. That is, the subject should have looked for negative evidence. It is easy to start out with a hypothesis that is too narrow and to miss the more general correct hypothesis. The only way to discover this error is to try examples that disconfirm one's hypothesis, but this is just what people have great difficulty doing.

In another experiment, Wason (1968) asked 16 subjects, after they had announced their hypotheses, what they would do to determine whether their hypotheses were incorrect. Nine subjects said they would only generate instances consistent with their hypotheses and wait for one to be identified as not an instance of the concept. Only four subjects said that they would generate instances inconsistent with the hypothesis to see if they were identified as members of the concept. The remaining three insisted that their hypotheses could not be incorrect.

Hypotheses About Personalities

In a series of experiments, Snyder and Swann (1978) showed that subjects have the same difficulties in judging hypotheses about the personalities of other people that they have in judging the more abstract number hypotheses in the Wason experiments. Snyder and Swann instructed one group of subjects to decide whether a person who was waiting in another room was an extrovert. Other subjects were asked to decide if the person was an introvert. Subjects were given a set of questions to choose from in interrogating the person. Some of these questions were classified as extroverted and some as introverted. Extroverted questions included the following:

What would you do if you wanted to liven things up at a party?

What kinds of situations do you seek out if you want to meet new people?

In what situations are you most talkative?

The important point about these questions is that they give the person an opportunity to display evidence of extroversion; they do not give much opportunity to display evidence of introversion. Thus, they serve as confirmatory evidence for the hypothesis that the person is extroverted. Using these questions is similar to testing the hypothesis in the Wason experiment with instances consistent with the hypothesis. If subjects were seeking negative evidence against the extroverted hypothesis they would have to ask introvert-based questions such as these:

In what situations do you wish you were more outgoing?

What factors make it hard for you to really open up to people?

What things do you dislike about loud parties?

These questions are like instances inconsistent with the mathematical hypothesis in the Wason experiment. If the people being questioned suggested ways to liven up a party, subjects might consider them to be extroverted; but if they also admitted to wishing they were more outgoing, subjects would realize that they were neither particularly extroverted nor particularly introverted.

To properly test the hypothesis, subjects would have to use both kinds of questions. However, subjects in the Snyder and Swann experiments displayed an overwhelming bias for confirmatory questions. That is, subjects evaluating an extroverted hypothesis asked mainly extroverted questions, and subjects evaluating the introverted hypothesis asked mainly introverted questions. Interestingly, independent judges listening only to the answers of interviewees to the subjects' (interviewers') questions concluded that interviewees for the extroverted condition were more extroverted than interviewees in the introverted condition. Thus, subjects were able to shape the behavior of the interviewees with their questions such that the interviewees give biased clinical evidence regarding their own personalities.

Hypothesis Evaluation

In the discussions of concept-identification and rule-induction tasks, the means of deciding if a hypothesis fit the facts and the degree to which it fit were fairly obvious. Consider, however, the following case. Suppose I come home and find the door to my house ajar. I am interested in the hypothesis that this might be the work of a burglar. How do I evaluate this hypothesis? The problem of hypothesis evaluation in this situation is more complicated than in a concept-formation experiment for two reasons. First, in concept-identification situations such as those discussed in the preceding section, each hypothesis (that it is a square, black, a triangle, and so on) is equally likely to be true from the beginning. This is not the case in the open-door mystery (where the two competing hypotheses are that the home has been burglarized and that it has not been burglarized). Before I noted that the door was open, I would have estimated the probability that my home had not been burglarized as high and the probability that it had been burglarized as correspondingly low. These unequal prior probabilities should have some influence on my hypothesis evaluation.

Second, the connection between hypotheses and observations is not absolute, as it is in a concept-identification experiment. In the latter, if the correct hypothesis is that the concept is black, then a large black triangle with two borders must be an instance of the concept. However, even if the hypothesis that my house has been burglarized is correct, it need not be the case that the door will be open. Perhaps the probability of this connection is only 80 percent.

Bayes' Theorem

Bayes' theorem provides a method for evaluating hypotheses in situations, such as that cited above, in which hypotheses vary in their prior probability and the connection between evidence and hypothesis is only probabilistic. The theorem is a mathematical prescription for estimating the *posterior probability* that a hypothesis is true from the *prior probability* that the hypothesis is true and the *conditional probability* of a piece of evidence given the hypothesis.

Prior probabilities are the probabilities that a hypothesis is true before evidence. Let us refer to the hypothesis that my house has been burglarized as *H*. Suppose that I know from police statistics that the probability *(P)* of a house in my neighborhood being burglarized on any particular day is 1 in 1,000. This probability is expressed as

$$P(H) = .001.$$

This equation expresses the prior probability of the hypothesis, or the probability of the hypothesis being true before the evidence. We will refer to this hypothesis as *H*. The other prior probability needed is the probability that the house has not been burglarized. This alternate hypothesis is denoted $\bar{H}$. This value is 1 minus *P(H)* and is

$$P(\bar{H}) = .999.$$

A conditional probability is the probability that a particular type of evidence is true if a particular hypothesis is true. Let us consider what the conditional probabilities of the evidence (door ajar) would be under the two hypotheses. Suppose I believe that the probability of the door being ajar is quite high if I have been burglarized, say 4 out of 5. Let *E* denote the evidence, or the event of the door being ajar. Then we will denote this conditional probability

$$P(E|H) = .8,$$

which should be read *the probability of* E *given* H *is true*. Second, we determine the probability of *E* if *H* is not true. Suppose I know that chances are only 1 out of 100 that the door would be ajar if no burglary had occurred (for example, by accident, neighbors with a key, and so on). This we denote

$$P(E|\bar{H}) = .01,$$

the probability of E *given that* H *is not true*.

The posterior probability is the probability of a hypothesis being true after some evidence. The notation *P(H|E)* is the posterior possibility of hypothesis *H* given evidence *E*. According to Bayes' theorem, we can calculate the posterior probability of *H,* that the house has been burglarized, in light of the evidence thus:

$$P(H|E) = \frac{P(E|H) \cdot P(H)}{P(E|H) \cdot P(H) + P(E|\bar{H}) \cdot P(\bar{H})} \qquad (1)$$

Given our assumed values, we can solve for *P(H|E)* by substituting into equation 1:

$$P(H|E) = \frac{(.8)(.001)}{(.8)(.001) + (.01)(.999)} = .074.$$

Thus, the probability that my house has been burglarized is still less than 8 in a 100. Note that this probability is true despite the fact that an open door is good evidence for burglary and not for a normal state of affairs *P(E|H) =* .8, and *P(E|$\bar{H}$) =* .01). The posterior probability is still quite low because the prior probability of *H—P(H) =* .001—was low to begin with. Relative to that low start, the posterior probability has been drastically revised upwards.

A formal derivation of Bayes' theorem is given in the appendix to this chapter. Table 11-3 offers an informal explanation of Bayes' theorem as applied to the burglary example (adapted from Hayes, in press). There are four

Table 11-3   An Analysis of Bayes' Theorem

Evidence	Burglarized *(H)*	Not Burglarized *(H̄)*	Sum of Probabilities
Door Open (E)	P(E|H) P(H) = .00080	P(E|H̄)P(H̄) = .00999	.01079
Door Not Open (Ē)	P(Ē|H)P(H) = .00020	P(Ē|H̄)P(H̄) = .98901	.98921
Sum of Probabilities	.00100	.99900	1.00000

possible states of affairs, determined by whether the burglary hypothesis is true or not and by whether there is the evidence of an open door or not. The probability of each state of affairs is set forth in the four cells of Table 11-3. The probability of each state is the prior probability of that hypothesis times the conditional probability of the event given the hypothesis. For instance, consider the upper left cell. Since *P(H)* is .001 and *P(E\|H)* is .8, the probability in that cell is .0008. The four probabilities in these cells must sum to 1. Given the evidence that the door is open, we can eliminate the two cells in the lower row of the table. Since one of the two remaining states of affairs must be the case, the posterior probabilities of the two remaining states must sum to 1. Bayes' theorem provides us with a means for recalculating the probabilities of the states in light of evidence that makes impossible one row of the matrix. What we have done in equation 1 in calculating the posterior probability is taken the probability of the upper left cell, where hypotheses *H* is true, and divided it by the sum of the probabilities in the two upper cells, which represent the only two possible states of affairs.

Bayes' theorem rests on a mathematical analysis of the nature of probability. The formula has been proven to evaluate hypotheses correctly; thus, it enables us to determine precisely the posterior probability of a hypothesis given the prior and conditional probabilities. The theorem serves as a *prescriptive,* or *normative, model* specifying the means of evaluating the probability of an hypothesis. Such a model contrasts with a *descriptive model,* which specifies what people actually do.

Deviations from Bayes' Theorem

It should come as no surprise to learn that humans typically do not behave perfectly in accord with the Bayesian model. Ward Edwards (1968) has extensively investigated how people use new information to adjust their estimates of the probabilities of various hypotheses. In one experiment, he presented subjects with two bags, each containing 100 poker chips. One of the bags contained 70 red chips and 30 blue and the other contained 70 blue chips and 30 red. The experimenter chose one of the bags at random and the subject's task was to decide which bag had been chosen.

In the absence of any prior information, the probability that the chosen bag contained predominantly red chips was 50 percent. Thus,

$$P(H_R) = .50 \quad \text{and} \quad P(H_B) = .50,$$

where H_R is the hypothesis of a predominantly red bag and H_B is the hypothesis of a predominantly blue bag. To obtain further information, subjects sampled chips at random from the bag. Suppose the first chip drawn was red. The conditional probability of drawing a red chip if most of the chips in the bag are red is

$$P(R|H_R) = .70.$$

Similarly, the conditional probability of drawing a red chip from a blue-majority bag is

$$P(R|H_B) = .30.$$

Now, we can calculate the posterior probability of the bag being predominantly red given the red chip by applying equation 1 to this situation:

$$P(H_R|R) = \frac{P(R|H_R) \cdot P(H_R)}{P(R|H_R) \cdot P(H_R) + P(R|H_B) \cdot P(H_B)}$$

$$= \frac{(.70) \cdot (.50)}{(.70) \cdot (.50) + (.30) \cdot (.50)} = .70$$

This result seems, both to naive and sophisticated observers, to be a rather sharp increase in probabilities. Typically, human subjects do not increase their probability of a red-majority bag to .70, rather, they make a more conservative revision to a value such as .60.

After this first drawing, the experiment continues: The poker chip is put back in the bag and a second chip is drawn at random. Suppose this chip too is red. Again, by applying Bayes' theorem, we can show that the posterior probability of a red bag is .84. Suppose our observations continued for 10 more trials and after all 12 we have observed 8 reds and 4 blues. By continuing the Bayesian analysis, we could show that the new posterior probability of the hypothesis of a red bag is .97. Subjects who see this sequence of 12 trials only estimate subjectively a posterior probability of .75 or less for the red bag. Edwards has used the term *conservative* to refer to subjects' tendency to underestimate the force of evidence. He estimates that they use between a half and a fifth of the available evidence from each chip.

Another problem is that subjects sometimes ignore prior probabilities. Kahneman and Tversky (1973) told one group of subjects that an individual had been chosen at random from a set of 100 individuals consisting of 70 engineers and 30 lawyers. This group of subjects was termed the *engineer-high group*. A second group, the *engineer-low group*, was told that the individual came from a set of 30 engineers and 70 lawyers. Both groups were asked to determine the probability that the individual chosen at random from the group would be a lawyer given no information about the individual. Subjects were able to respond with the right prior probabilities: the engineer-high group estimated .70 and the engineer-low group estimated .30. Then subjects were told that another person was chosen at random from the population and they were given the following description:

> Jack is a 45-year-old man. He is married and has four children. He is generally conservative, careful, and ambitious. He shows no interest in political and social issues and spends most of his free time on his many hobbies, which include home carpentry, sailing, and mathematical puzzles.

Subjects in both groups gave a .90 probability estimate to the hypothesis that this person was an engineer. No difference was displayed between the two groups, which had been given different prior probabilities for an engineer hypothesis. But Bayes' theorem prescribes that prior probability should have a strong effect resulting in a higher posterior probability from the engineer-high group than the engineer-low group.

The following sample description was also used by Kahneman and Tversky:

> Dick is a 30-year-old man. He is married with no children. A man of high ability and high motivation, he promises to be quite successful in his field. He is well liked by his colleagues.

This example was designed to provide no diagnostic information either way with respect to Dick's profession. According to Bayes' theorem, the posterior probability of the engineer hypothesis should be the same as the prior probability, since this description is not informative. However, both the engineer-high and the engineer-low groups estimated that the probability was .50 that the individual described was an engineer. Thus, they allowed a completely uninformative event to change their probabilities. Again, subjects were shown to be completely unable to use prior probabilities in assessing the posterior probability of a hypothesis.

The failure to take prior probabilities into account can lead an individual to make some totally unwarranted conclusions. For instance, suppose you take a test for cancer. It is known that a particular type of cancer will result in a positive test 95 percent of the time. On the other hand, if a person does not have the cancer there is only a 5 percent probability of a positive result. Suppose you are informed that your result is positive. If you are like most people, you will assume that your chances of having the cancer are 95 out of 100, and begin saying good-bye to your friends (Hammerton, 1973). You would be overreacting in assuming that the cancer would be fatal, but you would also be making a fundamental error in probability estimation. What is the error?

You would have failed to consider the base rate for the particular type of cancer in question. Suppose, only 1 in 10,000 people have this cancer. This

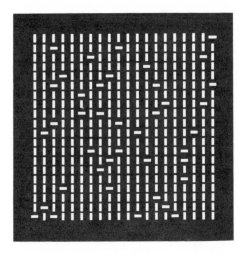

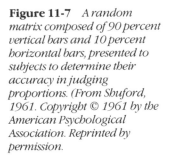

Figure 11-7 *A random matrix composed of 90 percent vertical bars and 10 percent horizontal bars, presented to subjects to determine their accuracy in judging proportions. (From Shuford, 1961. Copyright © 1961 by the American Psychological Association. Reprinted by permission.*

would be your prior probability. Now, with this information you would be able to determine the posterior probability of your having the cancer. Bringing out the Bayesian formula, you would express the problem this way:

$$P(H|E) = \frac{P(H)P(E|H)}{P(H)P(E|H) + P(\overline{H})P(E|\overline{H})}$$

where the prior probability of the cancer hypothesis is $P(H) = .0001$, and $P(\overline{H}) = .9999$, $P(E|H) = .95$, and $P(E|\overline{H}) = .05$. Thus,

$$P(H|E) = \frac{(.0001)(.95)}{(.0001)(.95) + (.9999)(.05)} = .0019$$

That is, the posterior probability of your having the cancer would still be less than 1 in 500.

Judgments of Probability

To understand why subjects do not operate according to Bayes' theorem in evaluating evidence, it is necessary to understand how they reason about probabilities. They certainly do not think about probabilities by performing mentally the kinds of arithmetic operations (additions, multiplications, and divisions) called for by Bayes' theorem. A number of experiments have asked subjects to make judgments of probabilities. In some circumstances they can do this quite accurately. Consider an experiment by Shuford (1961). He presented arrays such as that in Figure 11-7 to subjects for 1 second. He then asked subjects to judge the proportion of vertical bars relative to horizontal

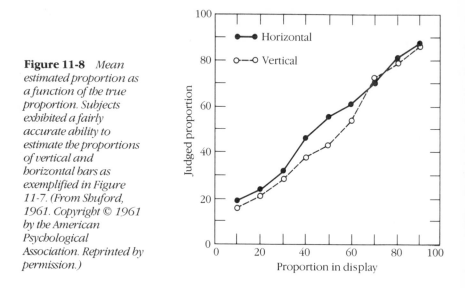

Figure 11-8 *Mean estimated proportion as a function of the true proportion. Subjects exhibited a fairly accurate ability to estimate the proportions of vertical and horizontal bars as exemplified in Figure 11-7. (From Shuford, 1961. Copyright © 1961 by the American Psychological Association. Reprinted by permission.)*

bars. The numbers of vertical bars varied from 10 to 90 percent in different matrices. Shuford's results are shown in Figure 11-8. As can be seen, subjects' estimates are quite close to the true proportions.

Another experiment to assess judgments as to proportion was performed by Robinson (1964). He presented his subjects with a sequence of flashes from a left light and a right light. The task was to estimate the proportion of left or right flashes in the sequence. Again, subjects were very accurate in making these estimates. Their estimates fell within .02 of the true proportions.

In both of these experiments, subjects were not actually estimating *probabilities;* rather, they were estimating the *proportions* of a type of event in a population. However, it seems that people think of probabilities in terms of proportion in a population—and, indeed, the mathematics of probability is based on a concept very close to this. In the two experiments cited, subjects were able to make an unbiased inspection of the population; thus, their estimates were unbiased. They could see all the instances. However, as we will see, in many probability-estimation situations, one does not have total and unbiased access to the underlying population. It is in such situations that distortions in probability estimates occur.

Availability

Consider the following experiment reported by Tversky and Kahneman (1973), which demonstrates that probability judgments can be biased by differential availability of examples: They asked subjects to judge the proportion of words in the language that fit certain characteristics. For instance, they asked subjects to estimate the proportion of English words that begin with a *k* versus words with a *k* in third position. How might subjects perform this task? One obvious heuristic is to briefly try to think of words that satisfy the specification and words that do not and to estimate the relative proportion of target words. How many words can you think of that begin with *k*? How many words can you think of that don't? What is your estimate of their relative proportion? Now how many words can you think of that have *k* in the third position? How many words can you think of that don't? What is their relative proportion? Subjects estimated that more words begin with *k* than have *k* in their third position. In actual fact, three times as many words have *k* in third position as begin with *k*.

As in this experiment, many real-life circumstances require that we estimate probabilities without having direct access to the population that these probabilities describe. In such cases, we must rely on memory as the source for our estimates. The memory factors we studied in Chapters 3, 6, and 7 serve to explain how such estimates can be biased. Under the reasonable assumption that words are more strongly associated to their first letter than their third letter, the bias exhibited in the experimental results can be explained in terms of the spreading-activation theory (Chapter 6). In the case of these gross overestimates of words beginning with particular letters, with the focus of attention on, say, *k,* activation will spread from that letter to words beginning with it. This process will tend to make words beginning with *k* more available than other words. Thus, these words will be overrepresented in the sample that subjects take from memory to estimate the true proportion in the population. The same overestimation does not occur for words with *k* in the third position, since words are unlikely to be directly associated to the letters that occur in their third position. Therefore, it is not possible to associatively prime these words and make them more available.

Similarity (The Gambler's Fallacy)

Other factors besides memory lead to biases in probability estimates. Consider another example from Tversky and Kahneman (1973). Which of the following sequences of six tosses from a fair coin is more likely (where H denotes *heads* and T *tails*): H T H T T H or H H H H H H? Many people think that the first sequence is more likely to occur, but the two sequences are actually equally probable. The probability of the first sequence is the probability of H on the first toss (which is .50) times the probability of T on the second toss (which is .50), times the probability of H on the third toss (which is .50), and so on. The probability of the whole sequence is .50 × .50 × .50 × .50 × .50 × .50 = .016. Similarly, the probability of the second sequence is the product of the probabilities of each coin toss and the probability of a head on each coin toss is .50. Thus, the final probability again is also .50 × .50 × .50 × .50 × .50 × .50 = .016. Why do some people have the illusion that the first sequence is more probable? It is because the first event seems similar to a lot of other events, for example, H T H T H T or H T T H T H. These similar events serve to bias upwards one's probability estimate of the target event. On the other hand, H H H H H H, straight heads, seems unlike any other event, and its probability will therefore not be biased upwards by other similar sequences. In conclusion, one's estimate of the probability of an event will be biased by other events that are similar to it.

Note that the effect of this fallacy is that subjects underestimate the frequency of runs of events, such as straight heads. This tendency to underestimate leads to a common phenomenon known as the *gambler's fallacy*. The fallacy is the belief that if an event has not occurred for a while, then it is more likely by the "law of averages" to occur in the near future. This phenomenon can be demonstrated in an experimental setting, for instance, where subjects see a sequence of coin tosses and must guess whether each toss will be a head or a tail. If they see a string of heads, they become more and more likely to guess that tails will come up on the next trial. Casino operators count on this fallacy to help them make money. Players who have had a string of losses at a table will keep playing, assuming that by the "law of averages" they will experience a compensating string of wins. However, the game is set in favor of the house. The dice do not know or care whether a gambler has had a string of losses. The consequence is that players tend to lose more as they try to recoup their losses. The "law of averages" is itself a fallacy.

The gambler's fallacy can be used to one's advantage in certain situations —for instance at the racetrack. Most racetracks operate by a pari-mutuel system, in which the odds on a horse are determined by the number of people betting on the horse. By the end of the day, if favorites have won all the races, people tend to doubt that another favorite can win, and they switch their bets to the long shots. As a consequence, the betting odds on the favorite deviate from what they should be, and one can sometimes make money by betting on the favorite.

Difficulty of Computation

Another reason subjects are off in their probability estimates is that the ease of computing the frequency of different events varies, and the more easily computed event will seem to be the more frequent. Consider the following example from Tversky and Kahneman. You want to form committees out of a group of 10 people. In one case, you want to make committees of 2 members each, and in the other case you want to make committees of 8 members each. The problem is to decide how many different committees of 2 and how many different committees of 8 are possible. Subjects ask to estimate the number of different possible committees of 2 came up with a median estimate of 70. Subjects asked to estimate the number of different committees of 8 came up with 20. Actually, in both cases the number of possible committees is 45. If one thinks about it in the right way, it is obvious that the number of commit-tees should be the same: each different committee of 2 defines a different committee of 8 which is the remainder of the 10 people after those 2 are subtracted out. However, clearly most subjects did not think about the prob-lem in this way. Tversky and Kahneman suggested that subjects tried to think of how many ways they could form different committees of 2 if that is what was asked or tried to see how many ways they could form committees of 8 if that is what was asked. They used their internal count as a basis for estimating the true number. For instance, a subject who could come up with 10 ways in a minute's thought might give five times this 10 as an estimate of all the possible ways. It is much easier to think up different ways of forming committees of 2 than committees of 8. The 10 members can be divided into 5 disjoint pairs in many ways. However, because any subset of 8 overlaps with any other subset of 8, keeping track of the different possible groups of 8 is difficult. It is the greater ease with which committees of 2 are computed that accounts for their higher estimated frequency.

Some strands of communality underlie all the types of distortions that Tversky and Kahneman found in subjects' estimates of probabilities and fre-quencies. In all cases, subjects must make estimates where they cannot get or do not know how to get unbiased access to the population they are estimat-ing. In this situation, such factors as availability, similarity, or difficulty of computation create distortions in subjects' perceptions, and most individuals do not know how to correct for these distortions. These distortions are like the distortion that occurs when one sees a stick that appears crooked in the water. A child who is educated as to the distorting effect of water on shape is eventually able to correct for the distortion. Similarly, we would hope that educating the general populace would help correct these common distor-tions in frequency and probability estimates.

An Explanation of Deviations from Bayes' Theorem

Now that we have identified the common distortions people experience in their probability and frequency estimates we can explain why their evalua-tions of hypotheses deviate from the normative prescriptions of Bayes' theorem. First consider conservatism, the tendency of most people not to use all the information available in an event in deciding on posterior probabili-ties. Let's consider again one of the standard Bayesian problems: subjects must decide whether the bag has 70 red chips and 30 blue or 70 blue and 30 red. After drawing 12 samples from a bag, they observe 8 reds and 4 blues. If they were to decide on the posterior probability of the red bag by relative proportion, they would have to compare the number of ways this event could occur given the red-majority bag with the number of ways with the blue-majority bag. Their probability estimates would be based on this relative proportion.

The problem with judging relative proportions is that it is quite impossible for a subject to estimate the number of ways in which the two types of events can occur. How many ways are there to get 8 red chips and 4 blue chips from the red-majority bag? On any draw from the bag there are 70 ways to get a red chip and 30 ways to get a blue chip, but how do you combine this information to get the number of ways for the full sequence of 12? Using a formula and a calculator, I determined that there are 3.3×10^{22} ways to get 8 reds and 4 blues from the red-majority bag and 1.1×10^{21} ways from a blue-majority bag. However, few subjects in the experiment would be in possession of the formula to make this calculation, and none would be in possession of a calculator. So, the first point to be made about subject's conservatism is that it arises from an inability to estimate the frequency of the relevant events, which leads to an inability to estimate the relevant proportion of one type of event to the other.

Unable to come up with a direct estimate of the proportion, subjects must fall back on some heuristic in attempting to estimate the proportion. It seems that subjects use some mapping of the relative ratio of red chips to blue chips. Consider the following three cases:

1. Six chips are sampled with replacement (i.e., a chip is put back into the bag after being sampled). Five are red and one is blue.

2. Twelve chips are sampled with replacement. Eight are red and four are blue.

3. Thirty-six chips are sampled with replacement. Twenty are red and sixteen are blue.

What is the probability that the bag is a red-majority bag in each case? Subject's estimates of the probability of the red-majority bag will decrease from the first case, where the ratio is 5 to 1, to the second case, where the ratio is 2 to 1, to the third case, where the ratio is 5 to 4. In fact, in all three cases the true probability is .97. It is an interesting consequence of Bayes' theorem that the absolute difference between red and blue chips is what is important, not the ratio. Therefore, subjects are doomed to conservatism because they use the ratio and pay little attention to the number of chips sampled.

In summary, conservatism arises for these reasons:

1. Subjects cannot calculate the frequency of the alternative events and so cannot make estimates of relative proportion.

2. Subjects choose a heuristic that incorrectly weights ratio highly and does not weight absolute difference.

Kahneman and Tversky offer an explanation of why subjects do not take prior probabilities into account in making predictions. When asked to judge whether a described individual is a lawyer or an engineer, subjects try to judge the number of lawyers versus the number of engineers that fit the description. In part, they may make this judgment by thinking of the numbers of lawyers versus engineers they know who fit the description. To use the terminology of Kahneman and Tversky, subjects try to decide how *representative* the description is of the lawyer versus the engineer. In making this representativeness judgment, subjects can only make a decision of how closely the description matches those of lawyers and engineers in the real world. No easy way exists for integrating the information about prior probabilities of the special sample into the representativeness judgment that is based on the real world.

The Implications of the Research on Induction

Bayes' Theorem and Probability Judgment

We have seen that people tend to judge probability by judging the relative frequency of different kinds of outcomes. Their probability judgments are distorted because they have difficulties in properly assessing frequencies of events that are not directly observed but that have to be remembered or imagined. This difficulty in making probability judgments results in a difficulty in making hypothesis evaluations in response to evidence. We reviewed two difficulties. First, people are too conservative in evaluating the impact of evidence. Second, they often ignore information about prior probabilities.

We are constantly being asked to evaluate hypotheses in the light of evidence. Therefore, it is important to try to avoid the errors in hypothesis evaluation reviewed in this chapter. One remedy is to memorize the Bayesian formula and use it whenever possible. However, the Bayesian formula presents a difficulty in that it requires one to come up with prior and conditional probabilities. Arriving at these probabilities is not always easy, and these estimates may themselves be subject to biases. Therefore, Bayes' theorem is not a total cure, though it can serve as a useful tool.

Also, in many situations doing the calculations required by Bayes' theorem is burdensome or impossible. To deal with this computational problem, Edwards (1962) introduced the idea of a probabilistic information-processing system, called PIP, that would mechanically aggregate subject-provided prior and conditional probabilities to produce posterior probabilities. It has been documented that despite the fact that PIP uses subjective prior and conditional probabilities, the system produces more accurate posterior evaluations of hypotheses than those arrived at by people evaluating evidence directly (see Slovic and Lichtenstein, 1971 for a review).

As already noted, even the Bayesian procedure requires that probabilities be estimated. Our capacity to evaluate hypotheses would be improved if our probability estimates were more accurate. About the only relevant advice I can think of for improving probability estimates is that one should be aware of the biases in such estimates and try to correct them. Just as we should correct judgments of the apparent shape of a stick in water by applying our knowledge of refraction, so we should correct our probability judgments by considering biasing factors such as differences in availability in memory, differences in similarity to other instances, differences in computational complexity, and differences in representativeness. As an exercise, consider the following questions and identify the biases that could lead to erroneous answers:

1. How easy is it to become a professional basketball player?
2. Is one more likely to be a victim of a crime in New York City or Scottsdale, Arizona?
3. Which birth order is more likely for 5 children in a family: boy, boy, girl, girl, girl or boy, girl, boy, girl, girl?
4. How likely is it, with 30 random people in the room, that at least 2 will have the same birthday?

One is likely to overestimate the ease of becoming a professional basketball player. The stories of those who tried and succeeded are well publicized and therefore highly available. What is not available are the stories of the tens of thousands who failed. Actually, Scottsdale, Arizona is supposed to have a higher crime rate than New York City. However, crime in New York City is much more frequently reported and dramatized.

The two birth orders given above should be equally likely (as are any other birth orders). However, the possibility of boy, girl, boy, girl, girl may seem more likely because it seems similar to other families of five. On the other hand, a run of boys followed by a run of girls seems quite unique. The gambler's fallacy seems to apply to expected birth order. If a couple has had two boys, the tendency is to believe that the third child will be a girl.

The probabilities are fairly high (70 percent) that with 30 random people at least 2 will have the same birthday. It is hard to realize that the probability is so high because it is hard to calculate the number of ways in which this event can occur. Taking the first individual, there are 29 different people he or she could share a birthday with; even if the first person did not share a birthday with any of these, the second person could share a birthday with 28 different people; even if the second did not, the third could share a birthday with 27 different people, and so on. Altogether, in a room of 30 people there are 435 different ways a birthday could be shared!

Scientific Induction

The research we have reviewed has been principally concerned with inductive reasoning as it occurs in the minds of undergraduate subjects. We found that such people exhibited major weaknesses in both their hypothesis formation and their hypothesis evaluation. Undergraduates as a group certainly are above average in intelligence, but they are not experts at induction. What happens when we look at people expected to be experts at induction? If any group is expert at induction it should be scientists. The scientist's job is induction pure and simple: he or she must look at the world, generate hypotheses about its operation, and test the validity of these hypotheses. However, the evidence shows that, the typical conceit of scientists notwithstanding, they are sometimes poor at hypothesis formation and hypothesis evaluation, and it is not clear whether they could improve significantly.

We saw that one common difficulty with subjects' inductive behavior is an inability to structure and search the hypothesis space properly. It is fair to say that this difficulty runs rampant among scientists. To date, no science has properly formulated to itself the hypothesis space it is searching.

Another problem we found with inductive reasoning was an inability to reason about the import of negative evidence. A related problem shows up in a misconception that is found in science, although almost every scientist has been taught about the misconception and understands, in the abstract, that it should be avoided: To understand the nature of this misunderstanding, one must appreciate the fact that hypotheses in science are usually stated as general laws, for example,

> The acceleration a of a mass m by an imbalanced force f is directly proportional to the force and inversely proportional to the mass.

Though scientists often view their efforts as attempts to prove such hypotheses, there is no way of proving that a general hypothesis is true. No matter how many particular situations have confirmed the law, it is always possible that another situation will fail to uphold the law. Particular experiments can never prove general scientific laws. On the other hand, while no experiment can prove a hypothesis, any experiment can disprove the hypothesis if the experiment comes out wrong. As Popper (1959) is famous for pointing out, what science does is try to disprove hypotheses in its experiments. One accrues support for a hypothesis by failing to disprove the hypothesis. This accrual of support can be seen to be an outcome of a standard Bayesian analysis: the posterior probability of a hypothesis is increased if an event is observed that has a very high conditional probability under the hypothesis (usually the probability is 1) but a relatively low conditional probability under alternative hypotheses. If the probability of the event under the hypothesis is 1, the posterior probability of the hypothesis is reduced to 0 if the predicted event does not occur.

This logic of supporting a hypothesis by failing to disconfirm it has a double negative embedded in it. While scientists can appreciate this fact, they typically fail to act in accordance with it. It is natural to think and write of a positive outcome as proving a hypothesis (which is equivalent to the fallacy of affirming the antecedent, discussed in Chapter 10). Indeed, the astute reader will note that this very logical error is at least implicit in much of the material presented in this book. In my defense, I might say that I deliberately made the error to facilitate communication, but this apology would be an acknowledgment and capitulation to the problem. The danger in capitulating to this error is that one comes to think of theories as *proven* and therefore *true* rather than as *not yet disproven* and perhaps *plausible*. The result is a lot of unreasonable dogmatism in science.

Many areas of science, such as psychology, do not deal in certain evidence, let alone certain hypotheses. Thus, in these fields it is necessary to reason probabilistically. There is ample evidence that the ability of scientists to reason about probabilities is only somewhat more sophisticated than that of the general populace. In psychology, researchers are taught elaborate statistical techniques for evaluating hypotheses. One function of these techniques is to protect the psychologist from the typical fallacies. To a degree these means do work but not to the degree one would like to see. Tversky and Kahneman (1971) have shown that trained psychologists are sometimes subject to only slightly more sophisticated versions of the common fallacies of induction.

The Tversky and Kahneman paper (1971) is essential reading for any serious cognitive-psychology student. Tversky and Kahneman found that professional psychologists made incorrect decisions about many example problems requiring judgments about probability or other statistical concepts. The paper should be read immediately after a course in statistics. At least an introductory statistics course is a prerequisite to understanding most of the examples cited. However, the following example is an exception:

> The mean IQ of the population of eighth graders in a city is known to be 100. You have selected a random sample of 50 children for a study of educational achievements. The first child tested has an IQ of 150. What do you expect the mean IQ to be for the whole sample?

Many psychologists believe that things will average out and that the mean should be 100. This is an example of the gambler's fallacy that we discussed earlier. In fact, conditional on the high IQ of the first child, the total sample should have a higher than average mean IQ.

Remarks and Suggested Readings

A good introduction to the philosophy of inductive logic is Skyrms (1966). A number of textbooks offer a thorough review of the concept-formation literature; these include Bourne (1966); Johnson (1972); Bourne, Ekstrand, and

Dominowski (1971); and Kintsch (1970). Levine (1975) provides a recent collection of papers spanning the history of research on concept formation. Bruner, Goodnow, and Austin (1956) remains a classic well worth reading. Simon and Lea (1974) provides a discussion of the similarity between inductive reasoning and problem solving. Tversky and Kahneman's (1974) *Science* article provides a good survey of their research on probabilistic judgment. The paper by Slovic and Lichtenstein (1971) contains an extensive review of psychological research on Bayes' theorem.

Appendix

A derivation of Bayes' theorem follows.

The posterior probability of a hypothesis if given evidence E is

$$P(H|E) = \frac{P(H \cap E)}{P(E)} \tag{1}$$

where $P(H \cap E)$ is the probability of both H and E being true and $P(E)$ is the probability of the evidence. We can express these as

$$P(H \cap E) = P(E|H)P(H), \text{ and} \tag{2}$$

$$P(E) = P(H \cap E) + P(\bar{H} \cap E), \tag{3}$$

where

$$P(\bar{H} \cap E) = P(E|\bar{H})P(\bar{H}). \tag{4}$$

In the above, $P(\bar{H} \cap E)$ denotes the probability of both the hypothesis being false and the evidence still obtaining; $P(E|H)$ is the conditional probability of the evidence if the hypothesis is true; $P(E|\bar{H})$ is the conditional probability of the evidence if the hypothesis is false; $P(H)$ is the prior probability of the hypothesis; and $P(\bar{H}) = 1 - P(H)$. Substituting equations 2, 3, and 4 into equation 1, we get the form of Bayes' theorem that we have been using:

$$P(H|E) = \frac{P(E|H)P(H)}{P(E|H)P(H) + P(E|\bar{H})P(\bar{H})}$$

Part V

LANGUAGE

Chapter 12

Language: An Overview

Summary

1. The linguist is concerned with characterizing our *linguistic competence,* which is our abstract knowledge about the structure of language. This concern contrasts with the psychologist's concern with *language performance,* which is how we actually use language.

2. The linguist wants to account for the *productivity* and *regularity* of language and the *linguistic intuitions* of language speakers. Productivity refers to the fact that it is always possible to generate novel sentences. Regularity refers to the fact that strict rules exist to determine what constitutes an acceptable sentence. Among the important linguistic intuitions are *judgments of paraphrase* and *judgments of ambiguity.*

3. The *surface structure* of a sentence is a hierarchical analysis of the sentence into phrases and subphrases.

4. Chomsky proposed a *transformational grammar* as a linguistic theory of the relation between *syntax, semantics,* and *phonology.* Syntax is concerned with rules of sentence form, semantics with sentence meaning, and phonology with rules of sentence sound. In Chomsky's proposal, syntax is central. It is because of the centrality of syntax that his theory cannot be used directly as a performance model.

5. Debate has long ensued as to whether language is dependent on thought, whether thought is dependent on language, or whether the two are independent of each other. The evidence is not decisive but favors the view that language is dependent on thought.

6. Human beings constitute the only species with a communication system that qualifies as a language. Recently, some efforts have been made to teach languages to apes, but so far these efforts have failed in transmitting to the apes full language facility.

7. Chomsky and others have advanced the claim that language is a unique system within human cognition. They point to evidence from language acquisition. However, the evidence is not convincing.

Of all of the human beings' cognitive abilities, the use of language is the most impressive. The difference between human language and the natural communication systems of other species is enormous. More than anything else, language is responsible for the current advanced state of human civilization. It is the principal means by which knowledge is recorded and transmitted from one generation to the next. Without language there would be little technology. Language is the principal medium for establishing religions, laws, and moral conventions. Therefore, without language no means would exist for establishing rules to govern groups ranging in size from tennis partners to nations. Language also provides people with the principal means of assessing what another person knows. So, without language human beings would experience countless more misunderstandings than they currently do. Language provides an important medium for art, a means of getting to know people, and a valuable aid to courtship. Therefore, without language much of the joy of living would be lost. In its written form, language enables humans to communicate over spatial distance and through time as this book demonstrates.

In this chapter, we will cover three general aspects of language. First, we will review the work in linguistics through which a characterization of the structure of language has been developing. Second, we will review the speculations and research about the possible relations between language and thought. Third, we will consider the issues surrounding the purported uniqueness of language to humans. With these general points as background, the following two chapters will explore in detail the two major aspects of language usage: comprehension and generation.

Throughout this chapter we will be discussing many ideas that were either proposed or strongly influenced by Noam Chomsky. Chomsky is an American linguist who began developing his theories in the 1950s at the University of Pennsylvania and then moved to the Massachusetts Institute of Technology, where he has been ever since. His work has had a revolutionary influence on linguistics, a powerful influence on cognitive psychology, and a lesser but important influence on other social sciences. He is also well known for his participation in the antiwar movement during the Vietnam War and his intellectual contributions to radical political causes. His ideas are difficult to comprehend, and the psychological implications of his claims often seem obscure. However, understanding his ideas is important not only because of their influence in cognitive psychology, but also because Chomsky is one of the major intellectual figures of our time.

The Structure of Language

Productivity and Regularity

The academic field of linguistics, which is distinct from psychology, attempts to characterize the nature of language. Although opinion and practice in linguistics vary widely, "average linguists" pursue their studies of language with little concern for how language is used. The fact that language is a functional human tool is largely irrelevant. Later in the chapter, we will discuss the competence-performance distinction, which linguists use to divorce their studies of the structure of language from the ways in which language is used. The linguist focuses on two aspects of language: its *productivity* and its *regularity*. The term productivity refers to the fact that an infinite number of utterances are possible in any language. Regularity refers to the fact that these utterances are systematic in many ways.

One need not seek far to convince oneself of the highly productive and creative character of language. One need only pick up a book and select a sentence from it at random. Suppose that, having chosen a sentence, an individual were instructed to go to the library and begin searching for a repetition of the sentence! Obviously, no sensible person would take up this challenge. But, were one to try, it is very unlikely that he or she would find the sentence repeated among the billions of sentences in the library. Still, it is important to realize that the components that make up sentences are quite small in number: only 26 letters, and 40 phonemes (see the discussion in Chapter 2), and 100,000 words are used in English. Nevertheless, using these components we can and do generate trillions of novel sentences.

A look at the structure of sentences makes clear why this productivity is possible. Natural language has facilities for endlessly embedding structure within structure and coordinating structure with structure. A mildly amusing party game is to start with a simple sentence and require participants to keep adding to the sentence:

The girl hit the boy.

The girl hit the boy and he cried.

The big girl hit the boy and he cried.

The big girl hit the boy and he cried loudly.

The big girl hit the boy who was misbehaving and he cried loudly.

The big girl with authoritarian instincts hit the boy who was misbehaving and he cried loudly.

The big girl with authoritarian instincts hit the boy who was misbehaving and he cried loudly and ran to his mother.

The big girl with authoritarian instincts hit the boy who was misbehaving and he cried loudly and ran to his mother who went to her husband.

The big girl with authoritarian instincts hit the boy who was misbehaving and he cried loudly and ran to his mother who went to her husband who called the police,

and so on until someone can no longer repeat the sentence.

The fact that an infinite number of word strings can be generated would not be particularly interesting in itself. If we have 100,000 words for each position and if sentences can be of any length, it is not hard to see that a very large (in fact, an infinite) number of word strings is possible. However, if we just combine words at random we get sentences like this:

From runners physicians prescribing miss a states joy rests what thought most.

In fact, very few of the possible word combinations are acceptable sentences. The speculation is often jokingly made that, given enough monkeys working at typewriters during a long enough time, some monkeys will type a best-selling book. It should be clear that it would take a lot of monkeys a long time to type just one acceptable *R@!#s.

So, balanced against the productivity of language is its highly regular character. One goal of linguistics is to discover a set of rules that will account for both the productivity and the regularity of natural language. Such a set of rules is referred to as a *grammar*. A grammar should be able to prescribe or generate all the acceptable sentences of a language and be able to reject all the unacceptable sentences in the language. Besides rejecting such obvious nonsentences as the one given above, grammar must be able to reject such near misses as

The girls hits the boys.

Did hit the girl the boys?

The girl hit a boys.

The boys were hit the girl.

The sentences above all contain *syntactic violations* (violations of sentence structure). That is, they are fairly meaningful but contain some mistakes in word combinations or word forms. Other nonsentences are possible in which the words are correct in form and syntactic position but their combination is nonsense. For instance:

> Colorless green ideas sleep furiously.
>
> Sincerity frightened the cat.

These constructions are called *anomalous sentences* and are said to contain *semantic violations* (violations of meaning). Still other sentences can be correct syntactically and semantically but be mispronounced. Such sentences are said to contain *phonological violations*. Consider this example:

The Inspector opened his notebook.

"Your name is Halcock, is't no?" he began.

The butler corrected him.

"H'alcock," he said, reprovingly.

"H, a, double-l?" suggested the Inspector.

"There is no h'aich in the name, young man. H'ay is the first letter, and there is h'only one h'ell."

[Sayers, 1968, p. 73]

To account for the regularity of language, then, linguists need a grammar that will specify *phonology* (sound), *syntax* (structure), and *semantics* (meaning).

Linguistic Intuitions

Another feature that linguists want a grammar to explain are the *linguistic intuitions* of speakers of the language. Linguistic intuitions are judgments about the nature of linguistic utterances or about the relationships between linguistic utterances. Speakers of the language are often able to make these judgments without knowing how they do so. Among these linguistic intuitions are judgments about why sentences are ill-formed. For instance, we can judge that some sentences are ill-formed because they have bad syntactic structure and that other sentences are ill-formed because they lack meaning. Linguists require that a grammar capture this distinction and clearly express the reasons for it. Another kind of intuition is about *paraphrase*. A speaker of English will judge that the following two sentences are very similar in meaning and hence are paraphrases:

> The girl hit the boy.
>
> The boy was hit by the girl.

Yet another kind of intuition is about *ambiguity*. The following sentence has two meanings:

> They are cooking apples.

This sentence can either mean that some people are cooking some apples or that the apples being referred to are for cooking. Moreover, speakers of the language can distinguish this type of ambiguity, which is called *structural ambiguity,* from *lexical ambiguity, in*

> I am going to the bank,

where *bank* can refer either to a monetary institution or a river bank. Lexical ambiguities arise when a word has two or more distinct meanings; structural ambiguities arise when an entire phrase or sentence has two or more meanings.

So, in summary, linguists strive to create grammars that (1) specify the nature of the well-formed sentences in a language; (2) specify which utterances are ill-formed and why; and (3) explain intuitions that speakers have about such things as paraphrase and ambiguity.

Competence Versus Performance

It should be clear, even from our brief discussion of the goals linguists have for the grammar of a language, that very little attention is given to how language is actually used. To be sure, linguists must reluctantly acknowledge that humans exist, if only because humans serve the function of what are called *informants.* If linguists want to develop a grammar for a particular language, they must go to a native speaker of the language, an informant, and ask the speaker for judgments about what sentences are acceptable in the language and for other intuitions. As often as not, the linguists will be trying to develop a grammar for their own languages, in which case they will use themselves as informants.

However, it is clear that in our everyday language use we do not always behave in ways we would judge to be correct if we were serving as informants. We generate sentences in conversation that, in a more reflective situation, we would judge to be ill-formed and unacceptable. We hesitate, repeat ourselves, stutter, and make slips of the tongue. We misunderstand the meaning of sentences. We hear sentences that are ambiguous but do not note their ambiguity.

Another complication is that linguistic intuitions are not always clear cut. For instance, we find the linguist Lakoff (1971) telling us that the first sentence below is not acceptable but that the second is:

> Tell John where the concert's this afternoon.
>
> Tell John that the concert's this afternoon.

People are not always reliable in their judgments of such sentences and certainly do not always agree with Lakoff.

Considerations about the unreliability of human linguistic behavior and judgment led Noam Chomsky to make a distinction between *linguistic compe-*

tence, one's abstract knowledge of the language, and *linguistic performance,* the actual application of knowledge in speaking or listening. In Chomsky's view, the linguist's task is to develop a theory of competence; the psychologist's task is to develop a theory of performance.

The exact relationship between a theory of competence and a theory of performance is unclear and can be the subject of heated debates. Chomsky has argued that a theory of competence is central to performance—that our linguistic competence underlies our ability to use language, if indirectly. Others believe that the concept of linguistic competence is based on a rather unnatural activity (making linguistic judgments) and has very little to do with everyday language use. One reason that this issue is so unclear is that linguists differ as to what should be covered under the topic of competence. Some want to cover topics such as mispronunciations or rules of conversation, which certainly seem to be parts of a performance theory.

In the remainder of this section we will take a rather traditional view of the function of a competence grammar and focus on proposals, largely derived from Noam Chomsky's theory, for how to formulate such a grammar for a language. A competence grammar has the virtue of identifying and articulating much of the syntactic structure of language. This material will prove particularly important in later chapters.

Surface Structure

One central linguistic concept is *surface structure.* Surface-structure analysis is not only significant in linguistics, but it is also very important to an understanding of the processes of comprehension and generation. Therefore, our coverage of this topic here is partially a preparation for material in subsequent chapters. Some readers who have had a certain kind of high-school training in English will find the analysis of surface structure to be similar to parsing exercises. For others, the analysis will be more novel.

The surface structure of a sentence is hierarchical division of the sentence into units called phrases. Consider this sentence:

The brave dog saved the drowning child.

If asked to divide this sentence into two major parts in the most natural way, most people would provide the following division:

(The brave dog)(saved the drowning child),

where the parentheses distinguish the two separate parts. The two parts of the sentence correspond to what are traditionally called subject and predicate, or noun-phrase and verb-phrase. If asked to divide the second part, the verb-phrase, further, most people would give

(The brave dog)(saved (the drowning child)).

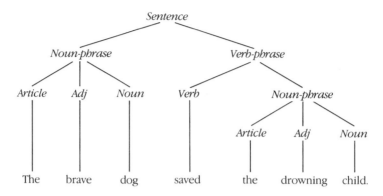

Figure 12-1   *An example of the surface structure of a sentence. The tree structure illustrates the hierarchical division of the sentence into phrases.*

Often this kind of sentence is represented as an upside-down tree, as in Figure 12-1. In this surface-structure tree, *sentence* points to its subunits, *noun-phrase* and *verb-phrase,* and each of these units points to its subunits. Eventually, the branches of the tree terminate in the individual words. Such tree-structure representations for surface structures are very common in linguistics. In fact, it is common to use the term *surface structure* to refer to such tree structures.

An analysis of surface structure can point up syntactic ambiguities. Consider again this sentence:

They are cooking apples.

Depending on the meaning, *cooking* is either part of the verb with *are* or part of the noun-phrase with *apples*. Figure 12-2 illustrates the surface structure for these two interpretations. In part A *cooking* is part of the verb, while in part B it is part of the noun-phrase.

Rewrite Rules

Note that the various nodes in the trees showing surface structure have meaningful labels such as *sentence, noun-phrase, verb-phrase, verb, noun,* and *adj* (for *adjective*), which indicate the character of these sentence units or constituents. Such labels can serve to form *rewrite rules* for actually generating sentences. Linguists formulate grammars for languages in terms of such rewrite rules. Table 12-1 consists of a set of rewrite rules indicating ways of rewriting these labels, or symbols. The symbol on the left can be rewritten as the symbols on the right. Thus, rule 1 says that *sentence* may be rewritten as *noun-phrase* plus *verb-phrase*. Rule 2A indicates that a noun-phrase can be rewritten as an optional article, an optional adjective, and a noun. The parentheses indicate that the article and adjective are optional. Rule 2B indicates that another way to rewrite a noun-phrase is as a pronoun. It is possible to

(A)

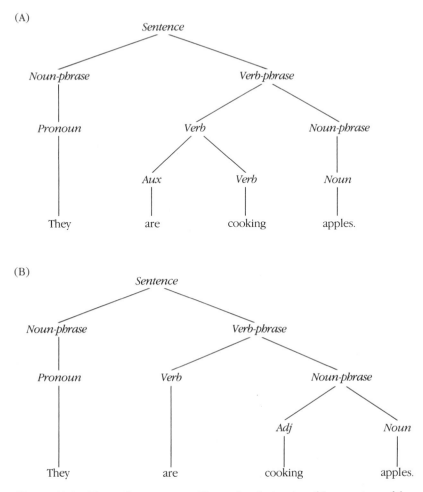

(B)

Figure 12-2 *The surface structures illustrating the two possible meanings of the ambiguous sentence* They are cooking apples. *(A) That those people* (they) *are cooking apples. (B) That those apples are for cooking.*

derive a sentence through these rewrite rules. For instance, consider the following sequence:

$$\rightarrow Sentence - noun\text{-}phrase + verb\text{-}phrase \tag{1}$$

$$\rightarrow article + adj + noun + verb + prepphrase \tag{2}$$

$$\rightarrow article + adj + noun + verb + preposition + noun\text{-}phrase \tag{3}$$

$$\rightarrow article + adj + noun + verb + preposition + article + noun \tag{4}$$

$$\rightarrow the + brave + boy + danced + in + the + river. \tag{5}$$

Table 12-1   Rewrite Rules for Generating a Fragment of English

Symbol	Rewrite as
1. Sentence	⟶ noun-phrase + verb-phrase
2A. Noun-phrase	⟶ (article) + (adj) + noun
2B.	⟶ pronoun
3A. Verb-phrase	⟶ verb + noun-phrase
3B.	⟶ verb + prepphrase
4. Prepphrase	⟶ preposition + noun-phrase
5A. Verb	⟶ aux + verb
5B.	⟶ hit, saved, cooking, danced
6. Noun	⟶ dog, child, boy, girl, apples, river
7. Article	⟶ the, a
8. Adj	⟶ brave, drowning, cooking
9. Pronoun	⟶ he, she, they
10. Preposition	⟶ in, by
11. Aux	⟶ was, were

In line 1, we rewrote *sentence* as *noun-phrase* plus *verb-phrase* according to rewrite rule 1. In line 2, we rewrote *noun-phrase* into *article* plus *adj* plus *noun* (according to rewrite rule 2A) and *verb-phrase* into *verb* plus *prepphrase* (according to rule 3B). In line 3, we rewrote *prepphrase* into *preposition* plus *noun-phrase* (according to rule 4). In line 4, we rewrote the *noun-phrase* from line 3 into *article* plus *noun* (rule 2A). Finally, in line 5, we replaced each of the symbols by words according to rules 5B, 6, 7, 8, and 10.

The tree representation of the surface structure of a sentence serves to illustrate derivation of the sentence through the rewrite rules. Figure 12-3 illustrates the surface structure of the sentence derived in Table 12-1. In such a tree structure, a symbol is connected below to the symbols that the rule rewrites into.

A set of rewrite rules is referred to as a grammar. Such rules constitute one way of specifying the acceptable sentences of the language. As such they provide a means of achieving one important goal of linguistics, which is to devise a grammar that (1) generates all the acceptable sentences of the language, and (2) that does not generate any unacceptable sentences. Can you find ways in which the simple set of rewrite rules in Table 12-1 fail to achieve these two criteria? While linguists have come up with grammars that are much more complex and comprehensive than the one in Table 12-1, they have not yet come close to achieving a grammar that completely satisfies criteria 1 and 2 stated above. Many issues in the field remain unresolved, including whether these two goals are realistic.

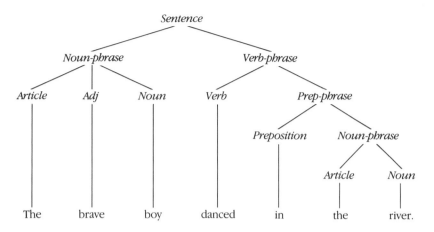

Figure 12-3   *The surface structure of the sentence* The brave boy danced in the river. *The branches in this tree derive from the rewrite rules in Table 12-1.*

Transformational Grammars

The rewrite rules in Table 12-1 are referred to as a *phrase-structure grammar*, because they define the phrases in a sentence such as the noun-phrases, verb-phrases, and prepositional phrases. Chomsky has argued (1957) that such grammars are inadequate as complete descriptions of natural language, since they fail to capture certain generalities and intuitions about natural language. A number of these intuitions involve the meaning of sentences. For instance, consider the following pair of ambiguous sentences:

1. They are cooking apples.
2. Visiting relatives can be boring.

We have already noted how the first sentence is ambiguous and how its ambiguity can be represented in its surface structure (see Figure 12-2). However, sentence 2 is also ambiguous: it can be boring to visit relatives or it can be boring to have relatives visit one. This ambiguity cannot be represented in the surface structure of the sentence, unlike that of sentence 1. In either reading of sentence 2, *visiting* would be represented as modifying *relatives*. To take an example of a different but related problem with phrase-structure grammars, consider another pair of sentences:

3. The cat chased the mouse.
4. The mouse was chased by the cat.

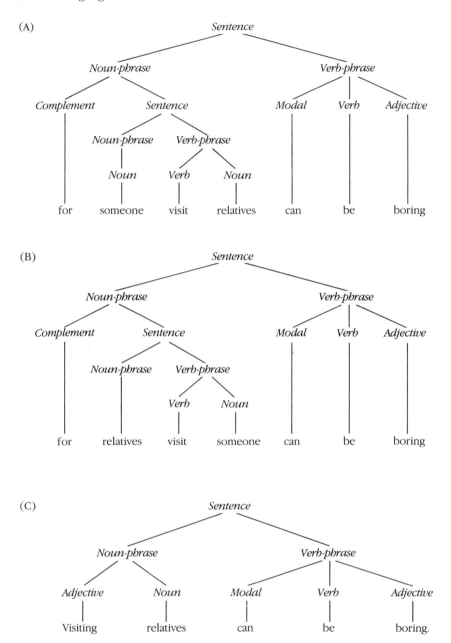

Figure 12-4   *The two possible deep structures of the sentence* Visiting relatives can be boring *in A and B are transformed into the surface structure in C. In A the relatives are the object of the visiting, while in B they are the subject of the visiting.*

These sentences have very similar meanings but their surface structures do not reflect this similarity.

The fact that such examples of ambiguity that cannot be represented in the surface structure of a sentence indicates the need for making a distinction between the *surface structure* and the *deep structure* of a sentence. In contrast to surface structure, which refers to the phrases in the actual sentence, deep structure refers to the phrases in an underlying hypothetical word string, postulated by Chomsky to more directly reflect the meaning of the sentence. Consider sentence 2. It can be analyzed as having two possible deep structures representing the two meanings of the sentence. Parts A and B of Figure 12-4 represent two deep structures (linguists will notice that many details are being glossed over in this general overview). The deep structure subject of Figure 12-4A is *for someone visit relatives* and the deep structure subject in Figure 12-4B is *for relatives visit someone*. The contrast between these two deep-structure subjects reflects the distinction between relatives being visited and relatives doing the visiting. These deep-structure subjects would not be syntactically correct if directly uttered as subjects of English sentences. The proposal is that different *transformations* relate these two underlying deep structures to the same surface structure. For the first interpretation of sentence 2 we have this transformation rule:

$$\text{For} + \text{someone} + verb + noun\text{-}phrase$$
$$\longrightarrow verb + \text{ing} + \text{noun-phrase}$$

For the second interpretation we have

$$\text{for} + noun\text{-}phrase + verb + \text{someone}$$
$$\longrightarrow verb + \text{ing} + noun\text{-}phrase$$

So, these transformation rules are rewrite rules that convert different deep structures into the same surface structure. They are similar to the rewrite rules of a phrase-structure grammar (such as those in Table 12-1), but they can have more than one symbol on their left-hand side. Basically, transformations serve to rearrange elements in a phrase. This surface structure is illustrated in Figure 12-4C. Thus, the deep structure is closer to the meaning of the sentence. As this example illustrates, in translating from deep structure to surface structure we can lose distinctions in the meaning of a sentence.

Sentences 3 and 4 displayed above, in the active and passive voices respectively, illustrate that in going from deep to surface structure it is also possible to create distinctions in form that have no consequence for meaning. Parts A and B of Figure 12-5 show the surface structures for these two sentences. Chomsky (1957) proposed that the deep structure underlying two such sentences was simliar to the active surface structure, in A, but that the passive

(A)

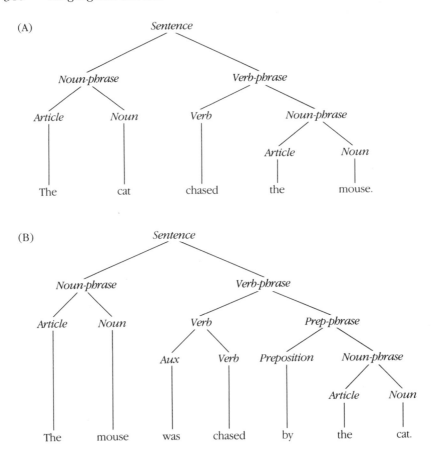

(B)

Figure 12-5 *The active and passive voice conveying basically the same meaning. The deep structure in A is transformed into B, which is the surface structure for a passive.*

surface structure, in B, was derived from A by means of an optional passive transformation:*

$$noun\text{-}phrase1 + verb + noun\text{-}phrase2$$
$$\longrightarrow noun\text{-}phrase2 + was + verb + by + noun\text{-}phrase1$$

---

*In the active case, a distinction was made between its deep and surface structure, but this subtlety is not critical here.

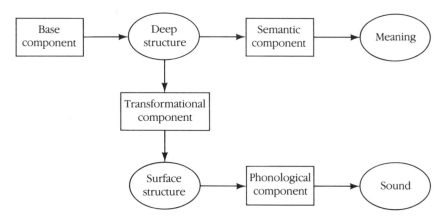

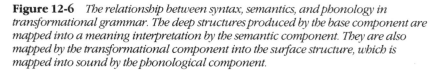

Figure 12-6   *The relationship between syntax, semantics, and phonology in transformational grammar. The deep structures produced by the base component are mapped into a meaning interpretation by the semantic component. They are also mapped by the transformational component into the surface structure, which is mapped into sound by the phonological component.*

The Three Components of Transformational Grammar

Transformational grammar, like many other linguistic systems, distinguishes between the syntax, the semantics, and the phonology of natural language. To reiterate, syntax refers to rules that specify what strings of words are structurally and positionally well formed; semantics refers to rules by which meanings are assigned to well-formed sentences; and phonology refers to rules for translating from surface structures to actual utterances. In our discussion of surface structure, deep structure, and transformational rules, we have been concerned with syntax, although some of the syntactic decisions had semantic motivations.

Figure 12-6 illustrates how syntax, semantics, and phonology are related in Chomsky's (1965) view of language. Two distinct syntactic components appear in the figure: a *base component,* which contains rewrite rules for the deep structure, and a *transformational component,* which contains the transformations relating deep structure to surface structure. The base component generates deep structures. From the deep structure there are two directions of processing. In one direction, the transformational component transforms the deep structure into surface structure, which is transformed into sound by the phonological component. In the other direction, the deep structure is assigned a meaning interpretation by the semantic component. The direct connection between the deep structure and the semantic component in Figure 12-6 reflects the central assumption that deep structure is closer to meaning than is surface structure.

Note that at the center of this scheme is the deep structure. Both meaning and sound derive from the deep structure. This aspect of Chomsky's scheme is sometimes referred to as the *centrality of syntax*, since the deep structure is part of the syntax. Because of the centrality of syntax, as opposed to semantics, it is hard to use Chomsky's linguistic proposal to develop a psychological model. The natural way to think of a process model for language generation would be to start from the intended meaning of the sentence and to transform this meaning into the syntactic deep structure, then into surface structure, and then into sound. Note, however, that deep structure is generated from the base-component rewrite rules without concern for meaning. Meaning is assigned to deep structure *after* the deep structure has been generated by the base component. Thus, the process flows from deep structure to meaning, not conversely. Consequently, this grammar cannot model language generation. It also cannot model language comprehension. In comprehension we would want to go from the sound to the surface structure to the deep structure. The direction is reversed in this model. The fact that this grammar models neither generation nor comprehension brings us back to the competence-performance distinction. A transformational grammar is not a model of actual language use (that is, it is not a performance model); rather it is a model of the abstract knowledge that underlies language use (that is, a competence model).*

One is naturally motivated to ask how transformational distinctions identified here manifest themselves in linguistic behavior. During the 1960s, many experiments were performed that looked for correlates of transformational distinctions in tasks involving paraphrase, memory, perception, and the like. A fair summary of this research is provided by Fodor, Bever, and Garrett (1974), who wrote,

> the experimental evidence for the psychological reality of deep and surface structure is considerably stronger than the experimental evidence for the psychological reality of transformations. [p. 274]

Given the close connection between deep structure and the meaning of a sentence, it is not surprising that there is considerable evidence for the existence of a deep structure. Indeed, much of the research in Chapter 4 on propositional codes can be construed as evidence for a deep structure. In

---

*One might think that the semantic interpretation assigned to a sentence could usefully be linked with the propositional networks discussed in Chapter 4. We used semantic networks there to represent the meaning of a sentence. However, linguistics has not used this kind of semantic interpretation. For a discussion of semantic analysis in linguistics, see the linguistics texts listed at the end of the chapter. A discussion of the various proposals would lead us far afield, and such material is not essential to subsequent discussions.

Chapters 13 and 14, we will review some of the ample evidence that surface structure is intimately involved in sentence comprehension and generation. The fact that little evidence exists for transformations, which form the heart of the Chomsky proposal, is symptomatic of the weak connection between transformational grammar and performance.

One should not conclude that transformational grammar is without psychological implications. Chomsky has used his transformational grammar to make strong claims about the uniqueness of language in human cognition and about how children acquire language. Ideas derived by Chomsky or psychologists influenced by his work will be cited throughout the subsequent sections in which these topics will be covered.

The Relationship Between Language and Thought

The Behaviorist Proposal

A wide variety of proposals have been put forth as to the connection between language and thought. The strongest such proposal was advanced by John B. Watson, the father of behaviorism. It was one of the tenets of Watson's behaviorism (Watson, 1930) that no such thing as internal mental activity existed. All humans did, he argued, was to emit responses that had been conditioned to stimuli. This radical proposal, which, as noted in Chapter 1, held sway in America for some time, seemed to fly in the face of the abundant evidence that humans can engage in thinking behavior (e.g., do mental arithmetic) that involves no response emission. To deal with this obvious counter, Watson proposed that thinking was just subvocal speech, that when people were engaged in such "mental" activities they were really talking to themselves. Hence, Watson's proposal was that a very important component of thought was simply subvocal speech. (The philosopher Herbert Feigl once said that Watson "made up his windpipe that he had no mind.")

This proposal was a stimulus for a research program that engaged itself in taking recordings to see if evidence could be found for subvocal activity of the speech apparatus during thinking. Indeed, often when a subject is engaged in thought one can get recordings of subvocal speech activity. However, the more important observation is that in some situations people engage in various silent thinking tasks with no detectable vocal activity. However, this finding did not upset Watson. He claimed that we think with our whole bodies—for instance, with our arms. He cited the fascinating evidence that deaf mutes actually make signs while asleep. (Speaking people who have done a lot of communication in sign language also sign while asleep.)

The decisive experiment addressing Watson's hypothesis was performed by Smith, Brown, Toman, and Goodman (1947). They used a curare derivative that paralyzed the human musculature. Smith was the subject for the experiment and had to be kept alive by means of an artificial respirator. Because his entire musculature was completely paralyzed, it was impossible for him to engage in subvocal speech or any other body movement. Nonetheless, under curare, Smith was able to observe what was going on around him, comprehend speech, remember these events, and think about them. Thus, it seems clear that thinking can proceed in the absence of any muscle activity. For current purporse, the relevant additional observation is that thought is not just implicit speech but is truly an internal, nonmotor activity.

Additional evidence that thought is not to be equated with language comes from the research on propositional memories that was reviewed in Chapter 4. There we discovered that people tend to retain not the exact words of a linguistic communication, but rather some more abstract representation of the meaning of the communication. Thought should be identified, at least in part, with this abstract, nonverbal propositional code.

Still more information comes from the occasional cases of individuals who have no apparent language at all but who certainly give evidence of being able to think. Also, it seems hard to claim that nonverbal animals such as apes are unable to think. Recall, for instance, the problem-solving exploits of Sultan in Chapter 9. It is always hard to determine the exact character of the "thought processes" of nonverbal subjects and how these differ from the thought processes of verbal subjects, since there is no language with which subjects can be interrogated. Thus, the apparent dependence of thought on language may be an illusion that derives from the fact that it is hard to obtain evidence about thought without using language.

The Whorfian Hypothesis of Linguistic Relativity

Linguistic relativity, or linguistic determinism, is the claim that language determines or strongly influences the way one thinks or perceives the world. This proposal is much weaker than Watson's position, because it does not claim language and thought are identical. The hypothesis has been advanced by a good many linguists but has been most strongly associated with Benjamin Lee Whorf (1956). Whorf was quite an unusual character himself. He was trained as a chemical engineer at the Massachusetts Institute of Technology, spent his life working for the Hartford Fire Insurance Company, and studied North American Indian languages as a hobby. He was very impressed by the fact that different languages emphasize in their structure rather different aspects of the world. He believed that these emphases must have a great influence on the way language speakers think about the world. For instance, Eskimos have many different words for snow, each of which refers to snow in a different state (wind-driven, packed, slushy, and so on), whereas English speakers have only a single word for snow. Many other examples exist at the vocabulary level. The Hanunoo people in the Phillipines have 92 names for different varieties of rice. The Arabic language supposedly has 6000 different ways of naming camels. Whorf felt that such a rich variety of terms would cause the speaker of the language to perceive the world differently from a person who had only a single word for a particular category.

Deciding how to evaluate the Whorfian hypothesis is very tricky. Nobody would be surprised to learn that Eskimos know more about snow than the average English speaker. After all, snow is a more important part of their life experience. The question is whether their language has any effect on the Eskimo's perception of snow over and above the effect of experience. If speakers of English went through the Eskimo life experience, would their perception of snow be any different than that of the Eskimo-language speakers? (Indeed, ski bums have a life experience that involves a great deal of exposure to snow and have a great deal of knowledge about snow.)

One fairly well researched test of the issue involves color words. English has 11 *basic color words*—black, white, red, green, yellow, blue, brown, purple, pink, orange, and gray—a relatively large number. These words are called basic color words because they are short and are used frequently, in contrast to such terms as saffron, turquoise, or magenta. At the other extreme is the language of the Dani, a Stone Age agricultural people of Indonesian New Guinea. This language has just two basic color terms: *mili* for dark, cold hues and *mola* for bright, warm hues. If the categories in language determine perception, the Dani should perceive color in a less refined manner than English speakers do. The relevant question is whether this speculation is true.

Speakers of English, at least, judge a certain color within the range referred to by each basic color term to be the best—for instance, the best red, the best blue, and so on (see Berlin and Kay, 1969). Each of the 11 basic color terms in English appears to have one generally agreed upon best color, called a *focal color*. English speakers find it easier to process and remember focal colors than nonfocal colors (e.g., Brown and Lenneberg, 1954). The interesting question is whether the special cognitive capacity for identifying focal colors evolved because English speakers have special words for these colors. If so, this would be a clear case of language influencing thought.

To test whether the special processing of focal colors was an instance of language influencing thought, Rosch (she has published some of this work under her former name, Heider) performed an important series of experiments on the Dani. The point was to see whether the Dani processed focal colors differently than English speakers. One experiment (Rosch, 1973) compared the ability of the Dani to learn nonsense names for focal versus nonfocal colors. English speakers find it easier to learn arbitrary names for focal colors. Dani subjects also found it easier to learn arbitrary names for focal colors than for nonfocal colors despite the fact that they have no names for these colors. In another experiment (see Heider, 1972), subjects were shown a color chip for 5 seconds; 30 seconds after the presentation ended they were required to select the color from among 160 color chips. English speakers perform better at this task when the chip they are to remember is a focal color rather than a nonfocal color. The Dani also perform better at this task for focal colors.

Thus, it appears that despite the differences in their linguistic terminology for colors, the Dani and English speakers see colors in much the same way. It appears that the 11 focal colors are processed specially by all people regardless of language. In fact, some facts about the physiology of color vision suggest that these focal colors are specially processed by the visual system (de Valois and Jacobs, 1968). The fact that many languages develop basic color terms for just these 11 colors can be seen as an instance of thought determining language.

Another test of the Whorfian hypothesis was performed by Carroll and Casagrande (1958). The Navaho language requires different verb forms depending on the nature of the thing being acted upon, particularly regarding its shape, rigidity, and material. Carroll and Casagrande presented Navaho-speaking children with three objects, such as a yellow stick, a piece of blue rope, and a yellow rope. The children had to say which of the two objects went with the third. Since Navaho requires that a different verb form be used for sticks (rigid) than ropes (flexible), the experimenters predicted that the Navaho-speaking subjects would tend to match the ropes and not match on color. They found that Navaho-speaking children preferred shape and that English-speaking Navaho children preferred color. However, in another study they found that English-speaking Boston children exhibited an even greater tendency to match on the basis of form. It seems that the Boston children's experience with toys (for which shape and rigidity are critical) was more important than the Navaho-language experience, although the language experience may have had some effect.

To conclude, the evidence tends not to support the hypothesis that language has any significant effect on the way we think or on the way we perceive the world. It is certainly true that language can influence us (or else there would be little point in writing this book), but its effect is to communicate ideas, not to determine the kind of ideas we can think about.

Does Language Depend on Thought?

The alternative possibility is that the structure of language is influenced by thought. Aristotle argued 2,500 years ago that the categories of thought determined the categories of language. There are some reasons for believing that he was correct, but most of these reasons were not available to Aristotle. So, although the hypothesis has been around for 2,500 years, we have better reasons for holding it today.

There are numerous reasons to suppose that the human's ability to think (that is, to engage in nonlinguistic cognitive activity such as remembering and problem solving) appeared earlier evolutionarily and occurs sooner develop-mentally than the ability to use language. Many species of animals without language appear to be capable of a complex cognition. Children, before they are effective at using their language, give clear evidence of relatively complex cognition. If one accepts that thought occurred before language, it seems natural to suppose that language is a tool whose function is to communicate thought. It is generally true that tools are shaped to fit the objects on which they must operate. Analogously, it seems reasonable to suppose that language has been shaped to fit the thoughts it must communicate. In addition to general arguments for the view that language depends on thought, a number of pieces of evidence to support the notion have been generated in cognitive psychology and related fields. I will review a few of the lines of evidence.

We saw in Chapter 4 that propositional structures constituted a very impor-tant type of knowledge structure in representing information both derived from language and derived from pictures. Every language has a phrase struc-ture. The basic phrase units of a language tend to convey propositions. For instance, *the tall boy* conveys the proposition that the boy is tall. Much of the discussion in the two chapters that follow will be concerned with how the phrase structure of language controls comprehension and generation. This phenomenon itself—the existence of a linguistic structure, the *phrase,* de-signed to accommodate a thought structure, the *proposition*—seems to be a clear example of the dependence of language on thought.

Another example of the way in which thought shapes language comes from Rosch's research on focal colors. As stated earlier, the human visual system is maximally sensitive to certain colors. As a consequence, languages have spe-cial, short, high-frequency words used to designate these colors. We noted that in English these basic color words are black, white, red, yellow, green, blue, brown, purple, pink, orange, and gray. Thus, the visual system has determined how the English language divides up the color space.

A related piece of evidence suggesting that thought influences language is that one finds highly differentiated terms for a category in a language only if instances of that category are relevant to the life experience of the language users. Thus, it is Eskimos who have many words for snow and Arabs who have many words for camels, not vice versa. Also, languages tend to evolve to encode differences important to the users. Thus, English-speaking skiers have developed their own dialect, which permits discriminations among many types of snow.

We find additional evidence for the influence of thought on language when we consider word order. Every language has a preferred word order for expressing subject (S), verb (V), and object (O). Consider this sentence, which exhibits the preferred word order in English:

Lynne petted the Labrador.

English is referred to as a SVO language. In a study of a diverse sample of the world's languages, Greenberg (1963) found that only four of the six possible orders of S, V, and O are used in natural languages and one of these four orders is rare. Below are the six possible word orders and the frequency with which each order occurs in the world's languages (the percentages are from Ultan, 1969):

SOV	44 percent	VOS	2 percent
SVO	35 percent	OVS	0 percent
VSO	19 percent	OSV	0 percent

The important feature is that the subject almost always precedes the object. This order makes good sense when we think about cognition. An action starts with the agent and then affects the object. Therefore, it is natural that the subject of a sentence, when it reflects its agency, occurs first. Also, as we will discuss more fully in the next chapter, sentences tend to be "about" their subject, and one naturally wants to establish first what the sentence is about.

Thus it seems that, in an important sense, Whorf's hypothesis reversed the actual relation of language and thought. The shape of language is determined in part by thought—just what we would expect if language were a tool designed to permit the communication of thought. However, it is possible to argue that language is much more intimately connected to thought than is a tool to its medium. This argument claims that the mechanisms underlying language use are basically the same in kind as the mechanisms underlying other aspects of cognition. It will be implicitly assumed that this claim is true in subsequent chapters, where production systems for language comprehension and language generation will be presented. This point, however, is by no means universally accepted as true. Linguists and psychologists from the Chomsky camp have claimed that language is a unique system and that linguistic processes are quite different from general thought processes. Their position on the language-thought issue, then, would be that the two systems are in some senses independent. The remainder of this chapter will be devoted to assessing the claims about the uniqueness of language.

Those language theorists propounding Chomsky's position insist that language is a very special facility in three senses:

1. Unlike most cognitive facilities, it is unique to human beings. No other species possesses a true language.

2. Special learning mechanisms exist for acquiring language that are different from the mechanisms underlying acquisition of any other cognitive skill.

3. The mechanisms for language comprehension and generation are unlike the mechanisms underlying the exercise of any other cognitive skill.

Most discussion in the field has concerned points 1 and 2 and these are the points that we will focus on.

The Uniqueness of Language to Humans

It is certainly not the case that humans have the only communication system. If you have had a dog or cat, you know all too well how much these creatures can communicate. Birds have songs to indicate sexual readiness and possession of territory. An interesting communication system is possessed by honeybees (von Frisch, 1967). A bee, upon finding some food, returns to the hive and performs a dance. The speed of the dance and the direction relative to the sun conveys information about the distance and direction of the food.

A Definition of Language

The question is whether any of these communicative systems qualify as language. To answer this question we must define what we mean by language. Hockett (1960) suggested some criteria for language that are worth reviewing and adding to:

1. *Semanticity and Arbitrariness of Units.* One feature of language is that its units (words) have meaning and the connection between the form or sound of the units and the meaning is arbitrary. There is no reason why a shoe should be called *shoe;* it just is. It appears that the warning calls of some monkeys (Marler, 1967) have this property of arbitrary meaning. The monkeys have different warning calls for different types of predators—a "chutter" for snakes; a "chirp" for leopards; and a "kraup" for eagles. The dance of the honeybee, described above, also exhibits this arbitrary feature. On the other hand, when dogs snarl and show their teeth to communicate hostility, they are not using an arbitrary communication system. Their teeth are very directly related to the message they are trying to communicate.

2. *Discreteness.* Language contains discrete units such as words. By this criterion, the bee dance system would be disqualified as a language because it does not contain any discrete units. On the other hand, the monkey warning system meets this criterion because each warning signal is a discrete unit.

3. *Displacement.* Language is generated in the absence of any direct controlling stimuli. Perhaps the bee dance meets this criterion in that the bee can communicate nonpresent food. But by this criterion, the monkey warning system cannot be considered a language because the monkeys only give their warning calls in the presence of danger.

4. *Productivity*. The productivity of language, discussed earlier in this chapter, is a very important feature. By using our verbal communication system, we can essentially produce an infinite number of novel expressions. This property distinguishes language from the monkey warning calls. Interestingly, it does not distinguish language from bee dances. In principle, honeybees should be able to convey an infinite variety of messages by slight changes in the speed and direction of the dance. Note, however, that "infinity" in this system is achieved because the dance is continuous and it is possible to make ever more refined discriminations in speed and direction. True languages achieve their infinity by means of the iteration and recursion of discrete symbols.

5. *Iteration and Recursion*. *Iteration* is the capacity for adding onto the ends of sentences or phrases to create new sentences. This iteration can go on without limit as in the following sequence:

The child breathed the air.

The child breathed the air and coughed loudly.

The child breathed the air and coughed loudly and felt sick.

Recursion is the capacity to embed one structure within the same kind of structure. Again, recursion can go on without limit, as in this sequence:

The child whom the mother loved breathed the air.

The child whom the mother whom the man
left loved breathed the air.

The child whom the mother whom the man
whom the police wanted left loved breathed the air.

And so on.

The last two sentences in the sequence above are interesting in that they are very difficult to comprehend; nonetheless most linguists would judge them to be grammatical.

To the best of anyone's knowledge, no natural communication system of any other species possesses property 5, and none possesses all four of the other properties listed. These properties appear to be essential to the concept of a language. Thus, humans are unique in having created language, and so far they are the only species to have used it. The interesting question is whether this says anything about the uniqueness of human abilities with respect to language. Could other species acquire and use a language? The effort to answer this question is one of the motivations for the many projects in which researchers have tried to teach language to apes.

Linguistic Apes?

There are good reasons for choosing apes in the attempt to teach language to another species. Apes are very intelligent and are the animals most like humans. A number of early attempts to teach chimpanzees to speak were total failures (Hayes, 1951; Kellogg and Kellogg, 1933). However, it is now clear (Lennenberg, 1967) that the human's vocal apparatus is specially designed to permit speech whereas the ape's is not. Thus, these early studies only provided information relevant to the physiology and musculature of apes, not to their cognitive capabilities.

While their vocal abilities are limited, their manual dexterity is considerable. Therefore, a number of recent attempts have been made to teach apes languages using a manual system. Some studies have used American Sign Language (Ameslan), which is used by many deaf people. It is clear that Ameslan is a language by the criteria set forth earlier. Therefore, if apes could become proficient in Ameslan, their capacity for acquiring a language would be firmly established.

One of the best-known research efforts inside and outside of psychology was started by Beatrice and Allen Gardner (Gardner and Gardner, 1969) in 1966 on a 1-year-old female chimpanzee named Washoe. Washoe was raised somewhat as a human child would be, following regimens of play, bathing, eating, and toilet training, all of which provided ample opportunity for sign learning. After 4 years, she had learned a vocabulary of 132 signs, was able to generate novel strings up to 5 signs in length, and was able to initiate conversation. She used order of sign in such utterances as *You tickle me* and *I tickle you* to distinguish subject from object. (See Figure 12-8 for other Gardner and Gardner subjects.)

David Premack (1971, 1976) developed an artificial language in which the "words" were colored plastic shapes that could be attached to a magnetic board. A chimp named Sarah was raised in a laboratory situation and was trained to use the symbols to make up "sentences" (see Figure 12-7). Because the chimp was raised in a laboratory situation, she never used her language in spontaneous, social situations as Washoe did. Sarah displayed considerable understanding of the significance of word order as well as control of a great many different constructions: yes-no interrogatives; negatives; class concepts of color, size and shape; compound and coordinate sentences; quantifiers (all, none, one, several); logical connectives (if . . . then); the copula (is); metalinguistic utterances (e.g., name of); and wh–interrogatives (what, where, when, etc.)

A great many experiments are presently being conducted on chimp language, and some of the more recent chimp studies have produced even more impressive results than the Washoe and Sarah studies. It is unclear just how far chimps will advance. Differences in brain capacity will probably mean that

Figure 12.7   *The chimp Peony (a successor to Sarah in Premack's lab) creates sentences by attaching plastic tokens to a magnetic board (Courtesy of David Premack.)*

chimps will never match humans. One of the interesting questions is whether these chimps will ever start teaching Ameslan to other chimps. B. T. Gardner (personal communication) reports some success in this direction (see Figure 12-8).

The critical question for our purposes is whether the chimp accomplishments indicate that the animals have acquired a language. If we apply the criteria of productivity, recursion, and iteration, it seems clear that chimps are not using a full-fledged language. They do not have productive control of the iterative and recursive features of language the way humans do. This is clear simply because their utterances are short and because they have not spontaneously generated new phrase structures that rely on iteration and recursion. For instance, they could not play the party game described earlier in which each participant built on a sentence. However, this interpretation may be unfair. Human children probably do not acquire full productive control of these properties of their language until after as much as ten years of language training. No ape has had this much training. One constraint is that chimps become dangerous as they mature. Also, it is difficult to provide learning situations that are interesting to older chimps. A related problem is that the

Figure 12-8 *Tatu, one of the new subjects of Gardner and Gardner, signing* drink *to her friend Moja. (Courtesy of B. T. Gardner.)*

concentration of linguistic exposure and practice during the chimps' years of linguistic training is not as intensive as that for a normal human during its years of linguistic learning.

Efforts to teach apes languages have come under serious criticism from various public and governmental sources. These projects are supported by government research grants, and critics characterize these experiments as the wasting of public tax dollars to develop circus acts. But these projects are important scientific research efforts. They are shedding light on questions such as the nature of language, its relation to thought, and what it means to be human. There is no doubt that these questions are abstract, but they are no more abstract and no less important than the questions regarding the nature of the universe investigated in the space program at much greater expense. It is important to be frugal in spending public money, and the scientific programs funded publicly should be carefully evaluated, but these considerations themselves suggest that we should be all the more careful not to fall victim to simplistic mischaracterizations of scientific research.

The Uniqueness of Language Within Humans

Another question, related to but independent of whether language is unique to humans, is whether language is unique among the human mental capacities—that is, whether special psychological principles are required to explain the acquisition and use of language. As we have noted, Chomsky and his followers have propounded the position that language is different from other cognitive faculties. The analogy is made to various body systems. We have one system for digestion, another for breathing, and another for circulation. While these systems have to interact, it is clear that the principles governing one are not the same as the principles that govern another. Similarly, it is argued that the human has separate systems for language, problem solving, reasoning, and so on. On the other hand, it can be argued that the analogy between language and physical body systems is poor, that it is hard to draw boundaries around language the way one can around the digestive system. Thus, the argument by analogy does little to help the uniqueness-of-language position.

The arguments cited earlier for the species specificity of language can be used to bolster the view that language is a unique system within human beings. Consider the argument that chimpanzees do not differ from humans qualitatively in their general intellectual abilities, only quantitatively. For instance, Bever, Fodor and Garrett (1974) argue that an adult chimpanzee has the same mental age as a 3-year-old child. However, the argument goes, 3-year-old children are highly verbal and adult chimpanzees are not. The research on ape languages is beginning to challenge the assumption that chimps cannot achieve the proficiency of a human 3-year-old in language. Further evidence that general intelligence and language development are correlated is the fact that retarded children have retarded language development (Lenneberg, Nichols, and Rosenberger, 1969; Lackner, 1968) and the fact that precocious children whose general intellectual development is accelerated also display accelerated language development (Luchsinger and Arnold, 1965). Thus, language appears to be highly dependent, not independent, of general intellectual facility.

Like the chimpanzee case, most of the other arguments for the uniqueness of language rest on various observations regarding language acquisition. We will review some of these arguments in the following subsection.

A Critical Period for Language Acquisition

A related argument for the uniqueness of language has to do with the claim that young children appear to acquire a second language much faster than older children or adults. It is claimed that there is a certain critical period, from 2 to about 11 years of age, when it is easiest to learn a language. If this claim were true, humans would be best able to learn a language when their intellectual faculties were least fully developed which would mean that language ability and intelligence are not correlated. However, the claim that young children learn second languages more readily is just folk wisdom. It is based on informal observations of children of various ages and adults in new linguistic communities, for example, when families are moved to a foreign country in response to a corporate assignment or when immigrants come to a country permanently. Young children are said to acquire a facility to get along in the new language more quickly than older children or adults. However, there are a great many differences among adults versus the older children versus younger children in terms of amount of linguistic exposure, type of exposure (for example, whether stocks, history, or marbles are being discussed), and willingness to try to learn (McLaughlin, 1978; Nida, 1971). In careful studies in which situations have been selected that controlled for these factors, a positive relationship is exhibited between children's ages and language development (Ervin-Tripp, 1974). That is, the older children (greater than 11 years) learn faster than younger children (the possible exception is phonology—younger children may learn to speak with less of an accent).

While the argument from second-language acquisition is weak, Lenneberg's (1967) observations about recovery from traumatic aphasias (aphasia is a loss of language function) are somewhat more convincing evidence that an early critical period does exist for language acquisition. Damage to the left hemisphere of the brain often results in aphasia. Children who suffer such damage before the age of 11 appear to have a 100 percent chance of recovering language function. For older asphasics recovery is 60 percent at best.

Considerable evidence (e.g., Gazzaniga, 1967) is converging to suggest that the left hemisphere is specialized in the adult for language function and other symbolic, analytic functions while the right hemisphere is specialized for nonanalytic, wholistic functions such as art appreciation. This process of the specialization of the hemispheres is referred to as *lateralization*. Lenneberg argued for a causal connection between lateralization and loss of ability to recover from aphasias. He claimed that this lateralization was complete by about puberty. Thus, he argued, before puberty the brain had not specialized, and in aphasics the right hemisphere could take over the language functions of the left hemisphere. After puberty and lateralization it was much harder for the now specialized right hemisphere to take over language function. This line of evidence appeared to indicate that the ability to acquire language is especially programed as a phase of our neural development, a suggestion that is certainly consistent with the view that language is a unique cognitive ability.

It appears, however, that Lenneberg considerably overestimated the period during which lateralization of the brain takes place. More recent evidence (e.g., Krashen and Harshman, 1972; Kinsbourne and Smith, 1974) has indicated that lateralization is complete somewhere between ages 2 and 5. Children show 100 percent recovery from aphasias after age 5. Thus, loss of ability to recover from aphasias does not seem to be related to lateralization. While loss of such ability undoubtedly has a physiological basis, it may not be part of a preprogramed developmental sequence for the brain.

Reynolds and Flagg (1977) have argued that the critical factor in success of recovery from aphasias is how well language is encoded. The brain of a post-11-year-old, having already acquired a language, may have restructured itself to the point at which recovering after damage would be difficult. So, in the view promoted by Reynolds and Flagg, it is experience and not age per se that is critical for relearning language. It follows that loss of ability to recover from aphasias is not part of a language-specific fixed sequence of neural development; rather, it is a consequence of the neural restructuring required to encode a very complex skill. In this view, a child who did not start learning a language until age 10 would probably recover completely from an aphasia after 15 or older. Similarly, losses of other highly learned complex skills sustained through brain damage would be permanent. For instance, the abilities of a chess master, which take at least ten years to develop, might be lost permanently due to neural damage.

The case study of Genie (Fromkin, Krashen, Curtiss, Rigler, and Rigler, 1974) provides an important test case for the hypothesis of Reynolds and Flagg. Genie had been locked in a tiny room until she was discovered and released at age 13 years, 9 months. She had had virtually no social contact. Her blind mother would hurriedly feed her. She was punished if she made any sound. Her father and older brother never spoke to her. Not surprisingly, she possessed no language.

While there are many sad aspects to Genie's history and many heartwarming aspects to the recovery attempts, the critical fact is that she had no opportunity to acquire a language until after the purported critical period. Fromkin et al. reported that in the two years after her discovery Genie showed considerable language-learning abilities. She was learning vocabulary more rapidly than a comparable child (i.e., a child of 3) but was learning syntax more slowly. In an updated report on Genie's development (1977), Curtiss noted that by age 18 Genie was able to speak in short sentences, to use a minimum of grammar, to understand English word order, and to use some prepositions. However, Genie has no generative control over many aspects of English syntax, even though her comprehension seems quite advanced. It is clear from her report that Curtiss believes that Genie will never gain full adult facility in the syntax of language.

To summarize the available evidence, the argument that a biologically determined critical period for language acquisition exists is only partially supported. Consequently, this argument provides only modest support for claims as to the uniqueness of language.

Language Universals

Chomsky has argued that special mechanisms underlie the acquisition of language. Specifically, his claim is that the number of formal possibilities for a natural language is so great that learning the language would simply be impossible unless we possessed some innate information about the possible forms of natural human languages. It is possible to prove formally that Chomsky is correct in his claim. While the formal analysis is beyond the scope of this book, an analogy might help. In Chomsky's view, the problem that child-learners face is to discover the grammar of their language when given instances of utterances of the language. The task can be compared to trying to find a book in a library by using sentences from the book. If the library contains enough books on similar topics, the task could prove impossible. Likewise, enough formally possible grammars are similar enough to each other to make language learning impossible. Thus, since language learning obviously occurs, according to Chomsky we must have special, innate knowledge that allows us to powerfully restrict the number of possible grammars that we have to consider. In the library analogy, the effect would be knowing ahead of time which shelf the book was on.

Chomsky proposes that *language universals* exist that limit the possible characteristics of a natural language and a natural grammar. He assumes that children can learn a natural language because they possess innate knowledge of these language universals. A language that violated these universals would simply be unlearnable. This means that there are hypothetical languages that no humans could learn. Languages that humans can learn are referred to as *natural languages.*

As noted above, we can prove formally that Chomsky's assertion is correct— that is, that constraints on the possible form of a natural language exist. However, the critical issue is whether these constraints reflect any linguistic-specific knowledge on children's part or whether they simply reflect general cognitive constraints of learning mechanisms. Chomsky would argue that the constraints are language specific. It is this claim of Chomsky's that is open to serious question. Stated as a question the issue is, Are the constraints on the form of natural languages universals of language or universals of cognition?

In speaking of language universals, Chomsky is concerned with a competence grammar. Recall that a competence analysis is concerned with an abstract specification of what a speaker knows about a language; in contrast, a performance analysis is concerned with the way a speaker uses language. Thus, Chomsky is claiming that children possess innate constraints about the types of phrase structures and transformations that might be found in a natural language. Because of the abstract, nonperformance-based character of these purported universals, evaluating Chomsky's claims about their existence has proven very difficult.

Although languages can be quite different from one another, some clear uniformities, or near-uniformities, exist among languages. For instance, as we saw earlier, virtually no language favors the word order subject-after-object. However, as we noted, this constraint (and many other limits on language form) appears to have a cognitive explanation. The literature is very thin on universal features of language that do not have general cognitive explanations. Indeed, in my opinion no convincing case exists of such a universal.

Often, the uniformities among languages seem so natural that we do not realize that other possibilities might exist. One such language universal is that adjectives occur near the nouns they modify. Thus, we translate *The brave woman hit the cruel man* into French as

La femme brave a frappé l'homme cruel,

and not as,

La femme cruel a frappé l'homme brave,

although a language in which the adjective beside the subject noun modified the object noun and vice versa would be logically possible. However, it is clear such a language design would be absurd in terms of its cognitive demands. It would require that listeners hold the adjectives from the beginning of the sentence until the noun at the end. No natural language has this perverse structure. If it really needed showing, I have shown with artificial languages that adult subjects were unable to learn such a language (Anderson, 1978).

To date, no convincing demonstrations have been offered to show that there is anything special about the universals of language. These constraints might better be called universals of cognition.

The Uniqueness of Language: A Summary

Little direct evidence exists to support the view that language is a unique system. There is only a little more direct evidence that language obeys general cognitive laws. In my opinion, the status of language is shaping up to be a major issue for cognitive psychology. The issue will be resolved by empirical and theoretical efforts more detailed than those reviewed in this chapter. The ideas here have served to define the context for the investigation of this issue. The next two chapters will review the current state of our knowledge about the details of comprehension and generation. Experimental research on all of these topics will finally resolve the issues about the uniqueness of language.

Remarks and Suggested Readings

A number of introductions to linguistics are available. These include Bolinger (1975), Fromkin and Rodman (1978), Langacker (1973), and Sampson (1975). Perhaps the best introduction to Chomsky's ideas is a book by Lyons (1970).

One should not get the impression that anything like unaniminity exists in linguistics regarding Chomsky's ideas or even that Chomsky still propounds all the details of the theory sketched in this chapter (which he developed between 1957 and 1965). However, that theory is essential to the understanding of many other developments in linguistics. Certain of the ideas comprised by the theory (transformations, distinctions between deep and surface structure) are important in their own right. Chomsky's more recent views on language can be found in his 1975 book.

Of interest are a number of fairly recent textbooks on the psychology of language, sometimes called psycholinguistics. These include Cairns and Cairns (1976); Clark and Clark (1977); Fodor, Bever, and Garrett (1974); Foss and Hakes (1978); and Glucksberg and Danks (1975). A great deal of research on language has been performed in artificial intelligence. The book by Charniak and Wilks (1976) provides an introduction to some of this work.

Fodor, Bever, and Garrett (1974) provide a strong argument for the uniqueness of language. Reynolds and Flagg (1977) provide arguments for the opposite position. Gardner (1975) discusses the effects of brain injuries on language and other facilities. Gazzaniga (1970) describes research in patients whose interhemispheric connections have been severed to arrest epileptic symptoms. This work is an important source of evidence for brain specialization. Roger Brown has done a great deal of research on child language acquisition; much of the research is reviewed in his 1973 book. Other reviews of first-language acquisition include Dale (1976) and deVilliers and deVilliers (1978). McLaughlin (1978) provides a review of research on second-language acquisition.

Chapter 13

Language Comprehension

Summary

1. Comprehension can be analyzed into three stages: *perception, parsing,* and *utilization.* Parsing is translation from the word representation to a meaning representation. Utilization is the use to which the comprehender puts the meaning of the message.

2. The comprehender parses a sentence by analyzing it into *phrases* or *constituents* and interpreting the meaning of each constituent. This process can be modeled by productions whose conditions describe constituent patterns and whose actions place meaning structures in memory.

3. Language comprehenders sometimes parse sentences by considering the meaning of the words alone and not the syntactic information conveyed by the sentence.

4. Comprehenders tend to choose just one meaning for ambiguous clauses. Consequently, they have to reanalyze the clause if later information indicates the original choice was wrong.

5. Part of the utilization process involves relating the information in the sentence to information already in memory. Languages have various syntactic devices for signaling *supposed* versus *asserted* information. Supposed information is material the speaker supposes to be already in the listener's memory. Asserted information is new information that the speaker wants to relate to the supposed information.

6. Linguistic units larger than sentences, such as paragraphs and texts, are structured hierarchically according to certain relations. Information higher in a text structure tends to be better recalled than that lower in the structure. Comprehension of a text depends critically on the perceiver's ability to identify the higher order structures that organize it.

7. Adults tend not to be limited in their reading ability by physiological or perceptual factors. Rather, they are limited by the extent of their general language-comprehension abilities and by their ability to adaptively control their reading rate.

A favorite device in science fiction is the computer or robot that can understand and speak language—whether evil, like HAL in *2001,* or beneficial, like C3PO in *Star Wars.* Workers in artificial intelligence have been at work to develop computers that understand and generate language. Some progress is being made, but it is clear from current research on language that actually inventing a language-processing machine will be a monumental achievement. An enormous amount of knowledge and intelligence underlies the successful use of language. In this chapter and in the next we will consider what is known about the human ability to understand and generate language. We start with comprehension because this aspect of language processing has been studied most thoroughly.

Language comprehenders unavoidably play a passive role. They must respond to what is said to them. In contrast, language generators play a correspondingly active role, in that they basically control the conversation. (Of course, in a typical conversation participants regularly switch roles according to prevailing rules of etiquette.) This asymmetry explains why we know more about the comprehension process than about language generation. Experimenters can exercise control over the material a subject is asked to comprehend, but gaining control over that which the subject generates is very difficult.

In discussing language comprehension, we will be treating comprehension as it is involved in both listening and reading. It is often thought that of the two the listening process is the more basic. Comprehension in reading involves the listening factors, but it is thought to involve other factors as well. Therefore, researchers give a primary emphasis in understanding the comprehension processes that are common to listening and reading. Research on basic comprehension processes can involve either written or spoken material. Researchers' choice of whether to use written or spoken material is determined by considerations of experimental tractability. We will review in this chapter what is known about the general language processes, and will close with a section on the factors that are unique to reading.

Comprehension can be analyzed into three stages. The first stage comprises the *perceptual processes* by which the acoustic or written message is originally encoded. The second stage is termed the *parsing* stage. Parsing is the process by which the words in the message are transformed into a mental representation of the combined meaning of the words. The third stage is the *utilization* stage, in which comprehenders actually use the mental representation of the sentence's meaning. If the sentence is an assertion, the listeners may simply store the meaning in memory; if it is a question, they may answer; if it is an instruction, they may obey. However, listeners are not always so compliant. They may use an assertion about the weather to make an inference about the speaker's personality, they may answer a question with a question, or they may do just the opposite of what the speaker asks. These three stages— perception, parsing, and utilization—are by necessity partially ordered in time; however, they also partly overlap. Listeners can be making inferences from the first part of a sentence while they are perceiving a later part.

This chapter will focus on the two higher level processes—parsing and utilization. The perceptual stage was already discussed in Chapter 2.

Parsing

Sentence Patterns

Language is structured according to a set of rules that tells us how to go from a particular string of words to an interpretation of that string's meaning. For instance, in English we know that if we hear a sequence of the form *A noun verb a noun,* the speaker means that an instance of the first noun has the specified relation (verb) to an instance of the second noun. In contrast, if the sentence is of the form *A noun was verbed by a noun,* the speaker means that an instance of the second noun has the specified relation to the first noun. Thus, our knowledge of the structure of English allows us to appreciate the difference between *A doctor shot a lawyer* and *A doctor was shot by a lawyer.* One way to represent our knowledge of such rules is as a series of productions, in which the condition of each production specifies the word pattern and the action builds into memory the meaning conveyed by that pattern. Such constructs are called *parsing productions.* We might represent our knowledge of the two English structures cited above with the following pair of productions:

IF   the sentence is of the form *A noun-1 verb a noun-2*
THEN   the meaning is that an instance of *noun-1*
        has the relation *verb* to an instance of *noun-2*

IF   the sentence is of the form *A noun-1 was verb by a noun-2*
THEN   the meaning is that an instance of *noun-2* had the relation
        verb to an instance of *noun-1*

In these productions, *noun-1, verb,* and *noun-2* serve to indicate whether the words should be nouns or verbs. The first production would apply if the

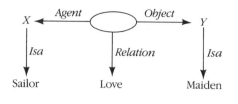

Figure 13-1   *The network representation of the meaning corresponding to the sentence* A sailor loved a maiden. *The letter* X *represents an instance of a sailor and* Y *an instance of a maiden.*

sentence was *A sailor loved a maiden,* and its action would be to build a representation of the sentence's meaning: that an instance of *sailor* had the relation of *loving* to an instance of *maiden.* (For simplicity we are ignoring the distinction between words and the concepts they refer to.) The effect of these productions can be represented as building propositional networks in active memory (see Chapters 4 and 6). So, for instance, the first production above applied to the sentence *A sailor loved a maiden* would build the network illustrated in Figure 13-1.

In learning to comprehend a language we acquire a great many rules that encode the various linguistic patterns in the language and relate these patterns to meaning interpretations. However, pattern rules that process whole sentences are not always possible because of the productivity of language discussed in the last chapter. Sentences can be very long and complex. A very large (probably infinite) number of patterns would be required to encode all possible sentence forms. Consider this example:

> There is a tendency in the average citizen, even if he has a high standing in his profession, to consider the decisions relating to the life of the society to which he belongs as matters of fate on which he has no influence.

A single pattern constructed to process this sentence might take the following form:

> There is a *noun preposition* the *adjective noun,* even if *pronoun verb* a *adjective noun preposition adjective noun,* to *verb* the *noun participle preposition* the *noun preposition* the *noun preposition relative–pronoun pronoun verb* as *noun preposition noun preposition relative–pronoun pronoun verb adjective noun.*

Note that most words in the sentence are replaced by classes such as noun, verb, and preposition. Thus, this pattern could characterize a large number of sentences, for instance,

> There is an inclination in the adult female, even if she practices a great deal of personal independence, to regard the officials participating in the government of the community in which she lives as men of character to whom she owes absolute allegiance.

While many potential sentences would satisfy this pattern, it is unlikely that we have encountered any of them. To see that this is so, let us calculate the number of different patterns 43 words long. We can do this by considering how many variations there are on the pattern above. At almost any point, this pattern could be continued in a variety of ways. For instance, consider the possible ways of continuing the sentence after the first three words, *There is a:*

1. With a noun, as in the original examples.
2. With an adjective, as in *There is a funny story....*
3. With an adverb, as in *There is a very funny story....*

Having chosen a noun for this position, consider the number of options we have for continuing *There is a noun:*

1. With a preposition, as in the original examples.
2. With the infinitive *to,* as in *There is a tendency to believe....*
3. With a relative pronoun, as in *There is a tendency that is hard to resist....*
4. With an article, as in *There is a tendency, a desire, and a compulsion....*
5. With a participle, as in *There is a tendency growing in our society....*
6. With an adverb, as in *There is a tendency, unfortunately, to construct....*

A conservative assumption might be that each fragment can be continued in three possible ways. Since there are 43 positions in the sentence, this assumption would mean that $3^{43} \cong 328,260,000,000,000,000,000$ different 43 word patterns possible in the English language. This number, a great deal larger the number of seconds in an average human life, is another testament to the productivity of natural language. It is by this reasoning that we can be certain that learned patterns do not exist in any language for every possible sentence structure within that language.

The Concatenation of Constituents

While we have not learned to process full sentence patterns such as the one above, we have learned to process subpatterns, or phrases, of these sentences and to combine, or *concatenate,* these subpatterns. These subpatterns correspond to basic phrases, or units, in a sentence's surface structure. These units are referred to as *constituents.*

Table 13-1 displays three productions capable of analyzing a variety of sentences by concatenating analyses of the sentence constituents. This production set uses the term *string* to refer to sequences of words that occur in

Table 13-1   Production for Parsing Various Sentence Constituents

Name of Production	Form of Production
NP	IF the string is of the form *A noun* THEN the meaning is an instance of *noun* and replace the string by this instance
RELATIVE	IF the string is of the form *person who verb object* THEN the meaning is that *person* had the relation *verb* to *object* and replace the string by *person*
MAIN	IF the string is of the form *person verb object* THEN the meaning is that *person* had the relation *verb* to *object*

the sentence. The productions look for various string patterns. Production NP will recognize some simple noun phrases; RELATIVE will recognize some relative clause patterns (that is, noun-modifying clauses such as *who ate the cheese, who loved a sailor*); and MAIN will recognize some simple subject-verb-object sentences. This set of productions can handle sentences composed from indefinite articles, nouns, verbs, and relative clauses. An example of such a sentence is

A princess, who loved a sailor, bought a ship.

The whole sentence can be regarded as a string of words; the productions in Table 13-1 enable the perceiver to pick out various constituents in the string.

The best way to understand such a set of productions is to apply it to an example. Figure 13-2 applies the productions in Table 13-1 to the sentence above. The figure shows how representation of the sentence's meaning is built up piece by piece. The first production to apply is NP. The NP production looks for a pattern of the form *a noun*. So, it matches *A princess*, which begins the sentence. The production replaces the string it matches by an instance of a princess. It does this by creating a new memory node to stand for this princess (referred to as *X*). Now the string has the form

X, who loved a sailor, bought a ship.

Figure 13-2B illustrates the state of memory at this point. Note that an *Isa* link has been encoded in memory asserting that *X* is a princess. This *Isa* structure is the meaning assigned to the noun phrase. This NP production will apply again, replacing *a sailor* with a new node (called *Y*). Now our string representation is

X, who loved Y, bought a ship.

(A)

Initial sentence

A princess, who loved a sailor, bought a ship.

(B)

NP applies

X, who loved a sailor, bought a ship

|Isa

Princess

(C)

NP applies

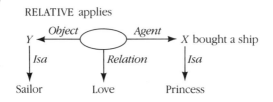

X, who loved Y, bought a ship

|Isa |Isa

Princess   Sailor

(D)

RELATIVE applies

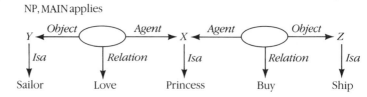

(E)

NP, MAIN applies

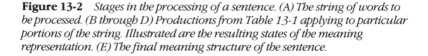

Figure 13-2 *Stages in the processing of a sentence. (A) The string of words to be processed. (B through D) Productions from Table 13-1 applying to particular portions of the string. Illustrated are the resulting states of the meaning representation. (E) The final meaning structure of the sentence.*

Figure 13-2C illustrates the structure in memory at this point. The production RELATIVE applies to the string *X who loves Y.* In its action, RELATIVE interprets this string as asserting that *X* had the loving relation to *Y,* and RELATIVE thus replaces the string by *X.* Now our string representation is

X bought a ship.

Part D of the figure illustrates that the meaning of the relative clause has been encoded by a proposition connecting *X* and *Y.* The NP production applies next, replacing *a ship* by a new node (called *Z*) and connecting the node to *ship* by an *Isa* link. Now our string representation is

X bought *Z.*

This string will be matched by the production MAIN. The production will interpret this string as asserting that *X* had a buying relation to *Z.* Figure 13-2E illustrates, in network form, the final meaning representation of this sentence.

The analysis above is a fairly elaborate example of language processing by means of productions. It is worthwhile to emphasize the important features of this example:

1. Language-processing productions look for typically occurring sentence patterns or constituents, such as *a noun* or *person verb object.*

2. The productions build in memory the semantic interpretation of these patterns.

3. A total sentence is processed through the concatenation of a number of pattern-recognizing productions.

Pattern-recognizing production systems are a means of implementing the idea that subjects have a set of strategies and rules for dividing a sentence up into constituents, identifying the character of each constituent, and applying a semantic interpretation to each constituent. Each production embodies one such rule. The productions rely for their success on the fact that sentences contain various clues (word order, key words such as *who,* inflections) that allow the constituents to be identified. This conception of parsing has been proposed by many researchers (e.g., Bever, 1970; Fodor and Garrett, 1967; Kimball, 1973; and Watt, 1970).

A similarity exists between pattern-recognizing productions and the rewrite rules that generate the surface structure of a sentence, discussed in the preceding chapter. The three rewrite rules that correspond to the productions in Table 13-1 are

SENTENCE → NP verb NP   (MAIN)

NP → NP who verb NP   (RELATIVE)

NP → a noun   (NP)

In applying these rewrite rules,* we would generate the example sentence—
A princess who loved a sailor bought a ship—in the following steps:

SENTENCE → NP *bought* NP	(apply MAIN)
SENTENCE → NP *bought a ship*	(apply NP)
SENTENCE → NP *who loved* NP *bought a ship*	(apply RELATIVE)
SENTENCE → *A princess who loved a sailor bought a ship.*	(apply NP twice)

Thus, parsing productions analyze a sentence by reversing the process of deriving a sentence through rewrite rules, interpreting the meaning of each phrase as they do so.

The Psychological Reality of Constituent Structure

The production systems examined above process a sentence in terms of constituents or phrases. If this analysis accurately models language comprehension, we would expect that the more clearly identifiable the constituent structure of a sentence is the more easily understandable the sentence would be. Graf and Torrey (1966) presented sentences to subjects just a line at a time. The passages could be presented in form A, in which each line corresponded with a major constituent boundary, or in form B, in which this was not the case. Examples of the two types of passages follow:

Form A	*Form B*
During World War II,	During World War
even fantastic schemes	II, even fantastic
received consideration	schemes received
if they gave promise	consideration if they gave
of shortening the conflict	promise of shortening the
	conflict

Subjects showed better comprehension of passages in form A. This finding demonstrates that the identification of constituent structure is important to comprehension.

In the parsing process, after a constituent has been identified, the production system replaces the exact sequence of words with an abstract symbol representing the meaning of that word string. Thus, we would predict that subjects will show poorer memory for the exact wording of a constituent after it has been parsed and parsing has begun on another constituent. An experiment by Jarvella (1971) confirms this prediction. He read subjects passages

---

*In Chapter 12, we followed the traditional linguistic practice of analyzing SENTENCE into SUBJECT + PREDICATE, SUBJECT into NP, and PREDICATE into VERB + NP. The subject–predicate distinction has been glossed over here for the sake of simplicity.

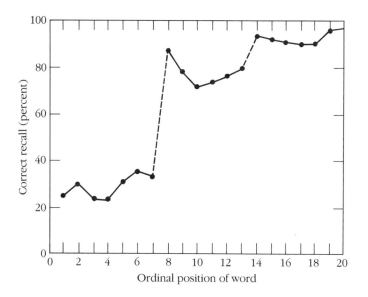

Figure 13-3 *Probability of recalling a word as a function of its position in the last 20 words in a passage. The dotted line shows jumps in recall at constituent boundaries. (Adapted from Jarvella, 1971.)*

that were interrupted at various points. At the points of interruption, subjects were instructed to write down as much of the passage as they could remember. Of interest were passages that ended with 20 words such as the following:

| 1 | 2 | 3 4 | 5 | 6 | 7 |

The tone of the document was threatening.

| 8 | 9 | 10 | 11 | 12 | 13 |

Having failed to disprove the charges,

| 14 | 15 | 16 | 17 | 18 | 19 | 20 |

Taylor was later fired by the president.

Each passage contained a seven-word sentence followed by a sentence composed of a six-word subordinate clause followed by a seven-word main clause. The two clauses are the two major constituents of the second sentence. Because the production-system model outlined above only retains a verbatim representation of the last constituent in the sentence it is currently processing, that model would predict that a subject would have better memory for the second constituent of the second sentence than for its first constituent.

Figure 13-3 plots probability of recall for each of the 20 words in a passage of the form shown above. Note that sharp rises in the function occur at two points—once at word 8, the beginning of the second sentence, and once at word 14, the beginning of the main clause. The graph indicates that subjects have the poorest memory for the first sentence, that a jump occurs to better memory for the first clause of the second sentence, and that a greater jump occurs to best memory for the most recent clause. Thus, these data reflect two effects. First, as expected, subjects show best memory for the last major constituent, a result consistent with the hypothesis that they retain a verbatim representation of the last constituent only. The second effect, the sharp drop-off at the sentence boundary, has a different explanation. It may be due to the fact that subjects work on a different meaning structure for each sentence. After finishing a sentence, they lose their access to that sentence's meaning representation. This effect would make reconstruction of the previous sentence quite difficult.

An experiment by Caplan (1972) also presents evidence for use of constituent structure, but this study uses a reaction-time methodology. Subjects were presented aurally first with a sentence and then with a probe word; they then had to indicate as quickly as possible whether the probe word was in the sentence. Caplan contrasted pairs of sentences such as the following:

1. Now that artists are working fewer hours oil prints are rare.
2. Now that artists are working in oil prints are rare.

Interest focused on how quickly subjects would recognize *oil* in these two sentences when probed at the ends of the sentences. The sentences were cleverly constructed so that in both sentences the word *oil* was fourth from the end and was followed by the same words. In fact, by splicing tape, Caplan arranged the presentation so that subjects heard the same recording of these last four words whichever full sentence they heard. However, in sentence 1 *oil* is part of the last constituent, *oil prints are rare,* whereas, in sentence 2 it is part of the first constituent, *now that artists are working in oil.* Caplan predicted that subjects would recognize *oil* more quickly in sentence 1 because they would still have active in memory a representation of this constituent. As he predicted, the probe word was recognized more rapidly if it occurred in the last constituent.

The Use of Syntactic Cues

Consider again the patterns in the conditions of the productions in Table 13-1. Note that function words, such as *a* and *who,* are very important to correct pattern recognition. Consider the following set of sentences:

1. The boy whom the girl liked was sick.
2. The boy the girl liked was sick.
3. The boy the girl and the dog were sick.

Sentences 1 and 2 are equivalent except that in 2 *whom* is deleted. Sentence 2 is a shorter sentence, but the cost of shortening is the loss of a cue as to how the sentence should be analyzed. At the point of *The boy the girl* it is ambiguous whether we have a relative clause as in sentence 2 or a conjunction as in sentence 3. If it is true that function words such as *whom* are used to indicate which parsing patterns are relevant, then constructions such as sentence 2 should be more difficult to parse than those similar to sentence 1.

Hakes and Foss (1970; Hakes, 1972) tested this prediction using what has been called the *phoneme-monitoring task*. They used doubly embedded sentences such as the following:

1. The zebra which the lion that the gorilla chased killed was running.
2. The zebra the lion the gorilla chased killed was running.

Sentence 2 lacks relative pronouns and so is easily confused with sentences having a noun-conjunction structure. Subjects were required to perform two simultaneous tasks. One task was to comprehend and paraphrase the sentence. The second task was to listen for a particular phoneme—in this case a [g] (in gorilla). Hakes and Foss predicted that the more difficult a sentence was to comprehend the more time subjects would take to detect the target phoneme since they would have less attention left over from the comprehension task with which to perform the monitoring. In fact, the prediction was borne out; subjects did take longer to indicate hearing [g] when presented with sentences such as sentence 2, which lacked relative pronouns.

Semantic Considerations

Semantic Patterns

While it is clear that people use syntactic patterns, such as those illustrated above, for understanding sentences, they can also make use of the meanings of the words involved. An individual can determine the meaning of a string of words simply by considering how they can be put together in order to make sense. Thus, when Tarzan says, "Jane fruit eat," we know what he means even though this sentence does not correspond to the syntax of English. We realize that a relationship is being asserted between something edible and someone capable of eating. Thus, the listener uses a semantic pattern to comprehend a sentence. This semantic pattern could be embodied by the following production:

EATING   IF   the speaker says *eat*
                and the speaker says the name of a food
                and the speaker says the name of a person
      THEN the speaker is asserting that the person eat
                the food

Translated, production EATING assumes that if the speaker mentions eating, an edible food, and a person, then the speaker means that the person ate (or should eat) the food.

Considerable evidence suggests that people use such strategies in language comprehension. Strohner and Nelson (1974) had 2- and 3-year-old children act out with animal dolls the following two sentences:

> The cat chased the mouse.
> The mouse chased the cat.

In both cases, the children interpreted the sentence as indicating that the cat chased the mouse, a meaning that corresponded to their prior knowledge about cats and mice. Thus, these young children were relying more heavily on semantic patterns than on syntactic patterns.

Fillenbaum (1971, 1974) had adults paraphrase sentences among which were "perverse" items such as

> John was buried and died.

More than 60 percent of the subjects paraphrased the sentences in a way that gave them a more conventional meaning, for example, here indicating that John died first and then was buried. However, the normal syntactic interpretation of such constructions would be that the first activity occurred before the second, as in

> John had a drink and went to the party,

as opposed to

> John went to the party and had a drink.

So it seems that when a semantic principle is placed in conflict with a syntactic principle the semantic principle sometimes (but not always) will determine the interpretation of the sentence.

Ambiguity

One of the problems a language comprehender must deal with is ambiguity. As we discussed in Chapter 12, two important types of ambiguity are found in language, *lexical ambiguity* and *structural ambiguity*. Examples are, respectively,

> John went to the bank.

> Flying planes can be dangerous.

It is also useful to distinguish between *transient ambiguity* and *permanent ambiguity*. The examples above are of permanent ambiguity. That is, the ambiguity remains to the end of the sentence. Transient ambiguity refers to sentences that are temporarily ambiguous but that are no longer ambiguous by the end of the sentence. An instance is

The old train the young.

Following the word *train,* it is unclear whether *old* is a noun or an adjective. The sentence could have continued to yield a sentence in which *train* was a noun:

The old train left the station.

This ambiguity is resolved by the end of the sentence.

Transient ambiguity is quite prevalent in language. Consider this sentence:

The model snapped the picture.

After *The model,* it is ambiguous whether the sentence refers to a person or an inanimate object, or an adjective, or a theory. After *snapped,* a great many interpretations are still possible. Consider the following alternative continuations:

The model snapped at the photographer.

The model snapped at by the photographer cried.

The model snapped on a dress.

The model snapped open and the parts spewed over the table.

Each of these continuations represents a different interpretation of the phrase *The model snapped.* Due in part to the ambiguity of natural language, efforts to develop computer programs that will understand natural languages have not yet been fully successful. Because a sentence can be interpreted in many ways at many points, it is difficult to program a computer to choose the intended meaning for a whole sentence. Often, programs must compute a large number of different meanings for sentences. As this number of meanings grows so does the cost of computation time.

We do not fully understand how humans deal with ambiguity in order to comprehend natural language. However, some of the mechanisms are clear. Humans make heavy use of contextual constraints in their efforts to select out a single meaning for each pattern to be interpreted. However, it appears that they only select one interpretation (their best guess) for a pattern and carry it through to the end of the sentence. If the best guess turns out to be wrong, their comprehension suffers and they have to backtrack and try another interpretation. Consider this example:

I know more beautiful women than Miss America
although she knows quite a few.

Such instances indicate that we can be misled in our initial interpretation of a sentence. It is sometimes said that the listener has been "led down a garden path." For this reason, the theory that we only consider a single meaning at a time is referred to as the *garden-path theory* of ambiguity.

Apparently, humans are affected by ambiguity while they are trying to interpret a sentence constituent but once they have interpreted the constituent, ambiguity has no further effect. Bever, Garrett, and Hartig (1973) had subjects complete the following four types of fragments:

1. Although flying airplanes can
2. Although flying airplanes can be dangerous, he
3. Although some airplanes can
4. Although some airplanes can be dangerous, he

Note that fragments 1 and 2 are ambiguous whereas 3 and 4 are not. Fragments 1 and 3 are very similar in structure but only sentence 1 is ambiguous. That is, in fragment 1 we can either be referring to airplanes that are flying or to the act of flying planes. If ambiguous constituents are harder to process because multiple meanings must be considered, subjects should take longer to continue fragment 1 than 3. This prediction was confirmed. Fragments 2 and 4 are also very similar except for the ambiguity of 2. However, in fragment 2, unlike 1, the ambiguity occurs in a constituent that has been completed. If subjects settle on a meaning after a constituent is complete there should be no difference in continuation time between ambiguous fragment 2 and unambiguous fragment 4. Again, this prediction was confirmed. Thus, it appears that we do consider the ambiguity of a constituent while processing it, but once we have finished with the constituent we settle on a particular interpretation. As long as we do not have to change our interpretation, the ambiguity has no further effect on sentence processing.

Utilization

Once a sentence has been parsed and mapped into a meaning representation, what then? A listener seldom simply passively records the meaning. If the sentence is a question or imperative, the speaker expects the listener to take some action in response. However, even for declarative sentences there is usually more to be done than simply register the sentence. Consider this sentence:

The General Assembly condemned Israeli occupation of Arab lands.

Figure 13-4A illustrates the propositional-network representation that might be assigned to this sentence by a set of parsing productions. However, a number of connections are necessary to relate this sentence to the listener's other knowledge. Figure 13-4B shows the memory structure after these con-

(A)

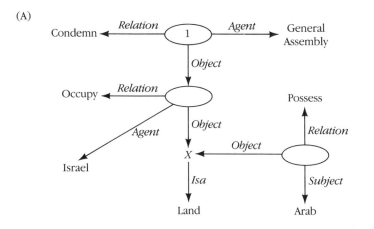

(B)

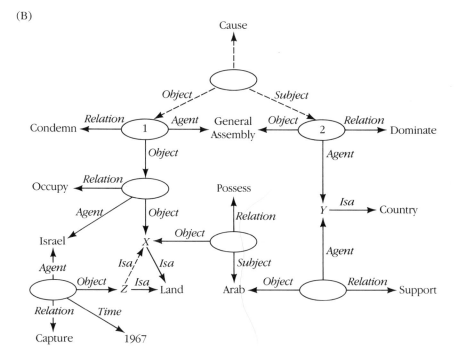

Figure 13-4 *(A) Construction of the meaning representation for the sentence* The General Assembly condemned Israeli occupation of Arab lands. *(B) Integration of this structure with past knowledge. The dotted lines indicate new links added to achieve this integration.*

nections have been made to integrate this new knowledge with existing knowledge. The dotted lines indicate additional connections. The listener will probably recognize the lands in the sentence as an entity already known—the lands captured by Israel in the 1967 war. Thus, a link will be established between the node, *X,* for the land mentioned in the sentence and node *Z,* representing the concept of the captured land, already in memory. Another connection relates the condemnation (proposition node 1) to the knowledge (proposition node 2) that the United Nations is dominated by countries supporting Arabs. Thus, at the very least, listeners try to relate the information in sentences to knowledge they have about the world. Basically, this task involves relating new information to old. Most sentences in a comprehensible communication contain both new and old information. This is because the speaker, in trying to assert new information, must relate it to old information that the listener knows. The speaker is said to *suppose* the old information in order to *assert* the new information. In the example above, the old information is that Israel occupied Arab lands and the new information is that the United Nations voted to condemn this.

Suppositions Versus Assertions

A number of linguistic conventions enable speakers to indicate which information they assume the listener knows and which information they are asserting as new. In this context, the term *supposition* refers to information assumed by speakers to be already known by listeners; the term *assertion* refers to information the speakers consider either new or warranting special emphasis. Among the devices used for signaling whether information is supposed or asserted are the following:

1. Supposed information tends to be contained in subjects of sentences; asserted information tends to occur in predicates. Also, various special linguistic structures exist for highlighting asserted information by emphasizing its predicate position.
2. Stress indicates asserted information.
3. The definite article *the* before a noun phrase indicates that the speaker assumes that the referent of the noun phrase is known; the definite article *a* indicates a new referent.

The devices for indicating whether supposed or asserted information is being expressed can be complex in their interactions, but generally their functions are clear.

Consider the following sentences, in which words in all capitals are stressed.

1. John hit BILL.
2. What happened to Bill was that JOHN HIT him.
3. The pilot caused an accident.
4. The pilot caused the accident.
5. The breed Bob likes is LABRADOR.
6. The one who likes Labradors is BOB.
7. The lawyer SHOT the sailor.
8. As for the shooting it was the lawyer who did it to the sailor.
9. A lawyer shot a sailor.
10. I am HONEST.
11. I am NOT a crook.

In sentence 1, *Bill* is stressed and occurs in the predicate. Thus, this sentence would probably be used when the listeners knew that John hit somebody and the speaker wanted to tell them whom. In sentence 2, a circumlocution is used to put *John hit* into the predicate position, where it is stressed. Thus, the sentence structure indicates the supposition that something happened to BILL and the assertion that what happened was that John hit him. In sentences 3 and 4 no stress is used, but in sentence 3 the indefinite article *an* occurs in the predicate position, while in sentence 4 the definite article *the* occurs. In both cases a definite article is used with the subject *pilot.* Thus, sentence 3 assumes that the listeners know of the pilot and asserts that an accident took place which the pilot caused. In contrast, sentence 4 assumes that listeners know of both the pilot and the accident and asserts that the first caused the second. Sentences 5 and 6 also illustrate redundant linguistic devices of stress and position for signaling supposed versus asserted information. Sentence 5 supposes that the listeners know Bob likes a breed and asserts that this breed is the Labrador. In contrast, sentence 6 supposes that someone likes Labradors and asserts that this person is Bob. Sentence 7 assumes that the listeners know both the lawyer and the sailor and asserts that one shot the other. Sentence 8, in addition to assuming that the lawyer and the sailor are known, also supposes that the listeners know of the shooting. Sentence 8 only asserts information about who was involved in the shooting. Sentence 9 is interesting in that it signals that the listeners should expect to know nothing—not who the lawyer is, who the sailor is, or that a shooting occurred. We might expect to find this kind of sentence at the beginning of a story.* Sentences 10 and 11

---

*However, in the modern literary style called *in media res* ("in the middle of things") such openings, which clearly acknowledge that the reader does not yet know anything about what is going on, are in disfavor. Rather, modern stories tend to open in the midst of things.

provide an interesting sociopolitical contrast. Sentence 10 simply asserts that I am honest. However, sentence 11 has a more complex structure although it conveys the same meaning. As we will discuss further shortly, sentence 11 supposes that it is reasonable to suppose that I am a crook but asserts that this is not true.

Evidence for the Supposition–Assertion Distinction

This supposition–assertion contrast constitutes part of what is called the *pragmatics* of language—that is, information conveyed by the sentence about how the sentence is to be used once its meaning has been extracted. One thing listeners must do with supposed information is to search for it in their memories, because the information should provide a connection between the sentence and past knowledge. Thus, we would expect a subject to be slow to comprehend a sentence when information was signaled as being supposed but the subject was unable to find a referent in memory for the supposed information. Haviland and Clark (1974) report an experiment directed at this issue. They compared subjects' comprehension time for two sentence pairs such as the following:

1. Ed was given an alligator for his birthday. The alligator was his favorite present.
2. Ed wanted an alligator for his birthday. The alligator was his favorite present.

Both pairs have the same second sentence. Pair 1 introduces a specific antecedent for alligator in its first sentence. On the other hand, although in pair 2 *alligator* is mentioned in the first sentence, a specific alligator is not posited. Thus, no antecedent occurs in the first sentence of 2 for *the alligator*. The definite article *the* in the second sentence of the pair supposes a specific antecedent. Therefore, we would expect that subjects would have difficulty with the second sentence in pair 2 but not in pair 1. In the Haviland and Clark experiment subjects saw pairs of such sentences one at a time. After they comprehended each sentence they pressed a button. The time was measured from the presentation of the second sentence until subjects pressed a button indicating that they understood that sentence. Subjects took an average of 1031 msec to comprehend the second sentence in pairs such as 1 above, in which an antecedent was given, but they took an average of 1168 msec to comprehend the second sentence in pairs such as 2 above, in which no antecedent for the definite noun phrase occurred. Thus, comprehension took over a tenth of a second longer when no antecedent occurred. This result confirms the hypothesis that comprehension is impaired if the supposed information is not available to the comprehender.

Another interesting aspect of the supposition–assertion distinction is that it implies that listeners should assume they know the supposed information and

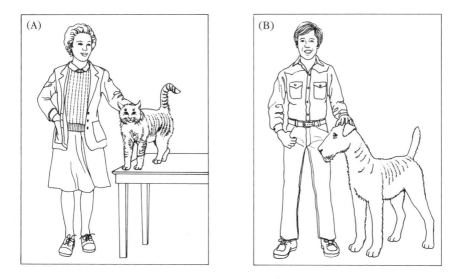

Figure 13-5   *Examples of pictures presented to subjects by Hornby to determine the effect of the supposition–assertion distinction on question answering. Subjects make more errors processing sentences about the pictures that contain an error in supposition rather than assertion. (From* Psychology *and* Language *by Herbert H. Clark and Eve V. Clark. © 1977 by Harcourt Brace Jovanovich, Inc. Reproduced by permission of the publisher.)*

apply their critical attention to that which is asserted. An experiment by Loftus and Zanni (1975) illustrates the power of suppositions in this regard. These experimenters showed subjects a film of an automobile accident and asked them a series of questions. Some subjects were asked,

1. Did you see a broken headlight?

Other subjects were asked,

2. Did you see the broken headlight?

In fact, there was no broken headlight in the film, but question 2 uses a definite article, which supposes the existence of a broken headlight. Subjects were more likely to respond *yes* when asked the question in form 2. As Loftus notes, this finding has important implications for the interrogation of eye-witnesses.

An experiment by Hornby (1974) also illustrates the importance of the supposition–assertion distinction. He showed subjects one of a pair of pictures such as Figure 13-5A and B and asked subjects to verify whether a sentence was true of it. The picture was only shown for 50 msec and the subjects therefore made many errors. Of interest was their error rate in responding to the following false sentences:

1. It is the BOY who is petting the cat.
2. It is the CAT which the boy is petting.
3. The one who is petting the cat is the BOY.
4. What the boy is petting is the CAT.

Sentence 1 supposes that someone is petting the cat and asserts that the someone is a boy; the same is true for sentence 3. In contrast, sentences 2 and 4 suppose that the boy is petting something and assert that the something is the cat. Each sentence matches one picture on its supposed information and contradicts it on its asserted information; the match is reversed for the other picture in the pair. Subjects made more errors when the sentence contradicted the picture on its supposed rather than its asserted information. That is, for sentence 1 they made more errors on picture B than A; for sentence 2, more errors on picture A than B; for sentence 3, more errors on picture B than A; and for sentence 4, more errors on picture A than B. It seems that subjects often did not bother to check the supposed information but only considered the asserted information. Overall, 72 percent errors were recorded when the supposed information was wrong but only 39 percent when the asserted information was wrong.

Negatives

Negative sentences appear to suppose a positive sentence and then assert the opposite. For instance, the sentence *John is not a crook* supposes that it is reasonable to assume *John is a crook* but asserts that this is false. As another example, imagine the following four replies from a normally healthy friend to the question *How are you feeling?*

1. I am well.
2. I am sick.
3. I am not well.
4. I am not sick.

Replies 1 through 3 would not be regarded as unusual linguistically, but reply 4 does seem peculiar. By using the negative it is supposing that thinking of our friend as sick is reasonable. In contrast, the negative in reply 3 is quite acceptable, since supposing that the friend is normally well is reasonable.

Clark and Chase (e.g., Chase and Clark, 1972; Clark and Chase, 1972; Clark, 1975) have been involved in a series of experiments on the verification of

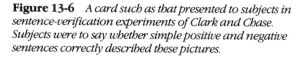

Figure 13-6 *A card such as that presented to subjects in sentence-verification experiments of Clark and Chase. Subjects were to say whether simple positive and negative sentences correctly described these pictures.*

negatives. In a typical experiment, they presented subjects with a card like that shown in Figure 13-6 and asked them to verify one of four sentences about this card:

1. The star is above the plus—true affirmative.
2. The plus is above the star—false affirmative.
3. The plus is not above the star—true negative.
4. The star is not above the plus—false negative.

The terms *true* and *false* refer to whether the sentence is true of the picture; the terms *affirmative* and *negative* refer to whether the sentence structure has a negative element. Sentences 1 and 2 involve a simple assertion, but sentences 3 and 4 involve a supposition plus an assertion. Sentence 3 supposes that the plus is above the star and asserts that this supposition is false; sentence 4 supposes that the star is above the plus and asserts that this supposition is false. Clark assumes that subjects will check the supposition first and the assertion next. In sentence 3, the supposition does not match the picture, but in sentence 4 the supposition does match the picture. Assuming that mismatches will take longer to process, Clark and Chase predict that subjects will take longer to respond to sentence 3, a true negative, than to sentence 4, a false negative. In contrast, subjects should take longer to process sentence 2, the false affirmative, than sentence 1, the true affirmative, because sentence 2's assertion mismatches the picture. In fact, the difference between sentences 2 and 1 should be identical to the difference between sentences 3 and 4 because both differences reflect the extra time due to a mismatch to the picture.

Clark and Chase developed a simple and elegant mathematical model for such data. They assumed that processing sentences 3 and 4 took N time units longer than processing 1 and 2 because of the more complex supposition-plus-negation structure of 3 and 4. Assume that processing sentence 2 took *M* time units longer than processing 1 because of the mismatch between picture and assertion, and similarly that processing 3 took *M* time units longer than processing 4 because of the mismatch between picture and supposition. Finally, they assumed that processing a true affirmative such as sentence 1 took *T* time units. The time *T* reflects the time used in processes not involving the negation and supposition mismatch. Let us consider the total time subjects should spend processing a sentence such as 3. This sentence has a complex supposition and negation structure, which cost *N* time units, and a supposition mismatch, which costs *M* item units. Therefore, total processing time should be $T + M + N$. Table 13-2 shows both the observed data and the reaction-time predictions that can be derived for the Clark and Chase experiment. The best-predicting values for *T, M,* and *N* for this experiment can be estimated from the data as $T = 1469$ msec, $M = 246$ msec, $N = 320$ msec. As the reader may confirm, the predictions match the observed time remarkably well. In particular, the difference between true negatives and false negatives is close to the difference between false affirmatives and true affirmatives. This finding supports the hypothesis that subjects do extract the suppositions of negative sentences and match these to the picture.

Problem Solving and Reasoning

Our discussion to this point seems to have implied that utilization involves only processes specific to analyzing language structure. However, much of the utilization process involves more general cognitive abilities. Consider the following passage:

> Mira was hiding in the ladies' room. She called it that even though someone had scratched out the word *ladies'* in the sign on the door, and written *women's* underneath. She called it that out of thirty-eight years habit, and until she saw the cross-out on the door, had never thought about it. "Ladies' room" was a euphemism, she supposed, and she disliked euphemisms on principle. [French, 1978, p. 7]

Language comprehenders might ask themselves the following questions in attempting to understand the passage:

1. What is Mira doing in the ladies' room?
2. Why was *ladies'* scratched off the door?
3. How old is Mira?
4. How could *ladies'* be considered a euphemism?
5. How does Mira respond to feminist issues?

Table 13-2   Observed and Predicted Reaction Times in Negative Verification

Condition	Observed Time	Equation	Predicted Time
True Affirmative	1463 msec	T	1469 msec
False Affirmative	1722 msec	$T + M$	1715 msec
True Negative	2028 msec	$T + M + N$	2035 msec
False Negative	1796 msec	$T + N$	1789 msec

Data drawn from Clark and Chase (1972).

Clearly, none of these questions are answered through processes specific to language. Rather the questions require a certain amount of world knowledge (in this case, about women's rooms and feminist issues) and an ability to solve problems and reason with this knowledge. Previous chapters were concerned with how knowledge is used and how we solve problems and reason. It is important to realize that language comprehension rests in part on nonlinguistic abilities and knowledge. Thus, one can be quite fluent linguistically and still fail to comprehend. For instance, it is hard to comprehend a text on a topic about which we have little familiarity even if it is well written.

Text Structure

So far we have focused on the comprehension of single sentences in isolation. Sentences are more frequently processed in larger contexts, for example, in the reading of a textbook. We consider now the effects on the utilization process of the structure of larger portions of text.

Text, like sentences, are structured according to certain patterns, though these patterns are perhaps more flexible than those associated with sentences. Much research has been conducted on the ways in which texts tend to be structured (e.g., Grimes, 1975; Kintsch, 1977; Kintsch and van Dijk, 1976; Mandler and Johnson, 1977; Meyer, 1974; Rumelhart, 1975; Thorndyke, 1977; van Dijk, 1977; van Dijk and Kintsch, 1976; and others). Researchers have noted that a number of recurring relationships serve to organize sentences into larger portions of a text. Some of the relations that have been identified are given in Table 13-3. These structural relations provide cues as to how a sentence should be utilized. For instance, the first text structure (response) in Table 13-3 directs the reader to relate one set of sentences as part of the solution to problems posed by other sentences. These relations can occur at

Table 13-3   Some Possible Types of Relationships Among Sentences in a Text

Type of Relationship	Description
1. Response	A question is presented and an answer follows, or a problem is presented and a solution follows.
2. Specific	Some specific information is given following a more general point.
3. Explanation	An explanation is given for a point.
4. Evidence	Evidence is given to support a point.
5. Sequence	Points are presented in their temporal sequence as a set.
6. Cause	An event is presented as the cause of another event.
7. Goal	An event is presented as the goal of another event.
8. Collection	A loose structure of points is presented. (This is perhaps a case where there is no real organizing relation.)

any level of a text. That is, the main relation organizing a paragraph might be any of the eight in the table. Subpoints in a paragraph may also be organized according to any of these relations.

To see how the relations in Table 13-3 might be used, consider Meyer's (1974) analysis of the following paragraph:

Parakeet Paragraph

The wide variety in color of parakeets that are available on the market today resulted from careful breeding of the color mutant offspring of green-bodied and yellow-faced parakeets. The light green body and yellow face color combination is the color of the parakeets in their natural habitat, Australia. The first living parakeets were brought to Europe from Australia by John Gould, a naturalist, in 1840. The first color mutation appeared in 1872 in Belgium; these birds were completely yellow. The most popular color of parakeets in the United States is sky-blue. These birds have sky-blue bodies and white faces; this color mutation occurred in 1878 in Europe. There are over 66 different colors of parakeets listed by the Color and Technical Committee of the Budgerigar Society. In addition to the original green-bodied and yellow-faced birds, colors of parakeets include varying shades of violets, blues, grays, greens, yellows, and whites [p. 61]

Her analysis of this paragraph is approximately reproduced in Table 13-4. Note that this structure tends to organize various facts as more or less major points. The highest-level organizing relationship in this paragraph is explanation (see point 3, Table 13-3). Specifically, the major points in this paragraph are (A) there has been careful breeding of color mutants and (B) there is a wide variety of parakeet color, and point A is given as an explanation of point B. Organized under A are some events from the history of parakeet

Table 13-4   Analysis of the Parakeet Paragraph

I. A explains B.
  A. There was careful breeding of color mutants of green and yellow-faced parakeets. The historical sequence is:
    1. Their natural habitat was Australia. Specific detail:
      a. Their color here is light-green-body and yellow-face combination.
    2. The first living parakeets were brought to Europe from Australia by John Gould in 1840. Specific detail:
      a. John Gould was a naturalist.
    3. The first color mutation appeared in 1877 in Belgium. Specific detail:
      a. These birds were completely yellow.
    4. The sky-blue mutation occurred in 1878 in Europe. Specific details:
      a. These birds have sky-blue bodies and white faces.
      b. This is the most popular color in America.
  B. There is a wide variety in color of parakeets that are on the market today. Evidence for this is:
    1. There are over 66 different colors of parakeets listed by the Color and Technical Committee of the Budgerigar Society.
    2. There are many available colors. A collection of which:
      a. The original green-bodied and yellow-faced birds.
      b. Violets
      c. Blues
      d. Grays
      e. Greens
      f. Yellows
      g. Whites

---

breeding. This organization is an example of a sequence relationship. Organized under these events are specific details. So, for instance, organized under A2 is the fact that John Gould was a naturalist. Organized under point B is evidence supporting the assertion about the wide variety and some details about the variation in color available.

Text Structure and Memory

Attempts to study the psychological significance of such text structures are still in their infancy. Considerable disagreement prevails in the field as to exactly what system of relations should be used in the analysis of texts, and uncertainty exists as to how such systems should be applied to a text. However, memory experiments have yielded evidence that subjects do, to some degree, respond to the structure of a text.

The kind of hierarchical structure exemplified in Meyer's analysis is reminiscent of the hierarchical structures we studied in Chapter 7 on memory. From the data cited in that chapter we would expect such hierarchies to have large effects on memory—if the subjects use these hierarchies in comprehension. Meyer has shown that subjects do display better memory for the major points in such a structure. For instance, subjects are more likely to remember that there was careful breeding of color mutants (point A) than that John Gould was a naturalist (point A2a).

Thorndyke (1977) has also shown that memory for text is poorer if the organization of the text conflicts with what would be considered its "natural" structure. This is clearly what we would expect given the results of Chapter 7 (consider, for instance, the experiment of Bower, Clark, Lesgold, and Winzenz, 1969, in that chapter). Thorndyke used a story that had a strong causal structure (relation 6 in Table 13-3). Some subjects studied the original story while other subjects studied the story with its sentences presented in a scrambled order. Subjects were able to recall 85 percent of the facts in the original story but only 32 percent of the facts in the scrambled story.

Such results are suggestive, but they tell us little about how often subjects perceive structure in text or how consistent their perceptions of text structure are with those of other subjects. If students often fail to correctly perceive the hierarchical structure of a text, then it would be quite helpful to train students to develop a structure based on relationships such as those in Table 13-3. Indeed, students are often urged to develop such a hierarchical structure in their note taking. One reason for encouraging this practice is to make students aware of the hierarchical structure in the material they are taking notes on.

Mandler and Johnson (1977) showed that children are much poorer than adults at recalling the causal structure of a story. Adults recall events and the outcomes of those events together, whereas children recall the outcomes but tend to forget how they were achieved. For instance, children might recall from a particular story that the butter melted but forget that this occurred because the butter was out in the sun. Adults do not have trouble with such simple causal structures, but they may have difficulty perceiving the more complex relationships connecting portions of a text. For instance, how easy is it for you to specify the relationship that connects this paragraph to the preceding text?

Meyer, Brandt, and Bluth (1978) studied students' perception of the high-level structure of a text—that is, the structural relations at the higher levels of hierarchies like that in Table 13-4. They found considerable variation in subjects' ability to recognize the high-level structure that organized a text. Moreover, they found that subjects' ability to identify the top-level structure of a text was an important predictor of their memory for the text. In another study, on ninth graders, Bartlett (1978) found that only 11 percent of the subjects consciously identified and used high-level structure to remember text material. This select group did twice as well as other students on their recall scores. Bartlett also showed that training students to identify and use top-level structure more than doubled recall performance.

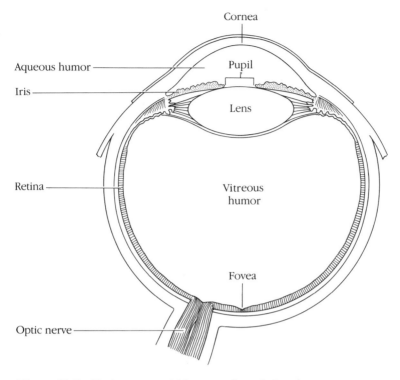

Figure 13.7   *The human eye. Light enters through the cornea, passes through the aqueous humor, pupil, lens, and vitreous humor to strike the retina, which registers the light. (From Lindsay and Norman, 1977.)*

Applications to Reading

In Chapter 7, we reviewed the PQ4R method for improving memory of text. However, it is safe to say that all the memory techniques in the world will have little effect if subjects are not comprehending what they are reading. Thus, it seems apt to close this chapter with a discussion of the implications of language-comprehension research for the reading process. First, however, it will be useful to review a few basic facts about the mechanics of reading. This topic has received a good deal of research in cognitive psychology.

The Mechanics of Reading

Fundamental to an understanding of reading is an appreciation of the mechanics of the human eye. Figure 13-7 is a schematic representation of the eye. Light enters the eye through a protective window (the cornea), passes through the aqueous humor (a jellylike substance), through the opening in the iris (the pupil), through the lens (which serves to focus), and through the vitreous humor, finally striking the retina (the back of the eye). The retina is the innervated portion of the eye, which actually registers light. The retina sends the registered light information to the brain through the optic nerve. A small portion of the retina, the fovea, is particularly sensitive to light and is the area of maximal acuity. Approximately 180 degrees of the retina is innervated, but the fovea occupies only about 2 degrees of the retina. In reading, we move our eyes so as to keep the fovea over the portion of the page we are attending to. In reading at a comfortable distance from the text the fovea spans about five letters. The sensitivity of the retina falls off gradually from the fovea, so the region just beyond the fovea is more sensitive than the rest of the nonfoveal retina. There is reason to believe that the fovea and immediately surrounding area is the only part on the eye sensitive enough to permit reading.

The eye is capable of moving in two modes. In following a moving object, the eye engages in *pursuit movement,* which is smooth movement designed to keep the object stable on the retina. However, when reading, the eye engages in *saccadic movements.* In this mode, the eye jumps approximately every 200 msec from one position to the next. This jump is called a *saccade.* The saccade has been termed a *ballistic movement* because the time to change position is very brief (only about 5 to 10 msec) and because it is not possible to change the direction of the saccade once it has started. Thus, in reading the pattern is jump, pause, jump, pause, and so on. It is generally believed that information is extracted from the text only when the eye is at rest. The pause while the eye is at rest and collecting information is called a *fixation.*

Readers of English normally proceed along one line at a time, fixating at various points on a line in a left-to-right fashion. In reading fairly difficult text carefully, many readers tend to fixate on almost each word once and often twice (Just and Carpenter, 1980). Such readers are making almost 20 fixations on an average line of text. However there is no really "typical" reading rate. Depending on the reader, the material, and the purpose in reading, number of fixations per line can range from a couple to more than 20. Both the number of fixations and the time per fixation tend to increase with the difficulty of the material. In contrast, the time for the saccades from fixation to fixation does not change. Occasionally, regressions occur in reading, in which the reader moves back to an earlier part of the line or an earlier line. Frequency of regressions also varies with difficulty of text. Thus, three eye measures vary with text difficulty: number of fixations per line, duration of fixation, and number of regressions. Of course, increases in all these activities slow reading speed. There is evidence to show that slow readers differ from fast readers on all three dimensions.

It is interesting to ask what the maximum possible reading speed is. An important issue in deciding the limits of reading has to do with the number of characters that we are capable of processing during any one fixation. Experiments by McConkie and Rayner (1974) and Rayner (1975) are particularly important in assessing this issue. McConkie and Rayner, using a computer-controlled system, manipulated the amount of text that the subject could see around a fixation point. The text around the fixation area was always well-composed and understandable, but the text in the periphery was mutilated (that is, a meaningless jumble of letters). The computer monitored the fixation point of the eye by taking a reflection off the cornea. The computer controlled what text was presented to the subject on a screen. Every time the subjects changed their fixation points, the computer advanced the readable portion of the text. McConkie and Rayner were interested in measuring the area around the fixation point that subjects could use. They reasoned that if mutilated information entered this area reading rate would drop. They found that subjects used information within an arc only about 5 degrees around the fixation point (this area represents the fovea and the immediately surrounding retina), or no more than 10 characters to the right or left of the fixation point. Mutilation of text beyond this range had no effect on reading rate. These findings imply that subjects can process only a relatively small portion (20 characters, 10 on each side of the fixation point) of the text at any one time.

Foss and Hakes (1978) offer a rather convincing demonstration of the limitations of a single fixation. When you finish reading this paragraph, turn to the next page and look at Figure 13-8. The figure consists of a series of words in a line with a circled X in the middle. You are to fix your vision on the X, the fixation point; when you turn to this figure (not yet), go directly to the X. As you fixate on the X, without moving your eyes, try to take in as much information to the left as possible. Then try to take in as much information to the right as possible. Remember: do not move your eyes. OK, try it.

You should have been able to make out about two words on either side of the fixation point. The third word to either side exceeds 10 characters (blanks count) and are therefore outside the boundary of perception. This exercise is an informal demonstration of McConkie and Rayner's more precise findings.

Determinants of Reading Skill

If one is able to process 10 characters on either side of a fixation point, then one can process about 20 characters a fixation, or about 3 words. Assuming 4 fixations a second, these figures imply a maximum reading rate of approximately 750 words a minute.* The average adult, in fact, reads at the rate of 200–400 words per minute (usually closer to 200 words). Therefore, it seems clear that our normal reading limit is not being imposed upon us by physiolog-

---

*Hakes and Foss, using estimates they admit are very optimistic, came up with a maximum of 1200 words.

| ONE | HOP | SILK | BUT | EYE | NOW | (X) | How | far | away | can | you | see? |

Figure 13-8   *Fixate on the X and see how far you can read on the periphery. (Foss and Hakes, 1978.)*

ical factors. Our reading speed is limited by the rate at which we can process information cognitively. This observation is important: the limits on adult reading speed tend to be *cognitive,* not motor or sensory. This conclusion is also implied by the results showing that duration of fixation, number of fixations per line, and number of regressions increase with the complexity of the text.

If the limits on reading are cognitive, are they related to speed of pattern recognition or to higher order language-comprehension factors such as parsing and utilization? There is no doubt that young children in the first years of reading are limited by their facility at the new perceptual skill. There is also no doubt that for some proportion of the population these perceptual problems remain in effect in adult life. However, general language comprehension abilities are now believed to be the most important factors controlling reading rate in most adults and children beyond elementary school (Miller, et al., 1974; Lesgold, Resnick, and Beck, 1978). The Lesgold, Resnick, and Beck (1978) study showed that in early grades (1 through 3) the most important determinant of reading skill is perceptual ability. At this stage, students are just learning to recognize letters. The experimenters found that in later grades, as letter recognition becomes more and more automatic, the important factor is general language ability. It is particularly likely that people with reading difficulties in a college context are experiencing the effects of language-comprehension factors and not perceptual factors. We often process written text much more rapidly than speech (which is seldom as fast as 200 words per minute). It is often very hard to follow a complex conversation. Therefore, it should come as no surprise that general language-comprehension factors prove to be the most important limits on reading skill.

Also relevant to this issue is the series of experiments by Sticht (1972), who compared learning by reading with learning by listening in adults (Army recruits). He found a high correlation between the two types of learning. People who were poor learners by reading were poor learners by listening. This result has been replicated a number of times (e.g., Jackson and McClelland, 1978). Again the implication is that most reading difficulties are comprehension difficulties and that the most effective way to improve reading skill is to improve language comprehension.

It is interesting to consider what the implications of knowledge about language comprehension might be for reading improvement. To start, let us review the various factors entailed in comprehension. First, we use our knowledge of the general syntactic and semantic patterns of the language to translate from words to meaning. Second, our general knowledge of the supposition–assertion distinction helps us to relate new information to old. Relevant also are such general cognitive skills as reasoning and problem solving plus general world knowledge. Finally, our knowledge of typical text structure helps us to perceive the relations between relatively large portions of linguistic input.

The extent to which adults use text structure in comprehension is unclear. As noted earlier, Bartlett (1978) was able to double the recall scores of ninth graders instructing them for just 5 hours about the relations used in text structure. It is possible that a relatively small investment in remedial training on text structure might also improve adult text comprehension considerably. It should be noted, however, that Bartlett's effect was on retention, not reading rate. With respect to the other knowledge and skill components involved in reading, it seems clear that any improvement will be slow indeed. These other components are already acquired and in some cases are fairly well learned. However, as we discussed in Chapter 8, the speed with which a cognitive skill can be performed will continue to increase with practice. So, to the extent that our reading comprehension is limited by slow linguistic procedures, this constraint is reducible by general linguistic practice. Chapter 8 also provided evidence for the diminishing returns of practice. Therefore, significant effects on reading rate may only occur after years of practice.

The Importance of Childhood Practice

The importance to reading of the practice of one's general comprehension abilities implies that childhood experience is critical to the development of reading skills. Children who have done a lot of reading, who have listened to a lot of verbal communication similar to that in text (for example, have had many stories read to them), and who have had the kind of upper-middle-class experiences assumed in most texts have had a good preparation (that is, a lot of practice) for reading typical high school and college texts. Durkin (1966) studied children who learned to read prior to entering school. She found that these children started with a large advantage over comparable students and maintained this advantage for the six years in which she followed them. In interviewing parents of these children, she found a higher tendency to encourage reading and to read to the children. The single most important environmental factor affecting reading skills is the amount of literacy in the home. Parents who read a lot and who buy lots of magazines, newspapers, and books have children who read well (Thorndike, 1973).

From this point of view, another conclusion seems unavoidable: that television, if it replaces reading and being read to, is harmful to the development of reading skills. Television is a relatively nonlinguistic medium. To the extent that linguistic communication is involved in television, it is communication of a simple dialogue structure—not particularly apt preparation for typical text structures. Speculation as to the relationship between television and the recent drop in verbal Scholastic Aptitude Test has been common. (Of course, the precise amount of reading and book listening that occurred before television appeared is unknown.)

The Effects of Culture and Dialect

If one accepts the premises that language-comprehension factors have the greatest influence on reading performance and that practice and experience are critical to language comprehension, then it would be expected that children who come from nonstandard cultures or who speak nonstandard dialects are at a disadvantage with respect to the reading of textbooks written in standard American English. Much research and speculation has been concerned with possible effects of black English, and English dialect spoken by 80 percent of the black population in America (Dillard, 1972), on the reading performance of its speakers. A host of factors distinguish standard* and black English. For example, at a phonological level, [i] and [e] may show no difference in black English; thus, *pin* and *pen* may be pronounced identically. At a slightly higher level, the copula may be deleted from sentences, resulting in such constructions as *He sick*. Consider another example, which would be incomprehensible to most speakers of white English, *You makin' sense but you don't be makin' sense.* This sentence might be liberally translated (Dillard, 1972) as *For once you've said something intelligent.* Obviously, such *differences* exhibited in black English are just that, differences, not instances of inferiority. However, these differences can create problems for comprehension of standard English. A speaker of standard English has difficulty in understanding black English; conversely, speakers of black English find standard English hard.

It is not the case that black-English speakers do not know standard English. In fact, many have fair ability to switch speech styles depending on context. So, in this sense black-English speakers are more capable and flexible than standard-English speakers who do not know the dialect. The problem is that they have had much less practice on standard English and lag behind when they have to comprehend standard English. In addition, the content of their life experiences tends to differ more from the content of standard reading material than does that of standard-English speakers.

Black students, on the average, score lower on standard reading-achievement tests than their white counterparts. However, the degree to

---

*It should also be noted that "standard American English," like all other dialects, is gradually changing. One of the ways it is changing is through the importation of black-English style and vocabulary.

which this difference is due to dialect variation is unclear. The fact that the gap increases in later school years, when general comprehension factors are more important, is consistent with the hypothesis that reading difficulty in those years is attributable to comprehension factors. However, other factors could be more important. Two major problems might be social conflict and a lack of understanding of black students by the typical school personnel. Piestrup (1973) studied the reading scores of black students whose teachers were more aware of and more supportive of cultural and linguistic characteristics of black students. Their reading scores did not lag behind the national average.

Some efforts have been made to create reading texts that reflect black culture and dialect. However, such texts might even accentuate the problem by giving black students still less practice in the standard English that typifies much of the important reading they will have to do in later years. Indeed, some black parents have complained about attempts to use such texts in schools, while other black parents have supported the use of such texts. Considerable controversy prevails as to the best course of action. It is not the role of cognitive psychology to make this decision, but research in the field should eventually be able to determine the consequences of the different courses of action. With all the data in, society would be able to make an informed choice.

Adaptive Control of Reading Rate

To this point, we have stressed the importance of language comprehension for reading ability, but other factors contribute significantly. One important factor is the voluntary, adaptive control of reading rate, that is, the ability to adjust the reading rate to the particular type of material being read.

Adaptive reading involves changing reading speed throughout a text in response to both the difficulty of the material and one's purpose in reading it. Learning how to monitor and adjust reading style is a skill that requires a good deal of practice.

Many people, even college students, are unaware that they can learn to control their reading speed. However, this factor can be greatly improved with a couple hundred hours of work, as opposed to the thousands of hours needed to significantly affect language comprehension. Many college reading-skills programs include a training procedure aimed at improving students' adaptive control of reading speed (e.g., Robinson, 1961; Thomas and Robinson, 1972). However, a number of problems are involved in successfully implementing such a program. The first problem is to convince students that they should adjust their reading rates. Many students regard skimming as a sin and read everything in a slow methodical manner. On the other hand, some students believe that everything, including difficult mathematics texts, can be read at the rate appropriate for a light novel. There seems to be evidence that people normally read more slowly than necessary. A number of studies on college students (e.g., Kintsch, 1974; Kieras, 1974) have found that when the students are forced to read faster than their self-imposed rate, there is no loss in retention of information typically regarded as important.

The second problem involved in teaching adaptive control lies in convincing students of the need to be aware of their purposes in reading. The point of adjusting reading rates is to serve particular purposes. Students who are unaware of what they want to get out of a reading assignment will find it difficult to adjust their rates appropriately. This point is related to the motivation for advance questions in the PQ4R method discussed in Chapter 7: the formation of advance questions helps the reader to identify study purposes. One should read more slowly those parts of the text that are related to the advance questions.

Once these problems of attitude are overcome, a reading-skills course can concentrate on teaching students the techniques for reading at various rates. Since most students have had little practice at rapid reading, most such instruction focuses on how to read rapidly. *Scanning* is a rapid-reading technique appropriate for searching out a piece of information embedded in a much larger text—for example, a student might scan this chapter for the effects of ambiguity on language comprehension. A skilled scanner can process 10,000 or more words a minute. Obviously, at this rate scanners only pick up bits and pieces of information, and skip whole paragraphs. It is easy for scanners to miss target information entirely, and they often have to rescan the text. Making quick decisions as to what should be ignored and what looked at takes much practice. However, the benefit is enormous. I would not be able to function as an academic without that skill because I would not be able to keep up with all the information that is generated in my field.

Skimming is the processing of about 800–1500 words a minute—a rate at which identifying every word is probably impossible. Skimming is used for extracting the gist of the text. This skill is useful when the skimmer is deciding whether to read a text, is implementing the preview phase in the PQ4R method, or is going over material that is mostly already known. In some applications, the reader must slow down when new important information is encountered.

Both scanning and skimming are aided by an appreciation of where the main points tend to be found in a text. A reader who knows where an author tends to put the main points can read selectively. Authors vary in their construction style, and one has to adjust to author differences, but some general rules usually apply. Section headings, first and last paragraphs in a section, first and last sentences in a paragraph, and highlighted material all tend to convey the main points.

In certain circumstances, we are able to deduce information that we have not read. For instance, in skimming or scanning experimental articles in fields with which I am familiar, I am able to know what methodology was used and what hypotheses were being tested just from reading the results sections, which do not contain this information. I am sufficiently familiar with the field that I can predict what I have not read. This ability is not just confined to academics. Suppose you are reading a popular novel and on one page you find this sentence:

> He asked her whether she would come up to his
> apartment for a nightcap.

Then you skip five pages and read this line:

> She helped him prepare breakfast the next morning.

You would probably have a fair idea of what went on in the intervening five pages. Basically, when the material we are reading conforms to our stereotypes, we are able to use this stereotypic knowledge in making predictions about the material rather than reading it fully. Thus, schematic knowledge (Chapter 5) proves to be important in yet another way.

Students in reading-skills programs often complain that rapid reading techniques require hard work and that they tend to regress towards less efficient reading habits after the end of the program. Therefore, it should be emphasized that the adaptive control of reading rate is hard work because it is a novel skill. Older reading habits seem easy because they have been practiced for longer. As students become more practiced in adjusting reading rate, they find it easier. I can report that after practicing variable reading rates for more than ten years, I find it easier to read a text using an adjustable rate than to read at a slow, methodical, word-by-word, rate. This is something of a problem for me because part of my professional duties is to edit papers that I would normally not process word by word. I find it very painful to have to read at this rate.

Speed Reading

As a final point, we come to the claims that have been made for speed reading by various commercial firms. In contrast to the responsible and modest claims of study-skills programs offered in colleges, commercial programs claim that with the investment of well under a 100 hours, students will be able to read at rates of 1500 words or more per minute and process every word. Our analyses of the facts about eye movement and amount taken in a fixation suggest an upper limit of about 750 words per minute. The eye movements of graduates from such courses are of the basic saccadic variety, although they are often quite unorthodox (for instance, going straight down one page and up the other).

The most well known of the commercial courses teaches students to read straight down pages using the hand as a pacer. It is claimed that students see large portions of the page, and that they read thought patterns and ideas rather than single words at a time. This particular course promises that students will be able to at least triple their reading rates, often to well over 1500 words a minute, with no loss in comprehension score. This claim probably indicates more about the nature of the comprehension test than anything else. The techniques taught appear to be appropriate for scanning or skimming. As long as the comprehension tests tap the kind of information that people extract when scanning or skimming (that is, the main points) no comprehension loss will be detected.

It seems very unlikely that speed reading involves anything more than skimming and scanning. These are valuable skills, but it is dangerous to overrate them. It is important to recognize that slow reading is called for by certain purposes and certain kinds of text. The consequences of speed reading a sales contract, for example, could be disastrous.

Remarks and Suggested Readings

The research on language comprehension is extensively reviewed in a text by Clark and Clark (1977). They make three independent distinctions that are similar to the supposition–assertion distinction used here. Their distinctions are new–given, subject–predicate, and frame–insert. Their text is a good source for students interested in a more detailed discussion of language comprehension than that provided here. Just and Carpenter (1977) edited a series of recent research papers on the comprehension process.

This chapter strongly emphasizes the connection between language and memory. This "memory-connection perspective" on language is found in my work (e.g., Anderson, 1976; Anderson and Bower, 1973) and in the work of others in the field (Kintsch, 1974; Collins and Quillian, 1972; Norman and Rumelhart, 1975). A number of schemes have been developed in artificial intelligence for parsing sentences besides the production-system proposal set forth here (e.g., Kaplan, 1973; Marcus, 1978; Riesbeck, 1974; Schank, 1975; Winograd, 1972; and Woods, 1973).

Gibson and Levin (1975) offer an extensive review of research on reading. Several recent papers are contained in Reber and Scarborough (1977). Just and Carpenter (1980) describe a detailed theory of reading based on the monitoring of eye movements. The books by Robinson (1961) and Thomas and Robinson (1972) both describe numerous study-skills techniques. As these writers emphasize, it is not enough just to read about the techniques— the techniques require *practice*. A word of warning: while such study-skill programs seem for the most part to be well founded, some aspects seem to be without good support. These texts lack much self-criticism, so the user is advised to take their recommendations with a grain of salt.

Chapter 14

Language Generation

Summary

1. Language generation can be analyzed into three stages: *construction, transformation,* and *execution.* Construction is the process of deciding on the meaning to be communicated. Transformation is the process of transforming the meaning into a linguistic message. Execution is the process of realizing the message in spoken or written form.

2. Construction can be divided into two stages: the planning of what is to be said and the planning of how it is to be said. In planning how to say a message, speakers must decide what they can *suppose* of their listeners so they can *assert* their intended messages. Successful communication also requires that speakers observe *conversational maxims* and the listeners understand these maxims.

3. In the transformation stage, sentences are generated in phrase-structure units. This generation process can be modeled by productions whose conditions specify pieces of meaning structure and whose actions create linguistic structures.

4. The writing process can be divided into three stages: *idea generation, composition,* and *rewriting.* A major problem in writing is the *coordinating* of multiple information-processing demands.

5. The writing stage of idea generation can be analyzed as a type of problem solving. This stage can be divided into the actual generation of ideas and the subsequent evaluation of the ideas.

The Stages of Language Generation

"Then you should say what you mean," the March Hare went on.

"I do," Alice hastily replied; "at least—at least I mean what I say—that's the same thing, you know."

"Not the same thing a bit!" said the Hatter.

"Why, you might just as well say that 'I see what I eat' is the same thing as 'I eat what I see'!" [Carroll, p. 80]

Alice is not the only one who has faced the frustration of intending to say one thing but of being misinterpreted. The path from thought to word can be tortuous and full of pitfalls. We will analyze this process of language generation by dividing it into three stages:

1. *Construction.* Building the meaning to be communicated in accordance with one's goals.
2. *Transformation.* Applying syntactic rules to transform the meaning into a linguistic message.
3. *Execution.* Realizing the message in some physical form (for example, speech or writing).

While the earlier stages must start before the later stages can begin, it is not necessary for one step to be completed before another begins. We all have had the experience of starting sentences before knowing how they would end.

It is interesting to compare the stages of generation with the stages of comprehension. In the previous chapter comprehension was also broken down into three stages:

1. *Perception.* Analyzing the linguistic message and identifying its units (e.g., words).
2. *Parsing.* Applying syntactic and semantic rules to extract a representation of the meaning of the analyzed message.
3. *Utilization.* Processing the meaning representation in accordance with one's goals.

Stage 1 of comprehension is analogous to stage 3 of generation, stage 2 of comprehension to stage 2 of generation, and stage 3 of comprehension to stage 1 of generation. While thinking of comprehension as simply language generation in reverse proves wrong, and while none of the comprehension stages is simply the corresponding generation stage in reverse, the kinds of knowledge required in the corresponding stages do overlap considerably. Perception, involving the eyes and the ears, obviously has to be somewhat different than execution, which involves the mouth and the hands. However, we have already seen that, at least with respect to speech perception (Chapter 2), the system seems geared to identifying sounds with respect to their articulatory significance. That is, we seem to perceive speech by perceiving the way in which speech is articulated.

This chapter will concentrate on the first two stages of language generation, construction and transformation, which involve high-level mental processes. We will show that the syntactic patterns used in transformation during generation are similar to those used in parsing during comprehension. However, parsing and transformation are not identical. For instance, the patterns apply in different orders.

Again, similarities and differences exist between the processes of construction and utilization. As an example of a similarity, both speakers and listeners must consider the supposition–assertion distinction. Speakers must decide what listeners do not know and what needs to be asserted. Correspondingly, listeners must decide how the information they know relates to that which they are hearing. On the other hand, little overlap exists between the motives and goals that lead speakers to generate a sentence and the motives and goals that govern the processing of the sentence by listeners. The distinction between constructing and utilizing questions serves as an example. Question construction involves deciding that one needs to know an answer and ascertaining that the listener might be able to provide the answer. The utilization stage in question comprehension involves deciding that one is willing and able to provide an answer and then making the mental or physical search for an answer.

While comprehension and generation exhibit some strong similarities, a significant unanswered question concerns whether the two activities use some of the same knowledge and processes. This chapter will treat the knowledge and processes involved in language generation as similar to but separate from those involved in comprehension. However, the two phenomena have not been shown to be entirely separate. To date, no incisive research has been addressed to the issue of whether comprehension and generation are distinct processes. The common wisdom seems to be that the two systems overlap a great deal, that training in one leads to improvement in the other, and that good readers are good writers. However, no hard evidence on the issue exists.

This chapter has three main sections. The first two review what is known about the construction and transformation stages of generation. The third covers the process of language generation during writing. Here we will be concerned with applying our knowledge of the process to the improvement of writing skills.

Construction

Deciding What to Say

Language generation is fundamentally a goal-oriented activity. People speak and write for reasons: to obtain information, to answer questions, to break the ice, to impress others with their linguistic virtuosity, to give orders, to be polite, to keep from being bored, to record information, to earn royalties, and so on. Sometimes people can easily see how to achieve their linguistic goals (as when they are deciding how to respond to the question, "What time is it?"); at other times, they have difficulty in seeing how to achieve their goals (say, in deciding what to write to win the Nobel Prize in literature). To the extent that achieving such goals is difficult, problem solving and reasoning processes will be important to the construction process. Therefore, much of the problem-solving analysis in Chapter 9 is relevant to language generation. We will return to this goal-seeking aspect of generation in more detail in considering the writing process.

Construction can often be divided into two substages: deciding which basic facts should be expressed and deciding how these facts should be structured and embellished. The former substage is the more complex and the less well understood. To illustrate what is involved in this stage, suppose a friend asks you, "What did you do today?" How would you go about deciding what to answer? (First, of course, you would want to decide what your friend really meant by this question—is the question well-meant, ironic, demanding? This interpretation of the question is really part of language comprehension, not language generation. But suppose you decide that there is no hidden meaning in the question and that you will try to be cooperative and provide an answer.) To begin the process of generating an answer, you might decide on a plan for searching memory. The obvious one is to start with the morning and trace your activities until the current point in time. For each activity you would have to decide whether you should report it. Would your friend want to hear such predictable facts as that you got out of bed, or is the question intended to elicit only nonpredictable facts—such as when you got to school, what classes you took, whom you talked to? Next you would have to resolve the question of detail: would it be enough to say that you went to math class or would you have to describe what was taught? In sum, to generate an answer, you would have to search through your day's activities, editing them for inclusion according to your goals and the listener's goals as you perceive them.

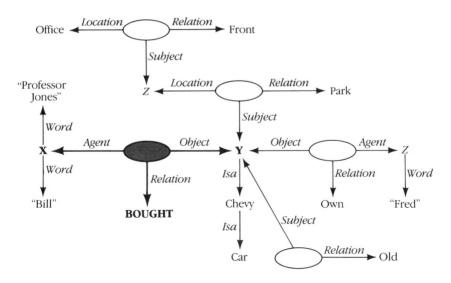

Figure 14-1   *A propositional-network representation of* Bill bought Fred's old Chevy. *A speaker saying this sentence is asserting* X bought Y *in this network but is supposing additional information from the network to make contact with the right nodes in the listener's network.*

Suppositions Versus Assertions

Assuming that a speaker has decided what to say, how does he or she go about structuring a set of facts for communication? Suppose the speaker wants to assert the proposition, represented in Figure 14-1, that *X bought Y*. The speaker may suppose that the listener does not know this and may want to convey the fact. Or the speaker may think that the listener knows it but may want to draw the listener's attention to the fact. Whatever the motive, the speaker cannot simply assert *X bought Y*. She or he must make contact with concepts *X* and *Y* in the listener's memory. This task involves diagnosing what the listener knows and making word choices accordingly. Suppose the speaker judges that this listener knows *X*'s name is Bill and that *Y* is Fred's old Chevy. Then the spoken form chosen might be *Bill bought Fred's old Chevy*. To another listener the speaker might have communicated the same proposition in this form: *Professor Jones bought the car that you saw parked in front of the office*. Thus, the speaker must decide what needs to be supposed about the listener in order to assert the desired proposition. This dual task, first to make contact with concepts in the listener's memory and then to structure the message around these concepts, is the origin of the supposition–assertion distinction, discussed from the listener's perspective in the preceding chapter.

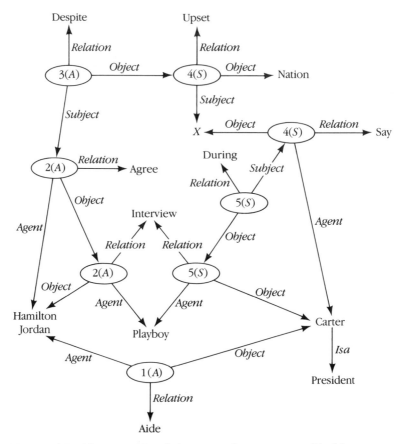

Figure 14-2   *The propositions being asserted versus supposed in this sentence:* Hamilton Jordan, President Carter's aide, has agreed to a *Playboy* interview despite the flap over Carter's statement during his interview with the same magazine. The assertions are labeled A *and the suppositions are labeled S.*

So, to generate a sentence the speaker needs to identify what is to be asserted and what needs to be supposed. This requires that the speaker must have a model of what the listener knows. We will assume that the speaker has in memory a representation of the intended message including certain propositions intended as to-be-asserted and others intended as to-be-supposed. To illustrate, consider the memory representation that might underlie the generation of this sentence:

Hamilton Jordan, President Carter's aide, has agreed to a *Playboy* interview despite the flap over Carter's statements during his interview with the same magazine.

Figure 14-2 illustrates what I assumed the writer's communicative intent to be in composing this sentence. The writer has some of the propositions intended as assertions and others as suppositions necessary for the communication of the assertion. I have indicated this distinction by labeling to-be-asserted propositions *A* and to-be-supposed propositions *S*. The asserted information includes these points:

1. Hamilton Jordan aids Carter.
2. Hamilton Jordan agreed to an interview with *Playboy*.
3. This is despite the fuss over Carter's interview.

Among the supposed information are these points:

4. The nation was upset by Carter's statements.
5. He made these statements during his interview with *Playboy*.

The use of the definite article *the* at the start of the phrase *the flap over Carter's statements during an interview with the same magazine* is evidence that points 4 and 5 are supposed (see p. 416). (I have omitted for the sake of simplicity some of the other low-level suppositions, such as that the term *Playboy* will identify the correct magazine for the listener.) In this case, the writer has included more supposed information than is strictly necessary to communicate the asserted information. The writer wants the reader to process the asserted information in light of other information that is being supposed. It is interesting to consider how the sentence would sound if the suppositions and assertions were reversed: Consider the following sentence:

> The president that Hamilton Jordan aids upset the nation by his statements during an interview with the same magazine that Jordan granted an interview to.

In this case the asserted propositions are

1. The president upset the nation by his statements.
2. He made these statements during an interview with a magazine.

The supposed information is

3. Hamilton Jordan aids the president.
4. Hamilton Jordan agreed to grant an interview to the same magazine.

The sentence built on the reversals of the original suppositions and assertions is a little bizarre because it assumes the listener knows information about Jordan, the aide, and needs to be told information about Carter, the president. For an illustration of the significance of the supposition–assertion distinction, see Figure 14-3.

Conversational Maxims

A number of principles control conversation. Consider the following conversation:

1. *Dumb:* I saw you sleeping during the lecture. I guess you thought it was pretty boring too.
2. *Weird:* No, it was a really exciting lecture.
3. *Dumb:* Why would you fall asleep during an exciting lecture? Didn't you get any sleep last night?
4. *Weird:* Can you tell me what time it is?
5. *Dumb:* I don't have a watch.
6. *Weird:* But you can read mine—the Seiko watch with a gold wrist band on my left arm just above the hand.
7. *Dumb:* It's 12 o'clock.
8. *Weird:* Actually the watch is broken.
9. *Dumb:* Then why did you ask me to read it?
10. *Weird:* Actually, if you appreciated Grice's maxim of quality you would have understood why I said the lecture was exciting.

This conversation between Dumb and Weird is clearly bizarre. The reason is the Weird is constantly violating what Grice (1967) called the *cooperativeness principle,* which states that speakers and listeners have to cooperate to succeed in communication. Grice suggests that, to satisfy the cooperativeness principle, the speaker has to satisfy at least four *conversational maxims:*

1. *The maxim of quantity.* Be as informative as is required, but not more informative than is required. Weird violated this rule twice in line 6. He implied that his watch was working, which it wasn't (not informative enough), and he gave an overly long description of the watch (too informative).
2. *The maxim of quality.* Be truthful. Weird violated this maxim in line 2 to create sarcasm. When an utterance is obviously false to both speaker and listener it is often intended for sarcastic effect. An obvious violation of truth can be acceptable in conversation, and would have been successful in this conversation had Dumb not been

Figure 14-3 *Illustration in terms of semantic networks of the importance of the distinction between supposition and assertion. The speaker's communication should add new structure (assertion) to knowledge that the listener already has (supposition). (From Lindsay and Norman, 1977, p. 466.)*

so obtuse. For instance, consider *The problem with Nixon was that he could never tell a lie.*

3. *The maxim of relation.* One should say things relevant to the conversation. Weird violates this rule twice, in line 4 and 10, where he introduces huge shifts in the conversation.

4. *The maxim of manner.* Be clear. Assuming that Dumb did not know Grice's maxim of quality, Weird was being unnecessarily obscure in line 10.

Of these four maxims, the maxim of quantity seems to be the most powerful in shaping conversation. Most sentences generated seem to be relatively bare-bones attempts to perform the two functions of supposition and assertion—making contact with concepts in the listener's memory and changing the state of the structure around these concepts. Speakers often choose the simplest sentence that serves these functions. They try to avoid being overly informative. Of course, speech can also be quite "flowery" when the goal of a speaker is more complicated than the simple communication of facts. However, more commonly, it seems, speech is not flowered with irrelevant information. Consider, for instance, the following sentence:

> Jimmy Carter, who is 53 years old and hails from Plains, Georgia, which is a small town, invited tall, balding Hubert Humphrey to Camp David, which is a presidential retreat.

In a newscast this sentence would strike us as odd, since the same assertion could be made this way:

> Carter invited Humphrey to Camp David.

Olson (1970) brings out these ideas in his analysis of the use of adjective phrases. He invites us to consider how we would refer to the same object in the three sets in Figure 14-4. For set A we would use the phrase *the white one,* for set B, *the round one,* and for set C, *the round, white one.* Using both adjectives only seems appropriate for set C, where both are needed to identify the object. Thus, a principle governing speech appears to be simplicity: only say what needs to be said to achieve a communicative intention.

Transformation

Constituent Structure in Generation

Once language speakers have decided what they want to assert and what they should suppose about their listeners' knowledge, they must translate these assertions and suppositions into sentential form. Recall that listeners seem to parse sentences in terms of multiword patterns such as noun phrases and prepositional phrases. The corresponding question naturally arises, How do speakers generate sentences? Do they generate them a word at a time or in clumps that constitute phrases? The evidence suggests that speakers generate language in phrases or constituents, just as listeners comprehend in constituents. For instance, Boomer (1965) analyzed examples of spontaneous speech and found that pauses did occur more frequently at grammatical junctures and that these pauses were longer than pauses at other locations. The average pause time at a grammatical juncture was 1.03 seconds, while the average was .75 seconds within grammatical clauses. This finding suggests that

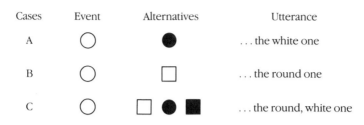

Cases	Event	Alternatives	Utterance
A	○	●	. . . the white one
B	○	☐	. . . the round one
C	○	☐ ● ■	. . . the round, white one

Figure 14-4 *Three arrays of figures and the noun phrases that are chosen to describe the left-hand circle in each. The chosen phrases suggest that simplicity guides speech. (From Olson, 1970. Copyright © 1970 by the American Psychological Association. Reprinted by permission.)*

speakers tend to generate sentences a clause at a time and often needed to pause after one clause to plan the next.

Grosjean, Grosjean, and Lane (1979) performed a careful study of pause structures during reading. They had subjects read paragraphs in which occurred critical sentences such as the two below:

(The agent) consulted (the agent's book) (in which (they)
  1   18   11   2   5   25 2   13   3
offered (numerous tours))
  10   10
(The expert) (who couldn't see (what to criticize)) sat back (in despair)
  3   14   2   4   11   7 3   41   5   7   3

The experimenters measured the percentage of total pause time that subjects spent pausing after every word. These percentages occur between each word on the line below each sentence. The major constituents of each sentence—noun phrases and clauses—are indicated by parentheses. Clearly, most of the pause time is spent before or after major constituents. It should be kept in mind that this reading task involves both comprehending a sentence and generating it. The pauses before major constituents indicate the planning that goes into the generation of the next phrase. It is possible that the pauses after major constituents reflect comprehension time to analyze the just processed component.

A Production System for Generation

The data cited above as well as other evidence reviewed below point to the conclusion that language is generated in terms of constituents, or phrases. The theoretical question raised by this conclusion is, What kind of system would generate language in phrase units? A production system for generation

Table 14-1 Productions for Generating Sentence Constituents

Name of Production	Form of Production	
MAIN	IF	it is to be asserted that a person performed a verb action on an object
	THEN	plan to say a string of the form *person verb object* and set FOCUS on the person
RELATIVE	IF	it is supposed that the FOCUS performed a verb action on an object
	THEN	plan to say after FOCUS a string of the form *who verb object*
NP	IF	it is supposed that the FOCUS is an instance of noun
	THEN	replace FOCUS by *the noun* and set FOCUS on *the*
SAY	IF	FOCUS is a word
	THEN	say FOCUS and shift FOCUS on the next item
END	IF	FOCUS is a word and nothing follows FOCUS
	THEN	say FOCUS and the sentence is finished

that would complement the production system described in the previous chapter for comprehension would, of course, be desirable. Table 14-1 gives a production set for generation that is analogous to Table 13-1, in which productions for comprehension were given. Like the production set in Chapter 13, this set has productions for generating main-clause constituents (MAIN), noun-phrase constituents (NP), and relative-clause constituents (RELATIVE). It also has two productions, SAY and END, for generating individual words. This production set assumes that representations such as the one in Figure 14-5, are active in the speaker's memory, setting forth what he or she wants to communicate. The term FOCUS in these productions refers to the point at which the speaker is in the process of sentence generalization. The elements after FOCUS refer to the portion of the message that the speaker plans to say.

Consider how the production system in Table 14-1 would apply to the network representation in Figure 14-5. The nodes labeled *RR, RS,* and *PN* refer to individuals. The speaker has decided that the following proposition represented is to be asserted.

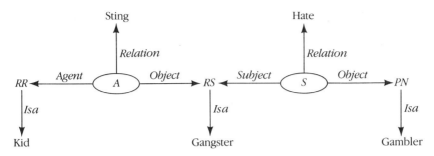

Figure 14-5   *The productions in Table 14-1 applied to this network representation generated by the sentence* The kid stung the gangster who hated the gambler.

1. *RR* stung *RS.*

This proposition is denoted by the *A* proposition node. The following information is supposed:

2. *RR* is a kid.
3. *RS* is a gangster.
4. *RS* hates *PN.*
5. *PN* is a gambler.

Production MAIN in Table 14-1 would be the first to apply. It looks for a to-be-asserted proposition, and in this case would match the proposition *RR stung RS.* The production sets the plan to generate a string of the form *RR stung RS. RR* and *RS* refer to two individuals that the system has not yet decided how to describe. The production sets FOCUS to the first element of this string, *RR.* At this point, production NP, which generates noun phrases, applies. Its condition matches the fact that *RR,* the focus, is a kid. It replaces *RR* by *The kid,* since the speaker supposes that this designation will identity *RR* for the listener. At this point, the sentence representation follows:

$$\downarrow$$
The kid stung *RS,*

where the arrow denotes attention FOCUS. Note that this is the representation of what the speaker has in mind and is intending to say. The words have yet to be generated.

At this point, production SAY will apply three times in a row, generating the words *the, kid,* and *stung* and moving FOCUS to be first nonword, *RS.* Once these steps have been performed, RELATIVE will apply. It will match the supposition represented in Figure 14-5 that *RS* hated *PN*. In its action, RELA-TIVE will add *who hated PN*. Now NP applies, adding *the gangster* as part of the description of *RS*. At this stage, the sentence representation is

The kid stung the gangster who hated *PN*.

Note that the words to the left of the arrow (FOCUS) are the only ones that have been generated. The word under the arrow and those to the right are words the speaker has in mind and is intending to say. Next, SAY applies four more times, to generate *the, gangster, who,* and *hated*. At this point, NP will apply again, replacing PN by *the gambler*. At this point the sentence representation is

The kid stung the gangster who hated the gambler.

Finally, SAY and then END will apply to generate the last two words, *the* and *gambler*.

More Evidence for Constituent Structure

The example presented in the subsection above illustrates that generation productions build a sentence in a manner analogous to that in which comprehension productions analyze a sentence—that is, a constituent at a time. Comprehension productions map constituent patterns into meaning representations, while generation productions do just the reverse.* If we accept that the system presented in Table 14-1 models language generation, we would predict that longer pauses would occur at constituent breaks than occur at other points in a sentence. Before a speaker could actually generate the words in a constituent, extra productions would have to apply to set forth the structure of this constituent. We saw that this prediction is confirmed by data such as those that form Boomer (1965) and from Grosjean, Grosjean, and Lane (1979).

Other research efforts have tested this constituent-generation theory. For example, Maclay and Osgood (1959) analyzed spontaneous recordings of speech to determine whether speech is generated in constituent units. They found a number of speech errors that suggested that constituents do have a psychological reality. They found that when speakers repeated themselves or corrected themselves they tended to repeat or correct a whole constituent.

---

*Clearly, production MAIN here corresponds to MAIN on Table 13-1. Similarly, the productions RELATIVE and NP in the two tables correspond. Note, however, that the productions apply in different order. If the comprehension productions in Table 13-1 were to parse this sentence, they would apply in the order NP, NP, NP, RELATIVE, MAIN whereas the generation productions apply in the order MAIN, NP, RELATIVE, NP, NP. This difference in order illustrates the general point that comprehension is not simply generation in reverse.

For instance, the following is the kind of repeat that is found:

Turn on the heater/the heater switch.

And the pair below constitutes a common type of correction:

Turn on the stove/the heater switch

In the preceding example, the noun phrase is repeated. In contrast, speakers do not provide repetitions such as

turn on the stove/on the heater switch,

in which the noun phrase and part of the verb phrase are repeated.

Other kinds of speech errors also provide evidence for the psychological reality of constituents as major units of speech generation. For instance, some research has analyzed slips of the tongue in speech (Fromkin, 1971, 1973; Garrett, 1975). Such errors are called *spoonerisms,* after the English clergyman William A. Spooner to whom are attributed some colossal and clever errors of speech . The following are among the errors of speech attributed to Spooner:

You have hissed all my mystery lectures.

I saw you fight a liar in the back quad; in fact, you have tasted the whole worm.

I assure you the insanitary spectre has seen all the bathrooms.

Easier for a camel to go through the knee of an idol.

The Lord is a shoving leopard to his flock.

Take the flea of my cat and heave it at the louse of my mother-in-law.

There is every reason to suspect that these errors were deliberate attempts at humor by Spooner. However, people do generate genuine spoonerisms, although they are seldom so funny.

By patient collecting, researchers have gathered a large set of errors made by friends and colleagues. Some of these involve simple sound anticipations or sound exchanges:

take my bike → bake my bike [an anticipation]

night life → nife lite [an exchange]

beast of burden → burst of beadan [an exchange]

One that gives me particularly difficulty is

coin toss → toin coss

The first error listed above is an example of an anticipation, where an early phoneme is changed to a later phoneme. The others are examples of exchanges in which two phonemes switch. The interesting feature about these kinds of errors is that they tend to occur within a single constituent rather than across constituents. So, one is unlikely to find the following anticipation,

1. The dancer took my bike → The bancer took my bike,

where an anticipation occurs between subject and object noun phrases. Also unlikely are sound exchanges where an exchange occurs between the initial prepositional phrase and the final noun phrase, as in

2. At night John lost his life → At nife John lost his lite.

Note that a production system such as that in Table 14-1, which generates language by constituents, only plans the words it will generate for the immediate constituent. Thus, sound exchange errors cannot occur across the relatively large distance exhibited in the example above. For instance, such a system would have already generated *night* in (2) above before planning *life*. *Life* would be decided upon after an exchange could occur. On the other hand, such a system might plan to say two words in a constituent, such as *night life,* before actually generating either word. Thus, an opportunity for the exchange *nife lite* would exist.

Another kind of speech error consistent with the constituent model is called the *stranded morpheme.* (A morpheme is a minimum unit of meaning. such as *trunk,* which indicates an object, or *–ed,* which indicates past tense.) Some examples are

> I'm not in the read for mooding.
>
> She's already trunked two packs.
>
> Fancy getting your model renosed.

This type of error exhibits two interesting features. First, like the other errors, this type tends to occur within a constituent boundary. Second, the content morphemes, such as *trunk* and *pack,* are always the ones that are switched. The functional morphemes, such as *ing, ed,* and *s,* stay put. Thus, one does not find such errors as

> I'm not in the mooding for read.

The phenomenon of the stranded morpheme seems to suggest that speakers first decide on the pattern they want to generate, for example, a phrase such as

> noun for verb + ing.

In the process of filling in the specific words of the pattern, however, the noun and verb get switched by mistake. In terms of a production system, this phrase might be generated by the following production:

IF   the FOCUS denotes a relation between a
       noun and a verb
THEN replace FOCUS by *noun for verb* + *ing*.

with a confusion occurring, however, as to the words assigned to the general terms in this production, *noun* and *verb*.

The Relationship Between Construction and Transformation

We have been describing language generation as if the speaker first planned the meaning completely and then transformed that meaning into linguistic form. However, speakers usually plan their meanings as they generate their sentences. Many of the awkward or grammatically deviant sentences that occur in discourse reflect the conflicting demands of these two ongoing processes of construction and transformation. Deese (1978) compared spontaneous speech, such as answers to unexpected questions, with prepared speech in which content (but not wording) was planned, such as seminar presentations. The latter, where content was planned, was much freer of grammatical and stylistic problems. A similar result is reported by Levin, Silverman, and Ford (1967), who found that children who are asked to generate simple descriptions of events exhibit fewer grammatical errors than children who are asked to give explanations of the events. Explanations are more demanding cognitively. Such research implies that processing capacity is limited and must be divided between construction and transformation. When the demands for construction (planning) increase, the quality of linguistic transformation suffers.

The Writing Process

Just as the research on language comprehension can be applied most naturally to reading, so the research on generation can be most naturally applied to writing. However, research on writing is more than just an applied arm of language-generation research. Writing appears to provide an important independent opportunity for the basic study of language generation. In this section, in the course of examining some recommendations for improving writing, we will develop some additional ideas about the nature of language generation.

The discussion in this section is based on two principles. The first is that the same basic processes involved in speech are involved in writing. Gould (Gould, 1978; Gould and Boies, 1977) in a comparative study of writing, dictating, and speaking, found a fairly high correlation among these three modes with respect to quality of composition. That is, people who were good speakers tended to be good writers.

The second principle is that the basic problem in writing is the coordination of the multiple, independent information-processing demands involved in creating good prose (this idea has been emphasized by Bruce, Collins, Rubin, and Gentner, 1979). In this discussion, the term *coordination problem* refers to this difficulty. A problem of coordination also arises in speech, but it is clearer when we consider writing.

Students were being taught to write long before cognitive psychology existed as a field of study. The suggestions in the following pages will draw heavily from the concepts developed in this pedagogical tradition. These concepts have been edited to reflect the general insights of cognitive psychology and elaborated with relevant findings in cognitive-psychology research. Currently, a surge of research is being experienced in America to further validate these ideas and to extract more ideas from cognitive psychology with respect to writing. I believe that these efforts will prove to be a notably fruitful application of cognitive psychology. The ideas of the field seem to be particularly relevant to writing, and people generally need to improve their writing skill, as this example, taken from an Internal Revenue Service tax form, suggests:

> Under the nonfarm optional method, you as a regularly self-employed individual may report two-thirds of your gross nonfarm profits (but not more than $1,600) as your net earnings from self-employment if your net earnings from such self-employment are less than $1,600 and less than two-thirds of your gross nonfarm profits from such self-employment. However, unlike the farm optional method, the nonfarm optional method precludes you from reporting less than your actual net earnings from nonfarm self-employment.

Some experimental data on writing exist, and it is to be hoped that a good deal more will soon be generated. Currently, however, much psychological information about writing comes from self-observation and informal reports. Written communication is an important part of science, and it is not unusual to find psychologists spending hours comparing and analyzing their writing experiences.

Stages of Writing

In a typical model of writing, the process is divided into three phases. First is an *idea generation,* or *prewriting,* phase, in which the writer decides on what he or she wants to say. Next is the actual *composition,* or *writing,* phase, in which the text is generated. The final stage is the *rewriting,* or *editing,* phase, in which the writer reworks the text to make it a more effective communicative device.

Recall the construction, transformation, and execution stages of language generation described at the beginning of this chapter. Clearly, the prewriting phase corresponds to construction, and both writing and rewriting are aspects of the transformation process. The aspect corresponding to execution would be the physical process by which the text is created—longhand writing, typing, dictating, and the like. This aspect is not trivial, and a whole technology has developed around manuscript preparation. With the continued elaboration of computer-based editing systems, this technology is becoming quite complex. However, it is typically ignored in analysis of writing because the major roadblocks to successful writing lie elsewhere.

In the following subsections, we will consider recommendations for the development of writing skills and the psychological bases for these recommendations with respect to each stage of the process. Although the discussion treats each stage independently, these phases are not necessarily discreet in the actual activity of writing. That is, prewriting is not necessarily completed before writing begins, and writing is not necessarily finished when editing begins. It is sometimes appropriate and even necessary to alternate among the phases. Properly relating these three stages is a major aspect of the coordination problem.

Prewriting: Idea Generation

Of the three, the prewriting phase involves creativity most. This phase tends to be shrouded with mystery and teachers tend to refrain from analyzing it in standard efforts at teaching English. A superstition has long prevailed that analyzing the creative act destroys it. Related to this mystique is a certain disastrous style of writing, practiced by some otherwise capable students, whereby they simply wait to be inspired by the gods. One healthy result of analyzing writing psychologically is the destruction of this aspect of the mystique of creativity. Generating ideas for writing is simply (or not so simply) the process of problem solving to achieve a goal. The problem-solving nature of the activity was emphasized by Flower and Hayes (1977). If one conceives of writing as problem solving, then it is natural to try to bring the various problem-solving techniques to bear. All such techniques require that one start with a definition of the goal. One could hardly hope to succeed in a problem-solving task without clearly defining the goal state that the problem solving is trying to achieve. Unfortunately, the goals of college students are often not well articulated—for instance, the goal of achieving an A in a course. The goals of more advanced writers are often ill-specified as well—for instance, the goal of writing a paper that can be published in a prestigious journal.

Let us consider some of the problem-solving techniques as they would apply to the writing process. For instance, recall the method of working backwards (see Chapter 9). Suppose one starts with the goal of getting an A on an essay about language generation. This goal requires choosing an innovative theme. Such a theme might be to argue that more is involved in creative writing than "just problem solving." The topic would be a subgoal in service of the main goal, getting an A. Thus, the writer has worked backwards from the main goal to a subgoal. He or she might work backwards again from this subgoal. For instance, the writer might decide upon a line of argument that would establish the point. One such a line of argument would be to present evidence that successful writers have experiences of "true inspiration." Thus, from the general subgoal of presenting a convincing argument, the writer would have worked backward to the additional subgoal of collecting testimonials for this point. A means-ends analysis might suggest that the writer go to the library to find books reporting the experiences of successful writers. And so one could go, setting subgoals and solving them until the essay was written.

Another method of problem solving discussed in Chapter 9 involves the use of analogy. This method seems to be the basis of the synectics techniques (a variety of brainstorming) advocated by Gordon (1961) and Prince (1970). A great many creative solutions result from the use of analogy. For instance, the Wright brothers based their work on the turning and stabilizing of an airplane on observations of how buzzards keep their balance in flight. Flower and Hayes (1977) suggest the following example of using analogy in writing:

> Suppose, for example, you are analyzing the operation of a university. It occurs to you that universities have much in common with big businesses. The potential connections between the two are numerous: the analogy could suggest that both need professional management, or that both would benefit from healthy competition, or perhaps that both turn out a product but seem to spend most of their advertising budget marketing a self-image.[p. 455]

Studies of Idea Generation

As noted earlier, the prewriting stage is the most creative phase of the writing process (see Chapter 9 for a discussion of problem solving and creativity). We turn now to a review of the research on the creativity involved in writing. The typical creativity experiment poses to subjects a rather open-ended problem. For instance, subjects might be given the plot of a story or movie and asked to write alternative titles for it. The titles would then be rated by independent judges who had been carefully trained and were in close agreement. This paradigm addresses the creativity involved in a much simpler task than the writing of an essay, but the results of such studies are nevertheless instructive.

One reasonable analysis of such tasks is what I refer to as the *generate-and-judge model*. In this model, the problem solving underlying the creative thinking required by the tasks is seen as a process of generating and judging possible solutions. In this view, the central issue is the relationship between quantity (how many ideas can be generated) and quality (how good the ideas are). That is, can one generate better ideas by trying to generate many or by inhibiting most and concentrating on trying to come up with one good idea?

Brainstorming, a creativity technique that has been advocated by some (e.g., Osborn, 1953), emphasizes the uninhibited generation of ideas. The goal of this technique is to postpone judgment, freeing the thinker's attention

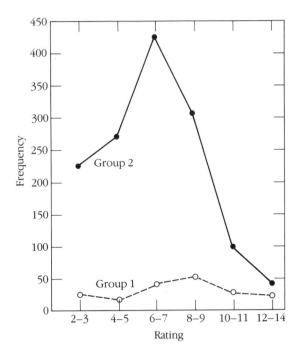

Figure 14-6 *Effects of instructions emphasizing quality (group 1) and quantity (group 2) on the frequency of solutions of varying qualities. (Data are from Johnson, Parrott, and Stratton, 1968.)*

for idea generation. The experiment of Johnson, Parrott, and Stratton (1968) is typical of the research into brainstorming techniques. It compared the effect of instructions that encouraged subjects to keep the quality of their ideas high with the effect of instructions that encouraged a lack of inhibition and the generation of many ideas. One group of subjects (group 1) was instructed to generate one best solution to creativity problems such as generating plot titles. The other group (group 2) was asked to write as many solutions as possible. Figure 14-6 illustrates the data from the quality group, group 1, and the quantity group, group 2. Two judges rated the quality of the solutions on a 1–7 scale with 7 indicating best. On the abscissa of the figure we have plotted the quality (the sums of two judges' rating) and on the ordinate the number of solutions with each quality rating generated in each group. Since the sum of two ratings are given, the range is 2–14 rather than 1–7.

A number of conclusions are evident from Figure 14-6. First, the quantity instructions certainly generated more solutions. Second, the mean quality of the solutions in the quantity group went down; that is, a majority of the solutions from that group got low ratings. Most important, however, was that the quantity group showed a greater number of superior solutions. So, *proportionally* the quantity group generated fewer good solutions but *absolutely* they generated more good solutions. Thus, in one sense, brainstorming does work in generating more good solutions.

It is interesting to ask whether the subjects in the brainstorming condition were able to judge which of their solutions were best. When asked, they tended to pick out better than average solutions, but not always the best. A comparison of the self-judged solutions in the brainstorming condition with the single solutions generated in group 1 yielded no difference in ratings (Johnson, Parrott, and Statton). It appears that subjects instructed to give just one best solution may implicitly generate many solutions and edit them, just as the brainstorming subjects are required to do overtly.

The analysis of these data confirms the idea that productive thinking has two major components: the generation of ideas and the judgment of the quality of the ideas. Thus, a researcher should be able to improve the quality of the idea chosen as best both by training subjects to generate more ideas and by training subjects to judge their ideas. This prediction was borne out in a study by Stratton and Brown (1972). They compared training techniques that emphasized quantity, quality, and both. The combined technique produced the most superior solutions to the plot-title problem.

Standard recommendations for idea generation in writing involve a variant of this first brainstorm–then-judge model. Students are encouraged to concentrate on generating ideas, reserving judgment for later. True, one naturally edits ideas as one generates them, choosing to set forth only those that seem good. However, students are encouraged not to concentrate on judgment in the initial stage, postponing it to the rewriting stage. Thus, under this recommendation, students are to write their papers from beginning to end, following their trains of thought and spurring themselves on whenever they hit a roadblock with problem-solving techniques designed to promote the generation of ideas. However, it should be emphasized that random association is not being recommended. All the ideas generated should be organized as solutions to explicit goals and subgoals generated in the writing process.

Composition

As Wason (1978) notes, in pedagogy one can find two rather contradictory models for relations between idea generation and composition. Under the first model, the writer generates ideas first, creating an outline of the paper to be written and then translating this outline into a first draft. Under the second model, the writer composes the first draft as he or she generates ideas. In the extreme case under model 1, no further ideas are generated once the outline is created. In the extreme case under model 2, no outline is made at all. It

"And don't forget the little pads, in case one of them has an idea."

Figure 14-7 *Creativity in business. (Drawing by Gardner Rea; © 1953 The New Yorker Magazine, Inc.)*

appears that good writers can be found who practice each of the extremes. However, most good writers represent some compromise between the two extremes. It is worthwhile reviewing the advantages for each model. Let us turn first to the model utilizing an outline.

Advantages of Model 1

1. Under this model, the writer can avoid wasting the effort of preparing a draft that might later be judged unfit with respect to the overall structure.
2. Ideas are often generated more quickly than they can be expressed coherently. Keeping up with the flow of ideas is easier if one need only take notes rather than write complete prose.
3. Attention to matters of writing style is not required. Such attention would detract from that given to the ideas. Again, this point relates to the coordination problem, identified earlier.

Now consider the advantage of the first-draft model.

Advantages of Model 2

1. Writers often do not know what certain points in their own outline really mean until they write the paper out. Thus, writers often complain that they cannot follow their outlines because the points, when expanded, do not fit together as they had intended them to.

2. The process of expanding a point often stimulates new ideas and new modes of organization. Thus, writers often claim that they do their thinking in the act of writing.

The arguments for both models are valid. Optimal writing requires free alternation between the two models. Achieving flexibility in alternating between idea generation and composition is important to solving the coordination problem. Having an outline—if only mentally—is always useful to writers in helping them to focus on their goals and to prevent them from going off on tangents. However, at the same time, writers need to be flexible regarding the outline and be able to reorganize it when necessary. They should never feel compelled to stick to the initial organization.

Thus, the composition process is inevitably intertwined with idea generation. This fact has an important practical implication: writers should not labor over the style and syntax of their writing in composing the first draft. The important task initially is to get ideas onto the paper. Content should be the focus of the first draft. The time to worry about style is during the rewriting phase.

Of course, the more poorly written the first draft the more time rewriting will require. In fact, most writers spend much more time on rewriting than they do in creating the first draft. The ability to write a final-draft-quality paper the first time through is an enviable skill, but few have it. A few of my colleagues claim that they only write one draft. Without exception, these are people whose spontaneous speech is of final-draft quality. This observation suggests that the quality of a writer's first-draft writing reflects his or her general linguistic skill at transforming ideas into words. Indeed, these colleagues' papers sound very much like their spontaneous speech.

It is usually true that content is more important than style. Of course, in some situations the reverse is the case, and one should be flexible and willing to sacrifice content for style. This consideration returns us to the principal moral of this section: always be aware of your goals in writing and of the means of achieving them.

Since many writers do emphasize content over style in first drafts, they tend not to practice the kinds of linguistic skills that lead to high-quality first draft. Thus, the stylistic quality of first drafts probably does not improve as quickly as it could. (Of course, by focusing on idea generation, writers improve the content of their first drafts.) Some veteran writers report that the stylistic quality of their first drafts does not improve much over the years although the quality of their final drafts does improve.

Rewriting or Editing

The first two phases of writing are intended to be relatively uninhibited. Their function is to get good ideas onto paper. It is in the third phase, *rewriting,* that the misjudgments made in the first two phases are corrected or edited. It is a maxim that subsequent drafts should be shorter than the first draft; a major goal at this stage is to cut out the poor ideas that got in because of the writer's low threshold for acceptance in the first two stages. In the framework of the generate-and-judge model of creativity discussed earlier, this is the stage in which judgment should be brought to bear. However, again flexibility needs to be emphasized. One should not fail to pursue a good idea just because it originates during rewriting—and good ideas do originate at this stage.

It is useful to review some of the major factors that usually need editing:

1. *Ideas.* Some of the ideas that seemed strong initially might really be weak or in conflict with other ideas. This problem gives writers particular difficulty. They find it hard to convince themselves that ideas should be thrown out after such a great effort was spent in generating them.

2. *Structure.* Since the structure of the text can change in the writing, the organization of the first draft is often mangled and in need of major restructuring. It is often necessary to rearrange sections to obtain a coherent structure. A useful technique is to develop a hierarchical outline of the paper after it is written, enabling the writer to inspect the structure. The structure should be clearly signaled so that it is apparent to the reader. Beginning paragraphs with main points, underlining, and using headings are all ways of highlighting the structure of a piece. A writer who is uncertain as to whether the structure is clear might begin with a paragraph explaining the text's structure.

3. *Connective tissue.* While the writer might see clearly how the ideas in a piece are related, a reader may not. It is sometimes necessary to write into subsequent drafts sentences or phrases (e.g., "On the other hand,") that indicate the relationship among ideas.

4. *Style.* Many problems arise regarding style in first drafts. In scientific writing, for instance, first drafts tend to be too verbose. Sentences are too long, too many abstract nouns occur where concrete verbs would do, and so on. Consider the following sentence, taken from a scientific paper: *In studies pertaining to the identification of phenolic derivations, drying of the paper gives less satisfactory visualization.* This sentence should have been edited to read, *Phenolic derivations are more easily seen and identified if the paper is left wet.*

5. *Grammar and spelling.* These errors occur with relatively high frequency in many first drafts (e.g., my own). Besides creating a poor
"public relations" image for the writer, such errors distract readers'
attention from the content of the passage.

Clearly, these errors are listed in order of decreasing complexity. The
simplest errors are easiest to detect and correct but they are also the least
important. Particularly with respect to the more complex errors, writers suffer
from problems of incorrect set (see Chapter 9). Their ideas and structure may
seem excellent to them, the connections among their ideas obvious, and their
style beautiful. The trick is to escape this egocentric perspective and perceive
the prose as another reader would. A number of solid recommendations can
be made about rewriting:

1. Again, as always, practice makes perfect. Earlier we noted that judgment training improves the mean quality of ideas. Analogously, training in editing improves rewriting. A particularly beneficial practice
   technique is rewriting someone else's prose. Editing someone else's
   material makes it easier to practice reading objectively and critically,
   finding problems, and deciding on solutions. A real advantage in
   multiple-author papers is that one person can edit another's writing.

2. If possible, writers should put their first drafts away for a while
   before rewriting. This time lapse allows all the little biases and self-
   understandings to dissipate. With a long enough lag between first
   draft and rewriting, rewriting one's own text will become like rewriting someone else's. The effect of this technique is similar to an
   incubation effect (discussed in Chapter 9).

3. Writers do well to try their work out on someone else. It is amazing
   how rapidly their golden prose crumbles before their eyes when
   they watch someone try to make sense out of it. One who cannot find
   a friend to suffer through first-draft scribble might imagine speaking
   the text to a friend. This practice alone often enables a writer to
   achieve objectivity.

4. Writers need to be their own critics, trying to poke holes in their own
   arguments, to make fun of their own styles, and so on. If one's ego is
   up to it, taking this perspective can also serve as a profitable way to
   troubleshoot prose.

5. Committing to memory the basic edits of style, grammar, and text
   structure is a necessity. Many texts on writing can serve as reference
   sources (e.g., Strunk and White, 1972; Woodward, 1968). These
   works also document the most common errors. For many points of
   style and grammar, writers can make accurate judgments when

forced to, but fail to recall these points unless specifically prompted. By committing these points to memory so they can be freely recalled, writers strengthen the representation of these points in memory and increase the probability that they will be activated when relevant in the rewriting process.

6. Another good technique is to practice speaking about complex topics. When one considers the nature of the writing difficulties discussed here, it becomes clear that many involve fundamental weaknesses in language-generation abilities. The inability to properly appreciate the reader's perspective reflects a weakness in developing suppositions and assertions. Some stylistic problems also reflect a lack of control over the necessary syntactic patterns. These language-generation deficits do not often show up in ordinary speech, since ordinary speech is not nearly so demanding as the typical essay topic. Typical discussions about movies, football, or the weather require a much less developed command of the language than an essay on the evidence for short-term memory. However, in certain circumstances oral discussion can be as demanding as an essay topic— for instance, in some college seminars. Clearly, entering into such discussions will help writers develop their language-generation skills.

7. Reading is thought to be good practice for writing (e.g., Haynes, 1978). As we mentioned earlier in this chapter, virtually nothing is known about the connection between language comprehension and language generation. However, it is generally believed that some connection exists between the two and that positive transfer should occur between one and the other.

8. The low-level skills, such as typing, spelling, and composing grammatical sentences, should be practiced until they become automatic. In Chapters 2 and 8, we saw how a task ceases to interfere with other ongoing tasks when it becomes automatic. Thus, it is wise to practice the low-level skills in preparation for the more difficult phases of composition. One might take the view that this function is served (or should be served) by the teaching of writing in grade school.

A number of researchers (e.g., Bruce, Collins, Rubin, and Gentner, 1979) have remarked that the central difficulty in performing, learning, or teaching writing is the coordination problem—the problem of integrating many levels at once. A common variation of the coordination problem is what Bruce et al. called *downsliding,* the tendency of writers to focus in the lower levels (e.g., spelling and grammar) to the neglect of the higher (e.g., idea generation and organization). Another phenomenon, which should perhaps be called *upslid-*

ing, is the focusing on higher levels to the exclusion of lower. Many of my papers are living proof of this. The researchers named above suggest training procedures in which students learn to do each level separately. This suggestion echoes the issue of part-to-whole training discussed in Chapter 8. To the extent that editing can be performed at various levels independently, it is efficient to learn to perform each level separately and then to integrate them rather than learning to perform all levels at once.

In fairness, a warning about overediting is in order. Up to this point, we have emphasized what can be done to get a paper into acceptable shape. But writers can polish their work forever, and some writers polish long past the point at which the improvement is still worth the investment of time. Thus, it is important to monitor one's editing and to note when the time being invested stops bringing in adequate return. At that point, one should stop working or at least to put the paper away until one can get a fresh perspective and see how to make valuable changes.

Remarks and Suggested Readings

As the reader may have noted, most of the recommendations on writing were based on general knowledge of cognitive psychology and not on specific knowledge about language generation. In fact, this knowledge is quite sparse. If cognitive psychology could come to a better understanding of language generation, much more could be said about improving writing skills. Perhaps, in this context, studying effective writing would be a good way to study language generation.

Writing is an appropriate topic with which to end the text. The study of writing is truly a frontier area for research and one that calls on many of the more established areas. In this respect, this area of study illustrates three important features of the current state of cognitive psychology: (1) many topics are ripe for research; (2) a clear challenge for the future lies in integrating the research that has been developed in many domains; and (3) extremely significant applications of our science may be less than a generation away.

For more reading on creativity and writing, see the texts by Johnson (1972) and by Hayes (1978) and the papers by Flower and Hayes (1977) and by Hayes and Flower (1980). A recent collection of papers on writing education was edited by Frederiksen, Whiteman, and Dominic (1979). Another was edited by Gregg and Steinberg (1980). The two-volume series by Stein (1975–1976) provides a survey of the many popular, but largely unproven, techniques for stimulating creativity.

References

Abelson, R. P. Script processing in attitude formation and decision-making. In J. S. Carroll and J. W. Payne (Eds.), *Cognition and Social Behavior,* Hillsdale, N.J.: Lawrence Erlbaum Associates, 1976.

Adams, J. A. and Dijkstra, S. Short-term memory for motor responses. *Journal of Experimental Psychology,* 1966, *71,* 314–318.

Adams, J. L. *Conceptual Blockbusting.* Palo Alto, Calif.: Stanford Alumni Association, 1974.

Anderson, J. R. Recognition confusions in sentence memory. Unpublished manuscript, 1972.

Anderson, J. R. Retrieval of propositional information from long-term memory. *Cognitive Psychology,* 1974(a), *6,* 451–474.

Anderson, J. R. Verbatim and propositional representation of sentences in immediate and long-term memory. *Journal of Verbal Learning and Verbal Behavior,* 1974(b), *13,* 149–162.

Anderson, J. R. *Language, Memory, and Thought.* Hillsdale, N.J.: Lawrence Erlbaum Associates, 1976.

Anderson, J. R. Arguments concerning representations for mental imagery. *Psychological Review,* 1978(a), *85,* 249–277.

Anderson, J. R. Computer simulation of a language acquisition system: A second report. In D. LaBerge and S. J. Samuels (Eds.), *Perception and Comprehension.* Hillsdale, N.J.: Lawrence Erlbaum Associates, 1978(b).

Anderson, J. R. and Bower, G. H. Configural properties in sentence memory. *Journal of Verbal Learning and Verbal Behavior,* 1972, *11,* 595–605.

Anderson, J. R. and Bower, G. H. *Human Associative Memory.* Washington, D.C.: Winston, 1973.

Anderson, J. R., Kline, P. J., and Beasley, C. M. A general learning theory and its application to schema abstraction. In G. H. Bower (Ed.), *The Psychology of Learning and Motivation,* Vol. 13, New York: Academic Press, 1979.

Anderson, J. R. and Reder, L. M. An elaborative processing explanation of depth of processing. In Cermak, L. S. and Craik, F. I. M. (Eds.), *Levels of processing in human memory,* Hillsdale, N.J.: Lawrence Erlbaum Associates, 1979.

Anderson, N. H. Information integration theory: A brief survey. In D. H. Krantz, R. C. Atkinson, R. D. Luce, and P. Suppes (Eds.), *Contemporary Developments in Mathematical Psychology, Vol. II: Measurement, Psychophysics, and Neural Information Processing,* San Francisco: W. H. Freeman and Company, 1974.

Anderson, R. C. and Biddle, W. B. On asking people questions about what they are reading. In G. H. Bower (Ed.), *The Psychology of Learning and Motivation, Vol. 9,* New York: Academic Press, 1975.

Anderson, T. H. Another look at the self-questioning study technique. Technical Education Report No. 6. Champaign: University of Illinois, Center for the Study of Reading, September, 1978.

Atkinson, R. C. and Raugh, M. R. An application of the mnemonic keyword method to the acquisition of Russian vocabulary. *Journal of Experimental Psychology: Human Learning and Memory,* 1975, *104,* 126–133.

Atkinson, R. C. and Shiffrin, R. M. Human memory: A proposed system and its control processes. In K. Spence and J. Spence (Eds.), *The Psychology of Learning and Motivation,* Vol. 2, New York: Academic Press, 1968.

Atwood, M. E. and Polson, P. G. A process model for water jug problems. *Cognitive Psychology,* 1976, *8,* 191–216.

Ausubel, D. P. *Educational psychology: A cognitive view.* New York: Holt, Rinehart, and Winston, 1968.

Baddeley, A. D. *The Psychology of Memory.* New York: Basic Books, 1976.

Banks, W. P. and Flora, J. Semantic and perceptual processes in symbolic comparisons. *Journal of Experimental Psychology: Human Perception and Performance,* 1977, *3,* 278–290.

Bartlett, B. J. Top-level structure as an organizational strategy for recall of classroom text. Unpublished doctoral dissertation, Arizona State University, 1978.

Bartlett, F. C. *Remembering: A Study in Experimental and Social Psychology.* Cambridge University Press, 1932.

Battig, W. F. and Montague, W. E. Category norms for verbal items in 56 categories: A replication and extension of the Connecticut category norms. *Journal of Experimental Psychology Monograph,* June 1969.

Baum, D. R. and Jonides, J. Comparative judgments of imagined vs. perceived distances. Paper presented at the meetings of the Psychonomics Society, Washington, D.C., November 10–12, 1977.

Begg, I. and Denny, J. P. Empirical reconciliation of atmosphere and conversion interpretations of syllogistic reasoning errors. *Journal of Experimental Psychology,* 1969, *81,* 351–354.

Benson, D. F. and Greenberg, J. P. Visual form agnosia. *Archives of Neurology,* 1969, *20,* 82–89.

Berlin, B. and Kay, P. *Basic color terms: Their universality and evolution.* Berkeley, Calif.: University of California Press, 1969.

Bever, T. G. The cognitive basis for linguistic structures. In J. R. Hayes (Ed.), *Cognition and the Development of Language,* New York: Wiley, 1970.

Bever, T. G., Garrett, M. F., and Hartig, R. The interaction of perceptual processes and ambiguous sentences. *Memory and Cognition,* 1973, *1,* 277–286.

Biederman, I., Glass, A. L., and Stacy, E. W. Searching for objects in real world scenes. *Journal of Experimental Psychology,* 1973, *97,* 22–27.

Bilodeau, I. McD. Information feedback. In E. A. Bilodeau (Ed.), *Principles of Skill Acquisition,* New York: Academic Press, 1969.

Bjork, R. A. Short-term storage: The ordered output of a central processor. In F. Restle, R. M. Shiffrin, N. J. Castellan, H. R. Lindman, and D. B. Pisoni (Eds.), *Cognitive Theory, Vol. 1,* Hillsdale, N.J.: Lawrence Erlbaum Associates, 1975.

Bjork, R. A. Information-processing analysis of college teaching. *Educational Psychologist,* 1979, *14,* 15–23.

Blackburn, J. M. Acquisition of skill: An analysis of learning curves. IHRB Report, 1936, No. 73.

Bobrow, D. G. and Winograd, T. An overview of KRL, a knowledge representation language. *Cognitive Science,* 1977, *1,* 3–46.

Bobrow, S. and Bower, G. H. Comprehension and recall of sentences. *Journal of Experimental Psychology,* 1969, *80,* 455–461.

Bolinger, D. L. *Aspects of Language.* New York: Harcourt, Brace, Jovanovich, 1975.

Boole, G. *An Investigation of the Laws of Thought.* London: Walton and Maberly, 1954.

Boomer, D. S. Hesitation and grammatical encoding. *Language and Speech,* 1965, *8,* 148–158.

Boring, E. G. *A History of Experimental Psychology.* New York: Appleton Century, 1950.

Bourne, L. E. Some factors affecting strategies used in problems of concept formation. *American Journal of Psychology,* 1963, *75,* 229–238.

Bourne, L. E. *Human Conceptual Behavior.* Boston: Allyn and Bacon, 1966.

Bourne, L. E., Dominowski, R. L., and Loftus, E. F. *Cognitive Processes.* Englewood Cliffs, N.J.: Prentice-Hall, 1979.

Bourne, L. E., Ekstrand, B. R., and Dominowski, R. L. *The Psychology of Thinking.* Englewood Cliffs, N.J.: Prentice-Hall, 1971.

Bower, G. H. Memo: Mnemonics and what to do about them. Prepared for SSRC. Committee on Learning and the Educational Process, September 27, 1969.

Bower, G. H. Analysis of a mnemonic device. *American Scientist,* 1970(a), *58,* 496–510.

Bower, G. H. Imagery as a relational organizer in associative learning. *Journal of Verbal Learning and Verbal Behavior,* 1970(b), *9,* 529–533.

Bower, G. H. Organizational factors in memory. *Cognitive Psychology,* 1970(c), *1,* 18–46.

Bower, G. H. Mental imagery and associative learning. In L. Gregg (Ed.), *Cognition in Learning and Memory,* New York: Wiley, 1972.

Bower, G. H. Contacts of cognitive psychology with social learning theory. Address to the Convention of American Association of Behavior Therapists, Atlanta, Georgia, December 9, 1977.

Bower, G. H., Black, J. B., and Turner, T. J. Scripts in memory for text. *Cognitive Psychology,* 1979, *11,* 177–220.

Bower, G. H. and Clark, M. C. Narrative stories as mediators for serial learning. *Psychonomic Science,* 1969, *14,* 181–182.

Bower, G. H., Clark, M. C., Lesgold, A. M., and Winzenz, D. Hierarchical retrieval schemes in recall of categorical word lists. *Journal of Verbal Learning and Verbal Behavior,* 1969, *8,* 323–343.

Bower, G. H., Karlin, M. B., and Dueck, A. Comprehension and memory for pictures. *Memory and Cognition,* 1975, *3,* 216–220.

Bower, G. H., Monteiro, K. P., and Gilligan, S. G. Emotional mood as a context for learning and recall. *Journal of Verbal Learning and Verbal Behavior,* 1978, *17,* 573–587.

Bower, G. H. and Trabasso, T. R. Reversals prior to solution in concept identification. *Journal of Experimental Psychology,* 1963, *66,* 409–418.

Bower, G. H. and Trabasso, T. R. Concept identification. In R. C. Atkinson (Ed.), *Studies in Mathematical Psychology,* Stanford: Stanford University Press, 1964, 32–94.

Bransford, J. D., Barclay, J. R., and Franks, J. J. Sentence memory: A constructive versus interpretive approach. *Cognitive Psychology,* 1972, *3,* 193–209.

Bray, C. W. *Psychology and military proficiency.* Princeton: Princeton University Press, 1948.

Brigham, J. C. Ethnic stereotypes. *Psychological Bulletin,* 1971, *76,* 15–38.

Brooks, L. R. Spatial and verbal components of the act of recall. *Canadian Journal of Psychology,* 1968, *22,* 349–368.

Brown, A. L. Theories of memory and the problems of development: Activity, growth, and knowledge. In L. S. Cermak and F. I. M. Craik (Eds.), *Levels of Processing in Human Memory,* Hillsdale, N.J.: Lawrence Erlbaum Associates, 1979.

Brown, R. *A First Language.* Cambridge, Mass.: Harvard University Press, 1973.

Brown, R. and Lenneberg, E. H. A study in language and cognition. *Journal of Abnormal and Social Psychology,* 1954, *49,* 454–462.

Bruce, B., Collins, A. M., Rubin, A. D., Gentner, D. A cognitive science approach to writing. In C. H. Fredericksen, M. F. Whiteman, and J. D. Dominic (Eds.), *Writing: The nature, development and teaching of written communication,* Hillsdale, N.J.: Lawrence Erlbaum Associates, 1979.

Bruner, J. S., Goodnow, J., and Austin, G. A. *A Study of Thinking.* New York: Wiley, 1956.

Buckley, P. B. and Gillman, C. B. Comparison of digits and dot patterns. *Journal of Experimental Psychology,* 1974, *103,* 1131–1136.

Cairns, H. S. and Cairns, C. E. *Psycholinguistics: A cognitive view of language.* New York: Holt, Rinehart and Winston, 1976.

Cantor, N. and Mischel, W. Traits as prototypes: Effects on recognition memory. *Journal of Personality and Social Psychology,* 1977, *35,* 38–48.

Cantor, N. and Mischel, W. Prototypes in person perception. In L. Berkowitz (Ed.), *Advances in Experimental Social Psychology,* New York: Academic Press, *12,* 1979.

Caplan, D. Clause boundaries and recognition latencies for words in sentences. *Perception and Psychophysics,* 1972, *12,* 73–76.

Carmichael, L., Hogan, H. P., and Walter, A. An experimental study of the effect of language on the reproduction of visually perceived form. *Journal of Experimental Psychology,* 1932, *15,* 73–86.

Carroll, J. B. and Casagrande, J. B. The function of language classifications in behavior. In E. E. Maccoby, T. M. Newcomb, and E. L. Hartley (Eds.), *Readings in Social Psychology* (3rd Edition), New York: Holt, Rinehart, and Winston, 1958.

Carroll, Lewis. *Alice's Adventures in Wonderland.* New York: Appleton, 1866, 1927.

Ceraso, J. and Provitera, A. Sources of error in syllogistic reasoning. *Cognitive Psychology,* 1971, *2,* 400–410.

Cermak, L. S. and Craik, F. I. M. *Levels of Processing in Human Memory.* Hillsdale, N.J.: Lawrence Erlbaum Associates, 1979.

Chapman, L. J. and Chapman, J. P. Atmosphere effect reexamined. *Journal of Experimental Psychology,* 1959, *58,* 220–226.

Charniak, E. and Wilks, Y. *Computational Semantics.* Amsterdam: North-Holland, 1976.

Chase, W. G. and Clark, H. H. Mental operations in the comparisons of sentences and pictures. In L. W. Gregg (Ed.), *Cognition in Learning and Memory,* New York: Wiley, 1972.

Chase, W. G. and Simon, H. A. The mind's eye in chess. In W. G. Chase (Ed.), *Visual Information Processing.* New York: Academic Press, 1973.

Cherry, E. C. Some experiments on the recognition of speech with one and with two ears. *Journal of the Acoustical Society of America,* 1953, *25,* 975–979.

Chomsky, N. *Syntactic Structures.* The Hague: Mouton, 1957.

Chomsky, N. *Aspects of the Theory of Syntax.* Cambridge, Mass.: MIT Press, 1965.

Chomsky, N. *Reflections on Language.* New York: Pantheon Books, 1975.

Chomsky, N. and Halle, M. *The Sound Pattern of English.* New York: Harper, 1968.

Christen, F. and Bjork, R. A. On updating the loci in the method of loci. Paper presented at the seventeenth annual meeting of the Psychonomic Society, St. Louis, Missouri, November 12, 1976.

Church, A. *Introduction to Mathematical Logic.* Princeton, N.J.: Princeton University Press, 1956.

Clark, H. H. Semantics and comprehension. In R. A. Sebeok (Ed.), *Current Trends in Linguistics,* Vol. 12, The Hague: Mouton, 1974.

Clark, H. H. and Chase, W. G. On the process of comparing sentences against pictures. *Cognitive Psychology,* 1972, *3,* 472–517.

Clark, H. H. and Clark, E. V. *Psychology and Language.* New York: Harcourt, Brace, Jovanovich, 1977.

Cohen, M. R. and Nagle, E. *An Introduction to Logic and Scientific Method.* New York: Harcourt, Brace, 1934.

Collins, A. M. and Loftus, E. F. A spreading-activation theory of semantic processing. *Psychological Review,* 1975, *82,* 407–428.

Collins, A. M. and Quillian, M. R. Retrieval time from semantic memory. *Journal of Verbal Learning and Verbal Behavior,* 1969, *8,* 240–247.

Collins, A. M. and Quillian, M. R. Experiments on semantic memory and language comprehension. In L. W. Gregg (Ed.), *Cognition and Learning,* New York: Wiley, 1972.

Conrad, C. Cognitive economy in semantic memory. *Journal of Experimental Psychology,* 1972, *92,* 149–154.

Conrad, R. and Hull, A. J. The preferred layout for numerical data entry sets. *Ergonomics,* 1968, *11,* 165–173.

Cooper, L. A. and Shepard, R. N. Chronometric studies of the rotation of mental images. In Chase, W. G. (Ed.), *Visual Information Processing,* New York: Academic Press, 1973.

Craik, F. I. M. and Jacoby, L. L. A process view of short-term retention. In F. Restle, R. M. Shiffrin, N. J. Castellan, H. R. Lindman, and D. B. Pisoni (Eds.), *Cognitive Theory, Vol. 1,* Hillsdale, N.J.: Lawrence Erlbaum Associates, 1975.

Craik, F. I. M. and Lockhart, R. S. Levels of processing: A framework for memory research. *Journal of Verbal Learning and Verbal Behavior,* 1972, *11,* 671–684.

Crossman, E. R. F. W. A theory of the acquisition of speed-skill. *Ergonomics,* 1959, *2,* 153–166.

Crowder, R. G. *Principles of Learning and Memory.* Hillsdale, N.J.: Lawrence Erlbaum Associates, 1976.

Curtiss, S. *Genie: A psycholinguistic study of a modern day "wild child."* New York: Academic Press, 1977.

Dale, P. S. *Language Development: Structure and Function.* New York: Holt, Rinehart, and Winston, 1976.

Darwin, C. J., Turvey, M. T., and Crowder, R. G. The auditory analogue of the Sperling partial report procedure: Evidence for brief auditory storage. *Cognitive Psychology,* 1972, *3,* 255–267.

Deese, J. Thought into speech. *American Scientist,* 1978, *66,* 314–321.

de Groot, A. D. *Thought and Choice in Chess.* The Hague: Mouton, 1965.

de Groot, A. D. Perception and memory versus thought. In B. Kleinmuntz (Ed.), *Problem-Solving.* New York: Wiley, 1966.

de Valois, R. L. and Jacobs, G. H. Primate color vision. *Science,* 1968, *162,* 533–540.

deVilliers, J. G. and deVilliers, P. A. *Language Acquisition.* Cambridge, Mass.: Harvard University Press, 1978.

Dickstein, L. S. The effect of figure on syllogistic reasoning. *Memory and Cognition,* 1978, *6,* 76–83.

Dillard, J. L. *Black English: Its History and Usage in the United States.* New York: Random House, 1972.

Dominowski, R. L. How do people discover concepts? In R. L. Solso (Ed.), *Theories in Cognitive Psychology: The Loyola Symposium,* Hillsdale, N.J.: Lawrence Erlbaum Associates, 1974.

Dominowski, R. L. Reasoning. *Interamerican Journal of Psychology,* 1977, *11,* 68–77.

Dominowski, R. L. and Jenrick, R. Effects of hints and interpolated activity on solution of an insight problem. *Psychonomic Science,* 1972, *26,* 335–338.

Dooling, D. J. and Christiaansen, R. E. Episodic and semantic aspects of memory for prose. *Journal of Experimental Psychology: Human Learning and Memory,* 1977, *3,* 428–436.

Doyle, A. C. *A Study in Scarlet and the Sign of the Four.* New York: Harper, 1904.

Duncan, C. P. Transfer after training with single vs. multiple tasks. *Journal of Experimental Psychology,* 1958, *55,* 63–72.

Duncker, K. On problem-solving (translated by L. S. Lees). *Psychological Monographs,* 1945, *58,* No. 270.

Durkin, D. *Children Who Read Early.* New York: Teachers College Press, 1966.

Ebbinghaus, H. Memory: A Contribution to Experimental Psychology (translated by Ruger, H. A. and Bussenues, C. E., 1913). New York: Teachers College, Columbia University, 1885.

Edwards, W. Dynamic decision theory and probabilistic information processing. *Human Factors,* 1962, *4,* 59–73.

Edwards, W. Conservatism in human information processing. In B. Kleinmuntz (Ed.), *Formal representations of human judgment.* New York: Wiley, 1968.

Eich, J., Weingartner, H., Stillman, R. C., and Gillin, J. C. State-dependent accessibility of retrieval cues in the retention of a categorized list. *Journal of Verbal Learning and Verbal Behavior,* 1975, *14,* 408–417.

Eimas, P. D. and Corbit, J. Selective adaptation of linguistic feature detectors. *Cognitive Psychology,* 1973, *4,* 99–109.

Erickson, J. R. A set analysis theory of behavior in formal syllogistic reasoning tasks. In R. L. Solso (Ed.), *Theories in Cognitive Psychology: The Loyola Symposium,* Hillsdale, N.J.: Lawrence Erlbaum Associates, 1974.

Ernst, G. and Newell, A. *GPS: A Case Study in Generality and Problem Solving.* New York: Academic Press, 1969.

Ervin-Tripp, S. M. Is second language learning like the first? *TESOL Quarterly,* 1974, *8,* 111–127.

Estes, W. K. *Handbook of Learning and Cognitive Processes, Vols. 1–6.* Hillsdale, N.J.: Lawrence Erlbaum Associates, 1975–1979.

Estes, W. K. Memory, perception, and decision in letter identification. In R. L. Solso (Ed.), *Information Processing and Cognition: The Loyola Symposium,* Hillsdale, N.J.: Lawrence Erlbaum Associates, 1975.

Falmagne, R. J. *Reasoning: Representation and Process.* Hillsdale, N.J.: Lawrence Erlbaum Associates, 1975.

Fillenbaum, S. On coping with ordered and unordered conjunctive sentences. *Journal of Experimental Psychology,* 1971, *87,* 93–98.

Fillenbaum, S. Pragmatic normalization: Further results for some conjunctive and disjunctive sentences. *Journal of Experimental Psychology,* 1974, *103,* 913–921.

Fitts, P. M. and Posner, M. I. *Human Performance.* Belmont, Calif.: Brooks Cole, 1967.

Flavell, J. H., Beach, D. H., and Chinsky, J. M. Spontaneous verbal rehearsal in a memory task as a function of age. *Child Development,* 1966, *37,* 283–299.

Flexser, A. J. and Tulving, E. Retrieval independence in recognition and recall. *Psychological Review,* 1978, *85,* 153–172.

Flower, L. S. and Hayes, J. R. Problem-solving strategies and the writing process. *College English,* 1977, *39,* 449–461.

Fodor, J. A., Bever, T. G., and Garrett, M. F. *The Psychology of Language.* New York: McGraw-Hill, 1974.

Fodor, J. A. and Garrett, M. F. Some syntactic determinants of sentential complexity. *Perception and Psychophysics,* 1967, *2,* 289–296.

Foss, D. J. and Hakes, D. T. *Psycholinguistics.* Englewood Cliffs, N.J.: Prentice-Hall, 1978.

Franks, J. J. and Bransford, J. D. Abstraction of visual patterns. *Journal of Experimental Psychology,* 1971, *90,* 65–74.

Frase, L. T. Prose processing. In G. H. Bower (Ed.), *The Psychology of Learning and Motivation, Vol. 9,* New York: Academic Press, 1975.

Fredericksen, C. H. Representing logical and semantic structure of knowledge acquired from discourse. *Cognitive Psychology,* 1975, *7,* 371–458.

Frederiksen, C. H., Whiteman, M. F., and Dominic, J. D. *Writing: The Nature, Development, and Teaching of Written Communications.* Hillsdale, N.J.: Lawrence Erlbaum Associates, 1979.

French, M. *The Women's Room.* New York: Jove, 1978.

Fromkin, V. The non-anomalous nature of anomalous utterances. *Language,* 1971, *47,* 27–52.

Fromkin, V. *Speech Errors as Linguistic Evidence.* The Hague: Mouton, 1973.

Fromkin, V., Krashen, S., Curtiss, S., Rigler, D., and Rigler, M. The development of language in Genie: A case of language acquisition beyond the "critical period." *Brain and Language,* 1974, *1,* 81–107.

Fromkin, V. and Rodman, R. *An Introduction to Language.* New York: Holt, Rinehart, and Winston, 1978.

Gardner, H. *The Shattered Mind.* New York: Alfred A. Knopf, 1975.

Gardner, R. A. and Gardner, B. T. Teaching sign language to a chimpanzee. *Science,* 1969, *165,* 664–672.

Garrett, M. F. The analysis of sentence production. In G. H. Bower (Ed.), *The Psychology of Learning and Motivation, Vol. 9,* New York: Academic Press, 1975, 133–177.

Gay, I. R. Temporal position of reviews and its effect on the retention of mathematical rules. *Journal of Educational Psychology,* 1973, *64,* 171–182.

Gazzaniga, M. A. The split brain in man. *Scientific American,* 1967, *217,* 24–29.

Gazzaniga, M. A. *The bisected brain.* New York: Appleton-Century-Crofts, 1970.

Gibson, E. J. and Levin, H. *The Psychology of Reading.* Cambridge, Mass: M.I.T. Press, 1975.

Gibson, J. J. *Perception of the Visual World.* Boston: Houghton, 1950.

Gibson, J. J. *The Senses Considered as Perceptual Systems.* Boston: Houghton, 1966.

Gilbert, G. M. Stereotype persistence and change among college students. *Journal of Abnormal and Social Psychology,* 1951, *46,* 245–254.

Glass, A. L., Holyoak, K. J., and Santa, J. L. *Cognition.* Reading, Mass.: Addison-Wesley, 1979.

Glenberg, A. M. Monotonic and nonmonotonic lag effects in paired-associate and recognition memory paradigms. *Journal of Verbal Learning and Verbal Behavior,* 1976, *15,* 1–16.

Glucksberg, S. and Danks, J. H. Effects of discriminative labels and of nonsense labels upon availability of novel function. *Journal of Verbal Learning and Verbal Behavior,* 1968, *7,* 72–76.

Glucksberg, S. and Danks, J. H. *Experimental Psycholinguistics.* New York: Halsted Press, 1975.

Glucksberg, S. and Weisberg, R. W. Verbal behavior and problem solving: Some effects of labeling in a functional fixedness problem. *Journal of Experimental Psychology,* 1966, *71,* 659–664.

Godden, D. R. and Baddeley, A. D. Context-dependent memory in two natural environments: On land and under water. *British Journal of Psychology,* 1975, *66,* 325–331.

Gordon, W. J. J. *Synectics: The development of creative capacity.* New York: Harper and Row, 1961.

Gould, J. D. An experimental study of writing, dictating, and speaking. In R. Requin (Ed.), *Attention and Performance VII,* Hillsdale, N.J.: Lawrence Erlbaum Associates, 1978.

Gould, J. D. and Boies, S. J. Writing, dictating, and speaking letters. IBM Research Report RC 6683 (No. 28698), August, 1977.

Graf, R. and Torrey, J. W. Perception of phrase structure in written language. *American Psychological Association Convention Proceedings,* 1966, 83–88.

Gray, J. A. and Wedderburn, A. A. I. Grouping strategies with simultaneous stimuli. *Quarterly Journal of Experimental Psychology,* 1960, *12,* 180–184.

Greenberg, J. H. Some universals of grammar with particular reference to the order of meaningful elements. In J. H. Greenberg (Ed.), *Universals of Language,* Cambridge, Mass.: MIT Press, 1963.

Greeno, J. G. Hobbits and orcs: Acquisition of a sequential concept. *Cognitive Psychology,* 1974, *6,* 270–292.

Greeno, J. G. Cognitive objectives of instruction: Theory of knowledge for solving problems and answering questions. In D. Klahr (Ed.), *Cognition and Instruction,* Hillsdale, N.J.: Lawrence Erlbaum Associates, 1976.

Greeno, J. G. Notes on problem-solving abilities. In W. K. Estes (Ed.), *Handbook of Learning and Cognitive Processes,* Hillsdale, N.J.: Lawrence Erlbaum Associates, 1978.

Greeno, J. G. Trends in the theory of knowledge for problem-solving. In D. T. Tuma and F. Reif (Eds.), *Problem Solving and Education: Issues in Teaching and Research,* Hillsdale, N.J.: Lawrence Erlbaum Associates, in press.

Gregg, L. W. *Knowledge and Cognition.* Hillsdale, N.J.: Lawrence Erlbaum Associates, 1974.

Gregg, L. W. and Steinberg, E. *Cognitive Processes in Writing.* Hillsdale, N.J.: Lawrence Erlbaum Associates, 1980.

Grice, H. P. *Logic and conversation.* In P. Cole and J. L. Morgan (Eds.), *Syntax and Semantics, III: Speech Acts,* New York: Seminar Press, 1975.

Grimes, L. *The Thread of Discourse.* The Hague: Mouton, 1975.

Grissom, R. J., Suedfeld, P., and Vernon, J. Memory for verbal material: Effects of sensory deprivation. *Science,* 1962, *138,* 429–430.

Grosjean, F., Grosjean, L., and Lane, H. The patterns of silence: Performance structures in sentence production. *Cognitive Psychology,* 1979, *11,* 58–81.

Guilford, J. P., Fruchter, B., and Zimmerman, W. S. Factor analysis of the Army Air Force's battery of experimental aptitude tests. *Psychometrika,* 1952, *17,* 45–68.

Guyote, M. J. and Sternberg, R. J. A transitive-chain theory of syllogistic reasoning. NR 150–412 Technical Report No. 5. New Haven, Conn.: Department of Psychology, Yale University, March 1978.

Haber, R. N. and Erdelyi, M. H. Emergence and recovery of initially unavailable perceptual material. *Journal of Verbal Learning and Verbal Behavior,* 1967, *6,* 618–628.

Hakes, D. T. Effects of reducing complement constructions on sentence comprehension. *Journal of Verbal Learning and Verbal Behavior,* 1972, *11,* 278–286.

Hakes, D. T. and Foss, D. J. Decision processes during sentence comprehension: Effects of surface structure reconsidered. *Perception and Psychophysics,* 1970, *8,* 413–416.

Hamilton, D. L. A cognitive-attributional analysis of stereotyping. In L. Berkowitz (Ed.), *Advances in Experimental Social Psychology,* Vol. 12, New York: Academic Press, 1979.

Hamilton, D. L. and Gifford, R. K. Illusory correlation in interpersonal perception: A cognitive basis of stereotypic judgments. *Journal of Experimental Social Psychology,* 1976, *12,* 392–407.

Hammerton, M. A case of radical probability estimation. *Journal of Experimental Psychology,* 1973, *101,* 252–254.

Harris, R. J. Comprehension of pragmatic implications in advertising. *Journal of Applied Psychology,* 1977, *62,* 603–608.

Hart, R. A. and Moore, G. I. The development of spatial cognition: A review. In R. M. Downs and D. Stea (Eds.), *Image and Environment,* Chicago: Aldine, 1973.

Hastie, R., Ostrom, T., Ebbesen, E., Wyer, R., Hamilton, D. L. and Carlston, D. (Eds.). *Person Memory.* Hillsdale, N.J.: Lawrence Erlbaum Associates, 1979.

Haviland, S. E. and Clark, H. H. What's new? Acquiring new information as a process in comprehension. *Journal of Verbal Learning and Verbal Behavior,* 1974, *13,* 512–521.

Hayes, C. *The Ape in Our House.* New York: Harper, 1951.

Hayes, J. R. *Cognitive Psychology.* Homewood, Ill.: Dorsey Press, 1978.

Hayes, J. R. *Problem Solving Techniques.* Philadelphia: Franklin Institute Press, in press.

Hayes-Roth, B. and Hayes-Roth, F. Concept learning and the recognition and classification of exemplars. *Journal of Verbal Learning and Verbal Behavior,* 1977, *16,* 321–338.

Haygood, R. C. and Bourne, L. E. Attribute- and rule-learning aspects of conceptual behavior. *Psychological Review,* 1965, *72,* 175–195.

Haynes, E. Using research in preparing to teach writing. *English Journal,* 1978, *67,* 82–88.

Heider, E. Universals of color naming and memory. *Journal of Experimental Psychology,* 1972, *93,* 10–20.

Henle, M. On the relation between logic and thinking. *Psychological Review,* 1962, *69,* 366–378.

Hilgard, E. R. *The Experience of Hypnosis.* New York: Harcourt, Brace, Jovanovich, 1968.

Hintzman, D. L. Theoretical implications of the spacing effect. In R. L. Solso (Ed.), *Theories in Cognitive Psychology: The Loyola Symposium.* Potomac, Maryland: Lawrence Erlbaum Associates, 1974.

Hintzman, D. L. Orientation in Cognitive Maps. Final report to the National Science Foundation, February 1979. Department of Psychology, University of Oregon.

Hochberg, J. *Perception.* Englewood Cliffs, N.J.: Prentice-Hall, 1978.

Hockett, C. F. The origin of speech. *Scientific American,* 1960, *203,* 89–96.

Holyoak, K. J. and Walker, J. H. Subjective magnitude information in semantic orderings. *Journal of Verbal Learning and Verbal Behavior,* 1976, *15,* 287–299.

Hornby, P. A. Surface structure and presupposition. *Journal of Verbal Learning and Verbal Behavior,* 1974, *13,* 530–538.

Hovland, C. I. and Weiss, W. Transmission of information concerning concepts through positive and negative instances. *Journal of Experimental Psychology,* 1953, *45,* 175–182.

Hubel, D. H. and Wiesel, T. N. Receptive fields, binocular interaction, and functional architecture in the cat's visual cortex. *Journal of Physiology,* 1962, *166,* 106–154.

Hunt, E. B. *Artificial Intelligence.* New York: Academic Press, 1975.

Hunter, I. M. L. Mental Calculation. In P. N. Johnson-Laird and P. C. Wason (Eds.), *Thinking,* New York: Cambridge University Press, 1977. (Originally published in 1966.)

Hunter, I. M. L. An exceptional memory. *British Journal of Psychology,* 1977, *68,* 154–164.

Hyde, T. S. and Jenkins, J. J. Recall for words as a function of semantic, graphic, and syntactic orienting tasks. *Journal of Verbal Learning and Verbal Behavior,* 1973, *12,* 471–480.

Jackson, M. D. and McClelland, J. L. Processing determinants of reading speed. *Journal of Experimental Psychology: General,* 1979, *108,* 151–181.

James, W. *The Principles of Psychology, Vols. 1 and 2.* New York: Henry Holt, 1890.

Jarvella, R. J. Syntactic processing of connected speech. *Journal of Verbal Learning and Verbal Behavior,* 1971, *10,* 409–416.

Jeffries, R. P., Polson, P. G., Razran, L., and Atwood, M. A process model for mission-aries-cannibals and other river-crossing problems. *Cognitive Psychology,* 1977, *9,* 412–440.

Jenkins, J. G. and Dallenbach, K. M. Obliviscence during sleep and waking. *American Journal of Psychology,* 1924, *35,* 605–612.

Johnson, D. M. Confidence and speed in the two-category judgment. *Archives of Psychology,* 1939, No. 241, 1–52.

Johnson, D. M. *A Systematic Introduction to the Psychology of Thinking.* New York: Harper and Row, 1972.

Johnson, D. M., Parrott, G. L., and Stratten, R. P. Production and judgment of solutions to five problems. *Journal of Educational Psychology,* 1968, *59,* Monograph Supplement No. 6.

Johnson-Laird, P. N. Models of deduction. In R. J. Falmagne (Ed.), *Reasoning: Representation and Process in Children and Adults.* Hillsdale, N.J.: Lawrence Erlbaum Associates, 1975.

Johnson-Laird, P. N., Legrenzi, P., and Legrenzi, M. S. Reasoning and a sense of reality. *British Journal of Psychology,* 1972, *63,* 305–400.

Johnson-Laird, P. N. and Steedman, M. The psychology of syllogisms. *Cognitive Psychology,* 1978, *10,* 64–99.

Jonides, J. and Baum, D. R. Cognitive maps as revealed by distance estimates. Paper presented at the fiftieth meeting of the Midwestern Psychological Association, Chicago, May 1978.

Just, M. A. and Carpenter, P. A. *Cognitive Processes in Comprehension.* Hillsdale, N.J.: Lawrence Erlbaum Associates, 1977.

Just, M. A. and Carpenter, P. A. *Cognitive processes in reading: Models based on reader's eye fixations.* In C. A. Prefetti and A. M. Lesgold (Eds.), *Interactive Processes and Reading,* Hillsdale, N.J.: Lawrence Erlbaum Associates, in press.

Kahneman, D. *Attention and Effort.* Englewood Cliffs, N.J.: Prentice-Hall, 1973.

Kahneman, D. and Tversky, A. Subjective probability: A judgment of representiveness. *Cognitive Psychology,* 1972, *3,* 430–454.

Kahneman, D. and Tversky, A. On the psychology of prediction. *Psychological Review,* 1973, *80,* 237–251.

Kaplan, R. A general syntactic processor. In R. Rustin (Ed.), *Natural Language Processing,* Englewood Cliffs: Prentice-Hall, 1973.

Karlins, M., Coffman, T. L., and Walters, G. On the fading of social stereotypes: Studies in three generations of college students. *Journal of Personality and Social Psychology,* 1969, *13,* 1–16.

Katz, D. and Braly, K. Racial stereotypes in one hundred college students. *Journal of Abnormal and Social Psychology,* 1933, *28,* 280–290.

Kaufman, L. *Sight and Mind: An Introduction to Visual Perception.* New York: Oxford University Press, 1974.

Keele, S. W. *Attention and Human Performance.* Pacific Palisades, Calif.: Goodyear, 1973.

Keele, S. W. and Summers, J. J. The structure of motor programs. In G. E. Stelmach (Ed.), *Motor Control: Issues and Trends,* New York: Academic Press, 1976.

Keenan, J. M. The role of episodic information in the assessment of semantic memory representations for sentences. Unpublished doctoral dissertation, University of Colorado, 1975.

Keeney, T. J., Cannizzo, S. R., and Flavell, J. H. Spontaneous and induced verbal rehearsal in a recall task. *Child Development,* 1967, *38,* 953–966.

Kellogg, W. N. and Kellogg, L. A. *The Ape and the Child.* New York: McGraw-Hill, 1933.

Keppel, G. and Underwood, B. J. Proactive inhibition in short-term retention of single items. *Journal of Verbal Learning and Verbal Behavior,* 1962, *1,* 153–161.

Kerst, S. M. and Howard, J. H., Jr. Mental comparisons for ordered information in abstract and concrete dimensions. *Memory and Cognition,* 1977, *5,* 227–234.

Kieras, D. E. Analysis of the effects of word properties and limited reading time in a reading comprehension and verification task. Unpublished doctoral dissertation, University of Michigan, 1974.

Kimball, J. P. Seven principles of surface structure parsing in natural language. *Cognition,* 1973, *2,* 15–47.

Kinney, G. C., Marsetta, M., and Showman, D. J. Studies in display symbol legibility, part XXI. The legibility of alphanumeric symbols for digitized television. Bedford, Mass.: The Mitre Corporation, November 1966, ESD-TR-66-117.

Kinsbourne, M. and Smith, W. L. *Hemispheric Disconnection and Cerebral Function.* Springfield, Ill.: Charles C Thomas, 1974.

Kintsch, W. *Learning, Memory, and Conceptual Processes.* New York: Wiley, 1970.

Kinstch, W. *The Representation of Meaning in Memory.* Hillsdale, N.J.: Lawrence Erlbaum Associates, 1974.

Kintsch, W. On comprehending stories. In M. A. Just and P. A. Carpenter (Eds.), *Cognitive Processes in Comprehension,* Hillsdale, N.J.: Lawrence Erlbaum Associates, 1977.

Kintsch, W. and van Dijk, T. A. Recalling and summarizing stories *(Comment on se rappelle et on resume des histoires). Languages,* 1976, *40,* 98–116.

Klahr, D. *Cognition and Instruction.* Hillsdale, N.J.: Lawrence Erlbaum Associates, 1976.

Klatzky, R. L. *Human Memory.* San Francisco: W. H. Freeman and Company, 1979.

Kleene, S. C. *Introduction to Mathematics.* Princeton, N.J.: Van Nostrand, 1952.

Koch, H. L. A neglected phase of a part/whole problem. *Journal of Experimental Psychology,* 1923, *6,* 366–376.

Köhler, W. *The Mentality of Apes.* New York: Harcourt Brace, 1927.

Köhler, W. *The Mentality of Apes.* London: Routledge & Kegan Paul Ltd., 1956.

Kolers, P. A. Reading a year later. *Journal of Experimental Psychology: Human Learning and Memory,* 1976, *2,* 554–565.

Kolers, P. A. A pattern analyzing basis of recognition. In L. S. Cermak and F. I. M. Craik, *Levels of Processing in Human Memory,* Hillsdale, N.J.: Lawrence Erlbaum Associates, 1979.

Kolers, P. A. and Perkins, P. N. Spatial and ordinal components of form perception and literacy. *Cognitive Psychology,* 1975, *7,* 228–267.

Kosslyn, S. M., Ball, T. M., and Reiser, B. J. Visual images preserve metric spatial information: Evidence from studies of image scanning. *Journal of Experimental Psychology: Human Perception and Performance,* 1978, *4,* 47–60.

Kosslyn, S. M. and Pomerantz, J. R. Imagery, propositions, and the form of internal representations. *Cognitive Psychology,* 1977, *9,* 52–76.

Kosslyn, S. M. and Shwartz, S. P. A simulation of visual imagery. *Cognitive Science,* 1977, *1,* 265–298.

Krashen, S. and Harshman, R. Lateralization and the critical period. *Working Papers in Phonetics,* 1972, *23,* 13–21.

LaBerge, D. Attention and the measurement of perceptual learning. *Memory and Cognition,* 1973, *1,* 268–276.

LaBerge, D. and Samuels, S. J. Toward a theory of automatic information processing in reading. *Cognitive Psychology,* 1974, *6,* 293–323.

Labov, W. The boundaries of words and their meanings. In C.-J. N. Bailey and R. W. Shuy (Eds.), *New Ways of Analyzing Variations in English,* Washington, D.C.: Georgetown University Press, 1973.

Lackner, J. A. A developmental study of language behavior in retarded children. *Neuropsychologica,* 1968, *6,* 301–320.

Lakoff, G. On generative semantics. In D. Steinberg and L. Jakobovits (Eds.), *Semantics—An Interdisciplinary Reader in Philosophy, Linguistics, Anthropology, and Psychology.* London: Cambridge University Press, 1971.

Langacker, R. W. *Language and Its Structure.* New York: Harcourt, Brace, Jovanovich, 1973.

LaPierre, R. T. Type-rationalizations of group antiplay. *Social Forces,* 1936, *15,* 232–237.

Lashley, K. The problem of serial order in behavior. In L. A. Jeffries (Ed.), *Cerebral Mechanisms in Behavior,* New York: Wiley, 1951.

Lenneberg, E. H. *Biological Foundations of Language.* New York: Wiley, 1967.

Lenneberg, E. H., Nichols, I. A., and Rosenberger, E. F. Primitive stages of language development in mongolism. *Disorders of Communication, Vol. XLII, Research Publications,* Baltimore, Md.: A. R. N. M. D. Williams and Wilkins, 1969.

Lesgold, A. M., Resnick, L. B., and Beck, I. C. Preliminary results of a longitudinal study of reading acquisition. Paper presented at the meetings of the Psychonomic Society, San Antonio, November 1978.

Lettvin, J. Y., Matturana, H. R., McCulloch, W. S., and Pitts, W. H. What the frog's eye tells the frog's brain. *Proceedings of the IRE,* 1959, *47,* 1940–1951.

Levin, H., Silverman, I., and Ford, B. Hesitations in children's speech during explanations and description. *Journal of Verbal Learning and Verbal Behavior,* 1967, *6,* 560–564.

Levine, M. Hypothesis behavior by humans during discrimination learning. *Journal of Experimental Psychology,* 1966, *71,* 331–338.

Levine, M. *A Cognitive Theory of Learning.* Hillsdale, N.J.: Lawrence Erlbaum Associates, 1975.

Lewis, C. H. and Anderson, J. R. Interference with real world knowledge. *Cognitive Psychology,* 1976, *7,* 311–335.

Lewis, D., McAllister, D. E., and Adams, J. A. Facilitation and interference in performance on the modified Mashburn apparatus: I. The effects of varying the amount of original learning. *Journal of Experimental Psychology,* 1951, *41,* 247–260.

Lindsay, P. H. and Norman, D. A. *Human Information Processing,* New York: Academic Press, 1977.

Lisker, L. and Abramson, A. The voicing dimension: Some experiments in comparative phonetics. *Proceedings of Sixth International Congress of Phonetic Sciences, Prague, 1967.* Prague: Academia, 1970, 563–567.

Loftus, E. F. Activation of semantic memory. *American Journal of Psychology,* 1974, *86,* 331–337.

Loftus, E. F. and Zanni, G. Eyewitness testimony: The influence of the wording of a question. *Bulletin of the Psychonomic Society,* 1975, *5,* 86–88.

Loftus, G. R. Comprehending compass directions. *Memory and Cognition,* 1978, *6,* 416–422.

Loftus, G. R. and Loftus, E. F. *Human Memory.* Hillsdale, N.J.: Lawrence Erlbaum Associates, 1976.

Lorayne, H. and Lucas, J. *The Memory Book.* New York: Stein and Day, 1974.

Luchins, A. S. Mechanization in problem solving. *Psychological Monographs,* 1942, *54,* No. 248.

Luchins, A. S. and Luchins, E. H. *Rigidity of Behavior: A Variational Approach to the Effects of Einstellung.* Eugene, Ore.: University of Oregon Books, 1959.

Luchsinger, R. and Arnold, G. *Voice, Speech, Language; Clinical Communicology: Its Physiology and Pathology.* Belmont, Calif.: Wadsworth, 1965.

Lynch, K. *The Image of the City.* Cambridge, Mass.: M.I.T. and Harvard Press, 1960.

Lyons, J. *Noam Chomsky.* New York: Viking Press, 1970.

Maclay, H. and Osgood, C. E. Hesitation phenomena in spontaneous speech. *Word,* 1959, *15,* 19–44.

McCloskey, M. E. and Glucksberg, S. Natural categories: Well-defined or fuzzy sets? *Memory and Cognition,* 1978, *6,* 462–472.

McConkie, G. W. and Rayner, K. Identifying the span of the effective stimulus in reading. *Final Report OEG 2-71-0531.* U.S. Office of Education, 1974.

McLaughlin, B. *Second-Language Acquisition in Childhood.* Hillsdale, N.J.: Lawrence Erlbaum Associates, 1978.

Madigan, S. A. Intraserial repetition and coding processes in free recall. *Journal of Verbal Learning and Verbal Behavior,* 1969, *8,* 828–835.

Maier, N. R. F. Reasoning in humans: II. The solution of a problem and its appearance in consciousness. *Journal of Comparative Psychology,* 1931, *12,* 181–194.

Maki, R. H., Maki, W. S., and Marsh, L. G. Processing locational and orientational information. *Memory and Cognition,* 1977, *5,* 602–612.

Mandler, G. Organization and memory. In K. W. Spence and J. A. Spence (Eds.), *The Psychology of Learning and Motivation, Vol. 1,* New York: Academic Press, 1967, 328–372.

Mandler, G. Organization and recognition. In E. Tulving and W. Donaldson (Eds.), *Organization and Memory,* New York: Academic Press, 1972.

Mandler, J. M. and Johnson, N. S. Some of the thousand words a picture is worth. *Journal of Experimental Psychology: Human Learning and Memory,* 1976, *2,* 529–540.

Mandler, J. M. and Johnson, N. S. Remembrance of things parsed: Story structure and recall. *Cognitive Psychology,* 1977, *9,* 111–151.

Mandler, J. M. and Ritchey, G. H. Long-term memory for pictures. *Journal of Experimental Psychology: Human Learning and Memory,* 1977, *3,* 386–396.

Marcus, M. A computational account of some constraints on language. *Proceedings of TINLAP-2,* 1978, 236–246.

Marcus, S. L. and Rips, L. J. Conditional reasoning. *Journal of Verbal Learning and Verbal Behavior,* 1979, *18,* 199–223.

Marler, P. Animal communication signals. *Science,* 1967, *157,* 764–774.

Massaro, D. W. *Experimental Psychology and Information Processing.* Chicago: Rand McNally, 1975.

Mayer, A. and Orth, I. Zur qualitativen untersuchung der Association. *Zeitschaft für Psychologie,* 1901, *26,* 1–13.

Medin, D. L. and Schaffer, M. M. A context theory of classification learning. *Psychological Review,* 1978, *85,* 207–238.

Melton, A. W. Implications of short-term memory for a general theory of memory. *Journal of Verbal Learning and Verbal Behavior,* 1963, *2,* 1–21.

Melton, A. W. and Martin, E. *Coding Processes in Memory.* Washington, D.C.: Winston, 1972.

Mendleson, E. *Introduction to Mathematical Logic.* New York: Van Nostrand, 1964.

Metzler, J. Cognitive analogues of the rotation of three-dimensional objects. Unpublished doctoral dissertation, Stanford University, 1973.

Metzler, J. and Shepard, R. N. Transformational studies of the internal representations of three dimensional objects. In R. L. Solso (Ed.), *Theories of Cognitive Psychology: The Loyola Symposium,* Hillsdale, N.J.: Lawrence Erlbaum Associates, 1974.

Meyer, B. J. F. The organization of prose and its effect on recall. Unpublished doctoral dissertation, Cornell University, 1974.

Meyer, B. J. F., Brandt, D. M., and Bluth, G. J. Use of author's textual schema: Key for ninth-grader's comprehension. Paper presented at the annual conference of the American Educational Research Association, Toronto, March 1978.

Meyer, D. E. and Schvaneveldt, R. W. Facilitation in recognizing pairs of words: Evidence of a dependence between retrieval operations. *Journal of Experimental Psychology,* 1971, *90,* 227–234.

Milgram, S. and Jodelet, D. Psychological maps of Paris. In H. M. Proshansky, W. H. Itelson, and L. G. Revlin, *Environmental Psychology,* New York: Holt, Rinehart, and Winston, 1976.

Miller, G. A. The magical number seven, plus or minus two: Some limits on our capacity for processing information. *Psychological Review,* 1956, *63,* 81–97.

Miller, G. A., et al. Report of the study group on linguistic communication to the National Institute of Education, January 1974.

Miller, G. A. and Isard, S. Some perceptual consequences of linguistic rules. *Journal of Verbal Learning and Verbal Behavior,* 1963, *2,* 217–228.

Miller, G. A. and Johnson-Laird, P. N. *Language and Perception.* Cambridge, Mass.: Belknap Press, 1976.

Miller, G. A. and Nicely, P. An analysis of perceptual confusions among some English consonants. *Journal of the Acoustical Society of America,* 1955, *27,* 338–352.

Minsky, M. A framework for representing knowledge. In P. H. Winston (Ed.), *The Psychology of Computer Vision,* New York: McGraw-Hill, 1975.

Moore, O. K. and Anderson, S. B. Modern logic and tasks for experiments on problem solving behavior. *Journal of Psychology,* 1954, *38,* 151–160.

Moray, N. Attention in dichotic listening: Affective cues and the influence of instruction. *Quarterly Journal of Experimental Psychology,* 1959, *11,* 56–60.

Moray, N., Bates, A., and Barnett, T. Experiments on the four-eared man. *Journal of the Acoustical Society of America,* 1965, *38,* 196–201.

Moyer, R. S. Comparing objects in memory: Evidence suggesting an internal psychophysics. *Perception and Psychophysics,* 1973, *13,* 180–184.

Moyer, R. S. and Landauer, T. K. Time required for judgments of numerical inequality. *Nature,* 1967, *215,* 1519–1520.

Murdock, B. B., Jr. The retention of individual items. *Journal of Experimental Psychology,* 1961, *62,* 618–625.

Murray, H. G. and Denny, J. P. Interaction of ability level and interpolated activity (opportunity for incubation) in human problem solving. *Psychological Reports,* 1969, *24,* 271–276.

Neisser, U. *Cognitive Psychology.* New York: Appleton, 1967.

Neisser, U. *Cognition and Reality: Principles and Implications of Cognitive Psychology.* San Francisco: W. H. Freeman and Company, 1976.

Nelson, T. O. Savings and forgetting from long-term memory. *Journal of Verbal Learning and Verbal Behavior,* 1971, *10,* 568–576.

Nelson, T. O. Reinforcement and human memory. In W. K. Estes (Ed.), *Handbook of Learning and Cognitive Processes, Vol. 3,* Hillsdale, N.J.: Lawrence Erlbaum Associates, 1976.

Nelson, T. O. Detecting small amounts of information in memory: Savings for nonrecognized items. *Journal of Experimental Psychology: Human Learning and Memory,* 1978, *4,* 453–468.

Neumann, P. G. Visual prototype formation with discontinuous representation of dimensions of variability. *Memory and Cognition,* 1977, *5,* 187–197.

Newell, A. Production systems: Models of control structures. In W. G. Chase (Ed.), *Visual Information Processing,* New York: Academic Press, 1973.

Newell, A. Reasoning, problem-solving, and decision processes: The problem space as a fundamental category. In R. Nickerson (Ed.), *Attention and Performance VIII,* Hillsdale, N.J.: Lawrence Erlbaum Associates, 1980, in press.

Newell, A. and Simon, H. *Human Problem Solving.* Englewood Cliffs, N.J.: Prentice-Hall, 1972.

Nida, E. A. Sociopsychological problems in language mastery and retention. In P. Pimsleur and T. Quinn (Eds.), *The Psychology of Second Language Acquisition,* London: Cambridge University Press, 1971.

Nilsson, N. J. *Problem-Solving Methods in Artificial Intelligence.* New York: McGraw-Hill, 1971.

Nisbett, R. E. and Ross, L. *Human Inference: Strategies and Shortcomings in Social Judgment.* Englewood Cliffs, N.J.: Prentice-Hall, 1980.

Norman, D. A. Memory, knowledge, and the answering of questions. In R. L. Solso (Ed.), *Contemporary Issues in Cognitive Psychology,* Washington, D.C.: Winston, 1973.

Norman, D. A. *Memory and Attention: An Introduction to Human Information Processing* (2nd Edition). New York: Wiley, 1976.

Norman, D. A. and Bobrow, D. G. On data-limited and resource-limited processes. *Cognitive Psychology,* 1975, *7,* 44–64.

Norman, D. A. and Rumelhart, D. E. *Explorations in Cognition.* San Francisco: W. H. Freeman and Company, 1975.

Olson, D. R. Language and thought: Aspects of a cognitive theory of semantics. *Psychological Review,* 1970, *77,* 257–273.

Osborn, A. F. *Applied Imagination.* New York: Scribners, 1953.

Osherson, D. Logic and models of logical thinking. In R. J. Falmagne (Ed.), *Reasoning: Representation and Process.* Hillsdale, N.J.: Lawrence Erlbaum Associates, 1975.

Owens, J., Bower, G. H., and Black, J. B. The "soap opera" effect in story recall. *Memory and Cognition,* 1979, 7, 185–191.

Paivio, A. Mental imagery in associative learning and memory. *Psychological Review,* 1969, 76, 241–263.

Paivio, A. *Imagery and Verbal Processes.* New York: Holt, Rinehart, and Winston, 1971.

Paivio, A. Perceptual comparisons through the mind's eye. *Memory and Cognition,* 1975, 3, 635–647.

Paivio, A. Images, propositions, and knowledge. In J. M. Nicholas (Ed.), *Images, Perception, and Knowledge,* The Western Ontario Series in the Philosophy of Science. Dordrecht, Holland: Reidel, 1976.

Paivio, A. Mental comparisons involving abstract attributes. *Memory and Cognition,* 1978, 6, 199–208.

Palmer, S. E. The effects of contextual scenes on the identification of objects. *Memory and Cognition,* 1975, 3, 519–526.

Palmer, S. E. Hierarchical structure in perceptual representation. *Cognitive Psychology,* 1977, 9, 441–474.

Palmer, S. E. Fundamental aspects of cognitive representation. In E. Rosch and B. Lloyd (Eds.), *Cognition and Categorization,* Hillsdale, N.J.: Lawrence Erlbaum Associates, 1978.

Parker, E. S., Birnbaum, I. M., and Noble, E. P. Alcohol and memory: Storage and state dependency. *Journal of Verbal Learning and Verbal Behavior,* 1976, 15, 691–702.

Penfield, W. The interpretive cortex. *Science,* 1959, 129, 1719–1725.

Perky, C. W. An experimental study of imagination. *American Journal of Psychology,* 1910, 21, 422–452.

Peterson, L. R. and Peterson, M. Short-term retention of individual items. *Journal of Experimental Psychology,* 1959, 58, 193–198.

Pew, R. W. Human perceptual-motor performance. In B. H. Kantowitz (Ed.), *Human Information Processing: Tutorials in Performance and Cognition,* Hillsdale, N.J.: Lawrence Erlbaum Associates, 1974.

Piestrup, A. Black dialect interference and accommodation of reading instruction in first grade. *Monographs of the Language-Behavior Research Laboratory, 4,* 1973.

Poincare, H. *The Foundations of Science.* New York: Science House, 1929.

Polya, G. *How to Solve It.* Garden City, N.Y.: Doubleday/Anchor, 1957.

Pomerantz, J. P., Soyer, L. C., and Stoever, R. J. Perception of wholes and their component parts: Some configural superiority effects. *Journal of Experimental Psychology: Human Perception and Performance,* 1977, 3, 422–435.

Pompi, K. F. and Lachman, R. Surrogate processes in the short-term retention of connected discourse. *Journal of Experimental Psychology,* 1967, 75, 143–150.

Popper, K. R. *The Logic of Scientific Discovery.* New York: Harper & Row, 1959.

Posner, M. I. Abstraction and the process of recognition. In G. H. Bower (Ed.), *The Psychology of Learning and Motivation, III,* New York: Academic Press, 1969.

Posner, M. I. *Cognition: An Introduction.* Glenview, Ill.: Scott, Foresman, 1973.

Posner, M. I., Boies, S., Eichelman, W. H., and Taylor, R. L. Retention of visual and name codes of single letters. *Journal of Experimental Psychology,* 1969, *79* (1, Pt. 2).

Posner, M. I. and Keele, S. W. On the genesis of abstract ideas. *Journal of Experimental Psychology,* 1968, *77,* 353–363.

Posner, M. I. and Keele, S. W. Retention of abstract ideas. *Journal of Experimental Psychology,* 1970, *83,* 304–308.

Posner, M. I. and Snyder, C. R. R. Attention and cognitive control. In R. L. Solso (Ed.), *Information Processing and Cognition,* Hillsdale, N.J.: Lawrence Erlbaum Associates, 1975.

Postman, L. Short-term memory and incidental learning. In A. W. Melton (Ed.), *Categories of Human Learning,* New York: Academic Press, 1964.

Postman, L. and Underwood, B. J. Critical issues in interference theory. *Memory and Cognition,* 1973, *1,* 19–40.

Potts, G. R. Information-processing strategies used in the encoding of linear orderings. *Journal of Verbal Learning and Verbal Behavior,* 1972, *11,* 727–740.

Potts, G. R. Bringing order to cognitive structures. In F. Restle, R. M. Shiffrin, N. J. Castellan, H. R. Lindman, and D. B. Pisoni (Eds.), *Cognitive Theory, Vol. 1,* Hillsdale, N.J.: Lawrence Erlbaum Associates, 1975.

Potts, G. R. Integrating new and old information. *Journal of Verbal Learning and Verbal Behavior,* 1977, *16,* 305–320.

Premack, D. Language in chimpanzee? *Science,* 1971, *172,* 808–822.

Premack, D. Language and intelligence in ape and man. *American Scientist,* 1976, *64,* 674–683.

Prince, G. M. *The Practice of Creativity.* New York: Harper & Row, 1970.

Pritchard, R. M. Stabilized images on the retina. *Scientific American,* 1961, *204,* 72–78.

Pronko, N. H. On learning to play the violin at the age of four without tears. *Psychology Today,* 1969, *2,* 52.

Pylyshyn, Z. What the mind's eye tells the mind's brain: A critique of mental imagery. *Psychological Bulletin,* 1973, *80,* 1–24.

Quillian, M. R. *Semantic Memory.* Cambridge, Mass.: Bolt, Beranak and Newman, 1966.

Quillian, M. R. The teachable language comprehender. *Communications of the Association for Computing Machinery,* 1969, *12,* 459–476.

Quine, W. V. O. *Methods of Logic.* New York: Holt, 1950.

Ratcliff, R. and McKoon, G. Priming in item recognition: Evidence for the propositional structure of sentences. *Journal of Verbal Learning and Verbal Behavior,* 1978, *17,* 403–417.

Rayner, K. The perceptual span and peripheral cues in reading. *Cognitive Psychology,* 1975, *7,* 65–81.

Reber, A. S. and Scarborough, D. L. *Toward a Psychology of Reading: The Proceedings of the CUNY Conference.* Hillsdale, N.J.: Lawrence Erlbaum Associates, 1977.

Reddy, R. (Ed.). *Speech Recognition: Invited Papers Presented at the IEEE Symposium.* New York: Academic Press, 1975.

Reddy, R. and Newell, A. Knowledge and its representation in a speech understanding system. In L. W. Gregg (Ed.), *Knowledge and Cognition,* Hillsdale, N.J.: Lawrence Erlbaum Associates, 1974.

Reder, L. M. The role of elaborations in the processing of prose. Unpublished doctoral dissertation, University of Michigan, 1976.

Reder, L. M. The role of elaborations in memory for prose. *Cognitive Psychology,* 1979, *11,* 221–234.

Reder, L. M. and Anderson, J. R. A comparison of texts and their summaries: Memorial consequences. *Journal of Verbal Learning and Verbal Behavior,* 1980, *19,* in press.

Reed, S. K. Decision processes in pattern classification. Unpublished doctoral dissertation, University of California, Los Angeles, 1970.

Reed, S. K. Pattern recognition and categorization. *Cognitive Psychology,* 1972, *3,* 382–407.

Reed, S. K. Structural descriptions and the limitations of visual images. *Memory and Cognition,* 1974, *2,* 329–336.

Reed, S. K. and Johnsen, J. A. Detection of parts in patterns and images. *Memory and Cognition,* 1975, *3,* 569–575.

Reicher, G. Perceptual recognition as a function of meaningfulness of stimulus material. *Journal of Experimental Psychology,* 1969, *81,* 275–280.

Reitman, J. S. and Bower, G. H. Structure and later recognition of exemplars of concepts. *Cognitive Psychology,* 1973, *4,* 194–206.

Reitman, W. *Cognition and Thought.* New York: Wiley, 1965.

Restle, F. The selection of strategies in cue learning. *Psychological Review,* 1962, *69,* 329–343.

Revlin, R. and Mayer, R. E. *Human Reasoning.* Washington, D.C.: Winston, 1978.

Reynolds, A. G. and Flagg, P. W. *Cognitive Psychology.* Cambridge, Mass.: Winthrop, 1977.

Reynolds, J. H. and Glaser, R. Effects of repetition and spaced review upon retention of a complex learning task. *Journal of Educational Psychology,* 1964, *55,* 297–308.

Richards, J. P. Interaction of position and conceptual level of adjunct questions in immediate and delayed retention of text. *Journal of Educational Psychology,* 1976, *68,* 210–217.

Richardson, A. *Mental Imagery.* New York: Springer, 1969.

Riesbeck, C. K. Computational understanding: Analysis of sentences and context. Stanford Artificial Intelligence Laboratory Memo AIM-238, 1974.

Rips, L. J. and Marcus, S. L. Supposition and the analysis of conditional sentences. In M. A Just and P. A. Carpenter (Eds.), *Cognitive Processes in Comprehension,* Hillsdale, N.J.: Lawrence Erlbaum Associates, 1977.

Rips, L. J., Shoben, E. J., and Smith, E. E. Semantic distance and the verification of semantic relations. *Journal of Verbal Learning and Verbal Behavior,* 1973, *12,* 1–20.

Robbin, J. W. *Mathematical Logic—A First Course.* New York: Benjamin, 1969.

Robinson, F. P. *Effective Study.* New York: Harper & Row, 1961.

Robinson, G. H. Continuous estimation of a time-varying probability. *Ergonomics,* 1964, *7,* 7–21.

Rock, I. *An Introduction to Perception.* New York: Macmillan, 1975.

Rosch, E. On the internal structure of perceptual and semantic categories. In T. E. Moore (Ed.), *Cognitive Development and the Acquisition of Language,* New York: Academic Press, 1973.

Rosch, E. Cognitive representations of semantic categories. *Journal of Experimental Psychology: General,* 1975, *104,* 192–223.

Rosch, E. Human categorization. In N. Warren (Ed.), *Advances in Cross-Cultural Psychology, Vol. I,* London: Academic Press, 1977.

Rosch, E. and Lloyd, B. B. *Cognition and Categorization.* Hillsdale, N.J.: Lawrence Erlbaum Associates, 1978.

Rosch, E. and Mervis, C. B. Family resemblances: Studies in the internal structure of categories. *Cognitive Psychology,* 1975, *7,* 573–605.

Rosenhan, D. L. On being sane in insane places. *Science,* 1973, *179,* 250–258.

Ross, J. and Lawrence, K. A. Some observations on memory artifice. *Psychonomic Science,* 1968, *13,* 107–108.

Rothkopf, E. Z. Learning from written instruction materials: An explanation of the control of inspection behavior by test-like events. *American Educational Research Journal,* 1966, *3,* 241–249.

Rothkopf, E. Z. Structural text features and the control of processes in learning from written materials. In R. O. Freedle and J. B. Carroll (Eds.), *Language Comprehension and the Acquisition of Knowledge,* Washington, D.C.: Winston, 1972.

Rothkopf, E. Z. and Coke, E. V. Repetition interval and rehearsal method in learning equivalences from written sentences. *Journal of Verbal Learning and Verbal Behavior,* 1963, *2,* 406–416.

Rothkopf, E. Z. and Coke, E. V. Variations in phrasing, repetition intervals, and the recall of sentence material. *Journal of Verbal Learning and Verbal Behavior,* 1966, *5,* 86–91.

Rumelhart, D. E. Notes on a schema for stories. In D. G. Bobrow and A. M. Collins (Eds.), *Representation and Understanding,* New York: Academic Press, 1975.

Rumelhart, D. E. *An Introduction to Human Information Processing.* New York: Wiley, 1977.

Rumelhart, D. E., Lindsay, P., and Norman, D. A. A process model for long-term memory. In E. Tulving and W. Donaldson (Eds.), *Organization of Memory,* New York: Academic Press, 1972.

Rumelhart, D. E. and Norman, D. A. Accretion, tuning, and restructuring: Three modes of learning. In J. W. Cotton and R. Klatzky (Eds.), *Semantic Factors in Cognition,* Hillsdale, N.J.: Lawrence Erlbaum Associates, 1978.

Rumelhart, D. E. and Ortony, A. The representation of knowledge in memory. In R. C. Anderson, R. J. Spiro, and W. E. Montague (Eds.), *Schooling and the Acquisition of Knowledge,* Hillsdale, N.J.: Lawrence Erlbaum Associates, 1977.

Rumelhart, D. E. and Siple, P. Process of recognizing tachistoscopically presented words. *Psychological Review,* 1974, *81,* 99–118.

Rundus, D. Analysis of rehearsal processes in free recall. *Journal of Experimental Psychology,* 1971, *89,* 63–77.

Rychener, M. D. and Newell, A. An instructible production system: Basic design issues. In D. A. Waterman and F. Hayes-Roth (Eds.), *Pattern-Directed Inference Systems,* New York: Academic Press, 1978.

Safren, M. A. Associations, set, and the solution of word problems. *Journal of Experimental Psychology,* 1962, *64,* 40–45.

Sampson, G. *The Form of Language.* London: George Weidenfeld and Nicolson, 1975.

Samuels, S. J., Dahl, P., and Archwamety, T. Effect of hypothesis/test training in reading skill. *Journal of Educational Psychology,* 1974, *66,* 835–844.

Santa, J. L. Spatial transformations of words and pictures. *Journal of Experimental Psychology: Human Learning and Memory,* 1977, *3,* 418–427.

Sayers, D. L. *Five Red Herrings.* New York: Avon, 1968.

Schank, R. C. *Conceptual Information Processing.* Amsterdam: North-Holland, 1975.

Schank, R. C. and Abelson, R. *Scripts, Plans, Goals, and Understanding.* Hillsdale, N.J.: Lawrence Erlbaum Associates, 1977.

Schneider, W. and Shiffrin, R. M. Controlled and automatic human information processing: I. Detection, search, and attention. *Psychological Review,* 1977, *84,* 1–66.

Schoenfield, J. R. *Mathematical Logic.* Reading, Mass.: Addison-Wesley, 1967.

Selfridge, O. G. Pattern recognition and modern computers. Proceedings of the Western Joint Computer Conference, 1955. New York: Institute of Electrical and Electronics Engineers.

Shaw, R. and Bransford, J. D. Introduction: Psychological approaches to the problem of knowledge. In R. Shaw and J. P. Bransford (Eds.), *Perceiving, Acting, and Knowing: Toward an Ecological Psychology.* Hillsdale, N.J.: Lawrence Erlbaum Associates, 1977.

Shaw, R. and Bransford, J. D. *Perceiving, Acting, and Knowing: Toward an Ecological Psychology. Hillsdale, N.J.: Lawrence Erlbaum Associates, 1977.*

Shepard, R. N. Recognition memory for words, sentences, and pictures. *Journal of Verbal Learning and Verbal Behavior,* 1967, *6,* 156–163.

Shepard, R. N. and Feng, C. A chronometric study of mental paper folding. *Cognitive Psychology,* 1972, *3,* 228–243.

Shepard, R. N. and Metzler, J. Mental rotation of three-dimensional objects. *Science,* 1971, *171,* 701–703.

Shepard, R. N. and Podgorny, P. Cognitive processes that resemble perceptual processes. In W. K. Estes (Ed.), *Handbook of Learning and Cognitive Processes,* Hillsdale, N.J.: Lawrence Erlbaum Associates, 1978.

Shiffrin, R. M. Short-term store: The basis for a memory system. In F. Restle, R. M. Shiffrin, N. J. Castellan, H. R. Lindman, and D. B. Pisoni (Eds.), *Cognitive Theory, Vol. I,* Hillsdale, N.J.: Lawrence Erlbaum Associates, 1975.

Shiffrin, R. M. and Schneider, W. Controlled and automatic human information processing: II. Perceptual learning, automatic attending, and a general theory. *Psychological Review,* 1977, *84,* 127–190.

Shuford, E. H. Percentage estimation of proportion as a function of element type, exposure time, and task. *Journal of Experimental Psychology,* 1961, *61,* 430–436.

Silveira, J. Incubation: The effect of interruption timing and length on problem solution and quality of problem processing. Unpublished doctoral dissertation, University of Oregon, 1971.

Simon, H. A. The functional equivalence of problem solving skills. *Cognitive Psychology,* 1975, *7,* 268–288.

Simon, H. A. Information-processing theory of human problem-solving. In W. K. Estes (Ed.), *Handbook of Learning and Cognitive Processes,* Hillsdale, N.J.: Lawrence Erlbaum Associates, 1978.

Simon, H. A. On forms of mental representation. In C. Wade Savage (Ed.), *Perception and Cognition: Issues in the Foundation of Psychology, Vol. IX,* Minnesota Studies on the Philosophy of Science, Minneapolis: University of Minnesota Press, 1978.

Simon, H. A. and Gilmartin, K. A simulation of memory for chess positions. *Cognitive Psychology,* 1973, *5,* 29–46.

Simon, H. A. and Lea, G. Problem solving and rule induction: A unified view. In L. W. Gregg (Ed.), *Knowledge and Cognition,* Hillsdale, N.J.: Lawrence Erlbaum Associates, 1974.

Simpson, M. E. and Johnson, D. M. Atmosphere and conversion errors in syllogistic reasoning. *Journal of Experimental Psychology,* 1966, *72,* 197–200.

Skyrms, B. *Choice and Chance: An Introduction to Inductive Logic.* Belmont, Calif.: Dickenson, 1966.

Slobin, D. I. Cognitive prerequisites for the development of grammar. In C. A. Ferguson and D. I. Slobin (Eds.), *Studies of Child Language Development,* New York: Holt, Rinehart, and Winston, 1973.

Slovic, P. and Lichtenstein, S. Comparison of Bayesian and regression approaches to the study of information processing in judgment. *Organizational Behavior and Human Performance,* 1971, *6,* 649–744.

Smith, S. M., Brown, H. O., Toman, J. E. P., and Goodman, L. S. The lack of cerebral effects of d-Tubercurarine. *Anesthesiology,* 1947, *8,* 1–14.

Smith, S. M., Glenberg, A., and Bjork, R. A. Environmental context and human memory. *Memory and Cognition,* 1978, *6,* 342–353.

Snyder, M. and Swann, W. B. Hypothesis-testing processes in social interaction. *Journal of Personality and Social Psychology,* 1978, *36,* 1202–1212.

Solso, R. L. (Ed.). *Contemporary Issues in Cognitive Psychology: The Loyola Symposium.* Washington, D.C.: Winston, 1973.

Solso, R. L. (Ed.). *Information Processing and Cognition: The Loyola Symposium.* Hillsdale, N.J.: Lawrence Erlbaum Associates, 1975.

Sommer, R. The new look on the witness stand. *Canadian Psychologist,* 1959, *8,* 94–99.

Spelke, E., Hirst, W., and Neisser U. Skills of divided attention. *Cognition,* 1976, *4,* 215–230.

Sperling, G. A. The information available in brief visual presentation. *Psychological Monographs,* 1960, *74,* Whole No. 498.

Sperling, G. A. Successive approximations to a model for short-term memory. *Acta Psychologia,* 1967, *27,* 285–292.

Spiro, R. J. Constructing a theory of reconstructive memory: The state of the schema approach. In R. C. Anderson, R. J. Spiro and W. E. Montague (Eds.), *Schooling and the Acquisition of Knowledge,* Hillsdale, N.J.: Lawrence Erlbaum Associates, 1977.

Staudenmayer, H. Understanding conditional reasoning with meaningful propositions. In R. J. Falmagne (Ed.), *Reasoning: Representation and Process in Children and Adults,* Hillsdale, N.J.: Lawrence Erlbaum Associates, 1975.

Stein, M. I. *Stimulating Creativity, Vols. 1 and 2.* New York: Academic Press, 1975, 1976.

Stevens, A. and Coupe, P. Distortions in judged spatial relations. *Cognitive Psychology,* 1978, *10,* 422–437.

Sticht, T. G. Learning by listening. In R. O. Freedle and J. B. Carroll (Eds.), *Language Comprehension and the Acquisition of Knowledge,* Washington, D.C.: Winston, 1972.

Stratton, R. P. and Brown, R. Improving creative thinking by training in the production and judgment of solutions on a verbal problem. *Journal of Educational Psychology,* 1972, *63,* 390–397.

Strohner, H. and Nelson, K. E. The young child's development of sentence comprehension: Influence of event probability, nonverbal context, syntactic form, and strategies. *Child Development,* 1974, *45,* 567–576.

Strunk, W., Jr. and White, E. B. *The Elements of Style* (Revised Edition). New York: Macmillan, 1972.

Studdert-Kennedy, M. Speech perception. In N. J. Lass (Ed.), *Contemporary Issues in Experimental Phonetics,* Springfield, Ill.: Charles C Thomas, 1976.

Sulin, R. A. and Dooling, D. J. Intrusion of a thematic idea in retention of prose. *Journal of Experimental Psychology,* 1974, *103,* 255–262.

Suppes, P. *Introduction to Logic.* Princeton, N.J.: Van Nostrand, 1957.

Taplin, J. E. Reasoning with conditional sentences. *Journal of Verbal Learning and Verbal Behavior,* 1971, *10,* 218–225.

Taplin, J. E. and Staudenmayer, H. Interpretation of abstract conditional sentences in deductive reasoning. *Journal of Verbal Learning and Verbal Behavior,* 1973, *12,* 530–542.

Taylor, S. E. and Crocker, J. Schematic bases of social information processing. In E. T. Higgins, C. P. Herman, and M. P. Zanna, *Social Cognition: The Ontario Symposium on Personality and Social Psychology,* Hillsdale, N.J.: Lawrence Erlbaum Associates, in press.

Taylor, S. E., Fiske, S. T., Etcoff, N. L., and Ruderman, A. J. The categorical and contextual bases of person memory and stereotyping. *Journal of Personality and Social Psychology,* 1978, *36,* 778–793.

Teborg, R. H. Dissipation of functional fixedness by means of conceptual grouping tasks. Unpublished doctoral dissertation, Michigan State University, 1968.

Tesser, A. Self-generated attitude change. In L. Berkowitz (Ed.), *Advances in Experimental Social Psychology, Vol. II,* New York: Academic Press, 1978.

Thomas, E. L. and Robinson, H. A. *Improving Reading in Every Class: A Sourcebook for Teachers.* Boston: Allyn and Bacon, 1972.

Thomson, D. M. Context effects on recognition memory. *Journal of Verbal Learning and Verbal Behavior,* 1972, *11,* 497–511.

Thomson, D. M. and Tulving, E. Associative encoding and retrieval; weak and strong cues. *Journal of Experimental Psychology,* 1970, *86,* 255–262.

Thorndike, R. L. *Reading Comprehension: Education in Fifteen Countries.* New York: Wiley, 1973.

Thorndyke, P. W. Cognitive structures in comprehension and memory in narrative discourse. *Cognitive Psychology,* 1977, *9,* 77–110.

Thorndyke, P. W. and Hayes-Roth, B. Spatial knowledge acquisition from maps and navigation. Paper presented at the meetings of the Psychonomic Society, San Antonio, Texas, November 9–11, 1978.

Tolman, E. C. Cognitive maps in rats and men. *Psychological Review,* 1948, *55,* 189–208.

Trabasso, T. R. and Bower, G. H. *Attention in Learning.* New York: Wiley, 1968.

Trabasso, T. R. and Riley, C. A. The construction and use of representations involving linear order. In R. L. Solso (Ed.), *Information Processing and Cognition,* Hillsdale, N.J.: Lawrence Erlbaum Associates, 1975.

Triesman, A. M. Verbal cues, language, and meaning in selective attention. *Quarterly Journal of Experimental Psychology,* 1960, *12,* 242–248.

Tulving, E., Mandler, G., and Baumal, R. Interaction of two sources of information in tachistoscopic word recognition. *Canadian Journal of Psychology,* 1964, *18,* 62–71.

Tulving, E. and Thomson, D. M. Encoding specificity and retrieval processes in episodic memory. *Psychological Review,* 1973, *80,* 352–373.

Turvey, M. T. and Shaw, R. E. Memory (or knowing) as a matter of specification not representation: Notes toward a different class of machines. Paper presented at the conference on Levels of Processing, Rockport, Massachusetts, June 1977.

Tversky, A. and Kahneman, D. Belief in the law of small numbers. *Psychological Bulletin,* 1971, *76,* 105–110.

Tversky, A. and Kahneman, D. Judgments under uncertainty: Heuristics and biases. *Science,* 1974, *185,* 1124–1131.

Ultan, R. Some general characteristics of interrogative systems. *Working Papers in Language Universals* (Stanford University), 1969, *1,* 41–63.

van Dijk, T. A. Semantic macro-structures and knowledge frames in discourse comprehension. In M. A. Just and P. A. Carpenter (Eds.), *Cognitive Processes in Comprehension,* Hillsdale, N.J.: Lawrence Erlbaum Associates, 1977.

van Dijk, T. A. and Kintsch, W. Cognitive psychology and discourse. In W. U. Dressler (Ed.), *Trends in Text Linguistics,* Berlin/New York: DeGruyter, 1976.

Vinacke, W. E. *The Psychology of Thinking.* New York: McGraw-Hill, 1974.

von Frisch, K. *The Dance Language and Orientation of Bees* (translated by C. E. Chadwick). Cambridge, Mass.: Belknap Press, 1967.

Wanner, H. E. On remembering, forgetting, and understanding sentences: A study of the deep structure hypothesis. Unpublished doctoral dissertation, Harvard University, 1968.

Warren, R. M. Perceptual restorations of missing speech sounds. *Science,* 1970, *167,* 392–393.

Warren, R. M. and Warren, R. P. Auditory illusions and confusions. *Scientific American,* 1970, *223,* 30–36.

Wason, P. C. On the failure to eliminate hypotheses in a conceptual task. *Quarterly Journal of Experimental Psychology,* 1960, *12,* 129–140.

Wason, P. C. On the failure to eliminate hypotheses in a conceptual task: A Second Look. In P. C. Wason and P. N. Johnson-Laird (Eds.), *Thinking and Reasoning,* Middlesex, England: Penguin Books, 1968.

Wason, P. C. Regression in reasoning? *British Journal of Psychology,* 1969, *60,* 471–480.

Wason, P. C. Specific thoughts on the writing process. Presented at the Cognitive Processes in Writing—Interdisciplinary Symposium on Cognition, Carnegie-Mellon University, 1978.

Wason, P. C. and Johnson-Laird, P. N. *Psychology of Reasoning: Structure and Content.* Cambridge, Mass.: Harvard University Press, 1972.

Watkins, M. J. and Tulving, E. Episodic memory: When recognition fails. *Journal of Experimental Psychology: General,* 1975, *104,* 5–29.

Watson, J. *Behaviorism.* New York: Norton, 1930.

Watt, W. C. On two hypotheses concerning psycholinguistics. In J. R. Hayes (Ed.), *Cognition and the Development of Language,* New York: Wiley, 1970.

Webster's Seventh New Collegiate Dictionary. Toronto, Ontario: Thomas Allen, 1963.

Weisberg, R. W. Sentence processing assessed through intrasentence word associations. *Journal of Experimental Psychology,* 1969, *82,* 332–338.

Welford, A. T. *Fundamentals of Skill.* London: Methuen, 1968.

Wheeler, D. D. Processes in word recognition. *Cognitive Psychology,* 1970, *1,* 59–85.

Whorf, B. L. *Language, Thought, and Reality.* Cambridge, Mass.: MIT Press, 1956.

Wicklegren, W. A. The long and the short of memory. *Psychological Bulletin,* 1973, *80,* 425–438.

Wicklegren, W. A. Single-trace fragility theory of memory dynamics. *Memory and Cognition,* 1974(a), *2,* 775–780.

Wicklegren, W. A. *How to Solve Problems.* San Francisco: W. H. Freeman and Company, 1974(b).

Wicklegren, W. A. Memory storage dynamics. In W. K. Estes (Ed.), *Handbook of Learning and Cognitive Processes, Vol. 4,* Hillsdale, N.J.: Lawrence Erlbaum Associates, 1976.

Wicklegren, W. A. *Cognitive Psychology.* Englewood Cliffs, N.J.: Prentice-Hall, 1979.

Winograd, T. Understanding language. *Cognitive Psychology,* 1972, *3,* 1–191.

Winston, P. H. (Ed.). *The Psychology of Computer Vision.* New York: McGraw-Hill, 1975.

Winston, P. H. *Artificial Intelligence.* Reading, Mass.: Addison-Wesley, 1977.

Wiseman, S. and Neisser, U. Perceptual organization as a determinant of visual recognition memory. *American Journal of Psychology,* 1974, *87,* 675–681.

Witkin, H. A. The perception of the upright. *Scientific American,* 1959, *200,* 50–56.

Wittgenstein, L. *Philosophical Investigations.* New York: Macmillan, 1953.

Wolford, G. Function of distinct associations for paired-associate performance. *Psychological Review,* 1971, *73,* 303–313.

Woocher, F. D., Glass, A. L., and Holyoak, K. J. Positional discriminability in linear orderings. *Memory and Cognition,* 1978, *6,* 165–174.

Woods, W. A. Progress in natural language and understanding: An application to lunar geology. *AFIPS Proceedings,* 1973 National Computer Conference and Exposition.

Woodword, F. B. *Scientific Writing for Graduate Students.* New York: The Rockefeller Press, 1968.

Woodworth, R. S. and Sells, S. B. An atmospheric effect in formal syllogistic reasoning. *Journal of Experimental Psychology,* 1935, *18,* 451–460.

Yates, F. A. *The Art of Memory.* Chicago: University of Chicago Press, 1966.

Name Index

Subject Index

Abstraction of schemas. *See* Schemas
Activation, 168–169, 186, 187
  fan effect, role in, 176–178
  probability estimates, 355
  problem-solving, role in, 288
  retrieval, role in, 169–187
  spread of, 172–175
Algorithms. *See* Heuristics
Ambiguity, 371–372, 374, 377–379, 412–414
Analog representations, 68–69.
  See also Imagery
Animal language, 389–393, 394
Artificial intelligence, 4, 10, 37, 401, 413.
  See also Computers, Propositional
    networks; Scripts
Attention, 26–32
  automaticity, 30–32, 41–42, 230–235
  divided-attention studies, 27–30
  Gestalt principles, relation to, 55–56
  pattern recognition, role in, 41–42,
    49–50, 231
  recognition of symbolic expression, role
    in, 232, 234
Auditory memory, 26–27
Automaticity
  skills, role in, 227–235, 252
  See also Attention

Bayes' Theorem, 348–353
  conservativism, 350–351, 357–358
  failure to use prior probabilities,
    351–353, 358–359
  implications, 359
  See also Probability judgments
Behaviorism, 8–9, 86
  imagery, 65
  language, 383–385
Bottom-up processing, 48–49
  See also Feature analysis

Categorical syllogisms. *See* Quantifiers
Categories. *See* Concepts; Schemas
Chimpanzee language, 391–393
Chunking, 167–169
  chess, 291–292
Cognitive maps. *See* Spatial cognition
Cognitive skills, 222–254
  acquisition of, 226–235
  generalization and discrimination of,
    247–249
  production-system models, 238–245
  representations of, 235–245
  short-term memory for, 245–246
  transfer of, 246–247
Color concepts, 385–386, 388